THE Catholic Vision

THE Catholic Vision

Edward D. O'Conner, C.S.C.

Our Sunday Visitor Publishing Division
Our Sunday Visitor, Inc.
Huntington, Indiana 46750

Nihil Obstat:
Archbishop John F. Whealon, Hartford, CT
Bishop Lawrence Riley, Boston, MA
Rev. John R. Sheets, S.J., Creighton University*
Rev. Richard Hire, St. Patrick's Parish, Fort Wayne, IN

Imprimatur:
John M. D'Arcy
Bishop of Fort Wayne-South Bend

The author is grateful to all copyright holders without whose material this book could not have been completed. Among them are those who are mentioned throughout this work. If any copyrighted materials have been inadvertently used in this book without proper credit being given in one manner or another, please notify Our Sunday Visitor in writing so that future printings of this work may be corrected accordingly.

ISBN: 0-87973-418-3
LCCCN: 91-66667

PRINTED IN THE UNITED STATES OF AMERICA

Cover design by Rebecca J. Heaston

418

* While this book was being set in type, Father Sheets
was ordained auxiliary bishop of Fort Wayne-South Bend.

To the generations of Notre Dame students, from the fall of '52 through the spring of '91, whose challenges, questions, and responses have contributed, directly or indirectly, to the shaping of this book.

TABLE OF CONTENTS

Part 6: The Church / 363

ABBREVIATIONS

CE — *The Catholic Encyclopedia* (New York: Encyclopedia Press, Inc., 1913-1915)

DS — *Enchiridion Symbolorum Definitionum et Declarationum de Rebus Fidei et Morum,* edited by H. Denzinger, revised by A. Schönmetzer, 32nd ed. (Freiburg: Herder, 1963)

JB — *The Jerusalem Bible* (London: Darton, Longman and Todd, 1966)

NABr — *New American Bible With Revised New Testament* (Nashville, Tenn.: Nelson, 1988)

NCE — *The New Catholic Encyclopedia* (New York: McGraw-Hill, 1967)

NEB — *The New English Bible* (New York: Cambridge University Press, 1971)

NIV — *The Holy Bible: New International Version* (Grand Rapids, Mich.: Zondervan, 1978)

RSV — *The Oxford Annotated Bible with the Apocrypha: Revised Standard Version* (New York: Oxford, 1965)

TCC — *Teachings of the Catholic Church*, by J. Neuner and H. Roos; edited by Karl Rahner; translated by G. Stevens (Staten Island, N.Y.: Alba House, 1967)

TCT — *The Church Teaches: Documents of the Church in English Translation* (St. Louis, Mo.: Herder, 1955)

WCE — *The World Christian Encyclopedia: A Comparative Survey of Churches and Religions in the Modern World, AD 1900-2000,* edited by David Barrett (Nairobi: Oxford University Press, 1982)

INTRODUCTION

A *summa* of theology is always needed, and more than ever as culture becomes more complex and diversified. This need is rooted in the profound thirst of the human spirit to see how things fit together. Unlike squirrels, whose instincts tell them to gather nuts in the fall and eat them in winter, we human beings need to know where we come from and where we are going, to make our own plans and decisions. Above all we require to know about that which is ultimate and to which everything relates.

But the world today, and even our Western world, no longer has the unity of culture that existed when St. Thomas Aquinas wrote his great *Summa*. There is no common faith, no common metaphysics, not even a common vocabulary. And the human sciences have multiplied beyond all comprehension! Not only have we a physics, biology, and chemistry unknown to the medieval scholar but each of the great disciplines has itself exploded into a shower of particles among which a scholar has to confine himself to a specialty that tends to alienate him from his colleagues.

Even within the confines of theology alone, no one any more can claim to be a competent master of exegesis, Church history, systematics, and ethics or even of a single one of those domains in its totality. This makes it infinitely more difficult to achieve a synthesis but all the more imperative to attempt one.

Thus the basic motivation of the present work is the same as that of all the *summas* that have gone before it: to map out the great structural lines of a theological vision of the universe. But the execution must respond to exigencies quite different from those of past centuries. On the one hand, a systematic acquaintance with philosophy, much less a firm grasp of metaphysics, cannot be presupposed. Hence, devoted Thomist though I aim to be, I have not, for example, followed St. Thomas's rigorously metaphysical exposition of the divine nature. Instead, adopting more popular views of the divine attributes, I have sought gently to refine them. Likewise, as noted in the text, I have slightly adjusted his concept of natural law to more current modes of thought.

On the other hand, this book ventures into terrains in which not only theology but also the sciences and humanities — especially astrophysics, biology, anthropology, history, comparative religion, and psychology — have a stake. (The last-named, however, will barely be touched on. To engage it seriously would require a special volume.)

Recognizing the impossibility of being an expert in all these areas gives one at least a certain freedom to experiment boldly. Theologians and scientists of the past hundred years have learned the hard way to respect the diversity of their disciplines; they have become very skittish about trespassing on one another's domains. (The occasional encounters, for example, between "creationists" and "evolutionists," have often been carried out — on *both* sides — by people ill informed about their counterparts.)

But disciplines that have a common interface can't go on indefinitely turning their backs on one another without a crippling effect on human intelligence. I was delighted a few years ago to hear the oceanographer Xavier Le Pichon insist that it was cowardly for theologians and scientists to ignore each other. What science tells us about the origins of the human species, for example, demands to be brought into conversation with what revelation affirms about creation; otherwise both scientist and theologian fall into a kind of "double-truth" mentality that is really a failure to take truth seriously. We can hardly hope to determine "Adam's dates"; however, the theologian needs to be aware that human history is not just a few thousand but more like millions of years old; and that human beings, for all their distinctiveness, are deeply rooted in the rest of the animal world. On the other hand, the anthropologist needs to have it pointed out that postulating a gradual transformation of brutes into human beings empties ethics of meaning and leads to an anthropology that is irrelevant to actual human affairs. The present work attempts to treat this matter in a spirit of tentative exploration, without claiming definitive results. (If, thanks to the critique of experts, a later edition can be refined, the author would find that much preferable to having launched a signal into empty space and getting no answer back!)

II

Outsiders sometimes regard Catholicism as a quaint way of life handed down from of old and enriched in the course of centuries with curious rituals, symbols, and customs, like one of those ancient Cambodian shrines encrusted with enough carvings to provide an antiquarian with years of delightful research. They do not suspect that Catholic theology has a coherent, intelligible vision of the universe that can give reasons for its positions. It is in fact the most intellectual and thoroughly thought-out religious tradition in the world. (It is no accident that the modern university is a by-product of medieval Catholicism.) Cultured people may be vaguely aware of the artistic, musical, and architectural wealth of Catholicism, but facile jibes about decadent scholasticism have permitted them to disregard the intense contemplation and critical reflection that have gone into the building and refining of Catholic theology. It was in it that the notion of "faith seeking understanding" originated, and that theological formulas which now seem banal were minted in the heat of intense debate. Even many Catholics who are familiar with the teachings and rituals of the Church often have no idea of the reasonable and intelligible coherence of their faith. They do not realize that the Catholic positions make very good sense.

It is therefore the aim of this book to give some indication of the *intelligibility* of the Catholic position. This will be done not so much by *argument* as by a peaceful statement of the defining features of the Catholic vision, out of a conviction that their intrinsic good sense is the strongest argument in their favor. Catholicism will occasionally be contrasted with other religious traditions not with the intention of denigrating the latter but simply as a way of highlighting the characteristic Catholic features.

No attempt will be made to present the latest theological speculations or in-house debates among diverse schools of Catholic thought; emphasis will lie in what is common and proper to Catholicism as such. As the work is addressed primarily not to professional theologians but to the educated public, technical language will be avoided as far as possible. (There are, of course, some technical terms which it is impossible to do without, and others which have special historical interest; but on the whole the language aims to be that of common intelligent discourse.) Topics will be treated as briefly as possible without oversimplification or illegibility. Footnotes will be avoided except where indispensable.

10

The history of doctrines will not be dealt with, except occasionally for illustrative purposes. This is not out of disdain for the great achievements of modern scholarship in disclosing the dynamics and meanderings of doctrinal development. Nevertheless, super-saturated with historical studies, theology today needs to be reminded of the permanent validity and distinctive value of an organic synthesis of the truth.

III

While insisting on the intelligible vision that illumines Catholicism, we must acknowledge, humbly and reverently, that this vision is confronted with a Mystery which transcends it. We are not seated on a mountaintop, surveying the plain below; we are plunged into a vast ocean into which we can peer only a short distance. Moreover, God's ways are not our ways, nor are his thoughts our thoughts. Christ crucified is a "stumbling block to Jews and foolishness to Gentiles, but to those whom God has called, both Jews and Greeks, Christ the power of God and the wisdom of God" (1 Corinthians 1:23f). The revelation given through Jesus Christ is a ray of divine light in which we can bask and rejoice, marveling at how it illumines the commonest, dullest realities. But it is not a specimen that can be dissected in the laboratory, nor even a philosophy that can be analyzed fully before being adopted. Faith possesses a person; to see by it, one must first live it. Even as believers and theologians, we remain confronted with something that eludes the grasp of our minds, and unceasingly beckons us onward by its inexhaustible riches.

IV

While the desire to make a simple, luminous presentation of the great lines of the Catholic vision was the original motivation behind this book, a second one took on increasing importance as the work progressed — that of *reaffirming some of the basic Catholic positions* that are being abandoned today.

American Catholic theology is going through a kind of adolescent rebellion. Fifty years ago, the Church in this country was faithful or at least conformist but largely devoid of intellectually serious theology. That began to change about the 1950s, with more serious studies, ecumenical ventures, and more audacious theological enterprises. Vatican II was not the cause but the occasion for an acceleration along all of these dimensions, with results that are a mixture of good and bad. One of the latter is that scarcely any doctrine is secure any longer against attack, denial, neglect, or a "reinterpretation" that is, in effect, an elimination. Catholic universities and seminaries are as likely as not to be the place where Catholic doctrine is mauled.

Although Europe is the source of most of the heretical innovations, it still has a corps of traditional theologians competently sustaining the great Catholic positions, and can swallow its Schillebeeckxes and Küngs without too serious a stomachache. But in this country, confronting a horde of starry-eyed young theologians who don't know their own tradition but adroitly invent overnight theologies to conform to each new situation, the defenders of tradition (not to be identified unqualifiedly with self-styled Traditionalists!) have been caught unequipped. They have either kept bitterly silent or have been muttering ineffectually to one another.

There is need, therefore, not to maintain the "old" against the "new" (I venture to hope that some new ideas will be found herein) but to reaffirm the essential and timeless Christian truths. In this too I have avoided argument as much as possible, not attacking errors but merely lingering somewhat over the biblical bases of those doctrines that are specially imperiled. Here, however, I may be permitted to point out that the biggest threat to Catholicism comes not from attacks on the outside nor even from dissent within but from a watery substitute which might be called *naturalistic humanism*. This is not a systematic philosophical position but an attitude or mentality which combines an admirable sensitivity to humane values with disregard for the supernatural. Where classic Catholic theology sees human life as determined by the three factors, nature, grace, and sin, naturalistic humanism honors nature but neglects grace and sin.

It is not secular humanism. It believes in God and in fact is somewhat pious, capable of producing impressive liturgies and architecture. It is quite appreciative of the cultural riches of religion. But what it esteems in religion is the latter's contribution to the fullness of human life, rather than the *divine* life which it brings to us. *Community* is the supreme value of naturalistic humanism, *love* its unique law, and *compassion* perhaps its principal virtue.

All three of these are precious indeed, but the good news proclaimed by Jesus is not that life would be wonderful if we would just get along harmoniously with one another. He declares that sin is the radical evil poisoning human life; that deliverance from it comes only through faith in him; and that we have been offered something much better than earthly happiness — the life of children of God, which begins now as communion with Father, Son, and Spirit, and attains its fulfillment in the beatific vision.

If naturalistic humanism is neglectful of grace, it has a real antipathy for the notion of sin, especially original sin. Striving to be "positive" and encouraging, it opposes any language that insists on evil or could seem to arouse guilt feelings. It instinctively resents any suggestion of a radical flaw in our humanity. Although deeply concerned with injustices, it tends to view them in a merely natural perspective and to combat them solely with human means. It does not recognize that evil has so radical a hold on us that we cannot be delivered by our own efforts but only by the grace of Christ. As a result, naturalistic humanism is inconsistent and deficient even as humanism; for an authentic appreciation of human nature must acknowledge its shortcomings as well as its glories.

However encouraging and timely it may appear, naturalistic humanism proves bankrupt in the end because it leans on a broken reed. It is a vision inspired by psychology and sociology more than by the Gospel. Its ultimate appeal is to the common consciousness of mankind rather than to the doctrine of the Lord. The Catholic vision, on the other hand, is out of sync with contemporary culture because it seeks not to be conformed to this age but to be transformed by the light of Christ. As a result it is somewhat more guarded in its optimism, for it knows of what we are made; subdued in its joy, for it follows its Master on the Way of the Cross; but its hope is solid, and its inspiration efficacious, because it arises out of the Word of God, which it seeks faithfully to preserve and earnestly to apply.

ACKNOWLEDGMENTS

Thanks are due to many people who have helped me in the preparation of this book:

In the first place, Sister Amata Fabbro, O.P., professor of theology at Aquinas College in Grand Rapids. Originally the two of us planned this as a collaborative venture. This turned out to be impossible, due to her time-consuming responsibilities; but she has gone through the manuscript many times and made valuable suggestions and criticisms, based both on her competence as an exegete, and on the reactions of her students at Aquinas, who used this text in a preliminary mimeographed form.

Rev. Charles Corcoran, C.S.C., read the entire work and gave me mountains of notes in his illegible microscopic scrawl! I had to elicit the gist of his observations by means of personal conversations. May his soul now rest in peace!

The four official readers appointed by Bishop D'Arcy, whose names are listed on the copyright page, besides judging the work in their capacity as censors, were exceedingly helpful and painstaking, calling my attention to flaws which I was happy to eliminate.

Several others have read and criticized portions of the manuscript: Dr. Joseph Bobik, professor of philosophy at the University of Notre Dame: Chapter 7; Dr. John Collins, professor of theology at Notre Dame: Chapters 6 and 15; Dr. Ruel E. Foster, chairman of the English Department at the University of West Virginia: Chapters 1, 7, 10, 16, 17, and 18; Rev. Patrick Gaffney, C.S.C., associate professor of anthropology at Notre Dame: the section on Islam in Chapter 1; Rev. Robert Krieg, C.S.C., associate professor of theology at Notre Dame: Chapters 16 and 17; Dr. Xavier le Pichon, professor of geodynamics at the Collège de France: Chapter 4; Dr. George Martin, editor of *God's Word Today:* Chapters 6, 15, and 16; Drs. Michael and Francette Meaney of Corpus Christi, Tex.: Chapter 12; Rev. Marvin O'Connell, professor of history at Notre Dame: Chapters 2 and 3; my brother Joseph, professor of history at Wittenberg University: Chapter 3; my sister Maria, pastoral assistant at St. George's Parish in Erie: the Introduction; my sister-in-law, Patricia, author of two insightful studies on St. Thérèse of Lisieux: Chapter 3; Rev. Herman Reith, C.S.C., professor of philosophy at Notre Dame: Chapters 4, 7, 10, and 11; Dr. Janet Smith, assistant professor of philosophy at the University of Dallas: Chapter 12; Dr. Joseph Tihen, formerly professor of biological sciences at Notre Dame: Chapter 4; Rev. Charles Weiher, C.S.C., assistant professor of philosophy at Notre Dame: Chapters 4, 7, and 9; Dr. John Yoder, professor of theology at Notre Dame: the section on Protestantism in Chapter 2.

Most of the drawings were done by Dr. Theodore Walker, who began them while a graduate student at Notre Dame and completed them as a member of the faculty of Perkins School of Theology at Southern Methodist University. In view of the pressures on a young teacher just beginning his career, this was an act of real generosity.

The drawings on pages 38, 55, 57, 58, 59, 60, 61, 62, 63, 216, 227, 278, 295, 357, 431, 432, 433, 441, and 457 were done by Mrs. Anne Newett Donovan while in the process of preparing for her marriage and then moving with her husband to Mainz, Germany. (Those on pages 357 and 457 were done originally for a Rosary booklet that is still to be published. With the gracious consent of Mr. Herbert Juliano, the main author of the booklet, I have been able to use them here.) Those on pages 205 and 449 are the work of my niece, Sister Alethaire Foster, O.P., who found time for them while busy teaching and working on a doctorate. That on page 377 was done years ago for a preliminary draft of this book by Rev. Joseph Keena, C.S.C.; may he rest in peace. In these too I appreciate not only the talent of the artists but the generosity of their collaboration.

Rev. James Flanigan, C.S.C., adapted some of the art to the special needs of this book, and drew the sketch of St. Thomas on page 113.

Dr. Jaime Bellalta, professor of architecture at Notre Dame, led me through numerous books of Church architecture in search of illustrations.

Teresa de Bertodano, free-lance editor, besides reading Chapter 12 and the last section of Chapter 7, made a very perceptive critique of the artwork.

Herbert Juliano, former curator of the International Sports and Games Research Collection in Notre Dame's Hesburgh Library, compiled the index, with help from Paul Radich, a Notre Dame student.

Dr. David Barrett, editor in chief of the *World Christian Encyclopedia,* was kind enough to direct me to the statistics needed in the first two chapters, and to review my use of them.

Mrs. Alma McClane of South Bend typed the original manuscript; Mrs. Cheryl Reed of the Notre Dame Steno Pool typed her way through many revisions and produced the final text.

Mr. Henry O'Brien of Our Sunday Visitor, Inc., made me the beneficiary of his many years of experience and his sharp eye for detail as he guided production of the printed work. Mrs. Monica Watts, also of Our Sunday Visitor, capably prepared the graphs and maps, and did many things necessary to adapt the drawings to the text.

The Congregation of Holy Cross was extremely generous in allowing me time to work on this book.

To them all, I am deeply grateful.

* * *

With few exceptions (which are indicated), Scripture texts in this work are taken from the *New International Version* (NIV), © 1973 by the New York Bible Society International. But regardless of the translation used, the name *Yahweh* has been retained in the Old Testament texts rather than being replaced with THE LORD as is done in several versions. Likewise, in the New Testament, the name *Paraclete* has been retained, as open to several meanings, in preference to the limiting translations *Counselor* (NIV) or *Advocate* (RSV, NABr).

Texts of Vatican II, except where indicated otherwise, are taken from *Vatican Council II: The Conciliar and Post Conciliar Documents,* edited by Austin Flannery (Collegeville, Minn.: Liturgical Press, 1975).

Bibliographies originally accompanied each chapter of this book. To be adequate, however, they would have to be enormous. As the book is already much longer than we would have wished, it has been decided to omit them altogether.

Edward D. O'Connor, C.S.C.
University of Notre Dame
November 11, 1991
St. Martin of Tours

PART 1
Perspectives

Before taking up Catholicism itself, it will be helpful to see where it stands in the general panorama of religions. We will first compare Christianity to the other major religious families and then Catholicism to the other Christian denominations. This is no simple undertaking. The number of religions that have appeared in human history is beyond counting. Furthermore, religions differ in such diverse ways that it is not easy to find a common ground on which to compare them. They do not just hold different doctrines; for many religions doctrine has not the importance that it has in Christianity and especially Catholicism. One religion may consist chiefly of ritual, and another of a code of morals. Their diversities are so radical and many-sided that it is a problem even to find a common definition that applies to them all. (As a working definition, we suggest the following: reverence for the sacred, expressed in symbols.) Finally, individual religions often have no fixed essence by which they could be defined. Most of the great religions are divided into sects, separated over issues that are often subtle, complicated, and difficult for an outsider to appreciate. Moreover, they change slowly but profoundly over the course of the centuries, like huge amoebas, extending pseudopods in various directions, sliding into some and pulling others back as they respond to various inspirations and historical encounters.

We do not therefore in these few pages undertake a general survey of world religions. Our intention is only to indicate some striking characteristics of the major non-Christian religions that will give perspective to our study of Christianity. We will try especially to point out those factors that seem to be roots from which a given tradition draws its initial dynamism; hence we will tend to focus on the early, or classic, phases, ignoring later developments.[1]

GEOGRAPHY OF WORLD RELIGIONS

1

CHRISTIAN

MUSLIM

HINDU

BUDDHIST

CHINESE
(Buddhist, Taoist, Confucian)

JAPANESE
(Buddhist, Shintoist)

LOCAL

This map, based on *The Times Atlas of the World*, gives only a gross indication of the dominant religions in the various parts of the world. Minorities can be found nearly everywhere, but to take account of them would make the map unreadably complex.

1
Christianity amid the world religions

The only generally acknowledged "world religions" besides Christianity are Islam, Hinduism, Buddhism, Confucianism, and Taoism. Even these tend to be located mainly in limited parts of the world (see Figure 1). Christianity is found chiefly in Europe and the Americas; Islam is centered in the Arab lands of the Middle East, from where it stretches west across North Africa and east to Indonesia. Hinduism is confined almost entirely to India; Confucianism and Taoism to China. Buddhism, which originated in India, has spread northward as far as Japan, and throughout Southeast Asia, while largely disappearing from India itself. Thus, even among these major religions, only Buddhism, Islam, and Christianity deserve to be called international.

So far as numbers are concerned, Christianity is by far the greatest, embracing approximately one fourth of the world population. This may surprise anyone conscious of the enormous populations of China and India; but the Chinese are divided in their religious allegiances, and neither the Chinese nor the Hindu religions have spread much beyond the land of their origin. Islam (a close cousin to Christianity) is second with about eight hundred sixty million adherents. Then follow the Asian religions as indicated in the chart below (Figure 2).

Besides the above religious families, there are tribal religions, found today mainly among the primitive peoples of Africa and Asia, and the Indians of North and South America. While few of them have attained any great numbers, and together they comprise less than two percent of the world population, they represent an important phase in the history of religions. Nature worship generally plays a large role in them; and as it also lies in the background of all of the great religions, it will be instructive to begin with it.[1]

NATURE WORSHIP

By nature worship, we mean veneration of the powers of nature. This can occur in an endless variety of ways. For example, the sun or the moon may be regarded as gods. Spirits dwelling in sacred mountains, rivers, trees, or rocks may be venerated or dreaded. A sacred animal such as the cow may be believed to stand in mysterious affinity with man. There may be deities that control the winds and the weather or give fertility to the crops. The great rhythms of nature, particularly those affecting humanity, such as the arrival of spring or the time of sowing and reaping, may be celebrated by religious festivals.

A relic of ancient nature religions still exists in our calendar week. The seven-day week (which was in use in the Near East before the Hebrews adopted it) probably originated from the fact that there are seven "movable stars" — the sun, moon, and five planets visible to the naked eye. To each of these heavenly bodies, regarded as a deity, a

day of the week was dedicated. English names of the days derive from the Saxon deities, sun, moon, Tiw, Wodin, Thor, Frigg, and Saetern. The last five correspond to the Roman gods, Mars, Mercury, Jupiter, Venus, and Saturn.

The category "nature religions" has been abandoned by many scholars in favor of "tribal" or "local" religions. However, it is not our purpose here to establish a category but to reflect on the implications of this fundamental dimension of religion, which is the veneration of the sacred as encountered in nature.

Nature worship gets visible expression in rituals such as sacrifice, dance, incantations, purifications, and the wearing of sacred garments, masks, amulets, etc. These rituals express man's acknowledgment of the sacred, and bring him into right relationship with it. Associated with the rituals are myths, which are typically stories about the gods, and explain things in our present world by what the gods did in the beginning of time. For example, evils were let loose by Pandora, whose curiosity made her open the box in which they had been confined. The fact that the Egyptians swathed the bodies of the dead in bandages was explained by the myth of Osiris, whose body, dismembered by his enemies, had to be bound back together.

Ritual and myth reappear in nearly all religions. Another very common factor is tradition. People do not ordinarily invent their own religions; they accept (or better, are assimilated into) the religious tradition of their people. Of course this is true of other factors in human culture also; but it is particularly important in the case of religion, which by its very essence is veneration of the sacred. That which has been handed down from of old tends to be looked upon as sacred; and the sacred becomes known to the great body of people not through an original personal experience but through tradition. (The shaman, who has personal experience of the sacred, tends to be an exceptional figure, even in those religions that recognize him.)

• *Ritual, myth, tradition*

These three elements of religion — ritual, myth, and tradition — are closely bound up with one another. Myth is typically an interpretation of the ritual, and ritual the acting out of myth. Both get their authority and power from tradition; and tradition expresses itself in them. In the early days of comparative religion, it was assumed that myth came first, and ritual arose as a way of representing it. Today, many scholars are rather inclined to see ritual as the original element, and myth as an attempt to explain it. This seems plausible, inasmuch as gestures appear to be a more primitive form of expression than words. In any case, the question is largely speculative, since the origins of religion lie in a remote past which we have no way of attaining historically.

Ritual and tradition play a very important role in the Christian religion, and especially in Catholicism. Whether myth also can be assigned a place is a delicate question which we will examine in Chapters 6 and 15.

• *The root of nature worship*

The sophisticated modern viewer is tempted to look with disdain at the crude superstitions, fantastic myths, and obscene rites with which nature worship abounds. Some theorists depict nature worship as the effort of an ignorant, prelogical mind to impose order on the world. Such appraisals are insensitive to the primal aspirations of the human spirit expressed in nature worship. The latter springs from a lively sense of the profound kinship of the human person with nature that helps to situate and so to define the person; it arises also from a deep awareness of the magnificence and goodness of nature that inspires awe. Awe is one of the chief roots of the religious spirit, even in its highest forms; the sense of kinship with nature is one of the main sources of the great moral systems that support the highest civilizations. The most refined religious thinkers have often experienced nature as the "envelope and manifestation" of the divine. Serge Bulgakov describes thus the first step in his conversion from Marxism to Christianity:

> I was twenty-four years old. For a decade I had lived without faith and, after early stormy doubts, a religious emptiness reigned in my soul. One evening we were driving across the southern steppes of Russia, and the strong-scented spring grass was gilded by the rays of a glorious sunset. Far in the distance I saw the blue outlines of the Caucasus. This was my first sight of the mountains. I drank in the light and the air of the steppes. I listened to the revelation of nature. My soul was accustomed to the dull pain of seeing nature as a lifeless desert and of treating its surface beauty as a deceptive mask. Yet, contrary to my intellectual convictions, I could not be reconciled to nature without God.
>
> Suddenly, in that evening hour, my soul was joyfully stirred. I started to wonder what would happen if the cosmos were not a desert and its beauty not a mask or deception — if nature were not death, but life. If he existed, the merciful and loving Father, if nature was the vesture of his love and glory, and if the pious feelings of my childhood, when I used to live in his presence, when I loved him and trembled because I was weak, were true, then the tears and inspiration of my adolescence, the sweetness of my prayers, my innocence and all those emotions which I had rejected and trodden down would be vindicated, and my present outlook with its emptiness and deadness would appear nothing more than blindness and lies, what a transformation it would bring to me!
>
> (A *Bulgakov Anthology*, ed. James Pain and N. Zernov, Philadelphia: Westminster, 1976, p. 10)

• *Shinto*

Today nature worship is confined mostly to primitive tribal religions. However, Shinto, the national religion of Japan, is heavily impregnated with it, which partly accounts for the delicate nature paintings for which the Japanese are famous, transmuting trees and mountains into symbols suggestive of sacred mystery. Moreover, the rich

Religious statistics of the world

It is extremely difficult to get reliable statistics on world religious adherence for many reasons. First, the task is too enormous to be done by any single agency; it is necessary to put together data from various sources, not all of which employ the same methods. Second, many religions have no formal criterion of membership; and in some regions, especially those of Asia, it is common for people to adhere to more than one. Third, outside the Christian world, and to some extent within it, religious bodies generally do not keep account of their numbers; hence only estimates can be made, and these often differ widely. Finally, official government disapproval of religion in the Marxist states has made it difficult to get information on which to base even an estimate. (The Muslim and Orthodox statistics are most affected by this difficulty.)

Figure 2 is based on estimates for the year 1990, compiled by David Barrett, published in *Our Globe and How to Reach It,* by Barrett and T. M. Johnson (Birmingham, Ala.: New Hope, 1990, p. 131). It has been supplemented by statistics, definitions, and methodological explanations given in the WCE.

For the sake of simplicity, Anglicans and Episcopalians are here counted with Protestants; for distinct statistics, see Figure 4, page 50.

Note that "Chinese folk religions," "New Religions," and "tribal religions" do not represent any single religious tradition but are merely categories embracing many particular religions.

The "New Religions" are mostly those that have developed in the Far East (Japan, Korea, China, Vietnam, and Indonesia) since the Second World War. They tend to be syncretistic (see WCE, p. 838).

"Tribal religions" (otherwise known as local religions) are usually confined to a single tribe or people, by contrast with religions open to everyone (WCE, p. 846).

Barrett gives no figure for the Taoists. However, as they used to comprise about ten percent of the "Chinese folk religions" (WCE, p. 231), one may conjecture that they numbered about eighteen million in 1990.

Since Confucianism is not so much a religion as an ethical system that affects all the Chinese religions, and even colors the attitudes of those who profess no religion, no global estimate for it is given by Barrett (WCE, p. 232). The *Encyclopedia Britannica Book of the Year for 1989* estimated some 5.8 million Confucians.

Shintoists are estimated by Barrett at about three million (WCE, p. 24).

THE MAJOR RELIGIONS OF THE WORLD

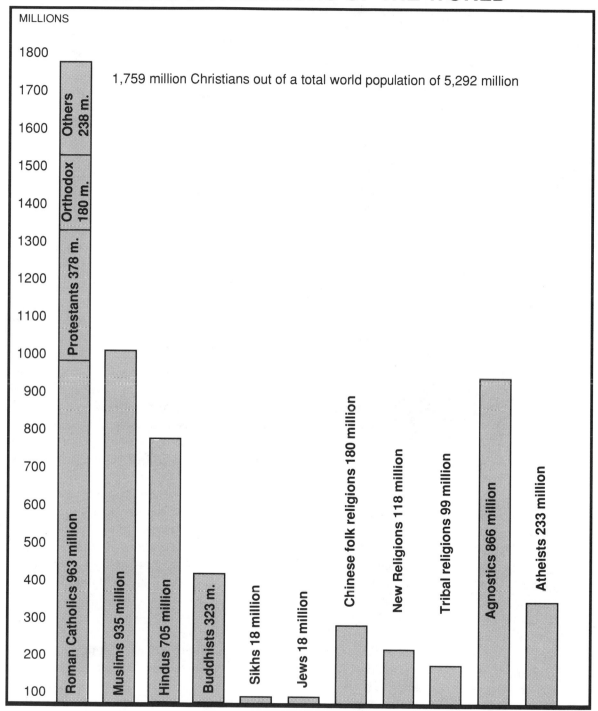

MILLIONS

1,759 million Christians out of a total world population of 5,292 million

Others 238 m.

Orthodox 180 m.

Protestants 378 m.

Roman Catholics 963 million

Muslims 935 million

Hindus 705 million

Buddhists 323 m.

Sikhs 18 million

Jews 18 million

Chinese folk religions 180 million

New Religions 118 million

Tribal religions 99 million

Agnostics 866 million

Atheists 233 million

polytheism which saturates Taoism, Hinduism, and Mahayana Buddhism is a derivative of ancient nature worship. All of the great monotheisms — Israel (this will be explained later on in this chapter), Christianity, and Islam — as well as Brahmanism and Taoism, have come into being in part by rejecting and in part by transcending the nature worship of the cultures in which they originated.

TAOISM

China is the birthplace of two great religions or quasi-religious ways of life: Taoism and Confucianism. They grew up together and in tension with each other. Taoism sprang directly out of nature worship, and can be understood as an effort to discover its profoundest underlying motivation. Confucianism, on the other hand, was driven by the conviction that nature needs to be tamed and governed. The opposition between the two is a classical example of the tension between nature and culture that perennially reappears in human society.

The Taoists had a simple, evident goal: to lengthen human life and enhance its quality. Some thought this was to be accomplished mainly by the kind of food they ate; they believed certain subtle elements in the body were immortal, and could be stored up by the eating of special grains or chemicals (especially cinnabar) or by the use of certain drugs. Others looked to physical exercises and breathing techniques. But the most significant line of Taoists developed a practice of meditation, and it is their theory of the universe which is preeminently called Taoism.

In this last sense, Taoism derives from the legendary teacher Lao Tzu, thought to have lived some six or seven centuries before Christ. Its chief expression is the book *Tao Te Ching*, traditionally attributed to him but probably composed about the fourth century B.C., when this school entered into its first philosophical phase. A second major source is the Book of Chuang Tzu, the latter being a sage who lived in the fourth and third centuries B.C.

• *The way of nature*

Tao means literally a way or road. For the Taoists, it refers in the first instance to the way of nature: the harmonious movement of the heavens, the regular succession of the seasons of the year, the orderly growth of living things, etc. This way is good and perfect and keeps all things in harmony when it is followed instead of being violated and disturbed by wickedness of men or demons. Chuang Tzu goes so far as to regard all art and civilization, including even the cultivated virtues of the Confucians, as a corruption of nature, a violation of the Tao. He looks back to an age of primeval innocence as the ideal from which the human race has fallen:

> At that time, there were no paths on the hills . . . no boats or dams on the lakes. . . . Birds and beasts multiplied into flocks and herds; the grass and trees grew luxuriant and long. In this condition, birds and beasts could be led about without feeling constraint; one could climb up to the nest of the magpie and peep into it.
>
> Yes, in the age of perfect virtue men lived in common with birds and beasts, and were on terms of equality with all creatures, as forming one family; how could they recognize distinctions among themselves between superior men and lesser men? Equally without knowledge, they did not depart from their natural virtue; equally free from desires, they were in a state of pure simplicity. In that state of pure simplicity, the nature of the people was what it ought to be.
>
> (Chuang Tzu, 9, 2; Legge trans. in The *Sacred Books of the East*, ed. Muller, vol. 39, Oxford, 1891; New Delhi reprint, 1968, p. 278; slightly adapted)

The way to obtain a long and harmonious life was to put oneself back in harmony with the way, the Tao, of nature, especially by renouncing busyness and bustle, retiring into solitude, and practicing meditation.

In their efforts to understand nature, Taoist philosophers asserted that all activity comes from the interplay of two opposite energies: Yang and Yin. They are contrasted with each other as light and darkness, heat and cold, action and passivity, male and female. (The Taoist symbol shown above represents the harmonious balance between the two.) Yin, however, came to be recognized as the original source of all things, to which all would eventually return. This female first principle was an all-embracing reality impossible to conceive or to name: a vast, impalpable matter, containing in itself the potential for all that comes into being. The term *Tao* was extended from the "way of nature," which everyone can observe and imitate, to this mysterious primal source from which nature and all beings originate but which is not itself a being, and must rather be called nonbeing. The Tao of nature was held to be only a manifestation of the original and unutterable Tao.

> Before Heaven and Earth existed there was something nebulous:
> Silent, isolated, standing alone, changing not,
> Eternally revolving without fail,
> Worthy to be the Mother of all things.
> I do not know its name and address it as Tao.
> If forced to give it a name, I shall call it "Great."
>   * * *
> The thing that is called Tao is elusive, evasive.
> Evasive, elusive, yet latent in it are forms.
> Elusive, evasive, yet latent in it are objects.
> Dark and dim, yet latent in it is the life-force.
> The life-force being very true, latent in it are evidences.

From the days of old till now its Names (manifested forms) have never ceased,
By which we may view the Father of All Things.
How do I know the shape of the Father of All Things?
Through These!

(The Wisdom of Laotse, trans. Lin Yutang, New York: Random House, 1948, ch. 25, p. 21)

• *Tao and God*

It would be an oversimplification to equate this notion of Tao with the Christian concept of God. Tao was not regarded as personal, nor was worship paid to it (although in modern times, there has been some development in this direction). Nevertheless, it cannot be denied that there is a striking parallel between this one original source from which all things derive, which underlies and pervades them all while transcending the limits of each, and the unique Creator God of the Hebrew and Christian religions.

Taoists believe also in personal deities that emanated from the Tao just as the universe itself did. Moreover, they regard the world as densely populated with spirits, demons, and all sorts of mysterious influences, good and bad. These beliefs derive from popular religions which seem to be distinct from and older than Taoist philosophy, even though they still commingle with it.

CONFUCIANISM

Like Taoism, Confucianism is a way of life, an ethical code, rather than the worship of a god. Unlike Taoism, it did not (at least in its original form and early phases) speculate about the ultimate nature, underlying basis, or original source of reality. It is simply a practical, unsystematic set of guidelines teaching how to live wisely and well. For example, we read in *The Analects of Confucius*:

> The Master said: "Make conscientiousness and sincerity your leading principles. Have no friends inferior to yourself. And when in the wrong, do not hesitate to amend."
>
> (IX, 24; Soothill trans., 2nd ed., New York, 1968)

Confucius, the principal authority for this teaching, did not invent it. In fact, he claimed to be only passing on the "way of the ancients," or "the way of the sages," handed down from an immemorial past. The dates usually assigned to Confucius are 551-479 B.C., making him slightly later than Lao Tzu, the chief of the Taoists. His most important disciple is Mencius, who lived two centuries later: 372?-289? B.C.

Confucius did not systematize his ethics, nor furnish a rationale for his maxims. Neither was he writing lessons in basic, universal righteousness for all people. He wrote for the aristocracy — the kings and nobles — to teach them behavior suitable to a Chinese gentleman. We might be tempted to call him the Emily Post of ancient China; however, he was not concerned just with superficial etiquette but with the behavior that characterizes "man-at-his-best."

• *Filial piety*

Filial piety is regarded by Confucians as the root of a virtuous life.[2] The "ancestor worship" for which the Chinese are famous (although they are by no means unique in this) is an obvious outgrowth of it. But so are all other virtues according to the *Hsiao Ching*:

> He who loves his parents does not dare to hate others. He who reverences his parents does not dare to act contemptuously toward others. By love and reverence being perfectly fulfilled in the service of his parents, his moral influence is shed upon the people and he becomes a pattern for all the border nations. This is the filiality [filial piety] of the Son of Heaven.
> (*The Hsiao Ching*, 2, Makra trans., New York: St. John's University Press, 1961, p. 5)

• *Not theistic*

Although Confucius did not discuss questions about the existence or nature of God, he did take for granted the worship of ancestral spirits and various divinities which were part of Chinese tradition, and gave prescriptions for right conduct in religious ceremonies. Moreover, he and Mencius refer to "the Will of Heaven" as determining that which should take place on earth. From this it can be argued that they believed in a personal God. Nevertheless, this point is vague and obscure, and the moral directives of the tradition were not motivated by obedience to a heavenly ruler, much less to a heavenly father (which, however, would have fitted so well into the framework of filial piety!). Neither did the Confucians promise longevity (like the Taoists) nor a future retribution (like the Hindus). Instead, it was to a sense of propriety (rooted in tradition) and of excellence that they implicitly appealed in summoning "superior men" to do what is becoming. Conversely, bad conduct was not represented as an offense against a divinity but simply as shameful.

In the course of the centuries, Confucius himself gradually became a cult figure; sacrifices were offered to his spirit. After the formation of the Chinese Republic in 1911, his cult languished. The Marxist regime introduced in 1949 by Mao Zedong actively

denigrated Confucius as an aristocrat and an idealist. It remains to be seen whether his spirit has thus been eradicated from the Chinese soul.

HINDUISM

Shinto is a religion, Taoism (at least that aspect we have examined) is perhaps better termed a philosophy, and Confucianism an ethical code. But all three took for granted the goodness of human life, which they sought to preserve and perfect. When we cross the Himalayas from China into India, we meet a very different atmosphere. More than any other part of the world except the Near East, India has been the cradle of great religions, the most important of which are Hinduism and Buddhism. But the classical Indian religions, ever since the sixth century B.C., have been inspired by the goal not of enhancing life but of escaping from it. For example, the sage Maitri sighs:

> In this ill-smelling, unsubstantial body, which is a conglomerate of bone, skin, muscle, marrow, flesh, semen, blood, mucus, tears, rheum, feces, urine, wind, bile and phlegm, what is the good of enjoyment of desires?
>
> In this body which is afflicted with desire, anger, covetousness, delusion, fear, despondency, envy, separation from the desirable, union with the undesirable, hunger, thirst, senility, death, disease, sorrow and the like, what is the good of enjoyment of desires? And we see that this whole world is decaying, as these gnats, mosquitoes and the like, the grass, and the trees that arise and perish. . . .
>
> In this sort of cycle of existence (*samsara*) what is the good of enjoyment of desires, when after a man has fed on them there is seen repeatedly his return here to earth?
>
> Be pleased to deliver me. In this cycle of existence I am like a frog in a waterless well.
>
> Maitri Upanishad, nos. 3-4; cited from *A Sourcebook in Indian Philosophy*, ed. Sarvepali Radhakrishnan and Charles Moore, Princeton, N.J.: Princeton University Press, 1957, pp. 93-94)

As a result of such a mentality, the religion and ethics of India are dominated by the goal of liberation from the evils of this present life and attainment of a state in which there will be no more suffering. The Hindus did not regard suffering as something that could be overcome by such means as improved medicine or a more equitable social order. They considered it endemic to man's situation in this world, so that the solution demanded separation from the world.

• *The true self and reincarnation*

India pullulated with philosophies seeking to explain the enigmas of life, but most of them agreed on two points: that the human being's true self was an inner reality, the soul (*atman*), rather than the total composite of soul and body; and that the death of the body did not mean the end of life but the transmigration of the soul into another body. Few religions have emphasized the primacy of the soul so much as those of India. Their symbol of human existence was a wheel endlessly turning (*samsara*: see the preceding illustration). If one lived a good life, he or she would be reincarnated in a higher form — for example, as a member of a superior caste. If his life had been evil, his reincarnation would take him into an inferior form, perhaps even that of a beast or an insect.

• *Ways to liberation: ritual, duty, asceticism*

The goal of life was not just to ascend higher in the scale of existence but to break out of the endless circle and attain the state called *moksha*, in which the soul was no longer incarnate, and would enjoy perfect serenity. There were different views as to how this could be accomplished. Some expected it to be brought about through performance of *religious rites*. A later view insisted more on performance of one's *duty* (*dharma*); for the

26

Hindus (like the Taoists) believed in a great cosmic order which ruled the activity of nature and of humanity, and even that of the gods. On the social plane, this order was expressed in the "caste system," according to which each person had a fixed place in society, determined by his birth. There were four major classes in Hindu society: priests, nobles, workers, and menials; each was further subdivided into innumerable castes. A person's duty was defined by his caste; and fulfillment or non-fulfillment of duty determined one's subsequent lot. Still another route to liberation was *asceticism*. Hindu ascetics are famous for the harshness with which they treated their bodies, deliberately subjecting themselves to extremes of heat and cold, hunger and thirst. Behind these practices lay the idea that desire for pleasure is what attaches a person to this world and so holds him prisoner in it. Utter detachment and indifference was the ascetic's aim, for thereby would come his liberation.

• *Yoga*

But the most famous way to liberation, and that which is the most original in Hinduism, is the way of *yoga*. The postures and breathing exercises for which yoga is known are only preliminary to meditation; their aim was to free the mind from its subjection to the body. Meditation was what led (through a series of degrees) to complete liberation. For the desires which make a person cling to the world are the result of ignorance about one's true self and about ultimate reality. Meditation is the way to discover the truth, and

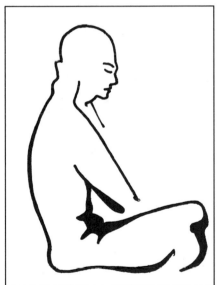

so divest oneself of all desire and attachment. Hindu meditation, however, is not philosophical inquiry or reflection on a doctrine. Whereas Christian meditation typically is rooted in the consideration of a text of Scripture, the meditation expounded by the classical yogi, Patanjali, was a deliberate effort to empty the mind of all definite thoughts, and ultimately of all consciousness of oneself as a distinct being. In other Hindu sects, meditation might consist in concentrating on a deity.

Yoga was based on the belief that the ultimate, underlying reality of all things is one — Brahman; and that the human soul is profoundly identical with Brahman. This is the truth that the yogi sought to realize through his meditation. He tried to rid his mind of all particular images and concepts because it is by these that things are identified with or distinguished from one another. For some schools of thought, the multiplicity of distinct beings in the world is pure illusion — *maya*; others recognized multiplicity as real, and explained that it had arisen out of a primal unity which had taken on various forms. In either case, the yogi's goal was to transcend multiplicity by emptying his mind of all the ideas and images (still more of the feelings of attraction and revulsion) by which he perceived things and related to them. Ultimately, he would lose even the sense of his own distinctness; he either merged into Brahman (according to the earlier view of the Upanishads) or achieved the total isolation of his soul in its eternal and timeless essence (according to the later Samhkya philosophy).

The story is often told of a Hindu monk bayoneted by a British soldier when India was still a British colony. As he began to topple over, the monk murmured serenely, "You too are it" — *it* referring to Brahman. The monk had attained the realization that all things were identical in Brahman, so that there was no real opposition between them, not even between himself and this soldier.

• *Brahman*

The idea of Brahman (if it may improperly be called an idea) is perhaps the summit of Hindu religious and philosophical thought. It is similar to the Chinese Tao, and in view of the diverse intellectual atmospheres in which the two notions arose, this resemblance is all the more striking. Like Tao, Brahman is an elusive notion that must be approached cautiously. The word itself means holy, or sacred; it was thus applied to the sacred scrip-

The sacred syllable OM, used in meditating on Brahman.

tures and rites of Hindu religion. Similarly, the priest who studies the scriptures and performs the rites is known as a brahman. But just as the Chinese sensed that behind the orderly way (*Tao*) of the visible universe there lay an invisible, all-embracing reality which could be called *Tao* in a deeper sense, so the Hindus perceived that scriptures, rites, and priests were sacred only in a derivative sense, by comparison with an absolute reality to which the name *Brahman* applies primarily. There is no simple, firm definition of Brahman in this ultimate sense. Brahman transcends all particular beings, and all definite conceptions of the human mind. Sankara (ninth century A.D.), perhaps the greatest Hindu philosopher, held that Brahman has no parts, no qualities, no limits, and no activity. Eternal and unchanging, permeating all things, it is the only true reality; all else is illusion (*maya*).

The resemblances between this and the Christian idea of God — especially as the latter has been expressed by the great mystics — are striking and profound. However, Brahman was not a creator or ruler of the world. Like Tao, it was often conceived as impersonal. In some views Brahman is the *only* reality, of which all else is an illusory veil or manifestation (pantheism).

• *Hindu gods*

Moreover, the emergence of belief in Brahman did not displace the cult of the gods, of which Hinduism has retained myriads (three hundred sixty-five million, it is sometimes said; one million for each day of the year). By far the most important gods are Shiva and Vishnu, although the former's wife, Durga (or Kali), also claims not a little devotion. Vishnu is thought to have come down to earth from time to time in the form of man or beast to aid suffering mankind. The two most famous of his incarnations, or avatars, are Rama and Krishna. The Hare Krishna movement is named after the latter, who is the main character of the *Bhagavad-Gita*, India's best-loved religious classic. There, in reply to a warrior's perplexity, Krishna gives instruction on how to attain liberation from the world while still fulfilling one's duty.

How the gods relate to Brahman and to one another is a question about which there are too many opinions to relate here. And besides the views sketched above about the relation of the soul to nature and to Brahman, there are numerous other schools of thought. Some very interesting developments led to the recognition of Brahman as a personal being, and to a warm personal devotion to the gods, especially Vishnu, as loving mankind and wanting to be loved by them. For Hinduism is not one doctrine but a variegated family of beliefs, with little that is common among them except the fundamental framework of the soul, Brahman, duty, retribution, reincarnation, and liberation.

BUDDHISM

The main lines of Hinduism were formed during the period 1500-500 B.C., which coincides almost exactly with the time when the Hebrew religion also was taking shape (see Figure 3, page 39). In the course of this development, Hindu thought became more and more philosophical, to a degree attained by few other ancient civilizations.

• *The Buddha*

About the time when the philosophical and ascetical tendencies of Hinduism had reached their peak intensity, there was born in the foothills of Nepal the man destined to

challenge both and modify them profoundly — Siddhartha Gautama, later known as the Buddha (approximately 563-483 B.C.). He tried living as a disciple of two gurus but later reacted against philosophical speculations as fruitless. Next he spent six years as an ascetic. When the rigors of his fasting led to a physical collapse, he recognized that excessive asceticism also fails of its goal. Finally, legend has it, after sitting forty-nine days under a *bodhi* tree in meditation, he experienced a remarkable enlightenment which gave him the essentials of his doctrine. Disciples gathered around him and formed the nucleus of the Buddhist monastic system, which eventually came to be known by the saffron robes and shaven heads of the monks.

These incidents illustrate the outstanding traits of Buddhism. It is basically Hindu, and takes for granted the ideas of duty, retribution, and reincarnation. Even more than Hinduism it insists that desire is the root of suffering, and ignorance the root of desire. It too aims at breaking out of the cycle of endless rebirths by attaining a state which it calls *nirvana*.

• *Nirvana*

Nirvana is impossible to define, and in fact there is little that can be said about it. It does not refer to a life of happiness in the next world, like the Christian heaven. It does not even have the positive sense of a perfect future existence, like the Hindu *moksha*. The Buddha did not believe in the existence of a soul (hence the question perennially addressed to Buddhists, what is it that transmigrates after death?). The Buddha also rejected as useless all philosophical speculation about the nature of ultimate reality. The word *nirvana* means literally extinction (it was used, for example, for the putting out of a flame). We may be tempted to suppose that, applied to human beings, it meant simply the absolute end of existence; however, the Buddha held that it transcended the duality of being and nonbeing. In any case, *nirvana* meant breaking out of *samsara*, that endless cycle of birth and rebirth, and liberation from all the evils of this life, through the extinction of all the desires that chained the person to it. To his disciple, Malunkyaputta, who was concerned with theoretical questions about the soul and the afterlife, the Buddha is said to have replied:

> Bear always in mind what it is that I have not elucidated and what it is that I have elucidated. And what, Malunkyaputta, have I not elucidated? I have not elucidated, Malunkyaputta, that the world is eternal; I have not elucidated that the world is not eternal; I have not elucidated that the world is infinite; I have not elucidated that the world is not infinite; I have not elucidated that the saint exists after death; I have not elucidated that the saint does not exist after death; I have not elucidated that the saint both exists and does not exist after death; I have not elucidated that the saint neither exists nor does not exist after death. And why, Malunkyaputta, have I not elucidated this? Because, Malunkyaputta, this profits not, nor has to do with the fundamentals of religion; therefore I have not elucidated this.
>
> And what, Malunkyaputta, have I elucidated? Misery, Malunkyaputta, have I elucidated; the origin of misery have I elucidated; and the path leading to the cessation of misery have I elucidated. And why, Malunkyaputta, have I elucidated this? Because, Malunkyaputta, this does profit, has to do with the fundamentals of religion, and tends to absence of passion, to knowledge, supreme wisdom and *Nirvana*.
>
> (*Majjhima Nikaya*, Henry C. Warren, *Buddhism in Translations*, Cambridge, Mass.: Harvard University Press, 1922, p. 122)

As a result of its founder's attitude, Buddhism was (at least in its initial thrust) very unphilosophical, confining itself to the practical question of the way for man to live, and resolutely disregarding all metaphysical questions about ultimate reality. It had much more to say about the path to be followed than about the goal to be attained.

• *Right living and meditation*

This path involved right living; and the Buddhist moral precepts coincide largely with those of the Christian world. Anger, lust, pride, the doing of harm to others, even in speech, were all condemned. But this is only the beginning of the path. Enlightenment is what brings a person to the goal. *Buddha* means enlightened one. Siddhartha, who is called The Buddha *par excellence*, is not the only one to whom that title can be given; in fact, the purpose of his instruction is to lead others to an enlightenment similar to his own. Meditation is the chief means to this, for the Buddhists even more than for the Hindus.

Meditation is the principal activity of Buddhist monks. The name *Zen*, given to a Buddhist sect which originated in China, is simply a corruption of *ch'an*, a Chinese word for meditation.

As the text cited above makes clear, the Buddha did not exclude belief in an ultimate reality. He simply put the question aside as insoluble and of no importance. He did believe in various deities but regarded them as of no use to human beings, who can and must attain *nirvana* solely by their own efforts. This attitude of complete self-reliance is one of the most striking traits of the Buddhist outlook in contrast with the Christian dependence on grace.

• *Mahayana Buddhism*

Several centuries after the death of the Buddha, a new type of Buddhism (Mahayana) arose, which ironically deified the Buddha himself. This type, which has spread much farther than the original (Theravada) form of Buddhism, embraces many diverse tendencies. In the more intellectual and critical ones, the historical person, Siddhartha Gautama, is not regarded as a god but simply as a symbol or embodiment of a transcendent, supramundane Buddha, who is eternal, infinite, omniscient, and all-powerful, forever engaged in a perfect act of meditation.

Besides the Buddha, numerous other buddhas and *bodhisattvas* as well as mythological feminine deities arose in the Buddhist pantheon — entities that can be summoned to the aid of the Buddhist struggling with the trials of this life. And besides the worship and invocation of heavenly figures, there came about an immense development of the ideal of *compassion* for all living beings. These changes make Mahayana Buddhism more like Christianity than the austere godless discipline of the Buddha himself. Some scholars wonder if they may not even be due in part to contacts with Christianity, since they took place largely during the first centuries of the Christian era.

ISRAEL

From the Far East and the Middle East, we pass now to the Near East. Three great religions — Israel, Christianity, and Islam — all originated in the rough oblong of largely desert land that was a crossroads between Africa, Asia, and Europe. The three religions compose one family of which Israel was the parent. Two characteristics distinguish these three from the other great religions of the world: monotheism and prophecy, both of which originated in Israel.[3]

• *Monotheism*

Monotheism was never actually attained by the ancient religions of Japan, China, or India, although some of them approached it. Emerging out of polytheistic nature religions, the ideas of Tao and Brahman implied a single, infinite source and ground for all reality; but it was not ordinarily regarded as a personal being (although occasionally, even in early texts, personal aspects were attributed to Brahman).

Moreover, Tao and Brahman did not displace the gods, who continued on in varied and ill-defined relations with them. Finally, Brahmanism was often understood in a pantheistic sense. It was Israel that gave the world belief in the "one God, besides whom there is no other," who is Creator of all else that is.

• *Prophecy*

Prophecy, the second feature of the Near Eastern religions, is less obvious but equally significant. A prophet is one sent by God with a message for the people. There is no such figure in the religions examined above. Their great teachers were men who, by the power of their insight, descried something of the mystery of the absolute; they did not claim to have been sent by a deity. Their doctrines eventually became venerable as representing the tradition of the ancients, not because they had divine authority. Their scriptures came to be revered but not the Word of God. When Moses came down out of the thunder, lightning, and clouds of Mt. Sinai, his face still glowing from his encounter with God, and declared, "Thus says Yahweh," he opened a new chapter in the religious history of mankind.

• *Influence*

In size and culture, the Israelites were an insignificant conglomerate of Semitic tribes, not to be compared with the great peoples of China, India, Persia, Babylon, Egypt, Greece, or Rome. They knew this well, for their own prophets continually reminded them: "It was not because you were more in number than any other people that Yahweh set his love upon you and chose you, for you were the fewest of all peoples; but it is because Yahweh loves you. . ." (Deuteronomy 7:7). Yet in the sphere of religious influence, they have had a greater impact than any other nation. However, since the main features of Israel have been assimilated into Christianity, we will examine them in Chapter 15, and need not elaborate here.

It cannot be emphasized too strongly that Christianity is not a religion totally diverse from that of Israel but a development of it. What distinguishes Christianity is the belief that the promises God made to Israel have been fulfilled in Jesus: that he is the Christ, or Messiah, the king anointed by God to bring about the Kingdom announced by the prophets. For the religion of Israel as held today by those who do not believe that Jesus is the Messiah, we will reserve the term *Judaism*, while using *Israel* for this same religion before it was confronted with the question of Jesus. We will not concern ourselves with the great diversity of belief and practice encompassed by the Judaic tradition today, nor with the fact that the question "Is Jesus the Messiah?" has no relevance for those Jews who no longer await a Messiah. The Jewish population today is still very small in comparison with its influence (see Figure 2, page 21).

ISLAM

The youngest of the major religions, Islam is nevertheless the second largest, surpassed only by Christianity in the number of adherents. This must be due in part to the fact that Christianity and Islam are the only missionary religions among the major religions of the world. Both hold that they have been divinely commissioned to go forth and proclaim the Word of God entrusted to them. Muslims date their origin from 622 A.D., the year in which Muhammad, driven out of the city of Mecca in Arabia, established the theocracy

which later reconquered Mecca and made it the holy city of the huge empire that developed during the following centuries.

Despite its numerical importance, Islam will be treated briefly here because it appears to be largely derivative from Judaism and Christianity (with elements taken also from Zoroastrianism and the tribal religions of Muhammad's Arabia). It starkly highlights the two great features of Western religion: monotheism and prophecy. Its message is simple: "There is no god but the true God, and Muhammad is his prophet." This teaching was vigorously proclaimed in opposition to the animistic and polytheistic cults of the native Arabs. Unflinching witness to the oneness of God is the trait which, more than any other, characterizes Islam in the panorama of world religions. (Muslims assail the Christian belief in the Trinity as a form of tritheism.)

Muslims acknowledge that God has spoken to mankind through many prophets, including Abraham, Moses, and Jesus; but they regard Muhammad as the last and the greatest of them. He has delivered God's final revelation, deposited in the Koran, every word of which has been dictated literally by the Holy Spirit (identified with the angel Gabriel). More than any other religion in the world, Islam is a religion of a book.

• *Islam: submission to Allah*

Submission to the will of God is the dominant attitude of the Muslim religious spirit. The name *Islam* means submission, and *Muslim*, "one who submits." The Koran lays so much stress on the will of God as determining everything which happens in the world that it hardly leaves any room for freedom. One of the questions which most occupied and divided the Muslim theologians of the Middle Ages was whether human freedom could be reconciled with the sovereignty of God. While the answers they gave — some insisting on freedom and others on determinism — were remarkably similar to those of Catholic and Protestant theologians in the sixteenth and seventeenth centuries, the overwhelming sense of God's absolute dominion has imbued the Muslim consciousness with a fatalistic outlook.

About death, judgment, heaven, and hell, the doctrine of the Koran could be regarded as a caricature of Jewish and Christian ideas. Heaven, for example, is represented in very sensual terms. It will be a lofty garden, containing a running fountain, and trees that bear their fruit close to the ground where it can be picked without trouble. The just, clad in garments of fine green silk and brocade, will recline on cushions and couches, attended by youths bearing silver goblets of fine wines and other liquors, of which one can drink as much as he desires. The torments of hell are proportionately vivid and horrifying. The popular imagination seized on these details and elaborated them still further, while a philosophical movement strove to give them a merely figurative interpretation.

CONCLUSION

As we pointed out in the beginning, the foregoing sketches are by no means an adequate presentation of the religions touched upon, nor do they give us grounds for generalizations about the nature of religion. They do, however, illustrate some important factors that help us perceive what is distinctive in Christianity.

• *The chief factors of religion*

From our survey of Asian religions, three factors emerge: (1) *Worship* or *fear* of mysterious, invisible deities, spirits, and demons. Expressed in traditional rituals and myths, this is particularly evident in the ancient tribal religions of India, China, and Japan as well as in modern Shinto, Hinduism, and Mahayana Buddhism. (2) Recognition of an *ultimate reality* underlying the particular beings of the phenomenal world, and the source of them (Tao and Brahman). (3) An *ethic* (prominent in Confucianism and primitive Buddhism but by no means absent from the other religions considered).

When we turn from Asia to the Near East and the Western world, what stands out first of all is that the above three factors are more closely linked together. In Judaism, Islam, and Christianity, ultimate reality is identified with the deity who is worshiped. The ethic is understood as the will of God. Moreover, God — although infinite, unchanging, and eternal — is personal. (The deities worshiped in the nature religions are often personal but not infinite; Tao and Brahman are infinite but not personal.)

• *Prophetic religion: a richer, firmer concept of God*

Because of their belief that God has spoken through prophets, revealing to man the secrets of his inner nature and of his plan for the world, the three great monotheisms possess richer, firmer, and more definite ideas of God than is to be found elsewhere. The myths of tribal and nature religions, although rich in color, tend to be vague, mutually incompatible, and subject to profound alterations in the course of time. Hence it is very difficult to determine exactly what they have to say about the deity. Taoism on the other hand, and to a lesser extent Brahmanism, are extremely laconic about the Ultimate Reality, insisting that it is unutterable. But in Judaism, Islam, and Christianity, God is recognized as infinite, eternal, immutable, all-knowing, and all-powerful, the just and merciful governor of creation. He has destined his creatures for beatitude and directs them to it by his providence. Rather than sitting afar off with placid indifference as they are swept along to their fate, he intervenes effectively to help and deliver them. In the end, he will judge, reward, and punish.

• *Christianity is Jesus Christ*

Christianity is differentiated from other religions above all by the figure of Jesus Christ. No comparable figure can be found elsewhere. Great teachers and personalities — such as Moses, Confucius, the Buddha, and Muhammad — may dominate the cult engendered by them, but these men are only teachers who show the way. None of them ever presumed to declare, as Jesus did, "I am the Way." Jesus is not just a prophet of the Most High; he is God's Son, come among us a man. It is true that the Hindu Vishnu is a deity

34

who appeared on earth and conversed with men. However, Vishnu has had eight or nine full incarnations, to say nothing of innumerable partial ones; whereas in Jesus God has appeared once for all. Moreover, the early incarnations of Vishnu as a Fish, Tortoise, Boar, and Man-lion are manifestly mythical. And if there is any historicity to Rama and Krishna, it can no longer be extracted from the myths and legends. Jesus, however, was definitely a historical person. We know when and where he lived, many of the things he said and did, and the names of some of his relatives and disciples. When Mahayana Buddhism began to deify Buddha, it also disembodied him. That is to say, the earthly, human person was regarded as a relatively unimportant symbol of the transcendent, divine Buddha. But Jesus is not just the earthly figure of a transcendent Christ; Jesus *is* the Christ. His human flesh is not set aside or transcended but adored as the body of God incarnate and partaken sacramentally as the Bread of Life. Belonging to his Church means identification with his body; eternal life is obtained by sharing in his resurrection through association with his death. We can perfectly well say that Christianity *is* Jesus Christ; one could never say that Buddhism is Siddhartha nor that Islam is Muhammad.

Consequently, besides the richness and firmness of prophetic religion, Christianity is characterized by familiarity with God. Jesus is God come among us under the sign of brotherhood; he walked our ways, conversing with those who came to him. He declared, "He that sees me sees the Father." Hence a kind of intimacy with God characterizes the Christian religion, especially in the case of the saints. And they have found a name for God not given in any other religion: God is love.

2

Catholicism amid the other Christian denominations

Christianity began with one hundred twenty disciples of Jesus. They had no written constitution, no formal protocol, not even an organization, except that the twelve apostles were their leaders, with Peter somehow the chief. As their numbers grew, it became necessary to develop an organization and to codify practices; we see this beginning to happen in the Acts of the Apostles with the appointment of seven (deacons?) to assume some of the apostles' burdens (Acts 6) and with the decision not to impose Old Testament prescriptions on Gentile converts (Acts 15). From Jerusalem, the Church spread by a kind of metastasis, as believers carried the word to other places where new churches sprang up. But all these churches remained in one great communion, one Church, whether they were in Egypt, Syria, Asia Minor, Greece, or Rome.

As this process went forward, disagreements also began to occur, the earliest we know of being a tension between the Greek-speaking and the Aramaic-speaking members of the primitive community in Jerusalem (Acts 6:1). Generally the differences were resolved, often by the intervention of those who held authority in the Church (for example, St. Paul in 1 Corinthians 3). But sometimes groups split off and formed separate communities.

Today there are over twenty thousand distinct Christian denominations. While the Catholic Church is the chief concern of this book, for it to be understood adequately, it has to be situated in relation to the other Christian bodies. Obviously these cannot be examined in detail but only in broad, general outline.

The most important occasions of division among Christians have been developments that have taken place in the course of the Church's growth. Christianity has been evolving from the very outset. Jesus did not set down a fixed and detailed blueprint which his disciples could simply follow faithfully; he gave pregnant indications, the implications of which would become manifest only gradually in the course of ages. He planted a tiny seed which has developed into a great tree, and still continues to grow.

Moreover, he taught in terms of Hebrew culture ("Two men went up to the Temple to pray; one was a pharisee and one a publican. . ."). As Christianity spread to the Gentiles, it became necessary to discriminate between what was essential and what was a Hebrew accident that could be discarded. Furthermore, each new civilization posed new problems for which a Christian solution had to be elaborated. Today, for example, we are struggling to formulate a Christian position on nuclear armaments. Finally, Jesus taught mostly in parables and practical examples that illustrated how to live but did not give a theoretical doctrine. Thus he summoned his disciples to put their faith in him, which they did, calling him Lord, Son of God, etc. But the question eventually arose: What exactly is the nature of his lordship? In what sense is he God's Son? The inquisitive character of the human mind made it inevitable that such questions be faced.

Another source of division lies in what is often called the pluralism of early Christianity. The Gospel of John depicts Jesus differently from the Synoptic Gospels. For example, in John, he speaks much about himself, whereas in the Synoptics he preaches almost exclusively about the Kingdom. Likewise St. Paul's doctrine that "a person is justified by faith apart from works of the law" (Romans 3:28, NABr) stands in tension with St. James's intransigent insistence that "a man is justified by what he does and not by faith alone" (2:24). But these are not contradictory versions of Christianity; they are simply the antitheses and incommensurabilities that inevitably result from efforts to formulate a doctrine so rich that it transcends any single conceptual expression. Rather than refuting the essential unity of Christian doctrine, they preserve it from narrowness by counterbalancing one another, as the wisdom of the Church has acknowledged in recognizing all of these various documents as inspired Scripture.

• *"Catholic"*

In answering such questions and in responding to new challenges, Christianity has been like an explosion in slow motion. Its energy comes from Jesus, but time has been necessary for it to take shape and define itself. Developments, however, often led to disagreement and the splintering off of particular sects from the great communion in which all the local churches were originally united. The term *Catholic Church* came into use to designate the body of those who remained in the original communion, and in continuity with the inherited traditions; those who separated from this unity were called heretics or schismatics.[1]

• *"Roman Catholic"*

The later term, *Roman Catholic*, derives from the fact that St. Peter, the chief of the apostles, established himself eventually in Rome. His successors, the bishops of Rome, came to be acknowledged as heirs to his authority over the universal Church. Occasionally at first, but more and more regularly as the pattern became established, appeal was made to them to settle disagreements that had arisen in other parts of the Church. Likewise the popes themselves began to take more initiative and intervene more actively in the affairs of the Church at large. This was not always welcomed by the local churches, and resulted in some of the most intractable separations. The term *Roman Catholic* has come to designate those who acknowledge the Pope, or Bishop of Rome, as having pastoral authority over the universal Church.

• *Catholic, Protestant, Orthodox*

Most of the groups that separated from the Church have disappeared or have left relatively small traces (for example, the Monophysites and Nestorians). But two separations have resulted in profound and lasting divisions in Christendom: that of the Orthodox in the eleventh century and that of the Protestants in the sixteenth (see Figure 3, page 39).

In order to show how Catholicism relates to these other denominations, it is necessary to point out some of the painful disagreements, and to make comparisons and contrasts. This will be done as objectively and irenically as possible, not with the intention of putting any belief in a bad light.

THE ORTHODOX

The separation of the Orthodox was preceded by several centuries in which different usages developed in Eastern churches (led by the Greeks) and the Western (Latin) church: different ways of calculating the date of Easter; the use of unleavened bread in the Eucharist by the Latins, whereas the Greeks used leavened bread, etc. These had little doctrinal importance but acted as irritants between Christians who did not always understand why the others were different. The most serious doctrinal debate came from a development in Trinitarian theology, which led the Latins to declare that the Holy Spirit arises from the Father and the Son *("Filioque")*, whereas the Greeks held that he arose from the Father simply. The development of Constantinople as a "new Rome," personal jealousies, misunderstandings, and difficulties of communication added to the complex of factors which finally led to separation between the "Orthodox" churches and the Catholic Church in 1054.

Orthodox and Oriental rite churches

Having rejected the jurisdiction of the Bishop of Rome, the Orthodox do not have any central authority to unite them in a single organization. They are divided into national churches: Russian, Rumanian, Bulgarian, Greek, etc. It is hard to say precisely how many distinct churches there are, because subordinate branches have taken on more or less independence from the original stem; some count fourteen distinct churches, others would say twenty-one. The largest Orthodox church is that of Russia (Moscow Patriarchate); Eliade's *Encyclopedia of Religion* (1987) estimates that about fifty million people are affiliated with it publicly and "untold others in secret."

Some sections of these Eastern churches, however, have returned to union with the Catholic Church while retaining their ancient rituals, languages, and customs. They belong to the Roman Catholic Church but not to the Roman rite. Hence the term *Roman* is usually avoided in references to them; instead, they are called, "Greek Catholics," "Ukrainian Catholics," etc.

• *Disagreement about the papacy*

Apart from the question about the Holy Spirit, the Orthodox hold by and large the same beliefs as Roman Catholics. Their fundamental disagreement is not over doctrine but over authority: whether the Bishop of Rome has authority over the other bishops

3
THE SPLINTERING OF CHRISTENDOM

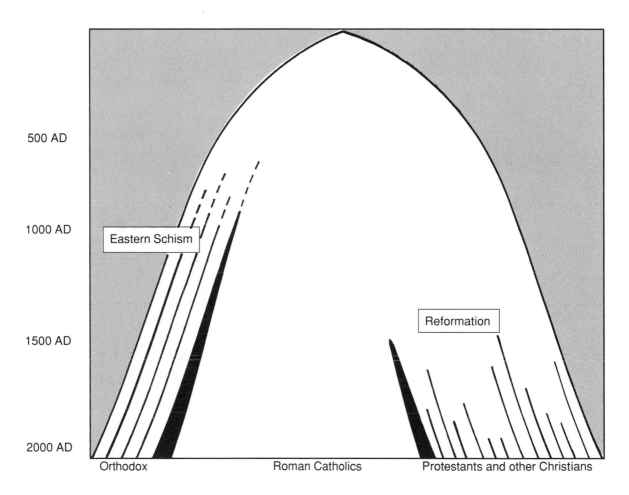

500 AD

1000 AD

Eastern Schism

Reformation

1500 AD

2000 AD

Orthodox   Roman Catholics   Protestants and other Christians

Down through the ages, many groups have separated from the one Church founded by Jesus. Many of them have disappeared; others are too small to be represented on this diagram.

The two main divisions, the Eastern Schism and the Protestant Reformation, are shown, with proportional space allotted to each. Additional lines are added to suggest the further subdivisions to be found in both the Orthodox and Protestant world but without any attempt to represent particular factions.

The distinctions between Orthodox churches go back of course to the earliest days of Christianity; however, at that time, they were all in communion with Rome and with one another. There is no way this graph can represent such nuances.

For more details, one may consult the diagrams given by David Barrett in the WCE and throughout many of his subsequent studies. However, in order to make space for the details, he has had to distort the proportions.

and their churches (dioceses). The Orthodox commonly admit that he has a certain primacy of honor but not of jurisdiction.

Several attempts were made during the late Middle Ages to heal the rift between Catholics and Orthodox, but all of them failed. In modern times, a new effort was initiated by Pope John XXIII. Its most dramatic moment came in 1964 when Pope Paul VI met Athenagoras, Patriarch of Constantinople, in Jerusalem, the Holy City revered by both of them. They embraced each other and withdrew the mutual excommunications which had stood between Pope and Patriarch ever since 1054. Theological discussions in view of restoring complete communion between Catholics and Orthodox are now being carried on very actively.

Because of their denial of papal authority, the Orthodox also object to the two modern dogmas defined by the popes: the Immaculate Conception and the Assumption. Ironically, however, it was in the East that these beliefs first developed, and from the East that the Latin West derived them.

PROTESTANTISM

Protestantism is not a single church, religion, or creed but a broad movement embracing numerous divergent tendencies. Its unity comes largely from reaction to the historical developments alluded to above. A rich body of customs, ritual, teaching, and structures had grown up, by which Christians sought to imprint the Gospel on their daily lives, and to draw out all its hidden potential. There were sacraments and sacramentals, vows, pilgrimages, penances, indulgences, and invocations of the saints, which, taken all together, represented an effort of the Church to draw upon all the resources of human nature in mediating the grace of Christ. Among them no doubt were exaggerations and excrescences calling for critical review and purification. Abuses also had insinuated themselves into Church life, particularly during that long, dark period when the appointment of bishops was largely controlled by lay princes.

• *The Reformation*

During the late Middle Ages, many people clamored for a reform, and many noteworthy reforms were in fact achieved — for example, by the Cluniac monasteries and the Clerks Regular as well as the Carthusian, Cistercian, Franciscan, and Dominican orders. But in a reality as human as the Church, the work of reform and renewal are never finished; and during the fourteenth and fifteenth centuries, complaints about the worldliness and corruption of the clergy became more and more frequent and bitter. Not all of the demands for reform need be regarded as the expression of wounded Christian piety; arrogance, bitterness, fanaticism, and hostility toward authority were at work then as much as now. Out of this tangle of motives, which we will not try to evaluate further, there accumulated a pent-up frustration which combined with extraneous factors, such as German and English nationalism, to produce that violent rupture known as the Reformation.

• *Challenge to tradition*

The intention of the Reformers was to restore Christianity to its primeval purity by the elimination of accretions and deformations. None of them wanted to found a new

Church; neither Luther nor any of the other leaders of the Reform could countenance the idea of several Christian churches not in communion with one another. But while some of the "reforms" demanded were justified and would eventually be accepted by the Catholic Church, others involved rejection of doctrines, rites, and principles of government to which the Church was committed. Taken as a whole, the stance of the Reformers amounted to a rejection of the actual Church of that day; they led their followers out of it into new "churches," which claimed identity with the primitive Church but lacked continuity with the Church which had come down through history.

The degree of rupture varied considerably among the four main branches of the Reformation. The Anglicans, at least in the beginning, were the most moderate. They cherished their religious traditions and objected only to the authority of the Pope. Luther tolerated established traditions so long as they did not seem to conflict with Scripture. Calvin was more severe in pruning away whatever was not apparently scriptural. The "Radical Reformers," particularly the Anabaptists and Puritans, sought rigorously to extirpate from Christendom whatever in their eyes could not be justified scripturally.

• *Scripture and Tradition*

In attempting to purify the Church, the Protestants in general adopted the principle that Scripture alone is the rule of faith. That is to say that whatever could not be justified on the basis of Scripture was either to be eliminated from religious doctrine and practice or, at most, tolerated as a human embellishment, lacking any binding authority. The Catholic Church, on the other hand, honored the beliefs and practices that had won acceptance throughout the Christian world ("Sacred Tradition") as authentic witnesses to divine

Scripture alone.

revelation, and precious aids to the interpretation of the Gospel. *Sacred Tradition* refers to the tradition of *the Church as such* and is to be distinguished from mere local or human traditions. Determining whether a given point belongs properly to Sacred Tradition or merely to human traditions within Christendom is often quite difficult, as witness the current debate about the ordination of women. But insofar as it can be recognized, Sacred Tradition is honored by the Church as an expression of divine revelation comparable to Scripture itself.[2] Its authority is not merely human but comes from the Holy Spirit who lives in the Christian community, gently pressuring the minds of the faithful to conform to the mind of Christ.

An important example is the notion of priesthood. In the New Testament, the pastors of the Church are not spoken of as priests but as elders and bishops; likewise the Eucharist is not called a sacrifice. In the course of the first few centuries, however, the sacrificial character of the Eucharist came to be recognized. By the same token, the bishops and elders who offered it began to be called priests, and the table on which it was celebrated, an altar. In the view of the Church, this represented an authentic insight into the nature of the Eucharist and the clerical office. For the Protestants, however, it was a corruption to be eliminated. (This is why, still today, the prevailing Protestant usage calls clergymen ministers but not priests.)

The principle that Scripture alone should be the rule of faith sounded simple and clear, but in practice it did not prove to be so, since there was not always agreement about the meaning of the biblical text. In Catholic practice, when disagreements arose, there were two major resources for settling them (besides theological discussion, which of course always had an important role). One was to look to the tradition of the Church, especially the teaching of the Fathers, such as St. Augustine, St. Gregory, and St. John Chrysostom. These were given great weight in determining the sense of the scriptural teaching. Secondly, the bishops of the Church were regarded as authorized by Jesus Christ to make decisions binding on all the faithful. Thus, when questions arose in the early Church about whether Jesus was truly God and truly man, all the bishops met together in council and settled the matter (see Chapter 18).

• *Divisions*

With the emergence of the view that Scripture alone has authority in questions of faith, the traditions of the Church ceased to have any great significance, and the pastors lost their authority to make decisions binding on the faithful. When disagreements arose, there was no way to settle them except by argument; and as arguments proved very ineffectual in bringing about agreement, Protestantism inevitably became divided into a multiplicity of denominations. From the beginning there were four major Reform movements: Anabaptist, Lutheran (evangelical), Calvinist (Reformed or Presbyterian), and Anglican.[3] Later splits occurred within each of these groups, especially when they spread to the New World. As a result, there are thousands of Protestant denominations today, to say nothing of countless local communities.[4]

• *The nature of the Church*

Thus the question about how disagreements among Christians are to be resolved leads to a question about the nature of the Church itself. This seems to be the most profound and lasting issue raised by the Reformation. In broad terms, it can be said that Catholics see the Church primarily as the work of Christ, and therefore stress its sacredness and sacramentality. Protestants see the Church more as a human work — a gathering of Christ's followers — and so tend to stress its frailties and sinfulness. Thus Catholics regard bishops as representatives of Christ, endowed with authority by him. Protestants typically view their ministers as fellow Christians devoted to a religious ministry but not qualified for it by any special sacredness or authority other than what they acquire by their natural talents and education. As a consequence of these differences, Catholic piety tends to be integrated into the Church community, whereas Protestant piety is more individualistic. (But these generalizations require many qualifications when applied to particular times, places, and denominations!)

• *Grace central for Luther*

In Luther's view, the principal issue was the doctrine of grace. It is the central teaching of the New Testament that everyone needs the grace of God to be saved; no one can achieve salvation by his or her own efforts. But how human efforts relate to the grace of

God is the point on which Luther took his stand against the Church. In Catholic thought, human beings have a responsibility to prepare for grace and cooperate with it. This means,  for example, repenting for past sins, striving to amend our lives, and doing the good works to which God summons us. We cannot live a good life without the grace of God, but by his grace we can, even though imperfectly. In the end, we will be judged according to how we have lived. As for the slight sins, which no one can avoid completely, we can atone for them by penance and good works, and those not atoned for will be purified away in purgatory before we enter into God's presence.

What Luther objected to above all in this teaching was the principle that we will be judged according to how we have lived. After years of anguish from fear of eternal damnation, he secured peace of mind in the idea, which he claimed to be that of St. Paul, that salvation does not depend on how we live but is simply the gift of God's grace, pardoning all those who believe in Jesus Christ:

> Christian righteousness consisteth in two things; that is to say, in faith of the heart, and in God's imputation. . . . Because of (my) faith in Christ, God seeth not my doubting of his good will towards me, my distrust, heaviness of spirit, and other sins which are yet in me. But because I am covered under the shadow of Christ's wings, as is the chicken under the wing of the hen, and dwell without all fear under that most ample and large heaven of the forgiveness of sins, which is spread over me, God covereth and pardoneth the remnant of sin in me: that is to say, because of that faith wherewith I began to lay hold upon Christ, he accepteth my imperfect righteousness even for perfect righteousness, and counteth my sin for no sin, which notwithstanding is sin indeed.
>
> . . .God winketh at the remnants of sin yet sticking in our flesh, and so covereth them, as if they were no sin.
>
> (*Commentary on Galatians*, ed. Watson, London: J. Clarke, 1953, pp. 223-226)

It should be noted that grace itself did not mean the same thing for Luther as for Catholics. For the latter, it was an action of God — healing, sanctifying, and helping fallen man. For Luther it was simply a divine decree forgiving the sinfulness that nevertheless remained. In other words, where Catholics saw grace bringing about a transformation that really (although imperfectly) delivers a person from his sinfulness, Luther saw it as a kind of veil, covering over the sin and assuring us that God no longer takes it into account. God declares man to be good ("just" in the language of St. Paul) in spite of the fact that he is really wicked. This explains the crucial function of faith for Luther: The sinner has to believe that he has been "justified" by the grace of God even though he can see that he is still really evil. Faith is thus the act whereby one accepts the gracious decree that declares him just. Hence Luther's motto, "Justification by faith alone." This means that what makes human beings just in the eyes of God is not the good life they lead but simply their faith in his grace.[5]

Luther did not deny that we ought to live a good life, to do "good works." He affirmed that anyone who really has faith will do so spontaneously out of love for God (even though his abiding sinfulness will continue to lead to evil deeds also). Luther accused Catholics of doing good out of a selfish desire to avoid hell and attain happiness, rather than out of love. Catholic theologians would agree that love of God is the highest motive of a good life; but few humans are capable of acting solely for that motive. If the lesser motive of saving our souls sustains our efforts, God does not condemn us for that; in fact, it is he himself who admonishes us that, as we have done to others, so it will be done to us.

Luther's position rejected the Catholic understanding of nature and grace. Where the Church viewed nature as essentially good, even though flawed by sin, Luther saw human nature as "totally corrupted" by sin. And where the Church saw grace as healing sin and elevating a person to a state of real holiness, Luther saw it as God's willingness to make no account of the sinfulness that remains.

An important corollary of Luther's position is the incapacity of human reason to deal with religious truth. It is (as Luther freely agreed) contrary to reason for one who knows himself to be a sinner to believe that he is just, or righteous, by grace. But, Luther affirmed, it is precisely the function of faith to believe doctrines that are contrary to reason. Reason has to be "sacrificed on the altar of faith." In the general corruption of human nature brought about by original sin, reason itself had been spoiled, at least in regard to its ability to apprehend religious truth. Catholic theology, on the contrary, has always maintained that the doctrines of faith, though they may transcend human reason, do not properly contradict it.[6]

• *Protestant and Catholic antitheses*

There were many other Protestant themes manifested in different degrees in the various denominations. The profound motive unifying them would seem to be a determination to give full credit to the grace of God that is offered through his Son and proclaimed in his word. But it was not this motive itself that divided Protestants from Catholics; rather, it was the *exclusive* way in which the former affirmed *grace, Christ,* and *Scripture.* The Protestants held *Scripture alone* as the Word of God, whereas Catholics held that God reveals himself also in *Sacred Tradition.* Thus the Protestants affirmed that the sinner is justified by *grace alone* or by *faith alone* (according as you refer to God's part or man's part); Catholics responded that *nature* must cooperate with grace, and that *good works* are not merely the expression of faith but are intrinsically involved in the work of justification. The Protestants saw salvation as accomplished by *Christ alone;* Catholics maintained that Christ had associated the entire Church — in particular, its *sacraments, pastors,* and *saints* — with himself in the work of salvation. *Alone* is the note that echoes throughout Protestant theology: God and his action are exalted in sacred solitude. "Glory to God alone" was the Protestant motto. *Together* with could be taken as the rejoinder of Catholic theology, which sees all of creation as touched by God's glory and enlisted in the preparation of his Kingdom. The difference between these two men-

Protestant and Catholic architecture

Some of the contrasts between Protestantism and Catholicism become palpable in church architecture, especially as it developed in the post-Reformation period. Catholic churches are rich with the deposits of an ancient tradition; Protestant churches, having eliminated much of that tradition, tend to be much simpler.

There are two chief areas of contrast. First, Protestant churches, especially those of the "reformed" type (for example, Presbyterian and Baptist), are conceived essentially as places for the congregation to listen to the Word of God. Hence they tend to have a single focal point: the pulpit. (Lutheran, Anglican, and Episcopalian churches, in addition to the pulpit, may also emphasize the Communion table, or altar.)

Catholic churches have three focal points: the altar, the tabernacle, and the pulpit. The altar is principal. The tabernacle, where Jesus in the Blessed Sacrament can be adored at any moment of the day, is likewise of major importance. (From about the thirteenth century onward, the tabernacle was usually placed on the altar, but since Vatican II it has been given a separate location.) The pulpit also used to be prominent and ornate, although this is less the case today, partly because microphones make a high, central platform unnecessary; also perhaps because of a growing preference for a more informal style of preaching.

Second, the walls and windows of Catholic churches tend to be enriched with sacred images. Besides the crucifix, which is primary, there are saints, angels, and incidents out of sacred history (particularly the Stations of the Cross). The images may be in the form of statues, mosaics, paintings, or stained-glass windows. (Confessionals add further to the variety of decor.) Protestants have almost none of this because they reject both the veneration and the use of "graven images."

Catholic churches have traditionally been rich in religious decor, and Protestant churches comparatively simple and stark. This contrast is illustrated by the two extreme examples pictured on the following pages, both built in the mid-eighteenth century. The majority of churches, whether Protestant or Catholic, would no doubt fall between these two extremes. Today, moreover, the differences are diminishing. Catholic churches are being simplified, especially by a drastic reduction of paintings and statues. Some Protestants, on the other hand, are giving increased importance to the altar and are modestly adopting sacred images.

Ottobeuren (1736-1766) ■ Belonging to one of the great Benedictine abbeys of Germany, this chapel is one of the finest productions of the Baroque period. Designed by Peter C. Vogt, it was constructed from 1737 to 1753, decorated from 1757 onward, and dedicated in 1766. — Photo courtesy of the Conway Library, Courtauld Institute of Art, London

King's Chapel in Boston (1749-1754) ■ Although constructed for an Anglican congregation, it is more typically Puritan (hence Protestant) in style. The busts honor early ministers of the church, not saints to be venerated. The tablets on the rear wall, inscribed with the Ten Commandments, the Our Father, and the Apostles' Creed, fix the parameters, so to speak, for the sermon. A stained-glass window, representing Jesus Christ, is hidden by the shutters over the window. Incidentally, it was in this chapel that American Unitarianism was born. — Photo by Leslie Larson, King's Chapel Archives, Boston talities can be seen in the contrast between the porticoes of later Gothic cathedrals or the interiors of baroque churches, with their exuberant armies of angels, saints, and struggling humans, and the stark Puritan meeting houses in which nothing but a lectern for the Bible emerges over the seats of the assembly (preceding photographs).

• *Catholicism, Protestantism, and world religions*

From these contrasts it can readily be seen that Catholicism is in many ways more congenial to the non-Christian religions of the world (except possibly Buddhism) than Protestantism is. The positive appreciation of human nature and of tradition, the rich use of symbols, sacramentals, and ritual, veneration of the saints, and the acceptance of the role of reason, which characterize Catholicism, harmonize with elements found in most religions and facilitate the transition from paganism to Christianity. They make possible a significant degree of "inculturation," that is, the adoption of traditional non-Christian religious expressions, into a Christian mentality. But to Protestant eyes, this makes the Catholic Church guilty of a kind of covert paganism. Classical Protestantism requires a much harsher rejection of the previous religious practices of its converts. In the Catholic perspective, nature is the subject of grace, and tradition the connatural educator of the human spirit, especially in the realms of religion and morality. Reason is the power to discern the hand of God. In classical Protestantism, nature is irredeemably spoiled by original sin, tradition is deposed as the normal educator, and reason's power to discover truth about God is denied. In most Protestant denominations today, these implications have not been expressly articulated nor carried to their ultimate conclusion; and they have been modified by other currents. Nevertheless, more or less universally operative as tendencies, they have marked the Protestant missionary effort.

THE UNIQUENESS OF CATHOLICISM

Our sketch of the relation of Christianity to the other religions and of Catholicism to the other Christian denominations can be summed up in terms of four main beliefs:

Belief in a personal God, distinct from the world, who has spoken to mankind through the prophets. This characterizes Christianity, Judaism, and Islam in contrast with the other world religions.

Belief in Jesus as the unique Mediator who relates man to God. This distinguishes Christianity from Islam and Judaism.

Belief that grace elevates nature but calls for its cooperation distinguishes Catholics and Orthodox from Protestants.

Belief that the concrete, historical Church shepherded by Peter's successor, the Bishop of Rome, is the work of Christ through his Spirit. This distinguishes Catholics from the Orthodox as well as from all other Christians.

Such doctrinal comparisons, however, need to be supplemented by a consideration of the unique coherence and unity of Catholicism as a religious body. Catholicism is not just an intellectual position, it is a Church, that is, a society united by a definite structure of doctrine, discipline, and government. It possesses a coherence not paralleled in any other religious tradition. Hinduism, for example, embraces so many varieties of belief, ritual, and ethics, all of which are in a constant evolution, that it defies summary. Buddhism, next to Christianity, has the best claim to being a world religion. But it has undergone such profound transformations in passing from the teachings of Buddha through Mahayana Buddhism to Japanese Zen that the bond tying the end to the beginning is very slender. Among the Muslims, there is fierce hostility between the Sunni and the Shi'ites, and there are various minor sects such as the Druzes; moreover, the essential creed of Islam is so brief, there is abundant room for variation in personal beliefs.

In the Protestant sphere, variations are so great that many deny that the term *Protestant* has any theological unity. Even within particular denominations, the divisions are deeper than is usually recognized. Thus the distance between "high church" Episcopalians and "evangelical" Episcopalians is greater than that between many diverse denominations. When Protestantism was transplanted to the New World, denominations began to proliferate. The fact that congregations had originated in various European countries and spoke different languages led to the formation of different churches within the same denomination. Doctrinal differences led to other splits, and the debate over slavery divided many denominations into northern and southern churches, which long remained separated from each other. Finally, new denominations arose, such as the Seventh Day Adventists, the Christian Scientists, and numerous forms of Pentecostals. On the other hand, there have been movements of reunion. In 1983, the northern and southern Presbyterians joined together again. In 1987, the "American Lutheran Church," the "Lutheran Church in America," and the "American Evangelical Lutheran Church" merged as the Evangelical Lutheran Church in America. It remains to be seen how durable these unions will be. Also not all Lutherans entered into their great union; the Missouri Synod does not even allow intercommunion with some of the other Lutheran bodies. Finally, Africa, in the last few decades, has given birth to many new sects that are hybrids of Christianity and native religions.

Among the Orthodox churches, the unity of doctrine and liturgy is much greater. Nevertheless, jurisdictional-territorial divisions are so sharp that it has never been possible to hold a Pan-Orthodox Synod. (There is hope, however, that the efforts to this end, which have been carried on ever since the First World War, may yet be fruitful.)

• *Catholic unity*

In the Catholic Church, there are of course differences of opinion about many topics. Nevertheless, there is a definite core of doctrine, clearly and firmly defined over the course of the centuries, which can unquestionably be pointed out as Catholic. Individual members may disagree with one point or another, and reinterpretations of the traditional beliefs are proposed from time to time. (We are living today in just such a time!) However, the overwhelming majority of Catholics in the world share a unity of belief more definite, comprehensive, and firm than can be found in any other major religious tradition. The famous debates between different schools of theology such as the Thomists and the Scotists or the Banezians and the Molinists have to do with *theological interpretations* of the same basic dogmas on which they all agree.

4
THE MAJOR CHRISTIAN CONFESSIONS (1990)

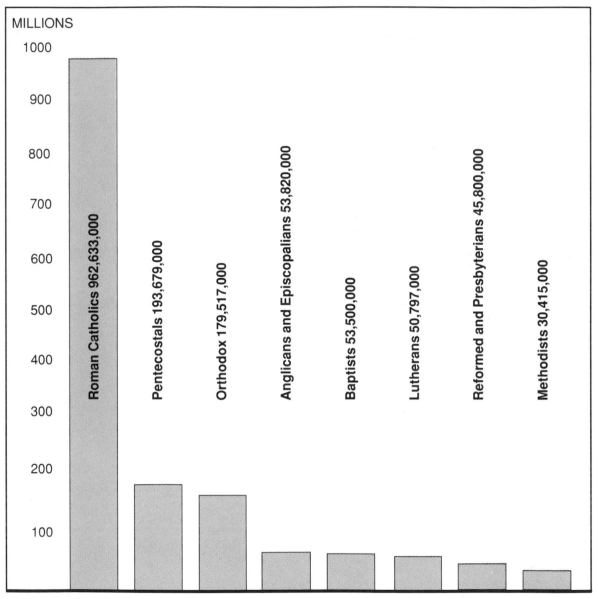

And while Catholic doctrine has evolved enormously in the course of history, from the earliest confession of faith, "Jesus is Lord," to the lengthy documents of Vatican II, it has maintained continuity and coherence. Each new doctrine has arisen out of the old, as a clarification or implication of it. The ancient Apostles' Creed and Nicene Creed remain valid affirmations of the faith of today.

• *Institutional continuity*

Similarly, in its governmental structure and corporateness, the Catholic Church has an unparalleled unity both historically and geographically. John Paul II is reckoned 264th in a line of popes going back to Peter.[7] Throughout the immense development from the little community of disciples led by Peter and the apostles, to the very complex system of pope, bishops, priests, curial congregations, chanceries, religious orders, and institutes that are found in the Church today, the continuity has remained unruptured. The other cultural or political institutions that existed in the time of Jesus, such as the Roman and Parthian empires or the great Chinese dynasties, have long since disappeared. *All* the governments, societies, and other institutions that exist today came into being long after the Church, which is simply *the oldest institution of any sort* standing on the face of the earth. It is composed of many local churches, or dioceses, each with a bishop at its head, and it embraces (and encourages!) a rich variety of liturgical traditions and local usages; yet it holds them all together not only in a spiritual communion but in practical collaboration under a single pastoral authority.

• *Size*

We have already noted that Christianity is the most widespread religious tradition in the world. But even the Catholic Church taken by itself is larger than any of the non-Christian religious groups, as can readily be seen from Figure 4.[8] And it is by far the largest distinct body within Christianity. All the Protestant, Orthodox, and other communities added together do not equal the Catholic Church in size. There were about 963 million Catholics in 1990. The largest Orthodox Church, the Patriarchate of Moscow, had perhaps 70 million or 80 million members. The largest Protestant denomination is

Lutheranism with about 51 million; and Lutheranism can hardly be regarded as one church. It is a group of churches having a common origin and tradition but which are now divided from one another — in some cases very sharply. The same applies to most other major Protestant denominations. Figure 4 is therefore misleading in representing them as solid blocks. A more realistic representation of the actual status of Christianity would show the Catholic Church as a great sun, around which the other denominations swing like planets and asteroids (the latter being understood as planets that have broken into fragments which retain similar orbits, while gradually drifting apart).

It will give some idea of the size of the Catholic Church to note that only one other organized society in the world is larger — the Republic of China. In 1990, the population of mainland China was estimated at just over a billion; that of India, the next largest country, at 850 million. (The United States had only 249 million.)

• *A unique phenomenon*

In conclusion, we must recognize that the Catholic Church is not just one religion among many; it stands apart as a phenomenon unprecedented, unparalleled, and unrivaled. Taken together with its Hebrew roots, it is probably the oldest extant religion (Figure 5). It is certainly the most widespread. Yet paradoxically it is also the most cohesive and united. Whereas religious traditions are usually vague and elusive in doctrine — immensely variegated in their ritual and ethics, subject to radically diverse interpretations, forever changing, evaporating, and reappearing in new shapes, like cumulus clouds in the wind, with no definite head or durable leadership, and therefore with an endemic tendency to split into sects — the Roman Catholic Church is an organic body that has held to a single, definite faith since its origin, and remains, after twenty centuries of constant growth and development, a community of people who profess the same faith, celebrate the same sacraments, and accept the same pastors.

In anything so old and big, it is inevitable that flaws appear. At times the Church seems outdated or lacking in vigor by comparison with more recent religious movements. Those close to it are painfully aware of its shortcomings. But that is like standing next to a giant sequoia and focusing on warps in the bark. When you step back and see how this tree towers over all others, you will then appreciate its grandeur. And when we consider that, notwithstanding the common human failings of its members, the size, cohesion, and stability of the Church transcend all the usual dimensions and trajectories of human religions, are we not compelled to pose the question: Must there not be hidden within it some mysterious, superhuman source of strength and vitality?

RELIGIOUS ORIGINS

	Israel and Christianity	Hinduism	Buddhism	Taoism	Confucianism	Islam
2000 B.C.						
1900						
1800						
1700	Abraham					
1600						
1500						
1400						
1300	Moses	Rig Veda				
1200						
1100						
1000						
900	David					
800	Elijah					
700	Isaiah	Brahmanism				
600	Captivity	Upanishads		Lao Tzu		
500			Buddha		Confucius	
400		Philosophers		Tao Te Ching		
300		Bhagavad-Gita			Mencius	
200						
100			Rise of			
100 A.D.	Jesus		Mahayana			
200			Transmission			
300			to China			
400						
500						
600			Transmission			Muhammad
700			to Japan			
800						
900						
1000	Eastern Schism					
1100						
1200						
1300						
1400						
1500						
1600	Reformation					
1700						
1800						
1900						
2000						

Dates of the foundational teachers, books, and events of the major world religions. (Those of Abraham, Moses, and the earliest Indian and Chinese figures are only conjectural and approximate.)

3
The modern religious atmosphere

The tensions between Catholicism and Protestantism today are by no means the same as in the sixteenth century. In fact, it takes a great effort for us to reconstruct the frame of mind in which the Reformation debates over nature and grace, faith and works, took place; or to take seriously the problems that violently sundered the Church of that time. We live in a very different intellectual climate.

The difference comes largely from the Enlightenment, a phase through which Western civilization passed during the eighteenth century, and which has left such a profound impression on our culture that we today are very much its offspring. It has made our outlook profoundly different not only from that of the sixteenth century but from those of all other cultures that have ever existed in this world. The secular humanism that dominates our intellectual horizons is a peculiarly modern and Western attitude, even though, due to the dominance of the West, it is now having a powerful impact on the East also. The atheism which is its sharpest expression is a new feature of human history. Most of mankind, for most of its history, has been religious. When Christian missionaries carried the Gospel to pagan lands, their task was not to persuade people to believe in God but to win them from false gods to the Father of Jesus Christ. Although there were occasional atheists among the ancients (for example, philosophical critics of popular religion), atheism was never widespread before the nineteenth century.

Primitive Buddhism did not include belief in God, but neither did it deny the deities with which Hindu society abounded. And the Mahayana Buddhists, unable to maintain the primitive agnosticism of Gautama, filled their pantheon with an abundance of gods, deifying even the Buddha himself! Modern man of Europe and North America is the first ever to have attempted, more or less systematically, to eliminate God from social and indeed from all human life. If ever we are surprised at the pervasive influence of religion on other cultures, we should bear in mind that we are the odd ones.

In this chapter we will try to indicate in broad outline how secular humanism has arisen. It is largely the result of four factors that led to or sprang from the Enlightenment: humanism, secularism, rationalism, and the development of science and technology (including the resultant industrialization and urbanization). After sketching the rise of secular humanism, we will look at its effects on both Protestantism and Catholicism.

1. THE RISE OF SECULAR HUMANISM

• *Theocentricity of the Middle Ages*

The Middle Ages were, at least at their peak, a very theocentric culture. God was recognized as the Creator from whom all things came, the Lord who rules over his creation, the Savior who opens the way to eternal life, and the Judge who will bestow our final recompense. The next world was recognized as of chief importance, and life in this world was seen as a struggle between sin and grace, in which man's future destiny is determined. Human life was filled with the signs of religion. Nearly every village of Europe had its church, the most impressive structure in it. The parish priest was one of the more important personages in the community; the numerous monasteries were often the centers around which towns grew. The bigger cities were for centuries occupied with the construction of great, beautiful cathedrals, the spires of which could be seen from a distance long before the city itself came into view. The Church bells rang not only to call people to Mass and prayer but also to announce other important events. Sundays and religious feast days were observed by practically everyone.

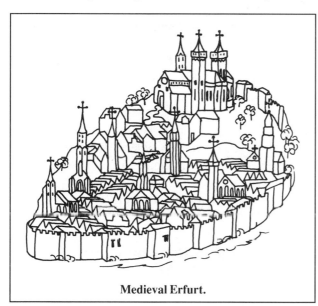

Medieval Erfurt.

This is not to suggest that all medievals were devout Christians. Criminals and hypocrites, the negligent, the indifferent, and the irreligious existed then as now. Nevertheless, the society and culture of the High Middle Ages (twelfth and thirteenth centuries) were imbued with a Christian vision which at least established the horizons of their outlook on the world. Nearly everyone believed in God, even those who sinned against him. Most people acknowledged the great religious dimensions of life, even if they did not live faithfully by them. One faith was shared by nearly all and could be taken for granted as the background against which daily life was lived and understood (the Jews had a different faith from the majority, but it too was religious). The fact that priests and monks were almost the only ones who knew how to read and write surely intensified the impact of religion on social life.

• *Fifteenth-century humanism*

Modern humanism can be dated approximately from the fifteenth century. The age of Christopher Columbus was one of adventure and discovery not only in geography (Africa, Asia, and America) and in economics (the development of commerce and the acquisition of unprecedented wealth with the rise of capitalism) but also in awareness of the resources of the human spirit. It involved a reaction against the God-centered culture of the Middle Ages, in favor of a new man-centered one. The humanists of fourteenth-century Italy led the reaction, followed before long by those of northern Europe. Delighting in the joys of this world, they angrily rejected the ideal of sacrificing for those of the next. Their scorn was directed particularly at the monks, whose life they often depicted as hypocritical and misdirected.

The humanists as a group were by no means crass voluptuaries. The earthly pleasures which they cultivated were chiefly those of poetry and art; it is they who gave us the term *humanities* for literary studies. Although they took the works of classic Greece and Rome as their models, and looked scornfully on the achievements of the Middle Ages, they were not pagans. They believed in God and professed a Christianity that seems to have been by and large sincere. What defined humanism was not any particular theory or philosophy of man but simply a greatly heightened emphasis on human values, particularly those of this life. Thus Petrarch (1303-1374) declared that "nothing is admirable but the (human) soul, in comparison to which, if it is great, nothing is great." Marsilio Ficino (1433-1499) emphasized human excellence in his *Platonic Theology*, while Pico della Mirandola (1463-1494) devoted one of his most famous orations to "The dignity of man." This humanism was not a rejection of God but a centering on man which tended to marginalize God.

The impact of humanism can be perceived in the contrast between the writings of Dante and Chaucer on the one hand, and Shakespeare on the other. The world of the former was essentially religious; the touches of malice in Dante or of bawdiness in Chaucer do not seriously distort a vision that gets its focus and direction from God. But Shakespeare's occasional touches of religion are hardly more than decor.

SECULARISM

While the humanist fever was raging among the intellectuals, *secularism* was making a less dramatic but steady progress on the social plane. *Seculum* is a Latin term used to refer to the things of this world, as contrasted with those of eternity; *secularism* means a tendency to divorce the activities of human society from any religious reference. Whereas *humanism* is a positive term, focused on human values, *secularism*, at least in its common usage, is more negative, emphasizing the exclusion of God and religion from human affairs.

Secularism is illustrated in the fact that schools, hospitals, orphan asylums, and the like — which during the Middle Ages had nearly all been founded by monasteries or other religious communities — began to be taken over by public authorities and carried on without a distinctively religious purpose or motivation. Sculpture, painting, and music had been cultivated during the Middle Ages chiefly for liturgical purposes; from the fourteenth century onward they were employed more and more to glorify statesmen and ornament palaces or for simple entertainment. The first and greatest medieval universities, such as Paris, Oxford, and Bologna, originated as schools for the training of priests; only much later did they become secularized. Medieval society regarded the ruler as in some sense a representative of God, and surrounded his office with religious trappings. Thus the Holy Roman Emperor was often consecrated by the Pope, and the King of France by the

Archbishop of Rheims. Such practices, inspired originally by deep faith, little by little became mere formalities, eventually abandoned. When Joan of Arc persuaded the reluctant Dauphin to be crowned in the cathedral of Rheims (1429), this rallied the people of France around him. But in 1804, when Napoleon, unwilling to allow the Pope to crown him emperor, seized the diadem and placed it on his own head, few people were troubled by this repudiation of the religious authorization of his office, which now was regarded in a secular light.

Whereas humanism burst like a fever upon the academic world of the fifteenth century and then abated, secularization had barely gotten under way in the fifteenth century. But it continued to gain momentum up through the nineteenth century, and even today sputters on in debates about prayer in the public schools or about Nativity scenes in civic settings. (The motto "In God we trust" engraved on our currency is one of many indications that America is not yet a totally secularized nation.) In the nineteenth century, the combined term *secular humanism* began to be used for an attitude that consciously affirms that man's fulfillment calls for the exclusion of God from human affairs.

Although the Reformation was in many ways quite opposite in spirit to both humanism and secularism, it reinforced their effect of breaking down the Catholic culture of the Middle Ages. Luther stressed not the dignity but the corruption of human nature. Yet in denying the human mind's capability of discovering the truth in religious matters, he rejected the synthesis of faith and reason which had developed during the Middle Ages, thereby becoming the unintentional ally of the humanists, who attacked scholastic theology for literary rather than theological reasons. Moreover, the religious divisions produced by the Reformation greatly accelerated the advance of secularism by making it expedient for politicians to dissociate themselves from any particular religious position in order to obtain a public consensus, and by leading people to suppress the external, visible marks of religious belief as something pertaining entirely to private life.

EARLY MODERN SCIENCE

While theological disputes (and military conflicts) dominated the stage of the sixteenth century (sometimes coinciding in religious wars), a few individuals were quietly pursuing their curiosity about natural science. Interest in them had been stimulated by the humanist movement and its rediscovery of ancient Greek scientists such as Galen and the Pythagoreans. The sixteenth century was punctuated by discoveries and inventions that laid the foundations of modern astronomy (Copernicus, Kepler, Brahe), mathematics, metallurgy (Agricola), medicine (Servetus, Paracelsus, Vesalius, Harvey), botany (Gesner's *Catalogue of plants*), biology (Gesner's *History of animals*), geography (Mercator), and chemistry (van Helmont). At the end of the century, Francis Bacon, with scornful contempt for the Aristotelian philosophy then dominant in the universities, formulated the demand that science be inductive, experimental, and utilitarian.

Newton.

This prepared for the seventeenth century, when empirical science began to be pursued systematically by many of the best minds of the Western world. The century began with Galileo's triumphant defense of the Copernican system, and ended with Newton, whose "Law of Gravitation" provided the framework within which scientists would work comfortably for two hundred years, fostering philosophical attempts to reduce the entire universe to matter in motion. The apparently unlimited capability of science to give an understanding of nature and to improve the world by technology electrified imaginations and stirred ambitions. The dreary concern of theologians with the depravity of human nature, and the futility of the interminable debates about grace and free will, now looked like a dark backdrop heightening the joyous excitement of the new discoveries and inventions. The temper of the times can be sensed in the awe with which Newton was pronounced the greatest and most fortunate genius that had ever lived. As Lagrange (himself a great mathematician) put it: "There is but one universe, and to be the interpreter of its laws can happen to but one man in the world's history."[1]

THE ENLIGHTENMENT

The eighteenth century prided itself on being the Age of Enlightenment. The light in which it basked complacently was that of human reason, the powers of which were now being displayed in the growth of empirical science. Philosophers turned this light on human affairs also, confident that, if reason could discover the secrets of nature, it could also direct human life to its betterment. In a world that had looked mostly to the past for guidance, the notion of *progress*, the conviction that the future can be expected to improve on the past, began to establish itself. The notion of *human rights* was contemplated with unprecedented intensity, and there developed the *humanitarian* ideal, with its spirit of *tolerance* for those of other persuasions (especially religious). People became sensitive to *liberty* as perhaps the chief sign of human dignity. In the name of humanity, they began to protest *against slavery,* which was still practiced in many places, notably in the New World. John Locke (1632-1704) argued persuasively in favor of *democracy* as the ideal political structure. Thus in various ways the Enlightenment is the direct descendant of the humanist movement of the fifteenth century; however, the sense of human brotherhood and love was an essentially Christian inspiration which the Enlightenment co-opted without acknowledging its true source.

The political thought which inspired the American Constitution was characteristic of the Enlightenment (Benjamin Franklin and Thomas Jefferson were both, in fact, deists.) Our Declaration of Independence enshrines some of the finer Enlightenment intuitions:

> We hold these truths to be self-evident: that all men are created equal and endowed by their creator with certain inalienable rights, among which are life, liberty and the pursuit of happiness.

The noble ideals of the Enlightenment were, however, sometimes deformed. Humanitarianism tended to become a *naturalism* that had little room or use for the supernatural. Love of liberty and confidence in reason led to an *antiauthoritarianism* in which all authority was felt to be an infringement on personal liberty and an affront to the power of reason to figure things out for itself. It is especially the *rationalism* of this age that had momentous consequences for religion.

• *Rationalism*

Rationalism denotes not merely the use of reason or esteem for it but the tendency to make reason the supreme guide, the absolute and self-sufficient standard of judgment in science, philosophy, religion, and human affairs. Whatever did not meet the standard of reason was dismissed as superstition and ignorance. Rationalism tends to be hostile to faith and tradition, disdainful of feeling, emotion, intuition. It resents mystery as a challenge to its own omnicompetence. Such an outlook could not fail to have religious repercussions. At first it entailed no overt hostility but rather an effort to produce an "enlightened religion." Where Luther wanted to sacrifice reason on the altar of faith, the rationalist theologians demanded that faith stand before the bar of reason.

• *Locke*

It was in England that the Religion of Reason was first fully elaborated, toward the

end of the seventeenth century. John Locke (1632-1704) characteristically entitled one of his works, *The reasonableness of Christianity*. He regarded religion as a branch of science with the purpose of supplying divine sanctions to make men behave as they should. It consists in a few propositions that appeal to everyone's reason: (1) There is an omnipotent God; (2) he demands that we live virtuously; (3) he will reward the good and punish the evil in the future life. For Locke and most of his contemporaries, reason was fully capable of demonstrating the existence of God, the immortality of the soul, the moral law, divine retribution, etc. Hence Locke declared, "There is little need or use of revelation: God having furnished us with natural and surer means to arrive at a knowledge of them."[2] "There can be no evidence that any traditional religion is of divine origin," he affirmed, "so clear and so certain as that of the principles of reason."[3]

The question concerning what to make of the Christian revelation greatly exercised and divided the thinkers of the age. The more orthodox, such as Locke himself, maintained that revelation was necessary for the majority of mankind, whose ignorance and prejudices made it too difficult for them to recognize their duties through reason alone. Locke also retained the classical position that miracles and prophecy function as signs to establish the Christian religion. He even acknowledged that there could be truths above reason, which could be known only by revelation, although he gave scant attention to them.

• *Deism*

The *deists*, on the contrary, denied that revelation was useful for anyone. Herbert of Cherbury (1583-1648) held that particular revelations were incompatible with the universality of God.[4] But even the deists were not formally antireligious. While they attacked institutional religion, especially the Catholic Church, they claimed to replace it with a better religion, that of nature itself, as interpreted by reason. They regarded religion as necessary to motivate people to be good, but they were convinced that reason by itself was capable of establishing religion. Declared Voltaire (1694-1778):

> The only gospel one ought to read, is the great book of Nature, written by the hand of God. . . . The only religion that ought to be professed is the religion of worshipping God and being a good man.

Newton himself, the hero of the Enlightenment, had argued that, as the watch implies the watchmaker, so the human body implies a designer. Voltaire developed this argument at length.

But after taunting and threatening Christianity with the weapon of "pure reason," deism itself was abruptly devoured by the monster it had unleashed. The later rationalists were more radical than their predecessors. Hume's *Essay on miracles* (1748) argued, with devastating effect, that no supernatural miracle could be established as a proof of the divinity of its author.

• *Kant on proofs for God's existence*

Finally Immanuel Kant (1724-1804), though a devout Christian himself, convinced the academic world that it was intrinsically impossible to prove the existence of God by pure reason. A relic of deism subsists, however, in his claim that *practical* reason could still maintain the necessity of postulating God to account for the "categorical imperative" which all men find inscribed in their conscience ("I am never to act otherwise than so that I could also will that my maxim should become a universal law").[5]

It is one of the ironies of intellectual history that the most rigorous proofs for the existence of God ever formulated — the "Five Ways" of St. Thomas Aquinas — were apparently quite unknown to Kant. But Kant's subtle, complex mind would probably have had little appreciation for the simplicity and directness of St. Thomas. In any case, it is due largely to Kant's influence that many philosophers of the past two centuries have denied that reason can demonstrate the existence of any realities or values that transcend empirical experience — in particular, the existence of God. The assumption that has become commonplace today that belief in God is purely a matter of faith is a legacy of Immanuel Kant, quite contrary to the news of the great Christian thinkers of the past.

THE RISE OF ATHEISM

• *Feuerbach*

The first major philosopher to adopt an overtly atheist position was Ludwig Feuerbach. His *Essence of Christianity* (1841), although not a work of great intellectual weight, set a pattern for others and was an important source for Karl Marx. Its strategy was not to refute the arguments for the existence of God but to explain the origin of belief in God in such a way as to make it untenable. God is said to be a fantasy of human excellence projected upon an infinite scale. It is man who has created God in his own image and likeness, only bigger and better:

> The divine being is nothing else than the human being, or rather the human nature, purified, freed from the limits of the individual man, [and] made objective — i.e., contemplated and revered as another, a distinct being.
>
> (*The Essence of Christianity*, New York: Harper and Row Torchbook ed., p. 14)

• *Freud*

The notion that God is a creation of the human spirit would be repeated over and over again. Sigmund Freud (1856-1939) explained it as the illusion of people frightened at the powers of nature and seeking a father figure for reassurance.

> When the child grows up and finds that he is destined to remain a child forever, and can never do without protection against unknown and mighty powers, he invests these with the traits of the father-figure; he creates for himself the gods, of whom he is afraid, whom he seeks to propitiate and to whom he nevertheless entrusts the task of protecting him.
>
> (*The Future of an Illusion*, tr. Robson-Scott, New York: Doubleday, 1927, p. 40; see also *Totem and Taboo*, New York: Norton, c. 1950)

• Darwin

Charles Darwin's *Origin of Species* (1859) did not directly attack faith in God; on the contrary, it took pains to point out that the theory proposed was fully in accord "with what we know of the laws impressed on matter by the Creator."[6] Nevertheless, Darwin's

explanation of the differentiation of species through natural selection was widely perceived, by believers and unbelievers alike, as eliminating a great part of the evidence for the existence of God, who was no longer needed to explain the variety and complexity of living things. At the same time, the evolutionary mentality which quickly took possession of nearly all branches of modern thought reinforced the idea that religion was simply a primitive stage in the evolution of reason's endeavor to grasp the universe. In this view, religious thought had been superseded by philosophy, which in its turn must now yield to positive science, the only fully and consistently rational world view. (The idea of the three stages of human thought derives from Auguste Comte [1798-1857], who termed them as theological, metaphysical, and positive.)

• Nietzsche

The quintessential atheist of the nineteenth century was Friedrich Nietzsche (1844-1900), the rebellious son of a Lutheran pastor. Not content to exult, "God is dead,"[7] he concerned himself with expunging the "shadow of God" that still hung over the European mind. He recognized with harsh lucidity that one cannot jauntily discard belief in God and continue living more or less as before; one's basic outlook on life has to be affected by such a step, especially one's moral values. Freethinkers such as Friedrich Strauss (author of *The Life of Jesus*) and Arthur Schopenhauer, after abandoning Christianity and theism,

thought they could retain the traditional moral values on the basis of reverence for nature, the authority of conscience, the "happiness of the greatest number," and suchlike. Nietzsche excoriated such positions; regarding himself as the only consistent, clear-sighted atheist of his time as well as a kind of anti-prophet, he proclaimed the collapse of the accepted value system, which the rest of Europe would need centuries perhaps to realize.

Thus he rejected the traditional moral virtues, particularly compassion, which he derided as a strategy of the weak to emasculate the strong *(Genealogy of Morals)*. The Superman of the future would be characterized by "naturalistic values," which Nietzsche defined as "whatever serves life." Deeply influenced by the Darwinian "survival of the fittest," he understood life to be a blind, instinctive "will to power."[8] Hence he proposed a "transvaluation of values," suggesting, for example, that such passions as hatred, envy, greed, and the impulse to dominate should be approved as "necessary in order to preserve the very nature of life."[9]

In a famous parable, Nietzsche indicates the consequences of consistent atheism. A madman goes about crying that the earth has been detached from the sun, and we can no longer say which way it is moving. "Backward, sideward, forward, in all directions? Is there still an up or down? Are we not straying through an infinite nothing?" (*Gay Science*, p. 181).

A man whose philosophy was inseparable from his passionate life, who fancied himself the Antichrist, Nietzsche became in his own person a living parable of humanity without God. He went mad at the age of forty-five, now identifying himself with both God and Christ. His condition was due partly to syphilis contracted in a brothel, and partly no doubt to the effect of living in a world in which there was neither up or down, right or wrong.

• *Marx*

Karl Marx (1818-1883) took over from Feuerbach the view that religion is a kind of alienation, in which man attributes his own best qualities to God. Marx's originality lay in connecting this view of religion with a social movement. The cruel and blatant exploitation of the laboring classes during the early stages of the industrial revolution was the supreme evil haunting and energizing him. He blamed it on the capitalist system which, by

allowing the wealthy to gain control of the means of production, compelled the laborer to sell his work for hire, thus alienating from him the fruits of his labor. The essential remedy, according to Marx, consisted in socialization of the means of production, through which would come about the ideal communist society, in which each person would work according to his abilities and be compensated according to his needs. Thus Marxism is primarily a socioeconomic theory for constructing the ideal human society. One could criticize Marxism solely on those grounds, and ask whether it does not presuppose a community of ideally intelligent and selfless human beings. In actual fact, does it not merely transfer the effective ownership of capital goods from one class of society to another, as Pope John Paul II suggested in his encyclical *On Human Labor* (no. 14)?

Marxism does not, however, confine itself to the plane of economics and social theory but regards the elimination ("critique") of religion as a necessary first step toward the emancipation of man. Religion is an opium which, by comforting the worker with the doctrines of divine providence and future reward, dulls his resentment at being enslaved and exploited. Moreover, religion itself is man's crowning alienation. So long as he worships a being superior to himself, man is not fully autonomous and free. Only a humanity liberated from servitude to God will be capable of realizing itself fully, and creating the perfect society.

Thus atheism was integrated by Marx into the system of "scientific socialism" which came to dominate Russia, China, and eastern Europe. It was by military force that Marxism was imposed on practically all the countries subject to it; nevertheless, its spread was undeniably prepared by the powerful fascination it exercises on many of the intelligentsia. But this appeal does not derive from any arguments against the existence of God, which Marx scarcely bothers with.

• *Christian-Marxist confrontation*

The debate between Christianity and Marxism is not therefore primarily or directly a philosophical argument about the existence of God. It is a practical confrontation between two visions of the ideal human society. The Christian vision is that of the Kingdom of God, in which man finds happiness and fulfillment in conformity to the will of God, and ultimately in full union with God. In the Marxist view, man himself is sovereign, capable of achieving fulfillment by the rational powers of his own nature. Submission to an illusionary higher being is degrading and enslaving. At this level, Marxism is opposed not only to Christianity but to Brahmanism, Taoism, Confucianism, Stoicism, and in general all religions which share the common insight that human perfection and happiness come from acceptance of one's rightful place in a higher order, whether the latter be called *dharma*, the Way of Nature, the Will of Heaven, or the will of the Father.

Thus the humanism of the fourteenth and fifteenth centuries, which began by diverting attention from God in order that human values might have more room for development, fructified in a social vision from which God has been totally excluded, so as to make man himself sovereign.

• *Decline of atheism*

There are some indications that the tide of atheism has crested, and that modern thought is drawing back from it. Reflective scientists have long been aware of the limits of scientific explanation. Analyzing the structure of matter, charting its movements, and measuring its infinitesimal particles or its immense vastness does not account for the pervasive fact of intelligible order. Explaining one part of the universe by another fails to satisfy the need for an explanation of the whole.

Moreover, the idea that technology is enough to equip us to achieve a good life has been shattered by the experience of two world wars, ecological disasters, and the threat of nuclear annihilation. Technology employed by the unwise or the selfish is like a power tool in the hands of an irresponsible boy. Scientists themselves, having "known sin," as Oppenheimer avowed after Hiroshima, are asking more and more, "Where do we find the wisdom needed to guide the power made available by our knowledge?"

Experience of a world that knows no God has left many people disturbed and disoriented, while others are nauseated at the hollowness and futility of a life centered on oneself. Even psychiatrists who hold the idea of God to be an illusion often find in practice that religious faith has a salutary effect which psychotherapy cannot achieve. It produces a sense of purpose, a personal integration, a joyous fullness and liberation. Is it plausible that an illusion should make a person better able to cope with reality than the truth does?

Marx claimed that experience would vindicate his thesis that emancipation from a

Supreme Being frees humanity to fulfill its own potential. Three quarters of a century of Marxist states has proven just the opposite. Their concentration camps, suppression of dissidents, manipulation of truth, and callous disregard of the rights of other peoples (among them Lithuania, Latvia, Estonia, Czechoslovakia, Hungary, Cambodia, and Afghanistan) as well as of individuals (Beijing), is evidence that denial of a Sovereign Lord opens the way to an alienation of the person and an oppression of the people far more hideous than those which Marx undertook to rectify. The Iron Curtain was not erected to keep outsiders from coming in but to prevent those enjoying the "blessings" of Marxism from getting out! The collapse of the Iron Curtain (which occurred as these pages were being written) has exposed to all the world the fact that even the most basic human promise of Marxism has not been fulfilled. Instead of ending the alienation of the laborer from the fruits of his work, it has left stores empty, productive farmers hungry, and earth, air, and water more polluted than anywhere else in the world.

• *Renewed attention to the spiritual*
Finally, there are indications of a resurgence of belief and interest in spiritual reality during the past two or three decades. What first attracted attention, in this country at least, was an unprecedented expansion of contemplative monasteries, especially of the Trappists, during the 1940s and 1950s. This was followed by a great number of new books on prayer and the spiritual life not just for religious houses and traditional centers of piety but for the public market. Interest in meditation and Oriental mysticism, which has been germinating quietly in small groups of Western intellectuals for over a century, has recently blossomed. The Pentecostal movement, which began at the turn of the century and at first seemed to be located among peripheral and bizarre Christian sects, is now firmly established (more often under the name *Charismatic Renewal*) in the most traditional and orthodox churches.

To complete the picture, we should take note also of the many testimonies to "life after death"; the claims to paranormal experiences such as extrasensory perception, psychokinesis, mind control, and astral projection; the recrudescence of ancient astrology and witchcraft; the spread of bizarre new sects and cults; renewed belief in ghosts, demonic possession, etc. In listing these phenomena together, we do not mean to suggest that they are all equally serious or healthy. However, they indicate that the spiritual realm is being taken more earnestly by society today than it was a few decades ago and that the religious instinct is irrepressible. It may be neglected or suppressed in individuals; stymied or discredited momentarily in a given society or certain layers of society; but eventually it will reassert itself. When its authentic expression is thwarted, it is liable to turn to covert and degraded forms.

2. CATHOLICISM AND PROTESTANTISM TODAY
Secular humanism, with the atheism, agnosticism, and indifference to which it leads, seems to be the chief enemy of Christian faith today. Its development greatly overshadows the division between Protestants and Catholics (or of Protestants among themselves). Only lately have Protestants and Catholics begun to realize that they are faced with a common

enemy that is a far greater threat to them both than they are to each other. This realization is stirring them toward efforts at mutual reconciliation. But both Protestantism and Catholicism have evolved considerably since the sixteenth century, and the tensions between them are no longer what they were. In order to understand the contemporary situation, we need to recall a few major developments of the past four hundred years.

For some three centuries after the Reformation, the issues between Protestants and Catholics remained essentially the same. Like the long-drawn-out trench warfare of World War I, interminable skirmishes kept hostility alive without significantly changing the situation. Eventually people grew weary of debate and began to ignore each other, so that their relations became more like the Cold War that followed World War II. This helped foster the development of secular humanism. Meanwhile, both Protestantism and Catholicism were undergoing their own inner development, especially in reaction to the Enlightenment. Although largely anti-Christian, especially in its later, most rationalistic phase, the Enlightenment has had a powerful impact within Christianity itself. In the Protestant world, it led to Liberal Protestantism, and in the Catholic world, to Modernism.

• *Liberal Protestantism*

The Reformation emphasis on Scripture stimulated the study of ancient languages (chiefly Hebrew and Greek), history, archaeology, and eventually anthropology for the light they shed on the biblical text. But attention to the natural and human aspects of Scripture had the unintended side effect of weakening belief in divine inspiration. Meanwhile rationalism was making the intelligentsia more and more uncomfortable with faith, while the post-Newtonian vision of a world machine seemed to exclude miracles and other divine interventions in history.

Liberal Protestantism, which took shape during the nineteenth century, was a reinterpretation of traditional Christianity to make it conform to the prevailing cultural outlook. There were many forms and degrees of Liberal Protestantism; among its dominant thrusts were abandonment of belief in the personal divinity and saviorhood of Christ, and a rejection of miracles. On the other hand, inspired by humanist ideals, Liberal Protestantism became more and more involved in social work, to such a degree that it has been charged with having commuted Luther's "faith without works" into a program of works without faith.

Although Liberalism dominated the Protestant intellectual world of the nineteenth and twentieth centuries, it has not gone unchallenged. There have been strong reactions, especially at the popular level, reaffirming biblical faith and a more classical Protestant interpretation of it (evangelicalism and fundamentalism).

MODERN CATHOLICISM

In the Catholic world, the main developments of the past four hundred years can be situated around three ecumenical councils: (1) Trent, which was the Catholic response to the Reformation; (2) Vatican I, responding to problems raised by the Enlightenment; and (3) Vatican II which was a response not to any attack from the outside but to a kind of sclerosis within.

66

The Council of Trent (1545-1563) ■ This anonymous engraving, based apparently on a painting by the Spaniard Vargas (who was living in Italy at the time of the Council), represents one of the sessions of the final period (1562-1563). A theologian (no. 3) is addressing the Fathers while a secretary (no. 2) takes notes. The most prominent position is occupied by the representative of King Philip II of Spain (no. 1). Six cardinals are seated at position no. 4; just above and behind them are the papal legates. Attendance at the Council varied greatly. At the opening session, only **34** voting members were present (in addition to **51** theologians and canonists). The final Acts , however, were signed by **255 prelates.** — Photo courtesy of the British Museum

• *Trent*

The Council of Trent (1545-1563) undertook to reaffirm the doctrines attacked by the Reformers, while defining them carefully so as to eliminate misconceptions or abuses. It produced the lengthiest and most detailed statement of Catholic teaching that had ever been drawn up by the magisterium; however, it treated only those topics that were under fire. At the same time, the Council had the delicate task of bringing about the reforms genuinely needed in the Church, while resisting the excessive and heretical demands made by Luther, Calvin, Zwingli, etc. The need for reform had long been recognized by earnest Catholics, many of whom, instead of breaking with the Church, worked fruitfully from within: Ignatius Loyola and the Jesuit Order founded by him (1540), Peter Canisius, Teresa of Ávila, John of the Cross, Robert Bellarmine, Charles Borromeo, Francis de Sales, Vincent de Paul, and many others. Their efforts largely fructified in or stemmed from this Council.

• *Vatican I*

The First Vatican Council (1869-1870) came during the combat over faith and reason generated by the Enlightenment. When rationalists demanded that all truth, including religious, be tested by human reason, fideists (from the Latin *fides*, faith) retorted that reason is of little or no use in matters of faith. In 1864, Pope Pius IX had issued a Syllabus of Errors, listing (somewhat globally) the chief aberrations threatening the faith in that day. The Vatican Council then drew up a carefully balanced statement of the mutual interdependence and complementarity of faith and reason.

The threat of rationalism was far from over, however. The cultural forces that produced Liberal Protestantism also affected Catholic intellectuals, leading to what was called Modernism. Under the guise of eliminating what was outdated, and rationalizing the ancient faith, this movement tended really to eliminate the supernatural. But the vigorous action of Pope Pius X with his encyclical Pascendi (1907) effectively put an end to the danger, at least for the time being.

The decrees of Trent and Vatican I as well as documents associated with the latter (such as the *Syllabus* and *Pascendi*) have been much criticized for their narrowness and rigidity. They were weapons of battle, however, issued when a strong reaffirmation of doctrines under attack was required. Given these circumstances, what is remarkable is their calm, firm, and balanced tone and, at least in the case of the conciliar decrees, an accuracy that has made them permanently valid.

• *Vatican II*

The Second Vatican Council (1962-1965) exudes a totally different atmosphere from its predecessors. It was not summoned to defend the Church against attack; it was a peaceful self-renewal of a Church confident of its heritage. After entering into the twentieth century in the posture of a besieged fortress, holding out against Protestantism on the one hand and Modernism on the other, the Church now took the stance of friendly and positive appreciation of the other Christian denominations as well as non-Christian religions. It likewise acknowledged many positive values in modern culture, especially its keen sense of the dignity and rights of the human person. Furthermore, the old battle lines between

The First Vatican Council (1869-1870) ■ **Six hundred ninety-eight prelates attended the first public session.** — NC Photo of a

Library of Congress engraving

The Second Vatican Council (1962-1965) ■ More than 2500 prelates entering for the opening session. (Throughout the Council, those present and voting usually numbered between 2200 and 2300.) — NC Photo

Protestants and Catholics had shifted considerably. In the sixteenth century, the controversies revolved around the three topics of Scripture, grace, and the Church. But today Liberal Protestantism has so undermined faith in Scripture, while the Catholic Church has strongly reaffirmed the inspiration of the Bible (see Chapter 6), that the real controversy is no longer between Protestants and Catholics but between those who believe in the Word of God and those who do not.

Likewise the interpretation of grace as justification imputed through faith alone has to a large extent been abandoned or forgotten by most Protestants; in fact, so little attention is paid any more to the very doctrine of grace, one is tempted to say that a new Martin Luther is needed to remind both Protestants and Catholics of it.

The Church, however, remains the main topic of theological differences between Protestants and Catholics. As in the sixteenth century, Catholics emphasize the holiness of the Church as a work of Christ among mankind, and Protestants put more stress on the Church's human limitations and defects. Protestants tend to regard the Church as the herald and servant of the coming Kingdom, whereas Vatican II speaks of the Church as "the Kingdom of God already present in mystery."[10]

An even more basic development is the fact that, weary of centuries of animosity, Catholics and Protestants have sensed the need of a greater openness to each other. The ecumenical movement, aimed at restoring unity among Christians, originated in the Protestant world but was embraced wholeheartedly by Vatican II. Since the Council, numerous bilateral commissions have been set up to discuss the differences between Catholics and Lutherans, Catholics and Presbyterians, Catholics and Orthodox, etc. Meanwhile, several Protestant denominations have joined together, as we noted in Chapter 2. The full unity of Christians still seems a long way off, but definite steps toward mutual understanding and acceptance have been made.

Vatican II took, as its main task, the updating *(aggiornamento)* of Catholic life. It decreed thoroughgoing reforms in the liturgy and law of the Church to put them more in tune with the conditions of the modern world. In so doing, it was accepting some of the worthy demands of the Reformers, such as the use of the vernacular (whereas previously the Mass and the sacraments of the Western Church had been celebrated in Latin) and Communion under the two forms of bread and wine. At the same time the Council freed these usages from the doctrinaire interpretations placed on them by the Reformers.

• *Post-Vatican II naturalism and rationalism*

Vatican II did not abandon any of the basic positions of Catholic tradition; on the contrary, it expressly reaffirmed them. Nevertheless, it was not rarely perceived as having lowered all barriers. Some (such as Archbishop Lefebvre) attacked it for "protestantizing" the Church, while others used the Council as a pretext to justify unauthorized innovations of their own. The rationalism and naturalism which had been effectively kept out of the Church by Vatican I and Pius X have since then invaded it like a flood, pouring over the sides and seeping through the cracks. "Pope John opened all the windows; Pope Paul had to put up screens to keep out the bugs," remarked one observer. The great question facing the Church today is whether it will be able to maintain the policy of openness to the value of other cultures without losing its own identity.

In any case, it is becoming more and more evident that a profound shift is taking place throughout Christendom. The most significant division is no longer between Catholics, Protestants, and Orthodox but between believers and secularists — that is to say, between those who live earnestly by faith in Jesus, and those who have accommodated their "Christianity" to a culture not based on faith.

• *Liberalism*

The necessity of keeping this account brief, and of painting in broad strokes, obliges us to ignore many nuances. This is painfully the case in regard to the term *liberal*, which has many references and connotations. By *Liberal Protestantism*, as the text above indicates, is meant a tendency to "liberate" Christianity from its great, characteristic doctrines under the influence of rationalism and secularism. But in the spheres of politics, economics, and social thought, the term *liberal* has other connotations, which do not enter into our present discussion. Similarly, *"Liberal Catholics"* are not just a Catholic analog of Liberal Protestants, and are not in question here. *Liberation theology* is bringing in still another raft of connotations.

SCIENCE AND RELIGION

One of the most powerful influences on modern culture has been the development of empirical science. We must ask whether it has contributed to the formation of modern atheism. In fact the view is widespread that religious belief and scientific thought are incompatible.

Why this should be so is not, however, obvious. Science itself cannot refute the existence of God; it is not even capable of formulating the question. Nearly all the founders of modern science were believers and regarded their scientific research as an exploration of the wonders of God's creation. Francis Bacon, the "prophet" of modern scientific method, proposed that Scripture and nature were like two books that God has given us to study: the book of his word and the book of his works, the former revealing his will, the latter his power.[11] Most of the scientific research for the next two centuries or more was conducted in this perspective. There is a long list of scientists, from Copernicus on, who have devoutly worshiped the Creator while contributing brilliantly to the rational analysis of his creation. There is an immensely longer list of scientists who, without making headlines or winning Nobel prizes, are equally at home in the laboratory and in church. In fact, the idea of an inherent conflict between science and religion is relatively new. In the English-speaking world, it was popularized chiefly at the end of the last century by two books: *History of the Conflict Between Religion and Science* by John W. Draper (1874) and *A History of the Warfare of Science With Theology* by Andrew P. White (1896).[12] But today many scientists, some with wide popular influence, such as Fred Hoyle, Carl Sagan, Richard Leakey, Donald Johanson, and Stephen Jay Gould, take it for granted that religion and science are more or less incompatible.

One reason for the apparent conflict lies in several highly publicized incidents pitting representatives of religion against representatives of science, with the latter emerging victorious. But these merely illustrate the fallibility and misunderstandings to which any human project is subject. (The Galileo case, moreover, has been monstrously oversimplified and distorted by popular caricatures.) They do not begin to counterbalance the fact that it was in a Christian culture that modern science originated and flourished (for seventeenth-century Europe was still predominantly Christian, and the product of centuries of Christian culture). Moreover, the Church has from early on been the patron of all forms of human culture, and of science in particular, through its monasteries, schools, academies, universities, and religious orders devoted to teaching. Nevertheless, the occasional dramatic conflicts have had more influence on the popular view of this matter than the thick archival records of quiet collaboration.

• *Scientific method*

If we ask whether there is anything in the very nature of science that inclines toward atheism, it should be noted that the scientific method deliberately sets aside any considerations not subject to empirical verification. It does not look for ultimate explanations or profound reasons. Since God is precisely the ultimate reality and the profoundest reason for all things, he is inevitably excluded from scientific investigation. This does not turn the scientist into an atheist; it means merely that, in his professional activity, he or she prescinds from questions that do not pertain to the discipline. However, there is a temptation to mistake the limitations of one's own discipline for the limits of truth itself. The habit of mind that rightly leads the scientist to prescind from ultimate questions while engaged in scientific research can have the effect of making him indifferent to such questions altogether. There is a famous (probably apocryphal) story that tells how Napoleon asked the mathematician-astronomer Laplace whether his research tended to confirm the existence of God. Laplace is said to have answered haughtily, "I have no need of that hypothesis!" In this sense science can foster atheism not of necessity but due to the narrow-mindedness of the one who cultivates it.

• *Miracles*

Another motive that may incline some scientists to atheism is that belief in miracles seems to imply an arbitrariness in nature. This would conflict with the idea of natural laws that hold necessarily and universally — something long held as a basic presupposition of science. It is out of such a mentality that Rudolf Bultmann quipped that no one who presses a switch to turn on electric lights can believe in miracles.[13]

But this objection is specious. Miracles are not the arbitrary manipulations of a whimsical demigod; neither are they on-course corrections made by an engineer who got the world off to a bad start. They are signs given by the Creator to assure us that he remains the Sovereign Lord of his creation. Far from negating the laws of nature, they have meaning only on the supposition that nature is ruled by law. If there were no recognized patterns of causality, miracles would lose all meaning. Hence belief in miracles does not conflict with a scientific mentality; rather, science helps us to discern what is truly a miracle (as at the famous Medical Bureau at Lourdes, which carefully scrutinizes all claims of miracles before they are accepted officially). And for those who reduce "laws of nature" to statistical probabilities, there can be no intractable objection against miracles.

• *Deficient notions of God*

Some of the tension between science and religion is due to a deficient notion of God. In the past, many people tended to use God to account for the marvels of nature that were to them inexplicable. God made the wind blow and the rain fall. Similarly, the regular motion of the stars was sometimes explained in the Middle Ages as brought about by angels, who kept the stars on their path and on time. This meant in effect that God was being used to plug the gaps in human knowledge; and in proportion as science advanced there was less need of this "God of the gaps," who was thus relegated more and more to the periphery of things.

Today, however, we have been reminded (most eloquently by Dietrich Bonhoeffer) that God is not needed just to fill the lacunae in human knowledge; he is needed everywhere. He is not simply the author of the extraordinary; he is equally necessary for the most ordinary and nonmysterious events. He is not called upon to explain certain special things but to explain the whole, and why there should be anything at all.

A second wrong idea, popular among the deists, represented God as the Grand Architect of this world or, more precisely, as its engineer. During the reign of mechanistic physics, the world was pictured as a great machine, operating flawlessly because of the cunning of its designer. Voltaire was only one of many who compared the universe to a clock, which could not have come into existence if there were not a Great Clockmaker who fitted its parts exquisitely together and started it moving.

This form of the "argument from design" ran into difficulty when science began to perceive indications of the immense role of chance events in the development of nature, especially of living things. As Stephen Jay Gould likes to point out, the history of evolution gives many evidences that the organs of present-day living beings have come about by adaptations in organs originally invented for quite a different purpose. For example, the hand of man, the paw of a cat, the hoof of a horse, and the wing of a bird all have the same basic structure, molded in each case to the special needs of the particular animal. It would appear as though one original structure was subsequently adapted for various functions, rather than each one being designed specially. Indeed, if we accept the widespread view that much of our back trouble comes from the fact that the spinal column originated in four-footed animals, and has not yet sufficiently adapted to being held upright on two legs, it would seem that we are far from possessing the optimum design. "If God had designed a beautiful machine to reflect his wisdom and power," Gould argues, "surely he would not have used a collection of parts generally fashioned for other purposes." Gould gives many other examples to show that living beings are examples of "messy engineering," contraptions indicating that nature is "an excellent tinkerer, not a divine artificer" (François Jacob).[14]

We will return to this argument in the next chapter. For the moment it is enough to note that what it refutes is not the existence of God but a superficial notion of God invented by deists who thought thereby to improve on the Christian faith. Their naïve vision of the world as a great machine, turning smoothly and inexorably, has been replaced by a vision of the universe in the process of dynamic and unforeseeable development. As a consequence, the notion of God as a master engineer has become incongruous. An intelligent engineer does not keep adjusting old machinery to new uses; he designs new equipment geared as specifically and economically as possible to its function. But a creator who endows his works with their proper natures and then allows them to enter upon the adventure of history, interacting with one another by their natural properties and powers, and thereby producing marvelous adaptations and innovations when conditions are right — such a notion is not refuted but rather illustrated by the findings of science.

• *Reduced awe of nature*

Another way science can affect religion is by altering our attitude toward nature. Since the dawn of consciousness, man has seen himself as a small factor in the great world of nature. The latter had powers that dwarfed his; its ways were beyond his understanding. It was, however, orderly and meaningful; it was on the whole beneficent, especially when he fitted rightly into its rhythm. Many cultures perceived a kind of sacredness about nature. They often deified its forces, and in some cases — for instance, Taoism and Stoicism — recognized in the ways of nature a kind of rule by which human conduct should be guided. Christianity saw nature as God's handiwork, governed by his wisdom, and used by him as a kind of sacrament to reveal himself.

Empirical science tends perhaps to eliminate the awe with which we regard the wonders of nature. It has "explained" the latter by reducing them to simpler components or assembling them into universal "laws." It has enabled us to forecast the movement of the stars and changes in the weather. Technology has harnessed natural forces. Our ancestors' day was regulated by the rising and setting of the sun; but electric lighting enables us to begin and end our day when we please. The cold of winter and the heat of summer no longer dominate our lives as they did in the days before central heating and air conditioning.

Such achievements have given us the sense of being master over nature instead of subject to it. Reinforced by the unbounded optimism of the nineteenth century, they aroused confidence that we are on the way to creating the conditions for an optimal life,

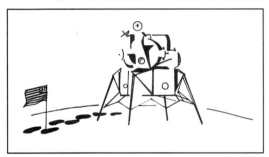

with no need of subservience to a supreme being. In 1969 Neil Armstrong put the first human footprint on the moon. That mysterious, ever-changing luminary which has fascinated the human mind since ancient times, standing for another world which we could only contemplate with wonder, which has been admired, hymned, and even deified, is now just another hunk of turf. And as nature lost its sacredness, so did nature's lord.

But if science has in some ways diminished our reverence for nature, we must not overlook the fact that it also gives us powerful new reasons to stand in awe of nature. Science reveals complex structures, beautiful designs, and great orders that are not evident to gross, untutored observation; and new discoveries, instead of settling our problems and eliminating the mysteries of nature, more often than not open fresh new fields of investigation. It has often been remarked that, in contrast with the arrogance and cockiness of second-rate scientists, great scientists tend to be humble and filled with awe at the uncharted vistas opening out before them.

• *Artificiality of modern life*

Finally, we should take note of a by-product of the scientific and technological revolution — the artificiality of modern life, which diminishes our contact with nature. More and more of mankind are living in big cities. We get food out of tin cans, milk out of waxed cardboard, water out of a spigot. Synthetic facsimiles replace wool, wood, leather, rubber, stone, and other useful products of nature. Entertainment is provided at the touch of a button. When we travel, instead of visiting the world as we walk, we speed along the expressway in an automobile or are catapulted over the clouds in hermetically sealed cabins. Even if nature has something to say about God, its message has difficulty reaching us. Ancient man, living in intimate dependence on nature and obliged to adapt himself to its moods, sensed the existence of an intelligent, purposeful source behind it, and spontaneously became religious. Modern man, living in an artificial environment of concrete, asphalt, brick, and plaster, sustaining himself on packaged food and conditioned air, using chemicals to purify a little drinking water out of rivers polluted by his industry, finding himself more and more engulfed by his own rubbish, abandoning the natural rhythms of life in order to satisfy the demands of cost effectiveness, has become atheistic.

PART 2
The sources of religious knowledge

Before going into the great questions of theology, we must examine briefly the sources from which religious knowledge can be sought. They reduce essentially to two: nature and revelation. Nature has often been perceived as a manifestation of God, and most of the classical arguments for the existence of God start from nature. But the Judeo-Christian tradition is characterized by the claim of having received a revelation from God himself, speaking through his prophets. This is not to deny that nature itself can be spoken of as a revelation; then the prophetic message might be called a *supernatural* revelation to distinguish it from the *natural* revelation provided by the world around us. But for simplicity's sake, we will speak here of the natural knowledge of God by reason in the one case (Chapter 4) and of divine revelation in the other (Chapter 5). The former can be envisioned as nature speaking to us about God, the latter as God speaking to us about himself.

Some people claim to know God by direct personal experience; others by a kind of innate knowledge or by a purely logical analysis of *a priori* philosophical propositions. It would require a long treatise to discuss such claims, and in the end, the result might be to reduce them all to these same two sources, nature (taken as inclusive of our inner nature) and (supernatural) revelation. Be that as it may, nature and revelation are the principal and classical sources of the knowledge of God, and it is these that we will now examine.

This brings us to grips with problems raised by the Enlightenment. We have seen how the Deists held that human reason, meditating on the facts of nature, is capable of attaining the knowledge of God; they saw therefore no need for revelation. The later agnostics, however, retorted that reason is incapable of demonstrating anything whatsoever about God. This impelled Fideists to take refuge in the position that he can be known only by faith.

The Church maintains that human reason is indeed capable by itself of attaining the knowledge of God; but that the revelation given to us through Jesus Christ and the prophets is nevertheless very useful. The First Vatican Council (1870) declared:

> God, the beginning and end of all things, can be known with certitude from created things by the natural light of human reason. . . . But God, in his infinite wisdom and goodness, has seen fit to reveal himself and the eternal decrees of his will to the human race in another way — one that is supernatural. . . .
>
> Thanks to this divine revelation, even those things about God which are within the reach of human reason are able to be known by all easily, with firm certitude and free from all error, even in the present condition of the human race. But this is not why revelation should be declared absolutely necessary; but because God, in his infinite goodness, ordained man to a supernatural end, namely, participation in the divine goods, which utterly transcend the understanding of the human mind.
>
> (Dogmatic Constitution *Dei Filius*, ch. 2; DS 3004f; TCC 31f; TCT 58f)

This text affirms both the possibility of natural knowledge of God, and the fact of a supernatural revelation. As regards natural knowledge, note that it does not say that the existence of God can be *demonstrated*; much less does it canonize any particular demonstration. Likewise it does not say that everyone actually has the natural knowledge of God. In very chaste language, and in the most general terms, it simply affirms the *possibility* of natural knowledge of God through reason.

As regards revelation, the Council says two things. First, that it is useful even in the case of those things that are within reach of our natural reason. Revelation enables us to know them *easily*, whereas without it the knowledge of God is quite difficult. "In the present condition of human nature" refers to the fact that our intellects have been darkened as a result of original sin. Likewise revelation enables us to have firm certitude instead of the hesitant, shaky notions that often characterize religious ideas. Finally, it gives us knowledge that is free of error, whereas even true insights in this matter are so often mingled with false notions. (In all this, the Council is obviously following St. Thomas Aquinas, *Summa Theologiae*, I, 1, 1.)

While these reasons help to explain why divine revelation is useful, they do not constitute the essential reason that makes revelation absolutely indispensable. This comes rather from the fact that God has, by a free "decree," called man to "participate in the divine goods, which utterly transcend human understanding." That is to say, mankind has a vocation that is supernatural, beyond the reach of mere natural human powers. This refers ultimately to the union with God which is to constitute human blessedness for all eternity. Without a revelation, we would not know that this has been offered to us; hence neither could we orient our efforts toward such a goal.

The part of this teaching most likely to meet resistance since the collapse of the Enlightenment is the assertion that human reason has within itself the capability of coming to a certain knowledge of God. And there is a kind of irony in the fact that, in an age skeptical about the power of reason to discover ultimate truth, it should be the Church that most stoutly defends the power of reason. Some may even sense a kind of contradiction when the Council teaches, *as a matter of faith*, that God can be known *without faith*. But the Council is not obliging anyone to believe that he sees what he does not see. It simply maintains the inherent potential of human reason to discover its Creator. This is one instance of many in which the Gospel comes to the aid of our bruised and wounded human nature and helps it to fulfill its potential; here the help consists in reassuring those who have grown diffident. In a world confused and hesitant about its capability of attaining truth, the message of the Church acts as a bracing tonic.

The Council bases its stand on the doctrine of St. Paul. In showing why Christ is needed as a savior, Paul declares that "the wrath of God is being revealed from heaven against all the godlessness and wickedness of men who suppress the truth by their wickedness" (Romans 1:18). This seems to refer especially to the idolatry of the pagans; it involves "suppressing the truth" because, as Paul goes on to say:

> What may be known about God is plain to them, because God has made it plain
> to them. Since the creation of the world, God's invisible qualities — his eternal power

and divine nature — have been clearly seen, being understood from what has been made.

In this, St. Paul was probably inspired by the Old Testament Book of Wisdom, which thus reproves the idolatry practiced by the Gentiles:

> If they had the power to know so much that they could investigate the world, how did they fail to find sooner or later the Lord of these things? (13:9). . . .
> From the greatness and beauty of created things comes a corresponding perception of their Creator. (13:5)

The teaching of Scripture and of the Council is confirmed by the religious experience of mankind. Some form of religion has arisen in practically every human culture. From time to time, anthropologists claim to have discovered in some remote part of the world a primitive tribe that is religionless. Even if true, this would be so exceptional as not to invalidate the general observation just made. But in actual fact, further inquiry has generally led to the recognition that the people in question were not without religion; rather, the anthropologists had simply failed to recognize the religious aspects of the culture on which they were reporting.

Evidently something in the nature and situation of mankind prompts people to believe in God. The notion they form of him may be crude or distorted; that is not surprising, given the difficulty of the subject. In some cases, there may not even be an explicit idea of God, yet what is said may point unmistakably toward him.

In some non-Christian civilizations, however, the notion of God has received a very clear and refined development. In the Western world, from Plato onward, philosophers have attempted to construct rigorous statements and even demonstrations about a supreme, ultimate reality. Plato conceived of "The Good" as the author of the being and essence of all things; as that which gives things their truth and beauty, and even confers the power of knowing on the knower. He added that The Good is not an essence in itself but far exceeds essence in dignity and power.[1] Aristotle argued for the existence of an "unmoved mover," which he said must be conceived of as "thought thinking itself."[2] The early Christian thinkers wholeheartedly endorsed the view that nature itself is a revelation of God; yet since they did not have to contend much with atheism but much more with false religions, their arguments for the existence of God were often left undeveloped. It was in the thirteenth century, at the crest of Christian philosophical reflection, that St. Thomas Aquinas (1224-1274) formulated the most stringent philosophical arguments for the existence of God.[3]

His *Summa Theologiae* gives five ways (I, 2, 3), each of which starts from a different observation of the natural world.

The first starts from the *change* observed in the world, and argues that all change presupposes ultimately a being that remains unchanged in itself, even while it is the source of change in other things — an "Unmoved Mover."

The second argument starts from the fact that the causes operative in our world each

depend on the action of some prior cause. This postulates a First Cause, that is, one which makes other causes operate without itself depending on the action of anything prior.

The third starts from the contingency of things. That is, they are able to be or not to be, since in fact they come into existence and subsequently perish. Beings with so frail a hold on existence postulate the existence of a Being that *necessarily is* — a being that by its very nature must be.

The fourth argument, the one which many find the most subtle, starts with what may be called the *varying degrees of excellence* in things. Some things are superior to others. It is not just that our subjective evaluations of them differ; there are objective differences in their intrinsic value. For example, a living being as such is intrinsically superior to an inanimate being. Such degrees of value imply an absolutely supreme entity in reference to which all others are measured, and from which they have their proper value.

The final argument is that from *finality*. Things in nature act in such a way as to show that they are aiming at an end, even though they do not have the intelligence to perceive an end. They must therefore be governed by an intelligence distinct from them, just as the arrow which flies toward the mark must be aimed by an archer. And since it is *by nature* that they act as they do, the intelligence governing them must be that which institutes their nature.

The above summaries are no more than an attempt to indicate in non-technical language the general drift of the five ways of St. Thomas. A rigorous study of his actual arguments would be too great an undertaking for the present work. Although not much longer than the above paraphrases, his arguments are stated in such technical, metaphysical language, and with such philosophical rigor, that a great deal of elaboration would be necessary to bring out their true sense. Modern intellectual culture has dulled our appreciation of metaphysical arguments and made us diffident of them to such a point that a vast preparation is often necessary to enable us to appreciate their force.

4

Nature speaks of God

The existence of God has been more or less dimly recognized by the majority of human beings in the most diverse cultures, without using philosophical arguments. In their vital, experiential interactions with the world around them, and in their simple, untrained musings, people have instinctively sensed that there must be some kind of Supreme Being. It ought therefore to be possible for us still today to recover this non-philosophical or non-academic way of approach to God.

Instead of attempting a rigorous proof therefore, the present chapter will offer what may be called *intimations of divinity* — delicate suggestions, discernible in nature or in human life, that point in the direction of God. They are merely half-open doors that invite us to enter and explore what lies on the other side. Perhaps they lie more in the domain of poetry than of philosophy. A philosopher might be able to elaborate them into a formal proof; but that will not be attempted here.

An excellent example of such an intimation can be seen in an old Chinese poem:

> I pluck chrysanthemums under the distant hedge,
> Then gaze long at the distant summer hills;
> The mountain air is fresh at the dusk of day.
> The flying birds two by two return.
> In these things there lies a deep meaning;
> Yet when we would express it, words suddenly fail us.
>
> (T'ao Ch'ien in *Anthology of World Poetry*, ed. Mark Van Doren, New York: Harcourt Brace Jovanovich, 1936)

It is indeed very difficult to articulate, let alone define, what the poet senses underlying the various facets of nature. Nevertheless, hedge and hills, flowers and birds, are powerful though mute witnesses to something profoundly meaningful that is expressed in them. This is what we are calling "divinity."

Without claiming to establish the existence of God rigorously or in any precise sense, we aim simply to call attention to indications which suggest a profound mystery latent in the universe, the nature of which will be left indeterminate for now. Accordingly, *divinity* here does not represent the divine nature taken in the abstract but what Paul Tillich calls the "dimension of depth." (Chapter 7 will attempt to consider the nature of God more exactly, drawing on the resources provided by faith.)

All of these considerations fall into the perspective of St. Thomas's fifth way, often called the argument from design. In this perspective, the question of God (or divinity) reduces to the question, whether the actual world is simply the result of the chance interaction of all the factors involved in it, or whether some kind of intelligence is at work in it. To say there is no God amounts to affirming that the world is purely the work of chance. If there are things that cannot be the result of mere chance but must have come about by design, some sort of intelligence must have produced them.

If we were walking through a jungle and came upon a house, we would be sure that human beings (or at least some kind of intelligent beings) had already been there. A house with windows and doors, or even a cabin of logs accurately cut and fitted together, does not come about by chance. So likewise, in contemplating nature, we must choose between chance and intelligent design. (Does "dumb matter" as it is found in non-intelligent beings behave as if directed by intelligence?)

To avoid misunderstandings, it is necessary to determine carefully what is meant by a chance event. It does not imply a haphazard, lawless world, with no fixed patterns or necessity. Chance presupposes multiple lines of causality, each operating according to its own inner necessity.[1] It is when two or more such lines intersect, without this intersection being intentionally planned, that we speak of a chance event. When a bullet hits the target at which it was aimed, that is not a chance event. But when a meteor strikes the earth, that is a chance event because it was not aimed by anyone. The fact that — given the position, direction, and velocity of the earth and the meteor a week earlier or even eons ago — the collision was inevitable does not take away from its being a chance event. Hence our question amounts to this: Can our world have come about simply by the chance interplay of the elements that make it up; or must there not lie an intelligent design behind it?

Likewise, when we speak of the universe as intelligible, or the work of design, we are not implying that it conforms totally to a rational plan (as the misleading term *universe* suggests). It is evident that contingency and chance play a very big role in the scattering and conglomeration of matter throughout space. Moreover, biologists have shown the immense role played by chance in the dynamics of evolution. There is not therefore some

evident master plan of the universe that argues for the existence of God. Instead, what we are asking here is whether, in this world that is largely the domain of contingency, there are not marks of intelligent design indicating amid all this randomness, the work of a purposeful agent. Those who deny the existence of God or of any sort of divinity are saying in effect that all is the result of chance. Life, including human life and even the human intellect (with its remarkable capability of making designs that are not by chance!) — all come from chance. On the other hand, those who will not admit that all is by chance are well on the way to acknowledging some sort of divinity.

With that as preamble, we will point out "intimations of divinity" at three diverse levels. The first consists in some practical attitudes that seem to imply the recognition of divinity even on the part of people who may not expressly believe in God. Second, we will look at some of the more common ways by which people have been led to believe in divinity. Finally, we will consider how science, rather than excluding divinity, strongly supports it.

IMPLICIT ATTITUDES

First, people commonly treat the world in a way that supposes an intelligent purpose in it. They may or may not be conscious of this implication; they may or may not believe in God; they may be convinced, like Einstein, of the existence of a "superior reasoning power"; or they may never have given thought to such a notion. But the stance they take in dealing with the world implicitly regards it as intelligent, meaningful, or purposeful. In the case of those who do not admit this implication, their attitude is all the more significant.

• *Meaning in life*

One such stance consists in attributing meaning to life, which occurs in many different ways. Some people are proud of having led a meaningful life; others are striving to make their life more meaningful. Some admire the meaningfulness they perceive in someone else's life; others are searching for the meaning of life as something they feel they ought to be able to discover. Some are deeply disturbed and desperate over the apparent meaninglessness of life — either their own or life as a whole. Underlying all of these attitudes is the conviction that life does have, can have, or ought to have, a meaning. This would not make sense if the world, and life in particular, were the work of chance. The fact that so many people — the overwhelming majority, it would seem — believe thus in the actual or potential meaningfulness of life shows unmistakably (and even if their conscious philosophy contradicts this) that for them the world is not reducible ultimately to the interaction of blind forces. Whatever be the "meaning" which they attribute to life — order, direction, or purpose (for most people, it is probably too vague to be articulated) — they have come to recognize, in the course of their observation of the world and involvement in it, that the universe somehow makes sense, that it is not all sound and fury signifying nothing but has something meaningful to say; and that they, as part of the world, are summoned to chime in with its meaning.

The existentialism of Sartre of course declares just the contrary: that reality is absurd, that it makes no sense, that the meanings we attribute to it are nothing but constructions of the human mind. But this is an *academic* position of a few philosophers, consciously rejecting the spontaneous convictions of the majority of mankind. Most people do see meaning in life, which would be strange if there were none. Furthermore, Sartre's existentialism is self-contradictory. What does it mean to call the world absurd? If all is swirling chaos and meaninglessness, nothing can be absurd. Absurdity presupposes a background of meaning or order, against which something can be measured as discordant, unfitting. Profound absurdity causes the human spirit (insatiably athirst for meaning — a fact, incidentally, which itself requires an explanation!) to react with disgust or nausea, something Sartre himself loved to dramatize. Yet if meaninglessness were absolute, the logical reaction would be not nausea but utter indifference. Suicidal nausea is the reaction of one who yearns for meaning but finds none. And to write books aimed at demonstrating rationally the utter irrationality of existence suggests that the author's "existentialism" is not very thoroughgoing. If nothing makes sense, why labor to correct the senselessness of those who think otherwise?

• *Confronting the world with confidence*

A second attitude to be considered here is that of confronting the world with confidence, security, and hope. If life were nothing but the product of chance, and therefore one enormous complex of accidents, the overwhelming probability would be that we and all our projects are doomed. To undertake anything meaningful would be foolish. It would make far more sense to crawl under the covers and hope to go out quietly and painlessly. This is in fact the route taken by some people; nothing motivates them to do anything.

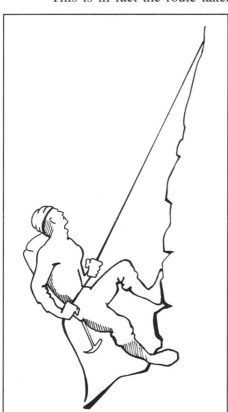

And because waiting for the light to go out is in fact an awful, distressing condition, some snuff out their own lives.

Most people, however, go on living, and do so with a hope, security, and expectation which implicitly acknowledge that the world is not just chaos. They live in the belief that something can be accomplished, that life can indeed be worth the effort. They meet with accidents and disappointments of course but do not take these as the fundamental truth and definition of reality. Instead, an indomitable hope welling up from the depths of their being makes them keep on trying, sometimes even in the face of crippling mishaps or apparently insurmountable obstacles. In people who consciously believe in God and his promise of a future reward, this behavior is understandable. But how explain this "hoping against hope" in those who lack such a belief? It is not by some argument that they have been persuaded to give life a try; their very experience of the world, in the course of their dealings with it, has led them to recognize that it is not just a meaningless, aimless swirl of stuff. The fact that they have no articulate belief makes them all the more convincing witnesses to what we have been calling divinity (or "dimension of depth") in the world.

We are not arguing that, because many people believe in the meaningfulness of life or the prevalence of the good, it must be true. But when great numbers of people from practically all cultures and walks of life, in their spontaneous reaction to the world through which they pass and with which they are in constant struggle, instinctively come to treat it as meaningful and hope-filled, there is probably an objective basis for their attitude. When belief in God is rightly presented to such people, it comes not as a *deus ex machina* urged upon them willy-nilly but as the one explanation which makes sense of their deepest convictions. To the man who is convinced that life has meaning and purpose or to the one who looks to the future with confidence, the existence of God makes his position intelligible and coherent. It is the denial of God that contradicts his deepest instincts and makes his outlook absurd and untenable.

SOME COMMON WAYS TO GOD

• *Beauty*

Three aspects of the world particularly solicit our attention: beauty, order, and goodness. There is beauty in the sunrise and sunset; in magnificent mountains and vast forests; in little lakes reflecting nearby hills. There is the gorgeous, spectacular beauty of the peacock's tail and of brilliantly variegated tropical fish swarming around a coral formation; there is also the gentle, quiet beauty of wild flowers or a bird's song. Wherever it be found, beauty thrills the human soul. It calls forth our admiration; it inspires some of the finer, nobler tendencies of our nature. In some way it fulfills and perfects us. It has a positive value, a life-giving, aspiration-fulfilling character that is lacking in things that are ugly. This admirable — are we not already tempted to say adorable? — quality of the beauty inherent in the world confronts us with the paradox that we, who consider ourselves superior to the natural world around us because of our intelligence, find in nature something we are bound to hold in awe, something we must look up to, treasure, and adhere to for the perfection and fulfillment of that which is finest in ourselves. This needs to be accounted for. We are not yet at the point of deciding whether "divinity" is merely an aspect of the world or a reality distinct from it. For the moment, it is enough to observe that beauty is there, and that the question of its meaning cannot be eluded. Beauty is just as real as molecules, atoms, electrons, and quarks; but information about the structure of matter does not explain why there should be beauty in it. This must be sought at another level, in some other dimension.

The objection is sometimes made that we call certain patterns beautiful and harmonious simply because we are used to them. A little reflection should show that this facile objection is completely unrealistic. Ugliness and banality are at least as common as beauty, especially in man-made environments, but that does not make them seem beautiful to us. Even when we get so inured to ugliness as to deaden our abhorrence, it does not become beautiful; in fact being confronted constantly with ugliness can make us revolt. It is also true that *styles* of beauty vary with culture; yet this is far from proving that beauty is nothing but a subjective evaluation.

• *Rhythm and order in nature*

Another intimation of divinity is provided by the rhythm and order apparent in the steady movement of the heavens, the alternation of night and day, and the annual pulse of the seasons. No doubt a scientist will insist that these are a necessary consequence of the natural properties of the matter of which the universe is composed and the events to which it has been subject. That merely situates the fundamental order; it does not refute the fact that it is inherent in the physical world. We will see below how the very possibility of scientific investigation is itself evidence for the existence of an intelligent creator. Here, we are considering only what can be sensed by anyone who marvels at the heavens or contemplates the encompassing world: It is indeed ordered and harmonious. But does this not suggest that somewhere out there — in matter or behind matter or before matter — there must be intelligence at work? And if matter itself is mindless, then where is this intelligence to be located?

Not only is nature orderly, in many ways it is our teacher. The age-old proverbs about the "wisdom of mother nature" express a lesson imprinted on the human spirit by a rich experience. There are rhythms in nature that set the tempo of authentic human life. The Taoists of China and the Stoics of Greece formulated a philosophy that had its roots in a kind of peasant wisdom that was more or less universal until the technological and industrial revolution: namely, that the right course for humanity consists in conforming to the patterns of nature. If scientific technology has tended to destroy this sense, replacing it with an arrogant pretension of being master of the universe, is not the ecological movement today an indication that we are relearning the old lesson on a new scale and in a negative mode: by disregarding the exigencies of nature, we stunt and destroy our own growth?

• *Goodness*

Third, the exuberant life that springs up out of the earth in forest, field, pond, and swamp — all the living things with their fantastic variety, abundance, their extraordinary adaptations and interactions — all this seems to suggest that somehow, in the depths of reality, there is a well of goodness and generosity, pouring itself out in beneficence.

> There lives the dearest freshness deep down things,
> And though the last lights off the black west went,
> Oh, morning on the brown brink eastward springs,
> Because the Holy Ghost over the bent world broods
> With warm breast and with — ah! — bright wings.
> (G. M. Hopkins, "God's Grandeur")

On a pleasant day, with the sun shining and a fresh breeze blowing, most people have the sense that there is something good about nature. We even say, "It is going to be a

good day." There are of course bad days too. And besides the fruits and vegetables which nourish us, there are poisonous herbs and noxious animals. These pose the problem of evil, with which we will deal in due course (Chapter 8). But the presence of evil does not negate the reality of good; in fact, evil is meaningless except in contrast with good (the converse does not hold!). Moreover, we are not asking in some kind of quantitative fashion, "When all is totaled up, does not the good outweigh the evil?" As if to say, "Are there not more good days than bad? Are there not more helpful microbes than noxious?" In a world that consisted of a meaningless chaos, neither good nor evil would have any meaning. But if there is something really good in the world, then all is not chance. There has to be some sort of "divinity" to explain the goodness that is there, whatever may be said about the badness or meaninglessness that encompasses it.

Some philosophers will object that goodness is nothing but an expression of the way we feel about things; but is there not an objective difference between things that foster our life and those that harm us? Evolutionists may maintain that we have simply adapted to conditions in our environment; but does that very speculative answer really account for the goodness we experience? Astrophysicists will observe that most of the universe is utterly inhospitable to life; that only reinforces the providential character of our world (see Chapter 9). We are not yet ready to conclude that "someone up there is smiling on us," but must we not at least admit that *goodness* is something real in the world?

• *The human mystery*

An entirely different sort of intimation is provided by the mystery of the human. This is a domain so rich and variegated, we cannot even make a general statement here but will only indicate a few suggestive examples: deep and lasting friendships that make people treasure each other to the point of sacrifice; intense love that binds two persons together in a union that transcends even friendship; the sense of justice that drives a person to fight against discrimination; the loyalty and patriotism that lead young men to risk limbs and

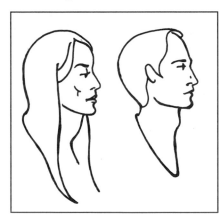

lives in defense of their homeland; the illumination that comes from the insights of great philosophers and poets; the light of the smile on a baby's face; the innocent delight of a child thrilled by a new experience; the horror of brutality committed against the helpless, etc.

These are only a few characteristic expressions of the human reality which we will appeal to later as signs of the distinction between man and beasts (see Chapter 10). Here, we are simply asking: Don't these things oblige us to acknowledge a level of being which cannot be reduced to matter and motion? If the world is nothing but a swirling galaxy of atoms, combining and recombining in various patterns according to the interplay of physical forces, then love is no better than selfishness; fidelity is not essentially different from lethargy; the most anguished cry of indignation or horror is comparable to a squeaking wheel; a baby's smile has no more meaning than the chance configuration of a passing cloud. That these things prove the existence of God we are not yet ready to say. But they are signs of a dimension of being, a mysterious depth of reality which cannot be denied except by stifling the voice of the human spirit and which cannot be accounted for in terms of material structures and forces.

GOD AND THE WORLD OF SCIENCE

The foregoing considerations arise directly out of our experience of the world and interaction with it. They are in a sense an attempt to recover the intuitions of prescientific mankind. But we are no longer primitives today. The results and methods of empirical science have created new perspectives in which all of us, whether professional scientists or not, do a large part of our thinking. Hence we must ask how this scientific perspective affects the question of God.

An enormous practical difficulty confronts such a project because few people have the double competence to speak both as theologians and as scientists. The following remarks are those of a theologian reflecting on the implications of what the scientists tell us about the universe. It is contended here that science, far from interfering with belief in God, provides a confirmation of it. This is not an attempt to prove the existence of God from science but, more modestly, to show that belief in God fits in with the scientific vision of the world far better than atheism does.

The question confronting us is, as noted above, whether the world to which we belong could have resulted from the various forces of nature interacting haphazardly or whether it postulates a directive intelligence. In other words, whether the factors that science can discern and measure suffice to explain what now exists through their random action or whether there is not evidence of a purposeful direction. In brief, is the world the product of chance or of design?

When considering the possibility of an intelligent designer, we need not imagine someone intervening extraneously in the universe to bring about results foreign to the natural workings of the material world. It is just such a notion, more appropriately called a demiurge, that has turned many scientists away from belief in God. We will suppose instead that whatever happens in the world (apart from the case of miracles, which are not in question here) is brought about by the natural operation of the factors that constitute the world. The intelligent designer for whom we would argue is not someone who interferes with nature in order to achieve effects alien to it but an *author* who allows the beings created by him to attain through their natural operation the goals set by him. (This will be examined further in Chapter 9.)

• *The scientific history of the universe*

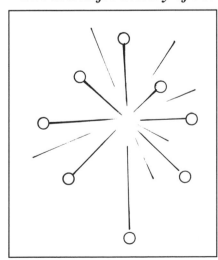

As an introduction to what follows, it may help to recall the broad outlines of the "history" of the universe as it has emerged in recent years out of the combined results of astronomy, geology, paleontology, biology, and auxiliary disciplines. There seems to be a fairly general consensus that the world we know has come into being in three major stages, which can be designated as the Big Bang, Galactic Ovens, and the evolution of life.

In this view, all that now exists originated as a single ball of plasma, in which the matter now scattered throughout space was compressed in a state so dense and hot that even basic atomic structures were untenable. This plasma exploded about fifteen billion years ago, spewing out its contents in all directions, in a movement that still continues today, as the stars and galaxies race farther and farther away from one another. As the plasma cooled, the particles of which it was composed began to coalesce in the form of hydrogen and helium. This condensed into galaxies and stars, in which more complex elements were formed. The stars in turn underwent secondary explosions, scattering debris which gathered into new stars in which still more complex forms of matter were forged. The solar system, and in particular our earth, are the result of several such recyclings.

Here on earth, thanks to conditions prevailing during its early millennia, a new type of process got underway. Complex molecules began to coalesce and then link together in greater complexes, from which resulted primitive living beings such as bacteria and blue-green algae. These in turn evolved into higher and more complex forms of life. The human race appears as the supreme product of the evolutionary process to date but not necessarily its ultimate term.

• *Theological reflections*

The above sketch is of course only a crudely simplified outline of an extremely complex process, not all the steps of which can be proposed with full assurance. Nevertheless, there seems to be a broad consensus that a development along such lines has taken place. While leaving it to professionals to criticize, refine, and elaborate this theory (or rather set of theories) according to the methods of their own disciplines, we can, in reflecting on it from a theological point of view, discover in it still further instances of what we have called intimations of divinity.

There is no need to challenge the history of the cosmos as sketched above. If the best scientific evidence indicates that this is approximately what happened, the theologian and the believer have no difficulty accepting it. (The reservations that need to be made about evolution will be pointed out in Chapter 8.) What we contend is that this very account of the cosmos at several points poses questions which oblige us to look for another level of explanation.

First is the obvious fact that it tells us nothing about what went on before the Big Bang or why the Big Bang took place. An explosion explains the fragments which follow, but it itself calls for an explanation. To avoid the intolerable abruptness of such a beginning, some have proposed a cyclic universe which alternately explodes and implodes upon itself, like an enormous accordion; but this theory seems to be chiefly the product of imagination seeking to evade a difficulty. It is not based on positive evidence, nor is there a theoretical principle to explain it. (Even if the quantity of matter is sufficient to make the exploding universe collapse eventually back upon itself, that does not imply an ongoing oscillation.)

Secondly, comparing the beginning and the present time of this process, we note that all the beings which now exist, including earth with its plants and animals, are composed out of particles blasted away from one another by the Bang, and subsequently recombined by the operation of the forces endemic to them. The electrons, quarks, neutrinos, etc., had to be assembled together in those delicately poised structures which we call atoms; to enter into such combinations, they had to be of precisely the right electrical charge and mass. The atoms in turn had to be able to bond with one another as molecules, sometimes of extraordinary complexity. These in turn, at least some of them, had to be capable of further assembly into the dynamic organizations which we call living beings, with all their own proper complexity and diversity, to say nothing of their interdependence. Is it conceivable that the primordial particles were susceptible of functioning as elements of so complex a structure by sheer accident, without being designed for that purpose? Could a skyscraper, an airplane, or a computer be constructed out of materials found haphazardly in a junkyard?

Again, we are not suggesting that these developments were directed by a demiurge who assembled things according to his plan, instead of letting them act out of their own inherent dynamism. We presume that electrons, quarks, and the like act according to their nature (even if their action is only statistically predictable), and that what has come about in the universe has been brought into being by the natural forces at work. What we are affirming is that somehow, somewhere in this process, there has to be room for a vast, architectonic intelligence governing the whole. If you wanted to build a house, and in looking around for materials, found stacks of brick, timbers cut to just the right dimensions, window frames already assembled as well as the pipes, wires, plumbing, and electri-

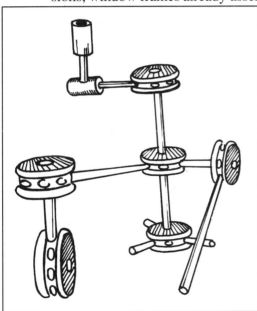

cal fixtures, furniture for the living room, dining room, bedroom, and kitchen, and even carpets and curtains, you would surely assume that someone already had the idea of building a house before you, and had prepared the materials with this in mind. It would be inconceivable that they had turned up by chance. But the complexity and design of a house are trivial by comparison with what we find in nature, especially in living beings. It takes a good deal of cleverness to design Tinker Toys, in which a few basic blocks, balls, and spokes can be joined into constructions of progressively greater complexity. Can it be supposed that particles capable of all the permutations and combinations required by the incredibly more complex constructions of the natural world simply happened to occur in the primordial plasma without any design, intention, or calculation?

• *The origin of life*

The third major point which seems to call for an explanation transcending the processes of nature is the origin of life. In the conditions which prevailed on the surface of the earth at the time of its formation, no form of life would have been possible. How did it get started?

A preliminary question that ought to be considered is whether a living being is simply a complex chemical. That is, is life only a complex coordination of simpler processes that can be found at the chemical level of being (along with the mechanical, electronic, etc.)? Those who hold for the spontaneous origin of life assume that this is so. This assumption can be challenged, as we will see below. But for the purpose of discussion, let us assume that life is nothing more than a special case of organic chemistry.

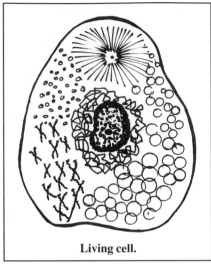

Living cell.

Then our problem is: Was it possible for the first living cell to arise spontaneously out of factors already given in inert matter? Even the simplest of living beings, the prokaryotic (that is, non-nucleated) cell is an entity of incredible complexity. It involves over a thousand different types of protein molecules, to say nothing of nucleic acids, fats, carbohydrates, and other elements. Chemists are still struggling with the problem of synthesizing the simplest proteins; they are nowhere near producing the more complicated ones. Yet the theory that life arose by chance requires that these diverse molecules be produced, gathered together, and assembled in the right order by accident. It means that organisms arose without organization. The components of a cell have to collaborate in performing all the vital functions of nutrition, growth, reproduction, sensation, and reaction. A cell wall has to be formed to keep the other molecules together and protect them; it must be endowed with the extraordinary discrimination of allowing nutriments to enter, excrements to pass out, and nothing else to go either way. Has this occurred without any plan?

• *Fred Hoyle*

The parameters of this problem were pointed out piquantly by the British astronomer Fred Hoyle. Until very recently, he says (writing in 1982), scientists could suppose that, even though the probability of a living cell arising by chance was extremely slight, the number of occasions in which it might have occurred in the billions of years available was extremely great. Hence they could maintain that, in the last analysis, the event was really not so improbable. But as the basic structures of the important biomolecules have become better known, more exact determinations of the probabilities are possible. For instance, enzymes are crucial for the functioning of a living cell. A typical enzyme is composed of ten or twenty different amino acids, most of which must be in the right position for the enzyme to function. Even if we neglect all other factors and consider nothing but the shuffling of amino acids needed to compose a given enzyme, there is only about one chance in 10^{20} (that is, 100,000,000,000,000,000,000) of getting them right. And as there are about two thousand enzymes, Hoyle concludes that the chance of getting them all in a random trial is only one out of $10^{40,000}$ (p. 24). This is a figure so rare that we cannot begin to form an idea of it. The total number of elementary particles in the entire visible universe is estimated to be about 10^{79}; yet this is only a minuscule fraction of $10^{40,000}$. Thus Hoyle is saying that the chance of getting all the enzymes right in a random trial is far less than that of striking one particular atom in all the stars of a universe, inconceivably greater than ours. And even if so utterly unlikely an event did occur, you would still not have life but

92

only enzymes. Other complex molecules are also needed for the living cell, such as histones, which serve as a structure for DNA at the time of cell division. There are five histones; the longest, H1, consists of over two hundred amino acids. Even if the latter were present in equal quantities (a highly unlikely supposition!), it would require about 20^{100} trials to obtain one histone molecule at random — another "figure larger than that of all atoms in the visible galaxies and stars" (p. 27). Finally, the enzymes, histones, and many other complex molecules would need to be assembled together — an operation probably far more difficult and unlikely than the formation of the molecules themselves (p. 130).[2]

Hoyle adds that the difficulty is aggravated by the shortage of time. It used to be supposed that enormous aeons were available for the play of chance in the "rich, hot, salty soup" which covered the face of the primitive earth. Recent research, however, has drastically reduced this estimate. The earth is about 4.5 billion years old. Fossil remains indicate that primitive forms of life were already present 3.2 (and most probably even 3.8) billion years ago. As conditions on earth were probably quite inimical to life for the first half billion years or so (due to lack of water, the heavy meteoric bombardment to which the earth, like the moon, was then subject, etc.) only about two hundred million years may have been available for the process leading up to the first living beings. This is an extremely short time for such a momentous development. As was remarked by Cyril Ponnamperuma, one of those who reported on the earliest fossil evidence for life, "We are now thinking, in geochemical terms, of instant life."[3]

For such reasons, Hoyle rejects as utterly unthinkable the supposition that life originated on this earth. He concludes that it must have come from elsewhere, and proposes that genetic material may have been brought to earth from outer space by comets, meteors, light waves, and other forces. As for how life originated in the first place, Hoyle, though an atheist, holds it much more reasonable to suppose that it was designed by some sort of superior intelligence, rather than coming about by chance. (Perhaps, he suggests, an intelligence based, like computers, on silicon, rather than on carbon, as our brain is.)

• *A series of events?*

Few scientists have been persuaded by Hoyle's idea that life came to earth from elsewhere, much less by his suggestion of a silicon-based intellect directing it. But twenty years before Hoyle, an American biologist, Quastler, had already declared:

> It is virtually impossible that life has originated by a random association of molecules; the proposition that a living structure could have arisen in a single event through the random association of molecules must be rejected.
> (*The Emergence of Geological Organization*, New Haven, Conn.: Yale University Press, 1964, p. 7).

Rather than conclude either to a creator or to the extraterrestrial origin of life, Quastler proposes that there must have been a long series of events by which the primitive living structures gradually came to be formed; and this would seem to be the position of most evolutionary biologists today. And laboratories all over the world are trying to discover the route this development might have followed.

But if the odds against the formation of a living cell by a single chance event are prohibitive, it is not clear how postulating a long series of fortunate accidents makes the outcome any less improbable. The chances of a wrong accident, that is, one that will interrupt the development, are nearly always far greater than the chances of a lucky accident that will carry it forward. Hence, the longer the series is prolonged, the more certain it becomes that a development left to chance will be destroyed rather than perpetuated.

• *Monkeys and typewriters*

In discussing this problem, people have endlessly had recourse to the imaginary example of a monkey playing with a typewriter, asking what are the chances of his writing *Hamlet*. Besides being trite, this example is prejudicial. In order to make the chances of the event calculable, it supposes an intelligently constructed machine (the typewriter) and a monkey trained to strike the keys. Moreover, the possibility of catastrophic endings (such as the monkey destroying the typewriter, or the ribbon jamming up) is disregarded. But in the real situation we are dealing with, the possibilities are incalculable and catastrophes frequent. A more realistic comparison would be to let a tribe of monkeys loose in a jungle, and ask how long it will take them to construct a typewriter. When you narrow the factors down to twenty-six typewriter keys being tapped with some regularity, you can calculate the probability of any combination of letters. But in the real situation of the monkeys wandering free, the probabilities are simply impossible to determine mathematically. What are the chances of monkeys manufacturing steel? How likely are they to cut and weld it into typewriter keys? How long would it be before they happened to come up with our alphabet? All of this, and all the other steps necessary to arrive at a Remington Rand, they could conceivably perform by a series of fortuitous accidents. But the statistical probability of their doing it cannot be put into even approximate mathematical figures because there are no firm parameters on which to erect calculations. It is not implausible that the monkeys would lose interest in their half-built typewriter and go eat bananas instead; or that they would take so long to complete their construction that the original parts would have rusted away to uselessness so that all the lucky progress that had been made would end at nothing. In the case of the evolving life-form, this would correspond to the possibility that, for a development taking place in the South Pacific, the potassium needed happens to be in Greenland. Or that an unfortunate event (always more probable than the fortunate ones) binds up the sodium in such a way as to make it inaccessible. Such things happen all the time not only in nature but even in the carefully controlled experiments of laboratories.

In the case of the monkeys, the long series of right accidents needed for their success would be far less, and the possibility of catastrophe probably greater, than in the case of the development of the first living cell. Moreover, in the case of the monkeys, we have the advantage of live operators, with nimble fingers, experimental curiosity, the sense of sight, etc., none of which would have been available to prepare the first living cell.

• *Life in the laboratory?*

A famous experiment by Stanley Miller in 1953 showed that amino acids, the building blocks of living tissue, could have been generated spontaneously in conditions similar to those supposed to have prevailed on the primitive earth. Many biologists are confident that, with enough such experiments, the route that led from inert matter to the living cell will one day be discovered. Up to now, however, no one has been able to devise a plausible route. The proposals that have been made are all very vague and general; as soon as they are made specific, they encounter contradictions and obstacles that no one is able to resolve. As we have noted, chemists are still struggling to synthesize the simplest protein molecules; they are nowhere near capable of the more complex ones, to say nothing of the innumerable other elements of the living cell (some of which may not yet even be known). And should the day come when all these elements are at hand, the task would remain of assembling and organizing them into an actual functioning cell-something that is completely beyond the horizons of our actual technological capabilities.

But even if the theoretical possibility of synthesizing life from inert materials could be demonstrated, that would not prove it actually feasible. How often have laboratory technicians been stymied by the fact that the diverse conditions required by their experiments are mutually incompatible, so that what is needed for one phase of the experiment prevents another, and what is theoretically possible is actually unrealizable? And if human calculations, dealing with comparatively simple problems, are often thus blocked, how can we suppose that random activity will solve problems of far greater complexity?

Supposing, however, that one day someone should succeed in producing life in a test tube, what would that prove? The fact that the combined efforts of thousands of trained intellects, investigating and experimenting for hundreds of years, had succeeded in synthesizing a blue-green alga — would this prove that it could have happened by chance? Would it not rather suggest that intelligence had been involved in the first production of life, just as it would be in this (hypothetical) second one? Scientific wit has produced the Cray computers; but who would take that as proof that a computer could have been assembled by the random interaction of all the iron, copper, nickel, and other materials available on the early continents? Yet a living cell is immeasurably more difficult to produce than the most advanced computer.

Note that the question here is not whether life has arisen from inert matter. It seems to be a fact of the history of the earth that this has indeed happened. The question is: "Did it come about by sheer chance or under the direction of some kind of intelligence?" Biology does not show that it *could* come about by chance; what it shows is the utter improbability of its having done so. From a purely statistical point of view, it would be far more plausible that the origin of living beings was guided by intelligence. When biologists affirm their confidence that it happened by chance, it is not on the basis of biology but for some other motive.

Often they seem to have excluded the possibility of God *a priori*. Then, given the fact that life has actually arisen on earth, they are compelled to suppose that it must have come about by chance. This means that they are accepting an improbability they would never tolerate elsewhere.

One reason why many biologists exclude the idea of divine causality is probably that they have in mind what we have called the action of a demiurge: one who intervenes in the world as human artisans do, artificially reworking his raw materials. However, it is not necessary to conceive thus of creation. Instead, one can accept that life arose from inert matter by a series of natural developments of the sort that the biologists suppose, and which they are in the process of tracking down in their laboratories. An intelligent creator does not imply someone interfering and doing violence to the nature of things but simply direction of the processes which lead to the intended result. If the original arrangement of things at the moment of creation was such that life inevitably arose in the course of time, through a sequence of events in which all the laws of physics and chemistry were operative so that the process of its origin could theoretically be traced by science in full detail, the process itself and the life resulting from it would still be the work of the intelligence that set everything in motion.

To hold that a living cell came into being by sheer chance (whether in a single step or by a long series of events) is to abandon the principle of causality that underlies all science. When an archaeologist looks at the artifacts of the most primitive hominids, he may be uncertain whether a given piece of stone is a tool fabricated on purpose or just a rock that accidentally broke in the right shape. But in the case of refined, beautiful instruments such as the Acheulean hand-axes, he is sure that they can only be the product of human industry. And if someone were to propose that the bisons of Lascaux were just the accidental results of the weathering process, he would be laughed out of his profession. But the wall paintings of Lascaux and the Acheulean tools are simplicity itself compared to the complex and dynamic structures of the most primitive living cell! If the principle of causality is respected in one case, it is hardly consistent to disregard it in the other.

Carl Sagan and others have excited the popular imagination by speculating about the number of stars likely to have planetary systems, the number of these likely to be suitable for life, the number of these on which life has probably actually evolved, the number of these on which it may have developed intelligence, and the number of these that may have developed a technology capable of communicating with others. Sagan suggests that within our galaxy, there might be about a thousand communicative civilizations.

Such speculations generate the impression that the spontaneous emergence of life from non-living matter is somehow scientifically assured. In fact, however, it has in no way been demonstrated; it has been taken for granted, and this in spite of its overwhelming improbability. And if it is utterly unlikely that life originated even once by chance, it is immensely more unlikely that it did so many times. In *The Emergence of Geological Organization*, Quastler remarks:

> . . .if life should have originated in this utterly improbable manner [by a single random event], then it is certain that no other life of independent origin exists either on earth or anywhere in space; if life of non-terrestrial origin is found on Mars, then the hypothesis of random association of molecules is disproved.

In conclusion: The existence of living beings, considered as nothing more than complex chemical structures, is strongly indicative that intelligent purpose is at work in the universe. Once again, we are not yet attempting to determine *where* this intelligence is located or *how* it operates. Likewise we are not postulating the intervention of some agent other than the forces of nature. We are saying simply that it is far more reasonable to suppose that a purposeful intelligence directed the formation of living organisms, than that they arose purely by chance.

• *Life not reducible to inanimate action*

Now we must reconsider the assumption underlying the calculations of the probability of the chance origin of life. As noted above, they assume that a living being is ultimately nothing more than a complex arrangement of molecules. But can this be taken for granted? Does not life involve a kind of activity and a mode of being of a radically different order from the mechanical, chemical, and electronic (even though it uses these, assimilating them into its own vital activity)? The difference is somewhat obscured today because we have been able to build robots programmed to perform certain operations which externally parallel those of living beings; but even without entering into the delicate philosophical question of the definition of life, is it not evident that the robot is not alive? It can be designed to react to certain rays of light or to shapes such as letters and numbers; but it does not *see* them or *know* them. It can be engineered to move toward certain objects and away from others; but that is not the same thing as hunger or dread. You could conceive of a robot that would react to certain situations by turning red or pale; that would simply be a demonstration of engineering virtuosity, it would not impart to the machine

the emotional experience of embarrassment or fear. We sometimes say that computers "remember" data; but this is an improper transfer of a name on the grounds of a superficial resemblance. The computer remembers nothing, just as it never knew anything in the first place; neither does it, strictly speaking, "obey commands" to retrieve information. Its operation is no more alive than that of a conveyor belt designed to pull a box of cornflakes off the shelf of a warehouse and bring it to the counter; only the computer works with electrical impulses rather than with real merchandise. (The expression *memory bank* is a significant, spontaneous effort to rectify the improper language used here by recalling that the so-called memory is only a bank — an electronic warehouse.)

The difference between living and non-living beings can perhaps be perceived most readily in the fact that a living being seeks its own welfare. It acts in such a way as to remain alive and healthy, to grow and reproduce. When injured, it repairs itself; when situations change, it adapts to them. The good of the whole organism is the goal of all its activities, and even of those of its parts. (When a part ceases to act for the good of the whole, as a gland that secretes too much or too little, this is a diseased condition that detracts from and may even destroy the life of the being.) For the living being is a true whole, we may even say a *self* (without meaning to suggest self-consciousness), with respect to which the parts are in the strictest sense *parts*.

The machine or electronic instrument, on the contrary, is only an assembly of pieces, each of which is more properly a whole than a part. The machine has no unity except that of being linked together; it has no self (the very idea is absurd!) which could even be conceived as seeking its own good. It simply persists in its operation (or rather the various operations of its components), even when this leads to its own destruction. If a part is worn or a bolt is loose, the machine does not make allowances for them but keeps right on functioning until it falls apart or becomes inoperative. If the road is hard on an automobile, the latter does not adjust to this but hurtles along until something gives. A dog with an injured paw will raise it off the ground and limp on the other three; but when did an automobile with a flat tire ever lean over and run on three wheels? The designer of the machine of course arranges the parts so that they will collaborate for the good of the whole; but that *intention* is in his mind, not in the machine. The difference between the machine and the living being can be summed up precisely in this, that the former requires an extrinsic designer (and an operator) to do for it what the latter does for itself.

To sum this up: Those who suppose that living beings arose by chance are not only postulating the occurrence of a very unlikely chemical event, they are wholly disregarding the qualities that make a living being radically different from a chemical compound. To account for life, we must account precisely for all those elusive, mysterious qualities that characterize living beings by contrast with chemicals.

• *Origin of life contradicts survival of the fittest*

Finally, in explaining the evolution of living things, Darwinian theory relies on the principle of the survival of the fittest. But the origin of life constitutes a major violation of that principle. *Fittest*, in this context, means fittest to survive; and rock and mud are far more fitted for survival than the fragile living beings that have emerged from them. On the principle of survival of the fittest, earth would have remained inert like the moon or Mars. The force that pressed bees, birds, and butterflies out of the edges of the primeval sea-lashed continents could not have been the struggle to survive! These things are irrefutable witnesses that tenacious clinging to existence is not the primal law governing evolution; but rather, deep in the bowels of nature, there must lie an even more powerful urge *to do something better*, to improve on that which is already there. We will return to this point in considering the implications of evolution. At the present moment of the argument, what is significant is that the origin of life violates the principle proposed as the driving principle behind all subsequent development. This wrecks all possibility of using the survival of the fittest in a consistent, comprehensive theory to explain both the origin and evolution of living beings.

• *Evolution of life*

Let us turn now to evolution in the strict sense of the emergence of newer forms of life from the old. Darwin accounted for it by his theory of natural selection. Many flaws have subsequently been pointed out in Darwin's theory, and modifications have been made in it. Paleontologists today are much more modest than they used to be in drawing up "family trees" to indicate the lineage of diverse species. But the fact that the forms of life inhabiting the earth today have, in general, evolved out of more primitive forms has been confirmed by so many converging lines of evidence that there seems to be no reasonable possibility of challenging it.

Supposing this to be so, we would now wish to argue that the history of evolution, insofar as it can be reconstructed, provides still another intimation of divinity — for this history does not have the lineaments of a haphazard sequence but those of a purposeful, directional thrust. It has indeed been heavily conditioned by chance but cannot be reduced totally to chance. If we limit ourselves to actual geological evidence, without speculating about the protobionts which may have preceded true life-forms, the story begins with the appearance of microscopic unicellular beings: bacteria and cyanobacteria. A stupendous advance occurred after more than a billion years, when some of these developed the process of photosynthesis; this was followed, half a billion years later, by the invention of nuclei to govern the cell's life processes; still later, some of them learned to breathe free oxygen, then to reproduce sexually. In another line of development, single-celled animals or plants began to live together in colonies, out of which genuine multi-cellular organisms apparently arose. From floating "jellyfish," the line of progress passes through hard-shelled mollusks to endoskeletal fish. These lead to reptiles and thence to birds. Meanwhile, along another lineage of uncertain derivation, furry little rodents develop into tree-swinging apes, among the likes of which man finally emerges. (About the essential discontinuity between man and his predecessors, something will be said in Chapter 10.) Despite many enormous lacunae, and granted the myriad little by-ways that intertwine with one another and often come to dead ends, there is an encompassing unity and coherence to this account. It is an awesome story, like the interminable sagas with which the Norsemen entertained themselves on long winter evenings. Although filled with random coincidence, it is held together and driven by a kind of primal thrust rising from deep within the heart of matter and moving inexorably forward, even though momentarily checked or reversed here and there. It turns corners, surmounts obstacles, makes numerous tentative efforts, mostly failing but exploiting its occasional successes as the basis for a new program of experiments. In some ways, it resembles an army moving forward along a broad front, meeting constant opposition but here and there achieving breakthroughs which allow battalions to pierce the line of resistance and open a new campaign.

The writings of authors who attempt to give a comprehensive account of evolution, such as Julian Huxley or Pierre Teilhard de Chardin, abound with images and language that illustrate this. The latter, for example, describing the development that takes place in a new phylum, writes:

> For a certain period of time [the phylum] devotes all its strength, so to speak, to groping about within itself. Tryout follows tryout, without being finally adopted. Then at last perfection comes within sight, and from that moment the rhythm of change slows down. The new invention, having reached the limit of its potentialities, enters its phase of conquest. Stronger now than its less perfected neighbors, the newly born group spreads and at the same time consolidates.
>
> (*The Phenomenon of Man*, p. 115; see also Huxley's essay "The uniqueness of man," in *Man Stands Alone*, New York: Harper, 1941)

Such accounts do not fit random events occurring to an entity drifting inertly on the sea of history. As the word *groping* indicates, they reflect a purposeful thrust, a tenacious insistence, an *élan vital* (Bergson). Not of course a calculated progression that keeps a set direction regardless of obstacles, nor the execution of a preconceived, fully detailed plan. The movement is subject to chance encounters; it can be deflected and thrown off course in many ways; it depends very much on lucky coincidences. It manifests great suppleness and adaptability, a readiness to make the most of each situation, a need to discover by "experiment" whether a given pathway is a blind alley or an opening to new opportunities. But always there remains an indomitable determination to go on and, what is even more significant, to go upward — to produce something superior to what is actually present.

• *"Survival of the fittest" does not explain evolution*

Earlier we pointed out that the principle of survival of the fittest does not account for the origin of life. Now we add that neither does it account adequately for the evolution of life. That it played a significant role is not in question; there is no reason to doubt that life-forms which were better equipped or better armed outlasted their competitors. But evolution has not led merely to forms more competitive and more durable; it has often led to forms which, being more complex, more gifted, and more beautiful, were also more fragile. (The most basic example of this is the passage from plant to animal life. This represented a great loss in survivability, for plants can endure more hardship, reproduce more abundantly, and live far longer than animals.)

Organizations produced by human efforts, whether they be a machine, an electrical circuit, a computer, a political party, or a chain store, when left to chance, do not improve with time. On the contrary, without constant maintenance, they degenerate. The more refined and highly organized they are, the more attention they need. The same applies to the individual living organism: In the course of time, it degenerates. Chance encounters do not improve things except exceedingly rarely; hence what is left to chance is in the long run destroyed. But in the case of life, there has been steady improvement in the course of time. Although each living being is quite vulnerable to accidents, the total realm of living things has thrived on them. Through three or four billion years of history, life has moved unstoppably forward, triumphing over obstacles, constantly rising to new achievements, perfecting itself, and exuberantly spinning off new forms, as if flaunting them in the face of the fiery extinction which, dour astrophysicists tell us, implacably awaits everything on the face of this earth. While holding in abeyance the twofold question "What is it all for? What purpose does it serve?" we are driven to the conclusion that the trajectory of life is not that of something agitated by the blind play of chance; it has a direction, an intention; it moves with a stubborn purposefulness.

• *Intelligence latent in the world*

We still are not ready to speak of God. This chapter leads us only to the point where we can say that in the world around us, particularly in the world of life, there is a latent intelligence and purposefulness. We might adopt provisionally the creed of Albert Einstein (who, in fact, did not believe in a personal God):

My religion consists of a humble admiration of the illimitable superior spirit who reveals himself in the slight details we are able to perceive with our frail and feeble minds. That deeply emotional conviction of the presence of a superior reasoning power, which is revealed in the incomprehensible universe, forms my idea of God.

(L. Barnett, *The Universe and Dr. Einstein*, New York: New American Library, 1952, p. 118)

Where this intelligence is to be located, how it can be accounted for, in what form it should be visualized — these are subsequent, more difficult questions, to which we will turn in Chapter 7, utilizing the light of faith. But before undertaking that, it was perhaps useful to pause at this halfway stage at which not only Christians, Jews, and Muslims but also Taoists, Hindus, and very many others who perhaps reject the notion of God may be able to agree.

5
God has spoken to us

Because nature's witness to the Creator is so difficult to interpret and so limited in scope, God has spoken to us about himself. This is the claim made by Christianity; one that is so familiar we may have lost sight of how stupendous and incredible it is. It means that the Supreme Being, the One for whom human language has no proper name, whose nature (if we even dare speak of nature here!) transcends the grasp of our brightest intellects, has revealed to us something of the secret of his inmost being. (Whether we should say *he, she,* or *it* of One who transcends all genders and all categories is itself a delicate question; but since, in the language of revelation itself, God is referred to as masculine, we will maintain this usage provisionally, and discuss it later — in Chapter 7.)

Christianity is founded on the belief that the Sovereign Lord of the universe has communicated to the world something of his inmost thoughts and intentions. He has not remained remote and unapproachable but has initiated a dialogue with us. The silence of the spheres has been broken by a word — a word addressed to us. This is the basis of Christianity's claim to be a religion of which God himself is the author. Natural religions are products of the human spirit in its search for God. But the flashes of intuition which occur even in the great religions of India, China, Persia, and Greece, to say nothing of the more primitive tribal religions, while sometimes very profound, are usually obscure, hesitant, confused, and contradictory. They differ from God's self-revelation to us as a footprint left in the sand differs from the look of a familiar face. They are indeed to be regarded with the greatest respect;[1] but the summits attained by the human mind trying to scale the steep cliff of the meaning of the world are far inferior to what has been given by the hand of God reaching down to us.

• *Revelation real or mythical?*

Rationalist scholars commonly treat divine revelation as a myth. It expresses perhaps the fact that the religious geniuses who first enunciated the basic Christian insights sensed that they had *received* these insights as a gift; but whatever be its rationale, the idea that God has imparted a message to certain chosen people is not to be taken literally.

Perhaps one could regard the Hindu Scriptures as myths and remain a Hindu; but to reduce the revelation made through Jesus and the prophets to myth is simply to reject the Christian faith. It is an essential element of this faith that God has really communicated with mankind, revealing himself and his gracious designs to us. "We did not follow cleverly devised myths when we made known to you the power and coming of our Lord Jesus Christ, but we were eyewitnesses of his majesty," declares the Second Letter of St. Peter (1:16, RSV). And St. Paul warns Timothy of the time "when men will not put up with sound doctrine. Instead, . . . They will turn their ears away from the truth and turn aside to myths" (2 Timothy 4:3f).

In Chapter 15 we will discuss the extent to which myth may be admitted in Christianity. Chapter 6 will examine Scripture, Sacred Tradition, and Church teaching, all of which modify our encounter with revelation. The present chapter will be confined to the fundamental structures of revelation, namely, *prophecy* and *faith*. It is by prophecy that revelation is presented to us, and by faith that we receive it.

PROPHECY

It is fact not sufficiently attended to, that Christianity gets one of its basic structures from the fact that divine revelation has been received by a few chosen prophets and has been accepted by others on their word. God could surely have illumined the hearts of all people equally. In fact, however, this is not how Christianity has come about. Instead,

there is a functional distinction between the prophets, who are enlightened to receive the revelation directly, and the disciples, who believe on the word of the prophets. (This does not mean that the prophet is the only one whose mind is illumined in this process. It will be seen below that the faith of the disciple also requires a light from God.)

Likewise there is no need to doubt that many people, whether outside or inside Christianity, have received private revelations. But in the case of the historic revelation which is constitutive of the Christian faith, it is a fact that it originated with a few from whom others received it. Accordingly, we have to look first at the function of the prophet, then at the faith of those who accept the prophetic message. Both depend on a divine illumination but not in the same way. The prophet is enlightened so as to perceive the truth directly;[2] others are enlightened so as to acknowledge what is uttered by the prophet.[3] The prophet has the role of articulating in human language the divine mysteries which others accept or reject as formulated by the prophet.

In popular thought, prophecy is usually taken as synonymous with prediction. This is a misconception, coming from the fact that the typical prophets are those of the Old Testament, whose most notable work, from a Christian point of view, consisted in foretelling the coming of the Messiah and his reign. But if we look attentively at their prophecies, we find them mostly concerned with the present, not the future, declaring God's judgment upon the people. And Jesus, although he came as the Messiah foretold in the Old Testament, was himself the greatest of all the prophets because he, more than any others, declared the divine mystery in the language of men.

There is also a tendency to apply the title of prophet to every critic of the social or religious establishment — for example, Mahatma Gandhi, Martin Luther King, or Daniel Berrigan. Some prophets did indeed engage in social or political criticisms; but what makes a person a prophet is not the content of his message — it is the fact that it originates not from him but from God. The prophet is *sent* by God to speak in God's name. "I will raise up for them a prophet like you [Moses] from among their brothers; I will put my words in his mouth, and he will tell them everything I command him" (Deuteronomy 18:18f).

Balaam, the pagan prophet described in Numbers 22ff, is a picturesque example. King Balak hired him to curse the Israelites, but Balaam declared, "I must speak only what God puts in my mouth" (22:38). Three times, at the king's bidding, he offered sacrifice and then, when the Spirit of God came upon him (24:2), prophesied blessings upon Israel. When the king protested, the prophet answered, "Even if Balak gave me his palace filled with silver and gold, I could not do anything, good or bad, to go beyond the command of Yahweh — and I must say only what Yahweh says" (24:13). In summary: "Yahweh put a message in Balaam's mouth" (23:5, 16).

BELIEF IN REVELATION

If revelation is the act by which God communicates to us the inner secret of his divinity, faith is the response by which we accept what he reveals. The terms *faith* and *belief* designate the fact that in this act, one gives assent to doctrines, the truth of which one is not able to see for oneself or to demonstrate. If someone who has been to a land you have never visited tells you stories about it and you accept his word, you are said to *believe* him: Whereas if you had gone and seen for yourself, you would no longer be believing this person, you would simply know the facts. In Christian faith, we believe the Word of God. Since divine revelation is not made separately to each individual but has been given to us through the prophets, and ultimately through Jesus the greatest of all the prophets, faith involves not only believing in God but also believing in the prophet as God's spokesman.

• *The term "faith"*

Faith is a term with a long, involved history. It has diverse connotations in diverse contexts. Even that faith on which salvation depends, according to the New Testament, has a rich variety of expressions. Sometimes it is clearly an attitude of belief, as when the Gospel of St. John says that "these are written that you may believe that Jesus is the Christ" (20:31). In other cases, faith appears as an attitude of trust in Jesus, without any clear conceptual formulation, as in the case of the many sick persons to whom Jesus declared, "Your faith has healed you" (for example, Matthew 9:22). Sometimes it is difficult to know how to classify it psychologically. We would contend that belief is always involved in it, even though the belief may be contained implicitly in some other, more manifest attitude such as trust.[4] Be that as it may, our intention here, in interpreting faith as belief, is neither to dismiss the other legitimate connotations of this polyvalent term, nor to reduce this rich personal attitude to a purely intellectual conviction. *Belief in what God has revealed* is the topic of our inquiry, and there is ample biblical warrant for calling this belief faith. Other dimensions of faith will be considered in Chapter 22.

• *The motives of faith*

What leads a person to make such an act of faith? This is indeed a profound mystery, and it involves one's entire life experience. We can, however, point out two important factors: *signs* presented to the rational mind to convince it, and *grace* by which God touches us in the hidden depths of our being.

It is normal for the prophet to offer signs as a guarantee that he has been sent by God. When Moses was sent to lead the Hebrews out of Egypt, he was afraid that the people would not believe God had sent him. So God gave him *miraculous signs* to work

(Exodus 4:1-9). Thus, after the pharaoh's army had been engulfed by the sea through which the Hebrews had passed dry-shod, "Israel saw the great work which Yahweh did against the Egyptians, and the people feared Yahweh, and they believed in Yahweh and in his servant Moses" (Exodus 14:31, RSV). Similarly, when the disciples of John the Baptist questioned whether Jesus was the Messiah, Jesus answered, "Go back and report to John what you have seen and heard: The blind receive sight, the lame walk, those who have leprosy are cured, the deaf hear, the dead are raised, and the good news is preached to the poor" (Luke 7:22).

Another kind of sign used by the prophets consists in foretelling future events which could not have been foreseen naturally. (It is this sort of prediction that is popularly and mistakenly identified with prophecy.) Thus Jesus foretold the circumstances of his death and resurrection: "The Son of man will be betrayed to the chief priests and teachers of the law. They will condemn him to death, and hand him over to the Gentiles; who will mock him, and spit on him, flog him and kill him; after three days he will rise" (Matthew 20:18f; Mark 10:33f; Luke 18:31ff). He also foretold the destruction of the Temple and of Jerusalem (Matthew 24:2ff; Mark 13:2ff; Luke 21:6ff).

Such signs confirm the prophet's claim to speak in the name of God. They are beyond natural power, and indicate that the Sovereign Lord of the Universe, whom all things obey, the eternal God to whom past, present, and future are all equally present, is vindicating the word of the prophet. They make faith reasonable, even when it assents to doctrines beyond the reach of reason. If a man claims to speak in the name of God, and produces signs that can come only from the power of God, it is reasonable to believe in him. Thus, while Christian faith embraces many doctrines which it is impossible to test or demonstrate, it is not irrational to believe them when you consider all the signs that Jesus gave to prove that he really was from God.[5]

• *Miracles today*

But a great difficulty with some of this evidence is its remoteness from us. We today are not able to see the miracles or hear the predictions of Jesus for ourselves, and we cannot help but wonder whether the reports handed down to us in the Gospels are reliable. To put the problem in another way, miracles do not seem to be happening in our presence. Consciously or subconsciously people are troubled by the oft-repeated objection, that our age of critical reason and scientific knowledge has either explained away or demythologized the things that used to be regarded as miraculous. If miracles do not occur in our culture, does this not suggest that the so-called miracles of biblical times were merely the fabrication of superstition and credulity?

The fact is that miracles have not ceased; it could indeed be argued that they are more abundant and more spectacular in the twentieth century than ever before. Certainly they are far better documented. Lourdes, for example, is the site of numerous miraculous healings, which are carefully examined and certified by a medical board composed of experts in various disciplines (these experts are not all Catholic; even atheists may be admitted to the staff). Apart from a few rare exceptions, no saint is canonized without several miracles having been worked through his intercession. The archives of the Congregation for the Causes of Saints are filled with accounts of miracles that have been scrutinized with utmost severity. At Fátima (Portugal) on October 13, 1917, the extraordinary "dance of the sun" was witnessed by a crowd of some seventy thousand to one hundred thousand persons, besides other people miles away. They saw the sun spinning in the sky, sending out rays of light of various colors, then plunging toward the earth in a way that terrified the observers and brought them to their knees. Even the journalists from the atheistic newspaper *Il Seculo*, who had come to deride the affair, were compelled to admit that they too witnessed this inexplicable happening.

The *tilma* of Guadalupe, bearing a miraculous image of the Blessed Virgin, has been submitted to rigorous scientific examination, which has astoundingly supported its authenticity. Stigmatics, such as Padre Pio, Teresa Neumann, Marthe Robin, and Alexandrina da Costa, were carefully observed in hospitals by doctors who testified that their wounds, which duplicated those of the crucified Christ, were genuine and naturally inexplicable (for example, not putrefying as prolonged wounds normally do); that their loss of blood was considerable without harm to their health. Moreover, several of them lived for years without taking any food other than the Eucharist. The blood of St. Januarius, kept in a vial in Naples since his martyrdom about 305 A.D., liquifies when it is brought near the relic of the saint's head. This occurs in a ceremony performed several times each year in the presence of great crowds of people, including the most skeptical. The bodies of SS. Catherine Labouré and Bernadette as well as many others have been found incorrupt after many years in the tomb, without having been embalmed.

The above examples are only some of the most famous and best established miracles of our time. We must also take into consideration the abundant reports of miracles associated with many lesser known shrines — for example, that of St. Anne de Beaupré in Canada; those which won the nickname "Miraculous Medal," for the medal of the Immaculate Conception; the great numbers of sick people cured by healers such as Brother

André of Montreal (1845-1937); the miracles and prophecies attributed to many mystics who, living hiddenly and quietly, have not yet become publicly known (for instance, Marthe Robin of Chateauneuf-de-Galaure in France, 1902-1981); the frequent reports of miracles in the context of the Charismatic Renewal or Medjugorje; and finally, countless others, not associated with any shrine, healer, or movement but which have come simply as an answer to the prayers of the ordinary faithful turning to God in their need. There is no way that all of these could be verified scientifically or critically so as to establish their authenticity beyond all doubt. Nevertheless, taken together, they add considerably to the weight of evidence that miracles cannot be relegated to ancient times of ignorance and superstition. They are still occurring today in comparative abundance (even though, by their very nature, they remain extraordinary and exceptional). And while we cannot summon up a miracle at will in order to prove a point or test a thesis, the more famous ones cited above have been well enough authenticated that they are available for the consideration of anyone who wants to study them seriously.

The idea that miracles belong only to the Dark Ages, and are not able to stand up under the scrutiny of the critical and scientific intelligence of the twentieth century, is itself a myth created by modern rationalism out of the very unscientific attitude of refusing to look at facts which disturb its assumptions. (People sometimes ask why these reports of miracles have not received more attention. This has not been for lack of evidence but because the communications media are reluctant to give them serious attention.)

Besides these public signs which can be examined by everyone, there are innumerable personal signs which may help to convince an individual, even though they have no such value for others. For example, a prayer that is answered, a chance word from a stranger that illumines my peculiar situation, a fortunate event that seems to be more than a coincidence — these and other things can be, in the context of an individual's life, signs of God speaking to him. Also, one person can be a sign for another. A saint or a very holy person is often convincing evidence of the presence and action of God for those who come into contact with him.

• *The Church as a sign*

Another sign, very different from those just discussed, is the Church itself. Chapter 2 suggested that, in comparison with other societies known to history, the Church appears as so extraordinary a phenomenon that one must ask whether recourse to some superhuman power is not necessary to explain it. However, the human imperfections of the Church are so disturbing that many find it an obstacle more than a support to their faith. But, taken in the right perspective, these human flaws really make the "miracle" all the more evident.

By all the ordinary laws of human development, the Church ought to have perished long ago, like all the other institutions contemporary with it. If we could draw up a vitality graph, it would probably indicate that after a frail beginning, the Church grew vigorously in spite of persecution until the fourth century. Then, once it had become accepted and favored by the state, a decline of fervor set in which worsened until, by the ninth and tenth centuries, the Church was in a truly miserable condition. Humanly speaking, it ought to have perished then. Instead a turnaround occurred in the eleventh century, with the result that the twelfth and thirteenth centuries were a time of impressive achievements. In the later Middle Ages another decline set in, and the Age of the Reformation appeared to threaten the demise of Catholicism once more. Instead, the seventeenth and eighteenth centuries were another period of reinvigoration. Even in the best moments, things are never completely *well* with the Church, and prophets of doom are forever predicting its approaching end, as is commonplace today. Nevertheless, the Church keeps on going, producing new and greater fruit. Must there not be a superhuman explanation for this mysterious, humanly inexplicable tenacity?

For the Church to have its full impact as a sign of divine revelation, it needs to be known well — not so much in an academic way, as by personal contact with its inner life. Is it not a fact that, in proportion as a person lives in sincere accord with its teaching, he or she finds his own life well ordered, sanctified and blessed, touched with grace, and at the same time more authentically human? The question could be rephrased schematically: Do we not find that the more we are *in* the Church, the closer we are to God and the truer we are to our own identity; whereas insofar as we withdraw from the Church, we lose contact with God, with our fellowman, and with our own true self? Obviously this is a question that each one must answer for himself or herself. It cannot be answered lightly or simply; it takes much testing and real living. But in the measure that it can be answered with a sure *yes*, the Church itself appears as a sign that God is speaking through it.

• *Scripture as a sign*

Finally, Scripture likewise is a sign of immense value for faith. Far from being a document which a person believes or rejects solely on the basis of extrinsic signs or evidence, Scripture is its own best witness. Those who heard Jesus preach were often convinced by this fact alone that he was of God: "We have heard for ourselves, and we know that this man really is the Savior of the world" (John 4:42). Similarly, on reading the New Testament, many people find in it a goodness, wisdom, and holiness that convince them of its profound truth and divine origin. This is not simply because it harmonizes with their previously held convictions; more likely, it convicts them of their wrongness. And it does so not by persuasive arguments but by an authority and power in which they recognize themselves as being addressed by Truth itself. Without perhaps knowing anything about theories of inspiration or the historical origins of this book, they recognize that God is speaking to them through it.

Scripture cannot of course exercise this influence on those who do not read it! To debate about Christianity without studying the New Testament carefully and thoughtfully is frivolous. Anyone who gives serious consideration to the Faith must examine its main piece of evidence.

What of those who read Scripture but are not impressed by it? It may be that their minds are so engrossed in material goods and sensual experience that they have become insensitive to the spiritual realm. Perhaps some form of pride keeps them from being open to what the Lord is trying to say to them. (Such was the case of St. Augustine when he first tried to read the New Testament.) Perhaps there is some other reason involving no fault at all. In any case, their negative experience in no way nullifies the positive experience of one who *does* encounter God in Scripture. Moreover, if they persevere humbly and prayerfully, often they too will eventually begin to perceive what they have been missing.

• *How to seek faith*

It is not necessary to find a single, absolutely convincing sign that suffices all by itself; the whole complex of signs occurring in an individual's life go together to give him the "evidence" he needs of divine revelation. A person seeking faith ought to study the New Testament at whatever level he is able, consider the Church, both in its history and in its present reality, associate with faithful members of the Church, and take note of whatever other signs occur in his life. Out of all these together he will form his judgment.

But are we to think that through such signs considered in a purely rational way, a person should be able to reach the certitude required for faith — a certitude that will enable him to commit his life to Christ without qualification? Jesus said that we must be ready to give up all things, even life itself, in order to follow him; that anyone who loves father or mother, brother, sister, wife, or children more than him is not worthy to be his disciple. The signs discussed hardly seem to lead to the kind of certitude necessary to commit one's life so absolutely. To understand how such certitude is actually attained, we must turn to the second factor mentioned above, the grace by which God induces us to believe.

THE GRACE OF FAITH

When arguing with people who did not believe in him, Jesus once pointed out various "witnesses" that supported his mission: John the Baptist, who was respected by all as a prophet; the Scriptures that foretold the one who was to come; the very works that Jesus himself was doing. Then he added: "And the Father who has sent me has himself testified concerning me. You have never heard his voice nor seen his form, nor does his word dwell in you. . ." (John 5:37f; see also 8:13). On another occasion, he said, "No one can come to me unless the Father who sent me draws him. . . . Everyone who listens to the Father and learns from him comes to me" (John 6:44f). This hidden witness of the Father is the decisive element in Christian faith, giving an absolute conviction, far beyond what we could get from any miracles or other signs taken by themselves.

• *The Father's witness*

The Father's witness need not be imagined in the form of apparitions or audible words. Immediately after one of the texts cited above, Jesus added, "No one has seen the Father except the one who is from God; only he has seen the Father" (John 6:46). The Father's witness is a secret, invisible, perhaps even unconscious, touch deep within a person, confirming that which is addressed externally to him. The classic illustration occurs in St. Peter's famous profession of faith. When Jesus asked, "Who do you say that I am?" Peter answered, "You are the Christ, the Son of the living God." "Blessed are you, Simon Bar-Jonah!" replied Jesus, "For flesh and blood has not revealed this to you, but my Father who is in heaven" (Matthew 16:15-17, RSV). Peter had seen the signs worked by Jesus

and had listened to Jesus' preaching; but all of this "flesh and blood" would never of itself have brought Peter to his act of faith. It was the inner witness of the Father that enabled him to believe in Jesus.

Peter was probably not conscious of having received a revelation; that is why Jesus had to declare it to him. Peter was conscious only of what he had heard and seen in Jesus. But in the light of an interior grace, to which Peter was loyal, these external signs took on a convincing power they would not have had by themselves, and Peter was able to perceive their true sense, and recognize Jesus as the Christ.

Similarly grace touches us as we read Scripture or contemplate the Church and enables us to recognize the hand, the voice of God amid the confusing welter of factors that attract and repel. The Father's inner witness makes it possible for people who have had no personal contact with the earthly Jesus to have a faith in him that is essentially the same as that of Peter and the apostles. When the early evangelists went proclaiming throughout the Roman empire that God had saved the world through a crucified Jew who had been raised from the dead, there was no way listeners in Greece, Rome, Egypt, Persia, etc., could verify the truth of this story. But just as God continued to work visible signs to confirm the word that was preached, so also he continued to give his inner witness. When St. Paul made his first missionary venture into the Western world, he found some women gathered in a place of prayer by the river outside the city of Philippi. Sitting down, he spoke to them about Jesus. Among his hearers was a woman named Lydia. "The Lord opened her heart to receive Paul's message" (Acts 16:14), and she and her household were baptized. Today it is still God's grace that makes people believe, even though it remains right and obligatory for us to do all we can by rational inquiry to verify the authenticity of the message. It often happens that our first instructions in the faith come from our parents or from others who may not be very learned. This does not detract from the quality of our faith, which is ultimately based not on the intelligence of those who instruct us but on the divine witness within us. Hence faith is essentially a living, personal response to God. In growing up we set aside the fairy tales told by our parents; we may receive more education than they had. But we need not outgrow the faith they communicated to us, because it is based not on them but on God.

The foregoing explanation does not of course "prove" the inner witness of the Father; it merely offers a theological analysis of what takes place in Christian faith. If someone does not have faith you cannot prove to him that God is speaking to him. Likewise there is no way you can prove to anyone — not even to yourself — that *your* faith is supported by the inner witness that you claim to have. Each one has to "hear the voice of the heavenly Father" in his own heart and for himself. We can bear witness to one another about what we believe, but the other will believe or not according to his own response to God.

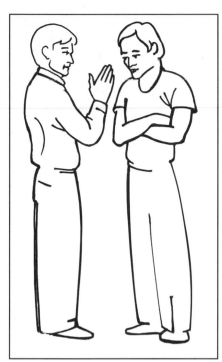

• *Human witnessing*

It follows likewise that, when we try to bring the faith to others, our role is limited essentially to that of bearing witness. In purely rational matters, we can give arguments to show the truth of our position. In matters of faith, although we may be able to show the reasonableness of what we believe, we can never properly *prove* it. Only the Father, by his inner witness, can convince a person that Jesus is the Son of God. Our human witness is of the highest importance because it poses the matter before the person's mind, and acts as a summons, an invitation, a sign, and a support for his belief. But we cannot convince the person directly; if he rejects our witness, we have no proof with which to defend our position. We can only trust that the Father will support us by his witness (and perhaps also by signs, though we never know when, where, or how these will occur). Jesus promised the apostles, "When the Paraclete comes, whom I will send to you from the Father, the Spirit of truth who goes out from the Father, he will testify to me; and you also must testify, for you have been with me from the beginning" (John 15:26f). Here, in terms of the Paraclete rather than the Father, is another assurance of the inner witness on which the apostles can rely.

Faith is not a function of our learning or intelligence; the uneducated and dull-witted have just as much access to faith as brilliant geniuses. On the other hand, neither is faith an irrational, emotional act; it is a judgment of the mind, and requires that we use our minds, considering the signs and evidence, resolving problems, etc. But whether or not we come to faith depends essentially on our loyalty to truth and our love of what is good and right, rather than on our intellectual power.

• *The sin of unbelief*

Conversely, the *sin of unbelief* is not just ignorance or mistaken judgment; it is a closing of one's mind to the light, that is, to the Father's witness. That is why it is a sin. It

need not be fully conscious and explicit. In fact, rarely does a person reject what he acknowledges to be the voice of God speaking to him. More typically, the one who closes his mind to the light denies that the light is there. This is why Jesus said, in the text cited above, "You have never heard his voice." Nevertheless, the person is really responsible for closing himself to the grace he is unwilling to receive.

We are not ordinarily in a position to judge anyone guilty of this sin. Because of the culture in which one has been raised or the psychological situation in which one finds oneself, a person may be closed to the truths of faith without sinning against the light. Hence we should normally suppose good will on the part of a non-believer. But this should not lead us to deny that there is a real sin of unbelief — the sin about which Jesus said some of his harshest words:

> If anyone will not welcome you or listen to your words, shake the dust off your feet when you leave that home or town. I tell you the truth, it will be more bearable for Sodom and Gomorrah on the day of judgment than for that town. (Matthew 10:14f)
> Whoever believes and is baptized will be saved, but whoever does not believe will be condemned. (Mark 16:16)
> God did not send his Son into the world to condemn the world, but to save the world through him. Whoever believes in him is not condemned, but whoever does not believe stands condemned already because he has not believed in the name of God's one and only Son. (John 3:16f)

• *Freedom of faith*

It is often said that faith is a free act; this is true, but it is likely to be misunderstood. It does not mean that a person normally deliberates about whether to believe or not and finally makes up his mind. Most people *find* faith within themselves or fail to find it. The decision has taken place in their subconscious, and has resulted from many little decisions to do right or wrong; to love the good or to abandon it. When they encounter the Church or the Word of God, they simply believe or do not believe, without knowing how or why. They have indeed made a free decision, but this decision took place in many other areas, long before it appeared as faith or unbelief. Similarly, falling away from the faith is seldom due to the reasons or problems we consciously declare; usually it is the result of living in discord with the faith we profess.

• *The claims of other religions*

Islam also claims to have originated in a prophetic revelation. Anyone wishing to inquire whether God has in fact spoken through Muhammad can study the life and writings of the latter and judge for himself. Our purpose here is not to refute the claims made by other religions but to expound those of Christianity. Because the certitude of faith comes essentially from one's personal experience of the Father's inner witness, it is quite possible and perfectly legitimate to be a believing Christian without knowing what to make of the claims of competing religions. However, it must be pointed out that, if Christianity is authentic, Islam cannot possibly be, for the one contradicts the other. Islam denies that Jesus is the Son of God, reducing him to the status of a prophet. Something similar could be said in the case of other religions which claim to have originated in a divine revelation, such as Mormonism, the Baha'i, and the Unification Church.

Note that the question is not whether God *could have* made other revelations but whether in fact he has. Without a doubt, God could have revealed himself in countless other ways; and so far as personal, or private, revelations are concerned, there is no need to deny that he has. But the question of a public revelation, as the foundation of a distinct religion, raises some very difficult issues. As we will see in Chapter 20, it is part of the

Christian revelation itself that what God has done in Jesus Christ is unique. He is the Only-begotten Son of God, the only mediator between God and mankind, the only Savior, the final and supreme Word of God. To propose therefore that other religions may enshrine a divine revelation just as Christianity does would be to deny Christianity.

Someone may object that millions of people read the Koran or the Vedas and claim to find God speaking there also. If we were trying to *prove* from Christian experience that God speaks in Scripture, this would be a valid objection. However, we are not offering a *proof* but an *invitation* to serious inquirers to read the Scripture for themselves. If they find that God does speak to them through Scripture, they do not have to refute or explain away the experience of others in order to acknowledge the value of their own experience.

There is undoubtedly genuine religious experience in other religions; we will consider its salvific value in Chapter 20. Here we are concerned simply with the Christian experience as evidence that God has spoken. Likewise there can be illusions and self-deceptions on the part of Christians, just as of others. This indeed makes us wary in judging so-called "religious experiences," but it does not exclude the possibility of authentic religious experience nor diminish the value of the experience one has had.

6
Scripture and the Church

Although many prophets spoke and acted without writing anything (for example, Elijah and Elisha), some wrote down their messages or had scribes write for them. The resultant literature has been collected in the volume we now call the Bible, or Sacred Scripture. The Bible is therefore not one book but a library — a collection of writings composed over a period of a thousand years. The "Old Testament" contains those Scriptures accepted as sacred by both Christians and Jews; the "New Testament," the distinctively Christian Scriptures. There is a slight disagreement over the contents of the Old Testament. Seven minor works, plus fragments of a few others, found in the Catholic Old Testament, are not in Jewish or most Protestant editions.

• *Deuterocanonical books*

The works in question, called "deuterocanonical" by Catholics, are: Tobit, Judith, The Wisdom of Solomon, Sirach (also called Ecclesiasticus), Baruch, and First and Second Maccabees, besides fragments of Esther and Daniel. All were written toward the end of the Old Testament period. Most were composed in Greek or Aramaic rather than in Hebrew, by Jews living in exile (for example, at Alexandria in Egypt). Some Jews accepted them as inspired; others did not. The latter eventually prevailed; not, however, until after the Christians had adopted the more inclusive version of the Old Testament; in fact, it seems plausible that the final Jewish canon was partially motivated by a reaction against the Christian practice. Some Christians, notably St. Jerome, aware that the deuterocanonical books were missing from the Hebrew Bible, expressed a doubt about whether they ought to be regarded as inspired; nevertheless, even Jerome retained them in his Latin translation of the Bible. The Church decided in favor of the disputed works, as will be described below.

In the sixteenth century, Martin Luther rejected the deuterocanonical works as not of divine inspiration, and in this he was eventually followed by most Protestant denominations. However, the Protestant Bibles continued to include these works in a separate section, commonly labeled "Apocrypha," until about the nineteenth century, when publishers began omitting them for economic reasons. Luther also wanted to reject certain parts of the New Testament, notably the Epistle of James, which he called "an epistle of straw" because of its doctrine that faith without works is dead. However, in this he has not been followed by any Protestant churches.

The disputed works are not of major importance (although 2 Maccabees 12:43-46 gives noteworthy support to the doctrine of purgatory, and the practical maxims of Wisdom and Sirach are much used in the liturgy). However, the disagreement raises the fundamental question "How is it determined what writings belong to Scripture, and what exactly is implied thereby?"

• *Origin of the Scriptures*

Among the Jews, as in most other religious traditions of the world, there was no formal method for deciding such questions. By popular acceptance, certain works came gradually to be revered as sacred, while others did not. Jesus spoke (for instance, in Mark 12:36) of the Holy Spirit as author of certain Old Testament passages but without making any general statement about the range or extent of this inspiration. Following him, the early Christians likewise acknowledged the Jewish Scriptures as inspired but also without any precise specifications. (However, the text they usually employed was the Septuagint, a Greek translation which normally included the deuterocanonical works.)

The New Testament began with letters written by St. Paul from about 51 A.D. onward to churches he had founded. The Synoptic Gospels seem to have been written shortly before or after the year 70. These and other writings, addressed mostly to particular communities, were received with veneration, then copied and circulated from one community to another. Selections from them were often read publicly at the Eucharist, along with passages from the Old Testament; thus the new writings were implicitly acknowledged as having been inspired like the old. Informal collections of new Scriptures began to form in various churches of the Christian world, and then to be amalgamated with one another. The greater part of the New Testament as we know it today (the Gospels and St. Paul) had been assembled in various places by 200 A.D., but the collections differed from place to place regarding the other New Testament books.

• *The official canon*

For, meanwhile, problems had arisen. Books claiming to be the work of apostles such as James or Peter appeared but were rejected by many Christians as not authentic. A heretic, Marcion (who died about 160), rejected the Old Testament, along with everything in the New Testament referring to it. Another, named Montanus, claimed (in 156 or 172?) to utter new prophecies of equal value to those of the Bible. It became necessary therefore to determine what should be regarded as Scripture and what not. Official lists ("canons") of the sacred writings began to be drawn up by various churches. There were discrepancies among them, however. For example, the Apocalypse (or Book of Revelation), the

Epistles of Jude, 2 Peter, 2 and 3 John, and the Letter to the Hebrews were omitted from some canons, while Pastor Hermas, Barnabas, and the Apocalypse of Peter were included in others. Finally, various provincial councils in 397, 418, and 692 as well as a letter of Pope Innocent I in 405 established the canon which the Catholic Church has followed ever since. The canon was not, however, defined solemnly until the Council of Trent (1546), when the Church had to deal with the omissions made by Luther and other Reformers.

Thus the determination of the books to be included in

Sacred Scripture did not come about by a formal process until toward the end. Individual books first won recognition by the authority of their authors or by their own intrinsic value. The discrimination took place at first more or less spontaneously in the Christian community, as in the Hebrew community before it. However, this was not by a merely popular, or "democratic," process. The various communities, especially among the Christians, were directed by pastoral authorities, who exercised a preponderant influence and made the final decisions. And behind these human decisions was the guidance of the Holy Spirit, about which more will be said below.

• *What is Sacred Scripture?*

What does it mean for a book to be recognized as Sacred Scripture? It is not easy to give a precise and complete answer to this question, basic though it be. The Christian community (like the Hebrew community) began to revere certain writings as sacred long before reflective thinkers undertook to define exactly what this implied. The Church today is still in the process of refining its understanding of the inspiration of Scripture, and of dealing with new problems raised by modern research. This is not surprising; it is normal for religious thought to begin with convictions that are deeply felt but only later and gradually come to be defined.

As the faith community attempted to put into words what it meant by Sacred Scripture, two notions emerged as of prime importance from early on: Scripture is *inspired by God*, and it is the *Word of God*. Both of these notions had been applied to the Hebrew prophets even before their message was put into writing. The Spirit of God was said to come upon them, and the Word of God to be given to them so they could declare it to others. When the message was put into written form — a form in which it could remain after the prophet had died, the written text itself began to be called the Word of God.

Two New Testament passages have governed Christian thought on the inspiration of Scripture. One has the form of an instruction given by St. Paul to his disciple Timothy:

> . . .from childhood you have been acquainted with the sacred writings which are able to instruct you for salvation through faith in Christ Jesus. All Scripture is inspired by God and profitable for teaching, for reproof, for correction, and for training in righteousness. . . .(2 Timothy 3:15f, RSV)

The other text, after describing the teaching of the prophets as a lamp shining in the dark, adds:

> No prophecy of Scripture is a matter of one's own interpretation, because no prophecy ever came by the impulse of man, but men moved by the Holy Spirit spoke from God. (2 Peter 1:20f, RSV)

In these texts, written before the New Testament had been compiled, "Scripture" refers to the Old Testament. But what they say was applied to the New Testament writings also as they came to be acknowledged. Thus the entire Bible was recognized as written under the inspiration of the Holy Spirit.

In attempting to represent graphically what this might mean, popular preachers and teachers (and even a theologian such as Bañez) sometimes spoke of the Holy Spirit dictating words to the inspired author. Such a notion, if taken strictly, would mean that the  human writer was nothing but a stenographer putting down words given to him; his own mind, sentiments, and culture would have had no significant role to play. Such an understanding of inspiration is not peculiarly Christian; we meet it in the Muslims of the seventh century and the Mormons of the nineteenth. It dominated the thinking of most of the Protestant Reformers, and is still held by Fundamentalists today. The dictation concept leads to an extremely literal interpretation of Scripture, and makes it impossible to accept many of the conclusions and insights of modern biblical scholarship. This has been a major factor in the crisis of faith which divided nineteenth-century Protestantism into liberals (who accept critical scholarship but often at the expense of biblical faith) and conservatives (who hold to the Bible but are often closed to scholarship).

• *Human factors influencing Scripture*

The intense investigations of the text and background of Scripture during the past two centuries have made it evident that a long, historical process and many very human factors went into the composition of the sacred books. For example, it is generally agreed that the stories given in the early books of the Old Testament must have been handed down by oral tradition for centuries before being written. Sometimes the same story (such as the creation or the flood) was recorded by several authors living in different communities, and their diverse accounts were subsequently combined (often very crudely) to form our present text. The writings of one prophet were often added to by others who came later; yet the whole was transmitted under the name of the original author. (Thus most of the "Psalms of David" seem to have been composed long after David's era; and about half of the "Book of the Prophet Isaiah" comes from someone other than the original Isaiah.) The religious literature of other Near Eastern peoples — for example, the Sumerians, Babylonians, Assyrians, Egyptians, and Hittites — contains striking parallels to the Hebrew Scriptures (for instance, stories of a universal flood). This suggests that our inspired writings arose by processes similar to the others, and probably even under the influence of some of them. The four Gospels were composed by men whose personality and culture obviously affected their writing: Mark is rough, blunt, and colorful; Matthew is a skillful teacher of moral lessons, indifferent to colorful details or the exact order of events; Luke is sensitive, refined, and concerned about historical accuracy; John is profoundly reflective.

Such facts are difficult to reconcile with the view that the human author was merely taking dictation from the Holy Spirit. But in reacting against the inadequacies of the dictation concept, some modern theologians have tended to go to the opposite extreme, abandoning all belief in the divine inspiration of Scripture or reducing it to a profound religious insight of the author.

• *The Catholic position*

The Catholic understanding of inspiration, although rooted in the writings of the early Church Fathers, and taking its key notions from St. Thomas Aquinas (thirteenth century), has received its fullest exposition only in the century that stretches from Vatican I (1869-70) to Vatican II (1962-1965). It can be summarized in two theses: (1) God is the principal author of Scripture; (2) the human writer is a subordinate but genuine author.

That God is the principal author means that he speaks to us through Scripture. Not, however, merely in the sense in which he speaks to us through nature or through the word of a friend who tells us something we need to hear. Nature is not properly a word but a *work*; only metaphorically can it be said to speak. Scripture is a true word, a communication of the heart and mind of one person to others. God is its author because God is the one who primarily and properly speaks what it says. Scripture can indeed be called the Word of God because it is a true word or speech, and the one who speaks in and through it is God himself.

The prophet or inspired writer articulates the divine message in human language. God does not use words to express his thoughts to himself (he has only a single Word, the substantial expression of himself, who is also his Son — see Chapter 17). It is for us that he formulates his intentions in human speech, and through an earthly spokesman that he does this. But even when this is done, God, and not the prophet, remains the principal author of what is said.

Note that Scripture is called God's *word*, and not just God's *idea* or God's *message*. God does not merely give the prophet an impulse or an idea, and then leave it to him to put it in words on his own. In that case, the sacred text would be in a sense inspired or stimulated by God, but it would not be properly his word. The human author is subordinate to God and acts as his instrument not only in receiving the message but also in the very act of articulating it. Only thus can the word that is produced properly be called *God's* word.

On the other hand, the human writers are genuine authors, even though subordinate to the principal author. Hence they write with their natural human characteristics. This point was expressed thus by the Second Vatican Council:

> To compose the sacred books, God chose certain men who, all the while he employed them in this task, made full use of their powers and faculties so that, though he acted in them and by them, it was as true authors that they consigned to writing whatever he wanted written and no more.
> (Dogmatic Constitution on Divine Revelation, no. 11)

At first glance, this may seem incompatible with the statement that the human writer acts as God's instrument. That is because we tend to think of instruments as inanimate and lacking in freedom. But even when acting freely, man can and should be the instrument of God; and God uses his instruments without depriving them of their freedom and human integrity. It is when man is rightly subordinate to God that he is most fully and truly free; and that is precisely the condition in which the inspired authors served as God's spokesmen.

In summary, Scripture is an authentically human word, and a truly divine word. Human, because the writers who composed it — for example, Isaiah or St. Paul — wrote out of their own mind and will, senses, sentiments, and experience, like any other author. Divine, because they were used by God to convey a message that originates in him, gets its authority from him, and, in the last analysis, is his more than theirs, although it remains truly theirs.

From a different point of view, the matter can be summarized thus: Everything in Scripture is of divine inspiration, and everything is the work of the human author. It would be a false escape from problems to imagine that certain parts were divinely inspired, and others merely human. In such a conception it could not be said that Scripture in its integrity is the Word of God (nor, for that matter, that it is all the work of its human authors). And the attempt to discriminate between the divine and human parts would, in practice, make the reading of Scripture entirely subjective.

• *Divine, human collaboration*

The collaboration between the divine and human authors was characterized thus by Pope Leo XIII:

> By supernatural power, God so moved these men and impelled them to write and so assisted them while they were writing, that the things he ordered and only those, they rightly understood, willed faithfully to write down, and finally expressed in apt words and with infallible truth.
>
> (*Providentissimus Deus*; TCC 100; TCT 110)

This statement, which must be read in conjunction with the text of Vatican II cited above, is not an attempt to describe the psychological experience of the biblical author but simply a specification of what is implied in saying that God inspired human beings to write his word.

These teachings do not imply that the "inspiration" is "equal" in all cases. One would be perfectly within his rights in maintaining, for instance, that St. John is more profound in his insights than the Synoptics or that the genealogies in the Book of Numbers are of less value than the account of creation in Genesis. The doctrine of inspiration allows for immense variation not only in the human qualities of the writers but also in the grace given to them. It simply affirms that their word is in truth God's word.

• *Inspiration and revelation*

Note also that inspiration is not the same as revelation. It was noted in the previous chapter that revelation means God communicating a "secret" which would otherwise remain hidden. Inspiration means God impelling someone to speak, write, or act. (Here, we are concerned only with writings.) God may inspire a prophet to write down something that has been given through a revelation, as in the case of Jeremiah and Isaiah. But he may also inspire him to write something known without any revelation. When St. Paul tells the story of his early years as a Christian (Galatians 1 and 2) or when the author of 2 Samuel recounts the adventures of King David, there is no need to suppose a revelation, for they

119

had seen with their own eyes the things they are writing about. God can also reveal something to a person without inspiring him to transmit it to others, as when St. Paul, in ecstasy, "heard inexpressible things, things that a man is not permitted to tell" (2 Corinthians 12:4).

The doctrine of the inspiration of Scripture does not imply that all inspired writings have been collected into Scripture but only that the scriptural writings themselves are all inspired. It is certain that the Holy Spirit continues to inspire people today in many ways (see Chapter 23), and there is no reason why he could not inspire their speech or writing. In fact, it is often suggested that *The Imitation of Christ* or the *Spiritual Exercises* of St. Ignatius or the *Dialogue* of St. Catherine of Siena or the *Revelations* of St. Gertrude were divinely inspired. The profit derived by immense numbers of Christians from these writings as well as the positive approval manifested by the Church itself gives abundant reason to believe that such is indeed the case.

But even if, as is most unlikely, the Church were one day officially to pronounce some of these later works to be divinely inspired, they would surely not be incorporated into the Canon of Sacred Scripture. For the latter is not merely a collection of inspired literature, it is that body of texts which have an official and, in a sense, foundational or constitutive role in the Church. ("In a sense," because, as explained below, the Church was fully constituted before the New Testament scriptures were written.) The Canon of Scripture is now "closed."

A second difference between Scripture and other inspired writings has to do with the kind of inspiration involved. Scripture can be called the Word of God, as we have seen. As such, it has a kind of infallibility. This cannot be said, it would seem, about any other inspired writings. Of course God could inspire a modern author in the same way as he did those of Scripture; in fact, however, this does not seem to happen. Other writings, however inspired and inspiring they may be, always seem to remain properly the work of the human author, and hence subject to the errors to which all human minds are prone. In other words, not only is Sacred Scripture inspired, as other writings might also be, but it is the product of a uniquely privileged inspiration which makes it the infallible Word of God in a way that other writings are not. We must now examine more carefully this very difficult notion of the infallibility, or inerrancy, of Scripture.

THE TRUTH OF SCRIPTURE

In recognizing the Sacred Scriptures as the Word of God, the Church by the same token affirmed them to be absolutely truthful. What God says cannot but be true. Insofar as he is the author of Scripture, the latter must be free from error. This firm conviction of the whole Church was expressed by St. Augustine in a letter to St. Jerome (the greatest Scripture scholar of the fourth century): "I have learned to pay such honor and reverence to the canonical books of Scripture as to believe most firmly that none of their writers has fallen into any error" (Letter 82, 1).

• *Problems raised by critical studies*

This remained the common and unshaken conviction of the Christian world, Catholic, Protestant, and Orthodox, until about the nineteenth century. As the newly developing methods of scientific history, archaeology, linguistics, and literary criticism began to be applied (often in a rationalistic and positively hostile manner) to Scripture, critics claimed to find errors of various sorts in the text.

In the first place are statements that seem to conflict with what is known from science or history. For example, there are passages in the Old Testament which represent the earth as resting on water (Psalm 24:2) or standing on foundations (Psalm 102:25; 104:5). Others speak of the sky as a firm dome separating the waters above it from those on earth (Genesis 1:6), with floodgates that can be opened to let the rain fall (Genesis 7:11). Such notions hardly conform to modern geology and astronomy. As for history, the Book of Daniel speaks of the Babylonian King, Belshazzar, the son of Nebuchadnezzar (5:2), whereas from other sources we know that he was the son of Nabonidus and that he never did reign as king. St. Luke says that Jesus was born at the time of a census taken by Caesar Augustus, when Quirinius was governor of Syria and Herod king of Judea. But Herod died in 4 B.C., while Quirinius did not begin to govern until 6 A.D. Moreover, Jesus seems to have been born well before Quirinius's notorious census of 7 A.D.

There are likewise texts of Scripture which seem to contradict one another. Noah was in the ark about a year, according to Genesis 7:11—8:13; but in Genesis 8:6-12, it would appear to have been between fifty-four and sixty-one days. The Gospels give varying accounts of Jesus' resurrection. Was there one angel in the tomb or two? Which women went there first? Did they report to the apostles what they had heard or not? Above all, did they return to Galilee and see the risen Lord there or did all of his apparitions take place in Jerusalem? The answers to these questions seem to differ from one Gospel to another. On a profounder level, St. Paul's doctrine of justification by faith appears at first sight to contradict St. James's teaching that "a person is justified by what he does, and not by faith alone" (James 2:24).

In the third place, Scripture sometimes narrates things which seem patently impossible, absurd, or legendary, such as Jonah's survival intact for three days and three nights in the belly of the "big fish" (Jonah 1:17), Lot's wife turning into a pillar of salt because of her curiosity (Genesis 19:26), or the striped sticks which Jacob set up in the sight of the sheep and goats in the breeding season, causing their offspring to be born with spots (Genesis 30:37ff).

Also to be noted is that writings attributed to Moses, David, Isaiah, or others seem, according to very serious indications, to have been composed by someone else centuries later; or that the Gospel of Matthew does not read like the work of an eyewitness but like something learned at second or third hand.

Such difficulties have led some people to abandon belief in the divine inspiration of Scripture, and others to engage in intense reflection and discussion on the nature and implications of inspiration.

• *Scholarship confirms historicity*

To put the matter in perspective, several points ought to be borne in mind. First, a certain malicious delight in shocking the faithful sometimes incites "scholars" (but more often mere popularizers of scholarship) to exaggerate the difficulties. They speak lightly of contradictions when dealing with what may be nothing more than the differences that occur whenever the same event is recounted by different observers. Second, the overwhelming majority of difficulties have to do with trivial details; only a few touch on the substance of the biblical message, and these can generally be resolved. Third, the overwhelming effect of historical and archaeological research has not been to create problems for the historicity of the Bible but rather to confirm it. The objections raised by critical scholarship seemed most devastating during the nineteenth century, when this scholarship was in its brash adolescence. Many of the objections have simply been eliminated by the progress of scholarship and more mature reflection. Once it was not uncommon for scholars to treat the Bible as containing little but myth and legend. Since then, as one major archaeologist has pointed out, "For the most part, archaeology has substantiated and illumined the Bible at so many crucial points that no one can seriously take this position."[1] Difficulties do indeed remain, but they do not preclude faith, which is capable of standing firm in the face of problems that have not yet been solved.

• *The Church affirms truthfulness*

While we cannot undertake here to go into particular exegetical problems, we will propose a few considerations which should help with them in a general way. The Catholic Church continues to affirm the truthfulness of Scripture, but it does so today in a more carefully nuanced way than Augustine did in the fifth century or even Leo XIII in the nineteenth. The Second Vatican Council declared its position in the following crucial statement, which is like the distillation of a century of discussion of this matter:

> Since, therefore, all that the inspired authors or sacred writers affirm should be regarded as affirmed by the Holy Spirit, we must acknowledge that the books of Scripture teach firmly, faithfully and without error the truth which God, for the sake of our salvation, willed to confide to them.
>
> (Dogmatic Constitution on Divine Revelation, no. 11)

• *Idiom not affirmation*

The essential assertion of this text is that what the inspired authors affirm must be true because it is affirmed by the Holy Spirit. The term *affirm* has been chosen precisely to indicate that not everything *said* in Scripture is actually *affirmed*. Any author is likely to employ ideas that are current in his culture, without intending to vouch for them himself. They are so much a part of the atmosphere in which he lives that he takes them for granted without even adverting to them. If he uses them, they can be regarded as part of the *idiom* in which he speaks, rather than *affirmations* which he makes. Thus it was surely not the intention of the author of Genesis to affirm that the stars were stuck onto the sky. This is how he spoke of them, and presumably how he, along with his countrymen, thought of them. But the statement that "God set [the stars] in the firmament" (Genesis 1:17, RSV) was obviously not a pronouncement about celestial architecture but a declaration that it was God who brought all this about.

Admittedly, it is sometimes difficult to determine what is being affirmed, and what belongs merely to the idiom. Likewise it is possible for someone to use this distinction as a pretext for arbitrary interpretations. But these are problems inherent in all human discourse; they are not peculiar to Scripture. To interpret any human document rightly we must read it with a certain sincerity; and the presence of occasional ambiguities does not keep us from profiting from what is intelligible in the work.

Secondly, the Vatican II statement declares that the Scriptures teach "without error that truth which God, for the sake of our salvation, willed to confide to them." It avoids saying that nothing erroneous whatsoever has crept into the text. If the author of the Book of Daniel, writing in the second century B.C., was a little hazy about Babylonian history of the sixth century B.C., that is altogether to be expected. And it seems quite unnecessary to suppose that the Holy Spirit, in inspiring him with a message of salvation for his contemporaries, would correct his historical notions when these were quite irrelevant to his message. (If Daniel were properly a historical work, the matter would be quite different; but we are taking for granted that it is not.)

Clearly Scripture was written not to satisfy human curiosity but to present "that truth which is for our salvation." It is in respect to this truth that Scripture is trustworthy. It was not written as a scientific treatise on astronomy, geology, or world history. Hence we need not be perturbed at the imaginary geography of the Garden of Eden (Genesis 3:10-15). Neither need we take the genealogies of the sons of Noah (Genesis 10) as a divinely guaranteed account of the origin of the peoples of the world nor the frequent explanations of the meanings of names as authentic etymologies. If we look in these works for something they did not intend to give, it is we, not they, who are guilty of error.

• *Scripture intended as history*

However, it would be going too far to conclude that there is no reliable history in Scripture, and that the stories it tells have only a symbolic value. Besides the fact, pointed out above, that the historical value of Scripture has been confirmed on many points, it is obviously the intent of the authors to narrate real events from the history of Israel and from the life of Jesus. To treat them as merely symbolic would be to disregard the manifest intention of the authors, and impose on them an alien sense.

But we must add at once that their notion of history was quite different from that of a modern professional historian. They were doing "popular" as opposed to "academic" or "scientific" history. Only what was considered memorable was passed on; the rest was forgotten. There were no journalists then to record things day by day (although from the time of King Solomon, there do seem to have been archivists in the royal palaces). The transmission was mostly by word of mouth, in stories told over and over "around the campfire" or in the marketplaces. (Storytellers have always had great importance in the social life of simple folk, as is still the case in parts of Africa, South America, and elsewhere.) Stories were told as they were remembered, that is, in a simplified form, without concern for precision. They were often arranged to heighten the dramatic effect. Things got out of sequence or into a wrong context. The ancient historians made little effort to adopt the detachment and objectivity prized (but how often actually attained?) by modern historians. Events were recounted from the point of view of the people of Israel (or, in the New Testament, of the followers of Jesus). Undoubtedly this put a certain coloring and bias into the story. The Assyrian invasion looks quite a bit different in the Book of Kings from the way Sennacherib describes it in his *Annals*. Such factors do not make the Bible unhistorical, but they oblige us to interpret it according to the kind of history written in those days, and not according to the canons of academic history developed in the last two or three centuries.

On the other hand, it is remarkable how sober, frank, and factual the biblical accounts are by comparison with the bombastic self-glorification of most ancient royal annals. If one were to do a history of the ideal of objectivity in historical writing, the books of Scripture — both Old and New Testaments — would probably appear as a major advance.

One characteristic of the biblical writings which often disturbs the modern reader unprepared for it is its free use of pseudonyms. It was noted above that much of the writing ascribed to Moses, David, Isaiah, and others was composed centuries after their time. In the case of the New Testament, it is freely debated whether any of the Gospels were actually written by the man whose name they bear. Similarly for some of the epistles, etc. The issue is not one of fraud or deception, however. Ancient peoples had none of our modern preoccupation with authenticity and documentation, and felt no scruples about adding supplements and explanations to ancient books as needed. They were not *falsifying* the work but helping the reader understand it. Moreover, reading and writing were esoteric arts, and authorship had an awesomeness even greater than it has today. A certain diffidence could make a person hesitate to publish a book under his own name. In any case, it was an accepted practice to present a new book under the cover of a great name from the past. (One might compare this to wearing a mask at a theatrical performance.)

• *Diverse literary types*

Diverse types of literary form are to be found in Scripture. While some books are genuinely historical, others are not properly historical at all. This is obvious in the case of hymns such as the Psalms; likewise of moral maxims such as Proverbs. To read the poetry of the Psalms or the wisdom of Proverbs as though they were narrating historical events would distort their meaning. In other cases, it is not so obvious whether the work has a historical intent or not; in any event, the aim of the reader must always be to read the text according to the mode and spirit in which it was written, remembering that each literary form can express truth but in its own proper way.

Is it possible to admit the presence of fables, legends, and myths in the Bible? It is common in all cultures to use stories to teach a lesson; Aesop's fables and Grimm's fairy tales are familiar examples. Similarly, the parables Jesus told about the Pharisee and the publican or about Lazarus and the rich man are not presented as historical accounts but as illustrations of humility and generosity. The Book of Daniel, the Book of Job, and the story of Jonah and the big fish would seem to be other obvious examples. The non-real character of the story is generally evident from indications in the text. The Book of Job, for example, opens with a dialogue in the court of heaven between God and Satan, and goes on to tell how Job's "friends" sat silently beside him for seven days and seven nights before beginning their long philosophical discourses. This tips the reader off that the story is not meant as history. There is *truth* in it — not the truth of history but a moral or doctrinal truth (for example, about how human suffering can be reconciled with the goodness of God).

When put thus in the abstract, and in general principles, the problem is not difficult; it is the evaluation of particular instances that is delicate. May we say that the stories of the risen Jesus appearing to the apostles were mere literary devices to express a profound interior experience? Is it legitimate to suppose that some of the sayings attributed to Jesus by the Gospels are really concoctions of the early Church put back on Jesus' lips in order to give them more authority?

This is not the place to attempt a final appraisal of such cases. They illustrate, however, that there must be a limit to our freedom in calling texts fictitious. To tell a parable or a fable in order to teach a lesson is a legitimate type of discourse. To summarize a person's statement in language different from his own is acceptable in popular history. But to propose *as history* a tale that is not, is simple dishonesty, which cannot be attributed to the Word of God. If we take seriously the belief that Scripture has been inspired by the Holy Spirit, there are types of fiction and error that cannot be ascribed to it because they are incompatible with the truthfulness of God. (They cannot be dismissed as incidental errors by the scribe, for they pertain to *affirmations* made, not just to the idiom used.)

Thus, in the case of the Resurrection stories, with their vivid details about the empty tomb, the conversations between Jesus and the apostles, the touching of his wounds, his eating fish, etc.: to say that these were only fictitious devices used by the apostles to express an experience that was purely interior would seem to involve a falsification that goes well beyond the limits of symbolic speech. To say that the early Christians, in reciting the teachings of Jesus, sometimes used language and expressions that belonged to their time rather than his is to attribute to them a very natural and legitimate transformation that occurs all the time in popular narrative. But to say that they made up new teachings and put them on the lips of Jesus in order to give them more authority would likewise entail a falsification incompatible with the Word of God. (Between these two extremes is the possibility of their concretizing his teaching, applying it to instances that he himself did not treat. In this area, it is difficult to draw a firm line *a priori* between what would be legitimate and what would be false.)

• *Unsolved problems and faith*

This leaves us with some unsolved problems; but the Church's conviction about Scripture as the Word of God is not conditioned upon having solved all the problems. This conviction arose in the Church long before most of the problems were perceived, and is grounded on something deeper than a rational solution of objections: namely, on a mysterious encounter with God that takes place mysteriously in the depths of the heart through the reading of his Word. This conviction need not be shaken or disturbed when difficulties arise. The Church does not disregard these difficulties, nor does it claim to have the solution to all of them; but it does have the assurance that the truth of Scripture is unassailable, and that solutions are somewhere to be found, even if not yet available. Like the Christians of early centuries, we today can read Scripture as the

Word of God, and encounter him therein, without having resolved all the problems.

Note that to hold some parts of Scripture as historical and others as fable is not to be arbitrary but to exercise discernment. The books of Scripture are distinct works, and to say that if one is symbolic they all must be would be like arguing that if *Huckleberry Finn* is fiction, the telephone book must be also. Each book, and sometimes each particular part of a book, must be judged according to criteria immanent in the work itself. We make such discrimination all the time in secular literature and conversation; there is no reason why it should not be called for in Scripture likewise.

TRADITION AND PASTORAL AUTHORITY

In dealing with religious questions, a Catholic looks not only to what Scripture says but also to the beliefs and practices of the Church, especially to decisions that have been made by the teaching authority *(magisterium)* of the Church. The classical Protestant approach, on the contrary, regards only the scriptural teaching as authoritative. Protestants pay heed to what Luther, Calvin, or Barth hold on a given question; but they see such men merely as expositors who can help us discover the sense of the scriptural teaching. Likewise the governing officers in certain Protestant churches have great weight in deciding what can be taught from their pulpits. Ultimately, however, *Scripture alone* has authority for them in matters of faith whereas, for Catholic thought, the Church has an authority of its own. This authority resides both in traditions that have become established in the Church (especially those of the primitive age), and in decisions made by Church officials.

Debates about this matter have produced in many minds a false dichotomy between Scripture and tradition; and the influence of fundamentalist and evangelical currents leads many people to suppose, as a self-evident principle, that Christian doctrine ought to be based totally and solely on Scripture. We must therefore take pains to note that such an attitude contradicts Scripture itself.

• *Jesus did not write a book*

There is first the basic fact that Jesus himself never *wrote a book*; all his teaching was by word of mouth. (The only writing he did was in sand which the wind blew away [see John 8:6]). For the instruction of his future disciples, he formed living teachers — the apostles — and sent them to proclaim his message by live personal contact. The earliest writings of the New Testament were not composed until twenty-five to thirty years later. Thus the Christian community lived for a generation without any of the New Testament and, as we have seen, for some centuries before the compilation of the full New Testament.

Secondly, not even the apostles made a book the basis of the churches they founded. Most of them never wrote anything so far as we know (they probably could not, since few people in those days knew how to read or write). When the apostles did write (usually with the aid of a scribe), it was on the occasion of a particular need: St. Paul's letters deal with problems in the communities he had founded. None of the writings in the New Testament attempt to give a complete summary of Jesus' teachings or a full account of his life. Meanwhile, the work of proclaiming Jesus as the Christ had gone on by means of oral preaching and teaching, and the Church lived and grew in this faith.

• *New Testament grew out of tradition*

Furthermore, the writings of the New Testament cannot be set in opposition to tradition, since they themselves arose out of the tradition which preceded them. One of the major achievements of modern Scripture studies has been the realization that the Gospels cannot be understood rightly unless they are seen as a deposit of the traditions of the early Church.

Even when the New Testament writings appeared, they were never taken as somehow annulling the authority of the oral teaching which preceded, engendered, and enveloped them. In his Second Letter to the Thessalonians, St. Paul tells them that they must hold fast to "the traditions which you were taught by us, either by word of mouth or by letter" (2:15); he condemns those who do not live "according to the tradition received from us" (3:6). Finally, as we have seen, it was the Church that determined the Canon of Scripture, recognizing certain texts as inspired and rejecting others. It was obviously not the Bible itself that decided what would go into the Bible! Hence those who accept the Bible as their rule of faith are following a Church tradition. They can hardly appeal to Scripture as grounds for disregarding that tradition.

• *Church teaching is also God's Word*

Not only the written Scriptures but even more the oral preaching of the Church is spoken of as the Word of God by the New Testament itself. Thus St. Paul wrote:

> We thank God continually because, when you received the word of God, which you heard from us, you accepted it not as the word of men but as it actually is, the word of God, which is at work in you who believe. (1 Thessalonians 2:13)

Similarly, in the First Letter of Peter we are told:

> You have been born again, not of perishable seed but of imperishable, through the living and enduring word of God. . . . And this is the word that was preached to you. (1:23-25)

In conclusion, we see that the Church is not founded on a book. It was by the oral teaching of living apostles that Jesus arranged for his doctrine to be passed on. The documents that came to be written later under the inspiration of his Spirit are precious aids for the instruction of the Church of subsequent ages, and we may indeed suppose that Jesus himself intended that they should eventually be written; but they do not nullify the value of the tradition which preceded them and expressed itself in them. This is frustrating to our natural desire to eliminate intermediaries, and go to the very words of Jesus himself. But such an ambition is unrealizable; there is no way Christian faith can circumvent the intermediary function of Church teaching. Rather than driving us to frustration, this should make us acknowledge that it is Jesus' own design that his doctrine be transmitted primarily by a living Church. To take "Scripture alone" as the basis of faith is to alter the regime established by Jesus and to contradict Scripture itself.

• *Religious traditions*

In this connection, it is interesting to note that the religions of the world generally tend to be very traditional. In nearly all cultures we find that religious practices have been handed down "from of old." It seems to be the nature of religion to be transmitted and molded by the tradition of the community. Even an innovator such as Buddha retained most of the traditional suppositions of Hinduism. It is likewise common for religions to continue to use language that is antiquated or has passed out of common use, as in the case of Hebrew, Aramaic, Sanskrit, Latin, the "language of the gods" in Homer's ritual, etc.[2] To want to purify religion of tradition, and to go back exclusively to an ancient text as the religious norm, as the Puritans had the ambition of doing, is to go against some very deep human instincts.

However, tradition creates problems, for it can distort and corrupt. History gives innumerable examples of how the insights and spirit of great masters have degenerated in the traditions of their followers. Jesus himself rebuked the Pharisees and scribes because, he said, "you break the command of God for the sake of your tradition" (Matthew 15:3).

But Church tradition is not to be put on the same plane as merely human traditions. In a later chapter we will study the nature of the Church and its offices and functions. Here, by anticipation, let us simply recall that Jesus put his Holy Spirit into the Church in order to keep it in the truth. He said to the apostles at the Last Supper:

> I will ask the Father, and he will give you another Paraclete, to be with you forever — the Spirit of Truth. The world cannot accept him, because it neither sees him nor knows him. But you know him, for he lives with you, and will be in you. . . . [He] will teach you all things, and will remind you of everything I have said to you. . . . He will guide you into all truth. (John 14:16, 26; 16:13)

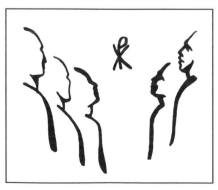

Sacred Tradition therefore is not merely a human reality but a product of the Holy Spirit's secret fermentation in the Church. Not that everything said and done in the Church is of the Holy Spirit; human beings retain their failings there too. We must distinguish between Sacred Tradition and lesser traditions in the Church. Discerning what is of the Holy Spirit and what is merely of the human spirit is a delicate, difficult operation, about which more will be said in the chapters on the Church. Here, to sum up the matter briefly, let us propose that wherever *the Church as Church* is speaking (as opposed to individuals or groups within it), the teaching of the Holy Spirit is expressed, and the tradition is to be held sacred.

THE MAGISTERIUM

Decisions about questions of doctrine in the Church are ordinarily made by councils of bishops who, as the pastors set over the flock by Christ (see Acts 29:23), meet together under the presidency of the Pope. Jesus promised that where two or three meet in his name, he would be present (Matthew 18:20). The most important of these councils, or synods, are called "ecumenical" (from the Greek *oikoumene* meaning the whole world) because they involve the bishops of the entire Church, not just of one region. A model for such councils appears in Acts 15, where the apostles and elders of the Church gathered to discuss whether the Gentile converts had to be circumcised. Since then, there have been twenty-one ecumenical councils.

The first, Nicaea (325 A.D.), affirmed the divinity of Christ in opposition to the Arians. The most important doctrinal council was that of Trent (1546-1563), which responded to the challenges of the Reformation by drawing up a lengthy statement of

Catholic doctrine on the Reformation issues. The most recent ecumenical council was Vatican II (1962-1965). It did not define any dogmas but was devoted to updating *(aggiornamento)* the teaching and practices of the Church to respond to the needs, problems, and aspirations of modern times.

Unlike the prophets, who were called to give a new Word of God to the world, the Church is minister of a word that has already been spoken. It has not the authority to propound a new teaching or a new revelation. It is the herald of the Gospel proclaimed by Jesus Christ and delivered through his apostles. It has to interpret the Gospel when questions arise, and apply it to new situations as they occur but not to alter or add to it. The Church regards the Gospel as the complete, sufficient, and final word of salvation from God to the world. It is as fruitful today as it was when Jesus spoke, and will remain so till the end of time. "Heaven and earth will pass away but my words will never pass away" (Matthew 24:25). When new situations or problems arise, the Church has to reflect on them in the light of the Gospel but not to invent a new Gospel. Hence Vatican II declared:

> The teaching office of the Church is not above the Word of God but serves it, teaching only what has been handed on, listening to it devoutly, guarding it scrupulously, and explaining it faithfully by divine commission and with the aid of the Holy Spirit. It draws from this one deposit of faith everything which it presents for belief as divinely revealed.
>
> (Dogmatic Constitution on Divine Revelation, no. 10).

The councils have at times defined new dogmas, but these have always expressed doctrines that lay implicit in the teaching handed down from the apostles. They were new only in the sense that they had not previously been officially articulated.

• *Apostolic rather than prophetic*

We noted above that God continues to raise up new prophets today, and to make revelations through them. But the Church never incorporates these revelations into its official teaching, even when it acknowledges their authenticity. In other words, the Church is characteristically *apostolic* rather than *prophetic*. A prophet declares a new word from God to the world. Even though the message may not be new (more often it is traditional), the *word* is new: God speaks in and by it. But an apostle is sent forth by Jesus to proclaim the word that has *already been spoken in and by Jesus*. This does not mean that there are no more prophets in the Church (even an apostle can also be a prophet) but that genuine prophecy today can be tested by its conformity to the apostolic word. Similarly, we can say that the Church is essentially traditional and conservative — not from inertia but from faithfulness to the word of Christ, in the conviction that this word remains valid and redemptive for every age.

But in another sense, the Church can be called prophetic, creative, liberal, revolutionary, even radical. For the Word of God is alive and speaks to each age a message that is ever new. Each culture that confronts it draws forth from it an answer, an implication, an application, that is new. Hence there is need of a constant attentiveness on the part of the Church to discern what the Word of God says to each new moment.

In the past, there was a tendency, especially in Europe, to identify the conservatism of Christianity with political and economic conservativism; to make the Church part of the *ancien régime*. Today, especially in Latin America, many link the Church with "liberal" social and political movements. But the conservativism and liberalism of the Church transcend all political, social, and economic projects; their source is the "ever ancient, ever new" Word of God.

PART 3
God the Creator

We have surveyed the major religious and irreligious viewpoints that compete with Catholicism. We have recognized that a Christian seeks religious truth not only by the efforts of reason but even more in the revelation that God has made of himself. These are the perspectives within which our work will continue.

Now we enter into the matter of theology proper. It has to do with four main topics. First of all, God himself. Second, creation. Third, Jesus Christ, the Mediator who reconciles creation with the Creator. Finally, the Church, that is to say, mankind reconciled to God and to one another by Jesus Christ.

God is the first and chief subject of theology. Everything else in this discipline is viewed in the light of God and in reference to God. Self-evident as this may appear, it has to be reaffirmed. For there is a widespread tendency among professional theologians today to concentrate on man — on psychological, social, and especially ethical questions — while taking God for granted. God is assumed as a kind of omnipresent background whose existence and nature need not be considered directly. This is not only an instance of the humanism of our culture (as pointed out in the Introduction) but also the result of weariness and frustration at the interminable and often fruitless debates about God in modern philosophy.

But it is absurd to treat other things in reference to God, without a serious effort to ascertain who and what God is in himself. And if God is the supreme reality, surely even the dimmest knowledge we can garner about him is of immense importance. We spend millions of dollars to research the distant galaxies; ought we not expend at least time and

reflection in an effort to know One who is infinitely more important than they, and far more intimately involved in our life?

There are many resemblances between the Christian conception of God and the Oriental notions of Tao or Brahman. But the Oriental philosophers insist above all on the incomprehensibility and "unnameability" of the Ultimate, who is mostly just alluded to in poetry and aphorisms. Christianity has produced a body of doctrine far more articulate, specific, organic, and detailed. One of the reasons for this is undoubtedly the fact that God has revealed himself in Jesus and has brought his people into intimate, personal relationship with himself. The Orientals are impressed above all by the hiddenness and transcendence of the deity; for Christians, God is one who has drawn close, and who is in a sense a familiar person.

There is, however, a certain danger in this familiarity. It

can betray us into thinking we know more about God than we do. It can make us lose the awe and the sense of mystery that should clothe our every approach to him. But this is a danger only for those whose contact with God is superficial. The saints and the great theologians have all had a profound sense of the weakness and inadequacy of our efforts to know God.

Two simplistic notions of God have done much harm in Christianity. One pictures God as a fearsome judge, glowering down from on high and watching for infractions to punish. Another represents him as a benign little old grandfather, who wishes us well but can't do much about it. These are corruptions of two profound truths: the Old Testament insistence that God requires moral uprightness of us, and the New Testament revelation of God as a Father.

These caricatures not only warp the religious thought of those who hold them; they also contribute to driving critically minded people into atheism. The latter are rejecting not the true God but inadequate notions of him. In attempting to form a right idea of God, we must indeed draw close to him, opening our minds fully to the revelation he has made of himself; but we must also retain a profound reverence and awareness of our utter inability to comprehend him.

Chapter 7 will take up the basic notions of God accessible to natural human inquiry (even though confirmed on many points by divine revelation). The more profound mysteries of the divinity, those known to us only through revelation, such as the Trinity and all that pertains to the mercy and grace of God, will be taken up later.

7

The divine nature

OUR KNOWLEDGE OF GOD

The things God has made point to him as to one immeasurably greater than themselves. Through them, we do not know God in himself but only as *the source* of the things we know directly. Is it possible then to form a true idea of him or to say anything about him that is not a lie? Instead of discussing him, ought we not to restrict ourselves to mute adoration?

The latter is, in a sense, the solution or at least the goal of Hindu yoga. The postures and breath control for which yoga is famous are only preliminary methods of freeing the mind from subjection to the body. The more advanced steps in this method seek to empty the mind of all ideas, and of all consciousness of distinction between the self and any object. The ultimate state to be attained is that of *samadhi*, in which there is no distinct idea, no consciousness of any distinct or particular object, a state in which the soul is immersed in a direct, total intuition of being. In this way the soul recovers its identity with Brahman, and is delivered *(moksha)* from the prison of this life. There is a striking parallel between this view and the traditional Catholic understanding of "infused contemplation" — a state of union with God in which love, rather than any distinct idea, is the means of union. However, infused contemplation is not something we can achieve by our own efforts; it is a gift of grace. And even when given, it does not nullify the validity of the knowledge we have of God through words and ideas. It gives us an intimate contact with God far superior to theology but does not prohibit us from turning back (outside of prayer) to the more rational type of knowledge proper to theology.

• *Analogous*

In the Christian understanding of things, it is indeed possible to know God and speak of him truly, provided we are aware of the limits of our knowledge. An oyster knows something real about the ocean, even though it doesn't begin to suspect how big the ocean is. Because God is the source of all else, whatever perfection or value there is in the world must preexist in him as an effect preexists in its cause.[1] Thus all that is tells us something of the One who made it.

It is possible therefore to say that God is wise and powerful, just and merciful, by analogy with the wise, powerful, just, and merciful people we know. However, his wisdom, power, etc., are not limited and defective like those of his creatures; for the cause is not confined to the limits of the effect. Created perfections are only weak, diminished reflections of the perfection of the Creator, and so do not give us the basis of an adequate knowledge of the latter, although they do enable us to know something true about them.

Thus three steps are involved in the application of human language to God: affirmation, negation, and transcendence. The first step is to affirm of God some perfection recognized in creatures — for example, wisdom. The second is to deny that God is wise in the way creatures are wise; his wisdom is not limited as theirs is. The third is to recognize that wisdom as it is in God infinitely surpasses any that we know on earth: God is wise in a way that utterly transcends any wisdom we are able to conceive.[2]

Rudolph Otto (followed by Karl Barth) speaks of God as the "altogether other." This is a forceful way of affirming the divine transcendence; however, it is misleading if taken as the first, or basic, proposition about God or even as strictly true. The resemblance between ourselves and God is more profound than the otherness. Not only are human beings made "in the image and likeness of God" (Genesis 1:26), all his works are a kind of reflection of his being; otherwise they could not exist at all. But granted this basic likeness which makes it possible for us to have a genuine knowledge of God, Otto's phrase can be accepted with the meaning that any perfection that is perceived in creatures and then predicated of God is found in him in a radically different way.

There is, however, an important distinction between two different ways in which the reflections of God found in creatures can be used to speak of God. When we say, "God is my shepherd" (Psalm 23), we are speaking in a very different tone from when we say, "God is wise." The first is *symbolic*, the second *analogical*. God is not properly a shepherd, but the way a shepherd guides his flock is an image of the way God watches over his creatures. God *is* wise; in fact, it is truer to say that God is wise than to say that Solomon is wise.

It is sometimes said that we can speak about God only symbolically or metaphorically because no matter what we say, we are applying limited, earthly terms to One who infinitely transcends them. What we call wisdom in God, it is argued, transcends earthly wisdom, just as much as the way God watches over us transcends the way the shepherd watches over his sheep. This is fallacious, overlooking an essential difference between the two cases. The term *shepherd* includes in its intended meaning material aspects, limits, and defects that cannot in any sense be attributed to God — all the very material things a shepherd does in tending the sheep: opening the pen in the morning and closing it at night after he has driven the sheep inside, etc. But the term *wisdom*, although derived from limited and imperfect human instances, does not *intend* to designate their limits. It designates a quality or value which in fact is realized only imperfectly, but it does not of itself designate the imperfection. The same cannot be said of *shepherd*; it refers directly to an activity which by its very nature includes material reality and is therefore incompatible with divinity.

It is very important that we can speak of God by proper analogies and not just symbolically. This makes it possible to philosophize genuinely and systematically (although always with humility!) about him. Thus we can discuss seriously God's goodness, knowledge, power, love, justice, creative activity, etc. If restricted to symbolic language, we would have religious poetry and rhetoric but hardly a systematic theology. Many people would doubtless be glad to settle for that; but then there would be no critical discussion, no synthesis, and no way to resolve the confusion that arises from the uninhibited use of conflicting metaphors.

On the other hand, symbol rather than analogy is the more ordinary vehicle of religious language. Scripture is full of symbols: "A mighty fortress is our God; our God is a consuming fire; the breath of God consumed the sinners; like a mighty warrior, God awoke from sleep and put his enemies to flight; God was sorry that he made man; God remembered Noah; God is the rock of my salvation; he is my shield and buckler. . . ." The very materiality of this language, which prevents us from attributing it to God properly, also makes it speak to us more powerfully. Likewise the evident impropriety of symbolic language guards us against the danger of supposing that we have a firm, comprehensive grasp on the divine mystery. It frees us to take advantage of all the gentle whispers and signals by which "the heavens proclaim the glory of God," without having to chasten our expressions to meet the exigencies of proper analogy — something most of us are most often unable to do.

Thus forewarned about the limits of our knowledge of God, let us examine the chief traits of the divine "portrait" as it has been drawn by Catholic theology. Most of the features are familiar — eternal, infinite, omnipotent, etc. What is difficult is to perceive the right sense in which to take them.

In what is perhaps the most profound, sensitive, and carefully nuanced treatise on God ever written, St. Thomas Aquinas begins his account of the divine nature (*Summa Theologiae*, I, qq. 3-26) by speaking first of the simplicity of God and then of his perfection. After that come the attributes of goodness, infinity, omnipresence, immutability, eternity, and unity. St. Thomas was writing for readers thoroughly versed in philosophy, and constructed his treatise in a rigorously philosophical order. Although we are following St. Thomas in regard to the substance of the doctrine, our aim is quite different. We do not expect most modern readers to have the philosophical preparation that could be assumed in medieval universities. Neither will we try to justify or demonstrate each point, except on certain particularly sensitive issues. Such an undertaking would require a much greater development than present limits allow. Our aim is simply to present the traditional Catholic understanding of God for intelligent and reasonably well-educated people, letting it speak for itself.

Hence a psychological rather than logical order that will be followed. Probably the most basic element of the popular notion of God is that he is eternal, and secondly that he is infinite. Upon this foundation of a being unlimited in time or nature, the remaining elements of the structure will be built.

THE BASIC DIVINE ATTRIBUTES

By "basic attributes," we mean those which, from a human point of view, seem to constitute the divine nature. "Moral attributes," such as justice and mercy, appear to us as built on to the former. This chapter will consider only the basic attributes; the moral attributes will be taken up in Chapter 9.

1. God is eternal. Perhaps what is most basic in the popular notion of God is that he has always existed. He did not come into being at a certain moment; there was never a time when he did not exist. If there had been, neither he nor anything else would ever have come into existence, since there would have been nothing to create anything. Likewise God always will exist; he will never cease to be.

"Always was and always will be" does not, however, sufficiently explain what is meant by eternity, which denotes that God necessarily is. God is a being that *cannot NOT be*. In the case of any other given thing, it is possible for it to exist or not; God is the one being who could not possibly not exist. If it were possible for him not to be — in other words, if he were a contingent being — he would need something else to explain his existence, and he would no longer be the ultimate reality, the ground, and explanation of all else.

Moreover, eternity is not to be imagined as a protracted duration without beginning or end: time without end. There are those who suppose that the world had no beginning but has gone on endlessly — perhaps in recurrent cycles, like summer and winter (as ancient philosophers conceived it), or exploding and contracting (as some modern scientists theorize). Even if that were the case, and if it were supposed also that the world will never end, that would not make it eternal in the sense in which God is eternal. Anything that exists in time has its being spread out over time; it does not exist totally at any one moment. What I once was, I am no longer; what I will be one day, I am not yet. Only a fraction of my full reality is actual at any given instant. (We do what we can to overcome this state, and to assure some future permanence to present enterprises, by making resolutions, promises, contracts, etc.; but how frail these bonds are to resist the alterations brought about by time!) God's eternity means that he is "all at once," that there is no future or past for him, simply an enduring present. This comes from the fact that there is no change in God, as will be seen below; for time depends on change.[3]

2. *God is infinite.* Infinite means without limit. All the beings within the realm of our experience have limits, first of all in a spatial sense: They are confined to a certain place. God, however, is not so confined; he is everywhere. But just as eternity does not mean endless time, so infinity does not mean extending outward endlessly in all directions, as we imagine when we try to think of an infinite universe. It does not mean that God takes up all of space; in fact, he does not take up space at all. Space is not the locus of his being, it is irrelevant to him. He is not spread out in dimensions any more than he is in time.

God's infinity has to do with something more fundamental than space. We are finite, that is, limited, not only in space but in our very nature. The nature of one thing is not that of another. Each being has a definite nature (the very word *definite* means delimited) that distinguishes it from other beings: men and angels; trees and flowers; birds, beasts, and reptiles — all of them are defined by a nature that limits them to a certain kind of being.

But God is not limited to a particular kind of being that can be compared or contrasted with others. God has the fullness of being; he is Being Unlimited. Each particular being possesses only a limited part of being (hence the term *particular*). But God has not just a part, he has the fullness. Each particular being is a reflection of some aspect of the divine nature; but God is the whole original that is partially reflected in them. Whatever exists is a being; every particular thing is some kind of being. But God is not just some kind of being, he is Being in its fullness, unlimited being.

A being that is eternal and infinite is impossible for us to imagine; we cannot even form a positive concept of it. A pair of pliers could take hold of the earth sooner than we could properly conceive of the infinite. What we can say is that things which come into being and perish postulate, for their explanation, something that does not begin or end, something that always IS. Likewise things that are finite postulate, as their ultimate explanation, something that is unlimited. In affirming the infinity of God, we are affirming merely that, in order to explain finite things, there must be something that does not have limits such as they do. This illustrates the incomprehensibility of God spoken of in the preceding section.

3. *God is perfect.* A being is said to be perfect if it lacks nothing that it ought to have, that is, if it has everything called for by its nature. Thus a perfect circle would be one in which every point was equidistant from the center, and a perfect square would be one with four absolutely equal, straight sides, meeting at right angles. To lack something not called for by its nature does not make a being imperfect. For a human body, to lack one leg would be an imperfection; but to lack antlers or hooves is not. The perfection of a being is therefore defined by its nature. But God does not have a particular nature or a particular kind of being, in reference to which we could say that his perfection calls for *a, b,* and *c* but not *d, e,* or *f.* God has the fullness of being; his perfection is his infinity — the fact that nothing in the order of being is wanting to him.

This does not mean, however, that God *is all things* or that he possesses, as "parts" of his being, all the particular kinds of being in the world: hands and feet, antlers and hooves, etc. This would be a crude kind of pantheism. As we shall see below, God's fullness of being is not a combination of multiple forms but utter simplicity. Other things differ from God by lacking something that he has, not by possessing something that he lacks. They are like partial reflections of the fullness that is his. They realize in a limited and partial way the Being that is fully realized in him. All the perfections that are found in them are already in him but in a higher way.

Hence the act of creation did not add anything to God. Similarly, when the Son of God became man, he did not add to his own being; he simply associated a finite human nature with his infinite divine nature. Or, to put it in another way, if it were possible to add all other beings and all possible beings together, this would not give an approximation of God but a conglomerate infinitely less than he.

4. *Immutability.* The impossibility of our forming an adequate concept of God appears strikingly when we reflect on the fact that he never undergoes change in any way whatsoever. This is declared vividly in Psalm 102:25-27:

> In the beginning you laid the foundations of the earth,
>> and the heavens are the work of your hands.
> They will perish, but you remain;
>> they will all wear out like a garment.
> Like clothing you will change them
>> and they will be discarded.
> But you remain the same,
>> and your years will never end.

Similarly, the Letter of James alludes to "the Father of lights with whom there is no variation or shadow due to change" (1:17, RSV). The law of process, according to which the living things of our world develop from infancy to maturity, and then decline with age, does not apply to God. He never was immature and in need of growing up; neither does he wear out, wither up, or run down.

This unchangeableness follows logically from his perfection and the completeness of his being. The fundamental reason why the beings of our world change is that they can fulfill their potentialities only in a limited way at any particular moment. When a man is sitting he cannot be walking; when a woman is fixing supper, she cannot be entertaining guests in the living room. Our life is a continual passing from one activity or state to another, as we attempt to unite in the course of time the multiple possibilities we cannot realize simultaneously. But in God there is no place for such transitions because all that he can be — which is to say, all the perfection of being — is already and eternally actual in him.

• *Creation not a new act*

Even when he creates, he is not doing anything new, so far as *his activity* is concerned. Creation implies on the part of the creature the coming into being of something which did not exist before; but it does not mean, on God's part, that he begins to act in a way he was not active before. His creative act is eternal and unchanging, though the changes it brings about take place only at the time willed by him. The same holds for God's "subsequent" interventions in the world, such as the call of Abraham or the miracles of Jesus. Change is always in the creature. It is caused by God but does not imply a change in God. Even when the Son of God "became" man, as we say, he did not begin to do something he had not previously been doing. Rather, a human nature came into existence and was united to his eternal actuality.

This is true even of mental states or psychic attitudes. God does not think first one thing and then another; in the fullness of his intelligence, all truth is perpetually present to his gaze. Likewise God does not feel angry at one moment and pleased at another; it is *we* who pass from the state of alienation from him to that of union with him and conformity to his will.

Scripture of course speaks without embarrassment or apology about God getting angry at the sinner, and being pleased with those who repent. It even represents him as changing his mind, as when Moses "persuaded" him not to destroy the Israelites for worshiping the golden calf (Exodus 21:14). But these are all anthropomorphic ways of speaking about God, as are those which speak of God's eyes and ears, mouth and breath, hands and arms, even of his heart and bowels. We cannot picture God except with human traits, and so to express the reality of his knowledge, of his love of the good, and of his hatred of evil, we use terms that connote change in him. But the change is always in the realm of creation; God remains eternally the same.

This may make his life appear like a boring, pointless existence. But we must remember that the reason we get bored with anything after a while lies in the poverty of our enjoyment. We have to pass from one activity to another because nothing that we have ever fulfills us completely. But God is completely fulfilled always; he is eternally brimming over with the joy and satisfaction of a perfect existence, such as we attain only at brief moments of success, and then quite imperfectly. Instead of imagining that his existence is boring, we should realize that our efforts to avoid boredom by turning from one thing to another are an attempt to imitate in time the fullness that God has in eternity.

5. *Simplicity*. God is utterly simple. "Simple" is the opposite of "complex"; it means, in basic terms, not divided into parts. The human person is quite complex because of the diverse factors such as mind, will, emotions, sensations, and instincts that compose us. In God there is no such diversity; all is one in an utter simplicity that defies our efforts to conceive it. The best we can do is to go through the various levels of complexity in ourselves, and recognize that God is without them. In him, there are no parts, no divisions, whatsoever.[4]

We have parts, first of all, in the sense that one organ of our body is distinct from the others. God has no such parts; in him, all is simply one. Our soul has parts in a more subtle sense, that is, faculties such as the mind and will. Although their distinction from one another is not visible, like the distinction of bodily organs, it is very evident because experience shows that to use our mind is not the same thing as to use our will. Knowing is not loving. I can develop my mind while neglecting my will or develop my will while neglecting my mind. But in God there is no such distinction. We speak of the mind and will of God only because we are unable to grasp his unimaginable simplicity. We can think of him only as similar to ourselves. In truth, however, mind and will are not distinct from one another in God, nor are they distinct from God himself. God is simply God.

Similarly, there are no distinct qualities in God. We use many different adjectives for him: powerful, wise, merciful, just, etc. We heap up these attributes in a vain attempt to describe the plenitude of his being, as someone might make a polygon of many sides in an attempt to represent the circle. As the white light of the sun is broken into red, yellow, and blue when it passes through a prism, so the simple light of divinity is refracted into diverse qualities by the crudeness of our minds. But in God these qualities are not diverse; God is simply God.

One of the complications that gives our life much of its color and variety comes from the domain of the accidental. We are not purely and simply what our essences define us to be; in each one of us, there are also many accidental features that differentiate individuals from one another, and lead to many unexpected events. One is short, another tall; one thin, another fat. In relating to people, it is not enough to know that they are human beings; we have to take into account the fact that one is sensitive, another callous; one is frank, another secretive, etc. In God, however, there is nothing accidental; he is purely his divinity. God is simply God.

In human beings (and in all creatures) there is a distinction between *the potential and the actual*. We all have potentialities that have not been actualized. Young people look to the future, wondering what they will become; the old ponder the past, and wonder what life would have been like if things had been done differently. At any given moment, no matter what I am actually doing, there are other things that I could be doing; these are all unactualized potentialities. But in God there are none of these; all is actual (in technical language, he is said to be "pure act"). God already is all that he ever will be and all that he ever can be; no future awaits him, no adventure lies in store for him.

This has an important bearing on how we conceive of God's activity. When *we* act, we pass from potency into actuality. For example, before I begin thinking, I have the potential to think; when I do think, I am actualizing that potential. As a result, my activity is a kind of increment to my being: The person acting exists more fully than one who is inactive. But God is simply, purely, and eternally actual. We have already seen that the various acts which we attribute to God, such as knowing, loving, and creating, are identical with one another. Now we must add that they are identical with God himself. Even in acting, God is doing no more than being himself. God is simply God.

This also affects our conception of God's power in a very important way. Power is predominantly a potential notion: The power to do something is potential for doing it, as distinguished from the actual doing. When we say that someone is powerful, we refer to what he *can* do, whether or not he is actually doing it. But God's power is completely actual. It is not an untapped potential which tomorrow, perhaps in answer to our prayer, will be brought into action. It is indeed legitimate to ask him to do something tomorrow that he is not doing today; but the potential to be actualized lies in us, not in him.

A final distinction to be eliminated from God is that between *essence* and *existence*. This delicate point was not perceived by any theologian or philosopher prior to St. Thomas Aquinas (1224-1274), and even for those who follow in his steps, it is difficult to grasp. The essence of a thing is that in it which determines *what it is*; its existence is its "act" of being. In any real being, both are present; however, we can know that something exists without knowing *what* it is, as when a hunter is not sure whether he sees a deer or another hunter. Likewise we can have an *idea* of something, and therefore know its essence but not know whether it exists or not. Hence we ask, "Are there really black holes? Does life really exist in other parts of the universe?" It seems inevitable that we think of things as essences that *have* existence. But that is not the case with God.

What this means can be put thus: On the one hand, the very essence of God includes existence. That is, he is a being that cannot *not* be. If we could grasp the essence of God, we would already know by that very fact that he does actually exist. Only because we do not have an adequate idea of God can we question whether or not he exists. On the other hand, to say that essence and existence are identical in God is to say that his essence is nothing but existence, that is, the fullness of being, as we saw earlier; for to exist means simply to be.

The early translators of the Hebrew Bible into Greek understood the sacred name *Yahweh* to mean, "He who is." If this is right, there is a remarkable coincidence between the name of God given to the crude desert nomads who followed Moses, and the supreme insight of the most refined metaphysics, that his essence is identical with his existence.[5]

This topic of the divine simplicity involves a startling paradox. In the material world, greater perfection usually involves greater complexity. Molecules are more complex than atoms; living cells more complex than molecules; the higher forms of life more complex than the lower. Man is the most complex of all. This led Teilhard de Chardin to propose the thesis that perfection and complexity are proportionate.[6] In God, however, the supremely perfect being is the most simple.

This is not, however, altogether alien to our experience. Other things being equal, a simple solution to a problem is superior to a complicated one. The geocentrism of Copernicus was recognized as superior to the complex system of spheres devised by the medieval astronomers precisely because it was more simple. The term *complex* is used in psychology to designate a personality disorder. A complicated person is difficult to deal with and usually ineffectual. There is a simplicity — involving frankness, straightforwardness, integrity, wholeness — that we highly esteem in persons. Above all, there is an amazing and beautiful simplicity in the saints that grace brings about, "decomplexifying" them. It is a kind of likeness to God. "Be wise as serpents and simple as doves," Jesus said (Matthew 10:16, RSV).

THE DIVINE PERSONALITY

The theological reflections of the Hindus led to a pantheistic conception of an Absolute that is identical with all reality; Brahman would seem to be nothing other than the depth-dimension of the real world. But Christian faith insists firmly that God is distinct from the world; moreover, that he is truly *personal*.

The belief that God is distinct from the world is anchored in three great facts given in Scripture. First, God made the world; he cannot be identified with his handiwork. Second, he has spoken and acted in the world: calling, encouraging, consoling, rebuking, helping, and directing us, intervening with "mighty deeds" on our behalf. Third, Jesus Christ is a divine person, who has come into the world. There is of course a danger of taking these statements in a gross sense that amounts to crude anthropomorphism. Any thinking person is sensitive to this danger. But granted that such terms as *making, speaking,* and *acting* have a different sense when applied to God from what they have in us, these basic affirmations of Christian faith oblige us to recognize that God is distinct from the world, and a person himself.

Even apart from the teachings of Scripture, reason itself supports this view. If you make the Ultimate Reality identical with the world or simply the "Dimension of Depth" in the world, you end up in absurdity. Either you deny the reality of the greater part of the world or you postulate as ultimate something that cannot possibly fulfill that function. The former is the route taken by the Hindu philosopher Sankara, who held that the multiplicity and change which appear in the world are all illusion. But that is simply denying the evidence that change does really occur and that reality is manifold; and if this evidence is denied, there is no basis left for affirming an ultimate reality at all. The second route, which holds that the divine does not refer to a being distinct from the world but simply to the deepest level or innermost core of all reality, is equally unsatisfactory. For the very reason why an Ultimate Reality must be postulated is that the things of our world cannot explain themselves, and therefore cannot be ultimate. In particular, matter lacks intelligence, and therefore cannot account for its own intelligent behavior. It calls for something of another order altogether. Similarly, multiple, limited, transitory things call for something one, unchanging, infinite, and eternal to explain them. This cannot be identified with them or even with the sum total of them; it must be "altogether other."

• *How can the infinite be personal?*

So much for God's distinction from the world. The *personality* of God is a more difficult notion to handle. What meaning would personality have in an infinite, unchanging being? Many who are ready to affirm that there must indeed be a mysterious and sacred "dimension of depth" to the world, a "ground of all being" that supports all observable beings, are unwilling to regard this Ultimate Being as personal. They consider this too to be an anthropomorphism.

Their objection would be valid if we made God out to be like a human person — a superman in the sky (as indeed Feuerbach imagined him). But that is not what is meant by calling God a person. Personality implies life, consciousness, and will. To say that God is personal is to say that the "ground of all being" is not an inanimate entity like some great block of translucent granite but is alive and full of life (indeed all in him is vibrant with life and *is* life, beyond anything in this world). It is to say that the source from which all things derive is not an unconsciously flowing spring but that he *knows* the things he has made, knows them totally and intimately. Finally, it is to say that the world did not emanate from him by a necessity of his nature but that he willed, and willed freely, to bring it into being, just as he still continues freely to intervene in it.

If God were merely an impersonal source and foundation of things, how could personal beings have come from him? If he lacked life, consciousness, and will, he would be inferior to us! Of all the modes of being known to our experience, personality is the finest and highest. If there is any attribute in this world which we dare attribute analogously to God, must it not be the highest perfection we have?

It is indeed difficult to conceive how an unchanging being can be alive and personal. But this only reminds us that life, consciousness, and will must have a different mode in God from what they have in us. A worm and a human are both alive, but it would be impossible for the worm, on the basis of his experience, to conceive of what life means at the human level. So likewise we must acknowledge that life, consciousness, and will are in God in an *eminent* way, compared to which we have only very rudimentary forms of them.

• *A masculine God?*

Finally we must ask what is to be made of the fact that, in Christian tradition, God is represented as masculine. The feminist movement has reacted strongly against this practice, which it sees as the expression of the patriarchal society in which the Scriptures were composed, and as a reinforcement of the attitudes of male dominance in our own culture. Several ways of counteracting this masculine bias have been suggested, such as: to speak of God as "her" or as him/her; to replace the notion of God the Father with God the Parent or, if the Father and the Son must be treated as masculine, to refer to the Holy Spirit at least as the "feminine principle in the divinity."

Perhaps the only point agreed upon by all is that God in fact transcends the difference between male and female. This biological distinction, based on the diverse functions of the partners in sexual reproduction, is irrelevant to God, who has no body. Although there is in God a mysterious engendering of an offspring by a parent, there is no union of male and female.

Hence the question of masculinity has to do not with the *nature* of God but with the *language* in which it is appropriate to speak of God. That is, there is no question about whether God is *in se* masculine or feminine but only about whether the traditional masculine language for God should be retained. Why Father and Son, rather than Mother and Daughter?

A second point that will be admitted by any Christian is that both man and woman are made "in the image and likeness of God" (Genesis 1:26f). It follows that, as we grope for an idea of God, we must employ both masculine and feminine traits. Thus the very masculine God of the Old Testament asks, "Can a mother forget the baby at her breast and have no compassion on the child she has borne? Though she may forget I will not forget you!" (Isaiah 49:14).

• *The language of Revelation*

Nevertheless, Christian tradition, both in popular piety and in academic theology, has been practically unanimous in using masculine language for God, until very recently when an issue was made of this matter. The basic reason for the unanimity of this tradition is undoubtedly the fact that God is spoken of as masculine in the language of Revelation.

The Old Testament speaks of God as a father to the people of Israel, also as a husband who takes Israel as his bride. It constantly refers to God as "him," never as "her." The few texts which attribute feminine qualities to God, such as that of Isaiah cited above, do not represent God as feminine; they simply insist that his care for his people is more faithful than the most faithful love known to human experience, that of a mother for her baby. Similarly for other texts of the same prophet: "As a mother comforts her child, so will I comfort you" (66:13). One may hold that "feminine" traits are being attributed to God here, but this does not refute the fact that God is visualized as masculine, any more than Paul denied his own masculinity when he exclaimed, "My dear children, with whom I am again in the pains of childbirth until Christ is formed in you" (Galatians 4:19).

In the New Testament, there are no texts that even qualify the unanimity of the use of the masculine. In the language of Jesus, Paul, and the other New Testament authors, God is consistently pictured as a Father and as a great king, never as feminine.

The authority of this biblical language is often discounted on the grounds that it simply reflects the patriarchal character of Jewish society. An expert on ancient Judaism has recently questioned whether this stock answer has any serious historical foundation; she sees it as an attempt by Christian scholars to shift responsibility for this masculine language from the New Testament writers to the Jews.[7]

Regardless of the verdict of historians on this issue, the decisive consideration for our question is the fact that Jesus always speaks of God as his Father. For anyone who regards him with the eye of faith, this cannot be dismissed as the result of a Hebrew prejudice. Jesus was sent to teach us the way to God. If the culture of his time included an unjust bias, would he not have corrected it? He denounced the hypocrisy of the scribes and Pharisees. He forbade the hatred of enemies that was usual in his day. He even broke with the so-called Jewish manner of disdaining women, as in the case of the Samaritan woman at Jacob's well (John 4). If therefore he did not oppose the Jewish way of speaking of God as Father but instead strongly reinforced it by using the notion of God's fatherhood more frequently, and with greater sensitivity, than anyone before him, his disciples can hardly dismiss his example as an uncritical acceptance of a culturally established bias.

In brief, Jesus taught us to address God as our Father; in fact, this is one of his most characteristic and precious teachings. If we are his disciples, we can hardly do otherwise.

Moreover, there is the fact that Jesus himself was a man. In his own person, he was God translated into human idiom. This does not imply a masculine character in his divinity; only in his humanity is Jesus a man. It does, however, mean that God, in revealing himself to us, in soliciting our love and devotion, took on a masculine form. "Whoever has seen me has seen the Father" (John 14:9). Hence we have to relate at least to God incarnate as a man. One can debate theoretically whether, within the Trinity, the second person could not be envisioned as a daughter; but our faith and worship are directed to Jesus as a concrete person, and there is no way we can leave open the option of regarding him as feminine, neuter, or indeterminate.

When we look at the alternative expressions proposed, we come up against the basic difficulty that our language has no term for a person who is neither male nor female. All human persons are one or the other. To refer to God as *It* would therefore depersonalize him — surely a worse evil than masculinizing.

There are, it is true, terms such as *parent* and *beget* that abstract from the question of gender. However, the very abstractness of the former makes it unsuitable for prayer, especially personal prayer. How many would be willing to accept the proposed version, "Our Parent who art in heaven"? It would also tend to make our relationship with God even more impersonal than it already is. Similarly, the practice of saying, "he or she": It can be done, but it would be repugnant as an expression of personal faith or personal prayer. A person can be visualized either as masculine or as feminine but not as alternatively one or the other. One can pray to God as a Father, and one could no doubt pray to God as a Mother; but our sentiments would be ill at ease treating the same being as alternately one and the other.

On another plane, it does not seem to be true that most women are uncomfortable addressing God as Father. For those who do find it so, there are perhaps just as many whose unhappy relations with their mothers would make them unwilling to address God as Mother.

To treat the Holy Spirit as feminine goes against the language of John 16:13f, where the Spirit is decisively referred to as masculine, despite the fact that the Greek word *pneuma* is neuter. In any case, a feminine Spirit associated with the masculine Father and Son still leaves a male-female ratio of two to one in the Trinity, which would not satisfy those who demand parity.

Finally, no matter what we theorize about why this masculine language originated (and that can never be more than speculation), it is in fact now firmly embedded in Christian tradition. To break with religious tradition is itself a grievous and painful step. There is a sacredness about religious observances which tends to keep them perpetual and unchanging; people instinctively resent any tampering with them. Where Church tradition is concerned, there is the quiet, constant action of the Holy Spirit to be reckoned with. This does not mean that there can never be reason to modify religious traditions (think of the *aggiornamento* of Vatican II), but it requires that we ask, "Would what is gained outweigh all the resentment, confusion, and disturbance incurred by this drastic alteration of the most basic term in our liturgy and our prayer?"

Moreover, Christianity is not just a religion; it is the grace of intimate, personal communion with God. The fact is widely attested that those who have developed a warm relationship with God the Father are deeply troubled by the proposal to call him Mother. Not because of any inferiority of motherhood to fatherhood but simply because you don't play around with warm personal relationships.

In conclusion, it seems to be universally agreed that God is in himself no more masculine than feminine. However, we have the need (and the grace!) to speak about God in our own language, and there is no human language capable of expressing the essence of the divinity as it really is. Divine revelation, on which the Christian religion is based, has presented God to us in masculine terms — both in words, and in the living person of Jesus of Nazareth. Guided by revelation, centuries of Christian tradition have spoken of God as masculine. Out of reverence for revelation, and in view of the wholly unsatisfactory character of any of the alternatives proposed, it seems better to maintain this tradition.

If men have taken advantage of their situation to oppress, exploit, and degrade women, that is an abuse to be corrected loyally and vigorously. If many women, resentful of the millennial belittlement to which they have been subjected, are determined to extirpate every vestige of patriarchal dominion, the justice of their motivation must be acknowledged. But there are bigger issues at stake here than human relations; and women's lot is hardly going to be enhanced by depriving them of a heavenly Father. For such reasons, it seems to us preferable to retain the traditional usage.

8
Creation

THE CREATION ACCOUNT OF GENESIS

The chief biblical account of creation is given in the first two chapters of Genesis, a book generally acknowledged to be a fusion of several earlier writings in which various traditions of the Hebrew people had been recorded. Chapters 1 and 2 were not originally successive chapters of a single book but two different accounts of The Beginnings, composed by different authors at different times.

Chapter 2 (beginning with the second half of verse 4) is older. It was composed around 950 B.C., during the period of the united Kingdom of Israel. It belongs to the "Yahwist" document, so called from its use of the divine name, *Yahweh*, which in most English translations is rendered as THE LORD. Primitive in style and anthropomorphic in its depiction of God, this account focuses on the story of the first man and woman, with only a single line about the creation of "the earth and the heavens." The same document continues on through Chapter 3, with the story of the first sin.

Chapter 1 (plus 2:1-4a) gives a relatively late account composed by Jewish priests after the time of the Babylonian exile (hence in about the fifth century B.C.). It describes the creation of the universe as taking place in six days, after which God rested on the seventh day (a point of great importance to the priests, who had to see that the holiness of the Sabbath was respected.) Brief creation accounts are also to be found in Psalm 33:6-10, Psalm 90:2, Psalm 95:3-5, Isaiah 40:12, 26 and in many passages of Job.

In simple, powerful language, these chapters declare that the heavens and earth and all they contain are the work of God; that he made them simply by calling them into being without any effort; that all the things he made were good; that he determined their natures and put them in order; that man is unique in all creation as being made in the image and likeness of God, having dominion over all other living things. Woman was made as "a helper fit for man," and their coming together was a part of the divine plan. Nakedness was no cause of shame for them.

• *The Enuma Elish*

The grandeur, beauty, and intelligence of this account appears sharply when it is compared with the creation myth of other religions — for example, the Babylonian *Enuma Elish*:

> This myth begins with two gods, Apsu (the river) and Tiamat (the sea). Apsu is male and Tiamat female, and their waters, mingling together give rise to other gods. When the noisiness of the god-children disturbed their parents, Apsu determined to murder them; instead, however, they killed him. Then Tiamat, the mother, set out to destroy her children. To assist in her murderous work, this huge, hideous ogre spawned

a horde of demons, such as the Viper, the Dragon, the Sphinx, the Great Lion, the Mad Dog, the Scorpion Man, the Dragon Fly, the Centaur and mighty lions.

Meanwhile, from the heart of the dead Apsu sprang Marduk, the god of the city of Babylon, who came to the defense of his brothers. He attacked their furious mother, who cried out like one possessed and took leave of her senses. She opened her mouth to swallow Marduk, but he drove the Evil Wind down her throat with such force that she could not close her mouth. The wind inflated her belly, into which Marduk drove his arrow, killing her. Standing over her carcass, he split it in two like a shellfish. One half he set up as the sky, and the other half he left prostrate to form the earth.

Then Marduk set about forming the world. He set up stations for the gods, and appointed stars to represent them. He likewise fixed constellations of stars for each of the twelve months and for the days of the year. Tiamat's belly he established as the zenith of the heavens. The moon he assigned to the night, giving it directions about when to be circular and when to have horns, so as to signify the time of the month.[1]

This myth seems to represent the world as a great battlefield between the forces of destruction and chaos, and the forces of order. Order was achieved by Marduk, the hero-god of Babylon, but it is continually threatened by the forces of destruction in the sea. In the biblical account, on the contrary, God is not merely one of the forces engaged in combat; he stands serenely above them all. He calls things into being with a word; no effort or struggle is involved in his work. Evil does not go back to the beginning, and is not in any kind of parity with God. Its origin is left unexplained, but man encounters it as a temptation. All subsequent woes result from man's having succumbed to the temptation.

It is a question of fundamental importance, whether Genesis 1-11 should be regarded as the Hebrew Myth of Beginnings, comparable to corresponding myths of other cultures. But the very meaning of such a view has changed radically over the past hundred years. In the last century, it would have meant, "Genesis is nothing but myth" — that is, the work of a primitive, undisciplined imagination. Since that time, however, anthropologists have learned to take ancient myths seriously as the symbolic expression of what may be very profound insights. In this perspective, the view in question would mean that, just as ancient people in America, China, Greece, Rome, and all over the world developed myths to express their sense of the ultimate meaning of things, so the Hebrews produced Genesis 1-11 as their mythical account of how the world began.

Since the Hebrews derived from Mesopotamia, and since the early chapters of Genesis at certain points bear some resemblance (very slight, it must be acknowledged) to the Babylonian myths (both, for example, tell of an ancient deluge from which their people were saved), many scholars consider it likely that the Hebrews reshaped the Babylonian myth (or perhaps a more primitive form of it), to make it conform to their own monotheism and moral standards.[2]

• *Symbol, myth, and legend*

In order to avoid confusion in this matter, it is important to distinguish between myth, legend, and symbol. *Symbol* occurs when one thing is taken to stand for something else, especially something physical for a spiritual or intangible reality. Thus the flag is a symbol of the nation and the governor's seal a symbol of his authorization of a document. Symbols are especially important in religion because God, being invisible, can be represented only symbolically. Likewise man's worship, being spiritual, can be expressed only through symbolic gestures, that is, rituals or ceremonies, such as kneeling, bowing, incensing, and marching in procession.

Myth is *one* form of symbolic expression. In the proper sense, it always has the form of a *story*. This story may be about how the world began, as in the Enuma Elish myth above. It may tell about the origin of the human race or of a particular race or tribe. The Shinto religion has a myth about how the sun god formed the Japanese people and their islands, and how the emperors descended from him. In any case, myths are usually about the origins of things, and explain them by a story about the gods, depicted more or less as human beings. Myths may also represent the human quest for happiness or the end of the world.

> Myth narrates a sacred history; it relates an event that took place in primordial Time, the fabled time of the "beginnings." In other words, myth tells how, through the deeds of Supernatural Beings, a reality came into existence, be it the whole of reality, the Cosmos, or only a fragment of reality — an island, a species of plant, a particular kind of human behavior, an institution. Myth, then, is always an account of a "creation"; it relates how something was produced, began to *be*. . . .
> (*Myth and Reality*, Mircea Eliade, New York: Harper, 1963, p. 5f)

Legend also is a story, the story of some marvelous event of the past. But whereas myth is situated in primordial time, before the beginning of "this world," legend is situated in historical time; what it recounts, however, is not historical but imaginary. Whereas myth is about divine beings, legends are about heroes or other famous people, such as Caesar or Napoleon, Washington or Lincoln, Daniel Boone or Knute Rockne. In both cases, the stories are hard to believe; but whereas the myths belong to an utterly different sort of world, legends tend to be merely marvelous cases or exaggerations of things that belong to this world: great feats of strength or cunning or bravery. There is often a kernel of history at the origin of the legend, but it has become exaggerated in the telling.

The line between myth and legend is not easy to define; the two are often blended together. Nevertheless, their motivation is quite diverse. Legend arises above all from the human enjoyment of a good story, especially a story that makes our country or our tribe look good, and discomfits the enemy. At its finest, myth is the product of the human spirit grappling with profound questions, especially about the why and wherefore of things. It attempts to declare in symbolic form an insight that cannot be expressed literally. At a lower level, myths are simply imaginary answers to questions about which people are ignorant (why the heavens are blue; why some stars wander, while others remain fixed, etc.); at this level, myth can be regarded as primitive science. Finally, some myths may be nothing but grotesque or obscene vagaries of fantasy.

In asking whether such categories can be applied to Scripture, it is important not to confuse them with one another. When the Psalms tell of God creating the world with the breath of his mouth or trampling his enemies underfoot, they are obviously speaking symbolically, but this is not myth or legend. When we read of Samson slaying a thousand men with the jawbone of an ass or Judith beguiling the general of the Assyrians and then cutting off his head when he had drunk himself to sleep, we may ask whether they are pure legends or have some historical value; but they clearly are not myths. The question which we are considering here is whether the creation accounts in Genesis should be called myths.

• *Symbol and myth in Genesis*

Obviously, many elements in them are symbolic: the tree of life, the tree of knowledge, the talking serpent, etc. The very name *Adam* is a Hebrew word for man, and throughout the first part of the story should probably be translated as "the man." Only from Genesis 3:21 on does it seem to be a proper name. Hence many interpret Adam as a symbol of mankind. But, as we have seen, symbolic language does not of itself constitute myth. However, other elements do seem to be mythical in the proper sense: for example, that snakes crawl on their belly and "eat dust" because God cursed the Serpent for leading Eve into sin (3:14); that the rainbow was placed in the sky as a sign of God's promise never again to destroy the world by a flood (9:12-17). From another point of view, the God who shapes man's body out of dirt like a sculptor working in clay, who breathes the breath of life into his nostrils, makes him a wife out of his rib, plants a garden for the two of them to dwell in, and then comes walking through the garden in the evening breeze — such an anthropomorphic God has much in common with the gods of myth.

What is meant then when it is proposed that the early chapters of Genesis are mythical in character, as even Pope John Paul has done?[3] It is first of all to say that the story of creation and the fall is not literal history but a symbolic story. The seven days are not a measure of the time in which the universe came into being but belong simply to the great metaphor which declares that God made all things. The formation of Eve from Adam's rib does not describe the process whereby she was formed but (perhaps) expresses the identity of her nature and his. The serpent who spoke to Eve was not a real talking snake but a symbol of the temptation to which mankind is subject. These particular interpretations are of course debatable; but they are meant only to illustrate the point that when the text of Genesis is called mythical, what is meant primarily is that it tells symbolically rather than literally the story of human and cosmic origins.

Such an application of the term *myth* is a very delicate matter for anyone who approaches Scripture with faith. It can easily be construed in a way that would be difficult to reconcile with Christian belief. Hence the following qualifications should be noted carefully:

1. Calling this text mythical does not mean that it is not inspired by the Holy Spirit.

Many anthropologists do speak of myth as simply the product of the human mind and imagination in its effort to express the inexpressible.[4] What they call myth is a purely natural creation of man, in which God has no part (or no more than he has in all human activity). But strictly speaking, myth designates one literary form among others. One who believes in the inspiration of Scripture will hold that, just as the Holy Spirit inspired various biblical authors to write in the form of history (for example, the Gospels), letters (the "epistles" of the New Testament), poetry (the Psalms), so he could also have inspired someone to use the form of myth. Thus Pope Pius XII said (in 1950) of the first eleven chapters of Genesis:

> . . .in simple and metaphorical language adapted to the mentality of a people of little culture, they both state the principal truths fundamental for our salvation, and also give a popular description of the origin of the human race and the Chosen People. And if the ancient sacred writers took anything from popular narratives which may well be granted — it must never be forgotten that they did so with the help of divine inspiration. . . .
>
> (*Humani Generis*, no. 38; TCC 126f; TCT 141)

2. The discussion of myth in Scripture focuses on Genesis 1-11, which deals with the origin of the world and of mankind as well as what may be called sacred prehistory (the Tower of Babel, Noah and the Flood, etc.). Chapter 12 of Genesis begins the story of Abraham, where we enter into the realm of history properly speaking. From this point on, it seems completely improper to speak of myth. Some (especially rationalist) authors do so, on the grounds that all stories about God intervening in the world of man are myth. But the intent of these books is obviously to affirm that God has in fact intervened; to speak of his interventions as mythical is simply to reject the biblical (that is, Hebrew and Christian) faith. The question to be asked about the historical books of the Old Testament is not whether they are mythical, but rather, whether they do not contain legendary material. It is generally recognized that they do; in other words, that the use of legends too can be inspired by the Holy Spirit. But this question does not concern us here (see Chapters 6 and 16).

3. Even when it is applied to Genesis 1-11, there is a problem with the term *myth* because of its opposition to history. As we have said, the stories of Adam and Eve, etc., need not be taken as history in the sense of a literal narrative of the events. However, it does seem that we must hold that they refer to *real* events, at least in the case of the sin of Adam and Eve. The account of this sin is obviously metaphorical; but, as will be explained more fully in Chapter 14 of this work, it is necessary to postulate that human sin originated in a particular human act. We cannot suppose that human nature, as originally created, was inherently sinful. That being the case, Genesis 1-11 is not myth in the usual sense of a story told to symbolize an ahistorical truth (as one may suppose that Marduk's struggle with Tiamat represents the perennial effort needed to preserve order amid chaos). Genesis is rather the story of a real event but told in symbolic language; in this sense, it has a certain historical character. Concretely, this means that there was a temptation and fall at the origin of human history, even though the "forbidden fruit," etc., is metaphorical language.[5]

150

4. Finally, it must not be forgotten that in popular usage, even among cultivated people, *myth* means a story or a belief *that is not true*. Thus people speak of the (Nazi) myth of Aryan supremacy, the myth of male superiority, etc., meaning thereby that these ideas are false. Robert Wilken has entitled one of his books *The Myth of Christian Origins* in order to indicate that "the apostolic age is a creation of the Christian imagination" (p. 158). The work of an investigative reporter is often represented as that of "debunking myths," which is to say that he discovers the facts which contradict what has generally been believed. Hence, no matter how carefully we qualify the proper, technical sense of myth, there is always a danger that people who hear that "the story of Adam and Eve is mythical" will understand this to mean that there is no truth in it or that it is, as *Humani Generis* says, "the product of an extravagant imagination" (no. 39).

In sum, it is obvious on the one hand that the stories of Genesis 1-11 are symbolic rather than literal. On the other hand, if we speak of them as myth, we must do so with care not to deny their divine inspiration or their realism which goes beyond that of pure myth. Finally, we must not use the notion of myth as a covert device for evading the affirmation of Hebrew and Christian faith that God has really intervened in the history of Israel and in Jesus Christ.

THE THEOLOGY OF CREATION

The basic teaching of the Genesis accounts is that God made the heavens and the earth, and all that is in them. Other religions have had very different conceptions of the relationship between the visible universe and the primal or ultimate reality. Some ancient Chinese believed in an original female entity (Yin — possibly a water or earth goddess) out of whose dark womb all things were born. Other myths tell of a god who made the world out of some material that was available to him, as, for instance, Marduk did using the corpse of Tiamat. With much greater sophistication, the Neoplatonists represented God as the original One from whom, by a process of emanation, all other things arose in a steadily descending order, with the material world being the lowest form, the farthest removed from the divine One. Some forms of modern pantheism conceive of the world as an expression of the inner life of the divine mind.

The Catholic theology of creation, as it has been fixed by centuries of reflection on the texts of the Old Testament, includes the following points:

1. God made the world. That is to say that all that is not God was brought into existence by God. There is nothing that has existence independently of God.

2. There is one God alone who is the Creator. A movement of thought that began in ancient Persia among the Zoroastrians, and has at various times had a powerful influence on Christians (for example, the Manichees with whom St. Augustine contended or the Albigensians of the Middle Ages), postulated two original sources of being. These were Mazda, the god of light and good, and Ahriman, the god of darkness and evil. But for Christianity, there is only one original source, God; everything else, even Satan, is his creature.

3. Creatures did not emanate from God as a stream flows from a spring or as rock comes from a quarry. In that case, the divine being would have been the *matter* out of

151

which particular creatures are fashioned. To say that God made things is to say that he is their *efficient cause*, as the carpenter is maker of the chair. The efficient cause is not the material out of which something is formed but the being by whose power they are brought into existence.

4. God made things out of nothing; or better, he did not make them out of anything, he simply called them into being. When God made things, he made them totally. Other efficient causes work on already existing matter, changing it from one form into another. People make clothes out of fabric, furniture out of wood, houses out of brick and mortar, or synthetic products out of minerals. There is always some previous matter out of which the new thing is made. But in the case of the divine act of creation, there was no previously existing matter. There was nothing; and God's creative act consisted in bringing the totality of things into being, not just in giving them a new form. (Beware of taking the phrase "out of nothing" as if to suggest that "nothing" is the *material* out of which God made things, as wood is the material out of which the carpenter makes furniture. The statement "God made things out of nothing" means simply that there was no material with which he worked.)

5. By the same token, the act of creation involved no *process*. There was nothing God had to *do* to bring about the world; there were no steps to be taken from nonbeing to being. As the Book of Genesis describes it, "God said, 'Let there be light,' and there was light." The act of creation was simply the divine command that something come into existence; at once, it was there: "He spoke, and it came to be; he commanded, and it stood forth" (Psalm 33:8, 9). (However, this does not exclude a process whereby the things originally created underwent developments leading to new forms.)

6. The act of creation was free. There was no necessity in God to create. The world did not emanate from him as a consequence of his nature, the way light emanates from the sun. He was free to create or not to. He could have remained in his eternal solitude with no loss to himself. And given the decision to create, he was free to create any world whatsoever. He did not have to create the world that actually exists. We cannot say that this is the only possible world, much less that it is the best of all possible worlds. Likewise there was no necessity that you or I be brought into existence. We and all creatures exist as the result of an utterly free, gratuitous divine decision.

7. But why, then, did God create at all? And what made him determine to create this rather than some other world? We must approach such questions very cautiously. Reasons and motives do not have the same meaning when referred to God as they do for us. This much, however, we can say, that God certainly did not create us because there was something he would gain thereby. He had absolutely no need of us, and no profit to be acquired by having us. There was no divine loneliness that called for companionship. Creation can be understood only as an act of sheer goodness. It was for our advantage that he brought us into being. He willed to share his infinite wealth and he brought us into existence in order that we might share it.

It is one of the most hallowed maxims of Christian spirituality that God made us for his glory. However, it would distort the meaning of this profound truth if we took it as giving God a motive for creating us. Then it would imply that what God ultimately wanted was someone to glorify him, as a politician might hire people to applaud at his speeches. The phrase "for his glory" should not be construed as the motive for God's act of creation but as the end to which our lives should be directed. We can and should glorify God in all that we do. We are in right order, and our existence makes sense, when we do this; not otherwise.

GENESIS AND SCIENCE

Genesis says that, on the first day, God created light; on the second, heaven; on the third, he divided the land from the sea and made vegetation spring up; on the fourth day, he created the sun, moon, and stars; on the fifth, birds and fish; on the sixth, animals and human brings.

Many readers of the Bible have taken this as a literal and essentially complete record of the way things happened. An Anglican bishop, James Ussher (1581-1656), by compiling all the ages and dates given in the Old Testament, came to the conclusion that creation occurred in the year 4004 B.C.;[6] from 1701 onward this date was mentioned in the margin of the Authorized (King James) Version of the Bible. Subsequently, Dr. John Lightfoot of Cambridge (1602-1675) argued that the creation of the first man would have taken place on the autumnal equinox (September 23), most appropriately at nine in the morning.[7]

Ussher and Lightfoot lived in the seventeenth century, when the era of modern science was just beginning. The development of science, especially during the present century, has led to a very different view of the origins of the world and of man. The universe is thought to be about fifteen billion years old. The earth was formed some four and a half billion years ago, and life has been on earth close to four billion years. Conjectures about the origin of human life have changed enormously in the past three decades; at the present time, Donald Johanson thinks that beings recognizable as human were walking the earth two million years ago.[8]

It is difficult for us to conceive of such long periods of time. If we let a single sheet of paper represent a million years, a volume of one thousand sheets (that is, two thousand pages) would represent a billion years. This is approximately the size of the *Oxford Annotated Bible*. Four and a half such bibles would represent the age of the earth. The entire fossil record of mankind would come on the last three sheets. If the pages are divided into two columns, with about fifty lines of print to a column (like the OAB), the last line of the last column of the last page would represent five thousand years, enough to include all recorded history (that is, from 3000 B.C. to 2000 A.D.); and that last line would not yet be completely filled out.

We have seen how the emergence of the theory of evolution created a crisis of faith during the nineteenth century for those who believed in God. An important factor in this crisis was the apparent conflict between the scientific view of the origin of the world, and that which we find in Genesis. Since then, this crisis has greatly abated, as it has become recognized that the Book of Genesis is not intended to give a geological or paleontological record. Rather, it is a religious statement meant to teach us about our relationships with God, not to satisfy curiosity about our connections with the rest of the world. Ussher and Lightfoot were trying to draw out of the Bible what it was not meant to give. Hence the enormous periods of time postulated by astrophysics and geology are not in contradiction with the "six days" of creation according to Genesis. The latter can be taken as nothing more than a framework on which to distribute the making of the universe as primitive people conceived of it. (For that matter, the first three days came before the creation of the sun; what would *day* mean under such conditions?)

• *Tension between scientists and believers*

Nevertheless, as we saw in Chapter 3, a tension still persists in many people's minds between "creationist" and "evolutionist" views. Popular Christian family magazines still print articles defending the former against the latter, and not a few scientists continue to speak derisively of the need to choose one or the other. Those who try to reconcile the two by pointing out parallels between Genesis and evolution (first plants, then birds and fish, then animals, and finally man) are only adding to the fundamental confusion that comes from reading Genesis as if it were meant to be a historical report on the process of creation.

A worse mistake is being made by some Christian intellectuals who "reconcile" their faith and science by letting science have the final say on all questions on which science and revelation seem to conflict. In effect, this means that they are willing to adapt their religious beliefs to the prevailing opinion in contemporary science (whereas genuine scientists tend to be very cautious about the claims they make even for their own theories). They forget that faith has an authority and certitude of its own. With regard to its proper message, the Bible has a certitude far greater than that of any human science, for it is the Word of God himself.

Ultimately, there can be no contradiction between revelation and science because truth does not conflict with truth. The God who created the world studied by science is the same God who speaks to us in Scripture. There can, however, be disagreements between scientists and theologians, both because they are prone to misinterpret one another, and because their grasp of their own discipline is only partial and feeble.

In actual fact, their realms are so diverse that there are not many points on which disagreement is even conceivable. There are a few points of tension, however, which need to be noted:

1. The general theory of evolution — namely, that life has evolved from lower to higher forms — poses no serious problem. Genesis affirms that God is the Creator of the entire universe. Whether he created all things directly or caused lower forms to give rise to higher ones is irrelevant. But in regard to human origins there is a serious problem. Paleontologists commonly take it for granted that the emergence of mankind is simply one more instance of evolution. Genesis, however, sharply differentiates human beings from other animals in declaring that they are made "in the image and likeness of God." In Chapter 10, we will see the grounds on which Catholic theology insists that the human soul, being spiritual, cannot simply emerge from an animal body. To hold that man evolved from simians is not so innocuous as to hold that mammals evolved from reptiles. A view widely adopted by Catholic anthropologists supposes that the human body was prepared by the evolution of the anthropoid body up to the point at which it was suitable to receive

a human soul, and that God at this point infused a spiritual soul into an animal that thereby became the first man. Thus Pius XII declared:

> The Teaching Authority of the Church does not forbid . . . research and discussion . . . with regard to the doctrine of evolution insofar as it inquires into the origin of the human body as coming from pre-existent and living matter — for the Catholic faith obliges us to hold that souls are immediately created by God.
>
> (*Humani Generis*, no. 36; TCC 205a; TCT 365)

2. However, this does not eliminate all the problems. The same pope went on immediately to warn against rashly assuming that the evolution of the human body had been established with certitude by the facts. He urged scholars to consider the reasons on both sides of the question "with the necessary seriousness, moderation and measure." This is sound advice not only in this question but in all anthropological studies. He called attention to the fact that "the sources of divine revelation require the greatest moderation and caution in this respect" (Ibid.).

These lines were written in 1950. The four decades that have elapsed since then have brought an immense amount of evidence from diverse lines of scientific investigation in support of the view that the human body has indeed emerged from that of its predecessors. Today, although caution is still in order, belief in the evolution of the human body from that of its predecessors is hardly to be considered a "rash assumption."

But there are other difficulties in the view that a human soul was infused into a body prepared by animal evolution. It would seem ridiculous to suppose that an apelike animal, in the course of its life, should suddenly have been endowed with a rational soul and thereby became human. It is more plausible to suppose that the infusion of the soul occurred at the moment of conception. But even that would imply a human child born to and raised by a mother that was a brute animal. In view of the human need for affection and communication, this does not seem acceptable either. Can we suppose that divine providence would have placed human beings in such a situation?

3. Moreover, paleontology is not totally confined to the realm of the body. Fossil tools and works of art are evidence of intelligence. Likewise the structure of the tongue and palate provide evidence of at least the potential for speech, which is one of the most important expressions of intelligence. Hence paleontology has important light to shed on the question when and how human intelligence arose.

If, in spite of the difficulties mentioned above, we suppose that the human body emerged gradually from that of beasts, and ask, at what point do we find evidence of a rational soul, paleontology provides evidence that is fascinating and perplexing but far too sketchy for a definite answer. The use of artifacts seems to be established as far back as 2.3 or even 2.5 million years ago — that is, about half a million years before *homo habilis*, the earliest being to whom the name *homo* is generally accorded. However, the manufacture of such crude tools is perhaps not beyond the capacity of irrational animals. On the other hand, *homo erectus* made tools systematically (not just opportunistically as did the Olduvans); he also used fire (perhaps 1.4 million years ago in Kenya), and established definite campsites. But works of art and burial of the dead do not seem to have been practiced before modern man (*homo sapiens*). Thus the fossil evidence does not indicate any point of sharp differentiation between a rational "homo" and the irrational hominids that preceded him. This difficulty will be treated further in Chapter 10.

4. A final set of problems has to do with the question whether the human race began with a single pair of ancestors or more. The doctrine of original sin (see Chapter 14) seems to presuppose the former. A few decades ago, many anthropologists were inclined to hold that human beings developed independently in various parts of the world, such as Indonesia, China, Europe, and Africa. (This view was known as *polyphyletism* — "many phyla.") Today, however, the fossils uncovered along the Great Rift Valley in Africa are so much older than all others, it is generally agreed that Africa is the cradle of humanity. Furthermore, the fact that all human races can interbreed makes it extremely unlikely that they could have had independent origins. Thus the advances made in paleontology itself have eliminated the problem which polyphyletism once posed for Catholic doctrine.

Polygenism, however, remains a problem. This is the view that the human race originated not in a single couple but through the gradual evolution of a population. Such would be the case, for example, if a tribe of chimpanzees in East Africa had little by little developed those traits which are recognized as human. This seems to be the normal way that evolution takes place; and biologists point out the extreme unlikelihood of two individuals, male and female, of a given species, both undergoing identical mutations decisive enough for them to be at the origin of a new species.[9] But this argument, which is based on the normal biological processes of evolution, would seem to be irrelevant if it be granted that the rational soul which specifies human beings requires a special creative act. Pius XII declared that, since polygenism appears irreconcilable with the doctrine of original sin, Catholics are not free to embrace it (*Humani Generis*, no. 37).

Thus between traditional Catholic theology and the current state of paleontology there are not precisely contradictions but tensions. Ready solutions for them do not seem available at the present time. They are pointed out here as examples of difficulties which the believing Christian has to live with in a scientific culture, and still more as topics on which the collaborative reflection of theologians and scientists is urgently needed. But it is not necessary to resolve them in order to have faith; on the contrary, they serve to remind us that faith is motivated by something deeper, stronger, and more reliable than scientific evidence — namely, God's own witness.

THE PROBLEM OF EVIL

If all things have been created by God, why is there evil in the world? This is one of the most ancient, persistent, and agonizing problems confronting believers. Sometimes it is posed implicitly: Why did this accident happen to me? Why did that fine man have to die so young? Other times it is more explicit: Why would God allow a mother to be afflicted with polio when her children need her? Massive human disasters such as the starvation of millions of people due to the drought in the Sahel or the killing and destruction involved in World War II are for some people grounds to deny the existence of God or to reject angrily a God who would allow such things to happen. Others find such grounds in the suffering of a single innocent child.

The Zoroastrians solved this problem by teaching that good things were created by Mazda, the god of light, and evil by Ahriman, the god of darkness. A less sophisticated form of the same basic attitude was that of the Delaware Indians who believed that God created most things, but that flies, midges, and the like were the work of an evil spirit. The Manichees, against whom St. Augustine reacted, held that all matter is evil, and spiritual realities alone are good. In such views, God is no longer the Creator of everything.

An opposite approach is taken by many evolutionists today, including, apparently, Teilhard de Chardin. In their view, *evil* refers simply to the numerous failures that are a necessary part of the evolutionary process, out of which a greater good is forever emerging. But apart from the fact that it hardly reckons with the danger of technology putting an end to all progress, such a view fails to take human malice seriously. Can cruelty and exploitation be shrugged off as nothing more than inevitable mishaps on the way to a better humanity?

The classic Catholic position on this question can be summarized thus: (1) Every creature is in itself good. Nothing is evil by nature. (2) Sin is the supreme evil; but it originates in the creature, not the Creator. (3) Suffering can be understood only in the light of sin, on the one hand, and of the redemptive use God makes of suffering, on the other.

Genesis tells us that "God saw all that he had made, and it was very good" (1:31); 1 Timothy declares, "Everything God created is good" (4:4). Such texts underlie the firm Christian insistence that nothing is evil by nature.

1. METAPHYSICS OF EVIL

• *Evil nature meaningless*

Even from a purely philosophical point of view, it can be recognized that the concept of a being that is evil by nature is meaningless. This can be seen by reflection on things classified as bad or evil.[10] They all fall into one or both of two types: failure to fulfill one's own nature or hindering another being from fulfilling its nature.[11] Examples of the former are a bad foot or a bad razor. Here *bad* indicates that the thing in question is deficient in respect to what its nature (or design) calls for. In the same perspective, that which does fulfill its nature or design is called good, as a good car, a good carpenter, or a good horse. Goodness is not some quality added onto the substance of a thing; calling it good is saying simply that it is fully itself. Similarly, calling it bad means that it is not all it ought to be; that it lacks something which, according to its nature, it ought to have. To be absolutely and totally bad, a thing would have to be nonexistent.

In this perspective, we can understand the famous position of St. Augustine, that evil is nonbeing. This insight, for which he was indebted to the Neoplatonists, does not mean that evil is unreal, as Hindu Vedanta would say. Paralysis and pain, disease and accidents, failures and frustrations, treachery and cruelty, are very real. But Augustine's point is that none of them imply an *evil nature*; all of them reduce to a deficiency in something which, of itself or by its nature, is good. A hole in a shoe is a model illustration of how evil, or badness, consists in nonbeing, that is, the lack of what ought to be there.

Sometimes the evil consists in having too much of something, for example, too much

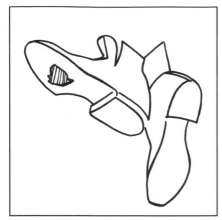

fat or an excessive secretion of a hormone. Yet even in these cases, it is not the superfluous being in itself that is properly evil but *lack of due proportion*. Proportion is a kind of *order*, and order is a real type of being, in comparison to which disorder is nonbeing. This point will become very important when we come to moral evil, which consists chiefly in disorder.

This distinction between good and bad is parallel to that which we have seen in Chapter 7 between the *perfect* and *imperfect*, and comes in effect to the same thing. There are of course differences in the way we use these two sets of terms. Whereas perfection has to do simply with the *being* of a thing, good and bad introduce the perspective of *love*. To say that a thing is good is to say that it is desirable or lovable; to say that it is evil is to say that it is undesirable, unlovable. But we are disregarding this nuance here, and taking good/bad as synonymous with perfect/imperfect. A thing is good insofar as it is perfect, bad insofar as it is imperfect.

It will be helpful for our discussion of sin to bear in mind that when a thing is called good or bad, usually its *functioning* is what is being evaluated. We speak of a bad arm or a bad leg when a limb is not able to perform its proper function or does so only painfully. A bad car likewise is one that doesn't run very well. But this bad functioning results from some incompleteness in *being*, so that *functional* good or bad ordinarily reduces to *entitative* good or bad.

• *Interference*

In the second sense of evil, one thing is said to be bad *for another* because it impedes the welfare of the other. Thus, whereas water and sunshine are good for the grass, salt and drought are bad. The lion is bad for the lamb, whereas lamb is quite good for lions. Fresh air and healthy foods are good for the body, but sugar is bad for the teeth, and smoke, as the U.S. surgeon general insistently reminds us, is bad for the lungs. This kind of badness, or evil, may be called *relative* because it implies not that the thing is deficient in itself but that it is harmful to some other being.

In sum, a thing is bad in the simple or absolute sense of the term when it is defective, failing to fulfill its nature. It is bad in the relative sense insofar as it interferes with the fulfillment of another being. Obviously, the relative evil reduces to the absolute. Because it is bad for a thing not to fulfill its nature (for example, for a body not to be healthy), whatever interferes with this fulfillment (for instance, smoking) is called *bad for* the thing.

While there are not many Zoroastrians or Manichees left today, a modern mind is likely to raise the question "How can carcinogenic viruses or *streptococcus bacilli* or, for that matter, even poison ivy, be conceived as good?" In terms of the above distinction, we must say first that only in relation to us are they called bad. In reference to their own nature, they are good in the measure that they live up to what a virus, a bacillus, or an ivy is meant to be. Even those which are the most noxious to us can, when considered in themselves, be recognized as entities of real quality and beauty. Furthermore, even in relationship to us, it may well be that these apparently malignant creatures are actually beneficial in the whole ecosystem. We know very little about the function which various beings serve in the overall economy of life on this planet. (It was somewhat belatedly that physiologists realized that many of the bacteria which inhabit our digestive tracts contribute to our well-being.)

In the light of the distinctions just made, it is evident that many things in the world are imperfect, defective, and therefore to that extent bad. In fact, it can be questioned whether anything existing in this material world is perfect. Not only human beings but animals and plants all seem to suffer from one defect or another. (It would be interesting to have a chemist's reflections on the question whether atoms and molecules or even subatomic particles can suffer from imperfections.) At any rate, imperfection seems to be endemic to the macroscopic world.

Does this mean that the Creator is an imperfect craftsman? Or may it not be that a world of imperfect beings, all striving for perfection, and succeeding more or less in the measure of each one's striving (dependent also on chance encounters), is the kind of world he intended? If every tree, every blade of grass, every horse and cow, every insect, and finally every human being were perfect, would there be any interest in living in such a world? It would certainly be lacking in the drama characteristic of our actual world. At any rate, the only perfect world attainable to us is the Kingdom of God, which will be brought about by the action of God at the term of our striving; and we cannot even imagine what it will be like. The form of evil that consists in deficiency seems to be part and parcel of our world as it was intended by the Creator.

In the second place, it is evident that the evil of *interference* is also endemic to our universe. That is to say, some beings are by nature inimical to others because their good involves the destruction of the others. Plants, for example, are needed as food by many animals; microscopic organisms provide nourishment for macroscopic organisms; certain beasts need prey to live. The soil on which our crops grow results from the decay of things that lived there previously. Even the coal and oil we burn for energy today derive ultimately from the decomposition or prehistoric forests. Thus particular beings contribute to the enrichment of the universe not only by the positive value of their own being but also in perishing so that others may live. The resulting world is greater, richer, and finer than one in which everything held on tenaciously to an endless existence.

Evil therefore in the metaphysical sense of the term belongs to the very nature of the world we live in. It is there by the will of God, who intended a universe in which things begin in an imperfect state and strive toward perfection, in the process of which some are destroyed by others. This kind of evil, considered in its generality, does not seem to pose a problem for the goodness and perfection of the Creator. It is not difficult to admit that, for the welfare of the whole ecological system, plants and animals need to nourish one another.

2. THE PROBLEM OF SIN AND SUFFERING

The "problem of evil," as it is ordinarily spoken of, has to do particularly with human beings. It concerns two specific kinds of evil: sin and suffering. Sin is certainly not in accord with the will of God; by definition it is the contrary. And for persons to suffer, especially when they are innocent, appears as a grave disorder, an evil that is difficult to justify by appeal to the greater good of the whole. These two evils therefore must be considered more carefully.

Moral evil, or sin, most often involves the second type of evil distinguished above, in which one being — here a person — interferes with the good of another. Thus acts of violence and other forms of injustice are likely to be the examples of sin that come first to our minds. But their sinfulness does not reside properly in the harm done to others; if it did, moral evil would be no different from physical evil, and the act of one person plundering another would not be significantly different from that of the lion preying on gazelles. Moral evil belongs primarily to the first type of evil, in which a being fails to fulfill the demands of its nature. Its fundamental wrongness consists in its being contrary to the authentic call of nature. Man sins by failing to live as man.

However, sin is not just deficiency in being — for example, having a retarded mind or disorderly emotions. Sin is always an *act*. But whereas animals or machines act badly as a necessary consequence of a defect in their being (for instance, an animal limps because of a bad leg), a sin is an act that goes *freely* and *willingly* contrary to nature. Gluttony, for example, consists in eating or drinking more than is good for one's health; but it is a sin only when done freely. If someone were force-fed to excess, it would be just as contrary to nature, but it would not be a sin on the part of the one "eating" because it was not done freely by him. (It would presumably be a sin on the part of those who force him because *they* would be acting freely and contrary to the authentic demands of human nature.) We will not take up here the immensely complex question, how to determine what accords with human nature; our present concern is how evil finds its way into a creation that was wholly good. In this perspective, what is important about moral evil, by contrast with the natural evils spoken of above, is that it is done freely and voluntarily. Man is the unique creature in this world who can act contrary to his nature.[12] Other beings are governed by their nature. If their natural endowments are deficient, their functioning will be correspondingly defective; but that is because they can do no better. Man alone is able freely to choose to act against his nature, and thus be the responsible author of evil. Furthermore, unlike the defects that belong to the natural order and as such are willed by God, sin is contrary to the will of God. God made us capable of sinning, but he did not will that we sin; in fact, the supreme evil of sin lies precisely in the fact that the creature is acting contrary to the will of the Creator.

God tolerates sin not because he is a defective craftsman, unable to make anything better, nor because he is a weak governor, unable to quell rebellion, but in order that there might be creatures that freely choose to fulfill his plan and enter into communion with him out of love. For there to be freedom, there must be the possibility of choice. Thus the hideous reality of sin is allowed — not directly willed! — for the sake of the magnificent reality of persons who serve God freely.

• *Suffering due to sin*

It is in the perspective of sin that human suffering must be understood. There would have been no suffering in human life had there been no sin. The suffering of persons does not belong to the original divine plan. It is not therefore positively willed by God but has been brought by man upon himself. The fact that sin is punished by suffering is one of the most persistent themes of the Old Testament. For example, after promising King David a son, God added: "When he does wrong, I will punish him with the rod of men, with floggings inflicted by men" (2 Samuel 7:14). Conversely, Isaiah affirms that obedience to God leads to the welfare of the nation:

> If only you had paid attention to my commands,
>> your peace would have been like a river,
>> your righteousness like the waves of the sea;
> Your descendants would have been like the sand,
>> your children like its numberless grains, . . . (48:18f)

We need not take these texts to mean a special divine intervention each time someone does what is right in order to reward him or to punish him when he does evil. Retribution is part of the natural order itself, which benefits those who harmonize with it, and injures those who resist. To understand this, we must examine separately the three ways by which suffering enters into human life: some, a person brings on himself by sin; some is inflicted on him by others; and some is brought about simply by natural factors, such as disease or accident.

The first way is illustrated by the fact that overindulgence in food or drink harms the body. (Hatred, resentment, and selfishness also degrade the person who harbors them and eventually make him miserable, but this is more difficult to see.) God is clearly not to be blamed for the suffering which we thus bring on ourselves. God wills our complete fulfillment and happiness as human beings. The fact that those who violate his law are thereby losers manifests his wisdom and goodness.

But this does not mean that anyone who suffers much must harbor some great, perhaps secret, guilt. When the disciples asked Jesus, "Rabbi, who sinned, this man or his parents, that he was born blind?" (John 9:2), Jesus replied that neither this man nor his parents were to blame. For besides the sufferings which a sinner brings on himself, there are also those inflicted on us by others, and those for which no one is at fault.

The sufferings that come into our life through the sins of others include first of all those which result from acts of selfishness or malice, in which one person deliberately harms another. Yet there are also the unintended but nevertheless real injuries that occur — for example, when drunken driving results in an accident or negligent parents cause their children to be unhealthy, uneducated, or undisciplined. This kind of suffering also comes from sin; but the one who suffers is not the one who sinned. Why God allows one person to suffer through the fault of another is one of the most difficult problems about divine justice.

• *Human solidarity*
We can gain perhaps a partial understanding by putting it in the perspective of the *solidarity of human nature*. Human beings are not isolated monads; there is an interdepen-

dence among us such that one person can attain his fulfillment only with and through others. We are brought into existence by others; in our immature years we are nourished, educated, and defended by others; even in adulthood we need the cooperation of others and find fulfillment in communion with them. It is the plan of God that we should thus all contribute to one another's welfare.

But it is the consequence of such a plan that when one fails to fulfill his role, those who depend on him are deprived of that which they were meant to receive. The individual sinner is not the only one injured by his sin; society too suffers. This is obvious in offenses such as violence, theft, slander, and, in general, every form of injustice. But even when the disorder is purely interior to the sinner himself, society is impoverished by having a member who fails to be all he ought to be. In other words, God's plan is for us to be a help and support for one another; when we are not, that is our fault, not his. Here, too, suffering is the result of sin.

While this explains how the suffering of the innocent comes about, it does not solve the problem, how such suffering can be reconciled with the justice of the Creator. Before taking that up, however, we must take note of the third class of suffering: that which comes about through purely natural causes or through accidents in which no one seems to be at fault.

In this case also, we must say that suffering is due to sin — not a sin committed by those directly involved in the misfortune but original sin, which affects the entire human race, and is the ultimate root of all the suffering we endure. Original sin will be the topic of Chapter 14. Here we will say only that the creative act of God produced a paradise in which human beings would not have had to suffer, had they been faithful to the divine order. God made the world for the good of its highest species, the human race, which alone is capable of recognizing the Creator, and referring all things back to him as Lord. The world was so designed and ordered by the providence of God that it would serve man's needs, and man could live in it *without suffering*. But when man sins, he discovers that the universe, which was designed to serve him as he walks in God's paths, resists him when he goes astray. It was through sin that death entered into the human world (Romans 5:12), and along with death, there came sickness, injuries, and all other kinds of human suffering.

In conclusion, human suffering is not due to some defect in the divine plan but to the disorder which human sin has introduced into that plan. Whether it be the hangover of a drunk, violence inflicted by a villain, or the starvation resulting from a famine, it was not directly willed by God but brought on man by man himself. Thus it is a negative sign of the wisdom and goodness of God, showing that when we refuse to be directed by him, we bring grief on ourselves.

That still leaves us with the question "Why did God allow it?" If he is all-knowing and all-powerful, could he not have prevented it? In this life, we will perhaps never have a completely satisfying answer to this tormenting problem. We can, however, see certain indications that point toward an answer — little glimmers of light that give assurance that there is a sun.

First, if God has allowed evil to occur, his goodness and wisdom will draw some greater good out of it. In some cases, we can see how this is. The suffering that we bring on ourselves by sin is directly designed to convert us back to his order. The sufferings we undergo through no fault of our own can, if we accept them humbly, serve as penance to atone for our sins and purify us of evil inclinations. Suffering also serves mysteriously to intensify our love. The greatest expression of love possible to us in this life is sacrifice, whereby we renounce some personal advantage for the sake of the one we love. In a world in which all was in perfect order, there would be little or no occasion for sacrifice. Finally, in the case of those whose hardness of heart rejects the forgiving grace of God, it can be recognized that the pains of punishment which they endure manifest the justice of God, just as those who accept his grace manifest his mercy (see the difficult passage of St. Paul, Romans 9:14-29).

With this, we are prepared for the mystery of the Redemption, in which the most awful sin of mankind becomes the occasion of God's supreme act of mercy (see Chapter 19). And it must not be overlooked that not only are the sufferings of Jesus salvific for mankind, but all the sufferings endured by his disciples, when borne in union with his, participate, as the work of his Mystical Body, in the redemptive value of his sufferings. "I rejoice in what was suffered for you," writes St. Paul, "and I fill up in my flesh what is still lacking in regard to Christ's afflictions, for the sake of his body, which is the Church" (Colossians 1:24). This is a dark mystery; but it is one of the surest and most basic principles of the Christian life.

Thus, even though suffering was not a part of the primeval divine plan, now that it is a fact of existence, God has integrated it into his plan so as to make possible an even more beautiful demonstration of his love. None of it therefore is in vain.

9

God and the world

Belief in God is not just an academic theory about the ultimate dimensions of the universe, like the theory that space-time bends back upon itself. God makes a radical difference in the meaning and tone of one's life. The existence of God means that, behind the mighty forces of the universe that dwarf our puny achievements, behind the great swirl of geological, solar, and galactic movements, which carry us along like a twig in a flood, behind the contending activities, interests, and potentialities of human existence, which often leave us disoriented and hesitant, there is an intelligent governor and a definite goal giving meaning and direction to it all.

It means moreover a living, conscious, loving presence that looks upon me and embraces me, imparting value and dignity to my existence. Tiny as I am in comparison with the seas and the mountains or the unimaginable extent of interstellar space, I am watched over more tenderly than a chick in the nest. The face of the sky is not a mask of leaden indifference but the smile of a benign Father. When lost and bewildered, I can remain calm because he has not lost sight of me.

This we now have to see in some detail. First, we will consider several attributes of God which concern his relationship with the world.

1. GOD SUSTAINS AND MOVES THE WORLD

It would be a mistake to suppose that the action of God is to be associated only with extraordinary things. He is not just the God of miracles but the ground of all that is and the source of all movement and energy. Awareness of God in ordinary things is a much more religious attitude, and a profounder expression of faith, than belief in his miracles.

In the first place, the work of creation is not terminated when creatures come into existence. They need to be sustained by the same creative power that made them, just as the light in the air must be sustained by the action of the sun. When a carpenter finishes making a chair, his causality ceases. The chair does not depend on him for its continued existence but only for the form he has imparted to the wood. The wood itself existed before he worked on it, and continues to exist after he has put it down. Yet creatures hold not just their form but their very *existence* from God; were he to let go of them, they would return to the nothingness from which they came.

Creatures depend on God likewise for their *activity*. He is the First Mover, the mainspring of all the activity in the world. The growth of a plant as it thrusts up out of the soil, the animal's pursuit of its prey, and the philosophical reflections of the human mind — to say nothing of the primordial attraction and repulsion of subatomic particles — all depend on the action of God constantly energizing the universe. The sinner cannot even violate God's command or hate God, except in virtue of an impulse received from God himself.

This does not imply that the existence of things is unreal, as in Hindu Vedanta; nor that creatures have no genuine power or action of their own. God's creative act brings real beings into existence and endows them with real powers. The universal, prime causality of God does not detract from the reality and responsibility of created beings; it means simply that their being and activity remain in constant dependence on the being and action of the Creator.

2. GOD KNOWS ALL THINGS

There is nothing of which God is ignorant; nothing in the world is hidden from him. This knowledge is not just vague and general; it is knowledge of things in particular, down to the least detail. When *we* look at a field of grass, we see the whole but only in a global way. We do not perceive each blade distinctly, so as to be aware, for example, which ones are tall and vigorous, which are short and undeveloped. Our minds would be overwhelmed by such a mass of detail. Hence the administrator of a large corporation, in order to give his attention to major policies, must entrust details to his subordinates. But God is not obliged to do that. Enormous as this world seems to *our* minds, it is very small in comparison with the infinity of the divine intelligence. God knows absolutely all that is in this world, including all its implications, all its hidden possibilities, in fact all that there is to be known in any sense whatsoever.

The limits of human intelligence appear also in the fact that, even among the things we know, we can give attention to only a few at any one time. Most of our knowledge has to be put out of sight, in the recesses of our mind, while we focus on the business of the moment. The divine mind does not suffer from such limitations. It is fully conscious always of each individual item; all stands directly under the gaze of its piercing eye.

God knows not only *things* and external, visible actions; he knows also the thoughts and sentiments of our heart: our inclinations, intentions, temptations, reactions, and impulses. No other person, neither our closest confidant, nor our guardian angel, knows us as he does. He sees plainly the depths of our soul that are hidden from our own observation, either by the camouflages with which we fool ourselves or because they are buried too deep for us to reach them. Nothing whatsoever is hidden from God's eyes.

> Yahweh, you have searched me and you know me.
> You know when I sit and when I rise; you perceive my thoughts from afar.
> You discern my going out and my lying down; you are familiar with
> all my ways. (Psalm 139:1-3)

Included among the things that God knows are those which for us still lie in the future. He knows how the world will end and all that each of us is going to do; he knows absolutely everything that is still to happen. (That is why he can on occasion inspire the prophets to predict the future, as a sign that the prophet is from God.)

165

• *Freedom remains intact*

This does not take freedom and contingency away from human events. We are still free in the decisions we make and the acts we perform, even though, before we act, God already knows what we will do. When I see a person do something freely, the fact that I know he is doing it does not detract from the fact that he does it freely. Action is one thing; knowledge another. When I look back over the past, I know things which were done freely. I now have certitude about them; it is no longer possible for them to turn out otherwise. But my certitude about what has been done does not take away from the fact that they were intrinsically free. Similarly, God's knowledge of human acts, whether past, present, or future, does not take away the freedom intrinsic to them.

The reason future acts seem to pose a special problem is that *we* are able to predict the future only by calculating from the operation of present causes. If we have sufficient information about the direction, speed, etc., of their movement, we can predict the trajectory of a missile or the collision of two automobiles. But we can do this only when there are no unknown agents capable of altering the course of things. It is of the very essence of freedom that the effect cannot be calculated from the cause. If God foresaw the future by calculating from present causes, then he too would be unable to predict free actions. However, God does not calculate from the present to the future. Nothing is future to him; all stands present before him. Hence he does not properly *foresee the future*; he simply *sees as present* things which are future to us.

• *God's knowledge causal*

There is, however, a deeper and more difficult aspect to this subject. In ordinary human knowledge, that which we know exists prior to our knowledge and is the cause of it. Thus the tree is there before I see it, and my seeing it depends on its actual existence. Even purely intellectual objects which I see within my mind, such as the truths of mathematics or the laws of logic, have an objective truth that is prior to my knowledge of them. I do not create or invent, I discover them. If I have ideas in my mind that do not reflect an existing reality, I am the victim of illusion or error or am indulging in imagination, not knowledge. God's knowledge, however, is not derived from things but is prior to them and the cause of them. His knowledge of us brings us into existence; it is not our existence that impresses itself on his mind.

There is an analogy for this in the knowledge by which we work. When I make something, whether it be as complicated as a house or as simple as the fold in a piece of paper, my idea precedes the object and is causative of it. That is, I first conceive what I intend to make, and then execute my design. Experience has of course taught us all how imperfectly our creations correspond to the ideas we had of them. Reality resists our plans, and obliges us to modify them, so that we seldom know exactly what we are going to do until after it is done. God's knowledge of creatures is like the artist's idea, in that it comes before the work of art and produces it. But God is an infallible artist who produces exactly what he intends.

This applies not only to created *things* but also to their *actions*. These too are a part of created reality, deriving their being from the Creator. Hence they too must exist in his mind before occurring in reality. Of them too it must be said that the conception God has of them is the cause of their real occurrence. In other words, not only does God know what I do before I do it, his knowledge is the First Cause of my doing it. This is where the problem of created freedom becomes most acute. For centuries, not only in the Christian world but also among the Muslims, theologians have debated the problem of how human freedom can be reconciled with divine foreknowledge.

A proper understanding of this matter would seem to lie beyond the reach of a created intellect. Just as we are incapable of comprehending the nature of God, so we are likewise incapable of understanding how he acts. When we hear that God causes our acts, we naturally tend to imagine this on the model of human causality. Certainly for us it is impossible to *make* someone do something while leaving him free. In our world, compulsion and freedom are mutually exclusive. But God's action is not limited like ours or confined to the modes we employ. His causation, like his nature, simply transcends our concept of it.

It is certain from both revelation and reason, that God is the sovereign First Cause of absolutely all reality beside himself; and that human beings are free and responsible. How these two truths can be fitted together in a single synthesis we will not understand until we understand God himself, in the beatific vision.

3. GOD IS ALL POWERFUL

God's power is infinite; he can do all things. A definition of omnipotence as good as any was given by St. Thérèse of Lisieux: Whatever God wills, he does. Or, since God does not have to *do* anything but simply to will it into existence, we can restate the principle thus: "Whatever God wills, happens."

In a negative sense, this means that nothing is impossible or even difficult to God. All conceivable "works" are finite; in comparison with the infinite power of God, they do not present any difficulty or resistance whatsoever. We have already seen that God did not have to create the present world. He could have made it differently; he could have made any other world he might have wished. Given the existence of the actual world, God's omnipotence means that he remains sovereign master over it. He is not limited or restrained by any of his creatures. He can do with them as he pleases. In particular, he is a God of miracles. He can intervene in the natural order so as to prevent a cause from having its connatural effect; for example, to prevent the flames from consuming the bush that Moses saw on fire. Similarly, he can bring about an effect without employing its natural cause; thus Jesus healed blindness, leprosy, paralysis, etc., by a simple command, instead of through the natural processes of the body.

Sometimes our way of speaking seems to imply God's inability to do something. For example, we say that he cannot be deceived; nor make a mountain so big he cannot move it; nor make a square circle. But it is only the deficiency of our language that structures these statements in such a way that they apparently detract from God's omnipotence. The first statement has nothing to do with power; it is simply denying a defect in God. The second is really affirming his infinite power in a negative way. The third says nothing whatsoever, for a square circle, being a contradiction in terms, is not anything. It is a meaningless conjunction of terms which we are able to put together simply because our language is not always bound by reality.

The omnipotence of the Creator does not mean that creatures have no real power of their own; it means simply that they do not limit him. In giving them their natural powers, he does not give up any of his. He is like a wise and strong governor who gives genuine responsibility to his subordinates while retaining the authority to intervene where he sees fit.

4. GOD IS EVERYWHERE

The omnipresence of God is one of the most important of his attributes for our religious life. It means there is nowhere we can go that God is not present. In the loneliest wilderness, the most inhospitable situations, or the most frightening predicaments, God is there. Even in hell he is present; in fact, it is his inescapable presence to those who have rejected him that may be what creates the essence of hell.

The presence of God is not, however, like that of material beings, which occupy space and are said to be present to the things contiguous to them. One who is everywhere can obviously not be thus "located." Neither is his omnipresence comparable to some kind of ether permeating all things. (As we saw in treating the divine nature, infinity does not mean extending outwardly in all directions.) God's omnipresence is simply a synthetic way of viewing the three truths we have just considered: namely, that God sustains all things in existence, knows them all, and has power over them all. For to see all that is going on in a place is one way of being present there. Likewise to have power over a place, to be able to intervene at any instant and change things according to one's will, is another kind of presence. Finally, the fact that God sustains all things in existence, that each of them is able to continue in being solely by reason of the constant influx of creative power from him, makes him present to them in the profoundest sense.

God is said to be absent from those who are in the state of sin, and present to those in the state of grace. This refers to the kind of presence that two beings have to one another through personal communion. We say that someone can be physically present but absent in spirit; or he can be physically absent but present in spirit. God is "physically" present everywhere; and this is the omnipresence considered above. But for those who are not in communion with him, he is in a very real sense absent; or, better, they are absent to him. This special presence of God that depends on the state of grace will be treated in Chapter 21.

5. GOD AS KING AND LORD: DIVINE PROVIDENCE

Not only is God present to all his creatures; he actively governs them. It cannot be otherwise if their existence and activity depend constantly on an intelligent creator. The scriptural way of indicating this is to call God King and Lord. These are not just titles of splendor and glory; they recognize God as the supreme governor of the universe.

That God is governor means that he has a purpose for the world, and directs his creatures so that this purpose will be achieved. This direction consists in the various natures and natural powers imparted to the diverse beings of the universe, the arrangement in

168

which they are associated with one another, and finally in laws enunciated for the guidance of rational creatures. Belief in God as governor implies that the universe is not a gigantic mixing bowl in which entities are scrambled haphazardly but a true cosmos moving with order and headed in a meaningful direction.

As we have noted before, this does not reduce creatures to puppets manipulated with no initiative or efficacy of their own. Each one has its proper nature, and acts out of the innate thrust of that nature. Apples are produced by apple trees, not hung there by God like decorations on a Christmas tree. Divine government is not imposed on the universe artificially, as chess pieces are deployed in a game; it uses their natural properties and functions, somewhat as a chemist uses the properties of the substances he works with. Thus we can suppose that God wanted the continents to be formed on earth as a habitat for humanity; but he brought this about through the volcanic activity, plate tectonics, etc., that are natural processes of the earth itself.

Moreover, the resultant order is not a simple, evident one that can be perceived by anyone who glances at it. A great part of our world consists of random activity, such as the waves lapping at the beach or plants competing in the jungle. There are natural disasters such as forest fires, hurricanes, and droughts. The purpose served by them in the total divine plan is not ordinarily apparent. But just as the chaotic medley of untamed nature springs from the interaction of a multitude of individuals, each of which behaves in an orderly way, so likewise all of nature is subsumed into a higher order intended by an intelligent creator. Like the rainbow that is perfectly arched and harmoniously tinted even though the millions of droplets that create it fall helter-skelter, so the divine plan achieves its goal beautifully and serenely in and through the randomness of creaturely energies.

Similarly, human history is the real result of the interplay of human activities, for which each person, in his own measure, is really responsible. Yet it is also governed by God not only in the sense that he makes laws for it and judges according to that law but also in the sense that he brings about whatever he wants to happen.

• *Providence*

Providence is one of the chief names given by Christian tradition to the divine government. Its primary intention is to affirm that God provides what is needed for the realization of his plans. It also connotes the wisdom and goodness of these plans. Jesus assured us of God's providence in some of the most touching of his parables, for example:

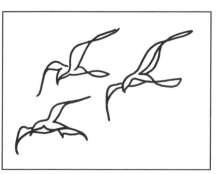

Look at the birds of the air; they do not sow or reap or store away in barns, and yet your heavenly Father feeds them. Are you not much more valuable than they? (Matthew 6:26)

Likewise, in sending the apostles out to preach the Gospel, Jesus told them not to take along any money in their belts, nor an extra tunic, sandals, or a staff (Matthew 10:9; see also Luke 10:4); they were to trust that God would provide for their needs. Afterward he asked them, "When I sent you without purse, bag or sandals, did you lack anything?" They answered, "Nothing" (Luke 22:35).

But providence is not a license to be negligent, as though we could count on God to care for us regardless of what we do. (Sometimes he does even that, but we cannot presume upon it.) It is through natural agencies that God ordinarily works, and our own planning and effort are among the natural factors he uses. If we neglect what depends on us, providence itself will let us fail, to teach us a lesson. But if we do our part, providence means that the Sovereign Lord of the universe is collaborating with us. All things are in his hands, and he will see to it that whatever we need — food or money, education or jobs, friends or assistance — is available. He does this sometimes in ways we could never forecast, and through coincidences we could not plan on. Thus, after Peter had fished all night in vain, Jesus told him where to cast his net, with the result that he made an enormous catch (Luke 5:4-7).

However, providence is not a guarantee that we will never go hungry or fall sick; it may be suffering and failure that are to bring us to the holiness God intends for us. We do not know what God's plan for us in this life entails; but we do know that he has a plan, that it is for our welfare, and that, so long as we do his will, everything necessary for the realization of that beautiful plan will be provided. "In all things God works for the good of those who love him" (Romans 8:28).

Hence a Christian can affirm with complete realism that this world is a garden spot in the universe, carefully nurtured by God to provide a home for mankind. We know, for example, that the temperatures of earth are very moderate compared to the wild extremes found elsewhere in the solar system (over 800 degrees Fahrenheit on the surface of Venus and 370 degrees below zero on Neptune's moon, Triton). The water that makes life possible, the oxygen-rich atmosphere which we need to breathe, the soil that has been prepared by the growth and decay of aeons of plants, insects, worms, moles, etc., the fuel stored in the ground and the food furnished by our vegetation — all of these are rightly seen as providential arrangements by our heavenly Father to make our home comfortable. What else is meant by the statement of Genesis:

> Now Yahweh God had planted a garden in the east, in Eden; and there he put the man he had formed. And Yahweh God made all kinds of trees grow out of the ground — trees that were pleasing to the eye and good for food. (2:8f)

We know the transcendent goal toward which God is directing the universe — the Heavenly Jerusalem, or Kingdom of God, which will be discussed in Chapter 28. We do not know the historical paths by which it will be reached, nor the earthly destiny of any particular individual; but we know that God's plan for each of us is one of grace and goodness, and that he really provides us with whatever is necessary for its attainment.

6. THE JUSTICE OF GOD

Divine government is characterized by justice and mercy, two of the qualities most frequently attributed to God in Scripture. God's justice must not be imagined like that of a human being who pays his debts. The one from whom all things come, and who rules over all things, owes no debts to anyone. "Who has given a gift to him that he should be repaid?" (Romans 1:35).

The only form of human justice which can be attributed to God is that of a ruler who deals fairly with his subjects; but even this analogy is severely limited. Human rulers stand under a law that determines what is just for them. Even a so-called absolute monarch is bound by the natural law and obligated thereby to respect the rights of persons under his rule. He *owes* them legitimate freedom and the fostering of the common good. For him to show favoritism is an injustice. But there is no law over God and no rights of creatures that he is obliged to respect. He does indeed respect the rights and dignity which he himself has conferred on them by his creative act; but this does not come from an obligation binding him — it simply expresses the consistency and faithfulness of his own action. God himself is the ground and source of all we have and all we are, and the basis therefore of the justice whereby we are bound.

To call God just is to affirm that he is not arbitrary in dealing with the world. In the first place, he does not demand what is beyond the capabilities of anyone. Before calling us to know and serve him, he supplies us with a mind capable of reasoning and a will that is free. The providence by which he furnishes us with what we need to carry out our functions belongs therefore to his justice. (Sometimes indeed he summons us to do things beyond our natural powers; but then by grace he makes us supernaturally capable.)

In the second place, divine justice rewards those who do right and punishes those who do wrong. This does not ordinarily imply special interventions, the way a parent punishes a child or the state a criminal. The justice of God is already at work in the fact that right action of itself tends toward good results, and wrongdoing to failure. Thus no divine intervention is required to prosper the work of the good farmer and hamper that of the lazy one. The very work of tilling the soil improves the crops, whereas neglect harms them. In other words, the justice of God resides in the first instance in the very order of the universe, which (as the Taoists saw so well) by its very nature rewards those who conform to it, and punishes those who do not.

• *The problem of injustice*

But it is precisely in this perspective that the classical problem of divine justice emerges. For in fact, success in human affairs is not always proportionate to hard work and right action. Some people are lucky and receive good things they have not earned; others labor industriously and wisely, only to lose the fruits of their labor to drought, pestilence, tornadoes, theft, or other factors beyond their control. Often it is dishonest merchants who make the most money, crooked politicians who win the election, people of loose morals who are the most popular. Sickness, accidents, and death seem to strike the good and the wicked indifferently. Where is there justice in all of this?

Such disorders are not due to flaws either in God's creative plan or in his justice. They result from mankind's failure to conform to the divine order, as we will see in connection with original sin. But the present life, being only a part of the total picture, has not sufficient scope to let us see the fulfillment of justice. In Chapter 28, when discussing eternal life, we will examine the final retribution by which the scales are finally balanced and ultimate justice achieved. Meanwhile, we are summoned to live justly as an expression of faith that the world is indeed governed by a just God.

Faith in divine justice is not primarily a threat of punishment for our sins but an assurance that our struggle to do what is right is not in vain. The fundamental temptation of human life is the impression that goodness is unprofitable and sin brings happiness. Faith in God's justice reassures us that, despite appearances to the contrary, "They are blessed whose ways are blameless, who walk according to the law of Yahweh" (Psalm 119:1).

And while our faith is often tested by momentary injustices, we are not left without signs of God's justice. Those who serve him faithfully receive the blessing of an inner peace and the confidence of a good conscience that enables them to rise even above grave troubles. Those who have gotten wealth, power, or pleasure illegitimately often betray, by their chronic dissatisfaction, that it has not brought them happiness. The deep joy shining from the wrinkled face of Mother Teresa of Calcutta, who gave up every comfort and security in devoting herself to the care of outcasts, makes an instructive contrast with the posed smile of Marilyn Monroe, the sexpot of the sixties, idolized by men and envied by women, who ended her life with an overdose of barbiturates.

7. THE MERCY OF GOD

The second quality of divine government is mercy. God's mercy is his willingness to forgive our sins and deliver us from trouble. Misery is the object of mercy; mercy is a particular manifestation of the divine goodness. It was out of goodness that God first brought his creatures into existence, since he gains nothing from them. When we get into difficulties, rather than coldly allowing us to suffer as we deserve, he comes to our aid; this is the act of his mercy. He showed mercy by taking pity on the people of Israel held captive by the Egyptians (Exodus 3:7ff); he showed mercy when David repented of his sin (2 Samuel 12:13). Jesus, moved to pity at the tears of the widow of Naim (Luke 7:13) and of the sisters of Lazarus (John 11:35), was the incarnation of divine mercy.

The vast ocean of suffering in which so many human lives are plunged does not contradict the mercy of God. As is pointed out elsewhere (Chapters 8 and 14), suffering did not belong to God's original plan for us; mankind brought it on by disobedience. But that being the case, God has integrated suffering into the designs of his goodness. He uses it to teach us our mistakes and turn us back to him. The Passion voluntarily undergone by Jesus becomes the means of Redemption for all humanity, and thereby the supreme sign of divine mercy and love. Likewise the sufferings endured by Jesus' followers are, by his grace, turned into a means of union with him, and of collaboration in his redemptive work

(Colossians 1:24). The only ones who do not profit by suffering are those who reject the mercy of God; and even their suffering serves as a display of divine justice. To Sister Faustina Kowalski, Jesus declared:

Jesus, I Trust In You!

I have opened My Heart as a living fountain of mercy. Let all souls draw life from it. Let them approach this sea of mercy with great trust. Sinners will attain justification, and the just will be confirmed in good. Whoever places his trust in My mercy will be filled with My divine peace at the hour of death.

My daughter, do not tire of proclaiming My mercy. In this way you will refresh this Heart of Mine, which burns with a flame of pity for sinners. Tell My priests that hardened sinners will repent on hearing their words when they speak about My unfathomable mercy, about the compassion I have for them in My Heart.

(*Divine Mercy in My Soul*, Sister Faustina Kowalski, Stockbridge, MA: Marian Press, 1987, nos. 1520, 1521).

Sister Faustina (1905-1938), of the Polish Sisters of Our Lady of Mercy, is the great apostle of divine mercy to the modern world. In 1931, she is reported to have experienced a vision of Jesus with red and white rays of light streaming from his heart. He instructed her to have a painting made of the vision, bearing the inscription "Jesus, I trust in you." He promised immense graces to all who would venerate this image or honor the Feast of Divine Mercy, which he wanted to be established to make sinners aware of the immensity of his mercy toward them.

Mercy is in no way the suppression of justice. Out of mercy, God is ready to forgive the sinner — but only on condition that the latter repent and, so far as he can, repair the injury he has done to the order of the universe. While this too is beyond our understanding, we know that the Passion, which Jesus voluntarily underwent as head of the human race, mysteriously serves to fulfill the demands of divine justice in making reparation for the sins of all those who through faith are identified with him (see Chapter 19). Mercy brings about a better kind of justice.

8. GOD ANSWERS PRAYER

Because God is a person, with knowledge and will, he can hear and answer the prayers we make to him. This is one of the chief ways his mercy is exercised.

The most vivid biblical example of prayer occurred when the Israelites were attacked by the Amalekites during the Exodus. While Joshua led the people in battle, Moses stood on top of a hill and prayed in the ancient Hebrew manner, with his hands aloft. So long as he kept this up, the Israelites were winning, but when he grew tired and let his hands droop, the Amalekites began to prevail. Aaron and Hur then had Moses sit on a rock while they supported his weary arms until victory was achieved (Exodus 17:8-13). It was not of course some magic in Moses' posture that brought this about; it was the power of prayer, expressed by his raised hands.

The power of prayer is not based on any kind of empirical proof but on faith in Christ's assurance:

> Ask and it will be given to you; seek and you will find; knock and the door will be opened to you. For everyone who asks receives, he who seeks finds; and to him who knocks, the door will be opened. (Matthew 7:7f)

• *Unanswered prayers*

Perhaps the most basic reason why many find it hard to believe in the efficacy of prayer is that often prayers don't seem to be answered. In such a case, it may be that we have not prayed very well. If we routinely mouth a formula, this is not prayer at all. If we pray without trust in God, our prayer will not be heard; for trust is the essence of prayer. But even if our prayer is all that it should be, the answer to it may not be evident. God *always* answers sincere prayer but not always in the way we anticipate. He answers according to his own wisdom; and if what we ask for is not in our best interests (or perhaps that of someone else), he will give something else that *is* in the best interests of all concerned. It should not be imagined, however, that the answers to prayer are so hidden that we can never expect to perceive them. Those who pray with humility and faith often receive very literal and obvious answers.

A more subtle reason why some do not believe in the power of prayer is the modern reluctance, which we have noted on other occasions, to believe that God intervenes to alter the course of nature. But that God does this is an article of Christian faith, often attested in Scripture and confirmed by the daily experience of the Church (see Chapter 3).

However, answers to prayer need not involve a miracle. The Lord of nature can arrange that nature itself, by its own workings, provide what we request. For example, when we pray for good weather and it arrives, perhaps against all expectations, this need not be due to a miracle. God knew, at the creation of the world, that we were going to make this prayer, and could have positioned the elements of the universe so that what we were to ask for would come about naturally. And it cannot be objected that, since the good weather was already in process of formation, the prayer made no difference; because God arranged this weather knowing we were going to pray for it. If we had not prayed, he would not have arranged things thus.

Perhaps the most hidden root of unwillingness to believe in prayer is the feeling that I am too insignificant for the Lord of all creation to pay attention to my personal requests. A mitigated form of this objection appears in people who believe in praying for important things but that we should not bother God about minor ones. Such an attitude comes from a very deficient idea of God. As was pointed out above, no detail is too small for God to take note of it. He is a Father who cares personally for each of his children, and provides for *all* their needs, great as well as small.

Prayer does not exercise a kind of power over God. Such a notion would belong to magic rather than to religion, as in the story of Aladdin's lamp where, when the lamp is rightly manipulated, the genie appears. Authentic prayer is a *request* addressed to God.

Neither does an answer to prayer imply a change in the mind of God. It is God who inspires our prayer and, in answering it, completes the work he began. It is not we who change God; it is he who changes us. Moses' prayer brought about victory over the Amalekites not because it prevailed upon God but because God used Moses to bring about what God himself intended.

But prayer does change the course of events. The things God gives in answer to prayer would not have been given if the prayer had been neglected. God does not need our prayer to bring anything about, but he does make many things conditional on prayer. Just as he makes tomatoes come from the tomato plant (although he could produce them without it), so he lets many of his gifts depend on our prayers: If we do not ask, we do not receive.

9. RELIGION

The divine attributes we have been examining up to now pertain to God in relationship to his creation. Speaking a little loosely,[1] we could say that they answer the question "What difference do creatures make in the life of God?" Now we must ask the correlative question "What difference does God make in the life of creatures?" That is to say, once we grant the existence of God, what consequences does this entail for us? They fall into two domains: religion and morality.

In ancient kingdoms, it was the custom for citizens to acknowledge their sovereign by kneeling before him or making some other act of obeisance. Religion is a similar expression of reverence for God as King and Lord of the universe. Modern democratic societies, reacting against the excessive pomp often associated with royalty, are less sensitive to the obligation of showing honor to those in authority. The vicious personal attacks of some of our electoral campaigns leave in the losers a residue of resentment toward the man elected; and as they begin laying the groundwork for the next campaign, they eagerly seize on any opportunity to criticize the incumbent. In spite of all that, there is a deep human recognition that the person who holds public office is on that account deserving of a certain honor. Even more readily, we sense the appropriateness of honoring those who have accomplished great things or have performed acts of outstanding courage or generosity. Nobel prizes, medals of honor, presidential awards, parades, etc., are among the tokens whereby such people are honored. Even in the domestic society of the household, parental authority should be honored, as is expressed in the fourth commandment, "Honor your father and your mother."

Religion is honor shown to God as the supreme monarch and transcendent reality. If kings are worthy of honor, the King of kings is more so; if greatness ought to be honored, how much more that greatness which surpasses all limits! But whereas human beings are uplifted by honor and are hurt by being dishonored, God is not thus affected by us. In honoring him, we put ourselves in the right relationship to him. To refuse to honor God is a kind of self-distorting impudence.

The heart of religion is the attitude of worship, whereby the created spirit, contemplating the Uncreated Spirit, declares, "You are my Lord." In the entire physical universe, man alone is capable of this. All other beings act within the confines of their nature, seeking nourishment, fleeing enemies, etc. Only man looks beyond the immediate concerns of this life, and in fact beyond the horizons of the whole universe, to recognize its author and relate to him.

Not to worship God is to be indifferent to the profoundest truth of one's situation. It is like tending a truck garden at the foot of Mt. Kilimanjaro, and having eyes for nothing but lettuce and tomatoes. To be human, to measure up fully to human stature, we need to discern the great dimensions of our situation, to take a reading on our location in the universe, and to orient ourselves consciously and deliberately in regard to it. This is the sense of religion.

• *Religious symbols*

Practically all religions embody their worship in ritual and symbol. Sacrifice, ceremony, masks, sacred vestments and ornaments, chant, dance, mime, ablutions, incensations, etc., are their common idiom. This may seem at first inconsistent with the fact that God is spiritual and worship an essentially interior attitude. What need is there of these externals? But it is precisely because God is invisible that we need symbols to represent him. Moreover we, as embodied spirits, need to express our inner sentiments in physical gestures. We spontaneously manifest joy and sorrow, love and hatred, and, in general, all of our strong feelings, by smiles, tears, embraces, scowls, etc.; it is natural and appropriate that adoration likewise should have bodily expression. There is also a social dimension to worship, for the social nature of man permeates all that he does. And to be social, religion practically has to be symbolic; how can a group worship together without some ritual to give common expression to what is in people's hearts? (Conversely, the need of visible expression reinforces the social character of worship; for the symbols with which we worship God tend to be addressed to our fellows as well.)

No doubt there is a constant danger that the ritual and social aspects of religion may overgrow and suffocate its meaningfulness, supplanting the personal sense of relationship with God. However, the remedy does not consist in purging the ceremony or scorning the religious society but in a constant concern to renew or recover the authentic religious sense that should inspire them.

The cultural forms of religion are of course quite diverse. Christian worship gets its distinctive character from the fact that the relationship between God and man is mediated through the person of Jesus Christ. Hence Christian worship is not just a symbolic acknowledgment of the omnipresent Creator but involves a recalling of what has been brought about in and by Jesus: doing this in remembrance of him (Luke 22:19; see also Chapter 19).

10. GOD AND THE MORAL ORDER

Belief in God is by no means the only basis of morality. Many people have a keen moral sense without such a belief — the Buddha, for example, and many contemporary secular humanists. As we saw in Chapter 8, moral evil can be defined without any reference to God, as an act discordant with the authentic demands of human nature. Things are not evil because God has forbidden them; rather he forbids them because they are intrinsically bad.

Nevertheless, belief in God has profound repercussions on our moral outlook. It implies that I am not the supreme norm for my own life, nor the center of my world. I owe my existence to the will of another who created me for a purpose which I need to discern and fulfill. I am not autonomous but have over me a Lord by whose decisions I am bound, and to whom I am accountable. Once it is recognized that the universe has a creator and governor, morality no longer means merely life in accordance with one's nature but fulfillment of the will of God. The law by which I am bound is personalized as the Father's will.

It is true that people who do not believe in a creator may nevertheless have a sense of existing for a purpose. But this seems to be a masked and implicit form of belief in a creator, as we noted in Chapter 4; the idea of being directed toward a goal is incomprehensible unless there is someone who directs. In any case, explicit recognition of a creator gives us a conscious and firm awareness that there is a purpose by which our lives will be measured. We are servants of God, sent to fulfill an assigned task.

From this it follows that *to do nothing is evil*; indeed it is one of the most radically evil postures one can adopt. The fact that I am not harming anyone else does not exempt me from the guilt of failing to fulfill the reason for my existence. The servant who, instead of trading with the master's money, hid it in the ground and returned it, received a severe judgment:

> Take the talent from him and give it to the one who has the ten talents. For everyone who has will be given more, and he will have an abundance. Whoever does not have, even what he has will be taken from him. And throw that worthless servant outside, into the darkness, where there will be weeping and gnashing of teeth. (Matthew 25:28-30)

Similarly, belief in a creator makes it evident that I have not the right to act as I please. I do not belong solely or primarily to myself but to the Lord. To injure oneself by drink or drugs, to experiment recklessly with new ways of "getting high," to take needless risks — such things are immoral not only because they are harmful to one's nature but because they violate God's creation, God's property. They cannot be justified on the pretext that "my body belongs to me," for my body belongs first of all to the Lord (see 1 Corinthians 6:13).

Moreover, the deepest dimension of sin is disclosed as disobedience. The sinner is not only doing something unreasonable, improper, and unjust; he is violating the law of his Lord. Only when we recognize a personal God whose plan governs the world, do we see the full hideousness of sin. Other creatures do God's will of necessity, following the natural drives he has implanted in them. We have the exceptional dignity of being able to embrace the will of God consciously and voluntarily. But we can also choose not to do so; and sin consists precisely in following one's own will in contradiction to that of God. Sin is the rebellion of the created, subordinate being against the rule of the Creator and source of all order.

When, moreover, as Christians, we realize that God is not only personal and sovereign but also a Father — that is, a God who, in his graciousness, has invited us into a filial relationship with himself (see Chapter 21) — then sin appears not only as disregard of the supreme wisdom but as ingratitude toward an incredible love.

• *Sin worse than suffering*

In today's world, evil is often identified with suffering. Such things as the pain suffered by innocent children or the terror and anguish endured by victims of war or of economic exploitation appear as the greatest of evils, and idealistic people make it their goal to eliminate them from the world. The avoidance of suffering for oneself and for others then becomes the supreme moral purpose. In this perspective, the question of whether to allow a terminally sick person to die by removing life-support apparatus or whether to permit a defective fetus to be born becomes simply the question about which course of action entails the least suffering. In such an outlook, a life of suffering seems unredeemable, and there is not much motive for heroism. A young man who has grown up viewing suffering as the supreme evil can hardly be expected to make a brave soldier, much less to endure torture rather than betray his country.

People with a refined moral conscience commonly recognize that some evils are so heinous that one ought never to commit them, even to escape suffering. But on purely philosophical grounds, it is hard to furnish a convincing reason for this. In a religious perspective, however, it becomes clear that sin is a far greater evil than suffering. Sin is a violation of the will of God, whereas suffering injures only the creature. Moreover, sin is an act freely chosen, whereas suffering does not necessarily imply a choice. Moral evil therefore has a dimension by which it utterly transcends suffering and all physical evil, and is incomparable with it.

This means concretely that it is never right to commit sin in order to save oneself or anyone else from pain. As every martyr recognizes, to deny Christ would be far worse than to be put to death for him. A businessman should prefer to let his business fail rather than to save it by a dishonest transaction. It would not be right for a woman to commit adultery in order to save her husband's job or even his life; or for a judge to condemn a single innocent man to death in order to avert a war which might entail thousands of deaths. In all these cases, the issue is not which course of action involves more suffering but the law of God which nothing authorizes us to violate.

• *Abortion and contraception*

Similarly, when a girl is pregnant out of wedlock, her counselors sometimes face the question "Which is the greater evil: destruction of an infant in the womb or the shame and anguish undergone by an unwed mother?" Often they opt for the former as "the lesser of two evils." But in perspective of the divine commandment "You shall not kill," this is clearly not the case. The shame, poverty, and other trials to which the mother is liable (as well as the mental suffering endured by an unwanted child) are indeed awful; but the taking of an innocent life is *sin*, and therefore a far greater evil.

This same principle is of capital importance for the question of contraception, so often recommended in order to protect the world or an individual family from overpopulation, to safeguard the health of a mother, or for some other such motive. These are indeed grave reasons; but if it be admitted, as the Catholic Church holds, that contraception is intrinsically immoral (see Chapter 12), then none of these dangers suffices to justify it.

In conclusion, belief in a personal God who stands behind the moral order both as lawgiver and as judge imparts to moral obligation a weight not to be found either in one's instinctive moral sense or in the most refined philosophical arguments. One who has faith in God reveres the Creator's law as absolute and inviolable, and arranges his life as best he can *within the limits of that law*. As for the problems that appear insoluble within those limits, he trusts in the wisdom and goodness of God, who knows what is truly good for us, who concerns himself not only with the order of the universe but also with the welfare of each individual; and who, finally, can draw good even out of evil. The person who attempts to solve a human problem by committing sin is saying in effect, "I have a better solution for this than God, from whom the moral law derives. My wisdom, for the conduct of my life, is superior to that of the creator and author of my life."

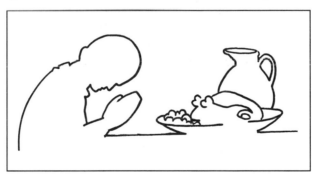

10

The uniqueness and mystery of the human person

Most people recognize a radical difference between man[1] and the other animals of this world. The murder of a human being is generally acknowledged as belonging to an entirely different order from the slaying of a beast (even our vocabulary differentiates them). The human person is regarded as the subject of rights in a sense that animals are not. (Even those who speak of the rights of animals do not ordinarily equate them with human rights.) Animals have no equivalent of what we call human dignity. Some things we recognize as beneath a person's dignity, and one of the worst things you can do to a human being is to deprive him or her of dignity (as is sometimes done in concentration camps to break a person's spirit). We sense that it is right to *use* animals but offensive to *use* a person or to treat persons as things. We feel embarrassment and shame when other persons observe us doing wrong; we have no such compunction in front of a dog or cat. All these points can perhaps be roughly summarized in this: The human person *has value in and for himself*; the plant or animal has not.

• *The modern challenge to human uniqueness*

Consciousness of the rights and dignity of the human person was fostered in Western society by Christianity, and given articulate expression by the Enlightenment. Today, however, it is being undermined by a settled and aggressive conviction of many biologists and anthropologists that between man, "the naked ape," and the other primates, there is no essential or radical difference but only a degree of evolutionary advance. It is commonplace for those who trace the development of prehistoric man through fossils to insist that we can expect to find no firm line of demarcation to mark the emergence of *homo* from the various hominoids and hominids that preceded him. While acknowledging the tentative character of many details, their accounts run along the following lines:[2]

Mammals began to flourish after the disappearance of the dinosaurs about 65 million years ago (MYA). Among the earliest primates were little tree-dwelling, insect-eating animals comparable to the modern tree shrews of Borneo. Life in the trees led them to develop prehensile fingers, stereoscopic vision, and other traits that brought about the formation of monkeys.

Some of these monkeys developed into apes, who came back down to the ground. Between 10 and 3 MYA, a group of apelike creatures in Africa acquired the ability to walk upright. This allowed their forelimbs to achieve far greater dexterity and develop into a hand. Meanwhile, the head became balanced atop the spinal column, while the mouth, freed from many occupations taken over by the hands, gradually retracted and acquired a form more compatible with articulate speech.

The most famous of these *australopithecines* is Lucy, an apelike being about four feet tall who lived some 3.5 MYA in Ethiopia. She is the earliest recognized hominid; but whether she belongs to the line leading to man or has already split off from it is debated.

Nearly 2 MYA there appeared in the Olduvai Gorge of East Africa a being about five feet tall with a brain considerably larger than that of the apes but smaller than that of modern man. His teeth also have some noteworthy resemblances to those of humans (sharper canines and smaller molars than those of apes). He is the earliest being generally recognized as *homo*. He sometimes adopted a fixed habitat and, because he used tools, has been named *homo habilis* ("handy man"). He lasted at least until 1.5 MYA.

The foregoing hominids were all confined to Africa. But *homo erectus*, who appeared about 1.6 MYA, spread from Africa to many widely scattered parts of Europe and Asia. He was slightly larger and still more humanlike than his predecessors. (The name, meaning "upright man," was given because, at the time of his discovery, he was the earliest known hominid that walked on two legs.)

Homo sapiens ("intelligent man") made his appearance about 500,000 years ago. Among the various transitional forms that developed, the most famous were the Neanderthals who existed from about 100,000 or 150,000 years ago until replaced about 35 or 40 thousand years ago by the Cro-Magnons *(homo sapiens sapiens)*, in whom modern man can be recognized.

While differing about the details of this outline, anthropologists generally agree that there has been a gradual development of human traits, rather than a sudden emergence. Thus, for example, the cranial capacity of *Australopithecus* was about 800 cubic centimeters (cc.); that of *homo erectus* lay between 700 and 900 cc.; modern man ranges between 1,000 and 2,000 cc. There has been a similar development of other human traits: bipedalism, hands suitable for grasping tools, arched feet, development of chin, nose, and tongue accompanied by a retraction of the mouth, bicuspid teeth, a U-shaped palate (in contrast with the V-shaped palate of the apes), the arched hard palate, etc., Johanson says:

> If one could assemble a complete series of mother-son skeletons covering a couple of million years of time, and in the process going from something that unmistakably was not human to something that unmistakably was, one would be hard pressed to place a finger on the approximate spot — let alone the exact spot — where the crossover to humanness took place.[3]

• *Human dignity in Scripture*

The Christian vision of the uniqueness of man is founded on the first two chapters of Genesis, which tell how God made man "in his own image and likeness" (Genesis 1:26f), something not said of any other creature. Moreover, the Creator gave man dominion over all the rest of creation:

Fill the earth and subdue it. Rule over the fish of the sea and the birds of the air and over every living creature that moves on the ground. . . . I give every green plant for food. (Genesis 1:28-30)

From this point on, God entered into manifold relationships with his human creatures, speaking to them, giving them commandments, punishing, rewarding, etc. Animals have value in Scripture chiefly in their relationships with man. The supreme indication of human dignity comes with the fact that the Son of God became man. Moreover, he invited all mankind to share in his eternal life with the Father, and poured out his Spirit upon them.

Belief in human uniqueness does not absolutely exclude an evolutionary view of human origins. It could be that the emergence of human beings was prepared by an evolutionary process that brought certain primates to the point at which they were ready to receive a human soul. All that Christian faith would seem to require is recognition of a decisive and essential difference between human beings and that which preceded them. This, in turn, would seem to suppose a special divine intervention, infusing a spiritual soul into each of the bodies thus prepared. We must not, however, minimize the considerable difficulty of conceiving concretely how this might have taken place. To suppose that an adult primate (akin, let us say, to the *australopithecines*) was suddenly "humanized" by the infusion of a spiritual soul would seem grotesque and contrived; more plausibly, the initial human beings would have been endowed with a soul from their conception. However, to imagine a human child as the offspring of beasts would not be very acceptable: A human being needs human nurture for its humane development. But this is not the place to pursue this extremely hypothetical topic.

The fact that paleontology finds no sharp differentiation between man and his predecessors is not an insoluble objection. The "stones and bones" which provide almost our only traces of early man are scarcely adequate to enable us to read what was going on in the human interior; and at the present time, fossil evidence is so skimpy that all theories about the interrelationships of hominid species are very conjectural.

THE SOUL

That which differentiates human beings from the rest of the animal kingdom is commonly referred to as the *soul* or, more precisely, a *spiritual soul*. By this is meant an invisible, immaterial component of the human person, the seat of intellectual activities, which persists even after the death of the body. Because of misleading connotations clinging to the word *soul*, some theologians today prefer to avoid it, and to speak of man as a *person* or a *subject* capable of self-consciousness and self-transcendence. But some term has to be given to the entitative factor which is peculiar to man, and as *soul* is the classical one, it seems better to use it with due caution rather than replace or circumnavigate it.

Belief in the existence of a soul distinct from the body, and even able to be parted from it, is by no means peculiarly Christian; on the contrary, it is widespread in the cultures of the world.

The ancient Egyptians believed in *Ka*, an invisible counterpart of the visible person.

The Malays believe in *semangat*: a little man, as big as a thumb, almost but not quite invisible and impalpable. It is a replica of the visible man, which departs from the body temporarily in sleep or a trance; permanently in death.

Similarly, the Nootka Indians of British Columbia conceived of a *manikin*, located in the crown of the head. When the manikin loses his upright position, the person loses his senses.

In a number of cultures, the soul is thought to be like a bird (Bella Coola Indians of British Columbia; Melanesians; Sumatrans).

The notion of spirits of the departed is so widespread that tabulation would be impossible. It has led both to the fear of ghosts, and to the veneration of the spirits of ancestors, as in China. The Egyptians and many others buried food, jewels, vessels, tools, and other things with the dead in order that their spirits might be provided for in the next world.

Among peoples of Brazil and Guiana, dreams are thought to be adventures of the soul that has departed momentarily from the body in sleep.

It is a common belief that the soul departs from the body through orifices such as the mouth and nostrils. Hence the Marqusans and New Caledonians would hold the nostrils and mouth of a dying person to prevent the soul's escape — or, after death, would plug up these openings to prevent the soul from emerging to hurt others.[4]

A much more refined idea of the soul was developed in Greek philosophy, particularly by Plato and Aristotle. The latter devoted an entire book to a study of the soul *(psyche)*.

• *The soul in theology*

The Old Testament speaks more or less interchangeably of the soul, spirit, and heart. Jesus does not insist particularly on the existence of the soul — a notion familiar to the people of his time, and unchallenged — but rather on the *resurrection of the body*, which was a debated issue (see Chapter 28). Yet he clearly alludes to the soul, as when he counsels us not to fear those who kill the body but cannot kill the soul (Matthew 10:28). St. Paul uses two terms, *soul* and *spirit*, but without giving them any philosophical precision. He likewise contrasts living in the body with departing to be with Christ (Philippians 1:22-24; see also 2 Corinthians 12:3). He speaks of the body as "the earthly tent in which we live," which will be replaced in heaven by "a building from God, an eternal house," which is at the same time "heavenly clothing" with which we will be clothed (2 Corinthians 5:1-4). Such language implies the existence of a spiritual reality that lives on after the body dies.

The development of Christian theology and philosophy stimulated efforts to define the nature of the spiritual soul and its faculties more precisely. The supreme achievement in this regard is to be found in the *Summa Theologiae* (I, qq. 75-90 and II, qq. 8-48), developing the *De anima* of Aristotle. Even though the notion of a soul inhabiting and en-

183

livening the body is by no means peculiarly Christian, the Church has become one of its chief defenders against the materialism of modern Western culture.

One of the greatest obstacles to our recognition of the existence of the soul comes from crude popular notions about it. Few people in modern Western society would go so far as to imagine it like a bird, a manikin, or any of the other forms from primitive cultures cited above. Nevertheless, the popular idea of soul commonly represents it as a distinct, complete entity that is only lodged in the human body. This has never been the view of Catholic theology, which insists that the soul is only a component factor of the human person; that is to say that neither body nor soul is complete without the other. Because of its spiritual nature, the soul continues to exist after the dissolution of the body; but then it is in an unnatural state, and needs the restoration of the body for its own completeness. This is why Christian belief in the resurrection of the body is important (see Chapter 28).

• *Evidence for the soul*

Although belief in a spiritual soul — or at least in an essential distinction between man and beast — is a matter of Christian faith, based on the texts indicated above, it is not purely a matter of faith, unable to be defended by simple reason. The fact that this belief is so widespread among human cultures is already an indication that we are not dealing here with something known through revelation alone. And since denial of the spiritual soul is one of the major obstacles to Christian faith today, it may be well (contrary to the policy generally followed in this book) to examine briefly the natural evidence for the soul (somewhat as we did for the "intimations of divinity" in Chapter 4). A comparison of human activity with that of beasts provides abundant evidence of a radical difference between them, postulating an essentially different principle. We will not try to define precisely what is meant by *spiritual* but will leave that implicit in the differences pointed out.

We must bear in mind, however, that man is indeed an animal and his basic psychic life is that of an animal. Serious research in the field of psychobiology has pointed out many points of animal behavior that strikingly resemble our own: displays of aggressiveness, of domination and submission, courtship rituals, territorial possession, etc. Hence, in the evidence we are about to consider, there are always traits common to man and beast in which we see their kinship; most human activities have analogs in the animal world. What is maintained here is that something in human life transcends that of the beasts, and postulates an essentially different sort of principle. The spirituality of the soul cannot be demonstrated by the kind of proofs usual in empirical science. It is hardly possible to furnish a concrete datum or a measurable fact that, taken simply as a fact, establishes the case. Instead, a kind of value judgment has to be made, about whether the human activity does not transcend the corresponding bestial activity, even though rooted in it; that it is essentially diverse even while remaining basically akin.

Four aspects of human activity are particularly significant as evidence for the soul: intelligence, love, freedom, and conscience. We will examine them briefly not merely as arguments for the existence of the soul but also as clues to what is distinctive of the human person. (Since freedom and conscience introduce the topic of morality, discussion of them will be reserved for the following chapter.)

INTELLIGENCE

It is in the domain of intelligence that the difference between man and beast is most obvious. No one denies that man is far more intelligent than other animals; the difficult question is whether the difference is only a matter of degree or whether it involves an essential distinction. We will consider this question in regard to three realms of activity: artifacts, language, and abstract thought.

• *Artifacts and technology*

Early on, of course, man learned to tame animals, and use their strength and speed for his own purposes. Then he learned to construct machines that move weights far more powerfully than an ox or an elephant; automobiles that move faster than horses or gazelles; planes and rockets that outstrip the birds. Hence man is sometimes characterized as a tool-making animal, in comparison with whom the beasts live essentially by their natural endowments. When you compare a city, built up by human beings and filled with their myriad artifacts, with the natural environment of the other animals, the evidence is overwhelming that a different principle is at work.

It may be objected that this difference is not radical or absolute because animals also use tools to a limited degree. Birds build nests, chipmunks burrow holes, beavers make dams. Monkeys have been observed using sticks to take honey from a beehive or leaves to ladle up water. But is there nothing more than a difference of degree between these rudimentary implements and the complex technology of human civilization? Man acts *by reason*, analyzing, calculating, and inventing; the other animals use only what we might call "natural" tools — things that are already at hand, for simple, direct, obvious functions. Through reason, man is able to have recourse to resources that have no obvious connection with the goal intended: mining a lump of iron ore, for example, in order to make a delicate needle. This use of reason is what makes the essential difference between man and beast. It may be capsulized in the observation that man is the only animal that makes tools which serve only to make other tools (a factory, for example).

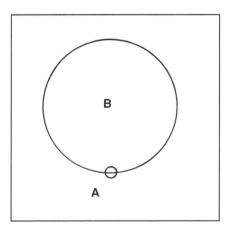

The fact that animal intelligence, at its supreme limits, approximates the most rudimentary works of human intelligence, so that it can be debated whether the rough hand axes found at Olduvai Gorge are the work of a clever *australopithecine* or a primitive *homo*, does not refute the radical difference between the two species. It only illustrates the Thomistic principle that the peak of a lower order touches the bottom of a higher order. To illustrate this graphically, we might say that the fact that the tiny circle *A* (representing animal artifacts) slightly overlaps the larger circle *B* (representing human technology) does not refute the fact that they have been generated by very different formulae.

A second objection comes from such marvels of engineering as the web of a spider, the honeycomb of the bee, etc. These can hardly be called crude; only the most sophisticated human intelligence can match them. How such abilities originated poses a problem for evolutionary theory more difficult than is generally acknowledged. (To ignore it is not to solve it!) But for our present argument, they do not create a serious difficulty, since the insects in question are obviously directed by inherited instinct, not by their own individual intelligence. They carry out a grand design but mechanically and unthinkingly; they are not designers. Human beings use lessons learned from their predecessors, but it was the intelligence of the ancestors that made the discoveries; and the deliberation, freedom, originality, and creativity with which the descendants use and improve them are a sign that they too are acting by intelligence, not mere instinct.

Furthermore, even the most intelligent animals continue to build their hives, burrows, etc., in essentially the same way today as they have done for millennia. But in the case of man, we see an inventiveness and resourcefulness that give man a true history (which animals have not), and a history marked by spectacular progress. This is another sign of the difference between acting by reason and by natural instinct.

However, the human technological inventiveness did not become apparent at once. Primitive man needed immense stretches of time to make the first rudimentary steps upward. Then each advance quickened the pace. It took perhaps a million years to move from the Oldowan to the Acheulean method of making stone tools, and more than another million to develop the more efficient Levalloisian technique. After that it was only a hundred thousand years or so before great varieties of techniques begin to develop in different places.[5] Similarly it took almost two and a half million years to domesticate the horse. Only a few thousand more years were necessary to pass from horse power to steam power; half a century was then enough to harness electricity; and another half a century to unleash the atom. A couple of decades sufficed to move from fission to fusion. Thus the history of man's technology can be represented as a curve that rises upward very slowly at first but faster and faster as time advances. (The corresponding graph for any of the animals would be practically indistinguishable from a horizontal straight line.)

This might seem to indicate that there was no sharp differentiation between primitive man and his predecessors. However, the slow beginnings of human progress can be explained by the fact that human intelligence (doubtless because it is situated in an animal body) needs stimulation and education to attain its full potential. Without them, even in the most advanced societies, children do not become intellectually alert and creative. Conversely, tribes that remained primitive right down to modern times (for example, American Indians, Australian aborigines, and various African peoples) have shown that, once emotional barriers are overcome, they are just as intelligent as those that have long been modernized. Thus, while the graph of human technology might be scarcely distinguishable from that of the other animals for the first million years or so, its later rise shows that it is governed by an essentially different principle. (Similarly, the graphs of two mathematical formulae may be almost indistinguishable for a short stretch but clearly show their differences when they are prolonged.)

Finally, while animals have been known occasionally to make chance discoveries, which are then passed on to others as learned behavior, they do not look for solutions deliberately and systematically, as humans do.

• *Language*

Language makes a more subtle but also more profound differentiation between man and beast. No doubt, many animals communicate through signals. A bee returning to the hive can let others know that it has found a good bunch of flowers, and in what direction they lie and about how far away. There are signs by which many species manifest hostility, submission, etc., to one another. Some animals mark off their domain by urinating around its borders. Here too the question is whether human language is simply a more highly developed exercise of the same activity or whether it entails a radically new factor.

The animal communications all seem to employ *natural* rather than *artificial* signs, and to manifest nothing but primal animal emotions. They involve nothing comparable to the complex grammar constructed by the human mind to express ideas, aspirations, projects, etc. We talk not only about what is but about what used to be, what has not yet happened, even about things that never could be. No animal has ever been found composing a poem, devising a mathematics, inventing a philosophy, or even conversing for the sheer love of communication.

People experimenting with chimpanzees have succeeded in teaching them to use a few artificial signs, in the sense that the animal learns which one to use when it is thirsty, which for a particular type of food, etc. But isn't the immense labor needed to produce such insignificant results the clear sign that this is simply one more instance of conditioned reflexes? And is it not noteworthy that it takes human beings to teach the animals? (Sometimes even a computer or other highly sophisticated equipment is used.)

In the education of infants, there is an initial period in which a child and a chimpanzee are comparable; the latter is even a little quicker to learn some things. But then there occurs a kind of "language explosion" in the child, in which it begins to acquire new words so rapidly and from so many different sources that it is impossible to keep track of them any longer; the child manifests a curiosity, originality, creativeness, and a simple *enjoyment* of talking, in comparison with which the chimpanzee is inert. This indicates that there is more than a difference of degree between them, that a radically new factor comes into play with the child.

• *Abstract knowledge of essences*

Our final point of comparison has to do with *knowledge*. The heart of human knowledge lies in the power to perceive essences. The animal, by its senses, perceives *individual things*, and by instinctual processes (which are little understood by us) evaluates some as good and attractive, others as bad and to be avoided or attacked. But the animal does not concern itself with the question "*What* is it?" That is a human question, one of the profoundest and most perennial of human questions. Man seeks to understand things, and this means, in the first place, knowing *what they are*. He is not content to know individuals and whether to approach or avoid them. He wants to analyze and define, and he is not satisfied until he can do so. And while his efforts are often incomplete and erroneous, the enterprise is fully and rightly done when, by his intellectual consideration, he succeeds in *abstracting* the essence of a nature from the particulars under which it is concretized in individuals. Thus he conceives of man, animal, plant, etc., devoid of individual traits. Similarly, he can conceive of the *ideal* form of things that never occur in an ideal condition (for example, a perfect circle); he can conceive of the infinite, and of *being* as being.

By the same token, the human mind wants to know the *reason* for things, and is capable of discovering it in many cases. Instead of being content to deal with the situation at hand, as the brute does, man experiences an imperious demand to understand *why* things are as they are: what brought them about and what purpose they serve. He asks these questions even when the answers are of no practical use, simply out of a desire to understand (as in the study of the stars).

Further differentiation of the human intellect from mere animal intelligence lies in the power to reflect upon oneself and to be conscious of oneself. This in turns opens the way to a whole world of interiority, on the one hand, and of self-transcendence, spirituality, and religion, on the other, that are completely unknown to the brute. But it would take too long to explore these and similar avenues of the human mind.

LOVE

The functions of making tools, using language, and inquiring into essences and reasons all result from intelligence and indicate that this is a power that radically differentiates the human person from the beast. A second indication, perhaps more readily accessible to intuitive reflection, is the capacity for love. This is a very mysterious factor in human life, difficult to define, impossible to analyze but undeniable in its importance and power. Love motivates people to the most extraordinary acts of devotion; lack of love can be devastating; the quest for love takes extraordinarily diverse and often perplexing forms and guises.

Love is not just the mating instinct, although closely connected with it. Beasts have the mating instinct but don't care who they mate with. Human beings can experience the mating instinct without love (an experience that is subhuman and debasing); they also have love without the mating instinct (as in the love of friendship, of brothers and sisters, the love of compassion for the needy, and the like).

There is of course an instinct that leads "social" animals, such as ants or wolves, to cooperate. Human beings experience this likewise, sometimes without any love (as among political allies). But even when they cooperate lovingly, human beings experience their love as something deeper and farther-ranging than collaboration. Love has a value in itself; it is not just the impulse to collaborate.

In a few of the higher animals, there seems to be a kind of affection that leads parents to care for their young, and can even lead a dog to become attached to its human master. Here perhaps is where animal affection approaches the closest to human love, and gives many of us an affection for animals. But has not human love a depth and a power that immensely surpass such affection? No doubt human attractions have a real kinship with those of animals; but out of the appetites and desires we have in common with brutes, mingled with and colored by them, there emerges in us a love that transcends sensory appetite. It is generally recognized that a person moved *solely* by animal appetites and instincts fails to exercise the very quality that differentiates him from the beasts; he is behaving "inhumanly."

• *"True love"*

Human love, at least at its finest, is characterized by a generosity and unselfishness that are inconceivable in terms of mere animal affection. (We sometimes call it *true love* to distinguish it from lesser affections, which are also called love, because it is the only one that is fully *true* to the potential and dignity of human nature.) Thus it is said that love makes me take another person as another *self*; or that it regards the other not as an object but as a subject. It identifies the other with myself in such a way that I regard the good of the other as *my* good, and the other's loss as my loss. This is just the opposite of appetite,

which is drawn to another insofar as the other is *good for me*. We say that love makes two hearts beat as one; the banality of this expression should not dull us to the precious reality to which it refers. Love can go even to the point of sacrifice, wherein I yield my interests for the good of the one I love. Perhaps the limit case of this is love of enemies — something surely not found in the animal world.

Love establishes a communion between two lovers, whereby they not only share with each other and experience a new and intense presence to each other but find themselves spiritually present *within* each other in a mysterious identity-in-mutuality, which is one of the most exquisite values in human life. The marital embrace is an external sign of a spiritual communion that is far more unifying. Appetite, by contrast, is simply an attraction toward something external to me.

Human love is of course always imperfect, troubled by the circumstances amid which it must be realized, especially selfishness. Still it *is* a reality, even if wounded, fragile, and short-lived. How often it appears to be attained for a brief, blissful moment and then lost! But not always; there are spouses who remain deeply attached to each other amid the infirmities of old age, and thus witness to the beautiful *faithfulness*, which is one of the traits of great love. And love is so firmly recognized as *the* goal — or at least essential to the goal — of human life, that each new generation, undaunted by the tragic failures of its forebears, goes untiringly in quest of it.

• *Materialist philosophers deny such love*

The above qualities are inconceivable in a purely material being as we may suppose a brute animal to be. For this reason, materialist psychologies, such as Freud's, deny their existence. Freud generates all human affections out of a primordial libido, which is essentially and wholly self-seeking. He holds that by imaginative calculation and self-discipline, this libido is sublimated so as to produce socially acceptable and productive conduct. The end result, however, is as selfish as the original drive, even if it is more sophisticated and indirect.

Similarly, popular psychology sometimes asserts that what appears to be generous activity is really selfish in its motivation: "You help the poor just because of the pleasure this affords you." But this completely unproven assertion does not really fit the evidence. It gets some plausibility from the common experience that what passes for generosity is sometimes hypocritical or illusory (as when I think I am acting for the good of my child but am really doing it for my own satisfaction). The ultimate basis of this view seems to be the supposition that, just as complex chemical compounds can be analyzed into their component atoms, so "higher" human activities can be reduced to simple animal desires and aversions. Self-seeking is assumed to be a simple, self-evident motivation, and concern for others a complex derivative from it.

Apart from the questionable philosophy underlying it, such an assumption disregards a large part of human experience. Anyone who has ever given or received unselfish love knows from experience that it is profoundly different from selfishness. This experience is simply being brushed aside by the person who claims that "generosity" is nothing but a more sophisticated form of self-seeking. No doubt there are cases in which one kind of love is mistaken for the other; no doubt we sometimes deceive ourselves about our own motivations; no doubt love is seldom pure but is usually mixed with selfish considerations. All of these factors being taken into consideration, it remains that true, generous love is a reality known to experience, and indeed one of the most noble and precious of human realities as well as one of the most characteristic. A philosophy that reduces all human life to sophisticated forms of self-seeking is simply denying a major part — in fact the finest part — of the life it pretends to explain.

• *Love supposes an immaterial source*

But if genuine love and generosity are a fact of human life, the human being cannot be reduced to matter. There must be some principle in human nature to explain it — something other than the body. That is precisely the meaning of the spiritual soul: an immaterial factor that is the source of those activities which cannot be explained by material forces and attractions.

Besides intelligence and love, two other human traits indicative of the spiritual soul are freedom and conscience. They will be treated in the following chapter as the foundation of moral life. But before turning to them, we must pause a moment to reflect on the significance of the body.

THE HUMAN BODY

In the effort to attain an awareness of the human soul, and to recognize its importance, many people, and even whole cultures, have been led to belittle the body as of minor importance. The idea that the spirit is the true human being, and the body only an inferior wrapping for it, may have originated in ancient Persia (modern-day Iran), from where it spread west into Europe and southeast into India. We have met it in the Hindu belief that only the *atman*, or soul, is the real self, which needs to be delivered from this bodily existence by recovering its identity with *Brahman*. In ancient Greece, Plato regarded the body as a prison in which the soul is confined.

Repeatedly in the course of its history, Christianity has been affected by spiritualist movements which, in one form or another, inculcated an attitude of contempt for the body: for example, the Gnostics (second and third centuries), the Manichees (fourth and fifth centuries), and the Albigensians (twelfth and thirteenth centuries). The Puritanism and Jansenism of the sixteenth and seventeenth centuries betray an influence of the same spirit. On each occasion, the Church has reacted by defending the body as an authentic part of the human person and a good creation of God.

It is striking that the earliest Christological heresy did not question the divinity of Christ but rather denied his humanity. The *Docetists*, feeling that it was beneath the dignity of a divine person to enter into a body of flesh, held that the human body of Jesus was not real but only an appearance. (*Docetism* comes from the Greek *dokein*, "to appear.") It is probably in reaction to this specious spirituality that the First Letter of John declares: "Every spirit that acknowledges that Jesus Christ has come in the flesh is from God, but every spirit that does not acknowledge Jesus is not from God" (4:2).

The soul is superior to the body and ought to govern it; but as the body's strong appetites make this difficult to achieve, some degree of *asceticism* is necessary for a well-ordered human life. Monasticism is famous for its ascetical practices. But disciplining the body is not to be confused with hatred or contempt for it. An authentic Christian attitude is inspired by the teaching of Genesis, that God made the body as well as the soul, and looking on his creation, "God saw that it was good." Unlike the Hindu yogi who strives to free his soul from the constraints imposed by the body, the Christian saint uses his body to do the will of the Father. The Holy Spirit sanctifies the body as well as the soul.

The Incarnation ("enfleshment") of the Son of God is for us the most convincing sign that the human body is good and belongs to the essential structure of the person. Accordingly, the eternal life promised us does not consist simply in the immortality of the soul but involves the *resurrection* of the body.

Likewise all the natural functions of the human body are good. The practice of celibacy, recommended by Jesus (Matthew 19:10-12) and St. Paul (1 Corinthians 7), is not motivated by the idea that sex is evil. On the contrary, conjugal union is highly honored by Jesus as inviolable, and is presented by St. Paul as a sacred replica of the union between Christ and the Church (Ephesians 5:21-33). Consecrated celibacy is rather a witness to (and a support for) this love relationship with Christ which for some people is so intense and personal that the single-hearted love normally directed to a spouse is focused on Jesus alone.

HUMAN BEINGS AS SOCIAL

Before leaving this topic, we should note that to conceive of human beings as composites of body and soul (or "rational animals") is still not adequate. The relations that bind people together in society must also be considered. Sometimes it is said that a human being is nothing but a center of interpersonal relations. While exaggerated, that expression underlines the essentially social character of human nature. A person cannot be evaluated in isolation; his relationships must be taken into consideration.

A human being is brought into existence by others, and for a long time needs to be nurtured by others. In this regard, he is much weaker and more in need of care than the lower animals that are born equipped to fend for themselves. Although the higher mammals are also born dependent, the human infant is by far the most dependent of all — a fact which imprints a social character very deep in the human psyche. Moreover, the care needed by the child is not just physical but also psychological. If deprived of affectionate cuddling, kissing, hugging, etc., the child tends to be retarded and warped in its development. The need to be loved is at the basis of human psychology.

As the child matures, it is deeply formed by parents, family, social situation, and environment. Even the mature human being continues to need others. No one can live all by himself, providing food, shelter, clothing, etc., except under very primitive conditions.

Moreover, to have a balanced psychological life, we ordinarily need contact with others. Very few people can endure complete solitude for any length of time. Solitary confinement is one of the worst punishments meted out to prisoners; it is reserved for the most hardened and intractable offenders. Without other people to discuss things with, we usually cannot think consistently, follow a line of thought to the end, or make balanced judgments. Deprived of the stimulus of others, we tend to become immobile.

The fact that human beings are dependent on the help of others for their own welfare provides a first level of explanation as to why they are social. On the basis of such considerations a whole political philosophy has developed, representing the state as the result of a pact made by free citizens, who give up some of their freedom for the sake of the benefits they derive from the society. But, contrary to the theory of Hobbes and others, human society is not adequately accounted for by this system of mutual self-serving and intelligent bargaining. There is another aspect of society rooted in the recognition that human beings have rights we are bound to respect. They are not just potential collaborators or rivals; they are *persons* with a value that makes them the subject of rights and gives *me* reason to promote *their* welfare. If they were of interest to me only insofar as I had something to gain from them, those who had nothing to offer me would have no claim whatsoever upon me. (There are indeed people who adopt such an attitude; but they are precisely those we condemn as inhumane.) To hurt another person willingly, to steal his property, to torment him, to do violence to him, and above all to kill him, is recognized as evil not just because it may put our own welfare in jeopardy but because it is wrong to treat human beings that way. There is a justice that ought to rule human relations, and though we may differ about details of its application, we recognize the claims of justice upon ourselves and upon all.

This appears above all in our instinctive abhorrence for taking the life of another person. Most people will agree that human beings ought to follow a philosophy of live and let live. There is a kind of sacredness of the human person, which is very difficult to articulate but which expresses itself in this abhorrence. This right to life lies at the foundation of human society but is being challenged today by those who defend abortion. In order to win public acceptance of abortion, they have had to take the stance (at least in this country) that the human fetus is not a person. And having won the "right" to kill the fetus, they are beginning to reason that if you can murder a baby in the womb, you can equally well kill one that has just emerged from the womb. There is a true logic in this; once the principle of the sacredness of the human person has been abandoned in the case of the fetus, there is no radical difference between it and the newborn that would forbid the further step. And if you allow murder of newborn infants, you will have to consider murder or murderous neglect of all the handicapped who are unable to defend themselves in human society. And soon after them go all the aged. And by then, what reason is there to respect the life of anyone who stands in the way of your advancement?

Not only is there an obligation to respect the rights of others; there is also a deeply felt summons to do positive good to them. This too is expressed in so many different ways that one has an embarrassment of examples to choose from. Take, for instance, the popularity of the famous "prayer of St. Francis": "Make me the channel of your peace. Where there is hatred, let me sow your love. . . ." This suggests that most of us recognize it as an authentic human ideal to contribute to the welfare of others; that it is good for one to do good to others. This is the very reverse of the radical selfishness and egotism assumed by Freud and the behaviorists. Instead of seeing others as good insofar at they benefit me, I recognize myself as good insofar as I benefit others.

An even deeper reason why we are social beings is that our perfection and fulfillment consist in friendship and love. Others relate to us not only as needful or as the subject of rights we ought to respect; they are also our friends and lovers. We need them for our own fulfillment not only in the sense that we depend on them but also because the love of others is itself a perfection of the human person. We become good not only by cultivating our talents but also by giving of ourselves. The one who gives away (supposing he gives wisely) becomes the richest of all. In part, this is because nothing is so precious as the love of another person, and this we cannot have except by loving likewise. But not only am I enriched by being loved, I am perfected by loving others.

• *The social economy of sin and grace*

In sum, we are social (1) because we need the help of others, (2) because we owe them respect and support, and (3) because love itself is a perfection. This social character of human nature will help to explain the entire economy of divine grace; for in dealing with his human creatures, God treats them according to their nature. Thus our sin and guilt affect others; they do not harm ourselves alone. Likewise our salvation and eternal life depend on another — Jesus Christ. We receive and live the life of grace in the fellowship of the Church, the communion of saints, in which love is the fundamental law. All this will be investigated in the coming chapters.

11

Morality: freedom, law, and conscience

Besides intelligence and love, another factor that differentiates the human race from other species is the realm of morality, or ethics. It would be hard to imagine anyone discussing the ethical behavior of dogs. When it is said that someone has the morals of an alley cat, this is a way of saying no morals at all. Morality is a peculiarly human reality, one of paramount importance for human life. Here we will seek only to indicate the fundamental meaning of morality as it has come to be understood through centuries of reflection by theologians, particularly of the Thomist tradition. We will offer a simplified, modernized statement of that tradition. It involves the closely interrelated factors of freedom, natural law, and conscience, each of which is complex and delicate. First, however, we must examine the special way in which the notions of good and evil apply to human beings.

In Chapter 8 we looked at good and evil on the metaphysical level, where they have to do with the fulfillment of the nature of a being. We distinguished between the goodness or evil of a being in itself, and its being good or evil in relationship to something else. *Relative goodness* applies to humans without difficulty. The person who benefits you is said to be good to you; one who harms you is bad to you. Sometimes there may be a question about who is really beneficial or harmful (as in the problem of indulgent versus strict parents), but that is merely a question about what really benefits a human being; it does not make a problem about the idea of relative goodness. When we tell a child, "Don't be bad," we usually mean don't do things which hurt or annoy others. When we regard murderers, thieves, and exploiters as bad, it is because they are interfering with the fulfillment of others. The term *benefactor*, on the contrary, means one who does good to others, that is, promotes their well-being.

• *What is a good human being?*

When we turn to *goodness in the simple sense*, however, the matter becomes much more difficult. What does it mean for a human being to be good not in relation to his friends and neighbors but simply in himself or herself? In the case of *particular functions* of the human being, the meaning is clear. For example, to say that a person is a good or bad carpenter is to say that he does or does not fulfill what is called for by the profession of carpentry. The same applies when we say that someone is a good athlete, artist, mother, or president. These are all cases of being good or bad in the measure that one fulfills the demands of a particular function. But to be a good carpenter or president is not the same thing as to be a good human being. There are good human beings who are poor carpenters,

and good carpenters who are bad human beings. What does it mean simply to be good as a human being? This is what is difficult to say.

By analogy with the other cases, we can say a good man or woman must be one who fulfills the demands of human nature, and a bad one, one who fails to do so. In classical thought, the good man is called *virtuous*. The Latin term for virtue (*virtus*) originally meant *manliness*, like the English *virility*. That is to say, a "virtuous" man was really and fully a man. The Greeks, on the other hand, spoke of virtue as "excellence," thereby indicating that the good man was an excellent man, that is to say, one who excelled *as a man*, that is, in fulfilling the demands of human nature.

This means that human nature is a kind of *criterion* by which the quality of the individual person can be measured. Just as the nature of a tree, a horse, or a car is a standard against which the individual of that species is evaluated, so it is with humans. There are of course immense differences between human nature and these other natures. The latter are rated chiefly on the basis of physical qualities; but man, because of his spiritual soul, is considered good or bad primarily on the ground of his spiritual qualities. And as human nature is radically social, a human being cannot be judged simply as an isolated individual. How he relates to others is one of the most important factors in determining his goodness, even in the simple sense. But even these differences illustrate the fact that the goodness of a human being is determined by his nature, just as is that of other beings. In all cases, nature is the standard of measurement of the goodness of the individual.[1]

To state in detail what constitutes a good (or virtuous or excellent) human being would requires a long treatise. Human nature calls for many virtues. People can be good in one respect and bad in another. A person who is good in regard to kindness might be bad in regard to wisdom; someone whom we dislike intensely (that is, whom we regard as bad) may nevertheless be very good at his profession. Thus also arises the paradox that a person can be good at something bad — for example, a good burglar.

The classical treatises speak of the *four "cardinal" virtues* of prudence, justice, fortitude, and temperance; but these need to be supplemented by many more. Furthermore, there are different evaluations of the virtues. The ancient Romans seem to have regarded courage and strength of character as the archetypical virtues. Our own culture would place a higher value on kindness and compassion. We will not undertake a detailed examination of the human virtues here. It is enough to recognize in a general way that a good or virtuous human being is one who fulfills what human nature calls for in his situation. Thus a good person is analogous to a good tree, a good horse, or a good car: In each case, the being is called good in reference to the fulfillment of the demands of its nature.

• *Natural law*

This is the core of the idea of *natural law*: that human nature is like a law determining what is good or bad for human beings.[2] We have already noted the ancient insight for which the Taoists and Stoics are particularly famous, that it is good for man to live in accord with his nature. (They wanted him to live in accord likewise with the whole of nature around him; but that is another dimension which we will not take up here.) Nearly all moral systems are based on a similar outlook, including the Confucian, the Buddhist, and

the Hindu, although their reference to nature is sometimes less explicit. They recog
that there is a type of conduct that becomes a human being, as there is also conduct th.
unbecoming, unfitting. That is to say, that a man ought to live *as* a man, in other words,
accordance with his nature. Thus nature is recognized as a kind of *law*, determining wh.
sort of activity is good and what is bad.

• *The will of God as the moral standard*

The Hebrew and Christian religions hold that God has spoken through the prophets,
revealing his will to mankind. Thus they have introduced a new and higher standard of
morality, namely, the *will of God*. We have already examined some of its implications in
Chapter 9. There is no conflict between nature and the will of God as moral standards.
God is the author of nature, and he makes his will known through nature as well as
through revelation. Likewise his will is not arbitrary. When he enjoins a certain conduct
upon us, it is always one that accords with our nature. St. Paul supports this when he says:
"When Gentiles, who do not have the |Mosaic| law, do by nature things required by the
law, they are a law for themselves, even though they do not have the law, since they show
that the requirements of the law are written on their hearts. . ." (Romans 2:14). The
revealed will of God reinforces and refines the natural law, it does not contradict it.

• *Freedom and responsibility*

Thus far we have stressed the analogy between human goodness and the goodness of
other species. Now, however, we must confront a radical difference which comes from the
fact of *human freedom*. Man, and man alone, chooses freely whether or not to fulfill the
demands of his nature. The donkey, the daisy, and the diamond cannot do otherwise than
act according to their nature (in interaction of course with their surroundings). Man is the

only being in this world that can decide to act contrary to his nature.

As a consequence, man has a *responsibility* for his actions which other beings have not. What a man does freely and consciously is in the fullest sense his action. It does not just flow from his nature; he himself determines to do it. If a dog or horse does something we don't want, we may be annoyed, we may even get rid of the animal, but we don't blame it. (When people scold their pets, it is because they are — consciously or unconsciously — treating them as if they were human.) But when a man does wrong freely and consciously, we blame him — we hold him accountable for his action.

By his freedom, man is, so to speak, the creator of his own life. If he does well, he is *the most beautiful being* in the universe because what he does is so truly *his* doing. If he does evil, he is *the monster of*

the universe. Other beings act badly because of a defect in their makeup for which they are not responsible; man alone is capable of the hideous deformity of doing what is evil while recognizing it as such.

It is to take account of this fact that we speak of the *moral order*. An act is good or bad according to how it harmonizes with human nature; it is *morally* good or bad only if it is freely (and hence consciously) chosen. Thus gluttony and drunkenness are *bad* because they are harmful to human nature; but they are *immoral* only insofar as a person is responsible for them. A child who overeats without realizing that this is harmful, or someone who gets drunk not knowing what he is drinking, is doing something bad for human nature but is not guilty of moral evil because he has not freely chosen what he did; he is not responsible for it.

FREEDOM

Because freedom is so crucial a human characteristic, we need to examine it further. It is a many-faceted reality. We speak of free speech, freedom of conscience, freedom of religion, freedom of the press, free love, and even of free samples, free wheeling, and free lunches. America prides itself on being "the land of the free," and the longing for freedom is one of the deepest, most powerful aspirations of the human spirit.

The root of all these various forms of freedom is *freedom of choice*. This is an inner power of self-determination, of dominion over one's own actions. To see precisely what it means, we must distinguish it carefully from more superficial kinds of freedom that are often confused with it.

In the first place, it is not the same as *freedom from constraint*. The latter means the absence of any compulsion or constriction upon you but has nothing to do with an inner power of the soul. A horse wandering "freely" in the meadow has freedom from constraint but not freedom of choice. A prisoner in irons is under constraint but retains his freedom of choice.

Second, freedom of choice does not necessarily mean that *many different possibilities* are available for a person to choose among: for example, to go to New York by plane, train, or automobile. This is a matter of external circumstances; freedom of choice is an inner power that does not depend on circumstances. Even if there is only one way to go somewhere, a person can still choose to go or not to go. So long as he retains the power to act or not, he has freedom. In the case of the prisoner who is prevented from doing as he pleases, his will at least remains free, and this is the essential faculty in freedom of choice.

Third, freedom of choice does not suppose the *possibility of choosing evil*. One can choose freely among various goods (as will be the case in heaven).

Fourth, freedom of choice does not mean *freedom from obligation*. On the contrary, only a free person can be subject to obligation. Obligation is a kind of moral bond or constraint. It implies a situation in which a certain conduct is right for me, and its opposite wrong, but without my being forced. For example, I *ought* to pay my debts; I *ought* to work for a living; I *ought* to honor my parents, love my children, and be loyal to my country. We are all bound by many obligations; no one but God is absolutely free of them.

197

But freedom of choice makes it possible for us either to fulfill or neglect our obligations. That is why, as we saw above, one who freely fulfills them (for example, a spouse who remains faithful in a marriage) is honored for doing a good thing. One who disregards his obligations (for instance, a neglectful parent or someone who does not pay a debt when he could) is blamed for doing evil.

As a corollary, note that being under the authority of another person is neither a contradiction to freedom of choice nor an offense against human dignity. Here is not the place to attempt a social philosophy that would show the necessity of authority in human society. We will assume as evident that authority is not the same thing as coercion. There are situations in which one person has authority to govern others, whether this be in the state, the family, a business corporation, the army, or a football team. The person who obeys unwillingly because he is afraid of the alternatives does indeed turn authority into a kind of coercion. By the same token, his submission is unworthy of a free man. But the intelligent and genuinely free person recognizes that rightful authority ought to be obeyed, and submits to it willingly and freely. Rebellion against legitimate authority does not come from our aspiration to freedom but from an egotistic pride that resents any kind of superiority on the part of others.

Finally, freedom is not to be confused with *arbitrariness.* To act arbitrarily is to act without reason; for example, to promote or demote people without regard for their just deserts. Freedom of choice is used well when exercised wisely, that is, in accord with reason, and badly when exercised unreasonably. I am free to eat or not, and to follow a balanced diet or not. To follow the laws of dietetics is not to abandon my freedom but to use it intelligently. If someone eats junk food in order to demonstrate his freedom, he is acting foolishly; moreover, he does not succeed in freeing himself from the laws of dietetics, as his state of health will eventually demonstrate. To use a cruder example: A person is free to come down from the thirteenth floor of the library either by taking the elevator or by jumping off the roof. If he is wise, he will ride down; if he jumps to prove his freedom, that would not make him more free; in fact it would promptly bring his freedom to an end.

From this, it should be clear that the fact that being bound to live a good life under pain of eternal damnation is not an infringement on our freedom. It simply implies that, just as a wise use of freedom brings us fulfillment, a misuse of it is damaging.

The significance of freedom of choice lies in the *self-determination* which it makes possible. Existentialists say that we create ourselves by our free decisions; that a human life is not just a realization of the human essence in particular circumstances but a *work* in which this person expresses himself. Provided they do not overlook the fact that one must have a definitely structured nature in order to be capable of free choice, the point is well made. The human being is not just a product of the factors that entered into his composition modified by the circumstances which he encounters. Each person, and in a sense each new decision, is a new beginning. Within the limits available, one chooses the path he will take; it is not predetermined for him. In freedom, he is responsible for what he becomes.

This does not deny that we are subject to powerful influences from the beginning of our life to the end. But freedom means that these influences do not determine us. They affect us, perhaps very considerably; but there remains within us the power to respond to them one way or another, even to react against and overcome them. Because influences are real, you can often forecast statistically what percentage of people are likely to act in such and such a way; but because the individual is free, you cannot say for sure which person will do what.

• *Behaviorist denial*

Behaviorist psychology, widely prevalent in American universities, denies free will. It claims to explain all human activity in terms of basic natural drives and learned reflexes. (Paradoxically, the behaviorists seem to join as much as anyone else in demanding freedom of speech, freedom of the press, freedom from oppression, etc. — all of which would be meaningless without the fundamental freedom of choice.) The profound motivation for their denial of freedom seems to lie in a materialist philosophical outlook. Matter as such is obviously incapable of free choices.[3]

Likewise the success of the atomic theory in explaining the behavior of matter has given the modern mind an unconscious expectation of being able to explain all macroscopic phenomena by the interplay of microscopic particles. But if what we call free acts were reducible to the interplay of non-free elements, by that very fact, they would cease to be genuinely free. Because freedom is incompatible with a materialist philosophy, and irreducible to lesser elements, the materialistic mind tends to deny freedom. But is that not simply to reject facts when they do not fit the theory?

• *Not proven but experienced*

It does not seem possible to demonstrate the fact of freedom; but neither can it be disproved. Those who deny it generally do not even pretend to have disproved it; they usually claim either that they can explain human activity without the "hypothesis" of freedom or that freedom is incomprehensible and hence absurd. But freedom is so big and evident a part of human experience, and so characteristic of human life, that to deny it or explain it away is simply to leave human reality out of consideration.

For freedom can be experienced in the act of choice. It may be an agonizing experience if the choice is momentous (for example, whether to accept a proposal of marriage); it may be an exhilarating experience — for instance, the decision to be loyal to a principle or faithful to a loved one in spite of great trials. The fact that we are proud of our good deeds and ashamed of bad ones implies that we acknowledge our responsibility for them (and therefore our freedom). The anger, resentment, and contempt we feel for others who do wrong (even when their wrongdoing does not affect us) reveals that we hold them accountable for what they have done. The law often voids acts done under duress or coercion; the priest at a wedding asks the couple whether they are entering freely into marriage. Likewise laws, persuasions, honors, and in fact an enormous part of human life bear witness to the general recognition that human beings act freely. Without freedom, no one could be given credit for anything, no one could be blamed. The criminal pervert would be no worse than the average citizen, the saint and the hero no better. There would be no use fighting for anything, and nothing to die for. All the earnestness would be gone from our striving, and all the sense from our living. (And those who say we are not free would, if they fully believed what they say, quit trying to persuade us because they would know we are not free to change our minds.)

The right starting point for a serious discussion of freedom is not some psychological theory or philosophy of nature but the fact that experience presents us with two very different kinds of acts, which we call free and non-free. This is a fact which any realistic science of humanity has to deal with. The right question is, "What characterizes the free act or choice in distinction from one that is not free or is not chosen?" To deny that there is a difference, to claim that the one simply reduces to the other, is to suppress one of the most widely attested and deeply experienced facts of human life. A psychology that suppresses freedom in its analysis of the human situation is like science fiction describing extraterrestrial robots that have little relevance to the human race we know and the life we lead. Freedom is indeed mysterious and difficult to understand. But if we are going to deny whatever we do not understand, we will have to do without electricity, gravity, quarks, quasars, and, above all, mankind itself!

In a *theological perspective*, the significance and purpose of freedom is clear. God could well have made a universe in which everything would do his will out of sheer necessity. But what would be the point of such a useless display of power? If he created beings that are free, it was in order that they might choose him and accept his will by a personal act of their own. He wanted someone who would do his will not out of necessity but by free choice. We could liken him to an army officer who has thousands of soldiers under his command but wants someone to love him.

CONSCIENCE

In addition to intelligence, love, and freedom, a fourth distinguishing mark of human nature, closely bound up with the other three, is conscience. It will hardly be maintained by anyone other than a hardened behaviorist that animals experience anything comparable to the human conscience. Our feeling *bound* to act according to our principles even when this is difficult, the abhorrence we feel for what we perceive as immoral (even though it may at the same time be very attractive because it is pleasant or expedient), the *guilt* or *remorse* we experience for having done wrong, our *satisfaction* at having done the right thing even when it was painful or costly, the *indignation* that rises up in us at the sight of injustice — all exemplify that peculiarly human function known as conscience. The fact that a well-trained dog, when he has done something wrong, sometimes slinks out of sight like a guilt-smitten child, is hardly serious evidence against the distinctiveness of the human conscience.

Two widely opposed interpretations of conscience are in popular currency today. One conceives of it as a "still small voice" implanted in our hearts by God, directing us about right and wrong. The other reduces conscience to a conditioned reflex.

The "still small voice" concept is current chiefly in popular Protestantism. Having rejected both natural law and the teaching authority of the Church, Protestantism attributed immense authority to conscience as the personal moral guide. There is indeed much truth to the view that God speaks to our hearts through conscience; however, the fact that different people get different readings in their conscience over controversial topics such as abortion, homosexuality, or nuclear armament makes it hard to identify conscience simply with the voice of God.

Behaviorist psychology, on the other hand, maintains that, just as a dog can be housebroken or trained to beg, so humans can be led to act in a desired way by rewards and punishments. In this view, conscience is nothing more than an attitude that has been made habitual through such conditioning. There is no denying that our attitudes are strongly influenced in this way. However, this theory fails to account for the fact that conscience often leads us to act in ways that bring us pain or deny us pleasure; or that children frequently perceive the wrongness of the behavior of their parents. No doubt a child needs instruction and discipline to help form it for a virtuous life; but its awareness of right and wrong is like an innate sense waiting to be informed, rather than a habit artificially imposed.

• *Reason appraising the moral character of an act*

Catholic moral theology, particularly that of St. Thomas Aquinas, regards conscience neither as an infallible inner voice implanted by God nor as an artificially induced attitude but as a natural function of human reason appraising the moral character of an act. The reason why the judgment of conscience seems to have a different character from other acts of reason is, on the one hand, that moral judgments are the gravest, most important judgments a person has to make. They determine the fundamental orientation of his life as good or bad. On the other hand, an inclination toward the good and away from evil is rooted in our very nature. Hence, when we recognize something as good, we experience an attraction toward it; when we recognize evil, we experience a revulsion. Thus the judgments of conscience have not the detached, objective character of other rational judgments; they are bound up with the basic dynamism of our being.

The most profound and powerful aspiration of our nature is toward its own fulfillment; in other words, toward its true good. The so-called "voice of conscience" is simply the recognition that a given act is in accord or discord with this deepest law of our being.

When we act against conscience, we are twisting a knife in our own heart, and remorse is the heart's cry of protest.

Why are human beings attracted toward something contrary to their own true good? It is because there are many different levels and diverse inclinations in human nature. Each of our faculties craves its own fulfillment, which is needed for the good of the whole. But our appetites are not capable of adjusting or measuring themselves in the way demanded by the welfare of the whole person. It is the function of reason, hence of conscience, to look to the good of the whole, the true good of the person. But like a government capitulating to pressure groups, reason sometimes follows the attraction of a particular appetite to the detriment of our overall welfare.

What we have said about nature aspiring to its own fulfillment must not be understood in an egotistic sense, as though it made each individual look solely to his or her own interests. As we saw in the preceding chapter, the human self finds its fulfillment chiefly in the love of others (and ultimately of God). Love is a kind of surrender and loss of self to another; hence the paradox, which holds even on a natural and human plane, "he that loves his life in this world (that is, selfishly) will lose it; but he that loses his life (that is, for the sake of love) will find it." That is, he that loves only himself ruins himself; he that loses himself in the love of another finds his own fulfillment therein.

To live in accord with one's conscience therefore means simply to do good and avoid evil insofar as we recognize them. This is rightly considered the description of a good human life. Few finer compliments can be paid to a person than to say that he is conscientious in all that he does. To say that a person should never go against his conscience is a tautology.

• *Erroneous conscience*

However, it would be an oversimplification to say that one who follows his conscience always does right. Like any other judgments of reason, those of conscience can be erroneous. Conscience can be falsified by a wrong education; it can be deadened by having its voice suppressed or disregarded. We must work to form a right conscience just as we have to make efforts at any other part of our education.

Judgments of conscience are not merely calculations of reason, they are also a function of what we love and desire. Love of what is truly good is the most important factor in the formation of a right conscience, as wrongly directed love is the chief (but not the only factor) that can distort it.

Conscience can err not only because it has been twisted or deadened but also due to purely innocent mistakes. As a result, a person can do something objectively wrong without guilt. For example, although abortion, as the taking of an innocent human life, is unequivocally evil, it is conceivable that a young woman, terrified at the consequences of an illegitimate pregnancy, and trusting the judgment of the United States Supreme Court Justices (in 1973), might in good conscience consider herself justified in destroying her baby. What she does is wrong, but she may be without guilt to the extent that the error is not due to her own fault. Here again, as in another context cited earlier, it is necessary to distinguish between the rightness or wrongness of the act considered in itself (that is, measured by the demands of human nature), and the guilt of the person who does it.

Conscience does not mean merely one's *personal opinion*, based on one's own experience and reflection. We are often in a situation in which we ought to be guided by the judgment of others more knowledgeable than ourselves or with authority over us. For example, suppose that an American politician, concerned about the energy shortage, came to the conclusion that, since America is rich in coal, the welfare of our country required that we burn coal in all our industries. But if it is the consensus of ecological experts that the long-term damage to the atmosphere from coal fumes would be far more serious than the energy shortage, the politician, even if unable to see this for himself, probably ought to follow their judgment rather than his own. That is to say, his judgment of conscience ought to take into consideration the advice of others, and not just his own personal opinions. Likewise a child normally ought to follow the judgment of its parents when theirs differs from the child's. One who recognizes that the Church has authority from Christ to define the moral law (as will be explained in Chapter 27), is bound by one's own conscience to submit to the Church's judgment, even when one's personal opinion differs (for example, on the subject of abortion or contraception). In all these cases, the person who submits is not acting against his conscience but rather is forming his conscience by respecting the expertise or authority of others.

12

Man and woman under God

A survey of Catholic moral doctrine would be too long for inclusion in this book. In order to give one concrete example, however, we will treat sexual morality. This topic has been chosen for several reasons. First, relationship with one's spouse is probably the most momentous relationship in the life of most people. Second, this is the area in which people commonly have the most frequent and severe battles of their moral life. Finally, it is on this topic that Catholic teaching is most fiercely attacked today.

Sexual morality is based not only on the natural relationship between man and woman but also on the fact that Christ has made marriage a sacrament. There would therefore be some advantages to postponing this chapter until after that on the sacraments. It is placed here, however, to exemplify what was said about moral principles in the preceding chapter. And in fact, the most controversial issues in this matter depend simply on the nature of human sexuality and marriage, independently of their sacramental character. Where sacramental principles are appealed to, this will be done with the proviso that they are to be explained in Chapter 26.

• *Catholicism restrictive?*

In a culture that constantly teases appetites with images of sex flaunted by television, movies, novels, songs, dances, styles of dress, etc., Catholic marriage doctrine appears prohibitive and restrictive. Furthermore, social pressure today is gearing moral standards and even public laws to the supposition that it is normal for people to have sex freely, so that we had better adjust to it by readily available contraceptives, unrestricted abortions (even for minors, without parental consent or information), easy marriages, no-fault divorces, etc. In such a climate, the doctrine that sex outside of marriage is immoral, and that even inside marriage it needs to be governed by the demands of its inner meaning and purpose, appears harsh and unreal. Young people in particular are tempted to see the Church as depriving them of the full joy of life.

On the other hand, many are beginning to sense that sexuality has become disoriented in our society and needs to recover meaning and direction. People expect happiness and fulfillment in marriage; but it is a cliché of modern literature that newlyweds quickly grow disenchanted. Over and over we hear of the tragedies of broken marriages with all the pain, anguish, bewilderment, and resentment experienced by the spouses as well as the hurt, deprivation, and emotional torment of children raised by a single parent or batted back and forth between a jealous, quarreling couple. In light of the flippancy, exploitation, perversion, and simple failure of sex in our society, some may be ready to recognize that the Church's defense of the holiness of marriage makes sense after all.

Catholicism does not promise unalloyed happiness to anyone in this world wrenched by original sin; but it does affirm that some of the most precious joys of human existence are to be found in the loving communion of spouses and in faithful parenthood. Moreover, these need not be short-lived; they can go on till the end of life, becoming daily more enriched. This requires, however, that the marriage be lived in accordance with its true nature and with the designs of the Creator. These we must now examine.

1. HUMAN SEXUALITY

Sexuality is common to most forms of life, both plant and animal. Asexual reproduction is found only in the lower, more primitive forms. Biologists used to explain the prevalence of sexual reproduction on the grounds that new genetic combinations produced through sexual union enrich the possibilities of life and thus promote evolution. In recent years, this explanation has been challenged, leaving the predominance of sexual reproduction a mysterious fact of the biological world.

Over and above its biological function, sexuality involves some of the highest and profoundest human sentiments and aspirations. No undertaking calls forth the deepest recesses of a personality more than the faithful living out of the responsibilities, difficulties, and joys of wedlock. Nevertheless, sex *is* truly a biological function, and to ignore this would be to detach it from its moorings and let it drift and bob on the waves of sentiment, where it would be impossible either to regulate it intelligently or even to understand it.

• *An expression of love*

Human sexuality has several characteristic features that set it apart.

1. The most important is that it serves not only for reproduction but also for the expression of love between the spouses. This more than anything else determines its distinc-

tively human character. As was noted in Chapter 10, other animals have no equivalent of love. Any affection that occurs among them seems to be nothing but a bonding to keep mates together for collaboration while the young are maturing. (It may of course endure even after the young have grown, as is said of swans; but that seems to be a kind of residue of the mating bond.) In most animals, there is no permanent bond between the mates; they copulate and separate. But among human beings love is a value in itself; it may even be said to be the supreme (natural) value of human life. And sexual union is a powerful support and expression of love, giving rise to a distinct kind of love, in fact the archetypal form of human love.

Among beasts there is often no difference between rape and normal sexual union; the male simply forces himself on the female. An authentically human sexual union involves the woman's loving acceptance. Even when the female also shares the mating instinct, animal mating is simply the result of an instinctual drive, and occurs between whichever couple happen to come together in propitious circumstances. This is hardly to be equated with human love, in which the couple, as they come to know each other, agree freely and consciously to a relationship. (There are of course humans who act at times more like animals; but that is precisely to act in a way unworthy of a human being.)

One of the most fundamental philosophical questions about sexual morality is why love and procreation are thus linked for human beings. Why does the supreme expression of love occur in the act by which new persons are begotten? One could imagine a world in which loving was one matter and having children another. Contraception and *in vitro* fertilization are beginning to offer the possibility of just such a world. We will not attempt a philosophical discussion of this difficult topic here. It is enough to note the fact that the two functions of love and procreation are in fact profoundly linked. Therein lies much of the pathos of human love and some of its most painful tensions but also some of its deepest joys.

• *Sacrament of matrimony*

2. Besides its two natural functions as a method of procreation and an expression of human love, sexuality has, as was noted above, been sanctified by Christ and transformed into a sacrament. Spouses are called not only to love each other and raise children but also to be the image of redemptive love. The union between husband and wife is a sacred sign of the bond between Christ and the Church (Ephesians 5:21-33). As God's love incarnated itself in Christ in order to impress itself on our dull human understanding, so Christ's love for the Church is incarnated symbolically in spousal love. The latter is a visible sign to all the world of how intensely and faithfully Jesus loves his people. It is the sacred and solemn vocation of Christian spouses to be not only devoted heads of their own household but also witnesses to society of the consuming and enduring *agape* of Jesus. Even more mysteriously, marriage is an earthly symbol of the eternal loving union between the persons of the Blessed Trinity.

The sacrament of matrimony has therefore a supernatural value and significance over and above those of natural marriage, profound as these are. Moreover, as a sacrament, it is an *efficacious* sign: It confers on the spouses grace to fulfill their high calling of imaging forth Christ's love. It makes the bond between them a permanent title to the grace needed for the difficult burden of remaining faithful, patient, and loving in their married life. In the friction and tensions that inevitably arise when two separate lives are melded into one, in the constant concern and self-sacrifice demanded by the care of small children, and in the awesome responsibility of making decisions that determine the future not only for oneself but for one's family, the grace of the sacrament is a constant, powerful resource for human weakness. Finally, it consecrates the deep joys of spousal and parental love by putting them in continuity with the Infinite Love from which they arise and back to which they flow.

3. Instead of being limited to a brief mating season as for most other animals, the human sexual drive is active all year round and, in a sense, all day long. As a consequence, human beings have to regulate their sexual activity. Other animals are sufficiently

guided by mating instincts; man is uniquely capable of excess and perversion — not only capable but very prone to them if he does not find a rule for right and healthy living. But regulation requires standards and principles; what is the standard by which to regulate sexuality?

Objective standards can be found in two sources, nature and Revelation. We must look to *nature* and ask, "What is the essential meaning or purpose of sex? How does it fit in with human nature as a whole?" And from *Revelation* we must ask, "What has been made of sex and marriage in the divine plan?" Neither of these questions is easy to answer, especially the former.

2. THE CRITERIA FOR SEXUAL MORALITY

Four basic principles determine the main lines of sexual morals as understood in Catholic tradition. The first two pertain to the whole realm of morality but are particularly challenged in the field of sexuality.

1. Sexuality is only one of many particular goods that need to be integrated together in a good and healthy life. It is not an absolute good or the supreme good. As a part of nature, it shares in the essential goodness of all of creation. God explained the creation of Eve by declaring, "It is not good for man to be alone; let us make him a helper fit for him" (Genesis 2:18). And when God said, "Let us make man in our own image and likeness. . . ," the sacred writer added immediately, "Male and female he made them" (Genesis 1:27). Because of the aberrations to which it is prone, sex often appears dirty and shameful. The Manichees held that sex, like everything involving the flesh, is intrinsically evil or at best only to be tolerated as a weakness. Less blatant forms of this disdain are likely to reappear in any age, including our own. The Church, however, has consistently repudiated such attitudes, holding that the union of man and woman has a right place in human life, and that in its right place it is good. In honoring the excellence of consecrated virginity, the Church has always insisted that this does not imply any evil in marriage but simply that the consecrated state facilitates a single-hearted devotedness to the Lord (1 Corinthians 7:32-38).

Sex is not, however, an absolute good: It is neither the goal of life nor its supreme value. It needs to be integrated with love, companionship, responsibility, achievement, justice, and all the other values that make a human life complete. The idea that sex, by itself, is the key to happiness is refuted by the numerous marriages that end in divorce (about one out of two in the United States now). In fact, inordinate sexuality is self-defeating. Whenever false expectations are unfulfilled, the resulting disappointment spoils even the limited good that is really present. Couples with nothing but sex to bind them together commonly end up hating each other. The human person is destined for something more than bodily pleasure and passionate love. He needs these too; yet if he situates his supreme goal in them, they do not fulfill but only frustrate him. The young Howard Hughes, with his innumerable Hollywood starlets, openly flouted the moral standards of society; but in his old age he hated women, and about the only pleasures remaining in his paranoid life were drugs and ice cream!

2. For sexuality to fulfill its purpose and yield the profound joy that it promises, it must be lived and used according to its nature, which means, ultimately, according to the

plan of the Creator. This of course is common to all human morality. Nevertheless, the most fundamental battle about sexuality today is over whether it is a meaningful element of human nature that needs to be governed by purpose and design, and therefore used in a spirit of responsibility, or just a form of fun, at which a person has the right to play as he pleases. The latter is essentially the position of those who hold, for example, "My body is my own, and I can do with it as I see fit." Such an attitude has led to the disorientation, trivialization, and human disasters mentioned above.

The Catholic understanding of sexuality implies that human beings are not autonomous in the use they make of it (or anything else). As parts of a universe created and governed by God, they are called to fit into the plan of the Creator by fulfilling the role assigned to them. They have of course a great deal of freedom to choose their particular path; the Kingdom of God is not run like a totalitarian state. Nevertheless, the right use of human faculties requires that they be exercised in accord with the divine design.

Since it is largely through nature itself that this design is manifested, we can put all of this briefly by saying that nature itself has the force of law. For a Christian, nature is the expression of the Father's will. This does not deny the human right to cultivate nature by art and technology (God himself has told us, "Fill the earth and subdue it" [Genesis 1:28]); but it means that to live in accordance with the authentic demands of human nature is not only self-fulfillment but the accomplishment of the will of God. The next two principles are more concrete applications of this to the area of sexuality.

• *Marriage*

3. For human beings sexual union is licit only in *marriage*. This means a permanent, monogamous, and exclusive bond between a man and a woman. Permanent: the bond lasting until death of one or both spouses. Monogamous: involving only one wife and one husband. Exclusive: prohibiting conjugal relations with anyone other than the spouse.

The rationale for marriage comes principally from the needs of the offspring. It is not sufficient for humans to be engendered, like turtles or tadpoles; as noted in Chapter 10, they need to be fed, clothed, protected, and educated. They have to be taught innumerable things, from the basics of personal hygiene to the subtle demands of interpersonal relationships. Their conscience has to be formed. They must learn how to earn a living, and how to develop their intellectual and social potential. Finally, they need a loving environment in order to learn to love others. All this calls for devoted care — care that none but the parents are likely to provide. It requires the combined strength and tenderness of a father and mother. In order that all this might be assured, the procreation of children needs to take place in the framework of a stable, personal union, which is what we call marriage.

Even apart from the needs of the children, spousal love itself strongly recommends such a union. The completeness and intimacy of the gift of self signified by the marital union calls for a bond that will remain unbroken. Casual sex is an intrinsic contradiction; the deep hurts, frustration, and disgust for which it is notorious are simply signs of this. Marital love is different from friendship, which can be more or less superficial, more or less transitory. There is no doubt a place for casual friendships in human life; but the human heart has need also for another kind of bond, stable and all-embracing: for a love given in such a way that it may never legitimately be retracted. Thus marital love has by its very nature the character of a complete and hence inviolable union. In this imperfect world of ours, spouses do of course fail in their fidelity, and a realistic social order has to have ways of dealing with these failures. But it also needs to acknowledge them as failures, not options.

Finally, the faithfulness of Christ's love for his spouse, the Church, obviously cannot be represented sacramentally in any but an unbreakable union.

Many sociologists speak casually of the breakup of the "traditional" family as nothing more than a cultural phenomenon to be contemplated with detached curiosity. The Church, however, holds that the family is not just a transitory cultural form but a natural and sacred necessity. Disintegration of the family is the degradation of human life.

4. The marital union is intrinsically ordered to procreation. We noted above the three goals, or ends, of human sexuality: procreation, the fostering of spousal love, and the representation of Christ's love for the Church. That the third of these presupposes the second is obvious: for if sexual union did not express love, it could hardly serve to represent Christ's love. But the connection between procreation and spousal love is the most fiercely contested principle in Catholic marriage teaching today.

Traditionally it has been an accepted principle of Catholic moral theology that procreation is the primary end of sexuality and marriage, whereas the fostering of mutual love is secondary. Because many objected to this "hierarchy of ends," Vatican II did not take a stand on this point. It did, however, in *Gaudium et Spes* (or Pastoral Constitution on the Church in the World) reiterate the basic principle that marriage is intrinsically ordered to procreation:

> By its very nature, the institution of marriage and married love is ordered to the procreation and education of the offspring and it is in them that it finds its crowning glory (no. 48).
>
> Marriage and married love are by nature ordered to the procreation and education of children. Indeed children are the supreme gift of marriage. . . . Without intending to underestimate the other ends of marriage, it must be said that true married love and the whole structure of family life which results from it is directed to disposing the spouses to cooperate valiantly with the love of the Creator and Savior who through them will increase and enrich his family from day to day (no. 50).[1]

This does not mean that a childless marriage is valueless. The Council declares expressly that "marriage is not instituted solely for the procreation of children," and that it retains its value "as a communion and all-embracing way of life"[2] even when children are lacking (no. 50). The point of the passages cited is that offspring may not be regarded as an accidental by-product or a merely possible option for married couples. By its very nature, and in the intention of nature's Creator, the conjugal union tends to be fruitful in children. They are its inherent goal, which man has not the right to frustrate artificially, as we shall see in the next section.

• *Unitive and procreative meanings inseparable*

Since the Council, the popes have repeatedly reaffirmed that the two goals of marriage may not be sundered. Thus Pope Paul VI, in the encyclical *Humanae Vitae* (1968), spoke of:

> . . .the inseparable connection, willed by God and unable to be broken by man on his own initiative, between the two meanings of the conjugal act: the unitive meaning and the procreative meaning (no. 12).

In making this solemn decision, the Holy Father did not attempt to explain the complex and subtle rationale behind it, which is in fact formulated differently by different theologians. We suggest the following line of explanation:

While the marital act is indeed an expression of love between the spouses, it cannot be made intelligible on this basis alone. If there were only the affection of two persons to be considered, it would make little sense for it to receive expression in such an act. There are many other gestures naturally expressive of human affection: hugging, kissing, holding hands, etc. But the complex system of organs, hormones, secretions, nervous and psychosomatic reactions involved in sexual union are obviously governed by the purpose of bringing about the fertilization of the ovum, and in a situation where its nourishment, maturation, and protection will be provided for. If the eye is obviously intended for seeing, and the digestive system for the assimilation of food, with even greater reason it must be admitted that the reproductive system is intended for reproduction. (The fact that biologists use the term *reproductive system* with complete unanimity is an implicit acknowledgment of the character they spontaneously recognize in it.) The only ones who can logically deny the procreative purpose of the marital act are those who reject absolutely all purpose and intentionality in nature. But that, as we saw in Chapter 4, involves the ultimate absurdity and anti-logic of holding that all the design in nature is the product of chance, and is not significantly different from pure chaos. Unless one is prepared to go that far, one must admit that the marital act is designed, in its basic structure, to lead to reproduction. That it serves to express love is something over and above its intrinsically procreative nature, and does not replace but presupposes the latter.

In confirmation of this argument, it should be recalled that in the life of plants and animals generally, procreation is obviously the purpose of sexuality. No other rationale for the coupling of male and female has ever been proposed by any biologist. However, to hold that sex is procreative in all the other animals and plants but not in the human race would be sheerly arbitrary and an abandonment of all rational and scientific thinking.

Hence, even though personal love is what normally leads a man and woman to embrace each other, by entering into a sexual relationship they participate in a movement and process far greater than their two selves and their plans. Sexuality is nature's way, and ultimately God's way, of carrying the human race forward, and it entails laws and exigencies of which the participants are not the authors, and to which they are bound to conform.

3. PRACTICAL IMPLICATIONS

From the principles just outlined, it becomes understandable that certain forms of sexual activity are immoral because they are irreconcilable with the essential finalities of sex and marriage. We cannot enter into all the arguments raised about some of them, particularly contraception; our intention here is merely to indicate a perspective in which their immorality becomes intelligible.

1. There are those acts which exercise sexuality while excluding its procreative function. Some do so by violating the integrity of the act of intercourse; thus: masturbation, homosexuality,[3] sodomy, oral sex, bestiality, necrophilia. All these acts involve a part of the sexual act but in alien circumstances that prevent it from being completed. This is a fundamental disorder. Sexuality is not just a way to have fun; it is a very serious function of human nature. Sexual pleasure is designed to encourage the conjugal union; to arouse it in ways that circumvent that union is to go against nature.

Artificial contraception in its crudest form — interruption of the act before its completion — belongs in the same category as the acts listed above. The more sophisticated methods of contraception leave the act intact but still prevent it from attaining its natural finality. Whether these means are medical (for example, progestin pills and the male contraceptives now under development), chemical (for instance, vaginal jellies and douches), or physical (for example, condoms and pessaries) makes no difference; their wrong consists in interfering with a natural act so as to prevent the attainment of its natural goal.

In the encyclical *Humanae Vitae* (1968), which has now become the classic statement of the Catholic doctrine on this matter (a doctrine, however, which goes back to the early centuries, and on which the Church has never wavered), Pope Paul VI affirmed that "each and every marriage act must remain open to the transmission of life" (no. 11). This excludes "every action which, either in anticipation of the conjugal act, or in its accomplishment, or in the development of its natural consequences, proposes, whether as an end or as a means, to render procreation impossible" (no. 14). Pope John Paul II (in many places, notably in his 1981 letter, *On the Family*) has reiterated this doctrine.[4]

• *Natural Family Planning*

There may be good reasons why a couple ought not to have more children (for example, the health of the mother or economic limitations of the family). In such cases, it is not wrong for them to restrict intercourse to the wife's infertile periods (as is practiced in what is called *Natural Family Planning*, or NFP). One may object that NFP leads to the same result as contraception, namely, sex without procreation; yet it is not the result but how it is attained that is at issue. NFP respects nature and is regulated by it; contraception manipulates and violates nature. In one case the couple modulate their conduct by the natural rhythms of the woman's body; in the other, they interfere with nature. Furthermore, contraceptive union is a kind of acted lie: The act signifies a total gift of self to the other whereas in reality something is withheld. In NFP, this is not the case. The gift of self is complete; but it is performed at a time when it will not lead to the formation of a child that ought not to be conceived.

It must be added, however, that for a married couple to exclude children arbitrarily or out of trivial or selfish motives is not legitimate. Because of the inherently procreative intent of marriage, offspring are not merely an option. Only when additional children would do grave harm to the existing family or to themselves is it legitimate to avoid them.

2. Another category of sins leaves the conjugal act and its goal intact but violates the requirement that sex belongs in marriage.

Extramarital sex (fornication) is wrong on three counts: (1) It runs the risk of engendering children outside of marriage (or, if this risk is prevented by contraception, then it is wrong because of the latter); (2) it cheapens and trivializes a most solemn interpersonal relationship by playing with it outside the firm union called for by conjugal love; and (3) it excludes the sacrament intended by Christ to protect, assist, and sanctify marriage.

Adultery is wrong for these same reasons, in addition to the fact that it makes the parentage of the children uncertain. Moreover, it offends against the second purpose of marriage, by violating the mutual love and pledged fidelity of the spouses. As a further consequence, it violates the sacramental function of representing Christ's love for the Church.

Divorce is breaking the faith pledged to one's spouse and to Christ. (Often it also involves severe harm to the children, who need the care of both mother and father, and the security of their faithful love.) If a marriage has broken down to the point that it is impossible or unwise for the spouses to continue living together, *separation* "of bed and board" can be tolerated; not, however, divorce. The couple remain sacramentally bound to each other, and are not free to remarry. The marriage bond is an objective and permanent one, which is not dissolved by the cooling of the partners' love. This position is based on the explicit teaching of Jesus:

> What God has joined together, let man not separate. . . . Anyone who divorces his wife and marries another woman commits adultery against her. And if she divorces her husband and marries another man, she commits adultery. (Mark 10:9-12; see also Matthew 5:32; 19:6-12; Luke 16:18; 1 Corinthians 7:10)

Separated spouses are allowed to get a civil divorce to protect themselves legally, but the divorce is not recognized by the Church. (An *annulment* is not a divorce but a declaration that there was never a valid marriage at all — due perhaps to the psychic incompetence of one or other party to make a responsible commitment.)

3. Impure touches, looks, and fantasies do not involve intercourse but seek to arouse sexual pleasure by images or suggestive approximations of the act. They include improper caressing, immodesty either in looking or in dress, and imaginary sexual activity (either simple fantasy or suggestive plays, novels, songs, jokes, stories, etc.).

Because such acts do not involve intercourse, much less the conception of a child, they are often taken lightly, and are accepted as an ordinary form of entertainment in our society. But they corrupt the sense of chastity and are severely condemned by Jesus, who said, "Anyone who looks at a woman lustfully has already committed adultery with her in his heart" (Matthew 5:28). Their immorality lies partly in the danger of inciting people toward sexual activity but also in the very fact of arousing and taking delight in disordered sentiments and passions. To take pleasure in the thought of evil is itself evil.

• *Beauty of marriage*

Sadly, it has taken longer to list the many ways of doing evil than to describe what is good and right. Let us close, at least, by recognizing that a good marriage is one of the

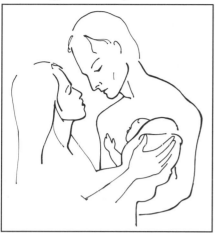

holiest, richest, and most fulfilling of human achievements. It is the communion — spiritual, psychological, and corporeal — of two persons in fully committed mutual love. It is a love made fruitful in the engendering of children, with the peculiarly holy joy of being entrusted with little ones, to protect, nurture, and gently guide their emerging personalities. Marriage brings couples the responsibility, the strength, and the joy of witnessing to God's faithful and all-embracing love in a world dominated by self-interest. While no marriage ever realizes these goals perfectly, even the flawed fulfillment that is possible by the grace of God is precious.

13

Spirits — good and evil

The idea that there are invisible spirits inhabiting this world is one of the most widespread of religious beliefs. It is found in all the religions we considered in Chapter 1 — nature religions, Shinto, Taoism, Confucianism, Hinduism, Buddhism, Israel, and Islam as well as countless others. Sometimes the spirits are thought of as utterly immaterial and invisible; more often as consisting of a vaporlike substance. Frequently they are diminutive copies of humans or other animals. They may be ghosts of the departed; they may be spirits animating rocks, trees, and forests; they may be degraded deities or entities on the way to becoming deities. (In polytheist religions, it is often difficult to distinguish between the lesser gods and the spirits.) Some spirits are hostile to man, others friendly; occasionally they are neutral or merely mischievous, as the poltergeists. It would be difficult to form a precise definition embracing the whole range of them. Spooks, goblins, elves, sprites, fairies, ghosts, trolls, pixies, kobolds, incubi, succubi, ghouls, mermaids, banshees, genii, leprechauns, and even the "little people" of Ireland are all remnants of the religious folklore of the world which can be classified loosely under the heading of spirits.

The fact that such beliefs are so widespread suggests that there is a serious motivation for them. Modern civilization has been hard on these beliefs but has failed to eradicate them; people cling to them tenaciously. And we should not overlook the irony of the fact that, after banishing angels and devils from his universe, modern man has hastened with unseemly credulity to fill the vacuum with UFO's and extraterrestrial entities.

In this perspective we can consider the traditional Christian belief in angels and demons. Perhaps no other element of the faith has suffered so much from the demythologizing tendencies of modern thought. It is true that there has been a resurgence of belief in the angels manifested, for example, by the Philangeloi ("friends of the angels") Society, and books such as *Angels* by Billy Graham (1975) and *A Rumor of Angels* by Peter Berger (1969). Popular concern with Satan has been manifested in movies such as *The Exorcist, The Omen*, and *Rosemary's Baby* as well as in the appearance of Satanic cults. Nevertheless, it seems fair to say that most educated Christians today, even if they hold on to the other Christian beliefs, are inclined at least to wonder whether angels and demons are not merely metaphors for the good and evil impulses we all experience. May Scripture not be using figures of speech adapted to the mentality of a primitive people, rather than affirming the objective existence of the angels and demons it mentions? (In the language proposed in Chapter 6, may they not belong to the idiom rather than the message of Scripture?) This question must be faced frankly but also with a desire to know what Scripture and the Church really teach on this subject rather than a determination to rid ourselves at all costs of a belief that is embarrassing in the eyes of the modern world.

ANGELS

• *In Scripture*

Scripture mentions both good and evil spirits; we will consider the former first. They are usually called angels (from the Greek *angelos*, messenger). This fits their most common function, which is that of communicating a message from God to man — as the angel Gabriel at the annunciation. Occasionally they serve in other ways, especially safeguarding individuals (for example, Abraham's steward [Genesis 24:7]) or nations (for instance, the angel of the Lord protecting the Hebrews from the Egyptian army that pursued them [Exodus 14:19]). These services are symbolized in Jacob's vision of angels going up and down a ladder which reached from earth to heaven. Angels are also depicted around the throne of God praising him (Apocalypse 5:12), whence the expression "choirs of angels." Hebrews 1:14 embraces all the activities of the angels under the term "ministering spirits."

Scripture gives very little concrete information about the angels. Only three have personal names: Michael, leader of the armies of God against those of Satan (Apocalypse 12:7); Gabriel, who announces the births of John the Baptist and Jesus (Luke 1:14, 26); and Raphael, who assists Tobias (Tobit 5:4). There is also mention of various classes of angels: seraphim (Isaiah 6:6), cherubim (Genesis 3:24; Ezekiel 1 and 10), and others (see especially Ephesians 1:21 and Colossians 1:16). It is hard to say what significance these classifications have.

Angels are prominent in the life of Jesus. They announce his conception (Luke 1:26) and birth (Luke 2:9); they safeguard his infancy (Matthew 2:13, 19); they minister to him at the end of his forty days' fast (Mark 1:13) and during his agony in the garden (Luke 22:43); they proclaim his resurrection (Luke 24:4). They are also referred to in his teaching (Matthew 18:20; 26:53).

The early Church continued to experience the intervention of angels. Twice they released apostles from prison (Acts 5:19; 12); they sent Philip on the trip that led to the conversion of the Ethiopian eunuch (Acts 8:26) and perhaps carried Philip off afterward (Acts 8:39). An angel was "distinctly seen" by the Roman centurion Cornelius, telling him to summon Peter to instruct him (Acts 10:3ff). Angels are mentioned also in the New Testament letters and Apocalypse.

• *Real, not figurative*

In many of these texts, it is undoubtedly possible to understand the reference as nothing but a figure of speech for the action of God; for example, the angel who strikes Herod dead (Acts 12:23). When an angel is said to speak to Philip and Cornelius, this might mean simply that they were divinely inspired (compare Acts 8:26 with 8:29 and 10:19). When Matthew says that an angel appeared to Joseph in a dream, instructing him to take Mary as his wife, to flee into Egypt, and to return to Nazareth (Matthew 1:20; 2:13; see also 2:12, 22), some might take this to mean simply that he dreamed it. However, there are certain texts which do not admit of a figurative interpretation. When Peter was freed from prison by an angel, the Acts of the Apostles tells us:

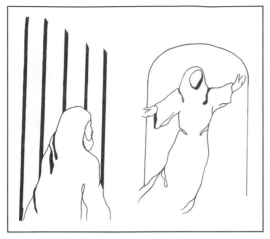

Peter followed him out of the prison, but he had no idea that what the angel was doing was really happening; he thought he was seeing a vision. (12:9)

After they had gone past two guards and through an iron gate that opened of itself,

. . .the angel left him. Then Peter came to himself and said, "Now I know without a doubt that the Lord sent his angel and rescued me from Herod's clutches. . . ." (12:11)

To deny the objective reality of the angel in such a case, one must dismiss the story as legendary. But is this not simply a refusal to accept what the Scripture is plainly affirming?

• *Experience of the Church*

Throughout history, the Church has understood the angels to be real beings of a personal but immaterial nature. Without ever formally defining the point (which was not challenged until modern times), it alluded to the creation of the angels in several solemn documents.[1] It celebrates feasts in honor of Michael, Gabriel, and Raphael (September 29) and the Guardian Angels (October 2). It has approved prayers especially to Michael and the guardian angels. Many Christians have had personal experience of angels. It was a seraph that pierced St. Francis of Assisi with the stigmata. St. Michael and other angels appeared to Joan of Arc. St. Frances of Rome continually saw her guardian angel. Catherine Emmerich and Padre Pio saw and conversed with theirs. All this evidence taken together would seem to confirm the existence of angels as real, objective beings.

One reason why angels are difficult to believe in is that artists since the late Gothic period have so often depicted them as chubby babes with red cheeks and fat round bottoms, hovering in the air on cute little wings. St. Thomas Aquinas has elaborated a far more credible portrait of them as pure spirits in the *Summa Theologiae* (I, qq. 50-64). Not being limited by a body, they have immensely greater intelligence and power than we have. They can make themselves present anywhere simply by willing it. If they sometimes assume human form, this is in order to manifest themselves to human beings.

In their scriptural appearances, angels always have the form of grown men, and often inspire fear in the beholder (for example, Ezekiel in Ezekiel 1:28, Mary and Zachary in Luke 1:11-20, 26-38). In modern times, however, they have often appeared as young boys: thus Michael at Fátima and Garabandal, and the guardian angels seen by St. Catherine Labouré, Catherine Emmerich, and Padre Pio. Was this perhaps adaptation to the appearance expected by these people?

Many imagine that the angels are in heaven as if it were their native land, just as human beings belong on earth. But heaven is not a "locale"; it is the state of being in the presence of God. And it is no more natural for angels than for us. They can be admitted to heaven only by grace. How this grace was bestowed on the angels, we do not know; but since they are intelligent, personal, and therefore free beings, we can presume that they had to make a choice, as we do. However, they would not have undergone a protracted lifetime of testing, as we do, in the course of which it is possible to change the direction of one's life. Being pure spirits, they would have made a single decision once and for all, which committed them totally and irrevocably either to accept God's will or to reject it. Those who sinned became the fallen angels; those who obeyed were admitted at once into the presence — that is, the vision — of God, where they form the heavenly court depicted by Isaiah 6, Ezekiel 1, and Apocalypse 4-5. Apocalypse 12 describes a great battle among the angels:

> There was war in heaven. Michael and his angels fought against the dragon, and the dragon and his angels fought back. But he was not strong enough, and they lost their place in heaven. The great dragon was hurled down — that ancient serpent called the devil or Satan, who leads the whole world astray. He was hurled to the earth, and his angels with him. . . .
>
> When the dragon saw that he had been hurled to the earth, he pursued the woman who had given birth to the male child. The woman was given the two wings of a great eagle, so that she might fly to the place prepared for her in the desert. . . . Then the dragon was enraged at the woman and went off to make war against the rest of her off-spring — those who obey God's commandments and hold to the testimony of Jesus. (Apocalypse 12:7-17)

We cannot of course imagine that warfare among pure spirits is comparable to the battles of earthly armies. How they fight we do not know. At least, this text can be understood as representing the choice that divided the two groups of angels, and their struggle to influence the fate of people on earth. Those who rebelled have become our tempters and adversaries; those who remained loyal are our allies. Besides bringing divine messages to us, they assist and protect us. The chief basis of this belief is given by the words of Jesus:

> See that you do not look down on one of these little ones. For I tell you that their angels in heaven always see the face of my Father in heaven. (Matthew 18:10)

217

• *Guardian angels*

It is commonly believed that each of us has an angel appointed to watch over him (although one might hold that a single angel could have the guardianship over a group or a society, as is suggested by Daniel 10:13-11). In any case, Church tradition strongly supports the practice of prayer to our guardian angel as well as to Michael, the great heavenly protector of the whole Church. Even though Jesus was the Son of God, he did not disdain the ministry of angels; with much less reason might we do so. And if these invisible allies aid us, especially in our struggle against invisible enemies, it is only appropriate that we call on them in time of need, and express our gratitude to them, just as we do with our human allies.

EVIL SPIRITS

Evil spirits have a larger role in Scripture than the good ones. Sacred history begins with the story of Adam and Eve being led into sin by the Serpent (Genesis 3). The last book of the Bible represents the course of history as a warfare waged by Satan against the followers of Jesus.[2] Here again we confront the question "May these not be mere figures of speech for the perverse inclinations which human beings experience within themselves?" Some of the language of Scripture, especially the wild imagery of the Apocalypse, does indeed favor a mythical interpretation; and liberal exegesis was dominated by this position for a century or so. But since the 1930s, there has been a growing recognition that evil spirits belong to the substance of biblical doctrine. There is not a single author in the New Testament who does not speak of them. It is evident that both they and Jesus himself believed in the reality of evil spirits.[3]

• *In Jesus' life and work*

In Jesus' life and work, evil spirits appear very prominently. During his forty days' fast, he was tempted by Satan (Mark 1:12; Matthew 4:1-10; Luke 4:1-13). Unless we are

prepared to admit that Jesus himself was subject to disordered inclinations and fantasies, it is difficult to see how a mythical interpretation of this passage would leave any serious sense in it. When these temptations failed, the devil left Jesus "until an opportune time" (Luke 4:13). This time came at the Passion, which Jesus called "the hour of the power of darkness" (Luke 22:53). Satan put it into the heart of Judas to betray Jesus (John 13:2), then he himself entered Judas's heart to assure execution of this evil design (John 13:27; Luke 22:3). Although apparently the hour of Satan's victory, the crucifixion was in reality his defeat: "The prince of this world now stands condemned," Jesus affirmed (John 16:11; see also 12:31).

Freeing people from demonic possession was a major part of Jesus' ministry (Luke 13:32). Evil spirits made people deaf, dumb, blind, and paralyzed (Matthew 9:32, 12:22; Luke

13:16), and caused convulsions (Luke 9:39). Frequently the demoniacs have an uncanny insight into Jesus' person and work, which they seek to disturb by crying out in untimely fashion that he is the Son of God or the Holy One of God (Mark 1:24, etc.). Mary Magdalene was in the clutches of seven demons (Luke 8:2).

The Synoptics tell at length the story of the demoniac who lived in the land of the Gerasenes. He spent day and night among the tombs and in the hills, shrieking and gash-

ing himself with stones. He "had often been chained hand and foot, but he tore the chains apart and broke the irons on his feet. No one was strong enough to subdue him" (Mark 5:2-5). At Jesus' approach, he cried out, "What do you want with me, Jesus, Son of the Most High God?" When asked his name, he replied, "My name is legion, for we are many." He implored Jesus not to torture him but to send him/them into a herd of pigs feeding on a nearby hillside. Jesus gave permission and the demons departed from the man, leaving him in his right mind. The pigs, however, rushed down the steep bank into the lake and drowned.

Jesus pointed to his victory over the demons as a sign of the coming of God's Kingdom. Once when he had cast out a demon that had made a man mute, his enemies retorted that he did this by Beelzebub, the prince of demons. After replying, "If Satan is divided against himself, how can his kingdom stand?" Jesus went on to insist, "If I drive out demons by the finger of God, then the kingdom of God has come to you" (Luke 11:14-20).

Jesus gave the apostles also the power to cast out demons. In fact this was a major part of their work (Matthew 10:1; Mark 6:7; Luke 9:1), along with preaching the Gospel and healing the sick. When his disciples reported that "even the demons submit to us in your name," Jesus replied, "I saw Satan fall like lightning from heaven" (Luke 10:18). But when, in one instance, the disciples were unable to free a possessed boy, and asked Jesus the reason, he replied, "This kind can come out only by prayer" (Mark 9:29).

The ministry of exorcism continued on in the Church after the departure of Jesus. When a girl with a "divining spirit" troubled the work of St. Paul, he ordered the spirit out of her (Acts 16:18). But when the seven sons of a Jewish priest tried to do something similar, a man with an evil spirit overpowered them all, giving them such a beating that they fled naked and bleeding (19:16).

• *Jesus' teaching*

Satan figures just as prominently in Jesus' teaching as in his activity. Jesus said that when the Gospel is preached, Satan snatches the Word out of people's minds to keep them from believing (Matthew 13:19; Mark 4:15; Luke 4:2). Where the Lord has sown good seed, the devil sows cockle (Luke 8:12). He tries to shake the disciples as wheat is sifted in a cribble (Luke 22:31). He is a liar and the father of lies; a murderer and the father of murderers (John 8:44).[4] Even after the evil spirit has left a man, it may return later with "seven other spirits more wicked than itself," and finding "the house unoccupied, swept clean and put in order," reenter it, making the last state of the man worse than the first (Matthew 12:43-45). Jesus calls Satan "the prince of this world" (John 12:31; 14:30; 16:11), as St. Paul would later call him "the god of this world" (2 Corinthians 4:4).

In many of these texts, it is evident that the reference to evil spirits cannot possibly be taken as a mythical expression for a person's evil inclinations. The exorcism stories especially, unless we dismiss them as purely legendary, oblige us to acknowledge the objective reality of evil spirits. In the teaching of Jesus, Satan is represented as the enemy *par excellence*, and the apostles obviously understand him literally. When the apostles misunderstood his parables, Jesus corrected and instructed them; but on the subject of Satan, instead of correcting them, Jesus reinforces their belief. To interpret Satan mythically would, in effect, declare Jesus himself to have erred; and if he erred on this point, how reliable would any of his teaching be?

Another interpretation frequently proposed is that demons are a primitive people's way of explaining illness, and that Jesus simply spoke the language of his hearers. May not the boy who kept falling into fire and water have been subject merely to epileptic fits (Matthew 17:15)? This interpretation is plausible for certain select cases, but it does not explain the superhuman strength of the Gerasene, for example, or the uncanny knowledge of many others, or why the demons often shrieked when being expelled. Moreover, there are two major reasons why this interpretation does not fit the work of Jesus. First, the Gospels generally distinguish clearly between people who are simply sick and those who are possessed. Luke 9:1, like Matthew 10:1, speaks of two powers given to the apostles, one to heal the sick, the other to cast out demons:

> When Jesus had called the twelve together, he gave them power and authority to drive out all demons and to cure diseases, and he sent them to preach the kingdom of God and to heal the sick.

Mark 6:13 adds:

> They drove out many demons and anointed many sick people with oil and healed them.

Second, Jesus addressed the demons he was expelling, sometimes dialogued with them, and finally ordered them to leave by an imperious command. This is not the way he dealt with simple illness, and it would have been a pure charade if nothing but illness were present.

• *Apostolic doctrine*

Jesus' teaching on evil spirits was perpetuated by the apostles; 1 John 5:19 declares that "the whole world is under the control of the evil one." The First Epistle of Peter warns us:

> Be self-controlled and alert. Your enemy the devil prowls around like a roaring lion looking for someone to devour. Resist him, standing firm in the faith. . . . (5:8f)

St. Paul exhorts:

> Put on the full armor of God so that you can take your stand against the devil's schemes. For our struggle is not against flesh and blood but against the rulers, against the authorities, against the powers of this dark world and against the spiritual forces of evil in the heavenly realms. (Ephesians 6:11-12)

The armor recommended by St. Paul is truth, righteousness, faith, prayer, the gospel of peace, and the Word of God. He also mentions the "helmet of salvation" (Ephesians 6:14-17). Note that the above text clearly states that the devil is not something belonging to human nature, which is comprised under "flesh and blood." Elsewhere we are told not to give Satan any occasion (Ephesians 4:27; 1 Corinthians 7:5). The devil was a sinner from the beginning, and those who commit sin are said to be from him (1 John 3:8).

In sum, it is the New Testament teaching, originating with Jesus himself, that man, in his struggle to live righteously, finds his efforts resisted not only by his own perversity but also by an Adversary. Abetted by an army of evil spirits, the devil tempts, obstructs, injures, and sometimes even dwells in human beings. So great is his power over the world that he can be called its prince. Jesus has defeated him; nevertheless, demons are still able to harass mankind, until the end of the present age. From the Apocalypse it appears that Satan will enjoy a moment of apparent victory over the Church, just as he did over Jesus (Apocalypse 13; see also 20:7-9). In the end, however, he will be cast into hell (Apocalypse 20:10), after which the heavenly Jerusalem will be revealed (Apocalypse 21:4).

• *Church doctrine*

Throughout its history, the Church has instructed and aided its members for the battle against Satan through its teaching, preaching, and liturgy, especially in connection with baptism. The "order" of exorcist was instituted as early as the third century to deal with the possessed. Since 1972, there is no longer a special order for this purpose, but exorcisms are still performed when needed by a priest authorized for this function.[5]

How are we to conceive of evil spirits? In the past, there have been several attempts to understand them as beings that are evil by their very nature. The Church has always resisted such Manichaean tendencies, which intend to free God from any responsibility for evil but in fact limit him by implying an order of reality that he did not create. The Catholic understanding of evil spirits is that they were created good, like the angels who are now in heaven — but by their own free choice have turned to evil. The chief scriptural basis for this position is the text cited above, about the war in heaven, in which Michael and his angels expelled Satan and his angels (Apocalypse 12:7-17). From this text as well as many others, it is also evident that the evil spirits are numerous.

• *Terminology*

The vocabulary in this realm is somewhat fluid and confusing. *Satan* is a Hebrew term which came to mean The Adversary. It is always used in the singular as the proper name of the principal evil spirit. *Devil* comes from the Greek *diabolos* (slanderer), which is ordinarily used in Scripture in the singular, as the equivalent of Satan. *Beelzeboul* (or *Beelzebub*) and *Belial* (or *Beliar*) are other proper names occasionally given to him in Scripture. Lucifer is not a biblical name for Satan. It is the Latin rendering of "bright morning star" in Isaiah 14:12-15. This passage was applied to Satan, first by the Jewish apocalyptic writers, later by the Christians, and had great influence on Christian thought about Satan.

The other evil spirits have no personal names in the New Testament. They are frequently called "unclean spirits," but this seems to denote nothing more specific than that they are evil. *Demons* is another common name for them, especially when they have entered into someone. Occasionally they are called *fallen angels* (Jude 6; 2 Peter 2:4) or *angels of Satan* (see Apocalypse 12:7, 9). There is also a cluster of names, such as principalities, powers, thrones, dominations, etc., applied to them in such a way that it is difficult to say whether they are merely synonyms or designations of distinct classes of evil spirits or classes of angels to whom an exaggerated cult is directed (see Ephesians 1:21; 3:10; 6:12; Colossians 1:6; 2:10).

While it seems appropriate to reserve the names *Satan* and *devil* to the chief of the evil spirits, and to speak of the rest as evil spirits, or demons, it must be borne in mind that the New Testament does not hold rigorously to this distinction. (On the pagan and Old Testament background for the idea of Satan, see Jeffrey Russell, *The Devil*, Ithaca, N.Y.: Cornell University Press, 1977.)

• *Satan and demons*

The relation between Satan and the other evil spirits is not clear from the New Testament; but the language of the Apocalypse would seem to imply that Satan is in some way chief of the others. What is in some places attributed specifically to demons in other places seems to be attributed to Satan (see especially Apocalypse 20:2, 7, 10).

Whereas many cultures, as we have seen, think of evil spirits as the cause of illness, madness, and other troubles, it is characteristic of the Christian view that the powers of evil are above all intent on leading us into sin. "Satan, who leads the whole world astray" (Apocalypse 12:9), tempts people to sin (1 Corinthians 7:5; 1 Thessalonians 3:5; Acts 5:3) and entraps them by his schemes and snares (2 Corinthians 2:11; 1 Timothy 3:7; 2 Timothy 2:26). To achieve this, he can disguise himself as an angel of light (2 Corinthians 11:14). He interferes with the work of the Gospel (1 Thessalonians 2:18).

According to St. Thomas Aquinas,[6] Satan is unable to act directly on the mind or will of man. He can, however, act directly on the imagination, thereby creating illusions. He can also excite passions and emotions (particularly hatred, lust, and depression), which may be so intense as to interfere with the activity of reason and powerfully sway the will. Like any spirit, he can exert physical power on material bodies; this makes possible the violence experienced by the Curé of Ars and Padre Pio as well as the demonically induced ailments mentioned in the New Testament. Satan can also assume a bodily appearance in order, for example, to tempt or to frighten — activities well attested in Christian experience.

• *Types of diabolical activity*

The devil attacks human beings in various ways, which can be classified roughly as temptation, obsession, harassment, and possession. (These are not mutually exclusive; and each could be further subdivided.) *Temptation* belongs to the human situation in this fallen world, and there is no need to blame all temptation on Satan. It can arise simply from our native weakness and concupiscence. However, by acting on our imagination or feelings, the devil is able to aggravate the temptation. Ordinarily, his role is hidden; but his influence is to be suspected when temptations are particularly perverse or unnatural, when they are excessively strong, or seem to go contrary to our natural temperament.

At times, however (and usually only in the life of someone who has been strong against ordinary temptations), the devil may manifest himself in visible form. He appeared to Catherine of Siena as a handsome young man offering her a magnificent wardrobe. For St. Anthony, he took the form of naked women. He appeared in innumerable forms to Padre Pio, once masquerading as his confessor. For Mirjana Dragicevic of Medjugorje, he took on a hideous bestial shape.

Obsession refers to temptations that are exceptionally powerful or insistent (as in some of the instances just cited). The obsessions dealt with by psychologists (as when they speak of an obsessive-compulsive personality disorder) are not necessarily diabolical; but at times they may very well be.

Harassment is not one of the standard terms in this subject matter; rather it is used here for actions which do not try to lead a person directly into sin but to injure him or interfere with his work. Thus the devil frequently beat Padre Pio physically; he shouted frightening threats at the Curé of Ars in an effort to intimidate him; he seems to have stirred up opposition of all sorts against Juliana of Liège. When a person cannot be tempted to sin, the devil will seek at least to prevent or discourage him from doing good. Depression and despair are among his most frequent weapons. Inducing people to commit suicide is one of his common strategies; he is not ordinarily allowed to kill anyone directly, but he can motivate them to kill themselves. When other tactics fail, Satan's hatred of the good is so great that he will sometimes stoop to injuring them physically (for example, Padre Pio).

Possession consists in Satan's control over the body of a person, so that he, rather than the person, is in control (at least at moments) of what the person does. This may be the result of someone's having allowed Satan to dominate him by sin; but there seem to have been instances of very holy people who suffered diabolical possession as a trial (for instance, the Carmelite nun Marie of Jesus Crucified).

Since pure spirits are far more powerful and intelligent than humans, it is no problem to know how they are able to act thus upon us. Rather, the question is, "Why do they not do so more often or with more devastating effect?" Ultimately of course it is by the providence of God that we are preserved from them; but what secondary causes are employed (for example, to what extent is the agency of the good angels involved?), and why the demons are given liberty to act in certain cases but not in others is very mysterious.

• *Remedies*

Whereas the action of the Holy Spirit is signaled by peace, love, and joy (Galatians 5:22), agitation and a troubled mind are often the signs of the devil's action. When his presence is suspected, it is not good to confront him directly and defiantly, for we are no match for him. Rather, we should have recourse to the saving power of Jesus, invoking the help of the archangel Michael, our guardian angel, and the Mother of God. Through Mary especially Jesus seems to be pleased to humiliate Satan, who, on his part, has a special abhorrence for her. Besides prayer, the reading of Scriptures is a powerful defense against Satan. The sign of the cross, blessed candles, the rosary, scapular, Miraculous Medal, holy water, and especially Lourdes water are also efficacious; the very humility of these means allows God to use them with greater power.

14
Original sin

The human combination of goodness and perversity, of promising potential and disappointing mediocrity, has perplexed and distressed the sages of all times. The human heart is perennially stirred by aspirations to excellence, nobility, beauty, and generosity; the human mind daily demonstrates anew its astounding resourcefulness in technological accomplishments; but human history is largely a record of violence, selfishness, pettiness, and ugliness. *Utopia* (literally "no place") is the name given by Thomas More to the design of an ideal society which, although theoretically conceivable, sad experience assures us will never become a fact in this world.

A typical illustration is the old communist settlement at New Harmony, Indiana. Convinced that "men were good by nature and needed only the proper environment to become virtuous, strong, intelligent and contented,"[1] Robert Owen, an enlightened advocate of human rights led eight hundred followers from Scotland in 1825 to establish a model community in America. Within one year, New Harmony was split by disharmony into several factions, which separated from one another and all dissolved within a few years. By the end of his life, Owen acknowledged the inadequacy of his earlier concept of the human potential.

St. Paul is voicing the experience of all mankind when he declares:

> I do not understand my own actions. For I do not do what I want, but I do the very thing I hate. . . . I can will what is right, but I cannot do it. For I do not do the good I want, but the evil I do not want is what I do. . . . For I delight in the law of God in my inmost self, but I see in my members another law at war with the law in my mind and making me captive to the law of sin which dwells in my members. (Romans 7:15-23, RSV)

The doctrine of original sin is the interpretation of this human condition by the light of revelation. However, the doctrine itself is an obscure one, still in the process of clarification. The story of Adam and Eve's sin is obviously not a literal account of a deed as it transpired but is highly symbolic. Its dark message has to do not merely with the beginning of human history but much more with mankind's present situation of sinful alienation from God. Theology is not yet in a position to define all the elements of this message, much less to fit them together into a fully coherent synthesis. Hence it will be necessary to proceed tentatively here, examining first the narrative of Genesis 3, then its interpretation by St. Paul and the Church, and finally theological reflection on it. This is a typical case of a truth of revelation which cannot be abstracted from the story in which it is communicated. But with all its obscurity, the mottled light of the doctrine sheds a precious illumination on the perplexing state in which we find ourselves.

GENESIS

According to Genesis 2 and 3, God put the first man and woman in the Garden of Eden (literally, "garden of delight") to cultivate it. Among the trees in the garden were the "tree of life" and the "tree of the knowledge of good and evil" (not, however, an apple tree!). God gave man permission to eat of all the trees but the latter:

> You must not eat from the tree of the knowledge of good and evil, for when you eat of it you will surely die. (2:17)

The Serpent, however, the "sliest" of all the wild creatures (but regarded as Satan here), said to the woman:

> You will not surely die. For God knows that when you eat of it your eyes will be opened, and you will be like God, knowing good and evil. (3:4, 5)

So the woman ate some of the fruit of this tree, and gave it to her husband who did likewise. Thus she who had been given to Adam as "a helper suitable for him" (2:18) became his temptress; and Adam, who had received dominion over all the earth, sought to become absolute master, like God.

Instead of making them like God in wisdom and sovereignty, the transgression brought about the immediate disintegration of their world. The first and immediate result was the loss of their original innocence. The man and woman experienced shame at their nakedness. They had come indeed to "know good and evil"; not, however, by the wisdom that knows how to discriminate between them but by the sad experience of one who has embraced sin and been ruined by it.

Further punishment soon followed. God passed sentence on each of the culprits: From now on the serpent will have to slither on its belly; the woman will suffer the pains of childbirth as well as subjugation to her husband; the man will find that the earth he tills resists his labor, which becomes disagreeable to him. Death is imposed on them all as the supreme punishment: "Dust you are, and to dust you will return." They are expelled from the Garden of Eden so that they may not eat of the tree of life and live forever.

The following chapters of Genesis (4 to 11) are an account of the multiplication of sin. Cain slays his brother Abel — the beginning of human conflict and warfare. But the spread of evil did not stop. "Yahweh saw how great man's wickedness on earth had become, and that every inclination of the thoughts of his heart was only evil all the time" (6:5). Consequently, God sends a flood to wipe out those who have offended him, the Creator, but saves those who "find favor in his eyes," namely, Noah and his family.

Compared to the myths of the ancient Near East literatures, the story of the Fall is remarkable for its sobriety, coherence, and realism as well as for the finesse of its psychological insight. It is free of the grotesque imaginations and aimless divagations abounding in the other literatures. Humanity has originally a peaceful, harmonious existence, in the situation Yahweh has fixed for it. The tempter, however, disturbs this harmony, first by arousing the desire for a better-than-human condition. He is also a deceiver, promising what he cannot give, and concealing the fatal consequences of his proposal. He approaches the woman who in turn seduces her husband. This portrayal of temptation, sin, and its sequels remains as fresh and instructive today as when it was first written.

Besides being a paradigm of the process of sin, Genesis 3 makes a theological statement about the human situation. It represents death and suffering as not belonging to man's primordial condition but rather as a punishment for sin. They pertain to a disorder disturbing the initial divine plan. It is one of the most difficult problems of contemporary theology to determine the precise import of this message, and especially to what extent it involves historical reference. Were Adam and Eve real, historical persons? Is Genesis telling us the story of a real sin — the first human sin — or is it giving us a parable about all sin? Did mankind exist for a while in a state of paradisiac harmony before losing it by the Fall? To treat these difficult questions we have to examine the interpretations of Genesis found in later texts of Scripture and in the teaching of the Church.

The old and new Adam.

ST. PAUL

St. Paul makes Adam a key figure of his theology, the negative counterpart to Jesus Christ:

> For since death came through a man, the resurrection of the dead comes also through a man. For as in Adam all die, so also in Christ all will be made alive. (1 Corinthians 15:21; see also vv. 45-49)

This doctrine is elaborated in Romans 5:12-21 (RSV), where the contrast between Adam and Christ is reiterated in diverse perspectives:

> . . .sin came into the world through one man and death through sin, and so death spread to all men because all men sinned. . . .
> . . .if many died through one man's trespass, much more have the grace of God and the free gift in the grace of that one man Jesus Christ abounded for many.

. . .the judgment following one trespass brought condemnation, but the free gift following many trespasses brings justification.

If, because of one man's trespass, death reigned through that one man, much more will those who receive the abundance of grace and the free gift of righteousness reign in life through the one man Jesus Christ.

. . .as one man's trespass led to condemnation for all men, so one man's act of righteousness leads to acquittal and life for all men.

. . .as by one man's disobedience many were made sinners, so by one man's obedience many will be made righteous.

In this tangled passage, St. Paul is not concerned primarily with expounding the nature and effects of Adam's sin, he is only using it as a backdrop to bring out the grandeur of the grace given through Jesus Christ. Nevertheless, he seems clearly to affirm that all mankind have been condemned, that is, accounted as sinners and sentenced to death, by reason of Adam's sin ("trespass," "transgression," or "disobedience").[2]

The rest of the New Testament, without focusing on Adam, is pervaded by the view that we all stand under the judgment of God as sinful until redeemed and reconciled with the Father by the work of Jesus Christ. While reference is made most often to the actual sins committed by individuals, there is the supposition of an underlying state, or condition, which inevitably leads everyone into actual sin. This state is spoken of, for example, as "sin" or "the law of sin" dwelling in our bodies (Romans 7:17-23), as a darkness in which we remain until we turn to the light of Christ (John 12:36; see also 1:5, 9; 9:5, 39; Colossians 1:13), as the power of sin under which all are held (Romans 3:9), as Satan's princely dominion over this world (John 12:31; 14:30; 16:11), as the great beast that has power over all the earth until it is slain by the Lord of Lords (Apocalypse 13-18), or simply as the fact that all are in need of salvation (see Chapter 20). In brief, we are all immersed in sin until Jesus sets us free; we are alienated from the Father until Jesus reconciles us.

CHURCH DOCTRINE

In synthesizing the teachings of Scripture and correlating them with human experience, the Church gradually put together a doctrine to which St. Augustine gave the name *original sin* (meaning, not the first sin, that which Adam committed, but that which his descendants inherit, which they have *from their origins*). The following consequences of Adam's fall are embraced by this doctrine: death, suffering, concupiscence, self-centeredness, loss of sanctifying grace, and, as a consequence of the others, inability to keep the moral law. Over and above these particular "wounds of nature," there is the state of sin itself. It is not readily apparent how sin can be inherited by children from their parents; yet a centuries-old Church tradition has confirmed the idea that what we inherit from our first parents is rightly called sin, it is not just the consequences of sin. How this can be, and how the *sin* in original sin relates to the above consequences, have been classical theological problems. Despite the intense reflection devoted to it, a fully coherent theology of this murky topic has never been achieved. However, certain points have been firmly fixed, and some enlightening connections established among them.

• *Pelagius and Luther*

In the sixteenth century, the Council of Trent defined the main lines of the Catholic position. This takes a middle way between Pelagius, who in effect denied original sin, and Luther, who exaggerated it. Pelagius held that the sin of Adam and Eve influenced their offspring merely in the way that bad example tends to lead others into sin. Modern rationalist theologians often revert to that position in a somewhat more sophisticated form, holding, for example, that original sin, renamed "sin of the world" (Schoonenberg), consists simply of the cumulative effects of all the sins of previous generations, poisoning the moral atmosphere in which we are born today. In response to Pelagius, the Church affirmed that, by his sin, the first man afflicted human nature with an injury that is transmitted "by propagation, not just by imitation."

Luther, on the other hand, held that human nature is totally corrupted by original sin. Perhaps this statement should not be taken literally; it would be wrong to treat Luther's rhetorical declamations as theological formulae. Nevertheless, some idea of his meaning can be gathered from his conclusions, that human reason is so clouded by original sin that, left to itself, it cannot attain a genuine knowledge of religious truth; and that the human will has been so perverted that all the deeds of pagans (that is, non-Christians) are sins (including even those which appear to be good deeds). Finally, Luther held that human nature is so impregnated with original sin that not even the grace of God removes it in this life. Those who have been justified by the grace of Christ retain their real wickedness, which God merely forgives: *"simul justus et peccator."* In response to this, the Church holds that human nature remains essentially good, even though injured by original sin; and that divine grace genuinely cleanses from the stain of sin, even though not removing all of sin's effects.

• *The Council of Trent*

The most important statements of the Council of Trent (1516) on this subject are the following:

1. *By his sin, the first man, Adam, harmed himself in both soul and body. His soul lost the holiness and justice in which it had been created. His body became subject to death.* (*Holiness* refers to man's relationship with God, and *justice* to rectitude in his human affairs. *Justice* in this sense is not confined to rendering to others what is due them but embraces the entire right order within a person; in brief, it includes all the virtues. Sin is directly contrary to holiness and justice thus understood.)

2. *Adam's sin affected not only himself but his descendants likewise. He transmitted to them not only death and bodily sufferings but also sin, which is death of the soul.* (Here the difficulty is just the opposite of that in the foregoing point. There it was obvious that Adam's sin harmed his soul, depriving him of holiness and justice; but how it harmed his body, making it subject to death, was difficult to understand. Here the fact that Adam's descendants inherit mortality and liability to other bodily ailments creates no problem, since this is evident. But that they inherit sin is a point of supreme difficulty. Even in regard to the body, this doctrine is not just a statement of the obvious. It implies that death and bodily ailments cannot be regarded *merely* as natural. They have the character of

punishment in us, since they involve the privation of the original gift of immortality. Thus the doctrine that we inherit sin is complemented by the doctrine that death and bodily ailments are a punishment for that sin.)

3. *Original sin is transmitted not by imitation but by propagation.* (That the bad example of parents influences their children is well known; but the Church insists that original sin cannot be reduced to this. We inherit it along with our human nature from those who engender us; it is in us even before we begin to act or imitate the actions of others. However, the Council did not mean to suggest anything sinful about the conjugal union through which the child is begotten. If there were, it would be a sin of the parents, not of the child. Original sin is like a wound in human nature, and is transmitted to us by our parents simply because it is from them that we receive nature itself.)

4. *Original sin is sin in the true and proper sense, and is taken away by the grace of Christ. But the concupiscence which remains after baptism is not sin in the proper sense.* (*Concupiscence* here designates all the unruly inclinations that tend to lead a person into sin. Luther identified original sin with concupiscence; and since the latter remains in the baptized, he held that baptism does not really take the sin away but merely pardons it. The Council recognizes that concupiscence is a factor in original sin but insists that there is a real difference — in fact, an infinite distance — between a person [even an infant] in the state of sin and one in the state of grace, though both are subject to concupiscence. Sin is a state of estrangement from God [in scriptural language, it is often called being hated by God], whereas grace is a state of loving union with God. In insisting that original sin is sin in the true and proper sense, the Council does not mean to equate it with actual sin [to which the term *sin* applies primarily] but to contrast it with concupiscence, which can be called sin only figuratively.)

5. *Even newborn infants, who have not yet committed any personal sin, are subject to original sin. For this reason, it is right to baptize them so that they may be cleansed from sin and reborn through the Holy Spirit.*

In brief, the Council of Trent holds that man was created in a state of justice, holiness, and immortality. By sin the first man lost these attributes not only for himself but also for his descendants. The latter are born in a state of sin, subject to concupiscence, suffering, and death. The grace of Christ, given in baptism, frees them from sin but not from concupiscence, suffering, and death.[3]

THEOLOGY OF ORIGINAL SIN

The Council did not attempt to provide a theoretical explanation of original sin but confined itself solely to defining those points which are essential to Christian faith. Theologians have looked for ways to make this doctrine intelligible but with limited success.

St. Augustine proposed the fundamental dynamics. So long as the human spirit was completely submissive to God, man's lower faculties were submissive to his reason. When the will of man rebelled against God, it lost dominion over its own passions and emotions, like a subordinate officer who cannot control the men under him without the full backing of a strong superior.[4]

This theory is supported by actual experience. When we are fully committed to the will of God, there results a kind of integrity in our psychological being such that evil has little attraction for us. Especially in moments of deep prayer and of strong, actual love of God, people often experience an inner peace and immunity to temptation. Conversely, when we turn away from God, our appetites again begin to grow unruly. It is reasonable to suppose that this would have been the case more radically for Adam than for us who have to struggle from the outset with disorders inherited from him.

• *Original harmony the work of grace*

St. Thomas Aquinas (*Summa Theologiae*, I, 95, 1) added that the harmony of Adam's nature before the Fall was not simply natural; otherwise children would be born with it still. It had to be the effect of a privileged grace. This grace was intended not merely for Adam personally but for the whole race that was to spring from him. In transmitting human nature to his descendants, he was meant to transmit it in a state of grace. But since, by his sin, he had deprived nature of grace in his own person, it was a graceless nature that he passed on. Thus our sufferings now, although natural in themselves, have the character of punishment, since we were meant to be preserved from them.

The fact that grace originally imparted a preternatural harmony to Adam's nature does not imply that the restoration of grace should *ipso facto* restore that harmony. When a complex whole has disintegrated because of the loss of one of its parts, restoring the part does not necessarily put the whole back in order. At its creation, nature was in perfect harmony due to grace; but now that nature originates without that harmony, the new harmony, of which grace is again the principle, is acquired only by a long and difficult process.

The foregoing accounts for the fact that human beings are now born without grace; it does not, however, explain why their state is one of *sin*. Grace does not belong to human nature; the latter has no claim on it. Hence a person does not deserve to be called a sinner simply because he comes into the world in a state of pure nature. Still less is it possible to reduce original sin to the limitedness of the creature in comparison with the infinity of the divine, as some theologians, more rationalist than Christian, have proposed. The biblical affirmation is that human beings descended from Adam and stand before God, by that very fact, as sinners. But to be sinful is not simply to be a creature; in fact, it implies discord with one's creaturely status.

• *The lack of due justice*

St. Anselm defined original sin as "lack of the justice one ought to have."[5] Here, as in the text of the Council of Trent cited above, *justice* does not mean the particular virtue which regulates man's dealings with others but stands for the complete rectitude of the human person. But what rectitude is wanting to the newborn infant? Clearly not that of good deeds, of which it is not yet capable.

St. Thomas Aquinas pointed out that, besides human acts, we must also take into consideration *dispositions* which affect the person for good or ill. He held original sin to be *a bad disposition*, meaning by that not a positive inclination to evil but simply an inner disorder resulting from the loss of the harmony conferred on Adam by grace (*Summa Theologiae*, I-II, 82, 1). What constitutes original sin is not properly the lack of grace but the *disorder* consequent upon the loss of grace. It includes concupiscence — the fact that our lower powers are not fully submissive to reason, making it impossible for anyone, left simply to his natural resources, to keep the moral law in its integrity. Moreover, our ability to love God has been lessened in two ways. First, we are unable to love God above all things (and by the same token to prefer the common good to our own private interests), as ought to be possible to an intact human nature; second, we are unable to love God with the love of charity, that is, the supernatural love that grace makes possible. As the latter is supernatural, its lack could not be held against someone created in a purely natural order; but in fact we are all called to love God with charity, by reason of the grace initially conferred on the human race in Adam. Not to be able to love him in this way is thus an instance of the "lack of the justice that ought to be there" by which original sin is defined.

• *Sin of nature*

Original sin has often been called a sin of nature rather than of the person, since it is a condition affecting human nature primarily, and only secondarily the persons who are subjects of that nature. As actual sin is an act of the person contrary to the will of God, original sin is a disposition of human nature contrary to the will of God.

But even the defects just listed may not seem to justify the term *sin*. The notions of sin and guilt would seem to be relevant only where there is freedom and personal responsibility. That which a person inherits, and which is present in him prior to any personal act, initiative, or self-determination on his part may be the result of someone else's sin; but how can it be regarded as this person's sin?

In reply, it must be noted first that the term *sin* is used here in an analogous sense. Its primary sense designates an act for which the agent is responsible, as we saw in Chapter 11; original sin is certainly not sin in that sense. It is a *state* rather than an act; a condition which affects a subject who is in no way responsible for it. But it is analogous to actual sin, first of all, because it is an *evil* state, one contrary to God's will for the person. An evil act is sin in the primary sense; this evil state is called sin in an analogous sense. Second, while the subject himself is not personally responsible, there *is* a human responsibility for it, namely, that of Adam. And if we bear in mind the mysterious solidarity that binds the human race together as one, we can say that just as the evil deed performed by my hand is a sin because of the impulse coming from my free will, so by analogy the evil state in which my nature originates is a kind of sin because the impulse to it came from the free will of the one from whom I derive my nature. Perhaps we could go so far as to maintain that the sinful character of our fallen condition does not appear when the individual is considered in isolation but only when he or she is taken in conjunction with the progenitors of the human race.

• *Alienation from God*

This sinfulness can be seen also in the fact of alienation from God. Born without grace, we are thereby strangers to that divine intimacy to which we have been called; so long as we remain in this condition, we are incapable of being admitted into the heavenly realm, which is the complete realization of grace. This alienation is certainly not to be equated with that of the actual sinner who has chosen to turn away from God. Neither does it mean that God withholds his love from the newborn child (it is precisely God's love for sinners that causes him to save them [Romans 5:8]). But it means that birth into human life is no longer entrance into an existence hallowed by grace. Each one must be born anew, "of water and the Holy Spirit," in order to be qualified for intimacy with God (John 3:3-8).

• *Human solidarity*

But why, we ask, should a baby suffer for the sins of its ancestors? And is it not arbitrary that a single mistake by one person should have such devastating consequences for his countless descendants? Such a question may not be fully answerable here below; but at least it should be approached with the awareness that it bears not only on original sin but on the fundamental rationale of human nature. Not only in the matter of sin but in countless other ways our situation and the quality of our life is affected by what has been done by our parents and our ancestors as well as our teachers, leaders, neighbors, and in fact all of our fellows. We can be gravely affected by decisions made in Teheran, Moscow, or Hanoi by people utterly unknown to us.

Among the members of a family, the sense of belonging to one another is perhaps the most powerful force for cohesion in human society. Among the members of a tribe or race, it is strong enough to lead to heroic acts of patriotism. That there is also a deep unity embracing the entire human race, difficult to account for but nonetheless powerful, is sensed by many people, and not just out of Christian motives. (It was the pre-Christian poet Terence who declared, "Nothing human is alien to me.") Solidarity is a fundamental even if mysterious law of humanity. Hence it is not arbitrarily but in accord with the deepest truth of our nature that God treats us as solidary with one another. And it is thanks to this same solidarity that we can all be redeemed by the sacrificial death of Jesus, and formed into one body by his Spirit. If solidarity has led to our woe, it also determines that our ultimate perfection will consist not in the cold contemplation of isolated hermits but in the communion and loving embrace of one another in the City of God, the Heavenly Jerusalem, which is at the same time the Body and Bride of Christ.

• *Genesis 3 and history*

Now we must return to the question raised at the beginning of this chapter: To what extent is a historical reference to be recognized in Genesis 3? Past centuries took for granted that the story of Adam and Eve, including their fall into sin, was entirely historical; but this was never defined as Church doctrine. Today, there is more and more a tendency to assimilate the account to the myths of other primitive peoples. But this can be done in many different ways and degrees. Here we will only suggest some limits within which a faithful interpretation must fall.

On the one hand, the story of the Fall can hardly be regarded as simple history. The obviously symbolic character of the text (the tree of life, the tree of knowledge, God walking in the afternoon breeze, etc.) preclude this. On the other hand, to dismiss the story as a mere product of the myth-making power of the human spirit expressing, for example, the tension between human conscience and concupiscence, is unacceptable to anyone who takes seriously the divine inspiration of Scripture. The story of the Fall is at the very least a teaching addressed to us by God, instructing us about the origin and place of evil in human life.

Between those two extremes is the theory that our text came about by a reworking of ancient Semitic myths in the light of prophetic monotheism. But besides the fact that no comparable myths have actually been found, this view neglects the fact that Genesis 3 speaks not only about God but also about sin. To regard it as the work of a pious Hebrew reflecting on the problem of evil in the light of his monotheistic faith would seem to empty its doctrine on sin of any divine authority. That contemporary myths furnished the idiom employed by the sacred writer is of course a possibility that archaeologists can explore; but it seems essential to hold that Genesis 3 is God's revelation, in story form and symbolic language, of how sin got anchored in our world.

How Genesis 3 relates to the historical event cannot be answered precisely. It would seem necessary to hold at least that the Fall was a real event occurring within human history. That is to say, there was a period of time in which mankind lived in a state of innocence prior to the Fall; and now we are living in a period subsequent to and conditioned by the Fall. There is no way of knowing how long the first period lasted; but obviously the second embraces almost the entirety of human history. (However, Karl Rahner's suggestion[6] that the first period lasted only for a moment or only until the first truly human act, which was also the first sin, seems more like a tactic designed to empty paradise of all practical significance, than a seriously grounded interpretation of it.)

Whether Adam and Eve were the first human couple is a more difficult problem. We do not of course mean whether they called each other by these two Hebrew names, Adam (= "man") and Eve (literally *Hawwah*, of uncertain etymology). The question is whether the doctrine of original sin implies that the entire human race has descended from a single couple. This is the natural sense of both Genesis and St. Paul, and seems to be presupposed by the doctrine that original sin is transmitted by generation, and is universal. Such a position meets resistance from modern evolutionary theory, which is more comfortable with the supposition that the human race developed in a large group of individuals over many generations. However, if the human soul did not emerge by natural evolution out of the purely animal world but resulted from a special creative act (see Chapter 10), this evolutionary objection becomes irrelevant. One might argue that the human race needed to begin as a community rather than as a single couple; but the supposition of a single couple coheres better with the doctrine of original sin.

• *The problem of paradise*

A final problem has to do with the state of the first human beings before the Fall. If death came into the world through Adam's sin, Adam must previously have been immortal. That would seem to imply immunity to illness also. And if human suffering in general is the consequence of sin (Chapter 8), then man and woman in paradise must have been secure from death, illness, and suffering. Theologians of past centuries had no difficulty with such a "paradisiac" state, and they sometimes elaborated lengthily and confidently on the privileged endowments of our first parents. The evolutionary mentality of our time makes many people reluctant to believe that the most primitive human beings were so far superior to their descendants. That in itself is not a decisive theological argument, however; for the divine intervention involved in the creation of the first human beings did not need to be bound by the patterns of evolutionary biology. Nevertheless, the human race is part and parcel of a biological universe in which all life has a limited span. Human life in particular is constantly threatened both by the great carnivores which devour and by the microscopic bacteria and viruses which infect — to say nothing of the discomforts inflicted by mosquitoes, poison ivy, and other noxious things. In such a milieu, is it conceivable that human beings were once immune to sickness, suffering, and death?

This topic undoubtedly needs to be rethought in the light of contemporary biology and paleontology — a vast project that cannot be undertaken here. We may, however, be allowed to suggest a few parameters for the discussion.

• *Church doctrine discreet*

In the first place, it should not be overlooked that the Church's official statements concerning the original human condition have been extremely reserved. About the only point defined is that Adam was afflicted with mortality because of his sin. Even that is being interpreted by some theologians today to mean that Adam's immunity to death did not have to do with biological death but only with the fearful character that death now has for us. But this requires attributing to St. Paul a subtle, spiritualized concept of death which accords ill with the physical realism of his language. And such a view seems manifestly incompatible with the doctrine of Trent cited above. As a minimum therefore, it seems necessary to hold that the original human beings were endowed with immortality.

In the second place, the problem is greatly illumined by St. Thomas's view that Adam's immortality was not natural but the result of a special grace which gave his soul a dominion over the body that his descendants, born without this grace, no longer enjoy. Such a view makes it unnecessary to attribute to Adam a biology different from that of today.

Likewise Adam's initial freedom from concupiscence which, though not defined, seems presupposed by the Council of Trent, is regarded by St. Thomas as the result of grace, not the connatural situation of human nature. This grace would have given Adam an inner harmony undisturbed by unruly appetites but would not have made him essentially different from us. It would also imply, incidentally, that the initial sin could not have been a "sin of the flesh" but must have been spiritual in nature (for example, pride). This suggests that the concupiscence which appeared in mankind thereafter belongs to our natural condition and would have been present in Eden too had Adam not been preserved by grace.[7]

There is no need, moreover, to imagine Adam and Eve as endowed with culture or to picture the Garden of Eden as a special place different in nature from our fields and forests. As the first human beings awakening to consciousness in an otherwise animal world, without benefit of tradition, education, or humane nurture of any sort, our first parents may have received a special divine illumination, which was all the more needful in view of their enormous responsibility as founders of the human race. Such a question is too speculative to be dealt with here; but whatever grace and light were conferred on Adam and Eve need not have been incompatible with the primitive cultural situation of hunters and gatherers or whatever the earliest human beings are presumed to have been.

The absence of suffering in paradise would not necessarily imply that the nature of man and his environment were radically different from what they are now; it suffices to suppose a human nature fully integrated by grace and harmonized with the world around it by a special providence. Human beings obedient to the law of God and of nature would have been free from all the effects of selfishness and immoderation. Healthy, vigorous bodies are naturally capable of resisting many illnesses to which the weak and defective succumb. Wild animals even now have an instinctive fear of man, which perhaps would have been greater had man not degraded his intrinsic dignity by sin. As for those dangers which cannot be avoided by natural human wisdom and virtue — earthquakes, tornadoes, and the like, and perhaps also some of the infectious diseases — one may suppose that a people docile to divine inspiration would have been preserved from them by divine providence.

By the same token, the curse that befell the earth because of Adam's sin need not be understood as some kind of agricultural blight; it would mean simply that labor became repugnant to man through the disorder in man himself. Even today physical labor and intellectual study can be either agreeable or disagreeable, depending on the attitude with which we undertake them. (What we regard as fun on the football field would be denounced as inhuman cruelty if required by a job!) Likewise the pains of childbearing are aggravated or diminished by the psychological state of the mother. It is possible to suppose that, for human beings free from all physical and psychic disorders, such natural functions would not have been painful or disagreeable.[8]

In brief, the paradisiac state need not imply conditions radically alien to those of our familiar world. It supposes only that humanity came into existence bathed in a divine grace that made possible a harmonious and fully integrated physical, psychic, and social development which would have continued up to the moment when people were ready to pass into the life of eternity.

CONCLUSION

The story of Adam and Eve seems to imply that mankind's fall into sin was a historical event but does not give us historical information about it. That sin and all the other evils afflicting human life originated with man, not with God, is the point of the story, not the details and circumstances of the first sin. Moreover, the doctrine of original sin is not a philosophical theory which can be demonstrated by pure reason or which solicits our assent as a fully intelligible and coherent account of the human situation. It is merely a humble, loyal statement of what the Church has learned from the Word of God about some very obscure aspects of our existence. It consists in a few rays of light directed into murky corners, not illumining them completely but indicating something about their dimensions.

236

And difficult though it be to conceptualize, this doctrine corresponds well with the facts of experience. It is not an absurd theory but a realistic declaration about the absurdity abounding in life. Mankind's ruinous proclivity to evil is an obvious fact. Anyone who rejects the doctrine of original sin has got to find some better way to account for the human condition.

Actually, only two such alternatives seem conceivable. One would be to say that sinfulness and suffering are simply part of man's natural condition. But this would make God responsible for our sinfulness (in which case sin loses all meaning), and would make human suffering part of God's design (which can hardly escape the objection that he is a cruel or imperfect creator). Another way would be to say that our troubles arise merely from actual sin, that is, from the wrongs freely and responsibly committed by human beings. But this fails to account for the universality of sin. In fact, such a view would imply that every person has the possibility of leading a sinless, flawless life, if he or she chooses to do so. This goes against all the evidence. It is axiomatic that no human is perfect. If we ever hear it said that someone is perfect, we spontaneously begin watching, confident that flaws will appear. If anyone claims that he himself is faultless, it is usually apparent to others that he is blind to his own defects, and guilty of pride, one of the most hideous defects of all. The view that any human being living under normal conditions of life in this world is capable of avoiding all sin is also clearly contradictory to the teaching of Scripture. "If we say we have committed no sin," writes St. John, "we make him [God] out to be a liar" (1 John 1:10). St. Paul has powerfully elaborated this theme in Romans 2 and 3, where he concludes:

> . . .all have sinned, and fall short of the glory of God, and are justified freely by his grace through the redemption that came by Christ Jesus. (3:23, 24)

• *Evil not part of original divine plan*

The significance of the doctrine of original sin lies chiefly in what it says about the place of evil in human life: namely, that it does not belong to the original divine plan for humanity but results from a disruption of that plan. God's will is always, in the first instance, for our welfare. If sin, suffering, and death have come into the world, this has been *our* doing, not God's. Given the fact of the Fall, God does indeed allow us to suffer as a punishment; but even in that he is acting out of justice and love. By the same token, the evil in the world is not a sign of the failure of divine wisdom but a confirmation of it: for mankind's refusal to be guided by the Creator is what got it into trouble. The doctrine of original sin enables us to maintain, on the one hand, that human nature is good in itself and that nothing truly natural is sinful; and on the other hand, that this nature comes to us in a flawed condition, due to a primordial fall which damaged it at its starting point.

Moreover, the wisdom of God has triumphed over the evil by not allowing it to ruin the divine plan utterly but rather incorporating it into a new plan, that of Redemption, in which suffering becomes the matter of sacrifice and thereby the expression of love and the means of a newer and more intimate union with God.

The doctrine of original sin ought never to be separated in our minds from the doctrine of Redemption. The first "theologian" to declare plainly the devastating effects of Adam's sin was St. Paul, who did so only to bring out the even more overwhelming grace of the Second Adam. As will be made clear in Chapter 20, despite the long road which history required to get from Eden to Calvary, there was never a time or place in which the saving grace of Christ was unavailable to the sinful offspring of Adam.

PART 4
Christ the Redeemer

Up to now, we have been examining the condition of mankind in its relationship with God. Our considerations have had a universal character, having to do with the religious and moral situation of all human beings. Now, however, we begin a very different sort of inquiry, one which is essentially historical. In the next two chapters we will be looking at the origin and development of the Hebrew people, culminating in the life of Jesus. We will be concerned with individual human beings and the experiences of a particular nation. We do this of course because they are of universal interest; it is for the sake of all mankind that God spoke and acted through Abraham, Moses, the prophets, and finally Jesus, his Son. Nevertheless, the concrete, historical character of the material we are now about to take up makes it quite different from what has been treated up till now.

Christianity is intrinsically historical. It is not a theory or a vision of the world that could be abstracted from the individuals who formulated it. It entails the belief that God has really intervened in history, through designated spokesmen and concrete events brought about and directed by him; that he has thereby revealed himself and offered his grace to us. Furthermore, being a Christian means involving oneself through faith with the historical personage, Jesus of Nazareth. An ahistorical Christianity is self-contradictory.

In treating the story of the Fall, we saw that it is legitimate to raise the question whether this text should not be regarded as myth. We pointed out some of the difficulties which such an approach would involve and the limits that would have to be observed if it were used. But when dealing with the properly historical part of the Old Testament, namely, that which begins with Genesis 12, the notion of myth must be excluded. To introduce this notion there would be, in effect, to say that God did not really call Abraham and promise him an offspring and a land; likewise that he did not speak to Moses on Mt. Sinai and give him the Law, etc. While it can be granted that the imagination of later generations has colored the accounts of these events, it is of the essence of Christian (and Hebrew) faith that God has really intervened in history. To apply the notion of myth to the great events that are foundational in the shaping of the People of God is not to reinterpret Christianity but to reject it.

One might be tempted to suppose that, while the historicity of the New Testament, at least in its essential lines, must be maintained, the Old Testament (the stories of which are much more embarrassing) could be treated as myth. This does not work at all. The activity of Jesus is inseparable from the history of Israel. He did not come as a radical innovator, founding something absolutely new, with no roots in the past. All four Gospels point out that Jesus fulfilled the prophecies of the Old Testament. Matthew in particular reiterates again and again, "This was to fulfill what was spoken through the prophet Isaiah. . ." (Matthew 12:17; see also 1:22; 2:5, 15, 17, 23; 3:3; etc.). Apologists of the past have no doubt exaggerated in creating the notion that the prophets foretold in detail all that

Jesus did and said. Without resorting to such a crude simplification, we must acknowledge that the New Testament insists on its own profound continuity and correspondence with the Old. To deny the historicity of the Old would therefore undermine the New. Thus Jesus instituted a New Covenant in his blood (1 Corinthians 11:25; see also Luke 22:20; Mark 14:14; Matthew 26:28) to replace that which Moses solemnized with the blood of the sacrificial victims (Exodus 24:4-8). How substantial is the meaning of the New Covenant if the Old was not a fact? Above all, Jesus came to fulfill the promises made to the Fathers, particularly Abraham (Luke 1:54-55; 1:72f; Rom 91:4f; etc.). What remains to the fulfillment if the promise was only a myth?

• *Popular history*

The narrative which begins in Genesis 12 with the story of Abraham is, to be sure, popular history. This means that it is simplified and colored by the perspectives of those who transmitted it orally, sometimes for centuries, before it was committed to writing. It is full of omissions, confusions, and maladjustments as various traditions and documents are brought together into one. But its main lines and great, substantive events are historical. For example, the migration of Abram, first from Ur to Haran and thence to the land of Canaan, can be traced on a map (Figure 6), and situated roughly between 2000 and 1500 B.C. The exact date is debated, as is likewise the date of the Exodus, but this kind of debate is normal concerning the events of ancient history. There is enough archaeological evidence to convince most scholars that the Exodus took place around the thirteenth century B.C., but whether the pharaoh "who knew not Joseph" should be identified as Seti I or Ramses II can be argued either way. It is fairly sure that David's reign began not long after 1000 B.C., and from then on most of the kings of Judah and Israel can be dated rather accurately. The great powers of Egypt, Babylon, Assyria, Persia, and Syria, whose titanic struggles constantly threatened the precarious existence of tiny Israel, are well known to us. There are even occasional references to the Hebrew people in the records of Egypt and Assyria. Archaeological research has uncovered countless confirmations of the biblical record. Even those who regard many details of the Old Testament as fabulous recognize that the account as a whole belongs to the domain of history.

To say that the story of Israel is history, however, is not to affirm that every narrative in it conveys historical fact. We have already seen, in Chapter 6, that the Hebrews included poetry, fable, legend, etc., in their sacred literature, just as other ancient peoples did. Often it may be hard to tell whether a given element of their folklore belongs to history or to fable. Few people would be inclined to take literally the account of Jacob getting spotted lambs by placing striped poles where the sheep would see them at breeding time (Genesis 30:37ff); or that of Samson losing his strength when Delilah cut his hair (Judges 16:17f)! In other cases, the distinction between historical fact and folk legend will be much more delicate to make, and the disagreements often impossible to resolve. But this too is normal in matters of history, and it merely confirms what we have seen already, that the story of the Hebrew people, like that of other ancient peoples, was preserved in the mode of popular history.

GEOGRAPHY OF THE OLD TESTAMENT

6

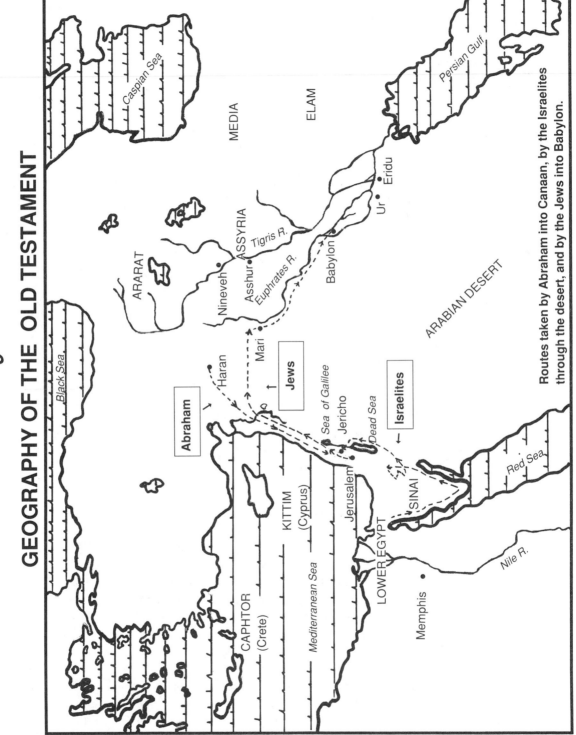

Caspian Sea

Black Sea

ARARAT

MEDIA

ELAM

Persian Gulf

Nineveh

Asshur

ASSYRIA

Tigris R.

Euphrates R.

Babylon

Ur

Eridu

Haran

Mari

Abraham

Jews

Sea of Galilee

Jericho

Dead Sea

Israelites

ARABIAN DESERT

CAPHTOR
(Crete)

KITTIM
(Cyprus)

Mediterranean Sea

Jerusalem

SINAI

LOWER EGYPT

Red Sea

Memphis

Nile R.

Routes taken by Abraham into Canaan, by the Israelites
through the desert, and by the Jews into Babylon.

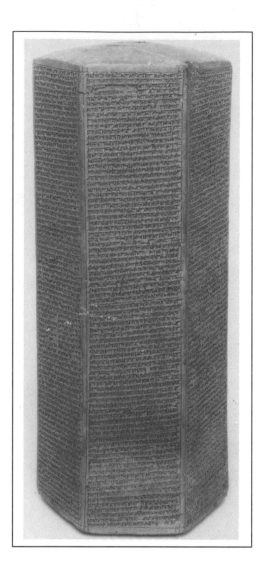

Sennacherib's prism is a monument inscribed with the exploits of the Assyrian king's expedition into Canaan. He boasts of having destroyed forty-six cities of Judah, laid waste the land, and carried off hordes of prisoners and booty. "As for Hezekiah of the land of Judah, who had not submitted to my yoke . . . I shut him up in Jerusalem, his royal city, like a bird in a cage." We read in 2 Kings 18 and 19 how Sennacherib laid siege to Jerusalem but failed to take it. — Photo courtesy of the British Museum

• *Faith-history*

Having insisted that the Old Testament is genuine history, we must add that it is history written *in* faith and *for* faith, and it is in this perspective that we will be examining it. We are not doing history as such or even the history of the Hebrew people for its own sake; rather, we are examining the Old Testament as background for the New.

To the eyes of faith, the events of history — especially of salvation history — have a meaning. In Scripture, aspects which are meaningful for faith are brought out; others are neglected. This does not mean that faith falsifies, fabricates, or distorts but that the narrator's point of view gives his tale a design different from what it would have if the same events were recounted by someone without this faith.

Thus, for example, the tradition that the Hebrew people are all descended from Abraham is questioned by some historians, who suggest that other Semitic peoples came to be incorporated into the little band led by Joshua. Other historians argue that, instead of one Exodus led by Moses, there were several migrations of Hebrews from Egypt into Canaan; or that the notion of the "Twelve tribes of Israel" is only an idealization never actually realized in history. These are legitimate and interesting historical questions, but they need not occupy us. We can consider what Abraham and Moses mean in the perspective of faith without getting into such questions, and without meaning to prejudice them either. Often the faith-meaning of persons and events is comparatively simple and sure, whereas the theories proposed by historians tend to be conjectural and are often impossible to prove.

In sum, we will be dealing with history not as historians but as theologians and people of faith — Christian faith. We will treat only those elements of the Old Testament indispensable for understanding the New. We will refer to the more objective views of modern history where this is useful and can be done readily but without excessive concern to determine what is historical fact and what is more the artistry of Hebrew tradition interpreting the facts.

15

Israel, the preparation for Christ

Since we are attempting to survey the great lines of the Christian vision as simply and briefly as possible, there is a strong temptation to omit the Old Testament. It is long and complex, hard to assimilate into a simple vision with broad outlines. And since the New Covenant has replaced the Old, we may imagine that the latter has been completely invalidated. The truth is, however, that the New springs out of the Old like a flower from its stalk, and is unintelligible without it. Jesus is indeed the shoot which comes forth from the stump of Jesse (Isaiah 11:1). The most basic formula of Christian faith affirms that "Jesus is the Christ." This means that he fulfills the messianic expectations of Israel. Without some knowledge of those expectations, and therefore of the history in which they were rooted, you cannot understand the meaning of that profession of faith. "Do not think that I have come to abolish the Law or the Prophets," Jesus himself declared. "I have not come to abolish them but to fulfill them. I tell you the truth, until heaven and earth disappear, not the smallest letter, not the least stroke of a pen, will by any means disappear from the Law until everything is accomplished" (Matthew 5:17f). Finally, Christians today are still "children of Abraham" (Galatians 3:7), looking forward expectantly to the fulfillment of the promises made to their ancient Hebrew father.

Moreover, the Old Testament retains for all time its intrinsic value as a revelation of God. For, as we have already noted (Chapter 5), God has revealed himself, especially his incredible grace and mercy, his enduring concern for the welfare of his people, and his fidelity to the Covenant, not so much in words as in deeds. The life of Jesus is indeed the chief of these revelatory deeds; but the centuries-long history of the Hebrew people adds a richness and color that help us to appreciate the incomprehensible grace revealed to us in Jesus, while the significance of the Old Testament revelations is enhanced in the light of their fulfillment in Jesus.

The story of Israel is, moreover, a revelation of the Church. There is a tendency of scholars today to claim that the Church was not founded by Jesus but sprang up on the initiative of his disciples. This view is motivated largely by the fact that Jesus seldom spoke explicitly about the Church as such. The truth, however, is almost at the opposite extreme. Jesus did not need to found the Church as something wholly new, because it had already been founded in the People of Israel. The Church is the flowering and prolongation of that people which God had formed for himself through Abraham and Moses, and which he has renewed through Jesus Christ. Jesus had only to retouch, gently but radically, what was already there, in giving it a new Spirit and a new covenant.

The history of Israel is also very instructive for the practical life of each individual. It is a divinely written paradigm, one composed in living letters of flesh and blood, of the interaction between God and humanity. St. Paul says, in reference to the Israelites, "These things happened to them as an example and were written down as warnings for us, on whom the fulfillment of the ages has come" (1 Corinthians 20:22). In the story of the Hebrew people, in their very flesh, we learn how God calls people, instructs, teaches, and blesses them, how they get into trouble when they wander away from him, how they delay their own fulfillment when they resist him, how he punishes yet also pardons and saves them. Only God can write a book in the very lives of people. This he has done in Israel, and the saints of the New Covenant have ever since found in the Old Testament a true sourcebook of instruction.

• *Salvation history*

The story of Israel, like that of Jesus Christ from which it is inseparable, is called *salvation history*. When rightly understood, this does not mean that the grace of God (who "wants all men to be saved" [1 Timothy 2:4]) is inoperative in the rest of human history or unavailable to the rest of mankind. But it means that God has brought about the salvation of mankind through particular individuals, and concretely through the children of Abraham, from whom is sprung Jesus, the Christ. "Salvation is from the Jews" (John 4:22).

The history of Israel, taken together with its culmination in Jesus, is salvific not only in the sense that it recounts the steps in the process by which salvation was brought about but also in the sense that when we contemplate this history with faith we thereby participate in the grace which it mediates. The revelation of grace that God makes through Israel and Jesus is not a theoretical message addressed simply to our minds — a kind of supernatural philosophy. It is the actual proffering of grace; when we open our souls to this revelation, we receive this grace.

• *God's Chosen People*

The promise made to Abraham and the Covenant given through Moses are the root of the idea of Israel as "God's Chosen People." It was a common thing for primitive peoples to believe that they were in a special relationship with some particular deity who was their heavenly patron; but Israel is the only race known to history which claimed to have been bonded in a special way with the one God, the Creator and Lord of the universe.[1] The prophets will amplify this notion: Israel has been allied with God by a unique covenant and appointed to be his servant, the bearer of his promise, and the witness to his glory. The prophets will also insist that it was not because of their own merits that the Hebrews had been chosen:

> You are a people holy to Yahweh, your God. Yahweh your God has chosen you out of all the peoples on the face of the earth to be his people, his treasured possession. Yahweh did not set his affection on you and choose you because you were more numerous than any other peoples, for you were the fewest of all peoples. But it was because Yahweh loved you and kept the oath he swore to your forefathers. . . . He is the faithful God, keeping his covenant of love to a thousand generations of those who love him and keep his commands. (Deuteronomy 7:6-9)

The modern mind, with its universalist outlook, is repelled by the idea that the God of the universe should single out a particular race as his special people.[2] It dismisses the idea derisively as a myth born of tribal parochialism and chauvinism. It can be answered of course that Israel was chosen not just for its own profit but for a universal mission. It was a messianic people, called to be God's witness and the bearer of his saving message to all the earth.

But the crucial issue is whether it is conceivable that God should make particular choices among his creatures. Here it is essential to recognize that choice is the characteristic act of a free person. If we believe that God is personal, we must be prepared to find him making choices. There can be no objection to them on principle but only from the pressure of a latent unwillingness to accept the personality of God with all its consequences.

A second root of this objection lies in the pseudo-democratic conviction that God must treat everyone alike. For him to choose someone for a special role, a special grace, or a special trial strikes many people as unfair. But it would be an enormous anthropomorphism to apply to God the same standards that apply to elected officials or to the umpire in a ball game. God has not been appointed to carry out the will of creatures; he is the Absolute Lord of all. As St. Paul says, "Does not the potter have the right to make out of the same lump of clay some pottery for noble purposes and some for common use?" (Romans 9:21). Likewise we have no "equal rights" that God is bound to respect. It is from him that we have all our rights as well as all that we have and are. As he destines one flower to be a rose and another a daisy or one animal to be a lion and another a mouse, so he destines various persons for various roles in the world. Our rights come *from* the nature and destiny he has given us, and do not precede them. This does not mean that he is an arbitrary despot. He plans all things with wisdom and love. His justice means that he treats us as we deserve; but what we deserve depends on how well we carry out the role he has assigned us. We have no claim over him prior to his free plan for us.

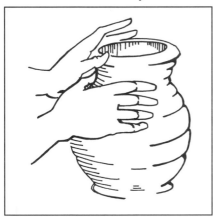

• *The structural texts of the Old Testament*

The following passages will give an acquaintance with the main events of the Old Testament needed for an understanding of the mission of Jesus:

1. The story of Abraham (Genesis 12-24)
    a. The call and promise of God (12)
    b. Abraham's faith (15)
    c. The Covenant of Circumcision (17)
    d. The birth of Isaac (21:1-7)
    e. The sacrifice of Isaac (22)
2. Moses: deliverance and covenant (Exodus)
    a. The call and mission of Moses (3, 4)
    b. The departure from Egypt and crossing of the sea (13:17-22; 14)

c. Mt. Sinai (19, 20): Covenant, Law, and Sacrifice (24:3-8)
3. King David (1 and 2 Samuel)
   a. Israel demands a human king (1 Samuel 8)
   b. Saul is rejected and David anointed (1 Samuel 15, 16)
   c. David promised a son who will reign forever (2 Samuel 7)
4. The Babylonian Captivity and its prophetic interpretation
   a. Prophecy of the punishment of sinful Israel (Jeremiah 5)
   b. Captivity of Judea and destruction of Jerusalem (2 Kings 24, 25; begin with the last two verses of Chapter 23)
   c. Promise of comfort and a New Covenant (Jeremiah 31, especially 31-34)
   d. Promise of a new heart and a new spirit (Ezekiel 36, especially 22f)
   e. The dry bones revived (Ezekiel 37:1-14)
   f. Cyrus sends the exiles back to Jerusalem (Ezra 1)
   g. Daniel's vision of the Son of Man and his everlasting Kingdom (Daniel 7)

ABRAHAM

The history of Israel is set in the land of Canaan — a tiny strip at the eastern end of the Mediterranean. This was almost a no-man's-land between Egypt and Mesopotamia — the two great powers of the ancient Near East. The existence of Israel was always conditioned by the activities of these two giants between which it lived precariously. Like froth on the windshield between two wipers sweeping alternately back and forth, it was forever on the verge of being wiped out, with no one but its God to sustain it.

The story of Israel, and in fact the whole of salvation history, begins with Abraham — whose original name was Abram. What comes before him in the Book of Genesis is only a preface, setting him in perspective. Abram's family was Mesopotamian. From Ur, one of the most ancient cities in the world, near the mouth of the Euphrates, they migrated north to Haran, perhaps in the nineteenth century B.C.

• *Migration to Canaan*

Archaeologists have discovered indications of kinship between the two cities of Ur and Haran that give a remarkable confirmation to this journey, and archaeology can give us scattered glimpses of the conditions under which nomadic herdsmen like Abram pursued their painful and perilous existence. But archaeology cannot do what the Book of Genesis does, disclosing the inner motive and theological meaning of Abram's second migration, which took him from Mesopotamia into the predestined land of Canaan:

Yahweh had said to Abram, "Leave your country, your people and your father's household and go to the land I will show you. I will make you into a great nation and I will bless you; I will make your name great, and you will be a blessing. I will bless those who bless you, and whoever curses you I will curse; and all peoples on earth will be blessed through you." (12:1-3)

• *God speaks to man*

Here God speaks to man. It is not like the enlightenment of a buddha, attained by the human effort of asceticism and meditation. It is God who speaks to Abram, not Abram who attains an insight into God. And what Abram receives is not some universal truth about the divine but a concrete, particular summons to an individual destiny. This is truly a *word*. Whether Abram heard it with his ears or experienced it interiorly is of no importance; it is speech in the sense of a free communication from one person to another, as contrasted with insight (which a person can have all by himself) or the kind of revelation that can be experienced by anyone anywhere contemplating nature. Those who label this account as mythical would say, at most, that Abram had an insight or, at the least, that an interpretation was put on his voyage by the narrator. Either interpretation dissolves the implication of this passage, that God took the initiative and communicated to Abram a message that nature could not impart. If there was no true word from God, there is nothing but illusion at the basis of the whole hope of Israel and of Christian faith.

• *The call*

God *called* Abram. He summoned him to a new destiny, not foreseen by himself, not imposed on him by events, but proposed by the Creator for his free acceptance. This first call, addressed to the patriarch of Israel, initiates a pattern that God will use in dealing with his people ever afterward. He called Isaiah and Jeremiah to be his prophets. Jesus called his disciples to come and follow him. Every Christian life originates in a personal call from the God who calls us "by name." Within the Christian life, there are more particular callings: for example, to the priesthood or to the religious state. (The term *vocation* properly means call, but its deep sense has been smudged and weakened by a usage that applies it to whatever a person does for a living.)

God called Abram *out of his own country*. He was inviting him into a better land, and to a much finer destiny; but first Abram had to let go of, to separate himself from, what he already had. This demanded immense trust. This aspect too is a type of the way people have been called ever since. The summons formulated by Isaiah 52:11 is applied by St. Paul to the whole Christian people: "Come out from them, and be separate, says the Lord" (2 Corinthians 6:17; see also Apocalypse 18:4).

• *The promise*

God's call was associated with a promise. In place of the land of his fathers, Abram would be given a new land — the one to which God would lead him. Moreover, he was promised a numerous offspring — that which a man of those days desired more than anything else. A man's sons were his security, his strength, and the only form of immortality to which he could aspire. This twofold promise is the taproot of the entire Hebrew and Christian religion. Israel was essentially a religion of hope, oriented to that future when the promises of God would be fulfilled. Christianity, while marked by faith that the promises have already been fulfilled radically in the person of Jesus, continues to look forward in hope toward the complete fulfillment. This Christian hope remains a prolongation and refinement of that which arose four thousand years earlier in the heart of the "wandering Aramaean" who became the patriarch of the Hebrew people. What we have to see in this and the following chapters is how the initial promise made to Abram was enriched, deepened, and concretized in the history of Israel and the preaching of Jesus.

• *Faith*

God's promise required faith of Abram: not simply some strong inner conviction arising from an unknown source but deliberate, conscious belief in the Word of God which had come to him — belief that God would keep his word.

> By faith Abraham, when called to go to a place he would later receive as his inheritance, obeyed and went, even though he did not know where he was going. By faith he made his home in the promised land like a stranger in a foreign country; he lived in tents, as did Isaac and Jacob, who were heirs with him of the same promise. For he was looking forward to the city with foundations, whose architect and builder is God.
> By faith Abraham, even though he was past age — and Sarah herself was barren — was enabled to become a father because he considered him faithful who had made the promise. And so from this one man, and he as good as dead, came descendants as numerous as the stars in the sky and as countless as the sand on the seashore.
> All these people were still living by faith when they died. They did not receive the things promised; they only saw them and welcomed them from a distance. And they admitted that they were aliens and strangers on earth. (Hebrews 11:8-13)

Today we can hardly conceive of the immense faith which it must have taken for a man to depart from his father's house and go into a strange land. There was no geography and no newspaper to inform a person about distant places, no police to guard the way, no concept of personal rights to give any assurance against being victimized by the natives. But Abram went, with his wife, his nephew, his herdsmen and flocks, into the land of Canaan. There were towns there — at Hebron, Beersheba, and Bethel, for example — with which Abram had some contact; but mostly he pastured his sheep and goats in the semidesert of the Negeb. The faith with which he responded to the promise of God was tested as the years passed and no child was born to his wife, Sarah. But God renewed his promise, and the earliest text of the Bible in which faith is actually named, says: "Abram believed Yahweh, and he [Yahweh] credited it to him [Abram] as righteousness" (Genesis 15:6).

• *Sacrifice of Isaac*

Eventually, when Abram was a hundred years old and Sarah ninety(!), their son, Isaac, was born. But the faith of the man now renamed Abraham ("a father of many nations" [Genesis 17:5]) still had to be tested again. God commanded him to take his son, the one in whom all his hopes were now vested, and offer him in sacrifice. In the supreme demonstration of his reliance on the inscrutable designs of God, Abraham set off to the mountain of sacrifice. As they trudged along, the boy asked, "The fire and the wood are here, but where is the lamb for the burnt offering?" "God himself will provide the lamb for a burnt offering," replied the stricken father. In fact, at the crucial moment, an angel of God withheld Abraham from slaying his son, and pointed to a ram that should be offered instead (Genesis 22). Thus did Abraham become for all subsequent generations the type of faith in God. And thus did Israel learn to celebrate God as faithful — one who keeps his word.

MOSES

In giving Abraham a son, Isaac, God had kept his word; but his promise was not yet completely fulfilled. A few hundred years later, Abraham's descendants had grown very numerous, but they did not yet possess the land of Canaan which God had promised them. Famine drove them into Egypt, where they found themselves an enslaved race, conscripted into hard labor. It is quite plausible that the grandiose building projects of the Pharaoh Ramses II (1290-1224 B.C.) were the occasion of their affliction.[3] When their misery had reached its depths, God raised up another leader to deliver them. Moses, a man of the tribe of Levi but educated as an Egyptian, had, while defending another Hebrew, slain an Egyptian. On this account he had to flee into the wilderness of Midian, in the Sinai peninsula, where he worked as a shepherd for the priest Jethro. While tending the flocks on Mt. Horeb (Mt. Sinai), he saw a bush that was on fire without being burnt up. Out of it, God called to him and declared:

> I have indeed seen the misery of my people in Egypt. I have heard them crying out because of their slave drivers, and I am concerned about their suffering. So I have come down to rescue them from the hand of the Egyptians and to bring them up out of that land into a good and spacious land, a land flowing with milk and honey. . . .(Exodus 3:7f)

Here the God of the Promise becomes the Savior God. Here, a new divine quality is manifested: that of compassion and mercy. Seeing the affliction of his people, God comes to their rescue. He also shows himself to be a God of power: "with a strong hand and an outstretched arm" (Psalm 136:12, RSV), he is going to deliver them from their powerful oppressor.

• *Mediator between God and man*

But he is going to do this through an intermediary. Up to now, God has dealt with individuals directly; Moses is the first true mediator between God and the people to appear in Scripture. From this point on, faith in the God of Israel will involve a collateral faith in his human representatives. Moses is not a natural leader; he was "very meek, more than all the men that were on the face of the earth" (Numbers 12:3, RSV). He was afraid of the mission the Lord gave him, and objected that he was not a very good speaker. But God insisted and so Moses, with his brother Aaron as spokesman, went back into Egypt.

To convince the Hebrews that the God of their ancestors had sent him, and to induce the pharaoh to let the people go, Moses was given a series of miraculous signs. What are we to make of these spectacular deeds, especially the ten plagues with which the Egyptians were afflicted? Presumably they have been exaggerated and dramatized in the course of being recited over and over again down through the centuries. Rationalist expositions dismiss them as mere legend; but this would seem irreconcilable with the sacred seriousness of the narrative. Ingenious attempts have been made to reduce them to natural phenomena — for example, a flooding of the Nile, leading to a great multiplication of mosquitoes and the consequent spread of a succession of diseases.[4] Such explanations, however, seem contrived and ultimately implausible. We can retain from the Exodus account the fact that God gave some marvelous signs to establish the credibility of his emissary, Moses; but a concrete image of "what actually happened" seems quite beyond our reach today.

• *The Exodus*

In any case, the Hebrews escaped from their servitude. After the most famous of the miracles, in which the Hebrews crossed the Red Sea dryshod, while their Egyptian pursuers were swallowed up in the waves, we read that "Israel saw the great work which

Yahweh did against the Egyptians, and the people feared Yahweh; and they believed in Yahweh and in his servant Moses" (Exodus 14:31, RSV).

Moses led the people back to the holy mountain where God had first spoken to him, and there, amid thunder, lightning, and smoke, occurred the great theophany which became the foundation of the covenant between God and his people. Moses went up the mountain to hear God's word, while the others remained terrified below. God said to Moses:

> You yourselves have seen what I did to Egypt, and how I carried you on eagles' wings and brought you to myself. Now if you obey me fully and keep my covenant, then out of all nations you will be my treasured possession. Although the whole earth is mine, you will be for me a kingdom of priests and a holy nation. (Exodus 19:4f)

• *The Covenant*

Already in dealing with Abraham, God had made a covenant; however, not until Sinai is there a covenant with the people as such. This solemn pact could be summarized in the words "I will be your God and you will be my people"

251

(Jeremiah 7:23; Ezekiel 11:20; Hosea 2:25; etc.). By the covenant, God pledged to be the protector and avenger of Israel, while they for their part promised to honor him and keep his law. This law, articulated in the Ten Commandments (Exodus 20:1-17), was supplemented by many other laws and prescriptions added in the course of Israel's history.

The Covenant of Sinai was ratified by a solemn sacrifice, in which Moses took the blood of oxen and other animals and threw it against the altar he had erected at the foot of the mountain. Then he read the "Book of the Covenant" to the people, who responded, "Everything that Yahweh said to us we will do, and we will be obedient." Finally Moses sprinkled the rest of the blood on the people themselves, declaring, "This is the blood of the covenant that Yahweh has made with you in accordance with all these words" (Exodus 24:3-8). Jesus alludes to this at the Last Supper when he calls his blood "the blood of the covenant" (Matthew 26:28; Mark 14:24) or "the new covenant in my blood" (Luke 22:20; 1 Corinthians 11:25).

• *God's name*

God's sacred name, *Yahweh*, is also to be associated with the Covenant, even though it had been given to Moses earlier, at the burning bush. The meaning of this name is much debated, and many different interpretations have been proposed, nearly all of which have to do with the idea of *being*, or *existence*. The traditional understanding, "He who is," is as probable as any other. What is significant, however, is not the meaning of this term but the fact that God gave his name to his people as a sign of their intimate relationship with him.

• *"Jehovah"*

Originally, only consonants were written in Hebrew; hence the sacred name was spelled YHWH or JHVH (in Hebrew, Y and J are the same letter; so likewise W and V). But reverence for the divine name grew to such a point that eventually the Jews avoided pronouncing it, instead reading "the Lord" *(adonai)*

 wherever *Yahweh* occurred in the text. When eventually the vowels came to be written, the scribes replaced the vowels of *Yahweh* with those of *Adonai*, as a reminder to the reader not to pronounce the word that was written but to say "the Lord" instead. For reasons too technical to be explained here, these vowels were construed as *e-o-a*, thus producing the form *Jehovah*. In time, the reason for this was forgotten, and Jehovah came to be regarded as God's proper name. It is still used, for example, in the King James version, but this is simply a mistaken form of Yahweh.

Whether the Israelites were already true monotheists at this date is debatable. Many indications suggest that they simply regarded Yahweh as their special god, just as other people had theirs; and that only later on, through the teaching of the prophets, this faith was gradually converted into strict monotheism. At any rate, they were forbidden to venerate any gods besides Yahweh — a discipline which differentiated them from all their neighbors, who generally took care to placate foreign gods as well as their own. Another striking difference about the Hebrews is that they were forbidden to make graven images of their God. This was probably a primitive way of teaching them that there is nothing in all creation that can represent him.[5]

Instead of images, the Israelites had, as their sacred symbol, the "Ark of the Covenant." This was simply a wooden chest containing the stone tablets on which the Law was engraved (Deuteronomy 10:1-5). It was kept in the "Tent of Meeting," where Moses went at times to consult God, and where God often manifested his presence in the form of a luminous cloud that settled over the Tent (Exodus 40:34-38; Numbers 11:25; 12:5; etc.).

• *The desert*

The Sinai experience can be said to have constituted Israel as a people — God's Chosen People. The first part of the promise made to Abraham was thereby fulfilled. However, they still did not have the land which God had promised, and the next great chapter in their history comprises their journey to the Promised Land. Through the desert  they went under the direction of God (Exodus 40:36ff) who on occasion provided water for them to drink (Exodus 17:2-7; Numbers 20:2-13) and a mysterious food, manna, for them to eat (Exodus 16:14-35). They went directly to the frontiers of Canaan; but frightened by the size of the Canaanites, they were unwilling to go further, and rebelled against the leadership of Moses. For this loss of faith, God condemned them to spend forty years in the desert until all the rebels had died off (Numbers 14). Here is a living parable of the Christian people, on its way to the Promised Land of heaven, called to live by faith in the God who leads, nourishes, and protects them but ever tempted to unbelief and rebellion, which in fact lead to detours, delays, and difficulties.

• *Conquest of Canaan*

Under Joshua, Moses' successor, the Israelites entered the land of Canaan and began to subdue it, beginning with the miraculous conquest of the city of Jericho (Joshua 6). With the occupation of this "land flowing with milk and honey," the second half of God's promise to Abraham was fulfilled, namely, the land of Canaan for his offspring to dwell in. However, this schematic view of things glosses over the fact that both the formation of the people of Israel, and their occupation of Canaan, were very gradual, complex processes. Moreover, each fulfillment of the prophecy was imperfect and incomplete, leaving a still further and better fulfillment yet to be realized. Thus Israel remained a people of hope. Their hope was forever based on the promises made to Father Abraham; but the shape of their expectations was gradually refined and concretized through the events of their history and through the teaching of the prophets who interpreted that history. We must now note a few high points of that history and its interpretation.

DAVID

• *The judges*

One of the developments that gave new form and color to the expectations of Israel was the rise of the monarchy. The "twelve tribes of Israel" that settled in the land of Canaan did not originally have a unified existence under a single ruler. They led their separate lives, warring with one another as well as with the Canaanite peoples, being only loosely bound together by a sense of kinship and by a common faith in Yahweh. Some of them merged with others and some split into distinct tribes, so that even the expression *twelve tribes* is probably a simplified idealization rather than a report on the abiding structure of the confederation. Their leadership came from "judges" — men stirred up by the Spirit of Yahweh in moments of need. Samson, Gideon, and Jephthah as well as the prophetess Deborah are the most famous of these transitory military leaders, around whom one or a few tribes rallied for as long as necessary to meet a crisis. Their exploits are recounted in the Book of Judges.

The idea of adopting a king in imitation of their Canaanite neighbors occurred at times to the Israelites. After Gideon had won a spectacular victory over the Midianites — fearsome bedouins who rode in on camels to harass the Israelite settlements — several of the tribes asked him to rule over them. He replied, "I will not rule over you, nor will my son rule over you; Yahweh will rule over you" (Judges 8:23). Gideon's son Abimelech succeeded by cruelty and cunning in having himself recognized as king; but his reign ended in three years with his untimely death (Judges 9:53). Meanwhile, a powerful new threat to Israel was developing: the Philistines, a race that came from "across the sea" and settled on the Mediterranean coast about the same time that the Israelites, coming up from Egypt, were settling in the highlands. More powerful than the native Canaanite peoples, and equipped with chariots, which the Hebrews lacked, as well as weapons of iron, which were then relatively new, they almost succeeded in subjugating the Hebrew tribes; instead, they drove them to monarchy.

The aging prophet Samuel was at that time widely accepted as judge in Israel. To him the elders of the tribes came, demanding that he appoint a king over them. Displeased at this, Samuel prayed to Yahweh about it, and received the reply:

> Listen to all that the people are saying to you; it is not you they have rejected as their king, but me. (1 Samuel 8:7)

Samuel therefore anointed Saul king over Israel. Although at first blessed by God and filled with the Spirit of God, Saul fell from grace and was defeated by the Philistines at Gilboa (1 Samuel 31). His successor, David, whose reign began about 1000 B.C., is the greatest royal figure in the history of Israel. He conquered the Philistines and the other enemies, and in doing so united the Israelites themselves into a single kingdom — the most powerful nation between Egypt and Assyria. It was under him that Jerusalem became the capital city. David was also renowned as a musician, and the Psalms — at least the earliest of them — are traditionally ascribed to him.

• *David plans a temple*

But the most memorable event in David's career, so far as his place in salvation history is concerned, was a project he never realized — that of building a temple. Since the  events of Mt. Sinai, the Ark of the Covenant had been the focal point of Hebrew worship (although there were periods when it fell into neglect). When David established his capital at Jerusalem, he had the Ark of the Covenant brought there, thus making the city the religious as well as the political center of the kingdom. At this time, the Ark was still housed in a tent, just as it had been during the wanderings of the Hebrews in the desert. The people themselves had by now for the most part abandoned their old tents for permanent houses of stone or mud brick. After subduing his enemies, David conceived the idea of building a temple for the Ark. When he spoke of this to the prophet Nathan, the latter returned with the following reply from Yahweh:

You are not the one to build me a house to dwell in. I have not dwelt in a house from the day I brought Israel up out of Egypt to this day. . . .

Yahweh will build a house for you: When your days are over and you go to be with your fathers, I will raise up your offspring to succeed you, one of your own sons, and I will establish his kingdom. He is the one who will build a house for me, and I will establish his throne forever. I will be his father, and he will be my son. I will never take my love away from him, as I took it away from your predecessor. I will set him over my house and my kingdom forever; his throne will be established forever. (1 Chronicles 17:4-14; see also 2 Samuel 7:5-16)

• *"Son of David"*

David is not to build Yahweh a house; but his generous intention will be rewarded by having Yahweh build him a house, that is to say, a household, a dynasty. Centuries earlier, God had promised Abraham offspring more numerous than the stars in the sky or the sands on the seashore; now to David, another shepherd who had become a king, God promises a royal lineage that will continue forever, and never be driven from the throne of Israel.

This promise is echoed in many other texts of the Old Testament, which glorify and magnify the "Son of David" until he begins to take on more than human dimensions. Yahweh proclaims:

I have found David my servant; with my sacred oil I have anointed him. . . . His line will continue forever, and his throne endure before me like the sun; it will be established forever like the moon, the faithful witness in the sky. (Psalm 89:20, 29, 36f)

The literal son of David who succeeded his father on the throne was Solomon (circa 961-922 B.C.). Taking advantage of the unity, strength, and peace which his father had brought to the kingdom, Solomon undertook to glorify his realm in a visible way. Importing craftsmen, cedar logs, and other materials from Hiram, the king of Phoenicia, and from many other sources, he undertook a vast building program, supported by an industry in wood, stone, and copper. Remnants of the cities built or reconstructed by his workmen have been unearthed by modern archaeologists, and their size and engineering is impressive. His greatest achievement was the Temple in Jerusalem, magnificently constructed and lavishly ornamented, the pride of the people of Israel. It gradually became the focal point of Israelite worship.

• *Kingdom divided*

But the heavy taxes levied by Solomon to support his projects were onerous to the people. Upon his death, the union forged by David between the northern and southern tribes came apart, never to be restored. For the next two hundred years, their history is one of rivalry between the larger kingdom in the north, which kept the name Israel, and the smaller one of Judah to the south, ruled by the house of David. This was also the great age of the prophets who, in both kingdoms, strove to keep the people faithful to the Covenant, warned them that their infidelities would be punished by Yahweh, and in the process purified and deepened the religious and moral ideas of the Hebrew religion. Amos, Hosea, Isaiah, and Jeremiah were the first to leave their prophecies in writing. Isaiah thus excoriates the kingdom of Judah:

> Ah, sinful nation, a people loaded with guilt, a brood of evildoers, children given to corruption. They have forsaken Yahweh; they have spurned the Holy One of Israel and turned their backs on him. (1:4)

A hundred years later, Jeremiah confirmed the portrait:

> Go up and down the streets of Jerusalem, look around and consider, search through her squares. If you can find but one person who deals honestly and seeks the truth, I will forgive this city. (5:1)

THE BABYLONIAN CAPTIVITY

• *Isaiah's prophecy*

The appeals and warnings of the prophets failed to arrest the wickedness of the people, and before long the threatened doom began to arrive. Achaz, the king of Judah, threatened with an invasion by Israel and Syria, turned for help to the mighty empire of Assyria. This great new power was expanding in the north of the Mesopotamian valley. Spreading east, west, and south under a series of brutal rulers, it ravaged the lands it overran, and systematically deported large sections of the conquered populations — particularly the leaders and craftsmen. By an alliance with them, the crafty Achaz thought he could forestall the threat of his more immediate neighbors.

While Achaz was overseeing the fortifications around Jerusalem, the prophet Isaiah was sent to warn him that if he relied on Assyria rather than on Yahweh, disaster would result. Isaiah assured the king, moreover, that the invasion threatened by Israel and Syria would fail. To convince the hesitant king, Isaiah invited him to ask God for a sign; when the king refused, Isaiah responded:

> The Lord himself will give you a sign: The maiden[6] will be with child and will give birth to a son, and will call him Immanuel. (7:14)

Exactly what these words would have meant to Achaz at that time is greatly debated; Matthew's Gospel (1:23) sees them fulfilled in a way that transcended, perhaps, even the vision of Isaiah. In any case, the king ignored the prophet's warning and went ahead with his appeal to Assyria. For a while, the strategy seemed to succeed; the Assyrians subdued both Syria and Israel. When the latter rebelled a few years later, the Assyrian army returned and subjected the capital city, Samaria, to a horrible siege that reduced the survivors to cannibalism (2 Kings 6:24-33). The city fell in 721 B.C., a large portion of its population was deported, and the kingdom of Israel disappeared forever. From that moment on, the history of the Hebrew people reduces to that of the single tribe of Judah, from which the terms *Judaism* and *Jew* are derived. Judah preserved its existence by becoming a vassal of Assyria. When the Assyrian empire began to weaken in the middle of the seventh century B.C., hope arose for a restoration of the old kingdom of David. But the prophet Jeremiah renewed the warning given earlier by Isaiah:

> "O house of Israel," declares Yahweh, "I am bringing a distant nation against you. . . .
> "They will devour your harvest and your food, devour your sons and daughters; they will devour your flocks and herds, devour your vines and fig trees. With the sword they will destroy the fortified cities in which you trust. . . .
> "As you have forsaken me and served foreign gods in your own land, so now you will serve foreigners in a land not your own." (5:15-19)

• *Fall of Jerusalem*

The Assyrian empire succumbed to another Mesopotamian people, the Babylonians. These conquered Jerusalem in 597 and carried off the king, the nobles, and the artisans into exile. An attempted revolt provoked a siege, just as in the case of Samaria, ending with the total destruction of the city in 587. The glorious temple, the royal palace, and all the houses were burned down, the city wall was demolished, and the remaining citizens taken captive to Babylon. For the second time in their history, the Hebrews were slaves in an alien land.

The Lamentations traditionally attributed to Jeremiah mourn over the Jerusalem that had not listened to his warnings:

How deserted lies the city, once so full of people! How like a widow is she, who once was great among the nations! She who was queen among the provinces has now become a slave.

Bitterly she weeps at night, tears are upon her cheeks. Among all her lovers there is none to comfort her, all her friends have betrayed her; they have become her enemies.

After affliction and harsh labor, Judah has gone into exile. She dwells among the nations; she finds no resting place. All who pursue her have overtaken her in the midst of her distress.

The roads to Zion mourn, for no one comes to her appointed feasts. All her gateways are desolate, her priests groan, her maidens grieve, and she is in bitter anguish. (1:1-5)

What can I say for you? With what can I compare you, O Daughter of Jerusalem? To what can I liken you, that I may comfort you, O Virgin Daughter of Zion? Your wound is as deep as the sea. Who can heal you? (2:13)

• *Prophets of encouragement*

The captivity lasted about fifty years (587-537 B.C.). New prophets arose; but instead of reprimanding sinners and foretelling punishment, their message consisted mostly of consolation and encouragement. An unknown prophet who added to the Book of Isaiah during this period begins his work thus:

Comfort, comfort my people, says your God. Speak tenderly to Jerusalem, and proclaim to her that her hard service has been completed, that her sin has been paid for, that she has received from Yahweh's hand double for all her sins. . . .

You who bring good tidings to Zion, go up on a high mountain. You who bring good tidings to Jerusalem, lift up your voice with a shout, lift it up, do not be afraid; say to the towns of Judah, "Here is your God!" See, the Sovereign Yahweh comes with power, and his arm rules for him. See, his reward is with him, and his recompense accompanies him. He tends his flock like a shepherd; he gathers the lambs in his arms and carries them close to his heart; she gently leads those that have young. (40:1f; 9-11)

Jeremiah himself, although not deported to Babylon, reassured the exiles in words that opened a new chapter in the expectations of Israel:

"The time is coming," declares Yahweh, "when I will make a new covenant with the house of Israel and with the house of Judah. It will not be like the covenant I made with their forefathers when I took them by the hand to lead them out of Egypt, because they broke my covenant, though I was a husband to them," declares Yahweh. "This is the covenant I will make with the house of Israel after that time," declares Yahweh. "I will put my law in their minds and write it on their hearts. I will be their God, and they will be my people. No longer will a man teach his neighbor, or a man his brother, saying 'Know Yahweh,' because they will all know me, from the least of them to the greatest," declares Yahweh. "For I will forgive their wickedness and will remember their sins no more." (31:31-34)

This text is the origin of the idea of the New Covenant (or, less properly, New Testament). It will be characterized by a mysterious interiority: The Law of God will be written on human hearts rather than on stone tablets; likewise there will be a knowledge of God not communicable in words.

The prophet Ezekiel, who was one of the exiles, developed this idea further with the following message from Yahweh:

For I will take you out of the nations; I will gather you from all the countries and bring you back into your own land. I will sprinkle clean water on you, and you will be clean; I will cleanse you from all your impurities and from all your idols. I will give you a new heart and put a new spirit in you; I will remove from you your heart of stone and give you a heart of flesh. And I will put my Spirit in you and move you to follow my decrees and be careful to keep my laws. (36:24-28)

It is the Spirit of God that will make hearts new, and inspire them from within to walk in the paths marked out by Yahweh.

Other prophets spoke of a time when God would restore the fortunes of his people and give them a blessed existence unmarred by any suffering or tears, a time of perfect prosperity and happiness. Frequently this was associated with an outpouring of the Spirit of God:

And afterward, I will pour out my Spirit on all people. Your sons and daughters will prophesy, your old men will dream dreams, your young men will see visions. Even on my servants, both men and women, I will pour out my Spirit in those days. (Joel 2:28f; see also Isaiah 44:3f)

• *Return of the Jews*

The prophecies about the restoration of Israel all included the basic assurance that the people would return to the land promised by God to their father, Abraham. This came about through an unlikely instrument: The Persian empire which, under Cyrus the Great (559-529), absorbed Babylonia. Cyrus was a remarkably humane ruler, who made it a deliberate policy to foster the religions of the peoples he conquered. Within a year after his occupation of Babylon, he issued an edict authorizing those who so wished, to return to

Jerusalem and rebuild the Temple of Yahweh (Ezra 1:2-4). The Jews, however, had by now become rather comfortably established in Babylon, and many preferred to remain there. The groups of over forty thousand who made the difficult and dangerous return to Palestine were soon disheartened at the hardships they met, the poverty of their situation, and the hostility of the neighboring Samaritans who jealously opposed the reconstruction of the city. Two new prophets, Haggai and Zechariah, encouraged them eloquently, however.

> "But now be strong . . . all you people of the land," declares Yahweh, "and work, for I am with you. . . . The desired of all nations will come, and I will fill this house with glory," says Yahweh the Almighty. (Haggai 2:3-7)

With such encouragement, the new Temple was finally completed in 515 B.C.; by the same token, the image of a new City of Jerusalem, restored by the hand of Yahweh himself (Isaiah 54; 60; Ezekiel 48:30-35) gained importance as the symbol of Jewish hope.

The expected restoration of the kingdom was not, however, forthcoming. The Persian empire succumbed to the Greeks, led by Alexander the Great (336-323 B.C.), whose subject Israel became. When the Alexandrian empire broke up, Palestine fell under the control of Egypt, then of Syria. King Antiochus Epiphanes of Syria (175-164 B.C.) attempted to suppress the Jewish religion by force and replace it with Greek rites. This, the first properly religious persecution of the Jews, provoked a rebellion led by the Maccabee brothers (see 1 Maccabees). They regained a fragile independence which collapsed before the allies of Rome in 63 B.C. Thus things remained until the time of Jesus. Later Jewish rebellions led to the destruction of the city and a final burning of the Temple in 70 A.D.

KINGDOM OF GOD AND MESSIAH

Out of this history and the teaching of the prophets emerge two ideas of special importance for an understanding of the message of Jesus: the Kingdom of God and the Messiah. We can say in brief that the Jews looked forward to the establishment of God's Kingdom among them through the Messiah; but it would be an oversimplification to suppose that these notions were definite and clear or that all had the same idea or even that all the Jews really shared in these expectations. The basic, original hope, based on the promise to Abraham had been colored and given new forms through the experience of the People of God down through the centuries. The ideas of the Kingdom and of the Messiah derived their basic shape from this common experience.

• *God and kingship*

The Hebrews were not the only people to see a connection between divinity and kingship; this association was common in the Near East, and is found in other parts of the world also (in Japan, the emperor was still worshiped as divine until the Second World War). Sometimes the king was venerated as a god, as in the case of the Egyptian pharaohs. Sometimes the god was pictured as a great king, as in the case of the Canaanite deity Moloch, whose name itself derives from the Semitic word for king *(melek)*. Both ideas merged in Mesopotamia, where Marduk, the creator god, was the origin of the kingship of the human rulers, who in turn participated in his divinity. Israel likewise came to look upon Yahweh as a great king, and to regard its human rulers as "sons of God." Which of these two ideas came first is not clear; at any rate, they developed together and influenced each other.

To call God a king expressed many things: that he had power over his people, that he would deliver them from danger, that he should be obeyed, that he was glorious, etc. The hymn in which the Israelites celebrated their deliverance from Egypt at the Red Sea proclaimed:

> Who among the gods is like you, Yahweh? Who is like you — majestic in holiness, awesome in glory, working wonders? . . .
>
> Yahweh will reign for ever and ever. (Exodus 15:11, 18)

After the downfall of the kingdoms of Israel and Judah, God's kingship came to be more and more celebrated:

> Say among the nations, "Yahweh reigns!" The world is firmly established, it cannot be moved; he will judge the peoples with equity. Let the heavens rejoice, let the earth be glad; let the sea resound, and all that is in it; let the fields be jubilant, and everything in them.
>
> Then all the trees of the forest will sing for joy; they will sing before Yahweh, for he comes, he comes to judge the earth. He will judge the world in righteousness and the peoples in his truth. (Psalm 96:10ff; see also Psalms 47 and 95-99)

• *The coming Kingdom of God*

The thought expressed in these last lines, that Yahweh *is coming* to judge (that is, to reign in power), is indicative of an important development taking place. Besides the conviction that God is actually king now, there is the expectation of a time to come when his kingship will be manifested gloriously before all the world. That was hardly the case at present; God's people was under the yoke of an oppressor. Even when Israel had been an independent kingdom, it was never free from injustice and oppression. But the time was coming when all wickedness and suffering would be eliminated from God's Kingdom, which, moreover, would be extended to the whole world.

• *"The Day of the Lord"*

As these glorious expectations were in stark contrast with the Jews' actual condition of humiliation and subjection, the coming of the Kingdom, or reign, of God implied a drastic reversal. This was often expressed by the term *"The Day of the Lord,"* meaning the day when the Lord would come to rectify things. At first this meant a day on which Yahweh would manifest his power and glory. However, the prophets, beginning with Amos, pointed out that it would not be so simple as that. For the wicked, the Day of the Lord would be a day of darkness and punishment, when Yahweh would purify his people. Ultimately, however, it would be a time of incomparable blessedness, when nature itself would cooperate bountifully in providing for the happiness of God's people:

> In that day the mountains will drip new wine, and the hills will flow with milk;
> all the ravines of Judah will run with water.
> A fountain will flow out of Yahweh's house. . . . (Joel 4:18)

• *God's son and anointed*

The kingship of Saul and his successors was sometimes interpreted as an offense to that of God; it had arisen from the people's unwillingness to rely on Yahweh alone as their king. Nevertheless, God had given his approval to these earthly rulers, and so the king came to be regarded as a sacred figure. Even the prophets looked upon him as God's chosen one and his representative. While never divinized like the kings of Mesopotamia and Egypt or the emperors of Rome, he was called God's son. Thus Psalm 2:1, 4-8, composed perhaps for the enthronement of a king, proclaims:

> Why do the nations rage and the peoples plot in vain? . . .
> The One enthroned in heaven laughs; Yahweh scoffs at them.
> Then he rebukes them in his anger and terrifies them in his wrath, saying,
> "I have installed my king on Zion, my holy hill."
> I will proclaim the decree of Yahweh:
> He said to me, "You are my Son; today I have become your Father.
> Ask of me, and I will make the nations your inheritance, the ends of the earth
> your possession."

• *Messianic expectations*

The Hebrew kings were installed in office by being anointed with oil (1 Samuel 10:1, 2 Samuel 2:4; etc.), rather than being crowned, as in Rome. The king therefore was often referred to as *the Anointed One* (in Hebrew, *Messiah*, and in Greek, *Christos*, from which the anglicized form *Christ* has derived).

God's promise that David's throne would pass to his son, and would be established forever, was the origin of the "messianic expectation." This came to be more and more celebrated in Hebrew thought and song, and took on superhuman dimensions, as we have seen. The idea of the glorious reign of an ideal Messiah merged with that of the Kingdom of God. Isaiah thus describes the reign of David's offspring:

> With righteousness he will judge the needy, with justice he will give decisions
> for the poor of the earth.
> He will strike the earth with the rod of his mouth; with the breath of his lips he
> will slay the wicked. . . .
> The wolf will live with the lamb, the leopard will lie down with the goat . . . and
> a little child will lead them. . . .

They will neither harm nor destroy on all my holy mountain, for the earth will be full of the knowledge of Yahweh as the waters cover the sea. (11:4-9)

• *Apocalyptic*

Remembering the great military exploits of David, and the heroism of the Maccabean "freedom fighters," many of the Jews expected that the messianic kingdom would be brought about by a military victory won by their armies under a great king. Another interpretation, which developed especially in the "apocalyptic"[7] literature, supposed that the expected kingdom could be brought about only by a cataclysm, with God intervening to establish an order radically different from the present one. It would be marked by signs in the heavens: The sun will be turned to darkness and the moon to blood, before the coming of the great and dreadful day of Yahweh (Joel 2:31).

The Book of Daniel, the chief apocalypse of the Old Testament, was very likely written during the terrible persecution of 167-164 B.C., which provoked the revolt of the Maccabees. One of Daniel's visions is of four hideous beasts, which seem to represent the four empires of the Babylonians, Assyrians ("Medes"), Persians, and Greeks. This last beast sprouted a horn (the Syrian king, Antiochus Epiphanes?) that warred against the saints of the Most High, prevailed over them, and blasphemously tampered with the sacred festivals and laws. Then:

As I looked, thrones were set in place, and the Ancient of Days took his seat.

His clothing was as white as snow; the hair of his head was white like wool. His throne was flaming with fire, and its wheels were all ablaze.

A river of fire was flowing, coming out from before him. Thousands upon thousands attended him; ten thousand times ten thousand stood before him. The court was seated, and the books were opened. . . . I kept looking until the beast was slain and his body destroyed and thrown into the blazing fire.

In my vision at night I looked, and there before me was one like a son of man, coming with the clouds of heaven. He approached the Ancient of Days and was led into his presence. He was given authority, glory and sovereign power; all peoples, nations and men of every language worshiped him. His dominion is an everlasting dominion that will not pass away, and his kingdom is one that will never be destroyed. (7:9-14)

The imagery of this vision, and especially that of the mysterious Son of Man, was to have many reverberations in the New Testament, particularly in the language of Jesus, who applied it to himself.

* * *

The history of the people of Israel is complex, like that of any nation. But throughout all of its twisting and turning, its startling rise and its tragic decline, amid all of its hesitations and apparent irrelevancies, one idea is tenaciously pursued, one hope is constantly reaffirmed: The promise made to Abraham is the hook that holds Israel together. The original, simple idea of a people and a land has now been transmuted into that of a kingdom — a perfect kingdom, with Yahweh himself ruling through a mysterious representative anointed by him. Various other notions enrich the picture: Son of God, Son of David, Day of the Lord, New Covenant, the outpouring of the Spirit of God. No one of them is susceptible of an abstract definition; they arose out of history and were freighted with historical connotations from which they cannot be separated. How they related to one another was likewise not clear. They could not be further interpreted until the One in whom they were to be realized came and disclosed their true meaning. This he did in a way no one had anticipated.

16
Jesus of Nazareth

Canaan, the land of Abraham, Isaac, and Jacob — after having been subject to the Babylonians, Persians, Greeks, and Syrians, and after a few years of independence won by the courageous Macchabeans — was finally incorporated forcibly into the Roman empire. The greatest empire history has ever known, the latter endured over a thousand years, and still stands in human memory as the archetype of empire. About 6 B.C., in what the Romans regarded as an insignificant outpost, was born a gentle, quiet man who, supplied with neither wealth nor arms, without calling for rebellion or even raising his voice in the streets, announced a new and greater empire — the Kingdom of God. The nervous political authorities quickly executed him for sedition; but the little band of disciples who had gathered around him rapidly grew into a great Church that has far outgrown and long outlasted the Roman empire.

• *The Gospels*

Our chief source for the life of Jesus consists in the four Gospels. The few references to him by pagan writers of antiquity such as Pliny and Tacitus do not inform us about any of the details of his life. Even the Gospels do not seem to be the work of eyewitnesses. The story of Jesus was passed down by word of mouth through various Christian communities, until several men were inspired to put it into writing. It seems clear that the incidents narrated in the Gospels were shaped by the countless retellings they had undergone. They are not in strict chronological order (for example, John puts the cleansing of the Temple at the beginning of Jesus' public life, whereas the others put it at the end). The words of Jesus are not always reported verbatim but have often been paraphrased; hence the Our Father and the beatitudes as reported by Luke vary somewhat from those given by Matthew, with which most people are more familiar. Written thirty or forty years after the events they report, the Gospels sometimes seem to use the language of their own time rather than that of the protagonists. For example, when Nathanael, at his first meeting with Jesus, is reported to have exclaimed, "Rabbi, you are the son of God; you are the king of Israel" (John 1:49), we may well wonder whether the language of the post-Resurrection Church is not being used here to express his incipient act of faith.

On the other hand, we should not exaggerate the separation between these books and the original eyewitnesses. Two of the Gospels were so closely associated with the apostles Matthew and John as to be called *theirs*; Mark was the immediate disciple of Peter; Luke took great care to compose a reliable and orderly account of things "just as they were handed down to us by those who from the first were eyewitnesses and servants of the word" (Luke 1:2). Hence, while it is impossible to compose a strict biography of Jesus,

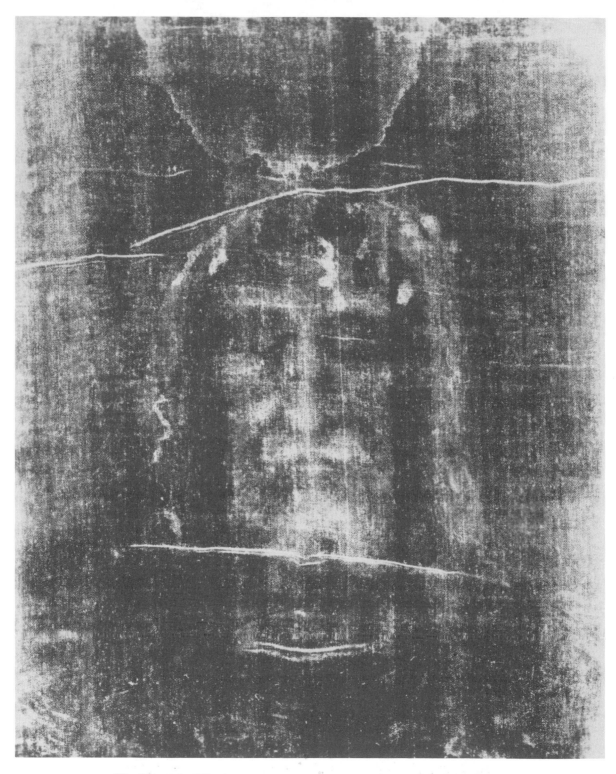

The Shroud of Turin. — Photo courtesy of the Redemptorist Fathers of New York

the broad outlines of his career can be sketched with sufficient certitude for our purpose.

We will look first at the external framework of Jesus' life (Chapter 16), then examine the question of his mysterious personal identity (Chapters 17 and 18), and finally consider his work (Chapter 19). However, these three topics are all interwoven: From his teaching we learn about his person and his work; teaching was also part of his work; and he taught not only in words but also by the example of his very person and his activity.

Today a great many of New Testament studies are conducted genetically. That is, they are concerned with determining where ideas originated, and how one developed out of another. Likewise most are careful to keep distinct the peculiar views and teachings of each of the New Testament authors — for example, distinguishing the "theology" of John from that of the Synoptics. Such methods are appropriate to academic studies of the history of ideas, but here we are trying to give a synthetic exposition of the life and teaching of Jesus. All of the Gospels, and the other New Testament writers as well, are authentic sources for this study.

It should also be noted that as soon as you undertake to get behind the actual Gospels to the objective historical data abstracted from the vision of faith, you get into an area that is highly conjectural. The doctrine of faith, on the other hand, consisting in the portrait of Jesus drawn by the evangelists, together with the interpretation of it forged in the life and thought of the Church as a community of faith, is comparatively definite in its essentials. It is with this that we are primarily concerned. The speculations of "detached" historians, interesting and valuable as they may be in their own right, are of secondary importance here.

AN ITINERANT PREACHER OF GOD'S KINGDOM

People often have a false image of the career of Jesus. He did not go about claiming to be the Messiah and offering signs to prove it; his messianic status became apparent only

gradually and indirectly in the course of his ministry, which was that of an itinerant preacher, proclaiming the imminent arrival of the Kingdom of God. The Gospel of Mark sums up his activity thus:

> After John was put in prison, Jesus went into Galilee, proclaiming the good news of God. "The time has come," he said. "The kingdom of God is near. Repent and believe the good news." (Mark 1:14)

Much of what Jesus says is about the Kingdom of God: He compares it to a net cast into the sea, a treasure buried in a field, a mustard seed, leaven in the dough, a wedding feast which a king held for his son, a household entrusted to the servants while the master goes on a journey, and so forth. The richest collection of parables about the Kingdom is given by Matthew in Chapter 13.

Where the other Gospels speak of the Kingdom of God, Matthew speaks of the Kingdom of Heaven. This does not mean "the Kingdom which is in heaven"; it is simply Matthew's way of referring to the Kingdom of God. He wrote primarily for Jews, who were inclined, out of reverence, to avoid using the name of God, and to replace it with paraphrases, such as Heaven or The Most High.

The prophets had foretold the coming of the Kingdom, and their message summoned people to hope. Jesus proclaimed the good news that this hope was now about to be fulfilled. He called, not so much for hope in something to come, as for *faith* in something present or about to become present. The central theme of his preaching therefore was not a doctrine about God nor a code of ethics but *news of an event* that was about to take place, and which implied the beginning of a new era in salvation history. All of his doctrinal and moral teaching was presented in function of this announcement.

• "Gospel"

That the Kingdom of God was near was good news. The word *gospel* (from the Anglo-Saxon, *god-spell*, "good tidings") referred originally to Jesus' message,[1] and only later came to be applied to the four books that tell about his career. It is an Old Testament term which Isaiah had already used to refer to the announcement of deliverance that would one day be proclaimed in Jerusalem (Isaiah 40:9 [cited in the preceding chapter, p. 258]; 41:27; 52:7; 61:1). Sometimes Jesus varied his terminology, and instead of speaking of the coming Kingdom, referred to the "coming of the Son of Man" or the "close of the age" (sometimes inaccurately translated as "the end of the world"). All these expressions referred essentially to the same event.

• *When is the Kingdom to come?*

When was the Kingdom, or the Son of Man, due to arrive? Jesus is not specific: ". . .is near," or ". . .is very close," indicates that it can no longer be put off into the far distant future; it evidently means that *now* is the time to get ready for the Kingdom, but no precise date is indicated. This was intentional, for whenever the apostles asked about the time, Jesus steadfastly refused to answer: "It is not for you to know the times or dates the Father has set by his own authority" (Acts 1:7). In fact, he declared, "No one knows about that day or that hour, not even the angels in heaven, nor the Son, but only the Father" (Mark 13:32).

The question about when Jesus himself expected the Kingdom of God to be realized has been one of the most passionately debated topics of New Testament scholarship since it was raised by Albert Schweitzer in 1899.[2] It is also an important key to our interpretation of the vision of Jesus. However, we must put off the answer to it until after we have examined his person and work.[3]

• *The Fatherhood of God*

The second major theme of Jesus' preaching is the fatherhood of God. Some scholars have even attempted to make this the essence of Christianity.[4] While that is an

268

oversimplification, there is no doubt that Jesus' presentation of the Father is one of the most characteristic notes of his work. "This is how you should pray: 'Our Father in heaven, hallowed be your name. . .' " (Matthew 6:8). He added:

> Do not worry, saying "What shall we eat?" or "What shall we wear?" For the pagans run after all these things; and your heavenly Father [who feeds the birds of the air and clothes the lilies of the field] knows that you need them all. But seek first his kingdom and his righteousness, and all these things will be given to you as well. (6:28-33)

The parable of the prodigal son represents God as a father who is not harsh with his wayward son but receives him with joy, *raises him up*, and throws a party for him (Luke 15). If earthly fathers, "evil" as they are, give good things to their children, "how much

more will your Father in heaven give good gifts to those who ask him" (Matthew 7:11)?

The idea that God is like a father to his creatures is not rare in the religions of the world. It is found, for example, in India, Babylon, and Egypt.[5] In the Old Testament, in particular, God sometimes speaks of Israel as his son, although not often. But in the Gospels, the term *father* is applied to God one hundred seventy times! Not only does Jesus speak about God as a father, but he addresses him as *Abba* (Mark 14:36). This was a familiar form of Aramaic for *father,* sometimes compared to the English *daddy* or *papa*. However, it was not just baby talk; older people used it as a title of respect for a venerable personage. All this goes to show that Jesus taught and fostered a uniquely intimate relationship with God. He depicted the Creator of heaven and earth, the Sovereign Lord of the universe, the almighty and all-holy God, as looking upon his people with the affection of a father, caring for them and cherishing them with a love that nothing can turn away, and that is always ready to forgive. This doctrine seems to have no parallel anywhere else.[6]

• *Jesus' message practical*

As Jesus' message was not just the exposition of a doctrine, such as a master of philosophy might give, but a summons and an exhortation, it is more properly called *preaching* or *proclamation (kerygma)* than simple teaching. Rather than discoursing about ultimate reality, Jesus told people how to be ready to enter the Kingdom of God, and how to live as children of the Father. "Be perfect, therefore, as your heavenly Father is perfect" (Matthew 5:48). Mark's summary of Jesus' message, after announcing, "The Kingdom of God is near," adds, "*repent and believe* in the good news." Repentance or conversion of hearts was the first and immediate requirement. It meant a turning of one's heart from evil ways, a turning to the Father. "Believe in the good news," is the second requirement.

Everything in Christianity (even repentance itself) is based on faith. Christianity is not just a humanism — a way of life suitable for human beings as such. It is a response to the Word of God that has come to man announcing pardon, grace, and love. For that word to produce any good in man, it must be believed.

But the supreme requirement which Jesus laid down for those who wish to live as children of the Father and be fit to enter the Kingdom is *love*. Love your neighbor as yourself, he taught (Matthew 19:19). Love one another as I have loved you (John 13:34). Love even your enemies, as your heavenly Father lets his rain and his sunshine fall upon the just and the unjust alike (Matthew 5:44-45). Love is the first and the greatest commandment (Matthew 22:38); love is the fulfillment of all the commandments (Galatians 5:14). God so loved the world that he sent his Son, so that the world might be saved through him (John 3:16-17). Love is poured forth in our hearts through the Holy Spirit (Romans 5:5), the Spirit Jesus imparts to those who believe in him (John 8:39). In the last analysis, God is love, and he who loves abides in God and God in him (1 John 4:16).

THE STYLE OF JESUS' PREACHING

Before leaving the subject of Jesus' preaching, we should note some remarkable features of its style. He taught "as one who had *authority*" (Matthew 7:29), not in the usual manner of the scribes. He spoke as one who knew what he taught, even concerning the Father (John 7:29). He interpreted the Law in ways contrary to Jewish tradition (Matthew 5:21ff; 15:2ff) and declared himself Lord over the Sabbath — the holy day, observance of which had been prescribed by Yahweh at Mt. Sinai (Matthew 12:8).

Moreover, his teaching had *power*. His words affected people like those of no one else. "No one ever spoke the way this man does," said the soldiers sent to imprison him, when they returned to the authorities (John 7:46). Peter exclaimed, "Lord, you have the words of eternal life!" (John 6:68).

• *Major sermons*

The most famous of Jesus' sermons, and the lengthiest, is the Sermon on the Mount (Matthew 5-7). It is presumably not the text of a single discourse, however, but a representative collection of teachings given in various situations. Another well-known sermon is that which was preached from the fisherman's boat to the crowd gathered on the shore (Matthew 13). The apocalyptic sermon of Matthew 24 and 25, on the destruction of Jerusalem and the end of the present era, gives a very different set of themes, less frequently noted today.

• *Parables*

Jesus made great use of parables. Some of these have been cited above. Their primary purpose was to make the lessons concrete and easy to grasp. At the same time they hid the doctrine from those who approached it in a wrong spirit — for example, Nicodemus, so disturbed about having to be "born again" (John 3).

This style raises a problem, however, because figures of speech are open to diverse interpretations, as in the case of the Kingdom of God. Even while Jesus was on earth, his hearers demanded in annoyance, "If you are the Christ tell us plainly" (John 10:24). Most of the disagreements among the Christian churches stem from diverse interpretations of Jesus' teaching by people, all of whom seek to be faithful disciples. If it is important for us to "know the truth," as he himself said (John 8:32), could he not have been more definite and precise, instead of speaking in a way that leaves so much to interpretation?

The problem of interpretation arises in the case of nearly all the other great religious teachers of mankind — Confucius or the Buddha or Muhammad or the anonymous authors of the Upanishads. The sacred teachings at the fountainheads of the great religions tend to be simple, forceful aphorisms that take hold of the mind of the disciple and inspire him but do not have the kind of clarity that enables one to define their meaning precisely. It seems to be normal that religious traditions are engendered by a charismatic figure who knows how to speak to the heart of his listeners but without precision; when a later generation of disciples tries to define his meaning and synthesize his insights, diverse interpretations develop.

We must recall first that Jesus was addressing people who, for the most part, were simple and uneducated. The parables he drew from nature — about the birds and the flowers, the flocks and the harvest — were easy for them to grasp; at the same time they had a profound truth and a perennial freshness that the most intelligent minds never exhaust. If he had defined himself in terms of person and nature, as the Council of Chalcedon was later to do, who would have understood him there by the Sea of Galilee? And if his message had been delivered in the refined language of intellectuals, would it not have been impoverished?

Furthermore, Jesus was a gentle, considerate teacher, who met people where they were and led them gradually forward. His immediate hearers were Jews, and he spoke to them entirely within the compass of their Jewish culture, appealing to what was finest in them, denouncing only the hypocrisy which they themselves could recognize as disloyal to their faith. In fact, his teaching was so homogeneous with Jewish tradition that its precise originality is hard to pin down. Jesus did not conduct himself as one founding a new religion but rather as one purifying the old and disclosing new depths in it. He was not like a contractor who razes one building in order to replace it with another; rather, he was like someone turning on a new but concealed light, softly illumining the familiar world of law and temple, priest and sacrifice, giving them new color.

Finally, and most important of all, Jesus' doctrine is one that needs to be entered into and lived in order to be understood. He was not communicating a philosophy to other intellects but leading disciples into a way of life. Those who respond in the right spirit will tend to understand his words in the right sense. Those who are unwilling to surrender their lives to him but scrutinize his doctrine with merely academic interest fulfill the prophecy of Isaiah 6:9f, cited by Jesus himself: "You will be ever hearing but never understanding; you will be ever seeing but never perceiving. For this people's heart has become calloused" (Matthew 13:14f). In short, Jesus taught in order to convert hearts; he was not interested in convincing minds alone.

This does not, however, entail the conclusion that academic theology is useless. Intellectual Christians need an intellectual appreciation of their faith — which is essentially

271

what theology amounts to. To be a Christian, one need not be an intellectual or a theologian; but if a person is an intellectual and a Christian, he needs in some measure to be a theologian. If he is not, his faith and his natural reason are not in communication with one another, and this will be to the detriment of both. Also, while an individual Christian does not need to be a theologian, the Church needs theologians among its ranks, and other Christians benefit from them.

JESUS AS A MIRACLE-WORKING PROPHET

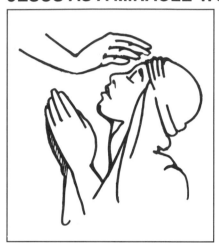

People were drawn to Jesus not only by the things he said (the good news of the Kingdom) but also by the things he did (the miracles that he worked). These were mostly acts of healing. He did not just encourage the sick with the assurance that they would eventually be healed; he actually made them well. He did not go about as a wonderworker, seeking to impress the public with his preternatural prowess. He avoided drawing attention to his cures, and often forbade the beneficiaries to speak about them. But compassion for the suffering impelled him to heal the deaf, the dumb, the blind, the lame, lepers, in fact, the ill of every sort. He even raised the dead to life (Lazarus, the daughter of Jairus, and the widow's son). Sometimes he healed by a touch, sometimes by a simple word of command, sometimes at a distance. Many got well by merely touching the hem of his cloak. Closely associated with these healing miracles was the casting out of demons.

There were also "nature miracles," such as stilling the storm on the lake or multiplying the loaves and fishes. While not acts of healing, they too were ordinarily done to rescue or help those in need.

The miracles of Jesus obliged his contemporaries to pose the question "What kind of man is this? Even the winds and the waves obey him?" (Matthew 8:27). For many, the answer was, "a prophet."[7] This was the one category furnished by the history of Israel that seemed to fit him. The prophets too had preached in the name of God, and had sometimes corroborated their words with miraculous deeds, as in the case of Moses or Elijah. Even one of Jesus' own disciples described him as "a prophet powerful in word and deed before God and all the people" (Luke 24:19).

• *Miracles a problem today*

For people today, the miracles of Jesus often seem to be a problem rather than a support for faith. The reason lies largely in that modern scientific consciousness of the laws of nature which, as we saw in Chapter 3, makes it difficult to believe that the natural order could be momentarily interrupted or suspended. Moreover, we are far removed from the actual witnesses of Jesus' miracles, so that it is difficult to verify satisfactorily that they really took place.

It is seldom proposed that the Gospels are deliberately perpetrating a fraud; they are also evidently the expression of the sincere belief of the early Christian communities. But appeal is made to the "legend-creating power" of faith. Stories passed on by word of mouth tend to grow, especially when they concern an admired personality. Hence it is suggested that Jesus may have done some remarkable things of a purely natural order which, in the retelling, were transmuted into miracles. For example, inspired by his generosity, others were led to share their food with one another, and thus arose the story of the multiplication of the loaves and fishes.

Aside from the fact that such an "explanation" contradicts many details in the account (in this case, the fact that the people had nothing to eat; that precisely five loaves and two fish were available; that these are what he blessed and distributed among the people; that the account manifestly intends to contrast the twelve baskets of remainders with the small amount with which the meal started; and that Jesus later refers explicitly to the fact that he provided food for the multitude out of this small amount [Mark 6:36-44; 8:1-9, 14-21]), this interpretation misses the fact that miracles are not just accessory ornamentations in the story of Jesus, they are an essential feature of his portrait. From the outset to the end of his ministry, the Gospels represent him as a miracle worker. This is what arouses the attention of the crowds, draws them to Jesus, and provokes their wondering questions; it also plays a major role in stirring up the enmity that led to his death. The soldiers who mocked him, the court of Herod that ridiculed him, the religious leaders that derided him as he hung from the cross — all alluded to the miracles he had done. It has several times been pointed out that if you take a New Testament and literally cut out all the miracle passages, you are left with nothing but shreds. There is no way to decontaminate the Gospels of the supernatural and retain their integrity and credibility. We must choose between accepting Jesus as a miracle worker, and abandoning the Gospels altogether as documents of faith.

Even though we today have not witnessed Jesus' miracles, and can take them only on faith, they are not useless as supports to our faith. If we recognize that the Gospels cannot be dismissed as vain legends, if the power of holiness and truth we experience in them convinces us of their seriousness, we must take seriously the fact that miracles constitute a major feature of Jesus' portrait, and of the idiom in which he is presented for our belief. We too must ask, as did his countrymen, "What sort of man is this?" But before attempting to answer this question, let us conclude the account of Jesus' life.

THE TWELVE APOSTLES

Jesus seems to have gained a great initial popularity by his preaching and miracles. Large crowds followed him, some of whom had come from a long distance away. They pressed so tightly around him that he was jostled, and those who wished to get to him often found it difficult. On some days, he scarcely had time to eat. When he tried to get away for a rest, the crowds would still follow; then, out of compassion for them, he would forsake his solitude and preach to them.

Looking at the crowds, Jesus said, "The harvest is plentiful, but the workers are few; ask the Lord of the harvest to send out workers into his harvest field" (Matthew 9:37f). Soon afterward he selected twelve of his disciples to assist him. After spending an entire night in prayer (Luke 6:12), he "called to him those he wanted" (Mark 3:13), and appointed them to accompany him and to go out preaching. He named them *apostles*, that is, emissaries, men sent on a mission (Luke 6:13).[8] "As the Father has sent me," he would tell them, "I am sending you" (John 20:21). He conferred on them power to heal the sick and to cast out demons (Matthew 10:1). From then on, the Twelve accompanied Jesus closely and were even sent out to preach on their own. Thus was established the basic shape of the Church: Jesus, the leader; the crowds of disciples attracted by his preaching; and, in between, the twelve apostles commissioned by Jesus to preach to the disciples (or future disciples).

THE CRUCIFIXION AND RESURRECTION

In spite of his initial popularity, Jesus also provoked enmity, especially among the religious leaders, who took him prisoner by night, put him through a hasty trial, stirred up the populace against him, and finally pressured the Roman authorities to crucify him.

Crucifixion was a form of execution used in the Roman empire chiefly for slaves. To crucify a Roman citizen was forbidden, except for very heinous crimes such as treason or rebellion.[9] In any case, crucifixion is one of the most brutal and humiliating forms of execution ever devised by human cruelty; that it should have been imposed on one who preached love for all and forgiveness of enemies is surely one of the supreme ironies of history.

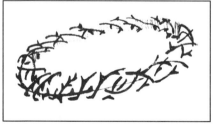

It was the imperial Roman authorities who executed Jesus, for they alone had authority to put a man to death. The reason alleged was that Jesus claimed to be a king; therefore, by implication, he was a rebel against Roman authority. This could explain the sentence of crucifixion; it also explains why the soldiers mocked him with a crown of thorns and a purple cloak (symbol of majesty), and upon his cross fixed the inscription "Jesus of Nazareth, King of the Jews."

The true instigators of Jesus' death, however, were the Jewish authorities. The accusation which they made against him was that of blasphemy — a religious rather than a political crime. Their deeper motive seems to have been resentment at his exposure of their religious hypocrisy. They too mocked him — but as a prophet rather than a king. His captors blindfolded and struck him, saying, "Prophesy! Who hit you?" (Luke 22:64).

• *Apostles proclaim the Resurrection*

In any event, the ignominious death of Jesus appeared to be the end of whatever he had begun, and a defeat for his "cause." It left his followers utterly dejected. "We had hoped that he was the one who was going to redeem Israel," declared the disciples on the way to Emmaus (Luke 24:21). But at this moment when all seemed lost, an extraordinary reversal came about. The cry went out among the disciples, "The Lord has risen and has appeared to Simon" (Luke 24:34). Simon Peter himself affirmed: "God raised him from the dead on the third day and caused him to be seen. He was not seen by all the people but by witnesses whom God had already chosen — by us who ate and drank with him after he rose from the dead" (Acts 10:40f). An early summary of the Christian proclamation declared:

What I received I passed on to you as of first importance: that Christ died for our sins according to the Scriptures, that he was buried, that he was raised on the third day according to the Scriptures, and that he appeared to Peter, and then to the Twelve. After that, he appeared to more than five hundred of the brothers at the same time, most of whom are still living, though some have fallen asleep. Then he appeared to James, then to all the apostles, and last of all he appeared to me also, as to one abnormally born. (1 Corinthians 15:3-8)

After the Resurrection, Jesus did not associate with the disciples in the same way as before. He was in a sense still on earth, for, as he said to Mary Magdalene, "I have not yet returned to the Father" (John 20:17). However, he was no longer living according to the natural conditions of life on earth. Over a period of forty days, he appeared at various times, abruptly and unexpectedly, then as promptly disappeared. Besides the appearances listed above, there were others that we know about (for example, to the disciples on the way to Emmaus, Luke 24:13-35) and presumably still more. During these appearances, the disciples could not only see and hear him but also touch him (John 20:27). Sometimes he even ate with them (Luke 24:42; Acts 1:4). Besides serving as evidence of his resurrection, these appearances were also the occasion of further instruction (Acts 1:3), in which Jesus opened the minds of the disciples to an understanding of the Scriptures (Luke 24:45).

• *The Ascension and Pentecost*

In the course of these instructions, Jesus told the apostles, "Do not leave Jerusalem, but wait for the gift my Father promised, which you have heard me speak about. For John baptized with water, but in a few days you will be baptized with the Holy Spirit" (Acts 1:4f). After forty days of this strange double existence, he led them up onto the Mount of Olives, where he blessed them, and then was lifted up bodily before them until "a cloud took him from their sight" (Acts 1:9).

Returning to the city, the apostles devoted themselves to prayer together with Mary and the other women who had accompanied them from Galilee. When the great Jewish festival of Pentecost came, some ten days later, the house in which they were staying was suddenly filled with a roar of wind. Tongues of fire appeared over each of them. At the same moment, they were filled with the Holy Spirit and began to praise the mighty works of God, using languages they had never learned (Acts 2). This noise drew a crowd, Jews from many countries who were celebrating the feast. These were amazed to hear the

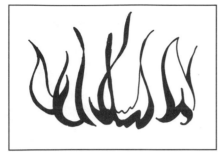

apostles speaking in their various languages. Peter then stood up and declared that Jesus, whom they had crucified, had been raised from the dead:

> Exalted to the right hand of God, he has received from the Father the promised Holy Spirit, and has poured out what you now see and hear. (Acts 2:33)

The apostles were permanently transformed by this experience. From frightened and confused men, they became intrepid, convincing preachers by whom Jesus Christ was proclaimed in tones that have never ceased to reverberate in the world.

SIGNIFICANCE OF THE RESURRECTION

We must give a more prolonged consideration to the Resurrection because, on the one hand, it is the linchpin of Christian faith, and on the other, because it is under renewed attack today. It is not merely the greatest of Jesus' miracles. If Jesus had not risen from the dead, his work would surely have ended with his death. His demoralized, frightened followers would never have carried his name across the Roman world and laid the foundation of that Church which has come down to us. As St. Paul declares:

> If Christ has not been raised, our preaching is useless and so is your faith. More than that, we are then found to be false witnesses about God, for we have testified about God that he raised Christ from the dead. But he did not raise him if in fact the dead are not raised. For if the dead are not raised, then Christ has not been raised either. And if Christ has not been raised, your faith is futile; you are still in your sins. Then those also who have fallen asleep in Christ are lost. (1 Corinthians 15:14-18)

It is not clear that the Resurrection ought to be regarded as a miracle of Jesus. The New Testament usually speaks of *the Father* raising him from the dead, as in the foregoing text. Jesus is represented as the recipient, the beneficiary of the miracle, rather than its author. A few times, the expression used is that Jesus rose.[10] The ultimate basis for the latter way of speaking lies in the words of Jesus himself: "I have authority to lay [my life] down, and I have authority to take it up again" (John 10:18). After the Arian controversy (Chapter 18), this way of speaking came to prevail in the Church, as a way of defending the divinity of Christ. It implied that the divine power that brought about the Resurrection belonged to Jesus himself. Nevertheless, the normal New Testament way of speaking is that Jesus was raised from the dead by the Father, and this seems a preferable way of speaking today, in accord with the renewed appreciation of the humanity of Jesus characteristic of our time.

The importance of the Resurrection does not lie merely in its vindication of Jesus' claim but also in the message intrinsic to it: that Jesus is victorious over death, that his work and life were not terminated by the crucifixion. He came to deliver people from death — death which is, in a certain human perspective, the ultimate enemy; yet he did so not by being invulnerable to death but by passing through it into eternal life. Thanks to him, this is the our destiny too, as will be seen more fully in Chapter 28. Jesus is the type or model to which we must be conformed. Belief in the Resurrection was often taken, in early Christian preaching, for the quintessence of Christian faith. Thus St. Paul writes:

> If you confess with your mouth, "Jesus is Lord," and believe in your heart that
> God raised him from the dead, you will be saved. (Romans 10:9)

Nevertheless, the Resurrection remains difficult to believe in, and is being challenged again today not only by those who reject Christianity but even by some who are trying to conceive of a resurrectionless Christianity. Without entering into a debate that has produced shelves of scholarly books, we will here recall, simply and naïvely, the substantial evidence for the Resurrection.

EVIDENCE FOR THE RESURRECTION

Our chief evidence is the witness of the apostles. They claim to have seen the Lord alive after his death and burial. He appeared to all of them except Thomas on Easter evening; a week later he appeared to all including Thomas (John 20:19-29), as he seems to have done repeatedly thereafter (Acts 1:3). He also appeared singly to Peter, James, and Paul (1 Corinthians 15:3-8). Besides the apostles, he was seen by the women at the tomb, the two disciples en route to Emmaus (Luke 24), and on occasion by more than five hundred persons at once.[11]

The accounts of these appearances are not easy to harmonize, a fact which is often used to refute them. However, the discordances are relatively slight. Perhaps the chief one is that Matthew situates Jesus' appearance to the apostles in Galilee, Luke situates it in Jerusalem, and John speaks of appearances in both Jerusalem and Galilee. Likewise Matthew has the risen Jesus appearing to two women, John speaks of Mary Magdalene alone, while Mark and Luke do not mention any appearance to women. But such discrepancies are to be expected when an event is reported by different witnesses, above all when it is an exciting and supernatural event. There are similar discrepancies in the accounts of how Pliny the Elder lost his life in the eruption of Mt. Vesuvius,[12] but no historian challenges the historicity of the fact.

Moreover, the witnesses did not merely see Jesus, they spoke with him. To dispel their fears that he was a ghost, Jesus invited them to touch him, and ate a piece of fish as they looked on (Luke 24:38-43). Thomas was absent from the first apparition. When he heard about it, he refused to believe, "unless," he said, "I see the nail marks in his hands, and put my finger where the nails were, and put my hand into his side" (John 20:25). When Jesus appeared to them again eight days later, he invited Thomas to do just that. Completely overcome, the latter responded, "My Lord and my God." The last apostle to believe in the Resurrection, Thomas was the first to profess explicitly the divinity of Christ.

Confirming the objectivity of the Resurrection is the fact of the empty tomb. The tomb had been sealed and kept under guard by Pilate's soldiers, yet the body of Jesus vanished from it in less than forty-eight hours.

Such are the accounts that the evangelists have left us. Anyone who denies the truth of the Resurrection must hold either that these accounts are fraudulent or that the disciples were deluded or something similar. Few critics suggest fraud. This would be hard to reconcile with the fact that the apostles and many other disciples endured martyrdom rather than deny Christ. Every indication suggests that they were sincere in their beliefs. Moreover, the New Testament summons people to honesty, holiness, and righteousness. It not only speaks in favor of these virtues, it breathes the very spirit of wisdom and goodness that it recommends. It is the most widely read and highly respected of all religious documents known to human history. That such a work could have been produced by scoundrels is not very plausible.

This is not a point that can be settled abstractly or in detachment from the Gospels themselves. It is one that each person must ponder while reading the Gospels for himself, and remaining open to their mysterious power to win belief. No doubt, history abounds with charlatans who have gulled the innocent under the guise of piety; but that does not mean that no book can furnish from within itself convincing proof of its own sincerity. Appealing to the evident sincerity of the Gospels may not be an effective argument for one who rejects the Resurrection as a lie; but immense numbers of readers will be ready to affirm that, whatever else must be said of them, the Gospels are not a hoax.

• *Realism of apparitions*

Another way of denying the Resurrection is to hold that those who testify to it, although in good faith, were victims of some kind of illusion. But this position likewise becomes implausible once it is examined concretely.

Wishful thinking can of course lead a person, especially in a moment of emotional stress, to imagine he sees something he intensely desires to see. But it is most improbable that whole groups should have such an illusion together and repeatedly over a period of a month and a half, in very diverse circumstances, and with different combinations of witnesses. That would be unlikely even if the apostles were mentally sick; and nothing indicates that they were. An illusion is the sign of a mind that has not a firm hold on reality; but these men, who earned their livelihood by fishing, although perhaps not particularly intelligent, were surely realistic. In any case, illusion might make a person think he sees a vision; it would hardly make a group agree about a conversation carried on with the apparition; much less that they had touched him, and felt the wounds in his hands and side. Above all, how could an illusion pick up a real fish and eat it, and how could an illusion taking place in the Upper Room explain the empty tomb at Calvary?

From another point of view, a cause must be equal to its effects. The apostles had been frightened and demoralized; at the death of Jesus they fled and hid. Something transformed them into fearless witnesses who could not be intimidated by imprisonment, beatings, or even death. They give a simple explanation of it: They have seen the risen Lord. If this explanation is rejected, another must be found. None is apparent.

• *Legend?*

A modification of the illusion thesis consists in holding that the Resurrection is a legend that arose gradually. However, we have many documents composed over a period of several decades of the early Church, and written in various places. Although traces of the most primitive Christian thought can be discerned in many of them (for example, the sermons reported in Acts), and a much later style of Christian life and thought can be recognized in others (for instance, the pastoral epistles), nowhere do we find the least vestige of a pre-Resurrection faith, nor do we find any variation of the essential theme *He is risen*. This becomes very striking by comparison with known legendary figures — for example, Asklepios, the healer born to the god Apollo and the human princess Coronis. The variations undergone by his story in the course of the centuries, and as it passes from one culture to another, betray its legendary or mythical character; but the story of Jesus' resurrection maintains its identity firmly.

• *Spiritual resurrection?*

A more subtle recent attempt to elude the historicity of the Resurrection stems largely from the German Lutheran exegete Willi Marxsen, whose work on this subject began to appear in 1964,[13] and has strongly influenced Catholic authors such as Hans Küng and Edward Schillebeeckx. They deny (directly or by implication) that the body of Jesus was ever brought back to life. Jesus has entered into "the realm of the Father" (Küng) and the disciples, beginning with Peter, realized this through some spiritual experience — for example, of forgiveness (Schillebeeckx). Their experience was really inexpressible; the only way to give others some inkling of it was to say that Jesus had risen. Hence the stories that appear in our Gospels. But it is simply not the case that an ongoing life of Jesus with the Father could not be expressed literally and directly; and it would have been a gross travesty on the part of the apostles to make up stories about things Jesus said and did on earth, if all they meant was that he now lives somehow with the Father in heaven. (Ascribing unreal deeds and words to a real person is not in the same category with telling fables to illustrate a moral truth.) The state of Jesus, in such a conception, would be no different from that of Abraham, Moses, etc. Finally, this view simply disregards St. Paul's formal teaching that our resurrection, which is modeled on that of Jesus, will involve restoration of *the body* to life (Romans 8:11).

* * *

The Resurrection is plainly inseparable from the Christian message; it is at the very heart of that message. In fact, one could say that all of Christianity reduces to the claim made by a dozen men, "Jesus has risen and we have seen him." There is no way we can get behind their testimony and verify the Resurrection directly for ourselves; but it is instructive that all attempts to explain it away lead to improbabilities more incredible than the Resurrection itself.

In any case, the question of Christian faith can be expressed thus: Do you believe what these men have said? If we do believe, our faith is not based merely on human credibility or on arguments such as those sketched above. It is the risen Jesus himself, who still lives today and is in living contact with the believer, who is the guarantee and persuader of our faith. To put it another way, it is not flesh and blood (see Matthew 16:17) that induce us to believe in the risen Jesus but the inner witness given by the heavenly Father (see John 5:37). The witness given by the apostles and evangelists was necessary to formulate in human language what is to be believed, but it is not the basis of our faith.

17

The Christ, the Son of God

From the externals of the life of Jesus, we turn now to the inner secret of his being: Who was he? What is the ultimate meaning of his life among us? These questions will occupy the next four chapters.

Although his identity is undoubtedly what interests us most about him, Jesus seems to have said very little directly on this subject. It is true that John's Gospel attributes many "I am. . ." statements to him: "I am the Bread of Life; I am the resurrection and the life; I am the way, the truth and the life; I am the true Vine; I am the Good Shepherd; I am the Light of the world"; etc., and especially the most mysterious statements of all, which declare simply, "I am."[1] There are many different views about what to make of these and other Johannine texts on the identity of Jesus. A strong evaluation would regard them as exceptional statements, not in the usual pattern of Jesus' preaching, retained only by John, the most perceptive and profound of the apostles. A weak evaluation would treat them as words invented by one circle of later Christians to express their own theology, and attributed to Jesus in order to gain authority.

The latter view seems incompatible with the divine inspiration of Scripture. The Johannine texts must be taken seriously as authentic expressions of Jesus' doctrine. How they are to be correlated with the Synoptic texts is a matter of historical speculation that need not be attempted here. We will assume, however, that the Synoptics represent the ordinary impression made by Jesus' preaching. This was focused, as we have seen (Chapter 15) on the imminent coming of the Kingdom of God. It contains no full and clear statement of what Jesus wanted his followers to believe about him. For that matter, even the Gospel of John indicates that his hearers were sometimes angered by the obscurity of his statements, for they demanded, "How long will you keep us in suspense? If you are the Christ, tell us plainly" (John 10:24).

• *Apostles had to discover his identity*

Jesus' way of revealing himself consisted in doing and saying things that raised questions in people's minds. Even the apostles were obliged to discover for themselves who he was. Then, when they put it into words, he ratified their statement, as when Peter avowed, "You are the Christ. . ." and Jesus replied, "Blessed are you, Simon Bar-Jona! For flesh and blood has not revealed this to you, but my Father who is in heaven" (Matthew 16:17, RSV). Similarly, when the high priest demanded, "Are you the Christ, the Son of the Blessed One?" and Jesus answered, "I am" (Mark 14:62).

It is instructive for us to review the major steps by which the apostles first came to discover the identity of Jesus and to formulate it in the language of their tradition; then

Jesus before the Sanhedrin.

how the early Church, immersed in a completely different culture — that of the Hellenistic world — forged other, less ambiguous expressions. We can of course make no more than a schematic outline of this living process which involved all that Jesus said and did, only a small part of which has been recorded. Moreover, the apostles' identification of Jesus came about through their personal involvement with him. Likewise it was not merely by an academic scrutiny of his words and deeds but much more by a living response to him that the later disciples came to know Jesus. Hence it is with all due caution that we dare to outline the following main stages in the development of the Christian faith.

At first, impressed by his preaching and stupefied by his miracles, the disciples asked such questions as "What kind of man is this? Even the wind and the waves obey him!" (Matthew 8:27) and "Could this be the Christ?" (John 4:29).

Then, drawing upon the categories furnished by the religious experience of Israel, they began to speak of him as a prophet (Matthew 16:16; Luke 24:19; etc.).

When their faith had fully matured, they called him the Christ (Messiah) and the Son of God. Thus, for example, Mark's Gospel opens with the heading, "The beginning of the gospel about Jesus Christ, the Son of God." The Gospel of John originally closed by saying, "These [things] are written that you may believe that Jesus is the Christ, the Son of God, and that by believing you may have life in his name" (John 20:31).[2] Matthew makes Peter's confession, "You are the Christ, the son of the living God," the crucial turning point in the development of the apostles' faith (see Chapter 5).

These two terms, *Christ* and *Son of God*, remained the principal New Testament expressions of faith. However, in a few rare instances the apostles went so far as to call Jesus simply God.

Finally, in a tough debate over the course of the next few centuries, the Church hammered out a precise and explicit statement of the sense in which Jesus was both divine and human.

Here, we will consider the three terms, *Christ, Son of God*, and *God*, as they were applied to Jesus.

THE CHRIST

Christ (in Greek, *Christos*) is the equivalent of the Hebrew *Messiah* (more exactly, *mashiah*), meaning "anointed." Originally a term applied to kings and priests, it came eventually to stand for *the* king whom the Jews expected to come and fulfill the promise made to David, to deliver Israel from its subjection to its enemies, and bring about the reign of perfect justice and peace (see Chapter 5).

Jesus seems generally to have avoided using this term for himself.[3] People sometimes wondered whether he might not be the Christ (John 8:41). But when others said it of him, he acknowledged the title, as we have seen. The reason for this way of procedure is evident. Jesus was indeed the Messiah but not the kind of messiah most people expected. When he fed them with bread in the wilderness, they wanted to make him king; he hid in order to elude their misdirected efforts (John 6:15). Some people expected him to gather an army and drive out the Romans (see John 11:48). (Even after the Resurrection, the apostles asked him, "Lord, will you at this time restore the kingdom of Israel?" [Acts 1:6].)

• Son of Man

Furthermore, Jesus reinterpreted the office of Messiah in two ways. First, he called himself the "Son of Man." This, his preferred way of designating himself, could be taken literally to mean simply a human being. However, the term has connotations deriving from Daniel's vision of one like a son of man, coming on the clouds of heaven, and receiving an everlasting kingship from God (Daniel 7:31, cited above in Chapter 5). Jesus designedly evokes these connotations when he speaks of "the Son of Man coming on the clouds of heaven with power and great glory" (Matthew 24:30). This makes it clear that he will not be a military or political leader, as many expected, but rather a "heavenly" messiah.

An even more radical, and in fact revolutionary, reinterpretation was involved in Jesus' announcement that suffering and death awaited him. This was completely alien to the messianic expectations of the time, which pictured the Messiah as a victorious and glorious figure. The apostles were so perplexed at Jesus' words that they could not take in the message (Matthew 16:22; Mark 9:32).[4]

• Isaiah: Servant of Yahweh

In effect, Jesus was identifying the Messiah with the mysterious Servant of Yahweh described in four passages of Isaiah (42:1-4; 49:1-6; 50:4-11; 52:13—53:12). The first of these begins in a way that can readily be appropriated to the Messiah:

> Here is my servant, whom I uphold, my chosen one, in whom I delight; I will put
> my Spirit on him and he will bring forth justice to the nations. . . . (42:1)

The fourth, however, describes the Servant as "a man of sorrows" who was "led like a lamb to slaughter." It declares that "Yahweh has laid on him the iniquity of us all." Hebrew commentators puzzled over the identity of this Suffering Servant, but none of them identified him with the Messiah.

It is Jesus who introduced the astounding paradox of the suffering Messiah. As Messiah, he is the fulfillment of God's promises: the agent of the establishment of God's Kingdom, the sign and guarantee of that ultimate justice by which the good will be rewarded and the wicked, if they are not repentant, will be punished. However, he is to accomplish all this not in a glorious and triumphant manner but through suffering and death. The cross was the ultimate sign of ignominy in the Roman empire, but Jesus turned it into a sign of blessing.

• *The coming of the Son of Man*

This reinterpretation led to another. Although Jesus regularly called himself the Son of Man, there were times when he spoke of the Son of Man as one who was still to come: "the Son of Man will come at an hour when you do not expect him" (Luke 12:40); "when the Son of Man comes, will he find faith on the earth?" (Luke 18:8). As the apostles came to recognize Jesus himself as the Son of Man and Messiah, they may have understood the future tense to refer to the establishment of the messianic kingdom. But then Jesus began to announce to them that he would be taken away from them and return to the Father. This filled them with grief (John 16:6; see also Matthew 17:23). They could not fit it into their expectations of a Messiah whose kingdom was to be everlasting. Jesus, however, did not explain his meaning; he merely assured them that it was good for them that he was going; otherwise the Paraclete would not come to them (John 16:7).

All this was clarified through the events of the Passion, Resurrection, and Pentecost. There are two comings of the Son of Man. He has already come once in humility and hiddenness, when he could be recognized as Messiah only by faith. The second coming will be in glory, at the time when the Kingdom of God is fully realized. Thus Christians, like the Jews of old, continue to be a people waiting for the coming of the Son of Man. The difference is that for Christians, he has made himself known already. We know for whom we are waiting. This makes us look all the more eagerly for his "Second Coming." The Church is a bride who knows her spouse and now longs for complete union with him; her constant prayer is, "Come, Lord Jesus" (Apocalypse 22:20). *Maranatha* is an Aramaic prayer used by the earliest Christian community, meaning, "Our Lord, come!" (1 Corinthians 16:22).

A major theme of Jesus' preaching was that the disciples should always be ready and waiting for the coming of the Son of Man. "You also must be ready; for the Son of man is coming at an hour you do not expect" (Matthew 24:44). "Watch therefore, for you know neither the day nor the hour" (Matthew 25:13). He will come like a thief in the night (Matthew 24:43f) or like a householder returning home from a wedding party (Luke 12:35-40); then again, he might come like a master returning from a long trip abroad (Matthew 25:14-30) or like the flood in the days of Noah (Matthew 24:37-39). "Blessed are those servants whom the master finds awake when he comes" (Luke 12:37). This was equivalent to telling them to be ready for the Kingdom of God. The prayer *Maranatha* is matched by a petition of the Our Father, "Thy kingdom come" (Matthew 6:10). The early Christians looked eagerly for the Lord's return. "Hasten the day of his coming," they were urged in 2 Peter 3:11. If Christians today do not pray for the return of the Lord and the coming of the Kingdom but rather fear this event or ignore it as something they need not be concerned about, they have lost one of the chief attitudes inculcated by Jesus. May they not be falling into that very unreadiness against which all the above parables were warning?

THE SON OF GOD

The second major faith-title given to Jesus is *Son of God*. It is not to be confused with *Christ* or *Messiah*. The Jews did not ordinarily refer to the expected Messiah as the Son of God, and they certainly did not expect the Messiah to be divine. Conversely, when the early disciples called Jesus the Son of God, they were affirming not merely his messiahship but something deeper. Eventually of course the two terms tended to be used interchangeably with one another,[5] but this was not so from the beginning.

The title *Son of God* was conferred on Jesus quite dramatically on two occasions. At his baptism, while the Spirit of God hovered over him in the form of a dove, a voice from heaven declared, "You are my beloved Son, with you I am well pleased" (Mark 1:11). Later Jesus was transfigured before three of the apostles: "His face shone like the sun, and his garments became white as light." Moses and Elijah, the two greatest figures of the Old Testament, appeared and spoke with him. Then a bright cloud overshadowed them all, and a voice from the cloud declared, "This is my beloved Son, with whom I am well pleased; listen to him" (Matthew 17:1-8).

• *Jesus as Son of God*

Jesus, however, did not ordinarily call himself the Son of God.[6] Rather, he intimated it, plainly but indirectly. "No one knows the Son except the Father," he said, and "no one knows the Father except the Son, and anyone to whom the Son chooses to reveal him" (Matthew 11:27). It is in the Gospel of John that the sense of this title is brought out most

fully and emphatically. Jesus said that he had come forth from the Father and come into the world; that he would leave the world and return to the Father (John 16:28). His doctrine was not his; he had received it from the Father (John 7:16). He did the works that the Father had given him to do (John 5:36).

Although Jesus taught his disciples to pray to God as their Father, he made it evident that he was God's Son in a way that no one else was. He spoke of the glory he had had with the Father before the world existed (John 17:5). He said, "He that sees me sees the Father" (John 14:9, RSV). The pinnacle of his association of himself with the Father was the declaration "The Father and I are one" (John 10:30; see also 17:22).[7]

• *Son in a unique and proper sense*

From such teachings, the disciples came to realize that Jesus was Son of God in a unique sense. This awareness is perhaps best summed up in this statement of St. John: "No one has ever seen God; the only Son, who is in the bosom of the Father, has revealed him" (1:18). The first chapter of the Letter to the Hebrews contains a prolonged meditation on the theme that no one else, not even the angels, has so excellent a name, even though the author is well aware that angels were commonly called sons of God (in a weaker sense) in the Old Testament. The idea underlying such statements is that Jesus is the Son of God in a unique and proper[8] sense, whereas others can be called sons of God only metaphorically. St. Paul brings this out in teaching that we become *adopted* sons by receiving the Spirit of Jesus, the *natural* Son:

When the time had fully come, God sent his Son, born of a woman, born under law, to redeem those under law, that we might receive the full rights of sons. Because you are sons, God sent the Spirit of his Son into our hearts, the Spirit who calls out, "*Abba*! Father!" (Galatians 4:4-6; see also Ephesians 1:5; Romans 8:14ff)

THE DIVINITY OF CHRIST

We can schematize the implications of the term *Son of God* in the following way: A son is of the same nature as his parents. If Jesus was the son of God in a strict and proper sense, it follows that he must be of the same nature as God, his Father — that is, he must be divine. Of course we cannot suppose that either the disciples of Jesus or the writers of the New Testament reflected academically on the distinction between proper and metaphorical uses of terms. But without any philosophical analysis, people who use metaphors (especially those who use them as lavishly and colorfully as did the Hebrews) are quite conscious of the fact that when you say that Simon is the son of John, you are speaking literally, whereas when you call him a son of Satan, it is only a figure of speech. In this perspective, we can say that when they heard Jesus spoken of (explicitly or implicitly) as God's Son, they may very well have taken it at first in a figurative sense. But the uniqueness, realism, and strength of all that was said about Jesus' sonship, by himself or others, gradually and cumulatively led them, as it leads us, to recognize that the term was meant strictly and properly (that is to say, as properly as any human term can be applied to God; see note 7). The ultimate implication of this language therefore is the divinity of Christ; as the Gospel of John puts it, "he was even calling God his own Father, making himself equal to God" (John 5:18). And Jesus' enemies declared, "You, a mere man, claim to be God" (John 10:33). Ordinarily, it was by means of this term, *Son of God*, that the New Testament expressed its faith on this point.

• *Jesus' implicit claims to divinity*

However, the logical implications of the title *Son of God* are by no means the only basis for belief in the divinity of Jesus. There are many other indications. Jesus made some extraordinary claims about himself which would seem to imply divinity. He represented himself as "Lord of the Sabbath" (Mark 2:28), with authority to set aside or to judge authoritatively about the sabbatical prescriptions, even though the Sabbath was the holy day instituted by the command of God. He held himself to be greater than the Temple, even though this was God's holy dwelling (Matthew 12:6). In the Sermon on the Mount, he declared repeatedly, "You have heard that it was said to the people long ago . . . but I tell you. . ." (Matthew 5:21ff). As what had been "said to the people long ago" was the law which came from God, this too suggests a claim to divine authority. He forgave sins (Mark 2:5; Luke 7:48) and, as his hearers did not fail to observe, "Who can forgive sins but God alone?" (Mark 2:7). Finally, he told the Jewish people, "Your Father Abraham rejoiced at the thought of seeing my day; he saw it and was glad." When his hearers scoffed at this because he was too young, he replied, "Before Abraham was born, I am" (John 8:58).

On another plane, Jesus demanded of his followers an absolute loyalty and devotion, such as no one but God could rightly claim. He required that we be ready to leave father and mother, wife and children, brothers and sisters, to follow him. In fact, we must be ready to deny our very own selves, and to lose our lives for his sake (Mark 8:34f). Who but God would have the right to make such demands? He claimed to give life to those who came to him: "Just as the living Father sent me, and I live because of [or by] the Father, so the one who feeds on me will live because of [or by] me" (John 6:57).

Besides the teachings and claims of Jesus, we have to consider also his deeds. The Gospels tell of him healing the sick of all sorts and even raising the dead, as we saw in Chapter 16. He healed them sometimes by a touch, sometimes by a simple word of command from a distance. Miracles had already been recorded of the prophets — but never such a proliferation of miracles as this. And the way he worked them, not beseeching God or invoking any kind of help (John 11:41 is a rare exception) but simply speaking with authority, suggests that the power he exercised belonged to him and was exercised in his own name. Finally, he himself, after being put to death, rose again. All this shows divine power at work in him in a way that was unique. If it doesn't prove that he himself was God, at least it gives divine confirmation to all that he said. And in some miracles, such as commanding the wind and the sea to be still, he acted in a manner that would seem appropriate solely to the author and Lord of nature.

• *Jesus called God*

The disciples' concept of Jesus arose gradually out of all these signs and indications. From regarding him as a prophet, they came little by little to see him not only as the Messiah but also as the Son of God in a unique and proper sense. Finally they went so far as to call him simply *God*. The first person to do this was Thomas, as we have seen (Chapter 16).

The most famous statement of the divinity of Christ is the prologue to St. John's Gospel:

> In the beginning was the Word, and the Word was with God, and the Word was God. . . . The Word became flesh, and lived for a while among us. We have seen his glory, the glory of the one and only Son, who came from the Father full of grace and truth. (John 1:1-14)

A few other New Testament texts which more or less openly declare the divinity of Christ are: 1 John 5:20; Romans 9:5; Philippians 2:6; Titus 2:13. But each of these texts would require a discussion too lengthy for us to go into here.

Such statements are, however, exceptional. In the ordinary language of the New Testament, following the usage of Jesus himself, the term *God* refers simply to the Father. Jesus is usually referred to not as God but as God's Son. This is understandable on purely psychological grounds. For people who had striven to maintain belief in an invisible, infinite, transcendent God in opposition to the anthropomorphic deities of the pagans, it was not easy to begin to apply the term *God* to a human being with whom they had been associating familiarly. But there was also a deeper, theological reason. Besides being related to the Father, Jesus had to be differentiated from him; it was therefore natural to continue to speak in terms of God and God's Son.

Another title which indicated Jesus' divinity is *Lord.* At first sight, this term may not seem very significant; and no doubt, the many texts which represent Jesus' contemporaries addressing him as Lord ordinarily mean this simply as a title of respect, very much as we say "Sir" in English. However, the Jews usually referred to God as "the Lord" (especially when reading Scripture passages containing the word *Yahweh*). Hence when, after the Resurrection, Christian Jews called Jesus the Lord, they were using a title which, in a religious context, ordinarily referred to Yahweh. This is especially striking when Old Testament passages referring to God are applied to Jesus. Thus Joel 2:32, "It shall come to pass that everyone who calls upon the name of the Lord shall be delivered," refers to Yahweh; but it is understood of Jesus in Romans 10:13.

* * *

In conclusion, the New Testament faith in Jesus is summed up chiefly in the two terms *Christ* and *Son of God*, supplemented by *the Lord. Christ* meant that he was the long-awaited Messiah. *Son of God* and *Lord* are elastic terms. They could be used in a way that implied little more than profound reverence, and no doubt this is how they were often understood at first. But each could also be used in a sense implying divinity: *Son of God* because of the implications of genuine sonship, and *Lord* because this was the usual name for God. From the various things Jesus did and said, his disciples gradually came to use these terms in a more and more profound sense that quite transcended the messianic expectations and indeed all human categories. This awakening realization comes to its fullest expression in the cry of Thomas, "My Lord and my God." Jesus is Son of God and Lord in so true and profound a sense that he himself can rightly be called God, like the Father. Nevertheless, the ordinary language of the New Testament continued to designate the Father alone as God, and Jesus as the Lord.

18

Father, Son, and Holy Spirit: the Trinity and the Incarnation

We have seen that in the teaching of the New Testament Jesus is "Son of God" in a unique and proper sense, with the consequence that he too can be called God, just as truly as the Father. Now we must examine more fully the meaning of this basic dogma of Christian faith. If the Father and Son are both God, how can there be only one God? Moreover, if Jesus is God, what is to be made of his humanity?

These problems did not trouble Jesus' immediate disciples. The gentle, concrete way in which Jesus made his divinity known allowed them to accept him and commit themselves to him without posing theoretical questions. (If he had followed the brusque, violent manner of the demoniacs, who called him Son of God from the outset, things would undoubtedly have been quite different.) The prevailing language of the early Christians, still preserved in the Creeds, speaks of "God the Father" and of "Jesus Christ his Son." Alongside that, however, the practice of speaking of Jesus himself as God little by little became established, as is witnessed in the letters of Ignatius, one of the earliest bishops of Syria (died circa 107). Likewise Pliny, the Roman governor of the northern part of Asia Minor, in a report describing the perplexing new sect of Christians, says that when they meet together, "they recite a hymn to Christ as God."[1]

Not until about the third century, when intellectuals began to come into the Church, and schools of theology began to form, theoretical statements about the nature of Jesus appear. This started a period of intense, and at times furious, theological reflection. At first, because Christianity was still outlawed and persecuted, the discussions were mostly confined to particular localities; but after the Edict of Milan (313) allowed Christians the freedom to take part in public life, it was not long before theological controversy embroiled the entire Church. Today we tend to take for granted the results of their intense debates. It will be instructive for us to review the main steps leading to these results.

TRINITY

If Jesus is the Son of God, this would seem to mean that in some sense he originates from God. And in fact he said, "I came from the Father. . ." (John 16:28). But would that not imply that he is subsequent to God, and therefore less than God? This would contradict the conclusion which, as we have seen, was drawn already within the New Testament, that Jesus was the son of God in so true and proper a sense that he himself can be called God.

• Arianism

The one who made this issue famous was Arius, a very learned and intelligent priest living in Alexandria (Egypt) at the beginning of the fourth century. A very ascetic man, he was highly regarded by his bishop, who put him in charge of an important parish. As Arius joined in the current theological reflections on the meaning of "Son of God," what impressed him chiefly was the fact that the Son had come forth from the Father. That being the case, "there was [a moment] when he did not exist." This was incompatible with divinity. Arius concluded that, since only the Father is without a beginning, only the Father is truly God.

"Son of God" can then be applied to Jesus in a sense not essentially different from the way we too are called children of God. Arius granted that the Son has a priority over all other creatures (for "through him all things were made" [John 1:1]). But in the last analysis, the Son of God was a creature, not the Creator. Arius favored St. John's expression, *the Word of God*, because it harmonized with the Platonic philosophy current at that time. He understood it in reference to the work of creation, which began with God uttering a creative Word, which in turn brought all other creatures into existence. The Word is from God and before all other creatures; this explains why divine honor is sometimes paid to him, and why St. John wrote, "The Word is God." But in the last analysis, the Word himself had been created.

• Council of Nicaea

This theory shocked Christians who had long been accustomed to venerate Jesus as true God. But Arius won many followers, and soon the eastern end of the Mediterranean was split by a bitter theological controversy. The emperor Constantine, who thought he had brought peace to the Church by the Edict of Milan, was perplexed to find Christians now in conflict with one another. In an effort to restore harmony to his domain, he summoned all the bishops of the Church to meet in 325 at Nicaea (a town close to his new capitol, Constantinople), and there settle this vexing question. Thus originated the first of the series of ecumenical councils.[2]

The First Council of Nicaea solemnly condemned Arius's position. One of its decisive considerations was the fact that for Arius the Son of God would not be truly and properly a son but rather a *work* of God, something quite different. He would have been *made*, not *begotten*. That which you make can indeed be said to come *from* you in a certain sense: The statue comes *from* the sculptor and the chair *from* the carpenter. But only in a metaphorical sense can such works of art be called the children, or offspring, of the one who makes them. As we have already seen, the biblical language about Jesus as Son of God has an earnestness and an emphasis which demand that it be taken as more than a mere metaphor. (In this connection, it is significant that Arius did not care much for the expression *Son of God*.)

What precisely distinguishes engendering, or begetting, from making? That which is engendered comes from the very substance of its parents, whereas that which is made normally consists of some other material; it does not arise out of the body of the maker. Second, that which is engendered is of the same nature as the parents who engender it; that which is made need not be. Finally, there is a vital continuity between the parent and the offspring which is not the case with the artist and his artifacts. The life of the child is like a continuation of the life of the parent, similar to a fire ignited from another fire.

To declare the Church's faith in the divinity of Christ, the Council took a profession of faith that was already in use (probably at Jerusalem) and added to it the phrases "God from God, light from light, true God from true God, begotten, not made." This was their way of insisting that the Son comes from the Father as a true and proper son, with the same divine nature as his Father.

But this raises another problem. When human parents engender a child, the result is another being of the same nature. Applied to the divinity, this would mean that Father and Son were two gods. (Taking the Holy Spirit into consideration would give three.) But it is the most fundamental affirmation of both Jewish and Christian faith that there is only one God. Our reason is utterly baffled by the problem of reconciling the oneness of God with the divinity of Father, Son, and Spirit. We have no earthly analogy for it (St. Patrick and his shamrock notwithstanding). We can only hold to both affirmations of Scripture and say that even though the Son comes forth from the Father, he remains one with him in so intimate a way that the two of them still constitute only one God. "I and the Father are one" (John 10:30), as Jesus said. We do not comprehend this; nothing in our experience can enable us to conceive of a Father and Son who are one and the same being. There is no way to explain, understand, or justify this doctrine about the mystery of divinity. It is an affirmation that can only be made in faith — faith in the divine revelation which teaches both that there is one only God, and that Jesus Christ is God's Son, and himself God.

The Council of Nicaea affirmed this by adding still another phrase to its description of the Son: "consubstantial *[homo-ousios]* with the Father." This means not only that he is of the same nature as the Father but that the two of them have identically the same substance. They are not only alike in nature (as are two human beings); rather, they are one and the same being.

• *The Nicene Creed*

Thus originated the "Nicene Creed" used in the Sunday liturgy:

> We believe in one God, the Father, the Almighty, maker of heaven and earth, of all that is seen and unseen.
>
> We believe in one Lord, Jesus Christ, the only Son of God, eternally begotten of the Father, *God from God, Light from Light, true God from true God, begotten, not made, one in being with the Father.* Through him all things were made.
>
> For us men and for our salvation he came down from heaven: by the power of the Holy Spirit he was born of the Virgin Mary, and became man. For our sake he was crucified under Pontius Pilate; he suffered, died, and was buried. On the third day he rose again in fulfillment of the Scriptures; he ascended into heaven and is seated at the right hand of the Father. He will come again in glory to judge the living and the dead, and his kingdom will have no end.

We believe in the Holy Spirit, the Lord, the giver of life, who proceeds from the Father and the Son. With the Father and the Son he is worshiped and glorified. He has spoken through the prophets. We believe in one holy catholic and apostolic Church. We acknowledge one baptism for the forgiveness of sins. We look for the resurrection of the dead, and the life of the world to come.

The italicized lines are those inserted by the Council of Nicaea. The Creed we use today is not identical with that promulgated at Nicaea. Besides containing several subsequent additions, it may have originated separately. Its traditional name, *Nicene*, can be justified by the fact that it incorporates the essential phrases of the Nicene doctrine.

Note that the translation in current usage, in order to avoid language obscure to most of the faithful, says, "one in being with the Father." But the actual term used by the Council, *homo-ousios* ("consubstantial") was a technical one, coined precisely for the purpose of expressing the Son's oneness with the Father. This was the first time in history that a philosophical term was adopted in an official document of the Church. This step was taken with reluctance, but there was no other way to exclude the error of Arius unmistakably. Since then, other councils have not hesitated to follow the same course.

• *Rational theology*

It is common today to belittle the doctrinal achievements of the early Church councils, with their precise definitions couched in philosophical language. Such a "Hellenization" of Christianity is sneered at as false intellectualism or an adulteration of the simple, robust faith of the first disciples. But man is naturally and inevitably an intellectual animal. He can be satisfied only for a while on rough statements and picturesque images such as those provided by Scripture. If a truth is precious to him, he wants to grasp it as exactly and understand it as fully as possible. There are of course some who, left to themselves, can get along indefinitely without theology and without posing intellectual questions; however, once a question has been posed, they need to have an answer. When wrong answers are being given, it is urgent to find the right one; good aspirations can be misdirected, and minds poisoned by bad theology. It was necessary therefore that rational theology develop in the Church. When questions about the faith began to be posed and answered, the Church immediately concerned itself with these theological debates and when necessary took a stand on them. For while official Church doctrine and academic theology are not one and the same thing, they are intimately and inseparably bound up with one another, in such a way that theological reflections are rooted in and subsequently have a considerable impact upon the beliefs and attitudes of the people.

• *The Son not inferior to the Father*

But what about the problem of eternity, raised by Arius? If the Father engendered the Son, it would appear that the Father came before the Son. But then the Son would not be eternal, and so could not be God. On the other hand, if the Son is divine, he must be eternal; but then how could he have been engendered by the Father? Here the solution is not so difficult. In God, the act of engendering a child is not an event that occurs in time as in the material world. Just as the Father is eternal, so is the Son and so also the act whereby the Father engenders the Son. In other words, the fathering of the Son is not an *event* that occurred at some past moment; it is an act that goes on eternally. The Father is eternally in the act of engendering a Son; the Son is eternally in the act of coming forth from the Father.

We should add that in our world, the offspring normally begins its career in a state of imperfection which we call infancy. It has to grow gradually to maturity. Ultimately it may surpass its parents, but at birth it is quite inferior to them. In God, however, the Son comes forth already equal to the Father. Both possess the same nature, the same properties, in fact, the very same being. All the divine attributes — omnipotence, omniscience, omnipresence, etc. — are attributes of the Son just as much as of the Father. "All that belongs to the Father is mine" (John 16:15). The only distinction between Father and Son is that they possess the divine nature or substance in two distinct ways: the one, as engendering, the other, as being engendered. But they are both divine and equal in every other respect. "Whatever the Father does, the Son also does" (John 5:19).

• *The Holy Spirit*

Besides the Father and the Son, *the Holy Spirit* must be integrated into this picture. What we know about him comes chiefly from the works attributed to him, such as teaching and sanctifying the disciples of Jesus which we will examine later (Part 5). From a careful study of these works, the Church of the third century recognized that he too, like the Son, had to be a divine person. (Otherwise, why would his presence make us a "temple" [1 Corinthians 3:16; 6:19; etc.]? And how could any but a divine being sanctify us?) Thus the Christian idea of God has not just two but three "persons" to reckon with.

Like the Son, the Holy Spirit comes forth from the Father; Jesus calls him "the Spirit of Truth who goes out from the Father" (John 15:26). However, he cannot be regarded as a second son. Nowhere in Scripture is he ever referred to as a son, whereas Jesus is called *The* Son as by his proper title, and even "the only Son" (John 1:18). The name *Holy Spirit* does not help us much here. It does not directly designate his relations with Father and Son but the role he plays among us creatures: that of inspiring. As regards his situation in the Trinity, we can say only that he comes forth from the Father like the Son but without being a son. Also, since the Son (as well as the Father) sends him to us (John 16:7), he must come forth not only from the Father but also from the Son; for the eternal relations of Son and Spirit are mirrored in the way these two divine persons are communicated to us on earth. This last point, which came to be recognized in the Western Church especially through the influence of St. Augustine, was not generally accepted in the East; and this disagreement was one of the points that contributed to separate the Orthodox from the Roman Catholics.

• *Not parts or manifestations*

We can sum this up by saying that in God, there are these three, Father, Son, and Holy Spirit, of whom the Son comes forth from the Father, and the Spirit from the Father and the Son together. But now we must ask the question "Three what?" If they are not three gods, are they parts of God? Are we to regard God as a troika, a triumvirate, a committee of three, none of whom by himself is God? This clearly will not work because, if there is anything evident from the New Testament, it is that the Father *is* God, not just a fraction of God. And it is certain also, as we have seen, that the Son is God, and the Holy Spirit likewise. We have to say that the Father is God, the Son is God, and the Holy Spirit is God; yet there is only one God.

May we say then that these are three manifestations of the one God? That he showed himself in certain circumstances in the role of Father, in others as our Brother, and finally as the Spirit who inspires us from within? This theory, concocted very early in the Church, is known as Modalism: one God manifesting himself in three modes. It reappeared in the sixteenth century in the wake of the Reformation, although rejected by all the major Protestant denominations, and led to the creation of the Unitarian (= anti-Trinitarian) Church, found chiefly in England and North America. It tends to be adopted, in one form or another, by theologians who are more concerned with creating a rational or philosophical theology than one that is completely submitted to Scripture (Paul Tillich is a major recent example).

• *Jesus distinct from Father and Spirit*

There is no doubt that the doctrine of the Trinity defies rational explanation and comprehension. However, it is equally evident that a modalist or unitarian interpretation of the Trinity does not conform to the teaching of the New Testament. Jesus tells us that he came forth from the Father and has been sent into the world by the Father. He prayed to the Father; he left the world to return to the Father, while sending the Holy Spirit to take his place. These things and many others like them imply that there must be a *real* distinction between Father, Son, and Spirit. Yet they are together one God.

• *Person*

We return therefore to the question "Three what?" If they are not three beings but are more than parts, aspects, or manifestations of one being, what term can be used for them? We are so accustomed to the formula "three persons in one God" that we may not be conscious of the hesitation with which the Church originally adopted it, after tentative experiments with other terminology. It has the disadvantage that, in the human world from which our language takes off, three persons are three distinct beings, which is precisely what we must avoid saying of God. St. Augustine declared that we say three persons simply because we have to say something, and have found no better term.

St. Thomas, however, was able to provide a rationale for this choice. *Person*, he said, is the term we use for individuals of an intelligent nature. Among men, as among angels, one who is distinct from others and cannot be subdivided further (that is, without being destroyed) is called a person. So, because Father, Son, and Spirit are distinct from one another, and cannot be subdivided any further, they are rightly called persons (*Summa Theologiae*, I, 29, 4).

There has been during the present century an intense philosophical and psychological reflection on the meaning and nature of personality, and the question has been raised whether we today ought to continue to speak of divine persons as the early Church did.

Father, Son, and Spirit at the baptism of Jesus.

Karl Barth, a Protestant, and Karl Rahner, a Catholic, have both suggested that the term *person* needs to be replaced by something else ("mode of being" and "mode of subsistence" are proposed as substitutes). Obviously, the Councils of Nicaea, Constantinople, Ephesus, and Chalcedon did not use the term with the meaning attributed to it by modern personalist philosophy; and many of the connotations taken on by the term today must be excluded from a definition of the Trinity. But this term has become so classical in the language of the Church that it would be extremely difficult to replace it; and its theological sense has been defined with such precision and agreement (something that cannot be said of modern philosophical terminology!) that it would seem wiser as well as simpler to retain the traditional language, while cautioning contemporary philosophers not to plug the Trinitarian doctrine uncritically into their language systems.

It is possible that modern personalism may lead us to new insights into the mystery of the Trinity. We must indeed be open to such developments. On the other hand, it must be borne in mind that new insights into *human* personality are not *ipso facto* transferable to the divine persons, who are called persons very improperly, for want of a better term.

• *Three persons, one substance*

While insisting on the distinction of Father, Son, and Spirit from one another, it is necessary also to maintain the unity of the Godhead. The language which was eventually established for this says that there are in God three persons but only one substance. As noted above, this conflicts with our earthly experience, in which distinct persons are also distinct substances; but we must recognize that all such terms, when applied to God, can at best be used analogically. They are not realized in God in the same way as in creatures.

When compared with one another, the three divine persons are alike in every respect except for the relationships, such as Father to Son and Son to Father, which differentiate them. The three are equally powerful, wise, good, etc. If one were less than another he would not be God. In the language of Jesus, this is expressed by various particular statements, such as, "The Son can do nothing by himself; he can do only what he sees his Father doing" (John 5:19); "My teaching is not my own. It comes from him who sent me" (John 7:16); and "All that belongs to the Father is mine" (John 16:15). These not only declare his *human* dependence on the divine, they also reflect the deeper truth that the divinity which is in him derives from the Father. This is the very Father-Son relationship which gives each of them a distinct character. Similarly, Jesus says of the Holy Spirit, "He will bring glory to me by taking from what is mine and making it known to you" (John 16:14). Scripture does not speak in terms of Trinitarian theology, but it is on the basis of statements such as these that this theology arose.

295

• *Appropriations*

Traditionally, different attributes have been associated with each of the three persons; for example, power with the Father, wisdom with the Son, and love with the Holy Spirit. This is a helpful way of concretizing the distinction between them, but it cannot be taken as a real differentiation whereby the Father would be the power of the Godhead, the Son wisdom, etc. In such a case, none of them would be fully God, and we would be back into a species of modalism. Each of the three is just as powerful, wise, and loving as the others.

In that mysterious inner activity which constitutes the life of the Trinity, whereby one person comes forth from another, their roles are distinct. But in the act of creation, and in all the activity by which God deals with creation, the three all act together. It is not only the Father who creates but also the Son and the Spirit; it is not only the Spirit who sanctifies but also the Father and the Son. Otherwise an inequality would be introduced among them.

This is more difficult to see in the case of the Son, who became man, lived among us, suffered, died, and rose again. These things cannot be said of the Father or the Spirit. However, all these events took place in his humanity, as we are about to see. They do not differentiate him, *in his divinity*, from the other two persons.

• *Special work of Son or Spirit?*

A more difficult question has to do with the "indwelling" of the Holy Spirit. The language of Jesus, declaring that the Spirit will dwell in us, teach us, bear witness to us, etc. (see John 14-16), is so strong that some modern theologians (especially since Scheeben) are unwilling to regard this as merely a way of "appropriating" to the Spirit a work that is really common to all three persons. On the other hand, it is certain that the Father and Son also dwell within us (John 14:23). It seems better therefore to maintain the traditional position that the three *always* act in unison.

It is even more important, however, not to get hung up on such issues, puzzling how three can be one and one can be three. From the outset, we should acknowledge that God is a mystery transcending the fumbling grasp of our reason. We could spend forever trying to figure him out, and make little significant progress. In effect, we would be turning the Trinity into a conundrum.

The diverse rays of light by which Jesus has given us a glimpse into the secrets of the divinity were not intended to challenge our intellectual ingenuity but to bring us into intimate, knowing, and loving contact with God. The life that Christ brought us is a participation in the interpersonal life of the three divine persons, and the teaching of faith is meant to acquaint us with these persons and with the life they share with us.

As in God the Son arises from the Father, so in the world the Son has been sent from the Father to restore what sin has disordered. And as the Holy Spirit arises from the Father and Son, so he has been sent into the world by the Father and Son to sanctify it. The grace we receive is a Trinitarian grace, in which the Holy Spirit identifies us with the Son so as to make us children of the Father. The eternal, inner "processes" by which the Son and Spirit proceed from the Father are mysteriously realized in us by grace. People who live

296

this divine life profoundly and sensitively — especially mystics — sometimes experience these "processes" within themselves. For example, someone who has been taught to pray to Jesus may find himself turning spontaneously to the Father in unison with the Son.

It is in this perspective primarily that we ought to view the Blessed Trinity; our knowledge of the Trinity ought to be chiefly the knowledge of those who enter vitally into its life. Then the conundrum aspect and the intellectual puzzles will become insignificant.

THE INCARNATION

From the Trinity, we turn to the mystery of the Incarnation. The former has to do with the three persons of the Godhead; the latter has to do with the second person becoming man. The term *Incarnation* originates from a line in the Prologue of St. John's Gospel (1:14): "The Word became flesh and lived for a while among us. . . ."

Incarnation means literally "enfleshment." (The root *carn-*, from which also the words *carnal* and *carnivorous* derive, means flesh.) It was coined to designate this unique event: that the second person of the Blessed Trinity, the Son (or Word of God), took upon himself human flesh and lived among us as the man Jesus.

The idea of a god taking on human form is not peculiar to Christianity; it appears in various religions. In Hindu mythology, the god Vishnu has appeared on earth repeatedly not only as man but also in the shape of various beasts. The most famous of these "avatars" is Krishna, from whom "Krishna consciousness" gets its name. In Roman mythology, Jupiter occasionally put on a human form in order to visit earth. On one occasion, accompanied by Mercury, he rewarded the hospitality of an old couple, Baucis and Philemon, by turning them into a couple of trees that lived on for ages at the gate of a temple to Jupiter.

In the study of comparative religion, these earthly appearances of divine beings are often called incarnations by analogy with the Christian Incarnation. But not only was this term coined originally by Christians to refer to Christ; the very concept of incarnation is quite different in Christianity from the mythological parallels. In the myths, the gods take on the appearance of human beings, but they do not ordinarily become genuine men. They want to appear as men and speak with men, perhaps to make a revelation. But when they have finished this escapade, they drop their human appearance and return to their divine state. They do not become really *involved* in human life. *Jesus*, however, is not just the mask of a halloweening god; his humanity is fully real. He is a historical person whose life can be dated and his footsteps traced like those of other human beings. Even at the end of his life on earth, he did not simply discard the body in which he had gone about; he keeps it eternally in a glorified state, as a pledge of the glory promised to all who follow him.

The fact that mythical religions have had beliefs in some way analogous to the Incarnation has nevertheless made some Christians uneasy over the thought that perhaps the Incarnation is only our peculiar form of a universal mythical type. But rather than an argument against the reality of the Incarnation, this fact can be seen as a sign of a deep and widespread human yearning for contact with God. "O that you would rend the heavens and come down," sighed the prophet Isaiah (64:1). What we see in Jesus Christ is that God has responded to this natural human aspiration.

• Reality of Jesus' humanity

Early Christian thinkers wrestled for several centuries with the mystery of the Incarnate Word, and the history of their reflections can help give us a right understanding of the humanity of Jesus and its union with the divinity. The first point to be established was that the humanity of Jesus was completely real, the very point which distinguishes the Christian belief from the myths. It surprises us, perhaps, that the earliest heresy about Jesus Christ did not assail his divinity but instead denied his genuine humanity. The Docetists held that the Word of God had taken on merely the appearance of humanity in order to deliver his message to mankind. They seem to have been motivated by the idea, which stemmed from the Zoroastrians of Persia, that there is something inherently evil and contemptible in flesh, making it unworthy for God to take upon himself. There were Docetists already in the first century, and it may well be that the Prologue of John was composed with the deliberate intention of rejecting their error. Even more vigorously, St. John's First Epistle declares:

> This is how you can recognize the Spirit of God: Every spirit that acknowledges that Jesus Christ has come in the flesh is from God, but every spirit that does not acknowledge Jesus is not from God. (4:2-3)

Accordingly, the Church holds that the flesh of Jesus was real and not just an appearance.[3] He made himself genuinely and fully our brother, and it was precisely as such that he brought about our salvation, as we will see in the following chapter. The Letter to the Hebrews sums the matter up forcefully:

> Jesus is not ashamed to call them brothers. . . . Since the children have flesh and blood, he too shared in their humanity so that by his death he might destroy him who holds the power of death — that is, the devil. . . . For surely it is not angels he helps, but Abraham's descendants. (2:11-16)

• Jesus' human soul

A second point about the humanity of Jesus that had to be affirmed very early was that it was *full and complete*. In attempting to visualize how the divine and human are united in Christ, one theologian of the fourth century, Apollinaris, took the text "The Word became flesh" to mean very strictly that Jesus had only a human body, and that the functions of the soul were carried on in him by the divinity. Whereas the Docetists denied the body of Jesus, Apollinaris denied his soul. This seemed like a plausible way to explain how he was both divine and human. But the Church reacted strongly against this theory also, because a body without a soul is not a human being. The soul is essential to our being human. In effect, Apollinaris's theory would make of Jesus an inanimate body being used by God to talk to men — a mere puppet. In that case there would be no true *Incarnation*. If Jesus was a genuine man, he had to have all that is essential to man.

In the seventh century, some Eastern theologians proposed that Jesus was a complete human being except that he did not have a distinct human will (hence their name,

Monothelites). They felt perhaps afraid that to speak of a human will in him, distinct from the divine will, would imply that, as man, he willed something other than what God willed. (In Greek, as in English, the word *will* is ambiguous, designating both the faculty and the act of willing.) The Church reacted just as in the previous case. It is essential to human nature that it include a human will; Jesus therefore, if he was a true man, had a human as well as a divine will. His sinlessness came about not by suppression of the human faculty of will but by the free and loving conformity of his human will to the divine.

• *Nestorius*

But if Jesus is a real and complete human being, how does this human being relate to the Son of God, who is an eternal divine person? A theory made famous by Nestorius, patriarch of Constantinople, proposed that the Son of God, or the "Word of God," inhabited the man Jesus somewhat as the Holy Spirit dwells in every Christian. The union between Jesus and the Word was more perfect and complete than the union between ourselves and the Holy Spirit; but it was, according to Nestorius, of the same general order. He held that the Divine Word entered into Jesus shortly after the latter was conceived by Mary; from then on, in all that he did, the man Jesus was guided by the Divine Word.

The views of Nestorius were drawn to public attention by an incident which may at first seem unrelated to it and inconsequential. Greek Christians had developed the habit of referring to the Virgin Mary as *theotokos*, that is, Mother of God (literally: "God-bearer"). Nestorius forbade the use of this term, explaining that Mary can be called mother of Jesus, or mother of Christ, but not mother of God. The people protested and a great public debate ensued, in which it soon became evident that the fundamental question was not about Mary but about Christ. If he was a combination of two persons, closely associated, as Nestorius held, Mary was obviously mother only of the human person, Jesus. But then you could not say that the divine person had *become* man but only that he had entered into a man.

• *Jesus only one person*

The instinct of the Church, voiced especially by St. Cyril of Alexandria, was to insist that Jesus Christ is only one being, one person. This person had existed from all eternity as God the Son. For our salvation, he became man and lived and acted among us as a genuine man. Hence one and the same person was both God and man. Jesus, though a real man, was also himself truly God. The apostle Thomas was right in calling him, "My Lord and my God." But if that is so, then the child born to Mary was God, and Mary can in full truth, without any exaggeration or imprecision, be called Mother of God. This does not mean that his divinity originated in her. In his divinity, he existed before her, and he created her. But in becoming man, the Son of God truly became the son of Mary because he drew his human nature from her just as every other child draws its nature from its parents.

By the same token, it is perfectly accurate to say that it was God who walked the roads of Galilee, who got thirsty and asked a drink of the Samaritan woman; God was scourged, crowned, and crucified; it was God who died on the cross. This does not mean that the divinity underwent change, or alteration, because all of these things took place not in his divinity, which is eternal and unalterable, but in his humanity, which is like ours. However, because that humanity belonged to the divine person, and not to some autonomous human person, all these things can be said to have happened to God. They did not change or affect his divinity in any way because they took place in his humanity, which is distinct from his divinity. But they do belong to him as the person to whom the actions and experiences must be attributed because he was only one person, one being, one "subject," even though living on two planes or in two realms.

Note that not even the Incarnation itself implied a change in God. If it did, it would be incompatible with divinity. But how can God really become man without changing? Here too the change takes place solely on the side of the human nature, which is brought into existence from nothing, and "attached," to put it crudely, to the second person of the Trinity, without that person undergoing any intrinsic alteration whatsoever. When God became man, God did not change, but man did — that man who was brought into being in order to embody the Son of God in his human existence. Human language fails miserably in attempting to express this, for we would never have thought of such a possibility had not the mystery of Jesus Christ placed it before us.

• *Monophysites*

The theory of Nestorius was condemned at the Council of Ephesus (431). However, some of his opponents, Egyptian theologians who had been the defenders of the unity of Jesus Christ, then went too far in the opposite direction, adopting the formula "one person and one nature." Where Nestorius had divided Jesus into two beings, they insisted so much on his unity that the distinction between the divine and human was lost. They seem to have thought that the human nature was somehow absorbed into the divine, thus leaving only one nature. We need not try to determine the exact sense in which they meant this. Various theologians had different interpretations; but they are all summed up under the term *Monophysite* (*mono* = one; *physis* = nature).

This ancient Egyptian heresy has a modern counterpart in people whose attention is so focused on the divinity of Christ that they lose sight of his humanity. (We have already noted those who, when someone speaks of God, think of Jesus; or who, when speaking about Jesus, call him God.) The humanity in Jesus was not suppressed or made unreal or nonfunctional, when taken on by a divine person. Jesus had genuine feelings and emotions like ours, except that they were not disordered by sin. He experienced pain, difficulty, and disappointment. The scourging and crucifixion really hurt him. (In fact, it can be argued that he would have been far more sensitive to pain than we are, mentally as well as physically, because he would not have developed the callousness with which we often shield ourselves.)

• *Not a hybrid nature*

The union of divine and human in Jesus Christ is entirely different from a blend, or union, of two natures. If you cross a horse and a donkey you produce a mule, which has

300

the size and strength of a horse, and the toughness of a donkey. And in many more familiar ways, we combine things of two different natures so as to produce a third (from oxygen and hydrogen comes water). Similarly, when the myths of ancient peoples tell of gods begetting children of mortal women, the offspring are commonly a kind of hybrid of human and divine. Thus Dionysus, son of Zeus and Semele, was a man who had wonderful powers, especially to destroy or make mad those who did not believe in his divinity. Asklepios, son of the god Apollo and the woman Coronis, had marvelous healing powers. But Christ cannot be conceived as a kind of hybrid, combining some properties of the divine with some of human nature. In that case, he would be neither God nor man but something else again. This would make him utterly useless for our salvation. The mystery of Christ is that he is both God and man, each fully and integrally, at one and the same time. Each nature remains distinct in itself, even while united with the other.

• *Definition of Chalcedon*

Monophysite theology was condemned at the Council of Chalcedon (451), which expressed its doctrine on Christ in the following terms, which have remained ever since the classical summary of the Church's position:

> With one accord, we all teach the profession of faith in the one identical Son, our Lord Jesus Christ. We declare that he is perfect [that is, complete] both in his divinity and in his humanity, truly God and truly man, composed [in his manhood] of body and a rational soul. He is consubstantial with the Father in his divinity and consubstantial with us in his humanity, and like us in every respect except for sin (Heb 4:15). We declare that in his divinity he was begotten of the Father before time, and in his humanity he was begotten in this last age of Mary the Virgin, the Mother of God *[theotokos]*, for us and for our salvation.
>
> We declare that the one selfsame Christ, the only-begotten Son and Lord, must be acknowledged in two natures, without any commingling, change, division or separation; that the distinction between the natures is in no way suppressed by their union with one another, but rather that the specific character of each nature is preserved. They are united in one person and *hypostasis* [= being]. We declare that this person is not split or divided into two persons, but that there is one selfsame only-begotten Son, God the Word, the Lord Jesus Christ. This the prophets have taught about Him from the beginning; this Jesus Christ himself taught us; this is the creed of the Fathers which has been handed down to us.
>
> (DS 301, 302; TCT 414; TCC 252)

• *Hypostatic union*

This union of the divine and human natures in Christ has come to be called *hypostatic union*, from the Greek term *hypostasis*, which means simply an individual subsistent being. If we want a diagram to help fix the different theories in mind, we might let a triangle represent the divine and a circle represent the human. The Nestorian view is represented by putting the triangle inside the circle (= the divine Word inside the man Jesus.)

The Monophysite and kindred views would combine the triangle and circle in a monstrous figure that would be neither (or, alternatively, in a triangle that so swallowed up the circle that nothing is left of the latter.) The true sense of the *hypostatic union* cannot possibly be represented by such a diagram because it would require drawing a triangle that is also a true circle; but the middle figure is meant to suggest this impossibility.

NESTORIANISM   HYPOSTATIC UNION   MONOPHYSITISM

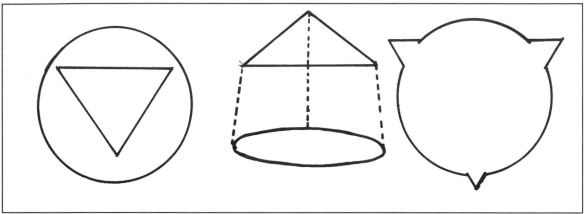

To express this as precisely and unmistakably as possible in human language, theologians adopted the terminology of person and nature, saying that Christ was one person with two natures (whereas in the Trinity, on the contrary, they recognized three persons with but one nature.) For a person is an individual being of an intellectual nature. But a nature is not a being; we never speak of a nature as an acting subject. Instead, we speak of the nature *of* a being; it is an aspect — *the* essential aspect — of the being. It is that aspect with which we are concerned when we seek to say in the most fundamental or substantial way, what kind of a being it is. To determine the nature of a thing is to determine *what it is*: It is a man, a beast, a plant, or an angel according to the nature it has. Furthermore, the nature of a being determines how it will act. A given being can act only according to the nature that it has: A dog acts according to the nature of a dog, and a butterfly according to the nature of a butterfly. (Being free, human beings can act in a way that discords with their nature; but for them too it is true that his possibilities of action are determined by his nature.)

There is no example we can offer from the natural world of a single being that has more than one nature. This is the unique mystery of Jesus Christ. If he had not been revealed to us, we would not even have known that such a combination is possible. And in speaking of person and natures in him, we do not pretend thereby to lift the mystery or to understand it. All we are doing is to indicate certain limits within which we must situate the mystery of Christ if we are to be loyal to all that Scripture tells us about him. If God really became man, while remaining God, there is hardly any other way to express this reality in our feeble language than to speak of one person with two natures. "Two natures" distinguishes between the divine and the human aspects of his being; "one person" maintains the unity of the being in whom these aspects are mysteriously joined.

The medieval theologians studied the metaphysical implications of the Trinity and Incarnation with great subtlety. Such inquiries are of less interest to most people today. It is sufficient to realize that God became man for our salvation; that he remained God while becoming truly man; that the divine and human remained distinct, while belonging both to the one person.

THE HUMAN PSYCHOLOGY OF JESUS

It is natural to want to know what went on in the mind and heart of Jesus but also very difficult. His inner life would surely have been quite different from ours. The Church has defined very little on this subject, other than the basic truth that Jesus had a complete human nature. There has, however, been a long history of theological reflection about the matter.

After the definition of Jesus' divinity by the Council of Nicaea, there was a tendency, especially in popular thought, to imagine him as God walking about on earth in human form. His human nature was not denied, but people tended to make little account of it, and to turn their attention directly to his divinity. Periodically, however, there have been reactions that sought to revalidate his humanity. One such period was the High Middle Ages, as represented particularly by St. Bernard and St. Francis of Assisi. (The Stations of the Cross were popularized chiefly by the Franciscans.)

Today we are in another such period. Theologians as well as preachers stress that Jesus was a human being like ourselves, except for his sinlessness. His weariness, his disappointments, his joys, are to be taken seriously as part of his sharing in the human condition. But there are two factors that pose a serious problem: sin and ignorance. Did Jesus share in them too?

• *Sin in Jesus?*

We need not spend long on the topic of sin, since no Christian theologian of any significance has ever held that Jesus sinned. Indeed, "meek and humble" as he was (Matthew 11:29), Jesus challenged his enemies to point out any sin in his life (John 8:46), and the Letter to the Hebrews declares expressly that "he was tempted like us in all things, without sin" (4:15). Sin is the evil from which God's Son was sent to deliver us, which he did by giving us, among other things, the example of a sinless life.

What we do need to note, however, is that this would have made Jesus' psychology quite different from ours. To say nothing of the fact that he was not burdened with any sense of guilt, there was in his life an integrity, a wholeness, and a freedom which we can scarcely conceive because he did not have to struggle with the dividedness and unruliness that sin has left in us. We have to struggle to "get our act together"; he, by contrast, was in serene possession of a harmonious inner unity. This did not make him inhuman; on the contrary, it is sin that dehumanizes. Jesus was able to be a fully authentic human being because his humanity, suffused by grace, was absolutely sinless.

• *Ignorance?*

The question of ignorance needs more discussion. Being God, did Jesus know all things? Or was his knowledge limited like that of other men? Did he have to learn and grow in knowledge? Clearly, as God he knew all things; but this applies to his divine mind. He also had a human mind, distinct from the divine, and limited. The questions just asked refer to it. Did not his human mind have to grow just as his body did?

The view which became established in the early Church, received its finest expression from St. Thomas Aquinas, and held sway almost unchallenged until the present century was that, even while on earth, the human mind of Jesus enjoyed the beatific vision, that is, he saw the heavenly Father face to face. Moreover, in his earthly life, his intellect was enlightened by "infused knowledge" from the outset, so that it knew all things and did not need to learn. (We can speak of this conception as the "omniscience" of Jesus, without meaning thereby to attribute to his human mind the infinite knowledge proper to the divine. If we suppose that he knew all that a human mind is capable of knowing, this can be spoken of as a relative omniscience.)

• *Modern view: Jesus needed to learn*

St. Thomas was the first to point out firmly that there was also an *experiential knowledge*, which Jesus acquired day by day through the things he experienced. This was a different way of knowing from that which he had by infused knowledge. For example, even before his first visit of Jerusalem, he had infused knowledge of the city and its Temple. But when he actually laid eyes on them, this was a new experience. This makes it possible to account for the fact that, even though he knew all things from childhood onward, still he conducted his life ordinarily by his experiential knowledge. As a child, he lived in the manner appropriate to a child, not as an adult.

In the present century, there has been a reaction to this traditional way of thinking, as making Jesus inhuman. The new approach, championed particularly by Karl Rahner, holds that, to be like us, Jesus had to begin his life in ignorance and grow through inquiry. In particular, it is said by some, he did not know the Father, and did not know himself as the Son of God, until later on in life (his baptism is often given as the moment the revelation was made to him). Some (not Rahner but, for example, Hans Küng) go so far as to declare that he made mistakes, for example, expecting the end of the world to come within a few years. Or that he expected to establish God's Kingdom by a glorious triumph, and was disconcerted when he came to the cross.[4]

In appraising such views, note first that the chief motivation for them does not come from Scripture but from the determination to make Jesus as much like us as possible. Such a motive, however, does not make a very sound principle of theology. In his essential humanity, Jesus was of course like us. Yet the fact that he was not only man but also God in person could hardly fail to give him a psychology different from ours. Moreover, if Jesus was without sin, even his intellectual life must have been quite different from that of people who struggle with disorderly passions, weakness, or self-centeredness of will, and hence confused and biased judgment.

• *Teaching of the Gospels*

Rather than project our psychology onto Jesus, a better method is to ask what Scripture tells us about him. While many questions will undoubtedly remain unanswered or uncertain, this much is clear: that the Gospels do not present Jesus as one who learned gradually and made mistakes like the rest of us. They represent him as a man endowed with supernatural knowledge that astounded others; one who always spoke with complete assurance and authority in his teaching, so much so that his hearers were deeply impressed by the difference between his manner of teaching and that of others (Matthew 7:29; Mark 1:22; Luke 4:32).

In the Gospel of St. John, Jesus repeatedly declares that he has been sent into the world by the Father, and that he is destined to return to the Father. "Jesus knew that the Father had put all things under his power, and that he had come from God and was returning to God" (13:3). He has come as a teacher from God, and teaches what the Father told him to (7:16ff; 12:49; etc.) He describes himself as "a man who has told you the truth that I heard from God" (8:40). "The Father is in me and I am in the Father," he asserts (10:38), and "I and the Father are one" (10:30). "Before Abraham was born, I am" (8:58). All this is well summed up by the statement of the apostles "Now we can see that you know all things and that you do not even need to have anyone ask you questions. This makes us believe that you came from God" (16:30). Similarly, Peter, after the Resurrection, declares, "Lord you know all things; you know that I love you" (21:17). And already at the beginning of the public ministry, the Gospel tells us, "He did not need man's testimony about men, for he knew what was in a man" (2:25).

Those who deny that Jesus enjoyed such (relative) omniscience dismiss these texts as the speculation of later Christians rather than a historical record of actual sayings. But no matter what one holds about the literary genre of this Gospel, if it is divinely inspired Scripture, it must be acknowledged as an authoritative and trustworthy interpretation of the person and life of Jesus. Historical accuracy of the words cited is not the decisive question here. Even if one holds that the later Christians made up these stories to illustrate their conception of Jesus, it is evident that they intended to represent him as omniscient. One can indeed disagree with them and reject their view; but then one is rejecting the divine inspiration of the Gospel of John and cannot claim to be basing his Christology on the New Testament.

The Synoptic Gospels do not express themselves so sharply and clearly as John, but they give indications that strongly confirm his portrait. As a twelve-year-old boy, Jesus amazes the teachers in the Temple by his understanding (Luke 2:47). This incident is surely intended to suggest an extraordinary knowledge, without however defining it precisely. And when, on the same occasion, the boy Jesus asks his mother, "Didn't you know I had to be in my Father's house?" the intention is evidently that he was affirming his divine sonship. This is another text, the historicity of which is commonly questioned; but then it becomes Luke's way of depicting Jesus, which one can reject only by discarding Luke likewise from inspired Scripture.

Jesus' knowledge of his divine sonship is even more strongly affirmed in the famous text "No one knows the Son except the Father, and no one knows the Father except the Son, and those to whom it pleases the Son to reveal him" (Matthew 11:27; Luke 10:22). This so plainly declares Jesus' awareness of his unique relationship with the Father that critics elude it by describing it as a Johannine text that has somehow found its way into the

Synoptics. But that is an *a priori* procedure. An objective view would recognize this as one more instance of what occurs so often: The Synoptics express in their laconic style ideas that John develops more fully and emphatically.

Furthermore, the Synoptics give many particular examples of Jesus knowing things that would be naturally impossible for a mere human being. He predicted his own passion, death and resurrection (repeatedly and in very concrete detail);[5] that Judas would betray him (Matthew 26:25; Mark 14:20; Luke 22:21), Peter would deny him (Matthew 26:34; Mark 14:30; Luke 22:34) and the others abandon him (Matthew 26:31; Mark 14:27; see also Luke 22:31). He announced the coming destruction of the Temple (Matthew 24:2; Mark 13:2; Luke 21:6) and of the city of Jerusalem.[6]

He knew the thoughts of men's hearts. Besides the mind of Judas, as already indicated, he knew the doubts, questions, and criticisms in the hearts of the Pharisees and others listening to him (for example, Luke 11:38; 14:3-5; 19:5). He was aware of the arguments and ambitions of the apostles as they followed him along the way (Mark 9:33).

Jesus also knew hidden facts about the world of nature: where the fish were to be found in the Sea of Galilee (when the experienced fishermen had been unable to find them [Luke 5:4-7; see also John 21:6]); that Peter would catch a fish with a coin in its mouth (Matthew 17:24-27); that when the apostles went into Jerusalem, they would find an ass tied, and would be questioned about their taking it (Matthew 21:2f; Mark 11:2; Luke 19:30); that they would meet a man carrying a water jug who would lead them to where a room was available for Jesus' Passover celebration (Matthew 26:17; Mark 14:12-16; Luke 22:7-13). Thus the Synoptics, without making a general statement like those of John but in their characteristically concrete and suggestive fashion, likewise depict Jesus as one who "knows all things."

• *Objections*

There are of course texts that pose objections to Jesus' omniscience. The most serious is his own statement about the time of the coming of the Son of Man: "No one knows about that day or hour, not even the angels in heaven, nor the Son, but only the Father" (Mark 13:32; see also Matthew 24:36). The strongest case that can be made from this text is that Jesus did not know the time of his return; but even if that be granted, it does not refute the evidence of the texts cited above to show that Jesus was endowed with supernatural knowledge, and in particular of his relationship with the Father. Moreover, since his colorful description of the End and of his coming (Matthew 24; Mark 13; Luke 21) indicate that he had a very full knowledge of these events, and since their importance would make it strange that he should be ignorant of them, there is considerable plausibility in the traditional view that his "not knowing" meant simply that he was not authorized to reveal it. One of Jesus' most emphatic teachings was that he would come unexpectedly,[7] taking the world by surprise. His statement about "not knowing" could be another way of saying the same thing.

St. Luke's summary of Jesus' childhood — "Jesus grew in wisdom and stature, and in favor with God and men" (Luke 2:52) — could be understood as implying growth in

306

knowledge; but even so, it would not put Jesus on a par with others, especially since it occurs immediately after the manifestation of Jesus' astonishing wisdom at the age of twelve. And in view of all the other indications of Jesus' supernatural knowledge, the most plausible interpretation is that it refers to his growth in *experiential* knowledge, and that he acted in accordance with the kind of knowledge appropriate to his age.

Finally, there is the fact that Jesus sometimes asked questions. "Why were you searching for me?" he asked his mother (Luke 2:49). "Who do people say the Son of Man is?" he asked the disciples (Matthew 16:13), etc. But this "Socratic" style of dialoguing and teaching is not necessarily an indication of ignorance on the part of the questioner.

• *Theological considerations*

Apart from the direct biblical evidence we have surveyed, there are strong theological reasons for holding that Jesus, even as man, was omniscient. He was one person, at once and together God and man. As God of course he knew himself fully. To suppose that his human mind was kept in ignorance of his divine identity would introduce a bizarre bifurcation into his psychology, making him in a sense inferior to us who in fact know our own identity. No doubt we are all more or less a mystery to ourselves; but that pertains to the natural depth and complexity of the human person, into which we penetrate in varying measures by experience and reflection. The thesis that Jesus' identity was concealed from himself would add onto this natural mystery an unbridgeable gulf making Jesus far more ignorant of himself than others.

It is true that for Jesus to know himself as God, and still more to know in advance all that awaited him in the future, would situate him very differently from us who have to advance stumblingly into the unknown. But it would not make him inhuman, any more than the beatific vision dehumanizes the saints in glory. They are enjoying the fulfillment and perfection of their humanity, toward which the confusion of this life is only an approach. And there is no serious theological objection to holding that Jesus, even during his life on earth, was in a state of perfection. His mission on earth was to bring others to perfection; he did not have to be one seeking it for himself.

Secondly, Jesus came as teacher of the things of God, a light shining in the darkness. But if he did not know the great truths of the Incarnation and Redemption (even if it were only for a part of his ministry), he was less informed about the plan of God than we are now. If, what is far worse, he had erred in his teaching (for example, about the time of his future coming), how can he be trusted as a faithful and sure teacher of the way of salvation?

• *Church tradition*

Finally, without making a dogmatic definition, the Church has taught with a considerable degree of solemnity that Jesus enjoyed the beatific vision while on earth. (Pius XII affirmed it in his encyclical on the Mystical Body, DS 3812.) Moreover, it is a commonplace in the writings of the saints, mystics, and spiritual writers that Jesus knew us individually as he hung from the cross or as he agonized in the Garden; that he knew our sins, our indifference, and also our efforts to make reparation. Such a testimony bears great weight in theological considerations; it comes close to making this point a doctrine of the Church. Contrary then to one of the strong currents of contemporary theology, it seems far more consonant with Scripture and the tradition of the Church to hold that Jesus, while on earth, enjoyed the beatific vision as well as complete knowledge of the world, past, current, and future.

19
Jesus, source of eternal life

The two preceding chapters were concerned primarily with the *person* of Jesus, who and what he was, including the Trinitarian implications of his divine nature. Now we turn to his *work*. In the history of his career (Chapter 16), we saw that, humanly considered, his life was that of a preacher and teacher. On this basis, Jesus can be compared to other great religious teachers, such as Confucius or the Buddha, who also taught their followers a way of life. Jesus taught his followers to live as children of the heavenly Father, and thereby to attain eternal life. He taught by example as well as by words: He lived as a son of man to show us how to live as children of God. But there is a mysterious power in his example that distinguishes him from any merely human teacher. By fixing our eyes on him, we find ourselves enabled to do as he did. We are joined to him and carried by his strength.

• *Revelation of the Father*

But Jesus' work quite transcended that of other teachers by the fact that it was a revelation of the Father. He was not merely a man who saw farther and deeper than others and shared his vision with his fellows; he was the Son of God who had been sent into the world to reveal what no human insight could ever discern. He was in truth a prophet but more than a prophet. The prophets uttered the Word of God in human language; but Jesus was in his very person the supreme Word of God incarnate in human flesh. "Anyone who has seen me has seen the Father," he said (John 14:9). He made the unexpected disclosure that God is a Trinity of persons. But what touches us perhaps most of all is that, to human beings troubled and depressed by a sense of guilt, he brought the message that God is a gracious Father, ready to receive back all who return to him. "There is more joy in heaven over one sinner who repents than over ninety-nine righteous persons who do not need to repent" (Luke 15:7). Jesus himself associated with sinners because he had been sent as a physician to save those who were sick. He represented himself as the Good Shepherd who leaves the flock of ninety-nine to go seek out the one sheep that is lost (Luke 15:3-6). His death is a sign, not so much of the wickedness of sin, as of the unquenchable mercy of God. When we contemplate Jesus, we see God's merciful love for sinners.

• *Mediation of divine grace*

But having given due credit to the immense importance of Jesus' teaching and revelation, we must recognize that neither of these constitutes his chief work, which is that of imparting divine life to mankind. "I have come that they may have life, and have it to the full" (John 10:10). "I am the way and the truth and the life" (John 14:6). "I am the bread of life" (John 6:35). "I am the vine, you are the branches" (John 15:5). "I am the resurrection and the life" (John 11:25).

The grace of God is not just God's graciousness toward us but the sharing of his life with us (Chapter 21); and Jesus is the Mediator (1 Timothy 2:5) through whom that life is given to us. Through him we attain union with God. Here is where the comparison between him and other great religious teachers breaks down altogether. Jesus does not merely show others the way to God; he himself *is* the Way (John 14:6). He does not merely reveal the grace of God, he imparts it. "If a man is thirsty, let him come to me and drink" (John 7:37). In Jesus, God and man are united in one being; and it is in and through his physical person that the rest of mankind are united with God.

The present chapter will consider what Jesus did to give us life. Grace, the new life principle which he imparts to us, will be taken up in Chapters 21-23. However, what he did and what we receive cannot be understood separately, since grace conforms us to him, as we are now about to see.

• *Three phases: Incarnation, Passion, Resurrection*

His saving work comprises three principal phases: the Incarnation, the Passion, and the Resurrection: (1) By becoming man, the Son of God made us his brothers and sisters; (2) by his death, he atoned for our sins; (3) by his resurrection, he restored us to life. Grace is a single vital reality in us, but it has diverse aspects deriving from these three diverse roots in the work of Jesus. In a sense, we can see visibly in him what he brings about in us: divine sonship, reconciliation with the Father, and resurrection. Thus not only does he "show us the Father" (John 14:8f) he also shows us ourselves — our destiny. We will consider each of the three phases in turn.

1. *The Son of God gives a share in his divine sonship to all who accept him by faith.* Jesus came into our world, taking on our nature and making himself our brother, so that we, as his brethren, might receive something of his nature. God did not will simply to give us grace from on high by a sovereign act of power; he sets up a new personal relationship between ourselves and him by a kind of interchange or transaction, in which he comes to us to lead us to him, and takes on our condition in order to give us something of his.

It is significant that the Son, rather than the Father or the Spirit, became man. His purpose is to make us sons and daughters of God. We are introduced into the life and intimacy of the Trinity but from the angle of the Son, so to speak. Hence it is the Son who comes to associate us with himself. We share in the divine life not as "fathers" or as "spirits" but as sons and daughters — as children of the Father imbued with the Spirit who identifies us with the Son. We are related to the Father by participating in the relationship of the Son. Jesus is the prototype of what we are called to be. He is the Son of God by nature; we are children by adoption. When we live as children of God, we are not just imitating him or pretending to be better than we are, we are living out the state into which he has really introduced us. (Our sonship will be considered in more detail in Chapter 21.)

We are related to the Spirit also of course; but he comes to us as the Spirit of the Son, making us like the Son, and thereby children of the Father.

When the time had fully come, God sent his Son, born of a woman, born under the Law, to redeem those under the Law, that we might receive the full rights of sons. Because you are sons, God sent the Spirit of his Son into our hearts, the Spirit who calls out, *"Abba!"* Father! (Galatians 4:4)

In the mysterious eternal life of the Trinity, the Son, together with the Father, breathes forth the Holy Spirit; on earth, the Son, together with the Father, breathes the Holy Spirit into our hearts. This is the fundamental structure of the grace given through Christ Jesus. It is not just a benevolent attitude on the part of God, forgiving our sins; God imparts his Spirit to change and renew us radically. Likewise the Spirit of Jesus, by whom the disciples of Jesus are "sealed" (Ephesians 4:30) or stamped, is not just a psychological attitude, like the spirit of Abraham Lincoln or the spirit of Notre Dame; he is a person — a divine person — who is communicated to us to conform us to Jesus by inspiring us from within.

However, the grace of divine sonship is not imparted automatically to all mankind by the mere fact that the Son of God has taken on human nature. A personal act of acceptance is required on the part of each one. This is the act of faith, whereby we acknowledge Jesus as the Christ, the Son of God, and accept him as our personal Savior. That is why Jesus said to so many of those who were beneficiaries of his saving acts, "Your faith has saved you." Not that our act of faith accomplishes our salvation; the Father does this by giving us his Spirit. But faith is the act by which we accept his gift.

2. *By the resurrection of Jesus, we are brought to life.* Jesus did not impart divine life to us simply by coming into the world but much more by what he did in the world. The most important of his deeds are his passion and resurrection. In them, Jesus underwent first, as pioneer and archetype, what we too must undergo in our own way.

The Passion and Resurrection together compose the Paschal Mystery (so called after the Jewish Pasch, or Passover, which foreshadowed what was fulfilled in Christ). Although the Resurrection came second chronologically, we will take it up first. Christianity is more the promise of eternal life than it is the annulment of sin through the cross. The original declaration of Christian faith was not "Christ has been crucified" but "Jesus is risen." Later piety tended to focus on the crucifixion more than on the Resurrection. This is understandable; for Jesus crucified is the supreme sign of God's love for us. Nevertheless, it is only in the perspective of the Resurrection that the sense of the crucifixion can rightly be appreciated.

• *The Resurrection for Jesus himself*

The Resurrection has its first level of meaning in the life of Jesus himself. It was the reward bestowed on Jesus the man for having fulfilled the will of the Father during his life on earth. By it he entered into the glory of the Father, "being placed at the right hand of the Father," as the apostles frequently put it (Acts 2:33, 5:31, 7:55; Colossians 3:1; etc.).

In his divine nature, as Son of God, Jesus shares the Father's glory from all eternity and he did not set it aside in coming to earth. But the human nature which he took upon himself was subject to the same conditions as ours (except for sin). Jesus as man moved along the same trajectory we do, from birth through labor to glory. He too longed for "the joy set before him" (Hebrews 12:2), and needed it to complete and fulfill his life. Thus as man he led a truly human life, a meaningful one, through which he merited the glory of heaven.

• *Archetype of our resurrection*

As the first of mankind to do so, he was the exemplar and archetype of all of us. "Christ has been raised from the dead, the firstfruits of those who have fallen asleep. . . . For as in Adam all die, so in Christ all will be made alive. . ." (1 Corinthians 15:20, 22).

The doctrine that those who believe in Christ share in his resurrection is indeed mysterious. One is tempted at first to understand it as a poetic metaphor. If we wish to fix its sense precisely, it seems necessary to distinguish several levels of meaning. Most basically it means that just as Jesus, after being put to death, was raised again to life, so we too after our death will, if we have been faithful to Jesus, be raised to life like him. He conquered death for us not by preserving us from it but by enabling us to rise out of it. His resurrection is the model, the type, the sign, and the guarantee of ours. In Jesus, God shows what he is doing for all who are united to Jesus.

But the resurrection of Jesus is not just the exemplar, it is the *cause* of our resurrection. Through it the grace of resurrection is imparted to us. The risen Jesus may be called the "sacrament" (that is, the efficacious sign) of our resurrection. It is by the Holy Spirit that we are brought to our resurrection, and the Holy Spirit was poured forth upon us through the resurrection of Jesus. The Spirit comes to us as an overflow of the Spirit given to Jesus; Jesus was not filled to overflowing until his resurrection.

The glorification of Jesus' body was the final work of the Spirit in him; and from the fullness of this glory he poured out the Spirit on his disciples. That is why St. Peter, explaining to the amazed inhabitants of Jerusalem the coming of the Holy Spirit on Pentecost, made the remarkable statement which we noted earlier:

> Exalted to the right hand of God, he has received from the Father the promised
> Holy Spirit and has poured out what you now see and hear. (Acts 2:33)

That explains why, at one point in Jesus' earthly life, St. John tells us that "the Spirit had not yet been given, because Jesus was not yet glorified" (7:39). Similarly, at the Last Supper, Jesus told the disciples, "unless I go away the Paraclete will not come to you; but if I go I will send him to you" (John 16:7).

Coming to us as an overflow of the resurrection of Jesus, the Spirit is given to bring about in us a resurrection modeled on that of Jesus. Thus St. Paul says:

> If Christ is in you, your body is dead because of sin, yet your spirit is alive because of righteousness. And if the Spirit of him who raised Jesus from the dead is living in you, he who raised Christ from the dead will also give life to your mortal bodies through his Spirit who lives in you. (Romans 8:10f)

312

• *Spiritual resurrection here and now*

Finally, besides the resurrection of our bodies, which will take place when the Lord returns to lay claim on the world he has redeemed, there is also a spiritual resurrection that takes place in us during this life. This is suggested in the above text, where it is said that even though our bodies are dead by reason of sin (that is, they are still subject to the dominion of death; the hand of death is upon them), our spirits are alive by reason of righteousness. Life has been imparted to our spirits by the Spirit of Jesus: a life stemming from a new vital principle, the Holy Spirit, dwelling within us and making us live by the life of God. When, in another text, Jesus says we must be "born again of water and the Spirit" (John 3:5), he is referring to the same reality which is here called a resurrection.

It goes without saying that our participation in the resurrection of Jesus is conditional on our faith in him. Faith is the act by which we accept what is given to us as a grace.

3. *By his passion and death, Jesus atoned for our sins.* When seeking to understand the role of Jesus' death, we must locate the explanation in the fact that we are sinners, and that his death delivers us from our sins. This was not implied in the two preceding points. Jesus' coming into the world could be understood simply as a way of imparting divine life to creatures. The fact that he is bringing us to a resurrection gives sense and meaning to his resurrection, which can be considered in abstraction from the fact of sin. (Of course, if we had not sinned, we would not have been doomed to death, nor would Jesus have been executed; but we can prescind from that in considering the Resurrection itself.) But there is no way that the meaning of Jesus' death can be understood, except as an atonement for sin. St. Paul says explicitly, "Christ died for our sins" (1 Corinthians 15:3; see also 1 Peter 3:18).

Thus Christ's death was not just a violent end to his ministry but pertained to its very substance. Neither was it just the death of a martyr. A martyr is one who witnesses to the truth even at the cost of his life. Jesus' death can of course be viewed in this light, but it was more. Besides witnessing to the grace of God, it was the *means* by which grace is imparted.

But how are we to understand that the death of Christ brings forgiveness and grace to mankind? Here we meet one of the most impenetrable mysteries of the Christian faith, and we must recognize from the outset that there can be no question of lifting the obscurity from it. Theologians have devoted immense reflection to this topic, and most of us have grown up familiar with some popular résumé of their theories. We may have the impression that all has been explained; but this would be an illusion. That the cross has become a sign of blessing is one of the greatest paradoxes in religious history; and those who *reject* the Christian teaching about the cross may have a keener sense of the mystery than those who find no difficulty in accepting it.

• *A mystery that illumines*

It is not of course necessary to explain the redemptive value of Christ's death in order to accept it. Those who accept it in faith discover that the cross sheds a mysterious light upon human life; without being understood in itself, it still makes many other things understandable. Nevertheless, it is helpful and rewarding for the believer to inquire rationally into this matter and seek some degree of understanding.

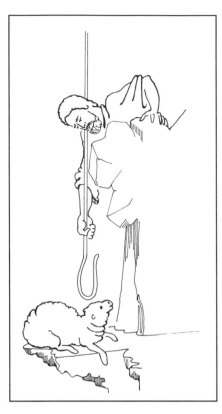

Scripture does not give us much by way of explanation. Most often it simply affirms that Jesus' death was *for our sins*, as indicated above.

Scripture also gives images which *suggest* the sense of the Passion but without properly explaining it. Thus Jesus spoke of his death as a *ransom*, or *redemption*, for sinners: "The Son of Man came to serve, and to give his life as a ransom for many" (Mark 10:45). Ransom is a price paid to release someone from captivity. In this figure, Jesus' death is the price by which we have been set free from captivity. This is clearly a metaphor, since there is no one to whom "payment" is made.[1] Similar is the metaphor of the "good shepherd" who lays down his life for his sheep, under attack by a wolf (John 10:11-15). Such images enable us to grasp the sense of the Passion, but they do not properly explain how it brings about its effect. They are a source and norm of our theology but do not replace the modest efforts of reason to attain a more rational and theoretical understanding.

• *Sacrifice*

A second way the salvific value of Christ's death is represented in Scripture is by the notion of sacrifice, which is one of the most widespread rites of worship in the world. Its meaning is not always clear; different cultures seem to have different understandings of it, and most peoples simply practice it without offering any articulate explanation.

The Hebrew people had a highly developed sacrificial system. There was a morning and evening sacrifice in the Temple; there were sacrifices of atonement for sin, the most solemn of which took place on the Day of Atonement (*Yom Kippur*, still a major Jewish holy day), when the high priest entered the Holy of Holies with the blood of the sacrificed animals and poured it on the altar.

One of the principal meanings of sacrifice is that of a *symbolic gift*. As we make gifts to our friends, and as subjects once made gifts to their lords in token of homage, so the religious person wants to offer a gift to his God. Of course it is impossible for man to make a true gift to the Creator; all things belong to him already. Nevertheless, by withdrawing something valuable from human usage, one at least symbolizes his desire to make a gift to God.

For the Hebrews, the blood of animals had special importance in this regard because blood represented life, the greatest of all God's gifts to his creatures. When Moses and the Israelites ratified their covenant with God, the blood of the sacrificial victims was dashed upon the altar and upon the people (Exodus 24:3-8).

At the Last supper, when he said, "This cup is the New Covenant in my blood which is poured out for you" (Luke 22:20), Jesus represented his death as a sacrifice ratifying the New Covenant with which he replaces that of Moses. The Letter to the Hebrews calls the Old Testament sacrifices mere shadows or images of the reality that came with Christ (8:5; 10:1). It points out that the blood of goats and bulls brought about only a bodily (that is, ritual) purification, whereas the blood of Christ effects a real purification from sin (9:14ff).

All of this was very meaningful for a people accustomed to worship God by bloody sacrifices of animals. It put the death of Jesus in a perspective with which they were familiar, as the perfect fulfillment of the weak and poor sacrifices which they offered from their herds. But for us today who are not accustomed to animal sacrifice (precisely because Christ's sacrifice put an end to them for his followers) this explanation is less meaningful. At least, however, it points to the fact that, like every act of external cult, the death of Christ draws its value from the interior attitude which it expressed. As the sacrifice of animals represented the worship of the Hebrews and their desire to offer something precious to their Lord, so the death endured by Jesus expressed his loving obedience to the Father.

• *Bearing and washing away sin*

Other New Testament texts speak of the blood of Jesus *cleansing* us from sin (1 John 1:7; Apocalypse 1:5), sanctifying (Ephesians 5:26; Hebrews 13:12) or perfecting us (Hebrews 10:1-14). These seem to be only variant expressions of the notion of sacrifice of purification. Fundamentalists however sometimes take them literally as they also do with 1 Peter 2:24: "He himself *bore our sins in his body* on the tree." But it is obvious that sin, being a moral and spiritual disorder, cannot literally be washed by blood or transferred to someone else's body. Such texts express vividly the truth that the death of Jesus liberates us from sin; but they do not give an explanation of how it did so.

Ransom and sacrifice are, in sum, the chief concepts by which the efficacy of Christ's atoning death is declared in Scripture. They are sacred notions to which faith must ever have recourse, and in which it finds an ever deeper and more precious meaning. Without abandoning them, the irrepressibly inquisitive human mind has throughout the centuries sought for other explanations that would be more rational, less metaphorical.

• *Satisfaction*

The theory of *satisfaction* developed by St. Anselm and St. Thomas Aquinas has generally been adopted in Catholic thought since the Middle Ages. Even it should not be regarded as a self-sufficient rationale but only an attempt by human reason to do what little it can to grasp the sense of a mystery that transcends it.

In this theory, Christ "satisfied" the Father for our sins by offering him something that pleased him more than our sins displeased him. What pleased the Father was the Son's loving obedience. This obedience was expressed in his enduring the sufferings of his passion and death. Note well that the Father did not put the Son to death. Neither should we conceive of him as *requiring* the death of his Son as the only satisfaction he would accept. It was sinful men, acting *against* the will of God, that were responsible for the crucifixion.

• *Calvary the sign of God's love*

Jesus had been sent by the Father to proclaim the good news of grace and the Kingdom. If those who heard this message had received it with faith instead of murdering the messenger, are we to think that the Redemption would have been thwarted? Jesus' loving obedience would have been just as perfect, and as capable of making satisfaction, as it was on Calvary. However, the intensity and generosity of his love would not have been so manifest to us. There is no more convincing and moving sign of God's love than the fact that Jesus endured excruciating sufferings and death for our redemption. "Greater love has no one than this, that one lay down his life for his friends" (John 15:13).

In the Garden of Gethsemani, Jesus prayed, "Father, if it be possible, let this chalice pass from me; nevertheless, not my will but thine be done." Here we see clearly his obedience to the Father; but this text also gives the impression that the Father was the one who insisted on the death of his Son. Similarly the words of the risen Lord on the way to Emmaus: "Did not the Christ have to suffer these things and then enter his glory?" (Luke 24:26). But these texts should be understood in the sense that the Father, knowing that men would react against his Son, required that the Son remain faithful even unto death, and accepted this death as the act of satisfaction.

Thus the ultimate explanation of the salvific value of Christ's death resides in love; but this love was embodied in the death on the cross in such a way as to make the latter effective for the atonement of sins. The love here was first of all the love of the Father that

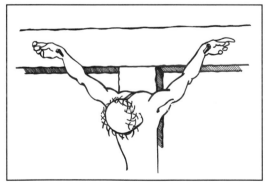

led him to send his Son into the world for our salvation, and deliver him up to death: "God so loved the world that he gave his only begotten Son, that whoever believes in him shall not perish but have eternal life" (John 3:16). Secondly, the cross expresses the love that motivated the Son to come and endure the Passion: both his eternal love and his human love for the Father and for us, his brethren.

The foregoing explanation is an adaptation of that of St. Thomas in the light of modern concerns and objections. It focuses not so much on the sufferings of Christ as on his love. This is to forestall the objection that the theory of satisfaction represents God as a terrible ogre taking delight in the suffering of a victim, and exacting a certain amount of it before he will be appeased. Such a notion of God has appeared in several barbarous religions which offered human sacrifice whenever the god seemed angry — for example, the Aztec cult of Huitzi-lopochtli. But such a notion of God and such a practice were vehemently rejected by Mosaic religion, and have nothing whatsoever to do with the Christian God, whose motivation is always and utterly love: "God is love. Whoever lives in love lives in God, and God in him" (1 John 4:16).

Nevertheless, it remains true that the passion of Christ is the very *means* of our redemption, not just a token of redeeming love. This point, more than any other, makes the doctrine of Redemption so difficult for human reason. But to present the death of Jesus as no more than a revelation of divine love fails to do justice to those texts, cited above, which speak of Christ bearing our sins in his body or washing us by his blood.

• *Substitutionary atonement*

In the Protestant Reformation, the notion of satisfaction was changed into that of *substitutionary atonement*. According to this, Jesus took the place of sinners and was punished in their stead. We are the ones who deserve to be punished; but the Father looked upon Jesus as though *he* were the sinner, and inflicted on him the punishment deserved by us. This seems to turn redemption into a charade, a game of make-believe. How can we conceive of God the Father being *angry* with his Son (as the Reformers asserted), and treating him as a sinner, when the Father himself declared, "This is my beloved Son"? And to punish the innocent while letting the guilty go free would be an act of injustice. In the theory of St. Anselm and St. Thomas, the Son is not punished by the Father but tormented by men; and it is not his suffering in and by itself that makes satisfaction but the loving obedience with which he endures the suffering inflicted on him.

• *Solidarity in redemptive love*

A second problem about the Redemption must now be considered. Why should what Jesus did and suffered be of value for others? His passion expressed *his* love for the Father and indeed merited *his* resurrection; but is it reasonable that *we* should be "justified" by it? In approaching this question, we should keep in the foreground the principle that God's love, by which we are justified, comes to us as a grace. It is not necessary to explain how we deserve to be justified; we don't. A loving and gracious God forgives and sanctifies us without our deserving it:

> Because of his great love for us, God, who is rich in mercy, made us alive with Christ even when we were dead in transgressions. . . . For it is by grace that you have been saved, through faith — and this not from yourselves, it is the gift of God — not by works, so that no one can boast. (Ephesians 2:4-9)

This is the fundamental Christian truth, the essence of the good news proclaimed by Jesus. But it is also a Christian dogma that the grace of God comes to us because of our association with Jesus, and in particular with his passion. Our question therefore is about the nature of this association.

To put the inquiry in perspective, we must recall the principle of solidarity men-

317

tioned in connection with original sin. Human beings are not entities completely separate from one another. Even on the natural plane a profound and mysterious bond unites them. This is particularly evident in the family, whose members feel deep, strong ties to each other, expressed in love, concern, and loyalty. Beyond the family, there is the nation. Patriotism is so powerful that it makes soldiers ready to sacrifice their lives in order that the country may endure. This makes no sense except on the supposition of a deep bond between a man and his country, linking fellow-citizens together. Still further, there is a sense in which all mankind are brothers. A profound humanism feels compassion and concern for everyone that wears a human face. "Nothing human is alien to me" (Terence). "Ask not for whom the bell tolls; it tolls for thee" (John Donne).

This profound affinity among human beings is difficult to analyze or explain; nevertheless, it is the reality on which human society is based. Simone Weil, a French Jewess living in England as an exile during the Second World War, had such a keen sense of fellowship with her countrymen suffering under the Nazi regime that she restricted herself to a starvation diet because she knew that *they* were starving. Not everyone experiences this fellow-feeling so keenly or draws such radical conclusions from it; nevertheless, it motivates a large part of the social activity of mankind. If our country sends medical aid to earthquake victims in Mexico or food to the famished in Ethiopia, this is an implicit acknowledgment of brotherhood with the people there. We recognize that in some deep, hidden sense, we are all one with the others; that what affects one, affects all. This natural solidarity of mankind provides a basis for explaining, at least in part, how one person can act in the name of all — especially one who is by his very nature the supreme human being, the type or model for all others, and the king of the universe.

For the fact that this man Jesus is, at the same time, God and Lord of the universe, makes him by nature the head and king of the human race, indeed of the entire universe. He has a primacy and authority over all others. This too helps to explain why his personal acts affect us all, and why he can act in the name of all.

• *Personal faith in Jesus creates a further bond*

However, neither our natural affinity with Jesus, nor his primacy over us, suffices to account for the fact that we are redeemed by his cross. We have to make a personal act of adherence to him. This act (as we have seen in connection with the Incarnation and Resurrection) consists in the fundamental Christian attitude of faith (faith engendering hope and charity). Only those who are bonded to Jesus by faith benefit from the fruits of his passion.

We also have to "die with him" in order to share in his resurrection (Romans 6:4-6; Colossians 2:12f; 3:1). Jesus himself had already announced, "If anyone would come after me, he must deny himself, take up his cross daily and follow me" (Luke 9:23). "Dying with him" embraces several factors.

Renunciation of sin, and of our sinful inclinations, is a kind of death of our "old self" (Romans 6:6, 8, 11-14, etc.). Secondly, we die with him in the sense that our act of faith in Jesus crucified is a way of appropriating his death, making it ours. Finally, the sacraments, especially baptism and the Eucharist, give us a participation in the death of the Lord (see Chapter 26). "Rising with him" is similarly complex as we saw earlier in this chapter. Part 5 will consider Christ's effects on us in detail. Here it is sufficient to recognize that a mysterious identification with Christ is at one and the same time a condition for, and result of, our being redeemed by his passion.

• *Identification with Christ by the Holy Spirit*

Finally, the Holy Spirit, the Spirit of Christ, whom the Father imparts to all who believe in Christ, brings about a further identification of Christians with Christ. Built on the natural bond among human beings, and on the supernatural bond created by faith, this goes even farther, bringing about what is traditionally called the "Mystical Body of Christ," in which Jesus is the head and the faithful are his members. This same relationship is expressed under another figure when Jesus says, "I am the vine, you are the branches" (John 15:5).

What has been said here has been intended to explain and clarify the essentially incomprehensible mystery that the divine life has been communicated to us through the person and the life of Jesus Christ. We should not expect such an explanation to have the self-sufficiency and completeness of a chemical theory explaining, for example, how hydrogen and oxygen form water. (One may wonder of course whether even chemistry really explains or only describes and measures what takes place regularly.) The only adequate explanation of what has been wrought in Christ is the merciful love of God, who has chosen to pour out his benefactions upon us. This love itself is beyond all explanation or comprehension, and provides the explanation for the grace that it imparts. It is because God has chosen the life, passion, and resurrection of Jesus as the instruments of his love that these have the effect of giving us life. Nevertheless, God's way of dealing with us is not arbitrary. There is a meaningfulness and appropriateness in the manner in which his grace is imparted to us, and it is this which we have attempted to explore, insofar as our weak human minds are able.

20

The one and only Savior

JESUS AS SAVIOR

Before the coming of Jesus, the Hebrew people had learned to look upon God as their Savior. The principal lesson by which they learned this was the Exodus, in which they had been delivered from captivity in Egypt by the mighty hand of Yahweh, acting through Moses. Many subsequent experiences, especially the Babylonian captivity, reinforced this lesson. The sacred writers declare over and over that Israel's salvation lies in Yahweh;[1] just as he alone is to be worshiped as God, so he alone is Savior (Hosea 13:4). In later centuries, Yahweh's role as the Savior of individuals, especially the poor and afflicted, is more and more emphasized. The Psalms frequently call him, "my saving God."[2] *Savior* is his most characteristic appellation in the Old Testament.

Human leaders were called saviors but always in the perspective that it was through them that Yahweh was acting. This was the case of many of the "judges" who were raised up by Yahweh to lead the people in their sporadic battles with neighboring tribes during the early years in Canaan; later, the title *Savior* was applied much more solemnly to the kings.[3]

In the New Testament, the term *Savior* is transferred to Jesus. The very name *Jesus* means "Yahweh is salvation." In explaining why this name was to be given, the angel told Joseph, "he will save his people from their sins" (Matthew 1:21). Likewise Jesus' birth was announced to the shepherds at Bethlehem with the statement "Today in the town of David, a Savior has been born to you" (Luke 2:11).

• *Yeshua*

Jesus is a Westernization of the Hebrew and Aramaic name *Yeshua*, which was Jesus' actual name. *Ye* or *Je* was an abridged form of *Yahweh*. *Shua* comes from the verb *yasha* in a form meaning set free, help, or save. *Yeshua* was a very common Jewish name in the first century. An early form of the same name, *Yoshua* or *Joshua*, was the name of Moses' successor.

• *The storm on the lake*

Salvation implies the presence of an evil from which one is to be saved: death, injury, illness, debt, or disgrace, for example. The Gospels frequently represent Jesus in a salvific role, healing the sick, freeing the demoniacs, etc. The most graphic instance is probably the storm on the lake. Experienced boatsmen though they were, the apostles were terrified that their boat was about to capsize. Jesus, exhausted from his preaching, had fallen asleep, so they woke him, crying, "Lord, save us, we're going to drown." He rebuked the winds and the sea, and there came a great calm (Matthew 8:23-27).

320

St. Paul represents Jesus as the one who overcame sin and death (for example, Romans 5, 6; 1 Corinthians 15:56f). Jesus saves from sin by reconciling sinful humanity with the Father. He saves from death by raising the dead to a life that will be everlasting. (These fruits of his work will be examined more fully in Part 5, below.) Sin and death are singled out because they are the two principal ills that threaten human happiness; but they connote all the other miseries that lead to them or flow from them: sickness, injury, pain, social injustice, failure, loneliness, etc. The list of human woes is long, and from them all, Jesus is Savior. "The Son of Man came to seek and to save what was lost" is Jesus' own summary of his mission" (Luke 19:10).

It is a mistake to think of Jesus as Savior from sin only. This entails a false spiritualization of Christianity, similar to that which sees only the soul as the person. Bodily ailments as well as psychological and social ills are genuine evils which threaten human happiness. Jesus has come to deliver us from them all. When he healed the deaf, the dumb, the blind, lepers, etc., these works were not just miracles intended to demonstrate his divine power — they were acts in which his saving mission was exercised. They were a true beginning of the salvation he brought. Just as Yahweh showed himself a savior by actually rescuing the Hebrews, so Jesus did likewise by succoring those in need.

On the other hand, it is equally clear that Jesus did not intend to achieve an immediate paradise. He did not heal all the sick, nor did he preserve his followers completely from suffering and death. This is because his saving work has only begun. He gave a few instances of it, and established its basic principles (above all, the grace of the Holy Spirit). Its complete accomplishment will come only with the full realization of the Kingdom of God. For now, we have only the firstfruits of our salvation (see Romans 8:23), with the promise of the rest. (Hence salvation requires faith: Only those will be saved who believe in the promise made by Jesus.)

• *Deliverance from sin primary*

Thus, while Jesus delivers from all the evils that afflict human existence, there is an order in the way he deals with them. Sin, or alienation from God, is the root cause of all human evil, and it is this that Jesus attacks first. To the paralytic, he said, "Son, your sins are forgiven"; not till later did he add, "Get up, take your mat and go home" (Matthew 9:1-7). Jesus' salvific work is aimed chiefly and most directly at eliminating sin; the rest will follow in time as a consequence. The present age, the age of the Church, is like the moment between the first and second injunctions addressed by Jesus to the paralytic. The Church's mission is to apply to everyone the words "Your sins are forgiven." When Jesus returns, all our other paralyses will likewise be removed.

NO OTHER SAVIOR

All Christians used to agree that salvation is possible through Jesus Christ alone. Catholics, Orthodox, and Protestants of every denomination, although they disagreed about many other things, were unanimous on this point, and regarded it as unassailable. Sometime they accused one another of neglecting it; for example, Catholic veneration of Mary and the saints was often interpreted as putting other saviors in the place of Jesus. This was due to a misunderstanding; the Church has tirelessly insisted that neither the saints nor the sacraments nor the clergy nor the whole Church have any power to save, except as communicating to us the saving grace that derives from Jesus alone. But the principle that Jesus is the only one who can save mankind from sin and its consequences was affirmed by all Christians.

• *Challenge of the Enlightenment*

Today, however, this agreement has been dissolved. The Enlightenment tended to cultivate the view that man needs to be saved from nothing so much as ignorance, which is the root of most of his other miseries: poverty, sickness, and even vice. Enthusiasm over the early successes of natural science generated indomitable confidence that all ignorance could be overcome, and that thus man would be his own savior. The evolutionary mentality which arose in the nineteenth century confirmed this assurance with the vision that progress toward a better world was inscribed in the very laws of nature. This era honored the "self-made man," and abhorred the notion of dependence on a savior.

Meanwhile, in consequence of the great explorations of Marco Polo, Christopher Columbus, and others, the Christian mind had been growing more and more conscious of the enormous masses of mankind, especially in the Far East, who have not accepted the Christian faith, and have hardly even heard of it. Is it to be supposed that all of them are irretrievably lost on account of the geographical accident of their birthplace? These various peoples have their own ways of worshiping God; recently we have begun to appreciate the sublime art, philosophy, and literature that have sprung from their religions. It seems narrow-minded to suppose that *our* religion alone offers a valid way to God.

Out of the confluence of such considerations, many Christians today have come to hold that mankind has developed diverse ways of attaining the Absolute (which itself has become more or less relativized!), all of which have their advantages and shortcomings, and none of which — not even Christianity — has the right to claim any exclusive privilege for itself.

Consequently, the traditional belief in Jesus as the unique Savior has been questioned by Liberal Protestant theologians for decades, and abandoned by many of them. Since Vatican II, Catholics also have begun to raise this question, and already not a few are taking it for granted that we can no longer speak in the traditional way or justify the missionary effort of the Church of past ages. Usually they grant (somewhat inconsistently, perhaps) that there is something unique about Jesus, and that his way is the best but not the only way to salvation.[4]

• *Doctrine of the New Testament*

We must therefore examine the basis and sense of the traditional doctrine, and then see how it is to be related to the modern objections. However, the New Testament is so impregnated with this doctrine that only a few representative texts can be cited here:

Jesus at the Last Supper: "I am the way. . . . No one can come to the Father except through me." (John 14:6)

Peter before the Sanhedrin: "Salvation is found in no one else, for there is no other name under heaven given to men by which we must be saved." (Acts 4:12)

Paul writing to Timothy: "There is one God and one mediator between God and men, the man Christ Jesus, who gave himself as a ransom for all men." (1 Timothy 2:5f)

• *Salvation only through faith*

Often this teaching is put in other terms, namely, that salvation (or justification, or eternal life) can be had only through faith, Christ being understood as the object of faith. Thus:

> God did not send his Son into the world to condemn the world, but to save the world through him. Whoever believes in him is not condemned, but whoever does not believe stands condemned already because he has not believed in the name of God's one and only Son. (John 3:17f)

> Go into the whole world and preach the good news to all creation. Whoever believes and is baptized will be saved, but whoever does not believe will be condemned. (Mark 16:15f; see also Romans 3-5; Galatians 2:15, 5:6; etc.)

This same teaching is also given frequently in the assertion that eternal life and/or justification can be had solely through Jesus, who is represented as the New Adam, who gives life to all, where the First Adam brought death (1 Corinthians 15:22, 45; Romans 5:12ff). Similarly, Jesus is declared to be "the head over everything" (Ephesians 1:22). This doctrine also appears as the implicit assumption underlying other things that are said. For example, about the early Church in Jerusalem, Luke tells us, "The Lord added to their number daily those who were being saved" (Acts 2:47). Paul says that the Gospel is "the power of God for salvation to everyone who has faith" (Romans 1:16). The reason Jesus sent the apostles, and the motive that drove them tirelessly in their strenuous and dangerous voyages, was that salvation might be brought to the world through the preaching of the Gospel. In short, it is the firm and universal teaching of the New Testament, expressly formulated and implicitly assumed, in actions as well as in words, that there is no other way to salvation but through faith in Jesus Christ.[5]

• *God's will to save all*

On the other hand, however, Scripture makes it clear that God loves all his creatures, and that he sent his Son for the salvation of all. St. Paul, immediately before his line about the one Mediator, speaks of:

> . . .God our Savior, who desires all men to be saved and to come to the knowledge of the truth. (1 Timothy 2:4)

If God sincerely desires the salvation of all mankind, is it conceivable that he would require as a condition of salvation something that is out of reach of the greater part of the human race? But if salvation is said to be available for everyone of good will, then what becomes of the saving role of Jesus? Is it not completely nullified?

A suggestion of a solution is given in the story of the Roman centurion Cornelius, who lived in Caesarea during the first years of the Church. He was a devout, God-fearing man, generous in giving alms and faithful in prayer. An angel appeared to him one day and said, "Your prayers and your alms have ascended as a memorial before God" (Acts 10:4). The angel instructed him to send for Peter; when the latter came and told about Jesus, Cornelius and his household were filled with the Holy Spirit and received baptism. It is clear that Cornelius was pleasing to God even before he received the Christian message. What else can this mean but that he had the grace of God? And would he not then have been saved even if he had died before Peter's arrival? And may there not be many other Corneliuses in the world who perhaps will never meet a Christian missionary but who live in the grace of God and will be saved? Such considerations have led the Catholic Church to hold that salvation is really possible, even for those who do not profess the Christian faith:

> Those who, through no fault of their own, do not know the Gospel of Christ or his Church, but who nevertheless seek God with a sincere heart, and, moved by grace, try in their actions to do his will as they know it through the dictates of their conscience — those too may achieve eternal salvation. Nor shall divine providence deny the assistance necessary for salvation to those who, without any fault of theirs, have not yet arrived at an explicit knowledge of God, and who — not without grace — strive to lead a good life.
>
> (Dogmatic Constitution on the Church, no. 16)

• *Saved by the grace of Christ*

Such people are not saving themselves. As the text just cited makes clear, it is by the grace of God that they are enabled to live the good life that brings them to eternal life. This grace, like all grace in the present order, has been merited for them by Jesus. These people are, without knowing it, beneficiaries of his passion and resurrection. Only when they enter into the light of glory will they discover their hidden benefactor.

> By himself and of his own power, no one is freed from sin or raised above himself, or completely rid of his sickness or his solitude or his servitude. On the contrary, all stand in need of Christ, their Model, their Mentor, their Liberator, their Savior, their source of life.
>
> (Decree on the Church's Missionary Activity, no. 8)

• *Implicit faith*

But are these "good pagans" saved without faith? Theologically, this is the most difficult part of the problem. The texts cited above insist that salvation comes only through faith in Jesus Christ. But how can we plausibly attribute faith to someone who never heard of Christ or has even rejected him? St. Thomas Aquinas solved this difficulty by pointing out that, besides the explicit faith of the one who acknowledges Jesus Christ as his Savior, there is the implicit faith of the person whose soul opens to and accepts whatever light God gives him.[6]

This does not come down to saying that faith really makes no difference. There is real faith in these people, even though in a larval form. Someone who has heard the Christian Gospel but, closing his mind to the light of grace, has refused to believe in Jesus, will not be saved as an "anonymous Christian." He is guilty of precisely the sin of unbelief which Jesus condemned. However, just as a professed Christian can be insincere, and will not be saved by his Christian label, someone who appears to be rejecting the Gospel may not really be guilty; he may be reacting to a caricature or a misunderstanding. God alone knows who is really responding to the light and who is not.

Thus the teaching of Christianity is that no one can be saved except through faith in Jesus Christ. This is a universal principle, to which there are no exceptions. However, what it means in terms of the fate of actual human beings, we cannot judge; God knows who has the requisite faith and who not.

> In ways known to himself, God can lead those inculpably ignorant of the Gospel
> to that faith without which it is impossible to please God.
> (Decree on the Church's Missionary Activity, no. 7)

Note finally that, even though the grace of Jesus had already reached Cornelius in a hidden way, Peter was sent to preach the Gospel to him. Salvation is possible for people who do not know Jesus; nevertheless, God wants the name of Jesus to be acknowledged by the entire world. It is possible to be saved by Jesus even without knowing him, but knowing him is a great advantage. It is hard to live a good life, not knowing what it leads to hereafter, and not supported by any awareness of the fatherly care of divine providence. The Gospel proclaimed by Jesus, the sacraments he established, and the community of believers he founded, are real helps to a good and holy life; that is why the apostles were sent to preach throughout the world.

• *The reason for Christian exclusivism*

Granted the fact of the New Testament doctrine, firmly reiterated by the Church, that salvation is possible only through faith in Jesus Christ, one may still inquire about the reason for it. Could it be a kind of parochialism or chauvinism inherited by Christians from the Jews, one of the innumerable instances of the common human tendency to regard our way as the best if not the only way?

No, the rationale for this exclusivist dogma lies in the human situation as it has been illuminated by the Christian revelation. It lies in the two complementary mysteries of sin and grace, which are like the two poles that define man's relationship to God.

• *Grace: supernatural participation in the divine life*

The mystery of grace will be explored in Part 5; here, by anticipation we can note that it involves a participation in the life of the Divine Trinity. This life, which will be enjoyed fully in the next world but already begins here below through faith, lies altogether beyond the possibility of attainment by man's natural resources. It is intrinsically and absolutely supernatural. Even the finest human being, an ideal person, perfect in every respect, would be naturally incapable of attaining divine life. This is a life of intimate relationship with God, and a participation in God's own inner life, into which a creature can be introduced only by a divine invitation and a divine enabling. This calling and enabling are extended to us through the Son of God, who became man precisely in order to associate us with him in his life as Son of the Father. Faith is the act by which we accept the grace proffered to us in Jesus, and are thereby associated with him.

This has nothing to do with whether a person is good or bad: It is a consequence of the infinite distance between the Creator and his creature. The Creator alone can bridge this chasm, and he has done so in sending Jesus Christ as mediator. The creature on his own is not capable of building a bridge.

Jesus is distinguished from the other great religious teachers of history by the fact that he is not just a genius emerging from the human race: He is the Son of God sent to us by his Father. The others may have had profound insights and noble counsels to offer; but being mere men, they could not be mediators capable of bringing the human race to God. The question is often asked, however, whether God may not have made other revelations in other cultures. Could he not even have sent other saviors to them? Hindus believe that the savior god Vishnu has manifested himself on earth in the form of various avatars, notably Krishna, who bears certain resemblances to Jesus Christ. Many Hindus regard Jesus as one more such avatar. Could not a Christian similarly be open to the possibility that Krishna and others were authentic savior figures?

Such an argument confuses two different orders: the interior order of grace and the exterior order of the Savior and his institutions. So far as the inner workings of divine grace are concerned, there is no question but that God reveals himself to people of every culture, and makes salvation accessible to them, as was explained above. But the possibility of other saviors is a different matter. It is excluded by divine revelation itself, in which Jesus is presented not merely as a savior but as *the only* Savior. The texts cited above show this plainly. He is the *only* Son of God, the *only* mediator between God and men; *no one* goes to the Father but by him. If he is genuine, there can be no others; if there are others, then Jesus is false, and thereby is no savior at all. No doubt God *could have* sent various saviors; however, our question is not about what God is capable of doing but about what he has in fact done. The Old Testament affirmed that there is but one God; the New Testament adds that there is but one Savior, around whom all of mankind is destined to be assembled in one body:

> There is one body and one Spirit — just as you were called to one hope when you were called — one Lord, one faith, one baptism, one God and Father of all, who is over all and through all and in all. (Ephesians 4:4-6)

• *Sin*

The second factor explaining why we can be saved through Jesus Christ alone is sin. Sin alienates from God, and only Jesus is capable of bringing about a reconciliation. *Sin* here means sin in the fullest sense of the word, namely, *mortal sin*. "Venial sin" does not separate us from God, even though it is inconsistent with our relationship to him; for that reason, it is not sin in the fullest sense (see Chapter 22).

We have explained why one who has sinned grievously needs Jesus as his Savior. But one may ask, are there not many people who have never sinned in this strong sense — who have led a decent, good life so that they cannot be classified properly as sinful?

This question obliges us to go deeper into the mystery of sin, and to recognize that sin is a reality greater than any single act, greater even than the life of any one person. It is an atmosphere enveloping the entire human race, and affecting us even before we begin to act. This is the mystery of original sin.

Without going back into a theoretical discussion of this difficult topic (see Chapter 14), we can note some of its concrete, practical implications, above all the *religious attitude* entailed by original sin. In their initial relationship with God, human beings do not stand as pure creatures but as *sinners*. There is no human being (apart from Jesus, kept sinless by the grace of his divinity, and Mary, preserved by a privilege [see the Epilogue]) that can come before God simply as an innocent creature, who has not yet done good or evil. Rather, everyone, in order to be drawn into union with God, must first be cleansed, absolved. The world is divided into those who have been cleansed of sin by the grace of God, and those who have not (though we are not able to determine who belongs in which class).

> Jews and Gentiles alike are all under sin. . . . all have sinned and fall short of the glory of God, and are justified freely by his grace through the redemption that came by Christ Jesus. (Romans 3:9, 23-24)

Being "under sin" means not only having committed sinful deeds but also being subject to that mysterious, all-pervasive condition known as original sin, the effects of which can be summarized thus:

1. All of us are subject to temptations. Even when we try to resist them, we find within ourselves a kind of complicity with them, like a fifth column sabotaging our efforts.

2. By our own strength, we cannot overcome them all completely, even though we are able to resist any particular temptation.

3. Consequently, we are unable on our own to make a success of our lives in any definitive sense. We may accomplish some of the goals we set out after; we may attain certain kinds of self-fulfillment (for example, becoming accomplished in some line of work, popular in human relations, wealthy, powerful, etc.), but in the complete picture, and in the long run, we cannot *succeed*. This is partly because our very successes are so limited and so flawed, partly because death comes to put an end to them all, and finally and above all because there is in fact no other fulfillment and happiness possible for man but that of eternal life in the Kingdom of God, from which we are excluded so long as this estrangement from God perdures.

We must linger a bit on this last point, which is not evident from the nature of man or discoverable by simple philosophical reasoning. From a merely rational point of view, it is very difficult to say much about what happens to man after death. That is a realm most cultures have dealt with by myths more than by sober reason. It is, however, evident that human life as we know it is terminated by death, and that fact alone suffices to limit the possibilities of success and happiness.

• *Heaven and hell the only possibilities*

But that after death, only two possibilities lie open for man — the Kingdom of God or the dominion of Satan; eternal life or a living death; light or "outer darkness" — this we know from revelation. In Chapter 28, we will examine these two ultimate states of humanity. Here, our concern is to note that there is no neutral ground between them, where one might suppose people who were neither good enough for heaven nor bad enough for hell could be placed. The only possible fulfillment for the human person consists in union with God in eternal life; whoever rejects this dooms himself to hell. This is the practical upshot of the doctrine of original sin. Note that it is not from some theoretical concept of original sin that we demonstrate the need of salvation by Christ. On the contrary, it is from the biblical teaching on the absolute need of salvation by Christ that we realize that man's initial condition is indeed one of *sin*.

• *Everyone has a choice*

One might wonder about a person who never was delivered from original sin (because he was never baptized) but who lived a reasonably good life, without ever committing a grave sin: Would such a one be condemned to hell? The fact seems to be that such a case could not arise. Everyone, when he becomes mature enough to make deliberate choices of his own, encounters the grace of God. If he cooperates with this grace and chooses the good, this very choice is an implicit act of faith and acceptance of grace, by which he is freed from original sin. If, on the contrary, he chooses evil, he is rejecting grace and confirming himself in sin, which then becomes mortal sin (see Chapter 21).

The individual may be only a child when he first makes this choice. It may be on the occasion of some apparently minor incident: for example, some instruction of his parents which he must decide to obey or disobey. What is significant is not the external occasion as measured by the mind of an adult but the fact that the child, conscious of the difference between good and evil, orients his life voluntarily and radically toward one or the other.

One might object that a child is not yet capable of such a radical personal choice. There are those who hold that even many adults are not really mature enough for it. Such objections seem to come from the idea that choosing between good and evil is a highly intellectual matter; on the contrary, it is one of the simplest, most primordial acts of the human person, and is a function of whether one loves good or evil, not of how fully informed one is. However, we do not need to determine the time when such a decision is made (which in any case will be different for different people). The point is that every person capable of free choice must make it, and this will be in reality a decision for grace or for sin. It goes without saying that this initial decision does not bind a person irrevocably for the rest of his life. One who first chooses evil can later (by the grace of God) repent, just as one who first chooses good can later fall away. But so long as a person persists in the radical choice of evil, he cannot live what was called above, "a reasonably good life."

If his deepest orientation is to evil, there will be evil in his life (even though he may successfully keep it hidden from human observation).

• *Problem of non-baptized infants*

The really difficult question has to do with those infants (or even adults) who have not matured sufficiently to make this radical choice between acceptance and rejection of divine grace. If they die without having been freed from original sin by the grace of baptism, it does not seem possible for them to enter heaven since, as Jesus said, "Unless one is born of water and the Spirit, he cannot enter the kingdom of God" (John 3:5). On the other hand, since they have not committed any personal sin, we cannot suppose that they would be made to suffer in the next world. Hence theologians have conjectured that they are in a state of natural happiness called limbo.[7] However this is purely speculative, not a dogma of the Church.

Some theologians, dissatisfied with the notion of limbo, have proposed that, at the instant of death, the infant receives a revelation allowing him to make that same choice that others make in the course of their natural life; but this too is pure speculation.

Without trying to resolve this difficult problem, we can note that it represents the hidden point of encounter between two great truths, both of which are absolutely certain. On the one hand, there is the loving mercy of God "who desires all men to be saved" (1 Timothy 2:4). On the other hand, there is the fact that salvation comes about solely through the one mediator, Jesus Christ (1 Timothy 2:5), and requires that we be united with him through faith and baptism. God alone knows how these truths apply to the case of unbaptized infants.

In summary, the grace of God is needed both for the overcoming of sin and for introduction into the state of divine sonship. These are two reasons why grace is needed; but the grace that responds to them is essentially one grace. This is the grace of divine sonship that delivers us from the state of sin. But it is only through Jesus Christ that this grace is given. Before being touched by the grace of Christ, we stand before God as sinful creatures; mere creatures, who are not yet children of God, and sinful creatures, who have been alienated from him in a state that leaves us moreover prone to aggravate our alienation by sinful acts of our own. God does not leave us in this condition; he pursues us with a love that incessantly endeavors to restore us to his grace. It is through Jesus, his beloved Son, that he does this — through Jesus, and no one else.

PART 5
The Holy Spirit, the Paraclete

Although Jesus is the unique Savior for all of humanity, it was not in the divine plan for him to proclaim the Gospel personally to everyone. Had that been the case, his ministry would have been far less human, since no human being lives forever or is in direct personal contact even with all his contemporaries. In coming to redeem the world in a human fashion, the Son of God took upon himself the limits of an ordinary human life; that made it necessary for him to send others to carry on his work, as other human masters likewise train disciples to transmit their doctrine.

Unlike others, however, Jesus was able to send forth a twofold mission. Besides the apostles, whom he sent forth visibly to proclaim the Gospel, there is also the Holy Spirit that he sends hiddenly and interiorly. At the Last Supper, in preparing the apostles for his departure, Jesus said:

> When the Paraclete[1] comes, whom I will send you from the Father, the Spirit of truth who goes out from the Father, he will testify about me; but you also must testify, for you have been with me from the beginning. (John 15:26f)

This double mission — of the apostles who bear witness to Jesus in words, and of the Spirit who confirms their witness in the hearts of the hearers — carries forward the mission of Jesus and creates the Church. We will examine first the interior action of the Paraclete, and in Part 6 the exterior proclamation of the apostles and its prolongation in the Church.

This is not meant to imply that the inner life of grace is something apart from the Church or that the Church consists only of external offices and functions. On the contrary, the interior and exterior have been wedded by Jesus into a single *mystery*, in which that which appears on the outside is the sign and instrument of that which takes place within. But the limits of human language require us to take up these diverse aspects of the Christian mystery one after the other.

The dramatic coming of the Holy Spirit culminated Jesus' earthly ministry (see Chapter 16) and launched the Church on its career. It marked the beginning of a new era in salvation history — the New Covenant, the era of the Holy Spirit. The New Covenant was of course inaugurated by Jesus; but the work of Jesus was not completed until Pentecost. Jesus stayed on earth only for a moment — long enough to institute the new regime, and then return to the

Father. The Holy Spirit is the permanent Paraclete, who abides with the Church forever. His public and visible coming was only the sign of an enduring Pentecost. The Spirit remains the perpetual source of animation for the Church as a whole and for each of its members.

• *The invisible focus of Christianity*

John the Baptist, sent to prepare the way for the Messiah and to point him out when he appeared, characterized him thus: "I baptize you with water, but he will baptize you with the Holy Spirit" (Mark 1:8), as if that adequately summed up Christ's entire ministry. Jesus himself spoke about the Spirit as *the* Gift of God (John 4:10), as if no other gift mattered. And although Jesus himself was the fulfillment of the promise made to Abraham and reiterated throughout the Old Testament, still he spoke of the Holy Spirit as "*the* promise of the Father" (that is, what the Father had promised [Acts 1:4]). He told the apostles, "It is for your good that I am going away. Unless I go away, the Paraclete will not come to you; but if I go, I will send him to you" (John 16:7). Even after Jesus had completed the instruction of the apostles, and after the Resurrection had given them a radically new perspective on the dynamics of his work, they still were not ready to begin their mission until they received the Holy Spirit. Jesus told them to wait in Jerusalem until they were "clothed with power from on high," for, he said, "you will receive power when the Holy Spirit comes on you; and you will be my witnesses in Jerusalem and in all Judea and Samaria, and to the ends of the earth" (Acts 1:8; see also Luke 24:47-49). All the activity of Jesus — not only his preaching and teaching, but even his birth, death, and resurrection — aimed at this one result: the imparting of the Holy Spirit to his followers.

• *Central reality of the New Covenant*

For the gift of the Holy Spirit is the chief and central reality of the New Covenant. Everything else in the Church and the Christian life is either a preparation for the gift of the Spirit, a consequence of it, or a framework in which to live it. Thus grace is simply the work of the Spirit within us. The sacraments get their power from him; or better, he uses the sacraments as instruments of the grace he imparts. Law in Christianity is only a basic instruction on how to live in accord with the Spirit, and is impossible to keep except with the Spirit's help; sacred doctrine takes hold on our minds only by the illumination of the Spirit. The Church is a community of those who live formed, animated, and united by the Spirit.

In other words, Christianity is not just a system of beliefs or a code of ethics or a body of ritual. It includes all these elements, but to reduce it to them turns it into a dead carapace. Christianity is essentially an anointing and animation by the Spirit of Christ; the other, structural elements are only the visible framework of the Christian life. "If anyone does not have the Spirit of Christ, he does not belong to Christ" (Romans 8:9).

Other spiritual or religious leaders of mankind are teachers and guides, who point out a way to go. But as human experience abundantly testifies, knowing the way does not necessarily enable a person to follow it. Jesus not only points out the way; by the gift of the Spirit he empowers us for it. The same Spirit that animated Jesus as he "went about doing good" is imparted to his disciples. The Spirit of Jesus leads them to accept and understand his teaching, and conforms them to him.

We also speak of a "spirit" imparted by inspirational human beings; for example, the spirit of the Pilgrim Fathers or the spirit of '76 or the spirit of Notre Dame. "John Brown's body lies a-molderin' in the grave, but his spirit marches on." *Spirit* in such cases refers to a mental and psychic atmosphere generated by the example or doctrine of influential persons. But the Spirit imparted by Jesus is a substantial reality, a dynamo of power, in fact, a person. He is the Holy Spirit: a divine person, like the Son himself. He is not just an occult power of the universe, like the spirits invoked in magic, witchcraft, or yoga. He is the Creator Spirit whose divine power brought the universe into being and still acts within it. He who proceeds from the Father and Son within the Trinity is sent into the world by them.

• *Divine secret at the heart of the universe*

Some of the late books of the Old Testament speak of the Spirit of God pervading the universe. "The Spirit of the Lord has filled the world," declares the Book of Wisdom (1:7). Many poets have sensed that the world is brimming with a sacred presence. Perhaps this is what St. Paul referred to when he reaffirmed in his own name the words of a Greek poet, "In him we live and move and have our being" (Acts 17:28). Whatever is to be said of this universal presence, however, it is not to be identified with the gift bestowed by Jesus, which is special to those who have faith in him.

The Old Testament also speaks of a special action of the Spirit of Yahweh on various leaders of the people of Israel. It gave Moses the wisdom and strength to conduct the Hebrews through the desert (see Numbers 11:25). It came upon the judges, stirring them up to lead Israel (Judges, *passim*). It came for a while upon King Saul (1 Samuel 10:1-13), then left him for David (1 Samuel 16:13-14). It was by the inspiration of the Spirit that the prophets spoke God's word, and the sacred writers composed the Scriptures (see, for example, Acts 4:25). The later books of the Old Testament coined the term *Holy Spirit*, which means, in effect, "divine inspirer," as we have already noted (Chapter 18). Nevertheless, Jesus' gift of the Spirit is so new that St. John can say flatly, "Up to that time, the Spirit had not been given, since Jesus had not yet been glorified" (John 7:39).[2]

• *Activity of the Spirit*

The most obvious characteristic of the New Testament gift of the Spirit is that it is not restricted to a few exceptional leaders but is "poured out" on the entire populace. St. Peter explains the Pentecostal events as a fulfillment of the prophecy of Joel, that God would pour out his Spirit "on all flesh" (Acts 2:16ff; Joel 2:28f). (This does not mean on all mankind indiscriminately but on all those who believe in Christ; for the gift of the Spirit was precisely the reward for faith. In explaining Jesus' promise of living water, John 7:39 [RSV] says, "This he said about the Spirit, which those who believed in him were to receive.")

A second striking fact about the New Testament gift of the Spirit is the rich and colorful variety of its effects. These are innumerable, but some of the more important are the following:

1. *Teaching.* "He will teach you all things, and will remind you of everything I have said to you" (John 14:26; see also 16:13; 1 John 2:27). Human evangelists and preachers can teach only externally. Before their work can bring people to real faith, it must be complemented by the interior teaching of the Holy Spirit. "No one can say 'Jesus is Lord,' except by the Holy Spirit" (1 Corinthians 12:3). The Spirit's teaching, moreover, is not confined to inducing people to accept the faith; it is a continuing light that enables them to grow in faith with an ever stronger and fuller grasp of its implications. The Spirit does not impart academic knowledge; he enlightens us by changing us and by taking possession of us.

2. *Guiding.* At times the Spirit directs us in very specific ways about actions we are to perform or decisions we are to make. He inspired Philip to speak to the Ethiopian who was studying Isaiah (Acts 8:29), Peter to respond to the invitation of the Roman centurion (Acts 10:19ff), and Paul not to preach in Bithynia (Acts 16:7).

3. *Strengthening.* Knowing what should be done is not enough to enable us to carry it out. For the demands of the Christian life and the apostolate, the Holy Spirit gives new strength, the supreme example of which was the transformation of the apostles on Pentecost Day (Acts 2ff). The text which sums this up most comprehensively is that of St. Paul: "I can do everything through him who gives me strength" (Philippians 4:13).

4. *Pouring forth* sentiments of love, joy, peace, etc., and giving a new freedom.

> The fruit of the Spirit is love, joy, peace, patience, kindness, goodness, faithfulness, gentleness, and self-control. (Galatians 5:22; see also 5:1; Romans 5:5; 8:14-16)

All the gifts of grace are appropriately viewed as flowing from the Holy Spirit who, as the supreme gift of God to us, is sometimes spoken of as "Uncreated Grace." In the next three chapters, we will examine the various orders of "created grace," or the work of the Holy Spirit within us. In the first place, there are the most fundamental aspects of grace: forgiveness of sin and divine sonship. Secondly, there is the *life* of grace, which consists principally in faith, hope, and charity. Finally, what are called "Gifts of the Holy Spirit" bring this life to its perfection. For while every grace can be regarded as a gift of the Holy Spirit, these manifest his presence in a special way. In other words, by *grace* he makes us children of God; by the virtues of *faith, hope,* and *charity* which he infuses in us, we *live* as children of God; by the *Gifts of the Spirit* (in the narrower sense), this life of children of God is *perfected.*

21
The dimensions of grace

If there is any one word that can express the entire Christian message, it is *grace*. That God is gracious to man is the essence of the good news proclaimed by Jesus. If Christianity can be summed up in the person of Jesus himself, it is because in his very person he is the supreme revelation of the gracious Father and the mediator through whom the Father's grace effectively reaches us. If God is revealed as a Father, this is first of all to say that he is kind, loving, and merciful, that is, gracious. If the fruit of Jesus' work is the imparting of the Holy Spirit, this is the expression of God's favor to us and the root of the transformation brought about in us. "All is grace," said Thérèse of Lisieux. Those who conceive of God primarily as a stern lawgiver or a threatening judge invert the Christian message, turning the good news into bad news.

Reflecting this message, the Christian attitude is characterized by joyous and grateful confidence. Joyous confidence because we know we have passed "from death to life" (1 John 3:14); grateful because it is not by our own achievement but by the grace of God that this has been brought about. But the consciousness of having been saved by grace is a difficult one to maintain. The human spirit is perpetually inclined to replace it either with the complacent assurance of one who has made it on his own or the despair of one convinced that salvation is beyond reach. It hurts our pride to accept a favor, and there are people who choose to reject the grace of God, rather than submit to the role of beggars receiving a gift. Yet acceptance of this stance is the indispensable condition of salvation through Christ: "I came not to call the righteous, but sinners" (Matthew 1:13).

It was Martin Luther's historic vocation to renew the consciousness of grace in the Church with power and eloquence. If his doctrine was, in the last analysis, untenable, this was not because of his stress on grace but because of an oversimplification that led him to deny human nature and the role of human works in collaboration with grace. In our own time, many Christians — even Lutherans — have lapsed again into a conception of Christianity as chiefly a style of human conduct. We need another Luther — but without Luther's one-sidedness — to reanimate our awareness of the grace of God given to us in Christ Jesus, our Lord.

• *Grace: good will or gifts?*

Basically, *grace* means favor, benevolence, good will toward someone. In this sense, St. Paul speaks of "the grace [of God] in which we stand" (Romans 5:2). And because good will commonly expresses itself in kindly deeds or gifts, the latter also come to be called graces. The word *favor* can mean either someone's favorable attitude (as when we seek to win his favor) or the deeds that result from it (as when we say, "Do me a favor"). Similarly, the term *grace* can refer either to God's graciousness (as in Romans 5:2 above) or to gifts given by God, as when St. Paul speaks of the grace he has received (Romans 1:5, etc.).

Whether in the mind or in the deed, grace is normally understood to be *undeserved*; this aspect is paramount in the grace that comes to us through Jesus Christ. It is a favor of which we are not worthy, a gift we have not merited. St. Paul insists on the point:

By grace you have been saved through faith; and this is not your own doing, it is the gift of God — not because of works, lest any man should boast. (Ephesians 2:8)

Catholics often tend to conceive of grace primarily as a *help* given by God in moments of temptation or trial. Such help is indeed one of the chief kinds of grace but does not define it. "Undeserved love" or "unmerited gift" should be in the foreground of our concept. Likewise the notion of meriting grace is so familiar that people commonly overlook the paradox it contains. The notion is justified, as we shall see, by the human cooperation demanded by grace; but this should not make us insensitive to the apparent incompatibility of grace and merit.

• *Grace in God, grace in us*

Corresponding to the two meanings of the word, divine grace can be seen either in God or in creatures. In God, it designates an attitude of benevolence, love, generosity, and readiness to forgive. In creatures, it refers to gifts received from God. Primarily, grace should be seen in God; for his favorable attitude toward us is the source of the gifts he bestows. In Scripture, the expression "the grace of God" usually refers to his graciousness toward us. Like children elated over presents they have received, we are often more attentive to God's gifts than to the love from which they originate. It was another of Luther's merits to insist on the primacy of grace in God; but here too he exaggerated and oversimplified by denying, in effect, the reality of the grace received by us. Catholics, on the other hand, in defending the reality of created grace, must take care to keep it in the perspective of uncreated grace.

In terms of the grace which is in God, Christianity is an affirmation that the ultimate truth of the universe lies not in the inexorable operation of the powers of nature but in a sweet, free graciousness that is ever within reach of our fingertips. The fertile abundance of the earth, the wild and playful varieties of living things, the mildness of our climate (which we can appreciate better now, having explored the harsh, inhospitable moon and planets), are signs of a Father's kindness. Moreover, when I have sinned, willfully contravening the order of nature and the deepest laws of my own being as well as the explicit command of my Sovereign, when I am conscious of having committed a wrong that cannot be righted, when guilt weighs crushingly upon me, there is a voice that says, "Turn back to me and you will be saved" (Isaiah 45:22). It is spoken softly; but its firm tones are able to quiet the clamor of the outraged universe calling for vengeance or the self-recrimination of my own wounded and disgusted heart. This is the message of grace.

• *God's grace effective*

But the grace of God is not mere benevolence; it is effective and creative. It really heals, helps, restores, and elevates us. God does not merely impute to us a justice and holiness we do not really have;[1] the effect of his grace is to give us a justice and holiness that are real. It does not sanctify us completely all at once; it calls for a response and a cooperation on our part in which we are all liable to fail. Not until the resurrection will we be brought fully into accord with the grace that has been given us: Meanwhile, its effects may at times be quite hidden by our imperfections and sinful tendencies. Nevertheless, the effects of grace are real, and the difference between the state of grace and the state of sin is radical. We must now examine these effects in some detail.

FORGIVENESS OF SIN

The grace received by us polarizes around two notions: forgiveness and divine sonship. They go together; however, we have to consider them one at a time. Although forgiveness is a familiar human reality, it is mysterious and difficult to analyze even on the natural level. It might be described as not holding against a person the wrong he has done to us. But in what does this "not holding" consist? We cannot deny the fact of what he has done. To put it out of our mind is a help to forgiveness (hence we say, "forgive and forget"), but forgetting the injury is by no means the same thing as forgiving it. Letting go of the resentment we feel is the way we most commonly experience forgiveness; but resentment is a feeling, or emotion, whereas true forgiveness is an act of will.

If human forgiveness is difficult to analyze, divine forgiveness is far more so. God does not have feelings, nor can he forget. Furthermore, he is absolutely unchanging. This means that when God is said to forgive us, it must be *we* who change, not God. On the other hand, God's forgiveness is not a figment of human imagination. It is real, and it literally makes the difference between life and death for us. It can be called a "reconciliation" (Romans 5:10, 11; 2 Corinthians 5:18-20; Ephesians 2:16; Colossians 1:20-22). It changes our relationship with God from alienation to friendship; it restores our status of sonship, like that of the prodigal son. We inevitably visualize this as a change in God; but in truth, it is in us that the change takes place. And yet God's forgiveness is not to be identified with our repentance: It is *God* who forgives us, not we who forgive ourselves. God is the one who produces the effect; but the effect is located in us.

• *Remission of punishment*

Three elements can be distinguished in the forgiveness of sin: remission of punishment, remission of guilt, and healing. Remission of punishment is the easiest to understand. As a human governor can, when appropriate, pardon a condemned criminal and release him from fulfilling all or part of the sentence imposed on him, so God, in pardoning the sinner, releases him from punishment he deserves. But this easy analogy would mislead us if we did not bear in mind the immense difference between the meaning of punishment in the two cases of divine and human justice. Punishment for sin does not seem to consist necessarily or primarily in God doing hurtful things to the sinner as human beings do hurtful things to those being punished. Divine punishment, for the most part at least, would seem to lie in the intrinsic consequences of the sin itself. God's law, that is to say the right order of things, is good and beneficial to those who abide by it. One who violates this order, by that very fact injures himself as well as others, and more than others (see Chapter 11). Whether there is still further punishment to be imposed by a special act of God is a question we can leave open; but the primary punishment consists in the damage one does to oneself by getting out of order.[2] Alternatively, it may be thought of as a repercussion of the violated order upon the guilty party.

When he forgives sin, God does not ordinarily release us from the kind of punishment just described, which is a part of the natural order of the universe (although sometimes, by exception, he does even that). The chief punishment from which he releases us is that of hell: the eternal separation from God merited by mortal sin. Between the eternal punishment of hell and the temporal punishment consisting in the natural consequences of sin, there is an intermediate type known as purgatory. This may be remitted completely, partially, or not at all, depending on the case. But that is a matter that will be understood better when we treat purgatory (Chapter 28).

• *Healing*

The second aspect of forgiveness is healing. Sin damages the sinner by creating a psychic disorder that makes him prone to sin again. This is very evident in the case of an addiction, in which there may even be a physical basis for the inclination. In a more subtle way, impurity destroys a delicate innate sense of modesty and leaves a person far more vulnerable to subsequent temptations. In general, it can be said that any sin leaves us inclined to further sin of the same sort; and this can be regarded as a wound or illness in the soul.

Divine forgiveness has a healing effect on such wounds. It does not merely gloss over our wrong deeds but affects us intrinsically, repairing the damage left by the sin. However, this is not accomplished all at once. The sinner, especially if he has a long-standing habit of sin, usually remains prone to the same sort of sin even after receiving forgiveness. Grace does its healing work only gradually in the course of a lifetime. Not until the final resurrection will it have its complete effect, when the Holy Spirit completely permeates and sanctifies every atom of our being. Meanwhile, there is a very real and progressive healing effect of grace that strengthens the sinner against temptation.

• *Cleansing from guilt*

Besides the remission of punishment and the healing of the wound left by sin, there is a more profound element of forgiveness, which is usually spoken of as cleansing from guilt. "Wash away all my iniquity and cleanse me from my sin," prayed the Psalmist

337

(51:2), and Yahweh, as if in answer, affirmed, "Though your sins are like scarlet, they shall be[come] white as snow" (Isaiah 1:18). The sinful act that has been committed cannot of course be annulled; it is an irrevocable fact of history. Likewise guilt cannot be removed in the sense of taking away one's responsibility for the sins one has committed. Nevertheless, grace does bring about a real cleansing of the soul of the sinner from the state of sinfulness that has been left by the act of sin. This sinfulness consists, on the one hand, in the inordinate attachment to some creaturely good — for example, sensual pleasure — which lay at the root of the sin. As the body is said to be soiled when alien matter adheres to it, so the soul is soiled when, through inordinate affections, it adheres to things it should not. Forgiveness requires that this affection be rectified, and grace brings about the rectification. Thus, if a person sinned by indulging in sensual pleasure more than is compatible with the love of God, grace cleanses him by causing him to put pleasure back into its due proportion in his life. (This occurs of course only through his free decision; but it is grace that enables him to make the decision.)

• *Reconciliation with God*

Secondly, "mortal sin" (as will be explained below) ruptures the relationship with God given by grace. It puts an end to one's status as son of God and makes one an alien — in fact, an enemy — of God (not that God hates him but that he in effect hates God). It makes him pass from light to darkness, for sin closes him to the light with which grace and charity had filled him. These effects will be more understandable after we consider the second major effect of grace, which is divine sonship. Here, the point to be made is that the grace of forgiveness includes the restoration to the status of sonship, which sin had terminated.

Cleansing, or remission of guilt, is not to be confused with deliverance from guilt *feelings*, although the latter may result from the former. There are three levels of guilt. The first is the *responsibility* for having done wrong, as when we say Brutus was guilty of murdering Caesar. The second is the *feeling* of remorse that often comes upon the person conscious of having sinned. The third is the *state of alienation* from God, of deprivation of the grace of God, which ends when grace is restored. Guilt in the first sense is a concern of the law; guilt in the second sense is a concern of psychology; guilt in the third sense is a concern of theology and pastoral ministry.

In conclusion, the forgiveness of sins involves three distinct elements: remission of the punishment due for sin (at least the eternal punishment), healing of the wound left by sin, and cleansing of the state of guilt. This last element coincides substantially with the second major work of grace in us, bestowal of divine sonship, which we must consider next.

THE GIFT OF DIVINE SONSHIP

Forgiveness of sins was the first major effect of grace in us; the gift of divine sonship is the second. (We become either sons or daughters of God, according to our gender. But since this relationship is a participation in the unique sonship of Jesus Christ, it may appropriately be called divine sonship in either case.) It is also called divine friendship (see John 15:14-15), divine indwelling (see John 14:23, 26), and union with God. These are all aspects of one same relationship with God that is conferred by grace. We will use the notion of sonship as the framework of our exposition, and supplement it where appropriate with the other notions.

The grace of forgiveness would not have been needed if we had not sinned; but we would still need grace for divine sonship. The latter is the principal and essential work of grace. For by nature, the human being is not a child of God but a servant, bound to do his Lord's bidding, having no entrée into the divine life. The wonder of grace consists precisely in this, that the servant has been brought into the master's proper family.

One might object that the simple fact of creation is grounds for regarding human beings as God's offspring; and, as we have seen (Chapter 16), many primitive religions — for example, in India, Babylon, and Egypt — have spoken of God as a father. But this way of speaking seems to be nothing more than a metaphor for the relationship between the artisan and his handiwork. At best, it would express an obscure intimation that human beings enjoy an affinity with the Creator that is unique in this material world. The grace of sonship that has been proffered to us through Jesus Christ is not just our natural relationship with God; it is a new gift, not *de facto* included in nature, and one which could not possibly be natural in any conceivable world because it is inherently divine. It is a free gift of God over and above nature and all that nature itself calls for.

> In love he predestined us to be adopted as his sons through Jesus Christ, in accordance with his pleasure and will — to the praise of his glorious grace which he has freely given us in the one he loves. (Ephesians 1:5)

The reality of this grace can be appreciated from the fact that it does not consist simply in God's acting as a Father toward us, nor in our "proving" ourselves to be his children by doing his will. These two aspects of divine sonship we have already seen in connection with the preaching of Jesus (Chapter 16). There are many other aspects and consequences of the grace of sonship. There is the gift of the Holy Spirit, "the Spirit of sonship," who bears witness to our spirits that we are children of God, who leads us in the life of children of God, and who is the source, hidden deep within us, of the cry "Abba, Father!" that springs from our heart (Chapter 23). There is the life which the Holy Spirit pours forth within us, which in this world takes the threefold form of faith, hope, and charity but which is properly the beginning of eternal life and a participation in the life of the Father, Son, and Holy Spirit (Chapter 22).

• *Sanctifying grace*

All of these things together pertain to the life of grace; they are its most salient aspects. The hidden link which binds them together is the mysterious reality known as sanctifying grace. This is simply the radical sanctification of our being to which St. Paul, for example, refers when he declares:

> . . .you were washed, you were sanctified, you were justified in the name of the Lord Jesus Christ and in the Spirit of our God. (1 Corinthians 6:11)

On the basis of this sanctification, Paul speaks of all Christians as "sanctified in Christ Jesus, called to be saints together with all those who in every place call on the name of our Lord Jesus Christ" (1 Corinthians 1:2). *Saint* here does not mean one who has entered into heaven, a connotation which it was to acquire in later tradition. St. Paul's idea is that every authentic Christian, by reason of his link with Jesus Christ, has a genuine, even if imperfect, sanctity, or holiness. Because he has it, not by nature but by grace, that which brings it about is called, in technical theological language, *sanctifying grace*.

Sanctifying grace is an effect of the Holy Spirit on us, making us, so to speak, a suitable temple for his abode. It is the most profound of all his effects; it is the root of the faith, hope, and charity by which we live the divine life. Faith sanctifies our minds; hope and charity sanctify our affections; sanctifying grace sanctifies not just an act or a faculty but our being itself. Without it the other sanctifications would remain relatively superficial and rootless. From another point of view, sanctifying grace is what gives us the quality of "image and likeness of God," distinguishing us from all other creatures in this world (Genesis 1:26). It is not just intellect and free will that qualify us as images of God, for in the state of sin we lose our godlikeness, and become a horrible caricature.

• *Participation in the divine nature*

The notion that most profoundly reveals the meaning of sanctifying grace is that of participation in the divine nature. The Second Epistle of St. Peter, in telling how God has granted us all that pertains to life and godliness, declares that "he has called us to his own glory and excellence," then adds:

> . . .he has given us his very great and precious promises, so that through them you may participate in the divine nature and escape the corruption in the world caused by evil desires. (1:3-4)

The phrase "participate in the divine nature" is the kernel around which reflection on the nature of grace has crystallized down through the centuries. It is also the key that explains and synthesizes the other aspects of grace reviewed above. We are "the image and likeness of God" to such a degree that we participate in his very nature. Being children of God means not merely enjoying an intimate relationship with him but that we have inherited his *nature*, as all offspring receive the nature of their parents. Sharing eternal life, that is, the divine life, can be seen as a consequence of this sharing in the divine nature. Our sanctification is not merely symbolic — like that of a church building, a chalice, or a sacred vestment, all of which are regarded as holy, or sacred, because they are set aside exclusively for religious use; it is much more substantial and real, involving a divinization of our very being.

A brief philosophical reflection may help to bring out the significance of this text of 2 Peter. (It would be an egregious error of course to read the text as though it had been composed in philosophical language; but it is legitimate to use philosophy to point up the implications of what is said.)

The nature of a being determines its operation. Chemicals interact according to their nature. Plants grow; animals run, fly, or swim according to their nature. Our rational nature enables us to think, to plan, to love; even though we are free to choose our acts, we can do so only within the limits of our nature. By an analogy that must be used with great caution, we may speak of the divine nature — which is not limited in any way whatsoever — as enabling God to do what he does, above all to live that life which consists in the mutual exchanges between the Father, Son, and Spirit. It is in the divine nature in this sense that we are said to participate by grace.

The comparison is often used, that if a dog were by some miracle given the power to think and speak like a man, he would then be sharing in human nature. This is a misleading comparison, however, because a dog could not be given such human powers without first being given a human soul; and then he would no longer be a dog but human (even though a freak). Hence we must stress that grace does not alter human nature but enhances it. A human being under grace is still man, simply and without qualification. (In fact, he is able to be more perfectly human, thanks to the healing and perfecting effects of grace.) His proper nature is still human nature; grace does not put him in a different category of being. If it did, there would have to be different definitions for the person who is in the state of grace, and the one who is not. Grace gives us a new resemblance to God, while respecting our distinctive essence as human.

• *The grounds of intimacy with God*

This resemblance consists concretely in being able to enter into communion with God by faith, hope, and charity in this life, and by the beatific vision in the next. It is the prerogative of the divine persons to live in full and intimate communion with one another. For us to be admitted into similar (even though imperfect) union with them is to be lifted above the realm of our nature, and to be given a share in the divine nature. Faith, hope, and charity, as will be seen in the next chapter, are the exercise of a supernatural communion with God; sanctifying grace elevates, adapts, and qualifies us for this communion. St. Thomas points out that the function of sanctifying grace is to make faith, hope, and charity connatural to human beings (*Summa Theologiae*, I-II, 110, 2). They are so intrinsically divine that they would be like an alien imposition upon us, were we not adapted to them by grace. Hence the latter can be described as a kind of "second nature"; without altering our essential nature, it nevertheless makes communion with God connatural to us.

The Greek tradition often expressed this truth by saying that we are divinized by grace. This did not mean some kind of apotheosis turning a man into a deity, nor a merging of ourselves into the divinity, entailing the loss of our distinct personality. The creature never receives more than a finite *participation* in the divine nature. But the godlikeness conferred by grace, in contrast with any natural endowment, is so proper that it can be called divinization.

• *The Holy Spirit and sanctifying grace*

Sanctifying grace is coterminous with the gift of the Holy Spirit. It is the direct and principal effect of his presence. If the Spirit be compared to a light, sanctifying grace is the resulting illumination. By the same token, it is lost when he departs. It is likewise inseparable from charity — that "love of God . . . poured forth in our hearts by the Spirit who has been given to us" (Romans 5:5). As grace results from the presence of the Holy Spirit, charity results from grace, the very meaning and purpose of which is to establish us in that communion with the divine persons which is brought about principally by charity. To abandon charity is to drive sanctifying grace out of one's soul just as surely as to stop breathing would drive the life out of one's body. Thus there is a kind of triangular relationship between these three terms: the indwelling of the Holy Spirit, sanctifying grace, and charity. The Spirit dwelling in us produces grace, grace generates charity, and charity is the act of communion with the Spirit by reason of which he is said to dwell in us. Obviously, the indwelling of the Spirit, grace, and charity are not to be conceived as events that succeed one another in time. Although there is a causal relationship among them, as we have indicated, they are simultaneous.

The Spirit can act upon us even when he is not dwelling in us. He touches the sinner with many actual graces (for example, repentance and prayer) that prepare for and lead up to the final act of charity in which the sinner receives sanctifying grace and the indwelling of the Spirit. Were this not the case, it would be impossible for a sinner to be converted. But it is only when the sinner has, by the grace of the Holy Spirit, turned to God in love, that we can speak of the Spirit as dwelling in him and putting him in the state of grace.

This helps to explain why we can have faith and hope without sanctifying grace. Although they too are effects of the Spirit in us, and pertain to our communion with God, they are only foundational for this communion which is realized in charity. They can be given to one who does not have charity or retained by one who has lost it. Every mortal sin implies a loss of charity, as we are now about to see; but mortal sin does not necessarily mean that the sinner has given up faith or hope.

MORTAL SIN

From the foregoing, we can understand the meaning of mortal sin. In brief, it means loving some created good in the place of God. It is a preference given to another value over God. Charity is the love-relationship with God into which we have been introduced by the grace of Christ. Mortal sin is a love-relationship with some other being — some creature — that is incompatible with the love of God. God is loved rightly only when he is loved above all else; when something else is loved more than God, there is mortal sin. It is a taking of something other than God as the supreme value in one's life — having "strange gods" before him.

This does not of course mean that the sinner declares this in words or even recognizes it consciously. Very commonly, he would wish to have the created good and God too, like an adulterer who doesn't want to lose his wife but wants a girl friend along with her. And just as a woman will not readily tolerate such duplicity on the part of her husband, so God, who in fact calls himself "jealous" (Deuteronomy 5:9), will not share his primacy with any other being. In fact, he often speaks of his grace-relationship with us not only as a fatherhood but also as a marriage.[3] Out of an infinite love that is beyond our comprehension he offers us not just his gifts but his own person in a union of which human marriage is only a weak image. The indwelling of the Holy Spirit is a divine embrace that will be consummated in the inseparable union of heaven. But this marriage demands of us a love that takes God as the supreme beloved.

Mortal sin does not necessarily imply the conscious rejection of the love of God but simply an actual love of something else that is incompatible with that love. In the concrete terms of our daily living, the love of God is expressed in the keeping of his commandments. "If you love me, keep my commandments" (John 14:15), Jesus demanded bluntly. In this perspective, mortal sin is that sort of disobedience to his commandments which implies that another love has taken command of our heart.

Thus it is not directly the magnitude of the harm done which determines when sin is mortal. This depends rather on whether the profound and ultimate motive of the wrongdoer has been to prefer something else to God, that is, to love something else more than God. If he gets drunk because he loves liquor so much that, when it comes to a showdown, drinking has a higher value in his life than doing the will of God, he has committed a mortal sin. But someone who has committed murder in a fit of passion, who would never do it in his right mind, and who did not really consider the implications and the consequences of his action — such a one might conceivably not be guilty of mortal sin. Such a distinction could never be made in the case of an angel, for a pure spirit perceives in an instant, and with full clarity, all the implications of what it does. But human beings are capable of such inconsistency, in acting contrary to their deepest beliefs and intentions out of thoughtlessness or weakness, that it is impossible to say, from a mere external examination, whether a given sin is actually mortal or not. Even the sinner himself, although able to look interiorly at his motives and intentions, is not always capable of appraising them objectively. One of the effects of sin is to make us blind to our own sinfulness; and most of us are inclined to seek excuses to justify what we have done. On the other hand, we can also judge ourselves superficially, and because something we have said or done had the aspect of revolt against God, we may consider ourselves as having sinned grievously when we did not.

• *"Grievous matter"*

By the same token, what is apparently very slight or trivial on the human plane may in fact express a very grievous affront to God. For example, a "harmless" lie or a curse, uttered as a deliberate gesture of defiance against God, by this very fact takes on a gravity that it would not ordinarily have, and thus can be a mortal sin. This does not contradict the traditional catechetical doctrine that for mortal sin there must be grievous matter. The "matter" in the case is not measured in terms of physical harm or social consequences but in terms of one's choice of the Supreme Good in his life, as this is reflected and expressed in the concrete human decision.

• *"Mortal"*

Mortal sin is so called because it puts an end to the life imparted by grace. One who abandons the love of God by turning to some other good in his place, by this very fact expels charity from his heart, and with it sanctifying grace. Such a person is then dead so far as the life of grace is concerned. He is, moreover, incapable of restoring himself to life.

Grace is beyond the power of human nature to attain or to merit. One who has lost it therefore cannot recover it for himself. Nothing he can do, not even giving up his life for his country or for a friend, is able, as a human act, to merit the restoration of grace.

This does not mean that he is hopeless but simply that his hope lies solely in the mercy of God. The loving Father who called us to be his children in the first instance wants nothing more than to restore us to that state when we have fallen from it. He is ever the father of the prodigal son (Luke 15). In order to obtain his pardon and the renewal of his grace, we must do all we can by way of repentance and the rectification of our lives as well as turning to him through prayer and the sacraments. It is precisely through such acts that we prepare ourselves for his grace and receive it. But the truth remains that grace is given out of God's generosity, not out of our merits: Grace is truly grace.

In brief, sanctifying grace is a real holiness bestowed by God. It cleanses and heals us as needed, but chiefly it gives us filial communion with him. It abides in us and tends to pervade us and all that we do, although our tepidity, infidelity, and inconsistency keep our lives from manifesting its effects fully. But sanctifying grace is best visualized as suspended between two loves: God's love for us, which causes it, and our love for God, which results from it. Sanctifying grace is a real quality abiding in us; but its existence is totally contingent on these two loves. And while God's love for us never changes, we can turn away from it just as we can turn our faces from the sun. This happens when we love something else in preference to God; and the blacking out of the light of his grace within us is the state of sin.

ACTUAL GRACE

Sanctifying grace is, as has been said, an abiding quality. There are other graces that do not abide but are simply transient helps given for a moment. For example, the light to know how to resolve a perplexity; the impulse to do something good we would not otherwise have done; the strength to persevere despite difficulties. Such graces are so diverse in form, the list of them would be endless. They are called *actual* because they are given directly in view of an act to be performed. Although sanctifying grace is the permanent basis of all the good we do in the order of grace ("meritorious works," as will be explained below), it does not directly cause us to act. It remains in us whether we are acting or not. Actual grace directly moves us to act, and lasts only while the act is taking place. In the last analysis, actual grace is nothing other than God moving us to act.

Even in the natural order, we can do nothing except by virtue of a movement imparted by God, the Prime Mover (see Chapter 9). With still greater reason, we can do nothing in the order of grace except as he moves us; and in this order, the movement or impulse coming from him is known as actual grace. Thus all that we do in our life as children of God is totally dependent on grace. Sanctifying grace establishes us in this life, and actual grace moves us to act in it. Jesus declared:

> I am the vine, you are the branches. . . . As the branch cannot bear fruit by itself, unless it abides in the vine, neither can you, unless you abide in me. . . . Apart from me you can do nothing. (John 15:4-5, RSV)

344

• *Dependence on grace*

In the natural order we can act without the grace of God. Not only can we commit sin, we can also do many good things: work and play, marry and raise families, build cities and write symphonies. But when we turn to the supernatural order — that is, to the life proper to us as children of God — there is nothing we can do without grace. And we need not only the sanctifying grace that has already been given to us but a new impulse of actual grace for each new act we are to perform. It may seem puzzling that sanctifying grace, which makes us children of God and enables us to live the divine life, is not sufficient for us to carry on the activity of that life. On a metaphysical plane, it could be shown that just as our natural activity supposes not only human nature but also actual energy coming from the First Mover, so it is with our supernatural activity. But here it is more important to stress that it is of the very essence of the life of grace to make us live in intimate relationship with God. Grace is not a power conferring on us some extraordinary type of autonomy; its effect is to relate us to God as our Father. This means not only turning to God in faith and love but also reposing in him, depending on him, and allowing him to act through us.

If one is dependent on actual grace for everything he does as a child of God, is he free? This question has occupied the Christian mind perennially, especially since the time of St. Augustine (354-430). Catholic doctrine maintains both the reality of human freedom, and the primacy of grace. Man is dependent on grace but free to cooperate with it or not. God is absolutely sovereign over human life, yet he deals with man in such a way as to leave the latter free. If we find it impossible to understand how this can be, that should not be surprising. If the nature of God is beyond our comprehension, it is natural that God's way of acting should be likewise. Just as it is a mistake to imagine God as one more being in addition to all those that make up the world, so it is a mistake to imagine God as interacting with us like the other persons and beings we have to deal with. God is the source of our being, himself the fullness of being, who nevertheless gives us distinct existence on our own; so likewise he is the First Mover, both in the world of nature and in the realm of grace, who nevertheless enables us to be the authors of our own acts.[4] More than this, it is difficult for us to say.

• *Grace and freedom*

The insolubility of the problem of grace and freedom is well illustrated by the famous debate between the Thomists, who insisted more on the efficacy of grace, and the Molinists, who stressed the freedom of man. Over a period of five years, in the presence of two successive popes (1602-1607), the argument was carried on by major representatives of each school. It terminated with the decree of Pope Paul V that both parties could maintain their own opinion, and that neither should call the other heretical.

In the Protestant world, specifically in the Reformed, that is, Calvinist churches, a parallel to this debate occurred at the very same time. Arminius, professor at Leyden from 1603-1609, rejected the Calvinist doctrine of predestination, and defended human free will. This produced a split in the Presbyterian and subsequently the Methodist churches.

Even in the Muslim world this debate had its counterpart. It is a fundamental dogma of Islam that all events in this world are absolutely determined by the will of Allah. But under the influence of Greek philosophy, the Mu'tazilites affirmed human freedom. The difficulty of reconciling these positions led to intense discussions during the High Middle Ages.

MERIT

The foregoing enables us to resolve the paradox of merit. By definition, grace means unmerited love and gift; so is it not a contradiction to speak of grace being merited? Moreover, it is basic Christian doctrine that salvation and eternal life come to us solely as a gracious gift of God. Do we not contradict this by speaking of meriting heaven? Even more fundamentally, the creature owes everything it has, including its very being, to God. How then can there be room for it to merit anything from God? This conglomerate of objections was one of the main issues of the Reformation, in which Luther assailed the Catholic teaching on merit as a travesty of the Gospel of grace.

• *Merit in Scripture*

But the notion of merit is commonplace in Scripture. The Old Testament taught that "God will render to every man according to his works" (Psalm 62:13; Proverbs 24:12; Sirach 16:14). The New Testament did not reject this axiom but reiterated it often (Romans 2:6; 2 Corinthians 5:10; 11:15b; Apocalypse 14:13; 20:12-15; etc.). Jesus declared that "the Son of Man is to come with his angels in the glory of his Father, and then he will repay every man for what he has done" (Matthew 16:27). In the parable of the Last Judgment, the Supreme Judge divides the "sheep" from the "goats" on the grounds of what they have done: "As long as you did it to one of the least of these, my brethren, you did it unto me" (Matthew 25:40). Innumerable other texts could be cited to illustrate the fact that there is a place in the Christian economy for retribution, that is, for reward or punishment in the next world (and in some measure, even in this one) according to the kind of life lived in the present. *Merit* denotes the relationship between the deed and its retribution. In the last analysis, it means that God is just, not arbitrary. After giving us grace that is undeserved, he rewards or punishes us according to the use we have made of it, like the householder in the Gospel who, on returning from a journey, rewarded or punished his servants according to the way they had invested his money (Matthew 25:14-29).

Absolutely speaking, we have no power to merit anything from God. In particular, the sinner has no way to deserve admission into the divine intimacy. But when we consider the order of the universe established by God, namely that each person will be rewarded or punished according to his deeds, then we are justified in saying that the latter merit the former. Merit is not a claim the creature has on God but a right conferred on the creature by the grace and justice of God. It is *by grace* that we are able to merit. As St. Augustine put it, "in rewarding our deeds, [O Lord,] you reward your own gifts."

Finally, the connection between good deeds and the reward they merit is not arbitrary. There is an intrinsic proportion between them because grace elevates human activity to the level of eternal life. All that we do out of sanctifying grace, which is to say all that we do for the love of God, is a genuine beginning of eternal life, and truly deserves the fulfillment that will be awarded to it in heaven. It is not insofar as they are *ours* that our works merit an eternal reward but insofar as they are the work of the Holy Spirit acting in us. And just as our cooperation with grace merits heaven, so it also merits further grace here on earth. When by the grace of God I do a good deed, he rewards me with further grace. Thus even that most outrageous of paradoxes, the notion of merited grace, simply expresses the order with which God lavishes his love upon us, the fact that his infinite generosity does not excuse us from the responsibility of collaborating with him, of "working out our salvation" (Philippians 2:12).

• *Primacy of sonship over forgiveness*

We have examined the two principal effects of grace: forgiveness of sin and divine sonship. As was pointed out earlier, the latter is greater and more characteristic. Even if we had not fallen into sin, grace would still be necessary to elevate us to the status of sons and daughters of God. The proper effect of grace is to make us participate in the divine life; the fact that grace also involves forgiveness is due simply to the state in which it finds us. In concrete actuality, however, the two effects go together. Grace takes the sinner and makes of him a beloved child of God. It makes him pass from death to life, from darkness to light.

One might wonder whether God could not pardon a sinner without going on to introduce him into the divine life. In other words, would it not be possible for us simply to be restored to an integral natural condition without any supernatural elevation? Theoretically, perhaps this is conceivable. But in dealing with the grace of Jesus Christ, we are not speculating about what God could have done in another order of things but what he has actually done in the real world. Nowhere in the teachings of Jesus or of the New Testament is there any hint of a neutral ground between the status of sinner and that of redeemed child of God. "He that is not with me is against me," Jesus said (Matthew 12:30).

The reason for this may be seen first in the close union between nature and grace. The latter is not a kind of divine afterthought; a remedy provided after nature had been wounded. Man was created from the beginning not simply to be lord of the material universe but to be the son of God. When grace was lost by the fall, it had to be restored by a redemption that included forgiveness; but grace as God intended and gave it from the beginning was the gift of divine sonship. Forgiveness became necessary when the prodigal son forsook his father's house; but sonship, not simply nature, is man's destiny.

In another way, we can understand this from the unity of divine love. God loves the sinner so much that he is willing not only to forgive but also to restore him to his household. For man to want to accept forgiveness, while rejecting the invitation to sonship, would be tantamount to rejecting divine love. There is one love with which God loves man, a love that is fatherly, and in its fatherliness, willing to forgive. Man can accept or reject that fatherly love; but he cannot carve it up, and take a portion of its effects while discarding others. In attempting to do so, he would reject the love itself and thereby all its effects.

22

Faith, hope, and charity: the life of children of God

"I have come," Jesus said, "that they may have life, and may have it more abundantly" (John 10:10). He spoke of this life as eternal life, but the Gospel of John makes it clear that eternal life already has its beginning in this world. "He that believes in me has eternal life" (John 6:47). This is the life of children of God: not merely human conduct befitting God's children but a radically new depth and power of life, for which we can be qualified solely by the Spirit of God. It requires that we be "born again" through the Holy Spirit (John 3:8). The foundation of this life is grace, by which we share in the divine nature as children of God, able to commune with the three divine persons. The activities in which this life is expressed consist essentially in the three "theological virtues" of faith, hope, and charity.

THE THEOLOGICAL VIRTUES

Faith, hope, and charity define the Christian life. Insofar as they pervade and inspire our life, they make it authentically Christian. Traditionally, they have been looked upon as virtues, but we must beware of letting this term obscure what is altogether distinctive and supernatural in them. In ordinary usage, a virtue is a human quality that results from living rightly, and which inclines, strengthens, and perfects a person to continue such a life. Justice is the most obvious example. Faith, hope, and charity, however, are not acquired simply by practice; they must be infused by the Holy Spirit; they are altogether beyond natural human power. They do not pertain simply to "right living" in a human sense, as justice does; they enable us to live in this world as children of the heavenly Father. This does not imply a life that is inhuman or unnatural; on the contrary, divine filiation brings human nature to a more sublime beauty and perfection even in its humanness. But the divine life transcends the power and measures of human nature; it is absolutely supernatural; it is a participation by mere humans in the life of God, as will be clearer when we examine each of these virtues in particular.

The theological virtues put a person in contact with God, and this is the chief reason for the name *theological*. God is beyond the reach of man, if natural human power alone be considered. Human activity, even its most sublime insights and noble aspirations, bears directly upon the created world, and attains God only indirectly through the medium of

348

creatures. From reflection on the created world, we can become aware of the existence of a creator and worship him. But in all this, God remains remote. The faith, hope, and charity infused by the Holy Spirit, however, attain God directly. This intimate and even familiar relationship with God is the privilege of the children of God. "This is eternal life," said Jesus, "that they may know you, the only true God, and Jesus Christ whom you have sent" (John 17:3). The knowledge that is here identified with eternal life is nothing other than the intimate contact of faith, hope, and charity given by the Holy Spirit.

"Living in the presence of God," a practice highly recommended by spiritual writers as an important source of spiritual growth, is nothing other than the deliberate, conscious exercise of this contact with the divine persons. It can of course be practiced at different degrees of perfection. The ordinary Christian who has little or no awareness of the presence of God, and the mystic plunged into profound union with God, both live by the same faith, hope, and charity. The difference between them is accounted for chiefly by the sanctifying gifts of the Holy Spirit (Chapter 23), which bring the virtues to their full perfection.

HOPE

People cannot live without hope. They have no motivation to do anything, no incentive even for continuing their existence. If they do not take their own lives, they live in misery or "quiet desperation," and the lack of motivation itself makes them all the more prone to illness and death.

Young people are generally hopeful by a kind of instinct of nature. As they age, however, they discover their limitations and meet with failure; then hope begins to wane in many. Those who are successful in the competitions of life have their spirit of hope and confidence confirmed for a while; but the eventual onset of old age, with its inevitable losses, mental and physical, sometimes plunges them into despondency greater than that of those who were inured to failure early. But there are also some blessed people who retain a hopeful and joyous spirit to the end of their lives, even amid overwhelming trials.

Most if not all religions hold out hope to mankind. The Buddhists hope for *nirvana*, the Hindus for *moksha*, the Muslims for paradise. Even the antireligion of Marx is motivated by hope for the ideal social order that is eventually to come. Christianity too is a religion of hope. Its hope is characterized by the *beatitude* hoped for, and still more by the *grace* of God which is the grounds of this hope.

• *Hope for the Kingdom of God*

Christian hope is rooted in the promise made by God to Abraham, and elaborated through the teaching of the prophets and the experience of Israel down through the centuries. By the time of Christ, it had taken the shape of hope for the coming Kingdom of God. The Kingdom does not consist primarily in sensual delights, like those of the Muslim paradise, nor does it imply an annihilation of the self, as in the Far Eastern religions; its essential beatitude, as explained by St. Paul and St. John, consists in a direct union with God, seeing him "face to face" (1 Corinthians 13:12; 1 John 3:2).

It belongs to the nature of hope to have a double object: the future good that is longed for, and the grounds on which we expect to attain it. Hope that has an inadequate basis is vain and doomed to disappointment. In most religions, the grounds for hope lie in our natural human resources, usually linked with some assumed order in the universe. If you live right, says Buddhism, and especially if you meditate well, you will attain *nirvana*. It is a deformation of Christianity (but a deformation that is not rare) to conceive its hope in the same pattern. The basis of Christian hope is not any power proper to ourselves but the grace of God offering us a beatitude of which we are naturally incapable and undeserving.

• *Beatitude possible by grace*

The beatitude of the Kingdom of God is intrinsically supernatural. Moreover, our sins make us still more unworthy of it. Original sin is already enough to disqualify every human being from admission to God's Kingdom, and by his personal sins, each one makes himself still more unworthy. Only the graciousness of God, as a Father superabundantly generous with his children and ever ready to pardon the prodigal son (Luke 15:20, 22) gives us grounds for hope.

This graciousness was already visible in the promise Abraham received without having done anything to merit it. It became more and more evident in the patience with which God put up with Israel's waywardness, and in his fidelity to the covenant despite Israel's infidelities. But the supreme and definitive manifestation of grace appears in Jesus Christ:

> God so loved the world that he gave his one and only Son that whoever believes in him shall not perish but have eternal life. (John 3:16)

This grace of God, imparted through the death and resurrection of Jesus, is the grounds of Christian hope:

> Because of his great love for us, God, who is rich in mercy, made us alive with Christ even when we were dead in transgressions. . . . For it is by grace you have been saved, through faith — and this not from yourselves, it is the gift of God — not by works, so that no one can boast. (Ephesians 2:4-9)

This does not make good works irrelevant or unimportant for salvation; on the contrary, they are required (see Romans 2). Nevertheless, it is not they but the grace of God that is the grounds of our hope.

Hope is so intrinsic to the Christian spirit that to fail in hope, to despair, is not only a misfortune, it is a sin. It is a failure to trust in the God whose grace is a sufficient and sure reason for hope. At the opposite end of the spectrum, the kind of hopefulness by which a person relies on his own resources alone, as if they were sufficient to bring his life to a successful fulfillment, is the sin of presumption. Trust in God, who has promised us a kingdom that is beyond our natural reach, is an essential Christian attitude. It is difficult to maintain when life is harsh and heaven seems quite distant; but we are sustained in it by the Holy Spirit. Thus Christian hope is not just natural optimism or self-confidence but an attitude of trust in God that is a primordial form of worship.

FAITH

By its hope in God's promises, Christianity is a prolongation of the Hebrew religion. But Christianity believes that the promises have already begun to be fulfilled by the coming of Christ and the gift of the Holy Spirit. Thus faith, which was only latent in the Old Testament (the Hebrew language did not even have a proper name for it) becomes one of the major terms of the New Testament.

Faith and hope are both forms of trust. Both involve a reliance on God for something that lies beyond human reach. But whereas hope looks to a good that lies in the future and relies on the power and goodness of God to grant it, faith looks to a truth that is beyond the grasp of reason and relies on the truthfulness of God who reveals it. Faith is belief in a truth revealed by God,[1] whereas hope is confidence of being saved by God. Since revealed truth is primarily about salvation, faith spontaneously engenders hope, and the two are, in actual life, almost inseparable. When the New Testament speaks of faith in Christ, it means not only belief that Jesus is the Christ (John 20:31) but also reliance on him for salvation (Mark 5:36) — in other words, faith flowering in hope.

• *Role of faith: entrance, foundation, first stage*

We have already seen something of the structure of faith as belief in the message of a prophet, based on the inner witness given by the heavenly Father (see Chapter 5); now we must examine its role in the Christian life. It is the entrance, foundation, and first stage of this life. In order to receive the salvation which God is bringing about through Jesus Christ, one must begin by *believing* in it. For God does not save us regardless of our cooperation; he requires that we respond to him willingly. He reveals his saving plan to us, and invites us to enter into it.

> He made known to us the mystery of his will according to his good pleasure, which he proposed in Christ, to be put into effect when the times will have reached their fulfillment — to bring all things in heaven and on earth together under one head, even Christ. (Ephesians 1:9-10)

But we have to recognize this plan before we can correspond to it. It is not an inherent law of the universe which we could discover by reflection; it hinges on the free, personal act of the Creator, who has graciously willed to repair the damage done by sin, and to invite his creatures into an unpredictable, unimaginable intimacy with himself. Only through his revelation, and therefore by *believing*, can we recognize it.

• *Acceptance of God's self-revelation*

At an even deeper level, we observe that what God is doing in Jesus Christ does not consist merely in a kind of rescue operation. It is his very self that God imparts to us, and the essence of his revelation is the disclosure of himself. As human relations, when they take on the character of friendship, involve the opening up of oneself to another, so God reveals not just his plan for our salvation but himself. For this reason too, we have to begin by believing. And just as people who cannot believe in the love of others are unable to contract a genuine friendship, so here one who is unwilling to believe in the revelation of divine love closes himself to the relationship with God that is offered to us in Christ.

Our culture tends to belittle the act of faith, or belief, on the grounds that what we *do* measures our worth, not what we think. But we should not overlook the fact that to take the word of another about a matter we cannot see for ourselves is a compliment to the other and a difficult thing for ourselves. Infants of course naturally and readily believe whatever they are told; but once the ego has formed, we experience repugnance for relying on the word of someone else. Especially in the case of the basic convictions that give direction to our lives, we want to make up our own minds. Of course laziness or gullibility inclines some people to believe anything they hear; but for a mature and responsible person voluntarily to accept another's word is not easy and is a great tribute to the other.

God does not demand faith merely as a way of putting us to the test; he uses it to enlighten us about truths that could not be known in any other way. But given the fact that faith is thus necessary, it becomes a radical act of worship. It is letting God be ruler of our minds, therefore of the most intimate and personal of all our faculties. It is letting oneself be taught by God: "they will all be taught by God" (John 6:45). It is an imprint of divine wisdom on the created intellect.[2]

• *Beginning of a personal relationship with God*

Hence faith is not merely an extrinsic precondition for eternal life, it is already the beginning of that relationship with God which characterizes the children of God. Faith does not result simply from human and rational reflections; neither is it merely the expression of our deepest natural instinct. It is an act of reliance on and trust in the inner witness of the Father. Faith is not a function of our intellectual ability. It is neither the achievement of a brilliant mind, nor the crutch of one unwilling to think for himself. The things to which faith assents are beyond the reach of all minds, even the most brilliant; and the basis of faith is worthy of the assent of all, even the most intelligent. Faith is a matter of personal relationship with God. The question posed by faith is: Are you willing to trust God and to take his word on matters which you cannot know except by his word? As in human affairs there are moments in which friendship is proven by willingness to trust another, so faith is an attitude of reliance upon God that is the first and fundamental element of a personal relationship with him.

We have seen that the New Testament insists on the necessity of faith for salvation (Chapter 20). If faith were a matter of intellectual power or if it amounted merely to a personal view about the mysterious depths of the universe, for salvation to hinge upon it would be incomprehensible and intolerable. But since the crucial element in faith is the acceptance of God's inner witness, it is understandable that faith determines one's most basic posture in regard to God. "Whoever hears my word and believes him who sent me, has eternal life" (John 5:24). Hearing the word of Jesus and accepting his testimony is not just a stance taken in regard to another human being; it is a response to that innermost and primordial action of God whereby, as Truth and Light, he touches the human soul. This is also why Jesus could condemn those who did not believe in him. He is not just another strongheaded man insisting that everyone see things his way; he is one whose doctrine coincides with Truth itself: "I am the way and the truth and the life" (John 14:6). Consequently, the stand people take in regard to his teaching expresses their stand in regard to Truth itself:

> Light has come into the world, but men loved darkness instead of the light. . . .
> (John 3:19)

CHARITY

If faith is the basis of the life of children of God, love is its pinnacle. Love pervades the entire Christian edifice and gives it a characteristic stamp. "God is love" (1 John 4:16)

is the ultimate Word of God's self-revelation. Out of love, "God gave his one and only Son, that whoever believes in him shall not perish but have eternal life" (John 3:16). Jesus, "having loved his own who were in the world, loved them to the end" (John 13:1, RSV), proving the greatness of his love by laying down his life for them (John 15:13). He loved them as the Father loved him, and he urged them to abide in his love (John 15:9). His parting injunction was that they should love one another as he had loved them (John 13:34; 15:12-17); by this all men would know that they are his disciples (John 13:35). Hence St. John can write that he who loves is born of God, knows God, abides in God, and has God abiding in himself (1 John 4:7, 13), and St. Paul that "the entire law is summed up in a single command, 'Love your neighbor as yourself' " (Galatians 5:14). Jesus' instructions to love not only our neighbor but also strangers (Luke 10:30ff) and even our enemies (Luke 6:27, 35) are famous.

It is not only Christianity that strongly recommends love. The Buddhist ideal of compassion entails love for all living beings. Concern for the welfare of society is the underlying motive of Marxism. But no teaching on the way of life for man or on the ultimate meaning of the universe has ever been so centered on love as that of Jesus, and no one has ever spoken the language of love as he.

• *Distinct character of Christian love*

However, it is not merely emphasis on love that distinguishes Jesus' teaching; the love he advocates — or rather breathes into the world — has a special character. This character derives from the total structure of the Christian mystery. The primordial love is that of the Father and Son for each other; but it is not confined to themselves. Besides the fact that their love is mysteriously personified in the Holy Spirit, the divine persons look also upon their creatures with the regard of love, which led them to send the Son and the Spirit for our redemption and sanctification. Coming into our world like lightning, this divine love has evoked sparks from the stony hearts of creatures.

St. Paul and St. John, the chief interpreters of Jesus' teaching, ordinarily designated love not by the usual Greek words *eros* (sexual love) and *philia* (love of friendship) but by *agape*, a term almost unused in secular literature. In Latin, this was rendered by *caritas*, from which we get the English word *charity*. The meaning of charity has been so distorted in our culture that the sense of love has almost been squeezed out of it; nevertheless, it needs to be retained as a technical term, and is a useful reminder of the special character of Christian love.

Consequently, our *agape*, or charity, is fundamentally a response to the divine love for us. "We love because he first loved us" (1 John 4:19); "God demonstrates his own love for us in this: While we were still sinners, Christ died for us" (Romans 5:8).

Our charity therefore is first of all love for God, the response of our love to his unmerited love. "Love the Lord your God with all your heart and with all your soul and with all your mind." This precept from Deuteronomy 6:5, Jesus calls "the first and greatest commandment" (Matthew 22:37-38). But charity is not just the love of creatures for their Creator; it is specifically the love of children for their Father. It is defined by the grace given to us in Jesus Christ making us children of God. Its characteristic cry is, "Abba, Father!" inspired in us by the Spirit of the Son who has been given to us (Galatians 4:6; Romans 8:15-16). Thus Christian charity does not spring simply from human nature; it does not correspond to our natural status as creatures. It is, so to speak, a *family* love that arises from and is characterized by the supernatural relationship with God into which we are introduced by the grace of Christ.

The need to love and be loved, to be joined with another in communion, is the deepest need of the human spirit (hence also the most radical source of human anguish). The astounding good news of Christianity is that the creature has been invited into a communion of love with the Creator. The infinity of God is a boundless ocean of love, not just extended to "mankind" in a general way but embracing each individual personally. The immense goodness and lovableness of God has been made accessible to the loving response of each of us. And this communion between God and man is not merely some metaphysical relationship that can be called love only by arcane analogy or poetic exaggeration; it is more genuinely and really love than any human affection, even though it is discovered to be such only by those who surrender themselves wholeheartedly to it. The countless human hearts suffering the anguish of loneliness even in crowded cities have here the reassurance that their yearning for love need never go unfulfilled. Those whose love has been wounded by the faults, unfaithfulness, and unresponsiveness of loved ones find in God a perfect lover who makes it possible for them in turn to love those that are imperfect.

• *Loving others in God*

But "whoever loves God must also love his brother" (1 John 4:21). The second commandment is like the first, "Love your neighbor as yourself" (Matthew 22:39). Like the love of God, love of neighbor is specified by the situation created by Christian grace. It is not merely humanitarian affection based on the fellow-feeling of one human being for 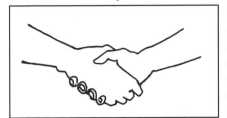 another. It is not merely the compassion that a Buddhist or an Albert Schweitzer would have us feel for all that lives. It arises from the supernatural relationships created by the grace of Christ. Being children of the same heavenly Father makes us brothers and sisters to one another. It is "in Christ" and "in God" that we love the others. These expressions which spring so naturally to the lips of the Christian but become so mysterious when you attempt to analyze them reflect the omnipresence of God and Christ who become like the atmosphere or milieu that makes Christian love possible. They also express the fact that love of God and of Christ is the primary motive of love of the brethren — not meaning thereby that we do not love others in themselves but rather that our love for them participates in our love for God. The self which we truly and really love in them is lovable as an image and likeness of God, a value which they have not from creation alone but from grace. Likewise the measure and model of our love for them is not merely our self-love but Christ's love for us. The Old Testament had already taught us to love others as ourselves;[3] but Jesus proposes as a model that incredible love that brought him into the world and drove him right to the arms of the cross: "Love each other as I have loved you" (John 15:12).

Although charity is properly love for those who share the life of the children of God as conferred by the grace of Christ, it is not confined to professed Christians. Like the love of God for us, which was given without our deserving it and before we had responded to it, our charity goes out to all, and where necessary seeks to communicate to them the grace of God which they have not yet acknowledged.

• *Infused by the Holy Spirit*

Such love cannot simply be demanded of human beings; it must first be given to them. Even the example of Jesus and the doctrine of faith do not suffice to engender a love that so far exceeds our native propensities. In fact, "God has poured out his love into our hearts by the Holy Spirit, whom he has given us" (Romans 5:5). Charity is not just the finest, noblest, most sublime of human loves; it is a participation in that eternal love with which Father and Son (to say nothing of the Holy Spirit) love each other; only the Spirit of the Father and Son can communicate it to us by a veritable infusion or outpouring.

* * *

Thus faith, hope, and charity characterize the Christian life, the life of those who have been made children of God through Jesus Christ. Faith is the substitute on earth for the light of glory we will enjoy in heaven. Charity on earth is essentially the same as the love we will experience in heaven; only now it is riddled with faults and hampered by weakness because it has to go by the dim light of faith instead of the full light of glory. By faith we live on earth, by love we are already in heaven. Hope is the bond that holds faith and love together. By hope, one caught in the darkness of the present looks forward to the light of the future. "And now these three remain: faith, hope and love. But the greatest of these is love" (1 Corinthians 13:13).

Faith, hope, and charity are meant to pervade the entire Christian life and define its spirit as one of total reliance on God by faith and hope, and of intimate union with him by charity. This is what it means to live as a child of God, as it also defines that childlikeness which Jesus called for when he said, "Unless you change and become like little children, you will never enter the kingdom of heaven" (Matthew 18:3).

23
The gift and gifts of the Spirit

The most important effect of the Holy Spirit, and that which seems to be most characteristic of the New Covenant, is *personal knowledge* of the Spirit himself, and through him, of the Father and Son. In telling his disciples about the "other Paraclete" that would be sent to take his place with them, Jesus said, "the world cannot receive him, because it neither sees him nor knows him; you know him, for he dwells with you, and will be in you" (John 14:17). It is therefore not merely by what they have been told that the disciples will know the Spirit but by an intimate, interior contact with him.

In this connection, it is striking that the Spirit was never recognized as a distinct person until the New Testament. When the Old Testament speaks of the Spirit of God coming upon particular leaders and stirring them up to carry out military exploits or to prophesy, one could well understand these statements as referring simply to the power of God acting in a special way in those called to an exceptional function.

Apostles receiving the Holy Spirit.

Only in the New Testament does he who gradually reveals himself as the Son of God (and therefore the second divine person) begin to suggest that the Spirit of God is also a distinct person. This appears especially at the Last Supper where, in the course of the most intimate revelation of his love for the apostles, Jesus also announces that he must now leave them. He reassures them, however, by promising to send in his place "another Paraclete" to be with them forever. He, "the Holy Spirit whom the Father will send in my name," will teach them all things and remind them of everything Jesus himself has said to them (John 14:16, 26). The personal character of the Spirit is already suggested by the fact that Jesus refers to him by a masculine pronoun, even though the Greek word for Spirit is neuter (John 15:26; 16:8, 13f). But it is above all the activity of the Spirit as teaching and guiding, bearing witness to Jesus (John 16:13), interceding for us (Romans 8:26f), grieving over our sins (Ephesians 4:30), giving us gifts, etc., that manifests his personal character.

• *Live contact with Father and Son*

This personal union with and intimate knowledge of the Spirit gives us also an intimate, live contact with the Father and Son. Our having God for a Father is not just a kind of legal relationship decreed by the Father and acknowledged by us. We have been given "the Spirit of sonship" (Romans 8:15), by none other than the Holy Spirit himself:

> God sent forth his Son, born of woman, born under the law, to redeem those who were under the law, so that we might receive adoption as sons. And because you are sons, God has sent the Spirit of his Son into our hearts, crying, "Abba! Father!" So through God you are no longer a slave but a son. . . . (Galatians 4:4-7, RSV)

Getting to know the Father is nothing other than entering into the sentiments of the Son and being mysteriously identified with him.

Likewise the Spirit of the Son gives us a personal intimacy with the Son. Some Christians complain that they do not have a truly personal knowledge of Jesus. Others for whom that situation has changed have confessed, "I used to know *about* Christ; now I *know* him." The latter echo the experience of St. Paul, who declared, "I consider everything a loss compared to the surpassing greatness of knowing Christ Jesus, my Lord" (Philippians 3:8). This too is the work of the Spirit through whom we are baptized into the body of Christ (1 Corinthians 12:13).

In sum, we are anointed as Christians by the same Spirit by whom Jesus was anointed as the Christ (1 John 2:21, 27; see also Luke 4:18). The transformation he brings about in us (2 Corinthians 3:18) is so profound, radical, and all-embracing that it is called a "new birth" (John 3:1-8), a "new creation" (2 Corinthians 5:17; Galatians 6:15; Colossians 3:10; Romans 6:4; Ephesians 4:23), or "regeneration"[1] (Titus 3:5). It does not, however, take place completely and instantaneously at the moment of his descent into us. The Spirit works in us gradually, like the yeast leavening a loaf, and only in the measure in which we allow him and cooperate with him. Most of us yield reluctantly to his action; we have to work to "purge out the old leaven" that we may become a new loaf (1 Corinthians 5:7).

THE GIFTS OF THE SPIRIT

Jesus speaks of the Holy Spirit as *the* gift of God (John 4:10). No other gift can be compared to this one; for the Spirit dwelling in our hearts is God himself given to us. Nevertheless, the Holy Spirit in turn bestows other gifts through which he works in us. "There are different kinds of gifts, but the same Spirit," declares St. Paul (1 Corinthians 12:4). Various lists of gifts occur in the New Testament, and their immense diversity makes it difficult to classify them. Without claiming to be exhaustive, we can note three main types: sanctifying gifts, ministry gifts, and sign gifts.

1. *Sanctifying gifts* are the traditional "seven gifts of the Holy Spirit," namely, wisdom, understanding, knowledge, counsel, fortitude, piety, and fear of the Lord. They are characterized by what may be called "amenability" to the inspirations of the Spirit. For example, in contrast with other forms of wisdom, the wisdom "given" by the Spirit is not a *possession* of those endowed with it; rather, it is the divine wisdom of the Holy Spirit conducting those who obey his inspirations. We do not know the whole plan of God, and hence are often unable to discern what is truly in accord with it. But by obedience to the

Spirit we can be led to act in accord with a plan that is hidden from us. Thus St. Paul set out on his second missionary journey intending to preach in Asia Minor. But the Holy Spirit would not allow him to do so (Acts 16:6), and Paul's obedience to the Spirit led to the evangelization of Greece. Why God intended for the Gospel thus to spread westward rather than eastward is a mystery; yet Paul cooperated "wisely" with it, by a wisdom that was not his own but belonged to the Holy Spirit who led him.

Similarly, the fortitude which is a gift of the Holy Spirit is not properly a strength of character on the part of the one who has it but the action of the Holy Spirit keeping him strong, perhaps in spite of personal weakness. This is surely how we are to understand the great courage shown after Pentecost by the apostles, who had not distinguished themselves for bravery before. Hence St. Paul gladly boasted of his weaknesses, which allowed the power of Christ — the fortitude given by the Holy Spirit — to dwell in him (2 Corinthians 12:9).

Something similar can be said about all seven of these gifts. They are not so much virtues of the human person as workings of the Holy Spirit. What they require of the recipient is above all a readiness to be led and moved by the Holy Spirit. (Incidentally, the number seven does not seem intended as a complete enumeration of this type of gift but only as a symbol for fullness or completeness.[2])

Everyone living in the state of grace has the sanctifying gifts of the Spirit. However, there is a great difference in the way people use them. The saints are led constantly by the Holy Spirit, fulfilling the word of St. Paul, "Those who are led by the Spirit of God are sons of God" (Romans 8:14). This does not of course mean that they cease to use their own minds but that in all their judgments they maintain a constant attention to the Spirit and a sensitivity to his gentle touch.

The mediocre Christian, on the other hand, is largely insensitive to the inspirations of the Spirit. He conducts his life mainly by the light of his own reason and feelings, taking into consideration perhaps even the major teachings of the faith. But he pays little heed to the living guide within himself, whose promptings would modify and powerfully sanctify the course of action taken by reason left to its own resources.

2. *Ministry gifts.* Another type of spiritual gift does not directly perfect or sanctify the recipient, but qualifies him for some work needed by the Church. These "ministry gifts"[3] in some cases give spiritual power to fulfill an office — for example, that of apostle (1 Corinthians 12:28) or that of bishop or elder (1 Timothy 4:14; 2 Timothy 1:6). These last are perpetuated today chiefly in the power of a priest to consecrate the Eucharist and absolve from sin. Other ministry gifts are not associated with a formal office; rather, they equip a person for some task. This may be very ordinary and inconspicuous; St. Paul lists service, acts of mercy, and the giving of aid as activities of the Body of Christ for which a person is qualified by special graces, or charisms (Romans 12:5-8).

3. *Sign gifts.* Some gifts have an extraordinary character that makes them, as St. Paul says, "manifestations of the Spirit" (1 Corinthians 12:7). The gift of healing has been a sign of God's action in the world since the time of the prophet Elijah. Another example is prophecy, which we have considered in Chapters 1 and 5, and which is by no means con-

fined to the Old Covenant. These more remarkable gifts or manifestations of the Spirit have tended to preempt the name charism, which originally meant simply "token of grace" or "work of grace" (*charis* is the Greek word for grace).[4] In themselves, they may be sanctifying gifts or ministry gifts; it is their extraordinary character that sets them apart as signs.

St. Paul gives a famous list of charisms in 1 Corinthians 12:8-11, which includes, besides prophecy and healing, "the word (that is, utterance) of wisdom," "the word of knowledge," miracles, discernment of spirits, various kinds of tongues, and the interpretation of tongues. Most of these are obviously ministry gifts; however, the gift of tongues, according to 1 Corinthians 14, seems to be given primarily for the good of the recipient, and only secondarily for the service of the community. It is a gift of prayer more than of preaching. Hence it is a sanctifying rather than a ministry gift.

• *New, abundant outpouring today*

Although these extraordinary charisms were apparently common in the early Church, later they became comparatively rare, confined mainly to the lives of the saints. Since the Reformation, the Catholic Church has been almost alone in recognizing that the charisms are still operative in the world. Most Protestant denominations, in rejecting the veneration of the saints, also took the stand that the charisms had been meant only for the earliest days of the Church, when extraordinary help was needed. In modern times, however, an abundant new outpouring of the charisms is occurring in nearly all the Christian denominations, in what is called the Pentecostal Movement or Charismatic Renewal. In it, the gifts of healing, prophecy, speaking in tongues, and many others are appearing in people of every rank and situation.

The Second Vatican Council expressed itself thus on charismatic gifts:

> It is not only through the sacraments and Church ministries that the same Holy Spirit sanctifies and leads the People of God as well as enriching it with virtues. Allotting his gifts "to everyone according as he will" (1 Cor 12:11), he distributes special graces among the faithful of every rank. By these gifts he makes them fit and ready to undertake the various tasks or offices advantageous for the renewal and upbuilding of the Church, according to the words of the Apostle: "To each one the manifestation of the Spirit is given for the common good" (1 Cor 12:7). These charismatic gifts, whether they be the most outstanding or the more simple and widely diffused, are to be received with thanksgiving and consolation, for they are exceedingly suitable and useful for the needs of the Church. Still, extraordinary gifts are not to be sought after rashly, nor are fruits of apostolic labor to be presumptuously expected from them. In any case, judgment as to their genuineness and proper use belongs to those who preside over the Church, and to whose special competence it belongs, not indeed to extinguish the Spirit, but to test all things and hold fast to that which is good.
>
> (See 1 Thessalonians 5:12, 19-21; Dogmatic Constitution on the Church, no. 12)

This doctrine is clearly in accord with that of Jesus and St. Paul, who spoke about the charismatic gifts as a normal factor in the Christian life, without ever suggesting that they would be limited only to the early days of the Church.[5]

GROWTH IN THE SPIRIT

Different people receive different gifts of the Spirit, and different measures of the same gift. This is due partly to the plan of God: "Each man has his own gift from God; one has this gift, another has that" (1 Corinthians 7:7). However, there are also differences coming from the person's receptivity. God gives the Spirit in proportion to our faith.[6] "According to your faith will it be done to you," Jesus sometimes said to those whom he healed (Matthew 9:29) and where he did not find faith, he normally did not heal (Mark 6:5). In the same way, the intensity of our faith is a measure of the work of the Spirit in our lives. Those who believe little receive little; by their timidity they paralyze the action of the Spirit. In those who have great faith, the Spirit works with great power.

The requirement that a person have faith in order to be filled with the Holy Spirit is not in conflict with the teaching that faith itself is a gift of the Holy Spirit (1 Corinthians 12:3; see also 12:9). Although faith is produced in us by the Spirit, apart from whom we could not believe as Christians, we consent freely to the grace he gives us.

• *"Baptism in the Spirit"*

Other factors also, such as our cooperation, greatly determine the influence of the Spirit in our lives. This explains why many Christians have so little experience of the Holy Spirit. Through faith and baptism, they have received the essential gift of the Spirit; but because their faith is slight and their cooperation stingy, the gifts of the Spirit are not very operative in them. Only in those who are attentive to his presence, obedient to his inspirations, and generous, strong, and faithful in carrying out what he asks of them, does the action of the Holy Spirit become manifest. At the beginning of our Christian life this action is normally hidden under the workings of our natural psychology. Only by a process of growth does it gradually begin to manifest its own distinctive character. Often there is a decisive step, sometimes spoken of as the "baptism in the Holy Spirit" (see Acts 1:5), in which a person yields wholeheartedly to the divine invitation, and begins to experience the inspiration of the Holy Spirit as a major factor in his life. But this more powerful action of the Spirit does not necessarily mean extraordinary charisms. These depend on the ministry or service for which the individual is destined. The principal works of the Spirit are such fruits as love, joy, and interior peace, which are always accompanied by humility, and may be hidden under a very inconspicuous exterior.

• *Conclusion: the Spirit as inspirer*

The supreme mystery of Christian grace is that the Divine Spirit has been given to be, we may say, *our* spirit, that is, the inner, vital principle of our life. He does not take the place of our natural spirit; on the contrary, he makes us more alive, free, and responsible than ever. But he becomes (in the measure in which we yield ourselves to his action) the first root, the initiator, of what we think and do. He inspires our thoughts, sentiments, words, and actions, so that while remaining fully human and fully ours, they nevertheless spring from him as their deepest source. Authentically human, they have divine value.

THE SPIRIT AND THE KINGDOM

Finally, the gift of the Spirit is the answer — or at least a major part of the answer — to the question raised earlier: When is the Kingdom of God coming? Jesus proclaimed that the Kingdom was near, and New Testament scholars have been debating for over a hundred years what he meant by that. The problem is made particularly acute by certain texts, such as Mark 9:1: "There are some standing here who will not taste death before they see the Kingdom of God come with power." This seems to mean that the Kingdom was to be expected during the lifetime of the first disciples. In fact, many of the early Christians did expect the end of the world to come in their lifetime, so that St. Paul had to write the Thessalonians a (second) letter, assuring them that the time had not yet come, whereas 2 Peter was a reply to those who had given up waiting for the Lord to come.

Some rationalist scholars affirm that Jesus himself was a visionary who, like many others in his day, mistakenly expected the cataclysmic "Day of the Lord" to come in his own lifetime, notwithstanding the fact that he declared that the date of his coming was known only to the heavenly Father (Mark 13:32; Acts 1:7). Also, St. Luke tells us that, when people supposed that the Kingdom of God was to appear immediately, Jesus told the parable about the nobleman who went to a distant country to receive kingly power, and gave his servants money to trade with in his absence (Luke 19:11-27). This would seem to imply that Jesus knew he was going to be gone for a long time (see Matthew 25:19), during which period the disciples would have work to do.

The solution to this dilemma seems to lie in the fact that the coming of the Kingdom, like the coming of the Son of Man, takes place in stages. The Kingdom was already planted on earth in the person of Jesus himself, the messianic king. It will be realized fully at the end of this world, when Christ is revealed in all his power and glory. Between these two visible comings of the Son, there is the time of the Holy Spirit, the Paraclete. He is what we may call the root principle of the Kingdom. The prophets Jeremiah and Ezekiel announced that the New Covenant would be marked by God's putting his Spirit in the hearts of the people. Isaiah 44:3 declares, "I will pour out my Spirit on your offspring, and my blessing on your descendants. They will spring up like grass in a meadow, like poplar trees by flowing streams." The prophet Joel characterized the Day of the Lord thus: "I will pour out my Spirit on all people; your sons and your daughters will prophesy" (2:28). St. Peter announced that the latter prophecy was fulfilled on the day of Pentecost (Acts 2:17). St. Paul declares that "the Kingdom of God is not a matter of eating and drinking, but of righteousness, peace and joy in the Holy Spirit" (Romans 14:17).

In other words, the Kingdom of God, while not yet fully completed, has already been established among us in power by the gift of the Holy Spirit. The gift of the Spirit is the chief reality of this Kingdom, and the root from which the rest will spring. Hence St. Paul calls him earnest money or a down payment or first installment on what is yet to come (2 Corinthians 1:22; Ephesians 1:14). Using a different metaphor, he says that what we have now is only the "first fruits" of the Spirit; that we wait for our "adoption as sons" to be completed by the "redemption of our bodies" (Romans 3:23).[7]

PART 6
The Church

The effect of Christ's redeeming activity does not consist merely in the inner renewal of individual persons. It has a social dimension, namely, the Church. However, the notion of Church turns many people off today, even some earnest believers. In fact, people who worship Christ but hate the Church are not uncommon. Their attitude is often caused by the faults of Church members, a matter that will be dealt with later. But it is also due to several misconceptions about the meaning of Church which it will be well to confront at once.

One misconception consists in identifying the Church with the clergy. *Church* then conjures up the image of a clan of severe old black-robed men, telling people what they ought to believe and how they ought to act. Even those who believe in the Church some-

times resent these authority figures. But the pastors by themselves are not the Church. They exist for the sake of the flock, and it is the whole Christian people, pastors and flock together, that constitute the Church. Without pastors, Christians would be a shapeless, directionless mass rather than an organic people.

A second misconception is to take *church* as meaning organized religion. Since organization seems to be the antithesis of spontaneity and interiority, *church* then comes across as hostile to an authentic religious spirit. Many sincerely religious people feel that they would rather worship God in their own way than follow a public ritual that does not appeal to them.

Here, as in the previous case, it must be said that organization is a fact about the Church but not its primary or characteristic feature. So far as the word itself is concerned, the English word *Church* or Scotch *Kirk* comes from the Greek *Kyriakon doma* meaning "the house of the Lord." Whether applied to the building or to the people who gather therein, it indicates faith in the Lordship of Jesus, not organization, as the defining factor. *Church* is not a general term for organized religion but refers to a unique historical phenomenon resulting from the ministry of Jesus.

• *Organization*

Church organization is needed in order for a large number of people to act in order and harmony. If they are to worship together in concert or act together as a body in any

363

other way, order is necessary; but this order and organization are only a means of implementing and protecting the essential communion in faith and love, which is what properly unites and defines the Church. A small number of people can sometimes maintain communion without any formal organization; but nine hundred million would inevitably degenerate into a vague, amorphous tradition or split into conflicting sects. (This has, in fact, happened in that part of the Christian world which rejects Peter as the principle of order.)

Organization as such does not suppress vitality and spontaneity but only when it is excessive and unintelligent. Life in this world presupposes organization. All living beings are organisms.

• *The Church as a religious society*

But even if it be admitted that organization is necessary for society, many today would challenge the assumption that religion needs to be embodied in a society. Might not an amorphous Christian tradition, which each one could interpret and express in his own way, be preferable?

We saw in Chapter 9 that religions have nearly always been social. Religious acts have predominantly been community functions in which a tribe (or sometimes a mere family or an entire race) gather together and by song, dance, processions, and ritual, worship the community's god. The idea that religion can and ought to be a purely personal and interior matter has arisen in the modern Western world chiefly as a way of escaping the conflicts originating in our religious divisions. It is a society weary of argument and bigotry that says, "Keep your religion to yourself!" But to deprive religion of common assemblies, solemn rites, and public demonstrations is to emasculate it. Human beings need a social expression of their most profound beliefs and sentiments. When you add to this the fact that God is an invisible spiritual reality difficult for us to appreciate, and more particularly the fact that Jesus has summoned us to a deep spiritual union with one another, it is readily understandable that religion as such, but especially the Christian religion, needs a communal, social expression.

The occasional emergence of solitary mystics is also a regular feature of religions. But even these individuals ordinarily spring out of the matrix of a social religion, and often originate new social movements, as in the case of the Buddha or Sankara Ramanuja. The Hebrew and Christian prophets, on the other hand, were by no means individualists; they had a mission to the community. Even the Christian hermits acknowledged and lived in a profound relationship to the Church.

On the other hand, it is evident that the Catholic Church has a degree of organization far beyond that of any other religion in the world (see Chapter 2). Its system for defining dogmas, promulgating laws, and regulating liturgy, to say nothing of the administration of the small congregations into which its members are grouped, has no close parallel anywhere. The notion that every new idea must come from Rome is of course a caricature; Catholicism has far more room for private initiative than critics recognize. But each initiative must take its place within the corporate whole. Historically, it has been a mark of the genius of Catholicism that the innovations of Francis of Assisi, Ignatius Loyola, or Vincent de Paul could be assimilated into the Church without creating a rift. To understand the reason for this aspect of Catholicism, it is not enough to appeal to the social nature of mankind; one must also look to the unique mystery of Jesus Christ, and the peculiar unity he forged among his disciples. That will be the main work of the next chapter; but before that, we must consider a third misconception, more subtle than the previous two.

• *The Church as an agency to spread the Gospel*

This views the Church as an agency for the spread of the Gospel, a kind of "Society for the Propagation of the Faith." Like the two preceding misconceptions, this touches on a real and important aspect of the Church, which is indeed missionary by its very essence. Jesus came with a message and a grace for all mankind; yet he could not, while living a natural human life, deliver his Gospel directly to everyone. It was necessary for him, like other great teachers, to form disciples and send them out as emissaries. Consequently, much of the Church's activity consists in the propagation of the Gospel to all mankind, and its transmission from generation to generation.

Nevertheless, to look simply at the missionary activity of the Church is to overlook its more fundamental reality as a community of those who *live* the Gospel. It is primarily a community, not an agency. Its success is measured chiefly not by its effectiveness in spreading a message but by the faithfulness of its members to the message. Obviously the two are connected: A Church with a vigorous inner life will tend to spread the Gospel; where the missionary spirit is lacking, the life of the Church is surely weak. Nevertheless, to see in the Church nothing but its missionary activity would be to overlook its substance.

In other words, the Church is not merely an instrument for carrying on the work of Jesus, it *is* his work. Church is what Jesus came to bring about: It is mankind liberated, uplifted, and united by and in Jesus Christ. It can be said to be the realization of the Father's plan for the consecration of the world, with this sole proviso: that the Church as we now know it is in an incomplete, imperfect condition, still waiting for its perfection. It is a pilgrim, weary, dirty, and stumbling, as it plods toward the Promised Land. It is the Bride of Christ still in the process of being purified and beautified for her Spouse.

In summary, the Church must not be identified with the clergy who govern it, nor the organization that structures it, nor the missionary dynamism incumbent upon it. The Church is the Christian people, with their limitations as well as their achievements, with their foibles, faults, and frailties as well as their noble aspirations, their beautiful liturgy, and their magnificent charitable enterprises. It is a complex, many-sided reality that includes both natural and supernatural aspects. It has all the rich color and warmth of humanity, but it is also mysteriously touched and ennobled with divinity.

24

The mystery of the Church

The Church is essentially and intrinsically mysterious: that is to say, a work of divine grace which, though acting among and through human beings, nevertheless produces in them a reality that transcends them. Scripture designates the Church by many names: *Body of Christ, Temple of the Holy Spirit, New Jerusalem, Household of God, Bride of Christ*, etc. Each of these terms casts a different light on this mysterious reality, and only by seeing it in the light of all of them together do we begin to get an inkling of its true dimensions. Here we can consider only a few of the more important terms. We will begin with the one that is most comprehensive, and was popularized by Vatican II.

PEOPLE OF GOD

The name *People of God* was first given to Israel under the Old Covenant (Chapter 15). Rooted in God's promise to Abraham, "I will make you into a great nation" (Genesis 12:2) and "I will establish my covenant as an everlasting covenant between me and you and your descendants after you for the generations to come" (Genesis 17:7), it was reiterated frequently by the prophets Jeremiah and Ezekiel in the formula "I will be their God and they will be my people" (Jeremiah 31:33; Ezekiel 11:20; etc.).

Israel can be called God's "special people" (Deuteronomy 7:6; 14:2; 16:18) first of all because God formed it by giving Abraham offspring when this was naturally impossible. Secondly, it is his people because he bound it to himself by a special covenant: The Hebrews were to serve him by keeping his law, witnessing to him, and glorifying him. On his part, God would care for them, as he demonstrated by delivering them from Egypt, leading them safely through the Red Sea, and providing them with manna in the desert and water from the rock. Moreover, he dwelt among them, as we will see shortly.

• *The Church prolongs Israel*

In the New Testament, the title *People of God* is applied to the Church (for example, 2 Corinthians 6:16-18).[1] The latter is not a new religion founded by Jesus; it is the prolongation and fulfillment of Israel. It is the very same people but renewed by the Spirit of God, and living under a new covenant, as the prophets of Israel themselves had foretold.[2] Jesus did not turn away from his fellow Jews; in fact his personal ministry was confined to them alone, proclaiming the realization of the Kingdom which they awaited. He did not come "to abolish the Law or the prophets . . . but to fulfill them" (Matthew 5:17). Accordingly, his disciples, good practicing Jews, continued to worship in the Temple and to observe the Hebrew rites. Even St. Paul, the great "missionary to the Gentiles," addressed himself first to Jews. Even after most of them rejected his preaching, compelling him to turn to the Gentiles, he still insisted firmly that the latter were aliens who had been admitted to the commonwealth of Israel through the blood of Christ (Ephesians 2:12, 13), wild olive branches that had been grafted onto the stock of Israel (Romans 11:17-24), whose faith made them children of faithful Abraham (Romans 5:11-18).[3]

Like Israel, the Church is the People of God first of all because it is primarily God's work rather than man's. In its most basic and fundamental reality, the Church is not a society formed by the followers of Jesus as a means to keep his memory and his spirit alive among them; it is God's own handiwork, his special creation.

In the first place, Jesus founded the Church. He took the initiative of calling disciples, training them, and sending them out as apostles. Although he did not draw up a formal constitution, he did give the Church its essential structures and components, by instituting the Eucharist, instructing his disciples to baptize, making the apostles pastors of the future flock, etc. Above all, by his passion and resurrection, Jesus was the source of the gift of the Holy Spirit, the vital energy that impels the Church ever forward in its mission to the world, and that keeps it living the life of the community of Christ.

It is not only at the beginning, or in its foundation, that the Church is the work of God in Jesus Christ. Throughout its history, the Church continues to be actually the work of God. Each person who enters it is called by an invitation of grace just as real as the "Come, follow me" to which the first disciples responded (Matthew 4:19; etc.). The part that each individual plays in the Church is determined ultimately by the personal grace given to him by the Spirit of Jesus.

> There are different kinds of gifts, but the same Spirit. . . . To each one the manifestation of the Spirit is given for the common good. (1 Corinthians 12:4, 7)

In particular, those who have a pastoral role in the Church are called to this task by God and qualified for it by a special charism:

> Not that we are competent to claim anything for ourselves, our competence comes from God. He has made us competent as ministers of a new covenant — not of the letter but of the Spirit. (2 Corinthians 3:5-6)

• *Human and imperfect*

Saying that the Church is the work of God does not imply that everything in it is perfect and holy. The fact that pastors are called and guided by the Holy Spirit does not mean that their decisions are always just and wise. This is the characteristic mystery of the Church, that the action of God is intermingled with the actions and the faults of human beings. Israel was a human society with the tragedy and irony, the carnality and inconsistency, of human life, even while being in full truth and in its deepest reality the People of God. The Church too has both martyrs and traitors. It flourishes in one century and declines in another; it is fervent in one region and tepid in another; it is perpetually in need of human energy and initiative to carry its work forward. The decisions made by popes, bishops, and individual Christians have a real effect on the way it develops and the shape it takes. Nevertheless, hidden under all this human activity, there is a mysterious action of God which is finally definitive of the Church and makes it in truth a people of God.

• *A people for God*

The Church is the People of God in a second sense, that it is *for God*. Israel was not called into being simply to add one more to the innumerable races in the world. Although living a fully human life like every other nation, Israel did not exist for this secular purpose but was defined by the holiness of its vocation: to be God's servant and witness in the world. At that solemn moment on Mt. Sinai when the Covenant was ratified with Moses and the people, God declared:

> If you obey me fully and keep my covenant, then out of all nations you will be my treasured possession. Although the whole earth is mine, you will be for me a kingdom of priests and a holy nation. (Exodus 19:5, 6)

Israel is here called to so holy a service of God that everyone in the nation is priestly. Worship is the chief function of a priest, and the worship of Yahweh the first reason for Israel's existence. Other peoples have worshiped other gods, each its own; Israel exists for the worship of Yahweh. When the Israelites left Egypt, it was not simply to flee. God summoned them to "hold a festival to me in the desert" (Exodus 5:1), which they did at Mt. Sinai (Exodus 24). Escape into a land of freedom came as a consequence of this first act of worship to the Lord. Thereafter, God called them his servant; and the service they had to give him was chiefly the liturgical service of worship. Later, when Israel's horizons were broadened to recognize God's salvific concern for the rest of the world, its vocation could be seen also as one of witnessing:

> "You are my witnesses," declares Yahweh, "and my servant whom I have chosen, so that you may know and believe me and understand that I am he. Before me no god was formed, nor will there be one after me. I, even I, am Yahweh, and apart from me there is no savior." (Isaiah 43:10, 11)

The First Letter of St. Peter takes up God's words to the people at Mt. Sinai, and actualizes them for the People of the New Covenant:

> You are a chosen race, a royal priesthood, a holy nation, God's own people, that you may declare the wonderful deeds of him who called you out of darkness into his marvelous light. Once you were no people but now you are God's people. . . . (2:9, 10)[4]

The Church too is a people but not on the same plane as secular nations, such as England, France, or the United States. It is not primarily a political or economic society, any more than Jesus was a rival to King Herod. It draws its members from all nations but leaves them citizens of their native lands, while making them at the same time members of a new republic which transcends all the others.

• *Functions*

The functions of this new People of God are, first, to proclaim the Gospel of Jesus to all the world; second, to impart the saving grace of Jesus, especially through the sacraments. Third, having brought people into saving contact with Christ, the Church assembles them together for worship, for the Eucharistic liturgy which is the supreme act of the Church as Church. In this perspective, Vatican II in its Constitution on the Sacred Liturgy declared:

> . . .the liturgy is the summit toward which the activity of the Church is directed; it is also the fount from which all her power flows (no. 10).
> . . .the principal manifestation of the Church consists in the full, active participation of all God's holy people in the same liturgical celebrations, especially in the same Eucharist, in one prayer, at one altar, at which the bishop presides, surrounded by his college of priests and by his ministers (no. 41).

In short, the Church is concerned with "the things of God" as these have been defined and interpreted by Jesus Christ; other peoples and nations have as their proper concern "the things of man."

• *The Church and social justice*

The Church also has a special concern for the needy and the oppressed but not in the same way that a political society does. The latter has as a normal part of its ordinary business the regulation of the exchanges that take place among its citizens, so as to ensure justice. The Church's characteristic concern, when it deals with human affairs, has generally been not so much to ensure justice as to promote charity. But more and more in our time it is being recognized that the state also has a concern with charity, in that it ought to provide, for example, welfare service for the unemployed, the handicapped, and the needy in general. Likewise it has long been recognized, and is more and more so today, that the Church has a concern with justice not only because it ought to teach the principles of justice but also because it should actively promote justice and protest against injustice. Thus there occur instances in which the activity of Church and state intersect one another, and in which it may be difficult to differentiate them.

Nevertheless, it is clear that their essential orientations are quite diverse. So far as the Church is concerned, it occupies itself with human affairs, (a) by teaching justice and charity, and thus encouraging people to do what is right and to care for one another; (b) by promoting direct works of charity, such as homes for the needy, hospitals, schools, etc. When injustice or irreligion is flagrant (for instance, racism or abortion), the Church also has the responsibility to denounce this. But it is evidently not the Church's affair directly to forge or to manage the political, economic, or social order. "My kingdom is not of this world," said Jesus (John 18:36), and early Christians were admonished, "Submit yourselves for the Lord's sake to every authority instituted among men: whether to the king, as the supreme authority, or to governors, who are sent by him to punish those who do wrong and to commend those who do right" (1 Peter 2:13f). The Church, as "People of God," does not supplant human governments.

• *The Church and the Kingdom of God*

One of the most fundamental questions about the Church is how it relates to the Kingdom of God. Loisy, who made the famous statement "Jesus proclaimed the Kingdom, and [instead] there arose the Church," meant this in a spirit of irony. To him the Church appeared as a poor substitute for the idealized Kingdom. Protestants tend to view the Church more as the herald of the Kingdom, sent to proclaim and prepare the way for it. They see the Kingdom as pure, ideal, and glorious, and contrast the poverty and sinfulness of the Church.

In the Catholic understanding, however, the Church is "the Kingdom of God present in mystery."[5] The Kingdom was inaugurated by the presence of Jesus; it has its first and chief element in the gift of the Holy Spirit; it is present and actual in the Church, and simply awaits its perfection and fulfillment in the age to come. The Church is compared to the Hebrew people on their journey through the desert; they had not yet reached the Promised Land, but they were already the People of God in spite of all their imperfections, formed and led by the hand of God.

Many of the parables of Jesus spoke of the Kingdom of God as undergoing development and being subject to trials and defects. The Kingdom is like leaven which needs time to raise the whole loaf, like a tiny mustard seed which will become a big tree, like a net cast into the sea that catches good fish and bad alike, like a field in which weeds are growing along with wheat (Matthew 13). St. Paul represents the Church as the Bride of Christ but still needing to be cleansed and beautified (Ephesians 5:25-27). The Apocalypse sees the "holy city, new Jerusalem, coming down out of heaven from God, prepared as a bride adorned for her husband" (Apocalypse 21:2); this is evidently identical with the Kingdom of God in its state of perfection. But the same book goes on to represent the Bride as praying "Come!" to her Lord (22:17): This is the Church in its present state.

Thus the Church as it is in this world, with all its "spots and wrinkles," etc. (Ephesians 5:27), is substantially identical with the promised Kingdom of God, only it does not yet have the perfection of holiness that is still to come. In this Kingdom, God reigns through his Spirit who has been poured into the hearts of all believers, inclining them (even though imperfectly) to walk in his ways. He reigns in all those who, led by the Spirit, seek his will in the affairs of this earth, even though at times they falter. In short, the Kingdom of God now consists in his secret reign in all who submit to him by faith; it will be transformed at the Parousia into the manifest and glorious Kingdom in which there will no longer be need of sacraments and offices; it will no longer be subject to the depredations of its enemies or the weaknesses of its citizens, but God will be "all in all" (1 Corinthians 15:2-8).

TEMPLE OF THE HOLY SPIRIT

A temple is a dwelling place for God. God's presence among his people under the Old Covenant was originally manifested by the cloud of glory which enveloped the "Tent of Meeting" in the desert (Exodus 40:34-38), and later the Temple of Solomon (1 Kings 8:10). Thus the Temple came to be regarded as the place of God's special dwelling, even though all the earth was his. The religious life of the Old Covenant was focused on the

Temple, where alone sacrifice could rightly be offered. (The *synagogues*, which developed after the destruction of the Temple, were simply assembly halls for instruction and prayer; they were not temples, and sacrifice was not offered in them.)

In the New Testament, the body of Jesus is the New Temple. The Holy Spirit descended on him in the form of a dove and remained on him (John 1:32). When Jesus told the Jews, "Destroy this temple, and in three days I will raise it up again," the evangelist explains that "he spoke of the temple of his body" (John 2:12-21).

When St. Paul began to identify the Church with the Body of Christ, he likewise represented it as the Temple of the Holy Spirit.

> We are the temple of the living God. As God has said, "I will live with them and walk among them, and I will be their God, and they will be my people." (2 Corinthians 6:16)

* * *

> Don't you know that you yourselves are God's temple and that God's Spirit lives in you? If any one destroys God's temple, God will destroy him; for God's temple is sacred, and you are that temple. (1 Corinthians 3:16-17)

> [In the latter text, the word *you* is clearly plural in Greek: *humeis*. Paul is therefore speaking of the community, not of the individual, as the temple. See also Ephesians 2:19-22 and 1 Peter 2:5 as well as the somewhat obscure text of 1 Corinthians 6:19f.]

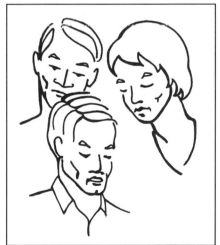

Chapter 23 examined the indwelling of the Holy Spirit in the individual Christian. Here we are dealing with something different: his presence in the Christian community as such. The one does not deny the other, but neither is reducible to the other.

This presence of the Spirit in the Christian community is the same as that of which Jesus spoke when he said:

> Where two or three are gathered in my name, there am I in the midst of them. (Matthew 18:20, RSV)

It is by his Spirit that Jesus is present among us; and what emerges from these texts is that the union of believers with one another is the locus of a special presence of his. It is in and among his people as such that God makes his dwelling place in the world.

• *Christian assemblies*

This helps to explain why the Church insists that its members gather together periodically, especially for the Sunday Eucharist. They are not just "going to Mass," they are gathering to express and realize their communion with one another. Besides being a sacrifice and the Bread of Life, the Eucharist also has the value of assembling believers together to benefit from a presence of the Holy Spirit that is not to be had otherwise. In addition to his "Real Presence" in the Eucharist, Jesus is present in the assembly as such.

This does not detract from the value of private individual prayer. (Did not Jesus himself say, "When you pray, go into your room, close the door and pray to your Father, who is unseen" [Matthew 6:6]?) But it affirms that, besides our individual relatedness to God, the communion of believers with one another is a sacred locale of communion with God. The New Testament word for Church, *ekklesia*, means assembly; it was used previously of all those assemblies in which Moses or Joshua and other leaders gathered the Hebrew people together to hear the Word of God, offer him worship, and make a covenant with him. And Vatican II's Constitution on the Sacred Liturgy (no. 41, cited above), declares that the Church is most truly and really itself, when the people are actually assembled around their bishop. Then the Holy Spirit is present among them, and they are indeed his Temple.

• *The Spirit makes the Church holy*

The presence of the Spirit makes the Church holy, no matter how sinful its individual members may be. Of course the Spirit is also at work sanctifying individuals; but they are more or less receptive to his influence, and always remain in some degree sinners. The Church as such has a holiness transcending that of its members.

Our sins do not reside properly in the Church, for the Church is not simply an empirical collection of human beings who profess the name of Christian. The Church is a mystical reality, formed in and among men by the Spirit of Jesus, with a holiness that comes from him. The sinfulness of its members lies outside the boundaries of the Church (Journet). Sin is that which has not been sanctified by the Spirit and which, by the same token, has not been integrated into the Church. This is not said to minimize the reality of sin or the responsibility for it; rather, it is to underline the fact that the Church consists properly of that which Jesus has made of us, fashioning a Temple for his Spirit out of human stones, and sanctifying this Temple by the presence of the Spirit.

The Spirit also keeps the Church in the Truth:

> When he, the Spirit of truth, comes, he will guide you into all truth. (John 16:13)
> When the Paraclete comes, whom I will send to you from the Father, the Spirit of truth who goes out from the Father, he will testify about me; but you also must testify, for you have been with me from the beginning. (John 15:26f, RSV)

This action of the Spirit coincides with the inner witness of the Father, which we considered in Chapter 5. We have already seen something of the Spirit's teaching and enlightening action in individuals (Chapter 23); here what needs to be noted is that he maintains the truth in the Church as a whole.

Individuals are not always obedient to the inspirations of the Spirit or receptive to his teachings; even though they have the Spirit, they can misinterpret the sense of the Gospel. But the Spirit does not allow the Truth to perish in the Church as a whole. This means not only that there will always be some members of the Church who are faithful but that, when the Church as a whole is united in its belief, the Spirit will not allow it to err. This is one of the most important points on which the Catholic understanding of the Church differs from that of all Protestant denominations. The conditions and implications of this "infallibility" of the Church will be discussed in greater detail in the following chapter.

The light which the Spirit gives to individuals, and that which he bestows on the Church as a whole, can be related in two ways. First, his action on individuals is like a pressure, urging them all in the same direction. Because of their personal waywardness, they will actually move in many different ways, like wavelets on a river; but their variations will offset one another, while the whole mass of the Church moves in the direction given by the Spirit.

Secondly, the Holy Spirit does not enlighten individuals in such a way as to make them independent of the teaching of the hierarchy. If that were the case, it would make no sense for Jesus to have sent out his apostles with the command to "make disciples of all nations, . . . teaching them to obey everything I have commanded you" (Matthew 28:19f). The work of the Spirit is to make individuals receptive to the message of the apostles, giving his interior confirmation to the word spoken externally, and helping the hearer to understand it in the right sense. Jesus sent the apostles as external, human teachers, and the Paraclete as the interior, divine enlightener.

The Spirit makes the Church a communion. Other societies are unified by common effort toward a common goal, but the Church is united by the faith, hope, and love given by the Spirit, and ultimately by the common possession of that one same Spirit. The common "spirit" which animates the members of a human community is a very precious unity of thought and sentiment. A common enthusiasm can fuse human hearts into a profound, mysterious communion not adequately accounted for if we reduce it simply to agreement of ideas or mutual affection. But whatever is to be said about this natural human communion, in the Church there is sharing of a single, personal reality: the Spirit of the living God, who is communicated to all alike, and makes the members of the Church one as no human society can ever unite them.

• *The Church cannot lose the Spirit*

The presence of the Holy Spirit can never be lost by the Church. He is "to be with you forever," Jesus said (John 14:16); and much earlier, Isaiah had given this assurance in the name of Yahweh:

> My spirit which rests on you and my words which I have put into your mouth
> shall never fail you from generation to generation of your descendants from now on-
> ward for ever. (59:21, RSV)

Any individual can lose the Holy Spirit by sinning against him, but the Church cannot because the Church is in the power of the Spirit. It is the Spirit who holds the Church together, who makes it Church. If we think of the Church as the Bride of Christ, the Holy Spirit is its dowry. Jesus, who has taken the Church for his Bride, does not divorce her; he does not withdraw his Spirit from her. Accordingly, the individual Christian turns to the Church lovingly and faithfully, as the locale where he can be surest of having contact with the Spirit of Jesus. The notion that the spirit of a founder is recovered only by individuals who, in a sense, isolate themselves from the community, is an unchristian notion. It may hold good for the typical secular community but not for the Church, which is not the product of the human persons who compose it but the work of Jesus and his Spirit. The general run of ordinary Christians can, indeed, drift away from their Master, so that the authentic Christian, the saint, often finds himself in isolation. But never from the Church as such; the saints have always been people who loved the Church and adhered to it, even when this meant suffering, because they recognized that it was in and through the Church that the Spirit of Jesus was to be had.

BODY OF CHRIST

Whereas *People of God* designates the Church in reference to the first person of the Blessed Trinity, and *Temple of the Holy Spirit* in reference to the third person, *Body of Christ* relates it to the second person, who took upon himself a human body in order to gather the Church around himself. The Church is like a body, of which Jesus Christ is the head:

> The body is a unit, though it is made up of many parts; and though all its parts are many, they form one body. So it is with Christ. (1 Corinthians 12:12)

When he wrote the above lines, and went on to compare the diverse functions in the Church to the hand, the foot, the eye, the ear, etc. of the human body, St. Paul was using a metaphor already familiar in the Roman and Hellenistic world. Plato had compared the citizens of a republic to the members of a human body.[6] Since then, the idea that a human society is like a body, with the ruler being the head, has become so ingrained in our thought and language that we are no longer aware of the metaphor that underlies such expressions as "the body politic," "the arm of the law," or "the head of state," to say nothing of less obvious terms such as captain (from *caput*, head), corporation (from *corpus*, body), etc.

• *The Holy Spirit its soul*

When applied to the Church this metaphor has a realism and a depth far beyond what it has for human society. Because of the Holy Spirit, the Church is a living body in a way the state can never be. The members of the Church are joined in one common life by the Holy Spirit who is given to all, who vivifies them all, and who pours forth in all the love which puts them in communion with one another. In short, he can be regarded as the soul which animates this body. The Church is in truth a single living organism. Hence the consequence drawn by St. Paul, "If one part suffers, every part suffers with it; if one part is honored, every part rejoices with it" (1 Corinthians 12:26), has far more truth in the case of the Church than in the case of secular society.

• *Jesus, head of the Church*

Likewise the Church has a head in a way that secular society has not. In the latter, the head is one who has (a very limited) authority to give a certain direction to the society, and to make decisions binding on it. In constitutional societies, it is common for the executive, legislative, and judicial functions to be separated, in order to safeguard against abuse by balancing the various powers against one another. But in the Church, all these powers are vested in Jesus, who is at once king, legislator, and judge: "All authority in heaven and on earth has been given to me," he declared (Matthew 28:18). Furthermore, as supreme prophet, he is the source of all the teaching by which the Church is directed, and as High Priest, he is its spokesman and mediator in offering worship to the Father. Now that he has been taken out of our midst, Jesus exercises his headship through representatives who direct the Church in his name. But it is not as though his activity had ceased, and has now been replaced by theirs. By his Spirit, he is the ever actual source of the spiritual energy by which the Church lives and acts, both in its official functions and in the personal Christian activity of each member.

• *Charisms in the Body of Christ*

Hence the collaboration of the various organs and members of the Church is a charismatic mystery that has no equivalent in secular society. St. Paul introduces his famous depiction of the Body of Christ by declaring:

> There are varieties of charisms, but the same Spirit; and there are varieties of service, but the same Lord; and there are varieties of working, but it is the same God who inspires them all in every one. To each is given the manifestation of the Spirit for the common good. (1 Corinthians 12:4-7, RSV)

Paul goes on to give the list of charismatic workings of the Spirit which we reexamined in Chapter 23. All these charisms and functions are meant to collaborate in the same purpose: the building up of the Body of Christ.

> His gifts were that some should be apostles, some prophets, some evangelists, some pastors and teachers, for the equipment of the saints, for the work of ministry, for building up the body of Christ, until we all attain to the unity of the faith and of the knowledge of the Son of God, to mature manhood, to the measure of the stature of the fullness of Christ; . . . we are to grow up in every way into him who is the head, into Christ, from whom the whole body, joined and knit together by every joint with which it is supplied, when each part is working properly, makes bodily growth and upbuilds itself in love. (Ephesians 4:11-16, RSV)

The magnificent metaphor of the Church as the Body of Christ seems to embrace and conceal another level of meaning that gives it still greater depth. When St. Paul says, "You are the body of Christ" (1 Corinthians 12:27), besides comparing the Church to a human body in which Christ is like the head, he is also affirming that identification of believers with Jesus which, as we have already seen (Chapter 19), is the root principle of the Redemption. We die and rise with Christ; we are ransomed by his death because we have been made one with him, with his very body. We are mystically but really identified with that body which was born of the Virgin Mary, crucified by the Roman soldiers, and raised by the Father. We *are* that body, and therefore we live by its life. It is in order to fulfill this identification that we receive the Body of Jesus sacramentally in the Eucharist, and are nourished by it.

> Because there is one loaf, we who are many, are one body, for we all partake of the one loaf. (1 Corinthians 10:17)

• *"Mystical" body*

In order to distinguish between the Church as Body of Christ, and the individual human body in which Jesus of Nazareth lived and died, the practice arose in the late Middle Ages of calling the Church the *Mystical* Body of Christ. *Mystical* here does not mean imaginary but a mysterious, supernatural reality of the order of grace. A secular historian can trace the history of the Church as a society, but only the vision of faith can recognize in it the mystical reality of the Body of Christ. Using this language, we distinguish two senses in which the Church is called the Body of Christ: The first is to say that the Church is *like a body* of which Jesus is the head; here we are speaking of the Church as the Mystical Body. The second is to say that the Church *is identified with* the individual body of Jesus of Nazareth; here we are not calling the Church a "mystical" body but are relating it to the real body of our Lord.

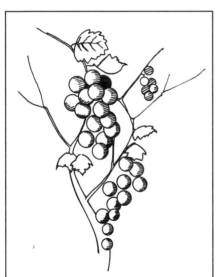

When Jesus says, "As the branch cannot bear fruit unless it abides in the vine, neither can you unless you abide in me. I am the vine, you are the branches" (John 15:4-5, RSV), he is using a metaphor very similar to that of head and body. *Vine* expresses above all the vital union between Jesus and his disciples, and the fact that he is the source of life and energy for them. *Body*, however, brings out better the variety of charisms that collaborate in the Church, and the ruling, governing role of Jesus.

Finally, the Church is also called the Bride of Christ to express the fact that its union with Jesus is one of love. The Covenant is not just juridical but a love-relationship. St. Paul, in speaking of the Church as Bride of Christ, links it inextricably with the image of the body:

> For the husband is the head of the wife as Christ is the head of the church, his body, of which he is the Savior. . . . In this same way, husbands ought to love their wives as their own bodies. He who loves his wife loves himself. After all, no one ever

hated his own body, but he feeds and cares for it, just as Christ does the Church — for we are members of his body. (Ephesians 5:23-30)

* * *

From what we have seen, it should be evident that there is an intrinsic contradiction in the attitude of one who claims to love Christ while despising the Church. If the Church is the Bride of Christ, we must love the Church as Christ loves her, and seek to identify ourselves with the Church in order to participate in the spousal love of Christ. If the Church is the People of God, the Body of Christ, and the Temple of the Holy Spirit, we cannot turn away from the Church without turning away from the Father, Son, and Holy Spirit. To the disciples he was sending forth to preach, Jesus declared explicitly, "He who listens to you listens to me; he who rejects you rejects me" (Luke 10:16).

When we look at the Church as it is actualized in our own parish or when we contemplate its past history, it is sometimes difficult to recognize the sacred character which faith attributes to it. But the defects we see do not give the lie to the doctrines of faith, any more than faith obliges us to close our eyes to the real disorders that are visible. Rather, we must realize that the work of Christ is one that is being brought to perfection in the course of time. It still awaits a drastic purification before its culmination in the Kingdom. On that day we will see the Church in all its beauty, as John saw it in his prophetic vision:

I saw the Holy City, the new Jerusalem, coming down out of heaven from God, prepared as a bride beautifully dressed for her husband. (Apocalypse 21:2; see also 21:10ff)

The intrinsic beauty of the Church is at present hidden under many blemishes. It is nevertheless a reality that can be perceived (not just believed!) by anyone who looks upon the Church with faith; and without faith, it is impossible to know the Church in its truth.

Also, we must take care not to exaggerate the blemishes. When you look objectively at the whole picture of the Church, the enormous number of people it has educated in the faith, the generosity of its missionaries carrying the Gospel abroad at the risk of their own lives, the faithfulness of pastors devoted to the daily ministry of their congregation, the intense spiritual life of the great religious orders, the heroism of the martyrs, the profound theology and beautiful art fostered by the Church, the innumerable schools, hospitals, and other works of mercy engendered by it — what other human organization can match its fruitfulness? The sins and the scandals that have occasionally embarrassed the Church are trivial compared to those of secular society. Those who are spoken of as "bad popes" were few in number compared to the good ones, and their sins peccadilloes compared to what we find in the histories of kings and presidents. Even when judged on purely secular terms, the Church stands out as by far the noblest society human history has ever seen.

Its blemishes distress us deeply because of the holiness to which the Church is called. Faults which we take for granted in secular society scandalize us in the Church. But then we must remember that it is out of mercy that Jesus puts up with human shortcomings, and leads us all gradually to the perfection he plans to achieve in us.

25
The identity of the Church

Once we have recognized the mysterious abiding presence of Jesus and his Spirit in the community of the faithful, the problem arises: How does this relate to the institutional aspects of the Church — so mundane, imperfect, and disappointing? Of course we must

take care not to exaggerate this problem (as many do) by disregarding the Church's magnificent historic achievements, such as nurturing great saints, diffusing a basic religious faith throughout the Catholic people, and arousing in the Western consciousness a sense of the dignity of the human person that many of the other great cultures of the world seem to lack. Along with that consciousness go all the hospitals, schools, asylums, and other works of charity that spring from it or support it. Much more could be added about the fruits of Christianity in various domains of culture — music, sculpture, painting, philosophy, and above all, theology.

But when due recognition is given to all this, the fact remains that in their day-to-day encounters with the Church — for example, in the parishes — people are often impressed more with the human ordinariness of the Church than with its divine holiness.

At the same time, innumerable churches and religious groups claim to be the authentic representatives of the Christian tradition. Hence the problem, how to correlate the New Testament's "mystical" vision of the Church as Body and Spouse of Christ, Temple of the Holy Spirit, with this somewhat disappointing and confusing human realization.

One way is to say that the "institutional" Church encountered in the parishes, dioceses, etc., is not to be identified with the "mystical" Church of the New Testament. The latter, the "true Church," is an invisible work of the Holy Spirit working secretly in the hearts of those who are truly faithful. The visible, institutional Church, on the other hand, is only the product of man's fumbling efforts to carry out the commission of Christ. In this view, the various denominations appear more or less successful, but none of them has any exclusive or permanent claim to be *"the Church,"* and each of them need to be complemented by the others to achieve a kind of approximation of the true, invisible Church. A kindred idea envisions the true Church as an eschatological goal that will not be realized until the end of time, while the present, empirical churches only aim at it without ever being able to attain it.

The attractiveness of these views lies in the fact that they allow us to retain the New Testament's mystical doctrine on the Body of Christ without obliging us to predicate it of any of those imperfect human congregations which simply carry on "Church services." Scripture, however, nowhere justifies such a distinction.

• *The Church in the New Testament*

First of all, throughout the New Testament, the Church and the Body of Christ are one and the same reality. "The church, which is his [that is, Christ's] body," we read in the Letter to the Ephesians (1:22-23; see also Colossians 1:18), and "his body, which is, the Church" in Colossians 1:24. The Body of Christ is not some heavenly ideal to which the Church on earth stands in relationship; the phrase "Body of Christ" affirms a mysterious identity of this earthly Church of ours with the person of Jesus Christ.

Secondly, *Church* in the new Testament always designates a definite congregation of real human beings. Simon Peter is pointed out as the Rock on which the Church is to be built (Matthew 16:18). When your brother has something against you that cannot be resolved privately, "tell the church," Jesus says, adding, "If he refuses to listen even to the church, treat him as you would a pagan or a tax collector" (Matthew 18:17). Such a counsel has meaning only in relationship to a definite, identifiable community. Elsewhere in the New Testament we see that the Church consists of the actual Christian believers who meet together to celebrate the Eucharist (sometimes too boisterously), who have families and arguments, who are tempted to divide into factions, who need to be encouraged, moderated, and directed. St. Paul can write letters to them; the heads of their pastors can be named: Timothy, Titus, Stephanus, Diotrephes, etc. The fact that the perfect holiness of the Bride of Christ has not yet been fully realized but is still in process (Ephesians 5:26-27) does not entitle us to refer what is said of the Church to some ideal or not yet existent entity. "*You* are the Body of Christ, and each one of you is part of it," St. Paul wrote to the very real and rambunctious community of Christians in Corinth (1 Corinthians 12:27). In sum, Vatican II says:

> . . .the society structured with hierarchical organs and the mystical body of Christ, the visible society and the spiritual community, the earthly Church and the Church endowed with heavenly riches, are not to be thought of as two realities. On the contrary, they form one complex reality which comes together from a human and a divine element. For this reason the Church is compared, not without significance, to the mystery of the incarnate Word. As the assumed nature, inseparably united to him, serves the divine Word as a living organ of salvation, so, in a somewhat similar way, does the social structure of the Church serve the Spirit of Christ who vivifies it, in the building up of the body (cf. Eph. 4:15).
>
> (Dogmatic Constitution on the Church, no. 8).

380

THE ROMAN CATHOLIC CHURCH AS THE CHURCH OF CHRIST

If the Church of Christ is to be sought in a particular, existing society, determining which it is becomes something of a problem, given the fact that some twenty thousand different denominations claim to be faithful heirs of Jesus. To make a systematic study of them all before adhering to any one would be practically impossible.

Most people bypass this problem by a practical, subjective approach. They look for that congregation in which the Christian spirit seems most alive and most accessible to them. They are not greatly concerned about the pedigree or official status of any institution. They may even be inclined to expect that fresh, new congregations will be more authentically Christian than the older establishments, given the tendency of all institutions to lose or degrade the spirit of their founder.

Such an attitude, however, implicitly views "churches" as congregations created by their members. It disregards the mysterious but firm New Testament teaching that *the Church* is the work of Jesus and his Spirit. Hence determining which is the "true" Church is not just a juridical issue; it is a matter of discovering where, in this desert of a world alienated from God, is the oasis flowing with the authentic "waters of eternal life." It may well be true that this can be discovered better by personal experience than by historical verification. Nevertheless, since "experience" is often very subjective and misleading, there is need also for some objective criteria.

The Catholic view is expressed thus by the Second Vatican Council:

> . . .the sole Church of Christ . . . constituted and organized as a society in the present world, subsists in the Catholic Church, which is governed by the successor of Peter and by the bishops in communion with him.
> (Dogmatic Constitution on the Church, no. 8)

The term *subsists in* was chosen deliberately, after much debate, in order to leave room for the recognition that many elements of genuine Christianity are to be found in other Christian denominations. The status of these non-Catholics will be examined in the following section; here we are concerned with the evidence that the Church Jesus founded subsists today in what is called the Roman Catholic Church. (Of course we can do nothing more than point out the main lines; a detailed examination of the evidence would fill volumes.)

There is first the basic fact that the Roman Catholic Church comprises the greater part of the Christian world. As we saw in Chapter 2, the other Christian communities are like small fragments broken off of this, the main block, or like little satellites orbiting around this sun. That already sets up a presumption that here is where the Church of Christ is to be looked for.

Secondly, the Church existing today is in historical continuity with the primitive Church. This can be seen not only in the succession of popes but also in the whole network of bishops who have been ordained by bishops who preceded them, back to those first ordained by the apostles themselves. Likewise there has been an unbroken continuity in the doctrine and observances of the Catholic people, who have passed them down through the centuries.

• *Protestant denominations*

The Protestant denominations originated chiefly in the sixteenth century and in subsequent subdivisions. It was not the intention of the Reformers to found new churches but simply to reform the existing Church. But is it not a historical fact that new churches or ecclesial bodies have resulted from their work? They can hardly claim continuity with what preceded them, for they came into being by a rupture with the Church of that day. They insist of course that the Church had become corrupt, and that they were simply returning to what Jesus intended. This claim needs to be examined seriously. No one doubts that there were many disorders in the Church of the sixteenth century (as also in that of the twentieth, and presumably every century). But it must also be acknowledged that the sixteenth-century Church was fruitful in great saints (among them Teresa of Ávila and John of the Cross) and new religious orders (notably the Jesuits, Capuchins, and Ursulines). In any case, the rupture of the sixteenth century was such that none of the Protestant denominations can make a plausible claim to have remained in unbroken continuity with the Church of the preceding centuries. And since many Protestants today seem to have abandoned Luther's thesis (namely, that justification comes about by faith alone, and that judgment will not depend on our works) they cannot even claim continuity with the Reformers of the sixteenth century. Finally, the innumerable divisions that have occurred in Protestantism since its separation from the Catholic Church suggest that the vital principle from which the Church derives its unity was lost through this separation.

Moreover, if the Church of the sixteenth century was so evil that its leadership had to be repudiated and a new beginning made, Christ would seem to have failed in his promises that he would remain with his Church forever (Matthew 28:20), and that the powers of hell would not prevail over it (Matthew 16:18).

• *The Orthodox*

The Orthodox churches, on the other hand, do have a continuous existence from the very beginning, and are acknowledged by the Catholic Church itself as genuine Christian churches. In their case, the principal issue is their refusal to accept the authority of the Bishop of Rome. We will examine this point in the following chapter; here it is to be noted that this authority had been acknowledged by the Orthodox in earlier centuries. It is also noteworthy that, since separating from Rome, the various Orthodox churches have never been able to unite with one another in an organic way. This suggests that they too have lost the principle of unity which previously they had had.

• *Faithfulness in doctrine*

The most important criterion for the authenticity of the Church is fidelity to the teaching of Jesus. This can hardly be dealt with globally; but it is, in a sense, what we have been doing throughout this book. Here we may add that Church doctrine has been in a constant state of lively evolution throughout its history. The rough, initial statements of the New Testament have had to be interpreted, their implications drawn out, and new applications made (see Chapter 2). But throughout all this process, the Church has never been obliged to retract any dogma to which it had committed itself. It has indeed, in response to new situations, adapted its customs, altered its procedures, and even revised the language in which its doctrines are expressed; but never has it had to renounce a principle formally adopted. When one recalls how often governments and other human organizations reverse themselves, even without having to contend with the multiplicity of cultures and extensive history of the Church, this constancy in doctrine is itself a remarkable feat.[1]

• *Fruitfulness in holiness*

A fourth criterion of the authenticity of the Church is its fruitfulness in producing saints. Good and holy people, even great heroes, are no doubt to be found in other religious traditions. But none of these can show anything comparable to the immense group of people canonized by the Church: martyrs and mystics; kings and queens faithful to justice and generous in charity amid their power and riches; humble peasants lifted out of obscurity by nothing other than their devoted prayer and service; stigmatics whose bodies bore the visible replica of Christ's passion; martyrs of love who reproduced the Passion invisibly in their hearts; courageous missionaries who left all things to spread the Gospel; quiet contemplatives whose life was poured out, like Mary's precious perfume, in a pure act of worship; miracle workers, charismatics, and agents of spectacular accomplishments, such as Catherine of Siena or Joan of Arc; but also ordinary faithful who simply did their secular tasks extraordinarily well, such as the lawyer Thomas More or the doctor Giuseppe Moscati (who died in 1927). The thousands who have been canonized by the Church have all been subjected to an intense scrutiny to ensure that they were not just spectacular in their accomplishments but were authentic in living the Christian virtues heroically.

There have also been sinners in the Church — even among the clergy, and even among the popes. These do not negate the presence of the Spirit in the Church, which has as its mission to gather sinners into its bosom in order to save them. If some, betraying the Church's own injunctions, revert to sinful ways, they do not nullify the fruits of grace in others; they stand simply as a reminder that the human will remains free, and a sign that the Church has been about its business of seeking to reform sinners — a work in which success is never complete.

• *Bad popes*

Since "bad popes" are brought up so often as evidence against the Church, it should be noted that, out of the two hundred sixty-six popes in history, only a small handful could be called bad. All of these came from an unfortunate period in which the pope was head of an important state and was being chosen in view of his capacity for administering secular affairs rather than for his suitability as a shepherd. The "wickedness" of these popes was not remarkable in comparison with that of secular rulers: A few had mistresses, some were addicted to luxury and ostentation, several behaved more like military leaders than religious pastors. And when the regrettable history of these few is weighed against the eighty recognized as saints and the much greater number of those who, like Benedict XV or Pius XI, without being "canonizable," were good and faithful shepherds, the popes as a group make a weighty witness to the action of the Holy Spirit in the Church.

In any case, it is not chiefly by historical investigation that anyone is likely to be persuaded of the authenticity of the Church but by direct personal experience of the Church's sanctifying power. It has already been pointed out (Chapter 5) that the Church is a convincing sign of its own authenticity when one discovers that, in following the Church, he is rectified in his human life and drawn closer to God, whereas neglect of the Church alienates him.

NON-CATHOLIC CHRISTIAN COMMUNITIES

The Second Vatican Council was a watershed in the attitude of the Catholic Church toward other religious denominations. The Church there adopted an attitude of friendly openness and positive appreciation which had not previously been the case.[2] However, the meaning of the Church's new posture has frequently been distorted and misinterpreted. Here we will not take up the subject of non-Christian religions but solely that of the "separated brethren," that is, those Christians who do not belong to the Roman Catholic communion.

• *Schismatics and heretics*

When the Orthodox were separated from the Roman Catholic Church in the twelfth century, they were classified by the Church as schismatics, and the Protestants in the sixteenth century as heretics. Schism and heresy are by no means the same thing. Schism denotes a split, a rupture of unity, in the community, but does not imply any disagreement about doctrine. And in fact, the Orthodox have on the whole maintained the traditional Christian doctrines, as their name itself is intended to affirm. Heresy, on the other hand, involves rejecting or changing the doctrines of the faith.

Both schism and heresy, when embraced knowingly and deliberately, are regarded by the Church as grievous sins. Schism offends against charity because it ruptures the unity of the Church; heresy is against faith because it alters the teaching of Christ. Both involve sin, not just legitimate differences of opinion, because they violate the order established by God himself in the Church.

In denouncing certain persons as schismatics or heretics, the Church does not claim to make a definitive judgment about their guilt in the eyes of God but simply to define their objective situation. In other words, whether Photius and Martin Luther were personally guilty of the sins of schism and heresy, the Church does not say but simply declares that their stance conflicts with the authentic position of the Church. Nevertheless, it would appear that Church leaders and theologians at the time of these two great ruptures commonly supposed that the men responsible for them were fully cognizant of what they were doing, and regarded them in effect as guilty of the *sins* of schism and heresy.

• *Vatican II*

Vatican II declares that, whatever be the guilt or responsibility of the original leaders, those people today who have grown up in the Orthodox and Protestant traditions ought not on that account to be regarded as guilty of schism or heresy. If they are in good faith, which is to be presumed, even though their objective situation is one of schism or heresy, they are not to blame for it.

This was not a radically new position, even though it had never before been declared by the official magisterium. Theologians and practicing Catholics everywhere, especially in those countries with a large Protestant or Orthodox population, had long come to realize that these people are generally in good faith, and should be treated with friendship and respect. Moreover, it was commonly recognized that their good faith was in fact supernatural or divine faith: an acceptance of the light of the Holy Spirit, through which they received the grace of God, by which they were linked invisibly with the Church, and on account of which they would be saved. This interpretation of the matter was even officially affirmed by the Holy Office, in a famous letter to Archbishop Cushing in 1949 about the case of Father Feeney.[3]

But in this view, no account was taken of the Protestant religious bodies as such. The individual members were regarded as linked with the Church and on the way to salvation because of their personal faith; but their communions were not recognized as churches, nor as contributing to the salvation of their members. Moreover, their ministries were regarded as invalid, their Communion services as nonsacramental, and even their baptisms were looked upon with such suspicion that, when a Protestant became a Catholic, he was usually baptized conditionally. Catholics were forbidden to take part in Protestant religious services or to marry Protestants (although permission to do so was ordinarily granted if requested). Likewise Protestants were not allowed to receive Communion in the Catholic Church (this was not a point that had to be insisted on, however, as there was so little inclination on the part of Protestants to do so).

The case of the Orthodox was different. The validity of their sacraments has always been acknowledged, including the power of their bishops to ordain priests and bishops. Their churches were recognized as true Christian churches, even though separated from the universal Church. Intercommunion, however, was forbidden because of the schism.

• *Originality of Vatican II*

Vatican II declared that non-Catholic Christians are genuine Christians, and are to be acknowledged as our brothers and sisters (Decree on Ecumenism, no. 3). The separation

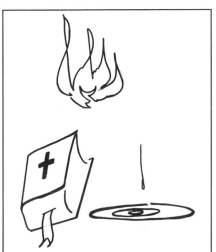

that exists between them and us was acknowledged but regretted. However, the originality of the Council does not lie in this friendly expression of esteem for individuals of other denominations; this merely gave official acceptance to what was already the common attitude of theologians and a large part of the faithful. The originality of Vatican II lies in its evaluation of the non-Catholic denominations as such. It attributed to them a worth such as had not been maintained by any but a few pioneering theologians. However, it is precisely on this point that the doctrine of Vatican II has been most distorted.

In speaking of non-Catholic "churches and ecclesial communities," the Decree on Ecumenism declared that they possess many genuine elements of the Church: Scripture, the life of grace, interior gifts of the Spirit such as faith, hope, and charity, and finally liturgical actions which contribute to the life of grace, notably the sacrament of baptism. From this follows the conclusion that these Christian denominations, although separated from the Catholic Church, are used by the Spirit of Christ "as means of salvation" for their members. In other words, a Lutheran or Presbyterian is not being saved merely by his good faith in spite of belonging to something other than the true Church; his religious community itself is an aid to his salvation (no. 3). This is quite new in official Catholic teaching.

The effect of Vatican II has been to foster an attitude of friendly, brotherly openness between Catholics and non-Catholic Christians as well as consciousness that the present divisions are contrary to the will of Christ, so that every effort ought to be made to overcome them and restore the complete unity of the Christian people that Jesus intended when he prayed "that all of them may be one, Father, just as you are in me and I in you: that they may be one in us" (John 17:21). The Council and subsequent popes have acknowledged explicitly that we Catholics, by our sins, share the blame for the divisions. All Catholics therefore are summoned to repentance and complete conversion of heart with a view to restoration of complete Christian unity (Ecumenism, nos. 4, 6-8).

• *The Church of Christ*

However, the Council did not take the stand, now implicitly attributed to it by many theologians, that the various Christian denominations are simply diverse (and presumably legitimate) traditions of the one Christian faith or parts of one Great Church. It did not recognize that there are many churches, all having, in principle at least, equal claim to the heritage of Jesus. It did not abandon the traditional claim of the Roman Catholic Church to be the one true Church of Jesus Christ. On the contrary, the Council reiterated that Jesus founded only one Church, which he placed under the government of the apostles, with Peter at their head. This Church still subsists today in the Roman Catholic Church, the bishops having succeeded the apostles, and the Pope St. Peter (The Church, no. 7; Ecumenism, no. 3).

This Church has been sent to all mankind, and all are called to belong to it. Belonging to it is in fact necessary for salvation, at least for those who are aware of this obligation (The Church, no. 14; Ecumenism, no. 3). Those who, in good faith, are not aware of it, can still be saved through whatever elements of Christianity they have; but by these elements, which "belong by right to the one Church of Christ" (Ecumenism, no. 3), they are linked with the Church itself (The Church, no. 15).

The Roman Catholic Church, says the Council, has within itself the fullness of the truth and of the means of salvation imparted by Jesus (Ecumenism, nos. 3 and 4). (It has them not as a human achievement due to the wisdom or fidelity of its members but due to the preserving action of the Holy Spirit that Jesus has imparted to his Church.) All those denominations that are separated from the Church are lacking in some of the heritage of Jesus. In particular, they lack that unity with the Church which Jesus desired for all (Ecumenism, no. 3).

For the above reasons, the Roman Catholic Church can rightly be called *the* Church, and not just one among many churches. Whenever the Council documents speak about *the* Church, this is clearly the reference intended. Thus the Bishop of Rome is spoken of as pastor over the whole Church, with "full, supreme and universal power over the Church" (The Church, no. 22). Likewise the Council is called ecumenical because it represents the whole Church.[4]

• *Particular churches*

The term *church* can also be used of particular congregations, as when we speak of the Eastern and Western churches (Ecumenism, no. 14) or the Church of Ephesus, the Church of New York, etc. However, the term *church* is not used by the Council as a common term that can be applied to any organized religious body. The theology of the local church is still being worked out; but it is clearly the intent of the Council that local churches are meant to be in communion with one another in the universal Catholic Church, with its head at Rome. In the case of the separated churches of the East, the Council has maintained the long-standing tradition of acknowledging them as churches. The same is not true, however, of Protestant denominations. Nowhere does the Council call them churches. It does not explicitly deny that Protestant communities are churches, but it avoids applying the term to them. It speaks of the "churches and ecclesial communities" of the West, without determining which denomination belongs in which category. The criterion for determining when a religious community can be called a church was not defined by the Council, but the presence or absence of a valid episcopate is very possibly the decisive issue.

* * *

In sum, the Council's vision of non-Catholic Christian denominations could be formulated thus: They are *fragments* of the Church. For whatever reason, they have been broken off from the one Church of Christ, while still retaining significant elements of it. The Roman Catholic Church, on the other hand, although surely wounded and impoverished by the loss of many it is called to embrace, is not a fragment because, thanks to the Holy Spirit, it retains the fullness of that with which Jesus endowed it for the salvation of mankind.

Such a position will seem arrogant if taken as a human community's appraisal of its own achievements. Centuries of history, colored with the invectives and blood of human rivalries, have taught the modern mind that all societies are a mixture of good and evil, that none dare propose itself as an absolute. However, the Catholic position is not the product of smug self-contemplation but of faith in Christ. His work, not mere human initiative, lies at the foundation of the Church, and he promised to protect it from the failure that would surely occur if all depended on our fulfillment of our responsibilities. It is with the shame of confessing that we have been unworthy of our calling that Catholics acknowledge the Church to be the People of God, the Temple of the Holy Spirit, and the Body of Jesus Christ.

26

The sacramentality of the Church

There are three factors which make the Church a visible, historical society: (1) the faith in Jesus Christ professed by all its members; (2) the pastoral authority by which they are directed and coordinated; and (3) the sacred rites in which they all take part. Faith has been dealt with throughout this book; hence nothing more need be said about it here except that Christian faith must be professed in an overt, public way in order to make a person a member of the Church. A society cannot be formed out of people who keep their faith secret in their hearts. For there to be a Church, Christians have to "confess" their faith before the world; and Jesus made this an important Christian duty.

> Everyone who acknowledges me before men, the Son of man also will acknowledge before the angels of God; but he who denies me before men will be denied before the angels of God. (Luke 12:8, RSV)

Hence also the Church has to have a creed: a formulation of the faith on which it is based. The other two factors which give the Church its visibility — its sacred rites and governing authority — must now be examined in detail.

• *The principle of sacramentality*

Sacramentality means God clothing the spiritual with the sensible in order to make it accessible to humanity. He does this in two degrees: first, by the natural reflection of himself that belongs to the essence of created things; and second, by choosing certain privileged creatures, namely Jesus and his Church, and using them in a way that transcends their natural endowments, to communicate himself. The Christian sacrament is not merely a symbol of the sacred, it is a historical reality, chosen and used by God as an effective sign of his presence and action. In this order, Jesus is the supreme sacrament, the archetype of all others. Subordinate to him, the Church in its entire being is a sacrament, as the efficacious sign of Jesus. It is "the universal sacrament of salvation."[1] The sacramental function of the Church, in turn, is realized chiefly in the seven official sacraments: baptism, confirmation, reconciliation (or penance), Eucharist, anointing of the sick, matrimony, and holy orders. These are all rituals performed in and by the Church, in which the sacramentality of the Church is particularly realized.

Nature itself is a revelation of God to man, a theophany, as we have noted in Chapter 1. The contemplation of nature is one of the chief roots of religion. The so-called "nature religions" — which worship the sun or moon or a mountain or forest — are crude examples; even though they confuse God with his handiwork, they have a valid awareness of

something sacred attained in and through this awesome symbol. It is a common religious experience today to perceive a beautiful forest as a kind of cathedral or to see the grandeur of the mountains and the infinity of the heavens as tokens of the greatness of God. All of this has to do with what may be called the sacramentality of nature itself.

In Jesus, however, a new order of sacramentality is introduced into the world. On the one hand, it is not natural symbolism. Although human beings, like the rest of nature, can function as symbols of the divine, the man Jesus presents God to us in a unique way that depends on a free intervention by God and not simply on the natural reflection of the divine inherent to human nature. In this sense, Jesus is like a *word* (from God to us) rather than a natural symbol. On the other hand, the divinity is communicated to us far more really and substantially in Jesus than in any mere symbol: "In Christ all the fullness of the deity lives in bodily form" (Colossians 2:9). The humanity of Jesus may be called an *efficacious sign* of the divinity: efficacious because Jesus effectively brings us into contact with God, instead of merely reminding us of him. This efficacity is characteristic of the Christian sacraments.

While Jesus is the essential and universal sacrament, his departure from our midst makes it necessary for him to be represented through the Church. If Jesus is the primordial Sacrament, the Church is the sacrament of the Sacrament. In the Church, Jesus is represented to us. And the Church does more than just symbolize and represent him; as Body of Christ, it makes him effectively present. To be incorporated into the Church is to be incorporated into Jesus; a member of the Church is a member of his body. Thus the Church also is an efficacious sign.

THE SEVEN SACRAMENTS

Rituals form a prominent part of most human religions. Sacrifice, procession, sacred dance and chant, purifications, sacred meals, fertility rites, initiatory rites, puberty rites, fetishes, mimic reenactments of myths — such are the stuff of which religions are made. What is common amid all their diversity is that they are symbols; and as religious rites, they are symbols of the sacred. For man has never been content with the natural sacredness of the world itself; he has never been satisfied with the theophanies provided by nature, though these are immeasurably more admirable than any of his petty little ceremonies. Everywhere that a deity is worshiped, and even where the religious instinct expresses itself without reference to a distinct god, sacred rites have been invented. For it is not enough for man that God be represented to him; he too must express his response to God. In addition to being sacred symbols, religious rites are something that *man does*.

The deep roots and profound bases of religious ritual are twofold: the hiddenness of God, who needs to be represented by a symbol, and the hiddenness of man's deepest sentiments, which need to be expressed in a gesture. On both sides, there is an embodiment of the spiritual in things sensible. In summarizing the dynamics of religion in the natural order, that is, prior to the Christian revelation, we may say that God reveals himself to man through nature, and man acknowledges and responds to that revelation by ritual.

In both of these movements, although religion has to do with the most sublime

values of the human spirit, the "embodiment" involved in its symbols makes it liable to corrupted into a subhuman degradation. When the symbol is identified with the Sacred, in the worship of the sun or a mountain or, worse, of a man-made statue, there is idolatry when the ritual is thought to have power over God or over the hidden forces of nature there is magic.

Christian sacraments belong to the genus of ritual. They fulfill in the Christian religion the role played by ritual in other religions. However, as sacraments, they are differentiated from other rituals in much the same way that God's revelation in Jesus differs from his revelation in nature. That is to say, the sacraments involve a positive intervention by God, choosing certain symbols for a privileged role, and imparting to them an efficacy they do not have of themselves. The sacraments have not been invented simply out of man's need to give expression to his religious sentiments. Unlike many other Christian rites that have arisen in this way — for example, the hymns we sing, the bows and genuflections we make, or the processions we hold — the sacraments have been appointed for us by an authoritative divine decision. They express not so much our sentiments toward God, as God's free graciousness toward us.

• *Institution by Christ*

Of course the gestures used in the sacraments may have been used prior to Christianity. Baptism seems to have been invented by John the Baptist; but it was Jesus who, by conferring on baptism the cleansing power of the Holy Spirit, turned it into a sacrament. Sacred meals are found in many religions, and Jesus and his disciples were possibly celebrating the Passover Meal at the Last Supper. But by the authoritative words "This is my body   this is my blood. , , , Do this in memory of me," Jesus changed the Jewish memorial into the sacrament of the Eucharist.

The institution of the other five sacraments by Christ is not so evident in Scripture, and hence most Protestant churches admit only the two sacraments of baptism and "The Lord's Supper." The Lutherans recognize also the sacrament of penance; some Anglicans accept the other five as "lesser sacraments." But Catholics and Orthodox hold that all seven sacraments were instituted by Christ,[2] although there are diverse opinions about exactly how some of them, notably matrimony, derive from him.

• *Jesus, agent in the sacraments*

Jesus, who instituted the sacraments, uses them to signify the grace he bestows. For example, one of the first effects of his grace is to cleanse us from sin. This is signified by the water of baptism, which washes the skin externally as a sign of the inner, spiritual cleansing of the soul. Another work of grace is to give us the life of children of God. Since human life is sustained by food and drink, bread and wine are used in the Eucharist to signify the nourishment of the spiritual life. If we were pure spirits, divine grace would presumably be imparted to us in some purely spiritual manner; but human beings need physical, sensible signs to help them perceive spiritual realities. Thus the sacraments are Jesus' way of humanizing the spiritual, adapting it to the manner of human beings. In talking to a little child, you use simple words and short sentences suited to his understanding

likewise, as far as possible, you don't merely speak, you *show* him what you mean. Similarly the sacraments are used by Christ to communicate with us in a way that speaks to our whole nature. Even children can understand them. For the same reason, the sacraments make use of some of the most basic human materials (water, bread, wine, oil) and some of the most basic human gestures (washing, feeding, anointing, blessing).

The sacraments are comparable to the gestures Jesus often used when healing or blessing people. He laid his hand on the eyes of the blind and said, "Receive your sight." He put his finger to the ears and lips of the deaf and dumb, saying "Ephphatha," that is, "be opened." This was not sympathetic magic but a way of helping people understand what he was doing. The sacraments of the Church may be compared to healing gestures left by Jesus for his ministers to perform, now that he is no longer visibly present.

Even more profoundly, the sacraments prolong the Incarnation itself. Jesus became man to make God visible, so that humans could more readily turn to him and love him. Similarly the sacraments give a kind of visibility to the works of grace done by Jesus.

• *Effective signs*

The sacraments are not only signs of what Jesus is doing by his Holy Spirit; they are also the means by which he accomplishes it. While on earth, his body was not merely a sign but the instrument through which he acted. When people touched him, power went forth from him and healed them (Luke 6:19), as we see most dramatically in the case of the woman with the flow of blood, who was healed by touching the fringe of his robe (Mark 5:25-34). So, in the sacraments, Jesus acts to cleanse, nourish, heal, etc. He does not merely cleanse the person *while* the baptism is going on, he does so *by means of* the baptism. He does not merely grant pardon when the priest is absolving the sinner or healing when the priest is anointing the sick person; he pardons *through* the absolution and heals *through* the anointing. Thus, at this level too, the sacrament is an *effective* sign: It not only signifies, it is the means used by Jesus to bring about what is symbolized by the sacrament.

Thus the connection between sacrament and grace is not arbitrary. The sacrament "shows" what kind of grace it is imparting; the grace is always represented by the sign. Observing the Eucharist, you can "see" that it is a sacrament of nourishment; observing a baptism, you can see that it is a cleansing. (Generally, however, the sacramental gesture is somewhat vague and generic, so that its precise meaning needs to be determined fully by the words that accompany it. From the mere fact that a person is being anointed with oil, you cannot tell whether the intention is to heal him from illness, ordain him a priest, or confirm him. The words that accompany the anointing, however, specify its meaning.)

• *Sacraments and magic*

The sacraments are sometimes scoffed at as "Christian magic," and at first sight may seem to resemble the potions of a medicine man or the incantations of a witch. In both sacraments and magic, there is the performance of a mysterious rite from which is expected an effect that is all out of proportion to that which is done. However, there is an essential difference between sacrament and magic. The magic rite is believed to produce its effects of and by itself; but the sacrament produces its effect only by the power of Jesus and as his instrument. In magic, the cause is inadequate for the effect; that is why magic is ultimately ridiculous. In the sacrament, the power of Jesus Christ is more than adequate to produce the effect. The sacrament is merely the instrumental sign of Christ's action. If there is any kinship between the sacraments and magic, it lies simply in the human need of symbolic expression, and confirms the principle that in Christianity divine grace is accommodated to human ways and needs.

Furthermore, the sacraments do not produce their effects automatically (as magic is supposed to do), regardless of our disposition or attitudes. They require a right intention on the part of the minister and faith on the part of the recipient. The sacrament is a sign of a spiritual reality which can be apprehended only by faith, and of a spiritual operation which can be recognized only by faith. To go through the motions of a sacrament without faith would be just an empty gesture. When the Iroquois poured boiling water over the head of the Jesuit missionary Jean de Brébeuf, in mockery of baptism, that was not a sacrament but a sacrilege. Furthermore, Jesus did not heal people unless they believed in him; so likewise his sacraments do not operate of themselves like natural causes; they are instruments used by Jesus to act upon those who believe.

On the other hand, it would be too little to say that the sacraments merely arouse our faith, and that Jesus acts in response to our faith. In that case, the sacrament would lose its inherent significance. Jesus would not be acting through it, and one who had sufficient faith would have no need of the sacraments. But Jesus said, "Whoever believes *and is baptized* will be saved" (Mark 16:16), and that a man must be "born again of water and the Spirit" (John 3:5), showing that the sacrament itself has a role. It must be used with faith, but when it is, it has an effect that goes beyond that of faith alone.

It is a common mistake to think that the sacraments are the only means of grace. God gives grace in countless ways, most of which we are unaware of. We can always turn to him to seek pardon or help, and he hears us. The sacraments were not intended to stop or to complicate this direct access to God but to add something lacking to it. An intimate personal relationship with an utterly invisible God is not easy to attain. God is everywhere; but being able to focus our attention on him in the Eucharist helps our adoration. God is always ready to pardon the repentant sinner; but it reassures our conscience to be told by his official representative, "Go in peace, your sins are forgiven."

Moreover, besides this psychological help, the sacraments also impart a grace not available elsewhere. The Eucharist as bread of life provides a nourishment not to be found in any natural food. The sacramental absolution given by the priest contains a healing grace that cannot be presumed when one simply repents. So with the other sacraments: It was not for nothing that Jesus instituted them but to help a people for whom it is hard to relate to God.

• *Signs of God's self-communication*

The grace symbolized and imparted by the sacraments is always some aspect of the divine life. Each sacrament has its specific meaning in relation to this life. Baptism brings about the beginning of the divine life in us; the Eucharist is its nourishment. Since the divine life as received in this world is subject to illnesses, two sacraments are medicinal: For the spiritual illness of sins committed, there is the sacrament of reconciliation, or penance. For physical illnesses, there is the anointing of the sick.

The remaining three sacraments are given primarily not for the life of the individual who receives them but to qualify him to foster the divine life in others. Confirmation strengthens him to be a witness of Christ to others; holy orders ordains him to administer the sacraments; matrimony sanctifies a couple for the work of bringing new members into the body of Christ and educating them in the faith. Thus all the sacraments have as their goal the fostering of the Christian life, either directly in the recipient or indirectly in those to whom he will minister.

• *Sacraments and the Church*

The sacraments can also be considered in reference to the Church, in which perspective they are signs indicating and effecting our relationship with the Church. Baptism and confirmation make us members of it; holy orders confer an office in the Church; reconciliation restores the wound we have caused the Church; matrimony makes a married couple a sacred sign of the Church. The anointing of the sick is a merciful gesture of the Church coming to the aid of one in need. The Eucharist is the supreme act in which the Church is realized. The Church could not be an authentically human society on the basis of exclusively spiritual realities such as grace; it needs external signs whereby people know where we stand.

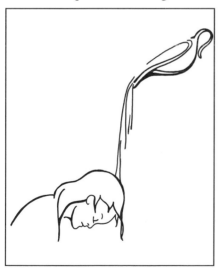

BAPTISM

Baptism is the fundamental sacrament, the entrance into sacramental life, because it is the act by which a person expresses his faith in Christ. Before being baptized, he is called to profess his faith; and the baptism formula itself summarizes the essence of the Christian faith:

> I baptize you in the name of the Father and
> of the Son and of the Holy Spirit.

There are several aspects to the effects of baptism: cleansing from sin, birth to life in the Spirit, and incorporation into the Church, the Body of Christ.

• *Cleansing from sin*

The principal gesture of baptism is that of bathing. Originally the one baptized was plunged completely into the water, as Jesus was in the Jordan River; but today most people are baptized by having water poured over their heads. This external bath signifies and brings about an interior cleansing from sin.

All sin is removed by this sacrament: original and actual, mortal and venial — and not only the guilt of sin but also whatever punishment is due for it. The recipient may have lived a life of utter wickedness; but if he has sincerely repented and adhered to Christ by faith, all of this is washed away in the waters of baptism. Were he to die immediately, he would be admitted directly into heaven like the "good thief" to whom Jesus said, "Today you will be with me in paradise" (Luke 23:43). For in the sacraments, it is not the merits of the recipient but the grace of Christ that produces the effect; and this grace is infinitely more abundant than all the sins in the world (Romans 5:15-17).

• *Infusion of the Holy Spirit*

The cleansing from sin in baptism is brought about by the Holy Spirit who is poured into the recipient, making him a temple of the Holy Spirit (1 Corinthians 6:19). More than a temple: He becomes a child of God, sanctified by grace and alive with the life of the Blessed Trinity (see Chapter 21). Hence baptism can be called a rebirth, as in Jesus' words to Nicodemus, "Unless a man is born again of water and the Spirit, he cannot enter the kingdom of God" (John 3:5).

Since the middle of the nineteenth century, some American evangelicals, particularly the Pentecostals, have come to distinguish between "baptism in the Spirit" and "water baptism." In this they are motivated largely by Jesus' parting words to his disciples, "in a few days, you will be baptized with the Holy Spirit" (Acts 1:5). This was fulfilled at Pentecost, when the apostles experienced the coming of the Holy Spirit with new power and gifts, such as speaking in tongues (Acts 2). Still in the Church today, many experience an outpouring of love, joy, and peace, as the Spirit comes to them in a new way, often accompanied by charisms such as tongues or prophecy (see Chapter 23). Why some have this experience and others do not is a difficult question that cannot be gone into here. Yet to treat "water baptism" as nothing but an external ritual in contrast to the experience of the fruits and action of the Spirit is contrary to the teaching of Jesus who speaks of being born "of water and the Spirit." Likewise the apostles baptized with water in order to communicate the Holy Spirit (for example, Acts 8:36). Hence the Church holds firmly that baptism with water is a sacrament by which the Holy Spirit is communicated to all who receive it worthily. And while personal experience of the coming of the Holy Spirit is not to be considered extraordinary, much less abnormal, neither is it a necessary sign of the validity of the sacrament.

• *Incorporation into the Church*

The third effect of baptism is incorporation into the Church. By this sacrament, a person becomes a member of the Body of Christ. Jesus saves us by gathering us into a people; that is why baptism is not just a personal act of repentance of sin and faith in Christ; it is the act of admittance into the People of God.

The key to this incorporation into the Church is the sacramental character. The word *character* is not used here in the psychological and moral sense as when we speak, for example, of "building character." It is closer to the characters on a printed page or the characters in a play. The sacramental character is a spiritual imprint of Christ upon the soul, marking the person as a Christian. It is a fundamental, indelible configuration to Christ to whom the person is from then on obliged to conform his way of life. If he does not live as a Christian, this basic configuration remains within him, to his shame. Even if he sins or renounces his Christianity, his baptismal character remains; later, if he returns to the Church and the Christian life, he will not be rebaptized but simply absolved because this character, though violated, has never been deleted.

The specific effect of the baptismal character is to conform the recipient to Christ *as priest*. By baptism a person is qualified and authorized to associate himself sacramentally with the sacrifice offered by Christ, the High Priest, by receiving the other sacraments. (These cannot be received validly except by one who is baptized; hence baptism is called the gateway to the sacraments.) Here is the foundation of the "priesthood of all the faithful," which fulfills the promise of God through Moses: "You will be to me a kingdom of priests. . . ." The priesthood of the laity is indeed exercised in every prayer and every good deed, according to St. Paul's injunction to "offer your bodies as living sacrifices, holy and pleasing to God, which is your spiritual worship" (Romans 12:1); but it is in the sacraments and liturgy that the priestliness of every Christian has its supreme expression.

• *Baptism of adults*

When an adult is baptized, he must already have faith in Christ, without which the "baptism" would not be a valid sacrament. If his faith is "living" faith, that is, animated by supernatural love, he is already in the state of grace, has the Holy Spirit, and is living as a child of God.

Nevertheless, baptism is not meaningless for him. It is the sign by which he testifies to his faith, and by which the Church receives him into its society. As we have already noted, a human community cannot have purely spiritual criteria; it needs signs to know who belongs to it and who does not. Finally, reception of the sacrament will bring new grace to him. The life of grace is always capable of being enriched and deepened, and every worthy reception of the sacraments graces the recipient. One who has been sanctified by the grace of the Holy Spirit prior to baptism is not yet a member of the Church.[3] He is living by that divine life which is the essential life of the Church; he is in profound communion with all his brothers and sisters in the Church (even though he may not know them as brothers and sisters); but he is not yet fully incorporated into the Church community.[4] He cannot share in the Eucharist or any of the other sacraments because he has not yet submitted himself to the pastoral direction of those who have the sacred office of representing Christ to his people. That whole human and social structure which Christ instituted as a framework and support, and as a vital source of nourishment, is not available to him.

• *Infant baptism*

The first recipients of baptism were no doubt adults — people converted by the preaching of the apostles. But the Church soon recognized that there was no need to delay baptism until adulthood because the effect of baptism is not due to the recipient but to the Holy Spirit. The baptism of infants probably began already in apostolic times; for when the New Testament speaks of households being baptized (1 Corinthians 1:16; Acts 16:15, 33), the presumption is that children were included.

Normally the recipient of a sacrament must be capable of making a free, responsible, personal act of faith in Christ; and this is required for the other sacraments. But they are received by one who is already a member of the Church, whereas baptism is an initiation into the Church; and in the realm of grace, the first initiative is always on the part of God. Our part is to respond to God's grace; and while the infant is incapable of any response at the moment of baptism, it will spend the rest of its life ratifying or failing to ratify what was done for it in baptism.

From another point of view, baptism is a new birth, and birth is something that happens to a person before his own activity begins. The child, born in the state of original sin, is reborn through baptism into the life of a child of God. The infant is not conscious of the change that has taken place nor is any change visible to the onlookers. Nevertheless, something profound and far-reaching has taken place — the most radical change that will ever occur in its life.

Some argue against the baptism of infants on the grounds that religion should not be imposed on a child, and that the latter ought to be allowed to make his own choice when he matures. But baptism does not impose anything; one baptized in infancy still has to take a personal stand for or against Christ when he comes of age. Baptism gives him a grace to help him to make the right choice. Moreover, if he dies in infancy, baptism assures him a place in the eternal Kingdom of God. What happens to the infant who dies unbaptized, we do not know; the traditional view consigns him to limbo[5] because of Jesus' teaching that no one enters the Kingdom unless he has been "born again of water and the Spirit." From this point of view, it is safer to have the child baptized. Finally, the importance of the preconscious and subconscious in the shaping of human psychology, which we are better aware of today than ever before, manifests the value of having a child's initial formation take place in the presence and under the influence of the Holy Spirit.

When Peter was telling the household of the Roman Cornelius about Jesus, the Holy Spirit fell upon his listeners with the effect that they began to speak in tongues and to praise God just as the apostles had on Pentecost (Acts 10:44-48). This did not deter Peter from baptizing them; on the contrary, it was a sign to him that they should be baptized. For the sacramental act whereby one is associated with the death and resurrection of Christ is never vain; through it, a new grace will be given to conform the person more perfectly to Christ.

CONFIRMATION

Baptism and confirmation are closely linked and give a person his complete status as a member of the Body of Christ and temple of the Holy Spirit. In the early Church, they seem to have gone together, as two parts of a single rite of initiation. In the story of the half-instructed Christians whom St. Paul met at Ephesus, we are told:

On hearing this, they were baptized into the name of the Lord Jesus. When Paul placed his hands on them, the Holy Spirit came on them, and they spoke in tongues and prophesied. (Acts 19:5-7)

In time, the two sacraments came to be separated from one another in the Latin Church, although the primitive practice of conferring them together is still observed by the Greeks. When and why the separation took place is not altogether clear; there is in any case a biblical precedent for it in the history of the Samaritans who were baptized by Philip and confirmed by the apostles Peter and John (Acts 8:14-17). At any rate it is certain that these two sacraments combine in giving the Christian his fundamental status as a member of the Church.

• *An anointing with the Holy Spirit*

The symbolism of baptism is primarily that of cleansing; for baptism purifies from sin. The symbolism of confirmation, an anointing with chrism, refers to the imparting of the Holy Spirit, by whom Christ was first anointed (Acts 10:38) and by whom the Christian is now anointed to be another Christ. However, it would not be right to suppose that the Holy Spirit is not imparted until confirmation, since baptism means being "born of

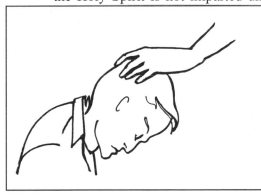

water and the Spirit" (John 3:5). Moreover, sin cannot be taken away except by the Holy Spirit. Hence the gift of the Spirit in confirmation can be only an additional gift, an increase or strengthening of the Spirit originally received in baptism (as fits very well with the term *confirmation*). In order to signify this, an anointing with chrism was introduced into the baptismal rite when it became separated from confirmation. Previously, when the two sacraments were joined in a single rite of initiation, there had been only a single chrismation.

• *Christian adulthood*

In distinguishing the effects of these two sacraments, traditional teaching holds that baptism, being a new birth, makes us children of God, and that confirmation gives us an additional spiritual strength, making us adults in the Christian life. Associated with the fact that baptism is most often conferred on infants, and confirmation on adolescents, this has led some people to view confirmation as a kind of Christian puberty rite.[6] In modern times, many have protested sharply against such a conception, which does not fit well with the origins of the Church, when most people were baptized as adults, nor with the later practice, still used in the East, of confirming infants. What is often overlooked on both sides of this discussion is the fact that the infancy and adulthood in question here do not refer to the natural development of the recipient but to the character of the grace bestowed. The grace of baptism is for the recipient, to give him a share in the Trinitarian life. This makes him a child of God, whether he is three days or thirty years of age, and is a grace he

397

never outgrows. The grace of confirmation is strength to enable the recipient to witness to Christ before others as well as to combat the spiritual enemies that beset every Christian life. Such grace pertains to a kind of adulthood (and to being a "soldier of Christ"), whether received in infancy or later. For the character imparted by this sacrament, like the baptismal character, is a permanent title to graces that will be conferred when needed.

> Bound more intimately to the Church by the sacrament of confirmation, they are endowed by the Holy Spirit with special strength. Hence they are more strictly obliged to spread and defend the faith both by word and by deed as true witnesses of Christ.
> (Dogmatic Constitution on the Church, no. 11)

One practical advantage of the separation of confirmation from baptism, which may help to account for it historically, is that it enables the bishop of a large diocese to confer the sacrament on all his people. The bishop is the principal priest of his diocese, as we shall see (Chapter 27); and when Christian communities were still quite small, the bishop celebrated the Eucharist for his entire flock, baptizing and confirming all newcomers. In our large dioceses today, it is no longer possible to have everyone at the same Mass; even in the parishes, it is ordinarily necessary to hold several different Masses to accommodate the crowds each Sunday. And it would not be expedient to defer all baptisms in a given parish until such a time as the bishop could be there; the Church wants infants baptized promptly after their birth. But confirmation can be deferred without serious disadvantage, thus giving the bishop a direct sacramental and priestly contact with each member of his flock. Even when confirmation is, in certain exceptional cases, conferred by a simple priest, the chrism used has been blessed by the bishop, as a sign of his pastoral headship.

THE EUCHARIST

• *A sacred meal*

The chief ritual of the Christian religion is a sacred meal. That the Eucharist is fundamentally a meal is a truth that became somewhat obscured in popular consciousness by secondary developments, especially stress on its sacrificial character. But that it is a meal

should be obvious from the fact that it arose from the Last Supper, and that it is essentially consummated by eating and drinking. Furthermore the Eucharist is celebrated at a table covered with a tablecloth, and set with a plate and a cup for the bread and wine which make up the simple menu. Knives, forks, and spoons as well as all the other little vessels of condiments which habitually accompany elaborate human banquets are radically eliminated from this meal, which does not require seasoning to bring out its flavor. On the contrary, this "Bread from heaven contains within itself all sweetness," as we say in an awkward English translation of a beautiful Latin responsory for Corpus Christi. Other foods and flavors would spoil your appetite for this bread and prevent you from appreciating it fully. Even a washing of the hands by the celebrant before the meal and a washing of the dishes at the end have been incorporated in all simplicity into the Mass liturgy. On the other hand, we do not disdain to burn two candles on the altar table as a little token of elegance.

In a banquet intended to honor a person or celebrate an event, it is customary to have an after-dinner speech to remind people of the meaning of the celebration and awaken in them the appropriate sentiments. This function is fulfilled at the Eucharist by two or three readings and the homily, which precede the meal. At the Jewish Passover, from which the Eucharist perhaps derives, the father would recount to his son the story of the deliverance from Egypt, to explain why the festival was being celebrated. However, the readings at Mass are not merely a presentation of the theme of this day's celebration. The Mass is a course of instruction as well as a banquet. It derives from the teaching services of the synagogue as well as from the Passover sacrifice. The readings therefore are organized so as to give a quasi-complete instruction in Sacred Scripture in cycles of two or three years,[7] and they are explained and applied by a homily. This is not in disharmony with the character of the Eucharist as a repast; instead, it means that the participants are nourished both on the sacrament and on the Word of God.

Insofar as it is a meal, the Eucharist is a thanksgiving dinner. Its central action begins with the summons "Let us give thanks to the Lord, our God," followed by the solemn prayer "We give thee thanks, Almighty and everlasting God. . . ," which is meant to set the basic theme of the entire Eucharistic prayer right down to the solemn conclusion "Through him, with him, and in him all glory and honor are yours, almighty Father." The central object for which we give thanks is the salvific death of Jesus Christ: "Whenever you eat this bread and drink this cup, you proclaim the Lord's death until he comes" (1 Corinthians 11:26). But because it delivers us from the captivity of sin, Jesus' death makes it possible for us to rejoice over the gift of creation, and over all the other gifts of God we have received. In the early Church, before the canon of the Mass became fixed and stylized, the celebrant freely recalled various gifts of God which were to be remembered with thankfulness. This is reflected today in the variety of Eucharistic prayers and prefaces in the Mass, which recommend different motives of thanksgiving corresponding to the diverse seasons and occasions. The name *Eucharist* itself comes from the Greek term for thanksgiving.

The sacred meal is a type of religious act widespread in the religions of the world, especially primitive religions. It generally seems to be understood as giving man communion with the deity and as sanctifying, that is, giving a sacred character to, human communion. (Here is another instance in which Catholicism manifests its kinship with primitive religions.) Whatever one may think about the value of pagan sacred meals, the Eucharist, as a sacrament, effectively brings about what it signifies; namely, communion of man with God, and of human beings with one another. Both are achieved through union with Jesus Christ in his sacrificial death.

• *The Real Presence*

After the miracle of the loaves and fishes, a crowd followed Jesus, looking for free food and stupendous miracles. Jesus took the occasion to admonish them not to be so concerned for the bread which perishes but rather to seek the true bread from heaven which he was going to give them. When they took this to refer to the manna of the desert, he went on to assert:

> I am the bread of life. He who comes to me will never go hungry, and he who believes in me will never be thirsty. For my Father's will is that everyone who looks to the Son and believes in him shall have eternal life, and I will raise him up at the last day. (John 6:35-40)

Here Jesus is represented as bread because he gives life; the way to "eat" this bread is to believe in him. This fundamental truth about the life-giving role of Jesus would hold even if he had not gone on to give it further expression in a sacrament. Jesus is bread inasmuch as he gives life to all who believe in him. But he went on to declare and repeat with insistence:

> This bread is my flesh, which I will give for the life of the world. . . . unless you eat the flesh of the Son of man and drink his blood, you have no life in you. Whoever eats my flesh and drinks my blood has eternal life, and I will raise him up at the last day. For my flesh is real food and my blood is real drink. Whoever eats my flesh and drinks my blood remains in me, and I in him. Just as the living Father sent me and I live because of the Father, so the one who feeds on me will live because of me. (John 6:51-57)

• *The Last Supper*

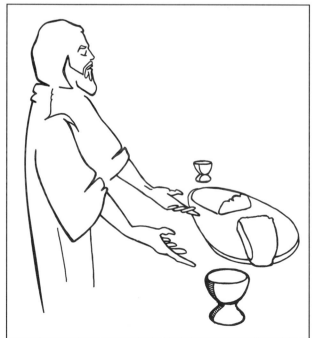

This statement, which shocked his hearers and drove many of them away, received its elucidation at the Last Supper. There, in keeping with the ritual of Jewish meals, Jesus blessed a loaf of bread, broke it, and gave it to the apostles, who were at table with him. But he added something that was not part of the traditional ritual: "Take it; this is my body." At the end of a solemn meal, the Jews passed around a cup of wine, over which three blessings were pronounced. It was at this point that Jesus declared: "This is my blood of the covenant, which is poured out for many" (Mark 14:22-24).

With nothing more than this laconic text to go on, a modern reader might wonder whether Jesus meant this only in a symbolic sense. But a letter of St. Paul, written about twenty-five years later, indicates clearly how the Eucharist was understood by the Christian community:

> The cup of blessing which we bless, is it not a participation in the blood of Christ? The bread which we break, is it not a participation in the body of Christ? (1 Corinthians 10:16, RSV)

All the indications we have of the faith of the early Christians confirm that the universal Church regarded the Eucharist as really, not just symbolically, the body and the blood of Christ. Not only is he *like* bread in the sense that he gives life to those who believe in him; he really gives his body and blood under the form of bread and wine as the means of a sacramental communion with himself.

Baptists generally regard the bread and wine as "emblems," that is, symbols, of the body and blood of Jesus. Lutherans traditionally hold that Jesus makes himself present *in* the bread and wine. But Catholics hold that the bread and wine are converted into the body and blood of Jesus by the consecrating words of the priest.[8]

• *Transubstantiation*

In technical theological language, this conversion is called *transubstantiation,* meaning that the substance of the bread is changed into the substance of our Lord's body, and the substance of the wine into the substance of his blood. The "accidents," however, or appearances — in other words, all that can be observed by the senses (shape, color, weight, taste, etc.) — remain those of bread and wine. There is no way other than faith that the body and blood of Jesus can be recognized in the sacrament; any physical or chemical test will always bear on the appearances of what is there, which will be those of bread and wine. Faith in the words of Jesus, and reliance on the Church's understanding of them, leads one to affirm that the reality present here, contrary to appearances, is the body of the Lord.

In recent years, Dutch theologians have proposed to replace the term *transubstantiation* with *transignification* or *transfinalization.* Several modern schools of philosophy have a great distaste for the classical distinction between substance and accident. The Holy See has insisted that we retain the term *transubstantiation,* however, even if we supplement it with others. For the consecration does not merely confer a new significance on the bread and wine; it changes them really and objectively into the body and blood of Christ. No other term expresses this fact so unambiguously as *transubstantiation.*

Some object fiercely to this term on the grounds that substance, as defined by Aristotle, no longer has meaning for modern philosophy. But besides the fact that that ephemeral reality, constantly in flux, known as "modern philosophy," has no claim to determine theological usage, the Church's use of *transubstantiation* does not imply a canonization of the hylomorphic theory of Aristotle. It is simply a historical fact that, after this term came to be adopted into the theological vocabulary, centuries of *Christian* usage hammered out its meaning and left it unambiguous — something that cannot be said of any competing term.

If, for the purposes of communication with other schools of philosophy, one wishes to experiment with a new vocabulary, no objection need be raised to that. But it would be a loss to drop the refined instrument we already possess.

• *The bodily presence of Jesus made available*

But what good is this mysterious change into the body and blood of Christ if, to all appearances, there is nothing but bread and wine? What is gained is the presence of Jesus in his physical reality, and hence the possibility of a real contact with him. When he was on earth, people sought to touch him because power flowed forth from him and healed them (Luke 6:19). His body is still the instrument used by his divinity to heal, to strengthen, and, above all in this sacrament, to nourish those who touch him with faith. This is what the Eucharist enables us to do. As God he is present everywhere; but his human body is present only in the Eucharist — this body which is our privileged means of access to the divinity.

We saw above that the human body of Jesus was the great sacrament of God's gift of himself to mankind, and of the healing action of his grace. Now in the Church, the body of Jesus continues to be the permanent source of life and grace for us. It is made available to us not through some stupendous miracle of preservation but by means of the simple signs of bread and wine. His presence can be recognized only by faith; but faith is, in any case, the condition for entering into life-giving contact with him. This sacrament of faith gives us the presence of Jesus really and effectively.

• *Eucharistic miracles*

Sometimes miracles occur in connection with the Eucharist as a confirmation of our faith. There are innumerable reports, some of them well documented, of hosts that have dripped blood or have taken on the form of the Infant Jesus, etc. At Lanciano in Italy, when a priest doubted the Real Presence, the host turned visibly into flesh. Preserved in a monstrance from the eighth century to the present day, it was recently subjected to scientific analysis, which determined that the relic consisted of flesh from a human heart.[9] Once a host left the altar and was carried to St. Catherine of Siena through no human hands.[10] Similar miracles are recorded of other saints. Such miracles are given as confirmations of faith in the Real Presence, but they are not the basis of faith, much less a proof that would make faith unnecessary.

The person receiving Communion does not ordinarily have a conscious experience of the presence of our Lord. Still it is not rare or extraordinary for someone to sense a deep peace and love or a quiet joy imparted by the sacrament. Yet the measure of its fruitfulness does not lie in such experiences but in the faith and the loving adherence to the will of God with which it is received. Those Communions which seem the most arid may in fact be the most fruitful.

The bread is changed simply into the body of Jesus and the wine into his blood. These separate consecrations represent the separation of Jesus' body and blood in death. However, the Jesus who is made present in the sacrament is the glorified Lord, in whom there is no longer any separation. Hence the whole Jesus is present, with his body and blood, soul and divinity, in either form. Someone who receives Communion under the form of bread alone (or even under the form of wine alone) receives Jesus in his entirety. But for the fullness of the sacramental symbolism, it is preferable to communicate under both forms.

• *The Eucharist as sacrifice*

In the course of the first two or three centuries, the Eucharistic meal came to be viewed as a sacrifice, and by the same movement of thought, the presbyters who presided over it began to be called priests *(hiereus, sacerdos)*.[11] This development seems to have been due to several factors working simultaneously. The Last Supper was either a celebration of the Jewish Passover sacrifice (as the Synoptic Gospels suggest) or at any rate closely connected with it (St. John). The language Jesus used about his body and blood was sacrificial language. The Eucharist, as St. Paul says, proclaims the death of the Lord (1 Corinthians 11:26); and Jesus himself associated the Last Supper with the death he was about to undergo (Luke 22:19f; Matthew 26:28; Mark 14:24). Since the Passion is emphatically represented as a sacrifice by the Letter to the Hebrews, the Eucharist likewise acquires thereby a sacrificial character. Finally, there is the simple fact that the Eucharist, as a sacred meal of communion with God, fulfills in the Christian religious life a function analogous to that of sacrifice in the Old Testament and in other religions.

This sacrificial character, which was instinctively perceived by the early Christians, has been confirmed by the Church in its theological reflection. In the Eucharist, we do not merely receive the bodily presence of Jesus, we are associated with him in his sacrificial death. Jesus offered himself to the Father once for all on Calvary; but in the Eucharist *we* are associated with that offering. The Eucharist is the Church's sacrifice not in the sense that it is a new sacrifice supplementing that of Jesus but in the sense that in it the Church renews, in its own act of worship, the offering that Jesus, as our head, once made for us. The sacrificial offering is the same: namely, Jesus in his death on the cross. Even the priest is the same; for the ordained priest consecrates the Eucharist in the name of, and as the representative of, Jesus, the great High Priest, who renews in his mystical Body the offering that he made on Calvary. In short, all the substance, value, and significance of the Eucharist comes from the sacrificial death of Jesus; but as a ritual enacted by the Church, the Eucharist enables the Church also to make an offering to the Father.

• *Veneration of the Real Presence*

The Eucharist is different from all other sacraments both by the fact that Jesus himself (and not simply some action of his) is received in it, and by the fact that the sacrament is a lasting reality, not just a transitory action. In the other sacraments, something is done which has a lasting spiritual effect, but the sacrament itself does not last. In the Eucharist, however, the body and blood of the Lord remain present so long as the sacramental appearance of bread and wine remain. (When they are digested or when, through any other natural process, the *sign* is destroyed, in other words ceases to have the appearance of bread and wine, then the sacramental presence likewise terminates.) This makes it possible to keep the Eucharist (or "Blessed Sacrament" as it is often referred to in this context) permanently as an object of veneration. The host is kept in the tabernacle so that people can go there to worship the Lord, and to benefit from his salutary presence. For here too it remains true that, while God is present everywhere and the Holy Spirit dwells in the hearts of all the faithful, the body of Jesus is the privileged means of access to the divinity. People find from experience that being in the presence of the Blessed Sacrament supports their prayer. There is nothing that personal relationship craves more than the presence of the loved one; hence those who love Jesus tenderly are instinctively drawn to abide in his sacramental presence, from which they go away comforted, strengthened, and renewed. This is particularly true when the Blessed Sacrament is not merely kept in the tabernacle but is exposed for adoration. As in Jesus' time on earth, it is still true today that power flows forth from him to heal those who touch him; and simply to look at the sacrament and to be in its presence with faith is a way of touching the Lord, and being touched by him.

RECONCILIATION, OR PENANCE

Sin is a pervasive fact of human existence. It includes that mysterious, primordial shadow that falls across every human life at its origins, and the fully deliberate embrace of evil that constitutes sin in the hideous fullness of its meaning (so hideous we seldom dare look it in the face). Between those extremes, it embraces an immense variety of misdemeanors, excesses and negligences, selfish demands and cowardly retreats, more or less aberrant, more or less deliberate, that tarnish even the most beautiful life.

The Son of God became man to deliver us from all this. He accomplished this task in root principle by "bearing our sins in his body on the tree" (1 Peter 2:24). The work will be fully achieved at the Parousia, when "they will neither harm nor destroy in all my holy mountain, for the earth will be full of the knowledge of Yahweh as the waters cover the sea" (Isaiah 11:9). Meanwhile, the Kingdom of God is in process, and the salvific passover of the People of God from captivity to freedom must be realized daily over and over again for each individual. Through baptism, the believer has been incorporated into Christ and cleansed from all past sin by the bath of water and blood flowing from the pierced heart of the Crucified. But even though, as a result, our "spirit is alive because of righteousness," our body remains "dead because of sin" (Romans 8:10). Consequently, even after our sacramental rebirth and resurrection with Christ, we fall again and need to be cleansed again. The summons "Repent, because the Kingdom of God is at hand" is addressed not merely to the unconverted man who has not yet obeyed the Gospel; it applies also to all those who, although justified, still fall many times a day. They are not, however, rebaptized. Christians who have sinned — which is to say all those in this world — are called to a repentance which is essentially an inner disposition of sorrow for their sins, a begging of God's pardon, and a determination to avoid sin in the future.

This disposition of contrition and repentance relates not merely to external transgressions but even more to the deep-seated interior attitudes — the "law of sin" in our members leading us to do the evil we do not want (Romans 7:19f). Although it should be an abiding factor of our religious stance as we relate to the all-holy God, contrition requires, on occasion, an external expression. Just as religion in general needs to be expressed in rites (even though the interior attitude is more essential and more permanent than they are), and just as the faith held in the heart needs to be confessed with the lips (Romans 10:9), so also repentance for sin needs to be manifested or declared. Sometimes this is done by penitential gestures; thus "to repent in sackcloth and ashes" is a stock biblical expression. Sometimes it is done by the confession of one's sins to a brother or sister in the Lord. "Confess your sins to each other and pray for each other, so that you may be healed" (James 5:16).

• *Sacramental penance*

But the attitude of repentance and the acts of penance and confession, which are already salutary by their very nature, have been elevated and given new power in the Christian order by being made into a sacrament. Traditionally known as the sacrament of penance, or confession, it was renamed "sacrament of reconciliation" by the Second Vatican Council in order to emphasize its healing effects rather than its somewhat unpleasant prerequisites. In it, the penitential acts of the sinner are used as elements of the sacrament, and thus take on a purifying value they do not have of themselves. Furthermore, to complete this sacrament, the priest is empowered to speak words of absolution in the name of Christ. This mysterious power was given to the apostles on the very day of the Resurrection. In his first appearance to the apostles, the risen Lord breathed on them saying, "Receive the Holy Spirit. If you forgive anyone his sins, they are forgiven; if you do not forgive them, they are not forgiven" (John 20:22-23). Earlier Jesus had told them, "Whatever you bind on earth will be bound in heaven, and whatever you loose on earth will be loosed in heaven" (Matthew 18:18). Those words affirmed the sacred, heavenly character of the authority given to the apostles but did not make it clear that even sins could be absolved. The Easter message shows that the authority of the apostles is not merely one of imposing (or releasing) obligations, it is the power to act as the instrument of divine grace, bestowing pardon.

"Who can forgive sins but God alone?" demanded the scribes and Pharisees when Jesus absolved the paralytic (Luke 5:21), and this same objection is unwittingly repeated today against the ministers of Jesus. The power of absolution does not mean that God has contracted out part of his work to subordinates. It is still true and absolutely without exception that absolution from sin can come from God alone; for the very essence of sin lies in the fact that it is not merely a transgression of a human standard but an affront to the Sovereign Lord of the universe. If a priest were fooled or cajoled or bribed into granting absolution to someone not sincerely repentant, the latter would not be forgiven by God, who knows the heart. But the power of absolution means that the priest's words of forgiveness are the instrument and channel of God's forgiving grace to all who receive the sacrament worthily. He speaks in the name of Christ, and his words, subsumed into the redeeming work of Christ, are bearers of a power that transcends the one who utters them.

Here above all applies the principle we have seen: Christianity gives a human face to the invisible grace of God. The Son of God became man so that in him we could more easily recognize God's merciful love for us. For the very same reason, his words of pardon are spoken to us in the human accents of his authorized representative.

Certainly we can always turn to God the moment we are conscious of sin, and ask forgiveness. Indeed we should do so; and if our dispositions are what they should be, he grants pardon at once. But it is not that easy to repent sincerely, especially of those sins for which we have a special weakness. It is very easy to mutter, "God, I'm sorry," without really changing our attitude. Although confession is not a sure guarantee of sincerity, the fact of having to admit our sins to another human being, and to submit our contrition to his authoritative judgment, helps considerably to keep us honest.

Likewise it is often difficult to believe in God's pardon, especially for sins of which we are profoundly ashamed. Our timid hearts receive a powerful reassurance when one authorized to speak for Christ declares, "I absolve you in the name of the Father, and of the Son, and of the Holy Spirit." Furthermore, not only does sin offend God, it also wounds the Church. Hence it is appropriate that we beg pardon not only interiorly from God but also exteriorly from a minister of the Church. But over and above all these considerations of appropriateness, there is the fact that God uses our confession and the priest's absolution as his sacrament, and through them confers upon us a grace that we cannot presume to obtain if we neglect the order of repentance instituted by him. (Because of this grace, it is a salutary practice to confess one's sins even more frequently than would be strictly obligatory.)

ANOINTING OF THE SICK

The last and least of the sacraments, in the general estimation, is the one which, in a sense, most obviously perpetuates the earthly ministry of Jesus: He went about healing the sick. And when he sent his disciples out on their mission, he commissioned them to do likewise: He "sent them out to preach the kingdom of God and to heal the sick" (Luke 9:1f; see also Matthew 10:1; Mark 6:7). St. Luke adds that they "went from village to village proclaiming the gospel and healing people everywhere" (9:6; see also Mark 6:13). The healing of the sick is put almost on equal footing with preaching the Gospel.

The apostles did not stop their healing mission after the departure of Jesus. Acts narrates some of the miraculous healings that occurred in the early days of the Church. Since then, the healing ministry has been maintained at three diverse levels. In the first place, there is simple prayer for healing (for oneself or for others). Where people pray with lively faith, healings do sometimes occur, sometimes very remarkable ones. Very often these prayers are associated with the invocation of the saints (for example, at shrines such as Lourdes), by the use of relics or blessed oil associated with the saints, or through novenas and other prayers addressed to the saints.

Secondly, there is a charism of healing with which some people (for example, Blessed Brother André of Montreal) are given a special power to heal. St. Paul speaks clearly of this charism in 1 Corinthians 12:9 and 30. For many centuries, it seemed as though this gift were given exclusively to the saints (which is no doubt part of the reason why they are so often invoked in prayers for healing). The Reformation churches rejected this charism along with veneration of the saints. In the nineteenth and twentieth centuries, however, there has been a rediscovery of the gift of healing by Protestants and Catholics alike (and to a lesser extent, by the Orthodox). Among Catholics, the Charismatic Renewal has led to a new realization that the gift of healing is not confined to the saints but may be simply a charism equipping a person for a special ministry to the sick. Among Protestants, this gift is commonly associated with popular evangelists (some of whom, unfortunately, prejudice it by supposing that all illness is the work of demons or that anyone with enough faith can be healed).

Finally, there is the sacrament of the anointing of the sick, in which the sick person is anointed with oil blessed by the local bishop for this purpose. Although in the form of a prayer, it is not merely a prayer for healing. As a sacrament, it has an intrinsic efficacy to bring about what it signifies. Neither does it involve any extraordinary charism; it is part of the ordinary ministry of any priest.

The apostles, from their very first mission, healed the sick by anointing them with oil (Mark 6:13). Later on, the Letter of James gave the following instructions, which have been followed by the Church ever since:

> Is any one of you sick? He should call the elders of the church to pray over him and anoint him with oil in the name of the Lord. And the prayer offered in faith will make the sick person well; the Lord will raise him up. If he has sinned, he will be forgiven. (4:14f)

Anyone can of course pray for the sick; and the practice of lay people accompanying their prayer by an anointing with blessed oil has been established since the earliest centuries. However, the sacrament of anointing can be administered only by a priest.

The Church does not allow this sacrament to be used for slight illnesses but only where there is danger of death. During the Middle Ages, this restriction was interpreted so severely that only those on the point of death were anointed, whence the sacrament came to be called "Extreme Unction," that is, the last anointing. Vatican II rejected this exaggeration and declared that "as soon as any one of the faithful begins to be in danger of death from sickness or old age, the appropriate time for him to receive the sacrament has already arrived" (Constitution on the Sacred Liturgy, no. 73). The phrase "*begins* to be" was chosen to indicate that it is wrong to wait until the person is about to die; as soon as there is serious danger, even though remote, the sacrament can be administered, for it is a sacrament of healing, not of dismissal from life.

The effects of the sacrament are carefully delineated in the Ritual of Paul VI:

> This sacrament gives the grace of the Holy Spirit to those who are sick: by this grace the whole person is helped and saved, sustained by trust in God and strengthened against the temptations of the Evil One and against anxiety over death. Thus the sick person is able not only to bear suffering bravely, but also to fight against it. A return to physical health may follow the reception of this sacrament if it will be beneficial to the sick person's salvation.[12]

HOLY ORDERS

Through a ceremony centering on the laying on of hands by a bishop, a man is ordained to sacred office in the Church. There are three such offices — bishop, priest, and deacon — conferred by the sacrament of holy orders. It is called *orders* because, in the ordered hierarchy of the Church, these are the three principal ranks; *holy* because these offices are not just administrative posts but involve a participation in the priesthood of Jesus Christ. Like baptism and confirmation, the sacrament of orders imparts a "character" — an indelible configuration to Christ's priesthood, involving a spiritual power. But whereas the baptismal character empowers a person to *receive* the spiritual goods of the Church, especially the sacraments, holy orders empowers a person to *confer* them.

Holy orders is the sacrament which qualifies a man to participate actively in the priesthood of Christ by administering the sacraments. Whereas the lay members of the Church participate typically as *recipients* of the sacraments, the ordained ministers confer the sacraments on others.

• *Universal priesthood and ordained priesthood*

It is true of course, and cannot be sufficiently emphasized, that the whole Church is a "priestly people," in which every baptized member participates in the priesthood of Christ. Yet the universal priesthood of Christians does not exclude but instead is strengthened by the special priesthood of those who are ordained. In the Old Testament, all Israel was a "kingdom of priests" (Exodus 19:6); nevertheless, Aaron and his descendants were designated as priests in a special way[13] because they offered sacrifice and led the Temple services.

Similarly in Christianity, the ordained priesthood involves a spiritual power not given to every Christian. The Eucharist is not something that anyone can celebrate on his own. It is not just a sacred meal expressive of Christian fellowship; its essence lies in the consecration of the bread and wine into the body and blood of Christ. This can be performed only by those duly authorized and empowered. Likewise not every Christian can forgive sins with the authority of Christ. The same applies to the other sacraments (except matrimony, which is conferred by the spouses on one another, and baptism, which in an emergency can be conferred by anyone). They presuppose supernatural powers not possessed by the ordinary Christian as such. When Jesus appointed the twelve apostles, he gave them powers not shared by the other disciples (Matthew 10:1; Mark 3:15; Luke 9:1f). At the Last Supper, he ordered them to do as he had done (Luke 22:19; 1 Corinthians 11:25). On Easter Day, he breathed the Holy Spirit into them with the power to forgive sins (John 20:22f). These are the powers perpetuated by holy orders.

From another point of view, holy orders implies that the priest is not merely someone designated by the community for a public function; he is consecrated by Jesus Christ to act as his personal representative to the community. The community of course may have a voice in selecting those who are to receive priestly orders (or better, in discerning who has been called by God for them); but by the sacrament of ordination it is Christ, not the community, who consecrates the man. In most Protestant denominations, the pastor has no special supernatural powers; hence he can be simply installed in office, without need of a sacrament.

The worship offered by the Christian community is complemented by the grace which God imparts to the community. While grace can be imparted by God in innumerable other ways as well, certain graces of special importance for the Church as such are given through the sacraments. And just as it pertains to the priestly function to offer the sacrifice by which the Church worships its Lord, so also it is a priestly function to administer the sacraments. The bishop, and in dependence on him, the ordained priest, is the ordinary minister of the sacraments. Hence the priest is sometimes defined as a mediator between God and man: offering sacrifice to God in the name of the Church, and returning blessings to the Church through the sacraments of God.

• *Bishop, priest, deacon*

A bishop has the fullness of the priesthood and can administer all the sacraments. A priest ordinarily administers all the sacraments except confirmation and holy orders. In certain cases, he is authorized to confirm; perhaps in a very exceptional situation, he could also ordain (that is not clear). A deacon is the ordinary minister of baptism, and can also impart liturgical blessings (including the blessing of marriage). All three are authorized to preach, but the priest and deacon may do so only under the superintendence of the bishop.

On account of the sacraments, the priestly office is sometimes referred to as the office of "sanctification" as distinguished from teaching and governing. However, it should be noticed that the priest does not properly have the power to sanctify. He is simply a minister of the sacraments; and in the sacraments, it is Jesus who, acting by the Holy Spirit, sanctifies the recipients.

• *Clerical celibacy*

St. Peter was a married man (Matthew 8:14) and most likely the other apostles were also. In the apostolic Church, bishops, elders, and deacons were normally married (1 Timothy 3:2-13; Titus 1:6; see also 1 Corinthians 9:5). However, the example of Jesus, Mary, and John the Baptist as well as the teaching of Jesus (Matthew 19:10-12; 22:30; Mark 12:25; Luke 20:36) and Paul (1 Corinthians 7:7, 32-38) inspired people to a life of complete chastity from the earliest years of the Church. Many priests in particular spontaneously chose a celibate way of life during the first three centuries. In some areas, this became so usual that people were unwilling to attend a Mass celebrated by a married priest.

At the beginning of the fourth century, the Council of Elvira made absolute continence obligatory for all the clergy of Spain. By the end of the century, this was the law of the entire Western Church, and it has remained so ever since. The Eastern Church likewise sensed the affinity of celibacy with the priesthood but was more moderate in requiring it only of those who had the fullness of the priesthood, that is, of bishops.[14]

The rationale behind a life of complete chastity is, as St. Paul explains, that it makes possible a single-minded devotion to the Lord, whereas those who are married are divided by their (rightful) anxiety to please their spouses. If there is anyone whose heart should be given undividedly to the Lord, surely priests ought to above all others. Celibacy permits them to be at the service of their flock far more than is possible for a man with wife and children to care for. Even more profoundly and intimately, because of his calling to be "another Christ," the priest needs to have a heart given over totally to the Lord. It is sometimes argued that allowing priests to marry would attract many more men to holy orders; but those unwilling to make the sacrifice of marriage might often be less ready for the sacrifice of one's personal interests that is constantly incumbent on the priest.

• *Women not ordained*

Women are not admitted to the priesthood in the Catholic Church. (Until the present century, most other Christian denominations likewise barred them from ministry.) In the past, theologians have generally held that ordination conferred on a woman would not even be valid. The feminist movement, however, has challenged this stand and accused the Church of unjust discrimination.

The Congregation for the Doctrine of the Faith, charged by the Holy Father to review this question, declared that "the Church, in fidelity to the example of the Lord, does not consider herself authorized to admit women to priestly ordination."[15] On a point such as this, the Congregation explained, the Church must seek before all else to be guided by the will of our Lord. Jesus never spoke directly on the subject, but there are in Scripture some indications of his mind on the matter. Although he showed the highest esteem for women, and did not hesitate to go against the traditional Jewish disdain for them (for example, engaging in conversation with the Samaritan woman at the well [John 4:9]), yet Jesus did not appoint any women as apostles. The apostles in turn never appointed a woman to public office in the Church, even though women were associated with them in the ministry. St. Paul teaches that women are not permitted to speak in Church (1 Corinthians 14:33; he is probably referring to public speeches, of the sort given by a preacher). "I do not permit a woman to teach or to have authority over a man," 1 Timothy 2:12 declares. This too probably referred only to ecclesiastical matters. Regardless of what may be said about possible cultural biases reflected here, these passages seem to exclude women from pastoral office in the Church.

In later centuries, this policy was followed without exception. Priestesses were not rare in the ancient world, but they are never found among Christians, except in schismatic or heretical sects. Canon law declares that only males can be ordained validly.[16] These facts take on greater weight when we bear in mind that Church tradition is one of the most authoritative guides to the right interpretation of Scripture.

• *Holiness and office distinct*

In seeking to understand this position, let us begin by noting that it does not imply that women are in a special way unworthy or unholy. Holiness and union with God are not a function of office, but of sanctifying grace which makes us children of God, members of Christ, and heirs of eternal life. In respect to this grace, men and women are equal ("joint heirs of the grace of life" [1 Peter 3:7]). The Church canonizes more women saints than men,[17] even though men have the advantage of holding the more prominent positions in the Church.

Conversely, the office one holds in the Church or the function to which one is called

410

is not indicative of one's merits or closeness to God. God assigns tasks according to his good pleasure and wisdom, not according to our merits. This is evident throughout the whole range of his works. For example, in the natural order women are, by the creative act of God, enabled to bear and nurse infants; men are not. In salvation history, the Hebrew people were chosen for a role not open to any other race. Mary was the holiest of all creatures and Judas one of the wickedest; yet he was made an apostle and she was not. Peter was appointed the chief of the apostles, even though he was not the Beloved Disciple. No one is worthy of the priesthood and no one has a right to it. At best, only a small percentage of Christians are called to it; those who are not called have no grounds for complaint.

Thus, in reserving ordination to men, the Church is not being guided by prejudice but is simply trying to be faithful to the intentions of Christ, as it understands them. If one asks why God willed things this way, the Congregation for the Doctrine of the Faith offers the suggestion that just as every sacrament has to have a natural resemblance to the grace which it signifies (thus the pouring of water signifies cleansing), masculinity gives the priest a natural resemblance to Christ, the bridegroom of the Church. (This is not just a sentimental, poetic fancy but a basic aspect of Christ's salvific role.) One might also seek to discern in the difference between male and female psychology characteristics that would make one more suited than the other for the role of shepherd of the flock. But such considerations are matters of speculation, not the grounds of the Church's decision.

27

The pastoral structure of the Church

Like any human society, once it has more than a handful of members, the Church needs officers to keep order and administer the common goods. But the Church is not simply a community of people brought together by natural motives; likewise it is not governed by coordinators deputed for this purpose by the assembly at large, as is theoretically the case in a democratic political society. The Church is directed by pastors commissioned and empowered to act in the name of Christ by Jesus himself.

This structure is adumbrated already in the primitive community of Jesus and his disciples. Jesus was not an elected leader; he came as one sent by the heavenly Father to speak "with authority" and to act with power as his disciples acknowledged. This original association, of Jesus and his disciples, remains the paradigm for the structure of the Church ever since. But since Jesus is no longer visibly present, he is represented now, not only by sacraments, as we have already seen, but also by pastors authorized to lead the flock in his name.

• *The apostles*

That this was to be the case became evident when Jesus first sent the Twelve to proclaim the Gospel. He gave them the name *apostle* (literally, "one who is sent") because, as he explained, "As the Father has sent me, I also send you" (John 20:21). He did not merely urge them, he *appointed* them to preach and teach, and gave them *power* to heal the sick and cast out demons.[1] This power and commission were not given to all the disciples but only to the Twelve.

In the course of time, Jesus specified the authority of the apostles in various ways. They were to do in memory of him what he had done at the Last Supper. They were empowered to forgive sins or refuse forgiveness (John 20:23). Their role was described as that of a shepherd or pastor (John 21:15-17). Their teaching authority is such that those who believe them will be saved and those who do not believe will be condemned (Mark 16:16). The link between Jesus and his envoys is so close that he could say, "He who receives you receives me."[2]

As the Father has sent me, I also send you.

• *Development of authority in the early Church*

After Pentecost, when the Church took on its definitive shape, we find it under the pastoral authority of the apostles from the outset: "They devoted themselves to the apostles' teaching and fellowship, to the breaking of bread and the prayers" (Acts 2:42).

As the Church developed, new forms and structures of authority became necessary. Thus we find the apostles appointing seven (deacons?) to assist them (Acts 6). Elders (in Greek, *"presbyters"*) help the apostles govern the Church in Jerusalem (Acts 15:6). Later, St. Paul appoints elders in charge of the churches founded by him (Acts 14:23). The development of Church government during those first decades is now impossible to trace in detail. At first there were no official names for the various offices; St. Paul tells the Thessalonians simply to hold in esteem "those who labor among you and are over you in the Lord and admonish you" (1 Thessalonians 5:12). Elsewhere he speaks vaguely of "helpers and administrators" (1 Corinthians 12:28).

By the end of the first century, however, the basic form of Church government was stabilized around three offices: bishop, presbyter (from which our word *priest* derives), and deacon. In each local church, there was normally one bishop assisted by a small group of presbyters and deacons. In all these forms, the Church is governed by pastors acting in the name of Jesus Christ, not as delegates of the community. Thus, when the question arose whether the Gentile converts had to be circumcised, the apostles and elders decided the matter in council, and then announced their (negative) decision in the words, "It has seemed good to the Holy Spirit and to us. . ." (Acts 15:28). St. Paul did not hesitate to declare that "what I am writing to you is a command of the Lord" (1 Corinthians 14:37), and to appeal to the authority which the Lord had given him "for building you up and not for destroying you" (2 Corinthians 10:8; 13:10).

• *Distinguishing clergy from laity*

In the course of the first few centuries, consciousness of the distinction between clergy and laity developed. Whereas the original apostles had been externally indistinguishable from the rest of the believers, gradually the clergy became differentiated in their style of dress, in living apart, and remaining celibate (in the greater part of the Church). Under various cultural pressures of the Middle Ages, the clergy tended more and more to become the active agents in the Church, with the laity as passive recipients and objects of their ministry.

Subsequently there came a reaction to this excessive "clericalization." Luther denied that the clergy had any power or authority other than what was delegated to them by the congregation. Although the Council of Trent reaffirmed the special sacramental powers of the ordained clergy,[3] malaise with excessive "clericalization" reappeared in modern times. In its more moderate form, this led to the rediscovery, beginning in the nineteenth century, of the "apostolate of the laity," and the various forms of "Catholic Action" which appeared in the twentieth century. More radical forms of anticlericalism that have recently appeared within the Catholic Church itself tend more or less to deny the sacramental power of the ordained priesthood, which is derided as a "mystification of the clergy."

• Vatican II

The Second Vatican Council strongly reaffirmed the dignity and responsibility proper to lay Christians, and on the theoretical plane sought to define more precisely the distinction and relationship between clergy and laity. Its most important documents on this subject are the Constitution on the Church, especially Chapters II, III, IV, and V; and the Decree on the Apostolate of the Laity. The Bishops' Synod of 1987 was devoted chiefly to the role of the laity.

The Church insists that all Christians are holy by the indwelling of the Holy Spirit; that all are called to be active organs in the Body of Christ; and that all participate in the priestly, prophetic, and even kingly role of Jesus Christ. The Holy Spirit imparts his charisms to laity as well as to clergy to empower them for the function assigned to them by Christ for the building up of his Body. The laity are not to be regarded as mere assistants to or collaborators with the clergy in a work that belongs properly to the latter. The laity have their own proper mission or apostolate, corresponding to the secular — that is, nonclerical — state of their lives:

> . . .by reason of their special vocation, it belongs to the laity to seek the kingdom of God by engaging in temporal affairs and directing them according to God's will. They live in the world, that is, they are engaged in each and every work and business of the earth and in the ordinary circumstances of social and family life which, as it were, constitute their very existence. There they are called by God that, being led by the spirit of the Gospel, they may contribute to the sanctification of the world, as from within like leaven, by fulfilling their own particular duties.
> (Dogmatic Constitution on the Church, no. 31)

On the other hand, the Council insists, there are offices in the Church established by Christ himself for the good of the whole Church and furnished by him with sacred powers in order to make their ministry efficacious.[4] Hence, although we can speak of a priesthood that is common to all the faithful, there is also a hierarchical or ordained priesthood which is essentially different.[5] It is characterized by the sacred powers received by the priest through the sacrament of holy orders, above all the power to consecrate the Eucharist[6] and to absolve from sin. It is the characteristic role of the ordained priest to act "in the person of Christ," according to the traditional expression.[7] That is to say, he acts as one sent by Christ to be his personal representative to the people — and to do this not merely symbolically but with real power, as Christ's effective instrument.

The Church takes this position in opposition to various currents of thought in the modern world which would hold that the priestly office simply grew up in the Church like offices in political society, that it represents merely a practical assignment of responsibility to certain persons who have special aptitude and training for it, and that the ordained priest is not in possession of any sacred powers essentially distinct from those common to all the members of the Church. That the external forms and style of the priestly function have undergone many developments in the course of history, and are liable to undergo still others, is not of course denied. But what the Church insists on is the essential structure established by Jesus when he called the apostles out of the general community of disciples, commissioned them to preach in his name, and gave them sacred power and authority to be effective pastors and ministers of his grace. This apostolic structure continues in the Church through those ordained to the pastoral office.

Hence the pastor of a Christian community is not merely one who leads or governs, he also has the priestly function of offering sacrifice and conferring the sacraments. The Church is primarily a worshiping community, and the principal responsibility of those who hold office in it is to lead the community in worship. In the complex organism of the Church, there are of course many positions of responsibility which do not suppose a priestly character — for example, administration of charity funds; supervision of schools and hospitals; and handling the finances of a parish. However, the essential ecclesiastical authority is always vested in a priest.

BISHOPS

The bishops of the Church have succeeded the apostles as pastors of the flock of Christ. As most people have more contact with their local parish priest than with the bishop, they are inclined to think of the former as "priest" and "pastor"; but in truth, it is the bishop who has the fullness of the priesthood, and who is properly the pastor of his diocese. "Simple priests" really have only a part of the priestly power. They cannot ordain other priests, and they do not have authority to make laws; only the bishop can do this. They function in the Church as the bishop's assistants and representatives to the local assembly of the faithful.[8] On the other hand, that "part" of the priesthood exercised by the simple priest is the most sacred and essential: consecrating the Eucharist and absolving sinners. The acts of authority reserved to the bishop in governing the diocese are not nearly so holy as these.

As the representative of Christ shepherding the flock entrusted to him, the bishop shares in Christ's triple office of prophet, priest, and king. This division of functions derives from the three types of leadership in the People of Israel, which can be seen as foreshadowings of the fulfillment that came in Jesus Christ. The *prophet* spoke God's message to the people; he was thus a teacher or preacher, calling men back to the Covenant. The *king* was not regarded as a mere political figure; he was God's representative, ruling in the name of God. Finally, the *priest* was the head and representative of the community in its worship. He offered sacrifice to God in the name of the community at large; he delivered oracles to those who sought the will of God in some affair; he gave instruction in the law.[9] In brief, he was the mediator between God and the people in religious matters.[10]

Like Moses, who exercised all three of these functions before they became differentiated, Jesus is at once prophet, priest, and king of the People of God of the New Covenant; bishops carry on these functions by teaching, governing, and administering the sacraments.

THE TEACHING OFFICE

The function of teaching and preaching is the most basic of all, and the first one committed to the apostles. It evokes and forms that faith which is the foundation of the en-

tire Christian life. The bishop does not teach merely as one who has studied a subject and therefore has something to say; his office in the Church is sacred, and his appointment to it, regardless of the human factors that may have entered in, comes ultimately from Christ. By the Holy Spirit, who endows everyone with the grace necessary to exercise the function to which he is called in the Body of Christ, the bishop is endowed with a special charism for teaching. This does not make him a skillful teacher, nor does it enable him to know the truth without having to study or reflect; but it assures him of the help of the Holy Spirit and imparts a sacred authority to his teaching which the faithful are bound to respect. Of a completely different sort is the natural authority that might be claimed by a theologian on account of his personal learning and intelligence. Thus when a bishop supervises the catechetical instruction given in his diocese, he is exercising his proper responsibility as pastor of the flock.

But it is only on matters pertaining to the Gospel, that is, faith and morals, that the episcopal authority bears. *Faith* here refers to the doctrines revealed through Christ, the apostles, and prophets; these form the doctrinal basis of the Church. *Morals* here includes all matters of right and wrong — not only what is revealed (such as the Decalogue given through Moses) but also matters of natural law not dealt with in revelation. For the pastoral responsibility of the Church is that of conducting people to the final goal of the Kingdom of God. Attainment of this depends on their doing what is right in their full life, not just in "supernatural" or religious affairs.

One might object that if there is a natural law, this ought to be evident to reason, and left therefore for each one to judge for himself, without the Church having anything to say on it. But it is obvious that natural law is not agreed upon by everyone; and this is not surprising, since human nature itself is very mysterious and diversely interpreted. Hence even in this realm there is need of pastoral direction.

• *Matters of natural law*

The Church has developed a doctrine about a great number of moral questions posed by modern life on which Scripture has no direct teaching, such as human rights, the mutual relations of capital and labor, the just wage, and the morality of warfare, abortion, sterilization, artificial insemination, masturbation, etc. The encyclical *Humanae Vitae* (1968), in which Pope Paul VI solemnly reaffirmed that contraception is intrinsically evil, is a famous recent example of the Church giving an authoritative moral teaching in the realm of natural law.[11]

The teaching authority of the Church does not extend into the realms of science, philosophy, history, economics, politics, etc. However, it is possible, and not at all rare, that issues of faith or morals come up in these areas. In such cases, the Church has authority to pronounce on the issue but only insofar as it involves faith or morals. For example, when a political and economic system such as Marxist communism postulates that there is no God above us, and no future life awaiting us, the Church condemns such a system as irreconcilable with the truths which it knows and professes. Similarly, if a psychological system treats man as a bundle of reflexes, without freedom of choice or responsibility, the Church can condemn it. In so doing, the Church is not speaking on psychological questions as such but is affirming a truth about man that lies within its proper domain.

Some protest that it is not the Church's business to concern itself with intimate details of personal life; but the Church is concerned with the entire moral life of humanity. Moreover, one must work out his salvation in the intimacy of his personal life no less than in public affairs, and hence needs guidance about right and wrong there too.

In discussing the teaching authority of the bishop, we have come to speak of the teaching of the Church. This is because it is the bishops who have authority to define the doctrine of the Church. However, the individual bishop has not the right to teach a merely personal doctrine of his own; instead, he must teach in concert with the entire college of bishops.

THE GOVERNING, OR PASTORAL, OFFICE

Like any organized society, the Church has to have authorities to coordinate and regulate its activities. The bishop is the principal one in whom this authority is invested. By this authority, the bishop participates in the royalty of Christ although, in the bishop,

this authority is better envisioned not as royal or even princely but as pastoral. He is a shepherd conducting the flock of Christ.

Here a distinction must be made between administrative decisions and the direction of Christian life. Administrative decisions are all those required by the Church as an organized society: for example, the appointment of pastors, the regulation of the hours of Church services, and decisions about opening or closing schools, hospitals, etc. While the bishop does not ordinarily make these decisions alone but with the collaboration of a complex array of counselors, diocesan synods, priests' senates, etc., ultimate authority for the decisions rests with the bishop. In such matters, the Church is quite comparable to any other society; there is simply the matter of determining what responsibility resides in each office.

Yet Church authority bears not only on the administration of Church functions but also on the direction of the personal lives of its members. Pastors exist primarily not to regulate the use of material resources but to guide their flock to the Kingdom of God. This does not mean that the Church can dictate any given decision in a person's private life; such authority is claimed by totalitarian states, not by the Church. But the Church can make laws governing the moral and religious conduct of its members even in their private lives. For example, the weekly "Lord's Day" prescribed in Exodus 20:8-11 was changed by the Church from Saturday to Sunday. Christ's general call to penance has been defined by the Church as applying especially to the season of Lent (and the laws for this too have been modified variously in the course of time). The general obligation to confess one's sins and receive Communion has been defined as requiring that the sacraments be received by everyone at least during the Easter Season each year. It is a Church law that requires celibacy of Latin-rite priests (as well as of bishops in the Eastern rites).

On most points, the laws of the Church are in such continuity with those of Scripture that it is difficult to make a precise demarcation between the function of transmitting the laws of Christ and that of making laws proper to the Church itself. Likewise the functions of teaching and governing often coincide. But distinguishing these various functions is usually of no great practical importance. It is important, however, to recognize in principle that the Church has authority both to declare what is objectively right and wrong (= teaching) and to make decisions determining certain things to be right and wrong for its members (= governing), in accordance with the teaching of Jesus, "Whatever you bind on earth will be bound in heaven; whatever you loose on earth will be loosed in heaven" (Matthew 18:18). In other words, the role of the Church in regard to the moral and religious life of its members is not confined merely to proposing ideals and exhorting people to live up to them; it defines with authority the standards by which its members are bound.

THE PRIESTLY OFFICE

By teaching and governing, bishops share in the prophetic and royal offices of Christ. They also share in Christ's priestly office, characterized by its involvement in worship.[12] A priest is the head of a worshiping community; however, not everyone who leads a group in prayer is called a priest.

It is very difficult to draw a satisfactory definition of priesthood from the practices of the various religions of the world, since they are so different. The shaman, the medicine man, the prophet, the scribe, the mystic — all are figures that partially overlap or are contiguous with priesthood, yet seem distinct from it. It seems safe, however, to say that the most characteristic act of priesthood is that of offering sacrifice in the name of the community. Thus Jesus, who did not belong to the priestly class of Judaism, and did not make use of any of the external trappings of priesthood, nevertheless came to be regarded as a priest by his disciples precisely insofar as his death was recognized as having the value of a sacrifice atoning for the sins of the world (Hebrews 3:10).[13]

His death is the unique sacrifice of the Church, offered "once and for all" on Calvary. But because this sacrifice is mysteriously renewed in the Eucharist, those who are empowered to consecrate the Eucharist have also come to be called priests. Thus the Christian priesthood is essentially sacramental: It is conferred by a sacrament and exercised chiefly through sacraments.

PAPAL PRIMACY

Bishops are the principal holders of the sacred power and authority by which Jesus Christ directs and sanctifies his Church. But there is one bishop who has authority over the others, and who is in his own person the principal sign and instrument of unity in the Church: the Bishop of Rome. He has this primacy as successor to St. Peter, the first bishop of Rome.

• *Peter head of the apostles*

In the Gospels, despite the frequent mistakes due to his impetuosity, Simon Peter appears constantly at the head of the apostles. His position is indicated above all by a statement Jesus made in response to Simon's profession of faith at Caesarea Philippi:

> Blessed are you, Simon Bar-Jona! For flesh and blood has not revealed this to you, but my Father who is in heaven. And I tell you, you are Peter, and on this rock I will build my church, and the powers of death shall not prevail against it. I will give you the keys of the kingdom of heaven, and whatever you bind on earth shall be bound in heaven, and whatever you loose on earth shall be loosed in heaven. (Matthew 16:17-19, RSV)

In the Aramaic language used by Jesus, the word *kepha* means rock; Jesus gives this name (often written *Cephas* in English) to Simon, as an indication of the role he is to play as the foundation of the Church. This does not conflict with the teaching of St. Paul that Jesus Christ is the sole foundation of the Church (1 Corinthians 3:11), for Peter's role is that of visible representative of Jesus, whence the term *Vicar of Christ on earth* that is now applied to the Pope. Peter is enabled to fulfill this role only by the strength he receives from Jesus, as another text declares:

> Simon, Simon, Satan has asked to sift you [plural] as wheat. But I have prayed for you [singular] that your [singular] faith may not fail. And when you [singular] have turned back, strengthen your brothers. (Luke 22:31; see also John 21:15-17)

St. Paul speaks of all the apostles (and the prophets as well) as foundation stones of the Church, with Christ Jesus the capstone or cornerstone (Ephesians 2:20). The general sense is clear: Jesus has given the apostles, and especially Peter, the role of foundation in the Church as it remains in the world after his departure. So long as the Church stands on this foundation, it will be based on Jesus himself, strengthened and protected by him. A church or part of the Church not built on the foundation stone of Peter will not stand firm, and in fact will not be what Jesus calls "my Church."[14]

Possession of the keys of the kingdom of heaven (Matthew's term for the Kingdom of God) implies the authority to admit people to and exclude them from the Kingdom. The popular image of St. Peter as doorkeeper at the "Pearly Gates" derives from this text. However, Peter does not admit people into heaven but only into the Kingdom as it exists in this world — namely, the Church. Moreover, the keys represent not merely the power to admit members or exclude them but more generally the supreme authority in the Church.

• *Vicar of Christ*

"Binding and loosing" was a Hebraism for holding authority. The text does not specify the nature of this authority; it simply gives the astounding assurance that the decisions made by Peter on earth will be ratified "in heaven," that is, by God himself. This is the fullest statement of what *Vicar of Christ* means. Christ once declared, "All authority in heaven and on earth has been given to me" (Matthew 28:18); here he makes Peter in a sense his plenipotentiary. Peter's authority is limited of course (unlike that of Jesus) to the domain of the Church; but within the Church, his authority is full and supreme.

The early chapters of the Acts of the Apostles give a vivid picture of Peter leading the primitive Christian community. Peter calls for and presides over the choice of Matthias to take the place of Judas (Acts 1); he speaks out on Pentecost Day to explain to the assembled crowd what has happened (2); he heals the lame man at the temple gate (3), and then addresses first the crowd, then the Sanhedrin (4) to explain it. He chastises Ananias and Sapphira for "lying to the Holy Spirit" when they try to deceive him (5). All the apostles witness to the Resurrection with great power (4:33), but it is to Peter particularly that the sick are brought for healing (5:15; 9:32-42). When the apostles are imprisoned, Peter is their chief spokesman, who gives the famous reply, "We must obey God rather than men" (5:29). It is Peter and John who investigate the conversion of the Samaritans and Peter who does all the speaking (8). Peter, inspired by the Holy Spirit, takes the revolutionary step of evangelizing the Gentile Cornelius and baptizing him (10).

The style of Peter's leadership is quite informal, as is to be expected in a small band of Christians instructed by Jesus and filled with his Spirit, but not freighted with the paraphernalia of an ecclesiastical organization for which there is as yet no need. One could not imagine Peter going about vested with miter and crosier! Likewise his mode of action is "collegial." All the apostles and elders together discuss the thorny problem, whether Gentile converts have to be circumcised. Peter's view prevails, with strong support from James, but it is as a group, a "college," that all together make the decision and send to the Church of Antioch the authoritative instructions, "It seemed good to the Holy Spirit and to us not to burden you with anything beyond the following requirements. . ." (Acts 15:28). And when Paul (Galatians 2:11) or others (Acts 11:2) think Peter has done wrong, they do not hesitate to criticize him.

• Primacy of Rome

Like all the other offices and ministries, however, the "Petrine ministry" developed as the Church itself grew. Because it was in Rome that Peter finally fixed his see, the bishops of Rome succeeded him in his role of Church leadership.

We have extremely little information about the details of Church government in the early decades. However, before the end of the first century, the so-called "First Epistle of Clement" witnesses to an intervention by the Church of Rome in the affairs of the Church of Corinth. Other indications that some kind of primacy of Rome was acknowledged by the other churches multiply with the passage of time.

"Whenever Rome does make an appearance she is engaged in this role peculiarly her

own, the role that is never denied her (though her exercise of it is sometimes resisted), the role that no other church even attempts to claim, the role, that is to say, of a general superintendence over all the churches of the Catholic Church."[15]

In the early centuries, the local churches in the various cities were almost completely self-governing, while taking great care, however, to remain in communion with one another and with Rome. Gradually, over the course of centuries, and above all during the Middle Ages when it became necessary to resist the encroachments of secular princes, the papacy assumed a more active role in legislating for all the churches (now called dioceses), and in appointing their bishops. This stronger Roman intervention was not always welcome, and was in part the occasion for the separation of the Orthodox churches (1054) and the Church of England (1531-1535) from Rome. The increased exercise of papal authority was also accompanied by a great development in the governmental structure of the Church. Besides the College of Cardinals, who convene only occasionally (especially for the election of a new pope), there is a large, complex staff of permanent offices in Rome, the Curia, which assists the Pope in the ordinary administration of the Church.

• Supreme pastor

The role of the Holy Father (the term *pope* comes from the late Latin *papa*, "father") is unlike that of any other ruler, secular or religious. In the first place, he is not simply an administrator charged with coordinating the activities of the various local churches, or dioceses. He is himself a pastor. Primarily, he is the Bishop of Rome, and relates to his diocese as does any other bishop. Hence the Orthodox regard him simply as *primus inter pares* ("first among equals"), that is, as having a place of honor but without juridical authority over the other bishops. The Catholic view, however, is that the Bishop of Rome, as successor to St. Peter, has authority over the whole Church. He has authority over the other bishops, and he has direct authority over each and every member of their dioceses.

(That is, his decrees are not directed merely to the local bishops, leaving to them the discretion about how to apply them to the people.) Thus the Pope is not only one of the pastors in the Church, he is the supreme pastor, to whom Jesus says, as he did to Simon Peter, "Feed my lambs . . . feed my sheep" (John 21:15-17). He is not only a personal representative of Christ, as is every bishop, he is the Vicar of Christ, endowed with the fullness of authority in the Church ("Whatever you bind on earth. . ." [Matthew 16:19]). But this authority is not for his personal glory or benefit, it is for the service of the Church, as is all ecclesial authority (2 Corinthians 13:10). Hence the title adopted by the Popes, "Servant of the servants of God." The warm personal devotion of the Catholic people to the Holy Father does not arise from awe at his hierarchical greatness or authority, however, but from the fact that he, more than any other, is the visible, personal representative of Jesus for them. "Christ on earth" is the name by which St. Catherine of Siena habitually referred to him (which did not prevent her from severely scolding the Avignon popes for having deserted Rome).

INFALLIBILITY

Infallibility is not merely or even primarily a papal prerogative. It is in the first instance an attribute of the Church as a whole; secondly, an attribute of the college of bishops; and only in the third instance an attribute of the papal teaching.

Fundamentally, infallibility implies that the Church is not just an association of Christians who do their best to follow their Master but that the Master himself supports and strengthens them in this endeavor, as he promised to do:

> Therefore go and make disciples of all nations . . . teaching them to obey everything I have commanded you. And surely I will be with you always, to the very end of the age. (Matthew 28:19-20)

How he would support them, he indicated at the Last Supper:

> The Paraclete, the Holy Spirit, whom the Father will send in my name, he will teach you all things, and bring to your remembrance all that I have said to you. (John 14:26, RSV alt)
>
> When the Spirit of truth comes, he will guide you into all the truth. (John 16:13)

Thus Jesus promised to remain with his disciples forever, and to give them the Spirit of Truth to preserve them in the truth. What has to be determined is what way and under what conditions this guarantee is operative. The Catholic understanding is that the Holy Spirit is active at the three levels distinguished above. In the first place, he dwells in each Christian, in order, among other things, to incline him toward the truth. This does not make the individual infallible in his beliefs because he can be unfaithful to the promptings of the Spirit or misinterpret them. But when the Church as a whole, that is, with moral unanimity, agrees about a matter of doctrine, this is a sure sign of the Spirit's inspiration. The Lord who gathered his followers into a community, and who wants them to live, act, and think as members of a body,[16] who gave his Spirit for the purpose of safeguarding his truth, will not let error prevail. In other words, the Church is not just a forum of human opinions but a reliable depository of Christ's teaching. It is, as the First Letter to Timothy says, "the pillar and bulwark of the truth" (3:13).

Hence "Church doctrine" does not mean simply the teaching of the bishops. On the contrary, the bishops recognize and respect an "instinct of faith" in the hearts of the faithful. They take very seriously any religious or moral convictions about which their people are in agreement. For example, the fact that Catholics all over the world had accepted belief in the Immaculate Conception was taken by Pius IX as the decisive indication that this was indeed the mind of Christ.

This does not mean that majority vote settles questions of doctrine. "Moral unanimity" is the sign of the Spirit's action. A simple majority or even a plurality on one side of a disputed question, where there are also strong voices on the opposite side, does not constitute moral unanimity. Likewise if one were to imagine a situation in which the majority of the laity believed one thing, while the bishops taught something else, this would not be moral unanimity.

• *Infallibility of the bishops*

The second level of operation of the charism of infallibility is that of the teaching office in the Church, exercised by the bishops. Here infallibility does not require unanimity on the part of the whole Church (it often comes into operation precisely on questions that divide the Church) but only on the part of the bishops. The Church is not a homogeneous community; it has a structure consisting of pastors, who have the office of teacher, and of the general faithful, who are to be led by their pastors. Jesus gave his apostles the commission to teach, and insisted that their teaching was meant to be believed.

> Go into all the world and preach the good news to all creation. Whoever believes and is baptized will be saved; but whoever does not believe will be condemned! (Mark 16:15-16)
>
> If [a man] refuses to listen even to the church, treat him as you would a pagan or a tax collector. (Matthew 18:17)

An individual bishop can err, as many have in fact; and they have been corrected eventually by their fellow bishops or by the Pope. But if the whole college of bishops were to err, there is no way the Church as a whole could be preserved from error. Thus Vatican II declares:

> Although the bishops, taken individually, do not enjoy the privilege of infallibility, they do, however, proclaim infallibly the doctrine of Christ under the following conditions: namely, when, even though dispersed throughout the world but preserving for all that amongst themselves and with Peter's successor the bond of communion, in their authoritative teaching concerning matters of faith and morals, they are in agreement that a particular teaching is to be held definitively and absolutely. This is still

423

more clearly the case when, assembled in an ecumenical council, they are, for the universal Church, teachers of and judges in matters of faith and morals. Their decisions must be adhered to with the loyal and obedient assent of faith.

(Dogmatic Constitution on the Church, no. 25)

• *Papal infallibility*

This unanimous teaching of the bishops is the normal locus of infallible teaching in the Church. However, issues can arise on which the bishops themselves are divided or on which for some reason it is more opportune for the Pope to pronounce on a matter in his own name. This he can do in virtue of his authority as supreme pastor. In so doing, he does not speak as the representative of the bishops, nor need authorization or confirmation from them. By virtue of his own office, as Vicar of Christ, he can make decisions in matters of faith and morals binding on the entire Church.

But not every official pronouncement made by the Pope is infallible. His ordinary teaching and decisions, given, for example, in encyclical letters or public addresses, although bearing the authority of his office, are not infallible. Vatican II carefully defined the conditions under which the charism of infallibility comes into operation for the Pope:

> The Roman Pontiff, head of the college of bishops, enjoys this infallibility in virtue of his office, when, as supreme pastor and teacher of all the faithful — who confirms his brethren in the faith (cf. Lk. 22:32) — he proclaims by a definitive act a doctrine pertaining to faith or morals. For that reason his definitions are rightly said to be irreformable by their very nature and not by reason of the assent of the Church, in as much as they were made with the assistance of the Holy Spirit promised to him in the person of blessed Peter himself; and as a consequence they are in no way in need of the approval of others, and do not admit of appeal to any other tribunal. For in such a case the Roman Pontiff does not utter a pronouncement as a private person, but rather does he expound and defend the teaching of the Catholic faith as the supreme teacher of the universal Church, in whom the Church's charism of infallibility is present in a singular way.

(Dogmatic Constitution on the Church, no. 25)

Papal infallibility is nothing other than the infallibility that resides in the Church as a whole. It is concentrated in the Holy Father by reason of his office as supreme pastor. Thus it is operative only in the exercise of this office: not when he is speaking as a private person, nor when he is speaking for some limited congregation, but only when he addresses the universal Church. Even then it is not infallible unless it has the form of "a definitive act," in other words, one that is final and irrevocably binding. For example, the definition of the dogma of the Immaculate Conception is worded thus:

> ". . .we declare, pronounce and define that the doctrine which holds that . . . Mary . . . was preserved from every stain of original sin has been revealed by God and is therefore to be believed firmly and constantly by all the faithful."[17]

Similar language occurs in the definition of the Assumption.[18]

The Pope's office is solely that of declaring the doctrine of the Church itself. He is not authorized to communicate new revelations, should he have any, or to alter the traditional doctrine of the Church. His infallibility comes into play because of some need either to reaffirm the Church's faith or to clarify its implications in regard to a new issue; in either case, it is *the faith already held by the Church* that he enunciates. On the other hand, every sincere member of the Church adheres to the teaching of the Church in intention, even when he happens to be mistaken or unsure about its implications on a given point. Thus even though some opinion I held was contrary to a doctrine that is later defined, it is still true that by the deepest intention of my faith, which was to accept the teaching of Christ and of the Church, I adhered to the doctrine which, in my conscious mind I rejected. Hence Cardinal Newman could write:

> Nothing, then, can be presented to me, in time to come, as part of the faith, but what I ought already to have received, and hitherto have been kept from receiving (if so), merely because it has not been brought home to me. Nothing can be imposed upon me different in kind from what I hold already, — much less contrary to it. The new truth which is promulgated, if it is to be called new, must be at least homogeneous, cognate, implicit, viewed relatively to the old truth.
>
> (*Apologia pro vita sua*, V, London: Longmans, 1875, p. 253)

And we can be sure that the grace which accompanies every proclamation of the Gospel and every act of the Church helps a person who was of a contrary opinion to recognize that the position to which he was opposed is indeed in accord with the truth to which he was attached.

• *Misconceptions*

Contrary to a widespread misunderstanding, infallibility has nothing to do with the personal life of the Pope but simply with his official teaching. In his personal life, the Bishop of Rome is subject to temptation and liable to sin like any other Christian.[19]

Secondly, infallibility is not a personal endowment of the Pope's, making him wiser or more learned than others or giving him the solution to problems without recourse to the normal means of study and investigation. Infallibility attaches to the *office* of the papacy, and ensures merely that in its most solemn exercise it will never proclaim any falsehood.

There are well-known cases of popes whose personal theological opinions were erroneous but who never imposed these officially on the Church. Thus Pope John XXII (1316-1335) held that the dead will not enter into heaven or hell until the final resurrection; but he did not require that others accept this position (which he himself retracted the day before he died!). Finally, infallibility is no guarantee that the Pope will know the answers to all questions, even in the sphere of faith. Over a period of several centuries, several popes refused to take a stand on the then disputed question of Mary's Immaculate Conception because, as one of them said, "The Holy Spirit has not yet opened to his Church the secrets of this mystery."[20] Later, after a long process of theological and spiritual decanting, the mind of the Church on this matter became so clear and unanimous that Pius IX did not hesitate to define the Immaculate Conception as a dogma of the faith (1854).

• *Authority of infallible teaching*

It is rarely, and only in matters of great importance, that the Church authority makes an infallible pronouncement. The earliest instance was the decision of the apostles and elders not to circumcise the Gentiles (Acts 15). The next was apparently the Council of Nicaea's definition of the divinity of the Son of God (325).[21] Since the definition of papal infallibility in 1870, the only dogmatic definition has been that of the Assumption (1950).

For the greater part of the Church's history, it is often difficult to determine whether a decision was infallible or not because relatively little attention was paid to this point before the nineteenth century. Popes and councils simply issued their decrees without precisely measuring their binding force. This fact itself is significant; what is important is not to have a complete list of infallible decrees but to recognize the principle that they can and do occur.

For the essential point is that the Holy Spirit does dwell in the Church to keep it in the truth; and that he assists the pastors particularly in their role of teaching and directing the faithful. By far the majority of their decisions are not infallible; nevertheless, even these have a sacred authority coming not only from the pastoral office but from the assistance of the Holy Spirit. Infallibility is only the supreme instance of the charism of truth by which the pastors of the Church are supported in the entire exercise of their office. Hence all of their teaching ought to be received with reverence; the fact that a teaching is not infallible does not mean that it is unimportant or not binding. The principle of infallibility functions as a hidden skeleton, giving firmness to the entire activity of the *magisterium.*

While infallible definitions are rare, the infallibility of the Church as a whole is in constant exercise. It is that firmness in the truth by which the Gospel of Jesus Christ continues to be believed, taught, and lived as it was in the beginning, and will be forever. It underlies all the ordinary activity of preaching, catechetics, and theology; even more, it is realized in that great body of doctrine which the members of the Church accept and by which they live. While there is no one act or person in whom this ordinary teaching of the Church may be found fully, adequately, and precisely expressed, and perhaps no one who adheres to it with perfect fidelity — still, in the living reality of the whole Church the teaching is there. Details may often be obscure, but in its main lines it has the solidity and certitude that comes from being held by so many with such diverse points of view. This "mind of the Church" is a reality, though diffuse and hard to finger. It gets its reality as well as its authenticity from the Spirit who enlightens the Church.

Finally, it is for the sake of the people, and not to reinforce the authority of the hierarchy, that the Church has been endowed with the charism of infallibility. Jesus came to bring truth to the world, to enlighten those who, without him, would be in darkness. Because his personal ministry was limited to a single lifetime, he deputed others to carry his message down through time. But it is very difficult for any human society to maintain the teachings of a great teacher in all their purity and authenticity. The higher and finer the doctrine, the more sure it is to be corrupted and distorted in the hands of inept disciples. Yet Jesus came to enlighten not just the original Twelve but all those who, until the end of time, should believe in him. Therefore he did what only he could do: Besides giving his followers the best instruction they were capable of receiving, he imparted his Holy Spirit to guarantee that the Church would always keep his doctrine inviolate for future ages.

28
The things that are to come

The question "What comes after death?" has long been a major human preoccupation. One of the earliest indications of religious belief consists in fossil evidence that the Neanderthals, unlike brute animals, did not leave their dead to rot where they died but buried them with care, and provided them with weapons, ornaments, and even flowers. Ever since, reverence for the dead as well as beliefs and speculation about their fate have played a prominent role in human culture. Only in modern Western civilization, out of a deliberate reaction, have there arisen sporadic efforts to strip funerals of religious ritual and of symbols of belief in an afterlife.

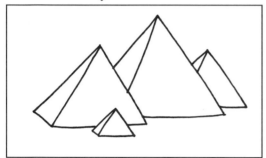

The search for some form of immortality is likewise a perennial human drive. The Taoists, especially in antiquity, were looking for what would prolong their human life as long as possible. It was the search for the "Fountain of Youth" that led Ponce de León to discover Florida. Today, attempts are being made to "freeze" the human body and preserve it for some future age when technology will be able to restore it to life. Some have sought for a kind of vicarious immortality by erecting monuments to themselves (the pyramids of the pharaohs), creating lasting works of art (Horace called poetry a monument more lasting than bronze), or great political structures (even David was promised a dynasty that would hold the throne of Israel forever). Among the early Hebrews, leaving a numerous family to perpetuate one's name was the kind of immortality most yearned for, and which every man could aspire to.

About the future lot of the dead, all the great religions have given answers, mostly vague and confused ones. The religions of India — Hinduism and Buddhism — hold to a series of transmigrations or reincarnations that will continue until one has finally been merged with ultimate reality or else lodged irretrievably at some inferior level of being. The religions of Greece and Rome had myths about the netherworld, a dark, unpleasant realm governed by Pluto. The ideas of the ancient Hebrews were not too different from those of the Greeks and Romans; but shortly before the time of Jesus, belief in a bodily resurrection began to emerge.

Modern secularism has gone directly against the mainstream of human tradition by insisting, on the grounds of alleged scientific reasoning, that nothing remains after death but a disorganized collection of molecules. But the sudden popularity in recent years of works about "life after life" is an indication that the longing for immortality has not been expunged even in our society.

THE KINGDOM FULLY REALIZED

The promise made to Abraham, that from him would arise a great nation in whom all the peoples of earth would be blessed, was elaborated and enriched by the prophets into expectation of the messianic Kingdom. Jesus' central message was that this Kingdom was about to appear. In fact, he himself inaugurated it; his Church is a mysterious beginning of the Kingdom.

If Christians await something further, it is because the Kingdom is not yet fully realized; it exists in a flawed, imperfect condition due to the remnants of sin still present in the world. But Jesus will come again in the glory of the Father, and bring about the complete fulfillment of the promises, the perfect realization of God's Kingdom. The *Parousia*, or Second Coming of the Lord, is not a mythical construct of the primitive community, which an enlightened Christianity can set aside; it is a basic dogma of Christian faith and the proper focal point of Christian hope.

THE ANTICHRIST

Before Christ returns, however, there will be a time of terrible trials for the Church. Seated with his disciples on the Mount of Olives overlooking the Temple, Jesus spoke of the time when not one stone would be left on another:

> . . .those will be days of distress unequaled from the beginning, when God created the world, until now — and never to be equaled again. If the Lord had not cut short those days, no one would survive. But for the sake of the elect, whom he has chosen, he has shortened them. (Mark 13:19f; see also Matthew 24:21f; Luke 21:23f)

It is not easy to interpret this Last Discourse, recorded by all three Synoptics, in which the fall of Jerusalem seems to be taken as a figure of the "end of the age," and described partly in images taken from Israel's past. It is clear, however, that the tribulation will be due in part to false Christs and false prophets, attempting, by means of signs and wonders, to lead people astray (Matthew 24:5, 23f; Mark 13:6, 22; Luke 21:8).

This same theme reappears in the Apocalypse, in symbols derived from the Book of Daniel. A hideous beast, empowered by Satan, will succeed in having himself worshiped by all the inhabitants of the earth except for those whose name is written in the Book of Life. He will make war against the disciples of Jesus and conquer them. In this, he will be seconded by another beast, whose number is 666 (Apocalypse 13). In the end, they will be overcome by the Lamb who is Lord of lords and King of kings (Apocalypse 16:14).

St. Paul apparently refers to the same theme when, speaking about the Day of the Lord, he says:

> . . .that day will not come until the rebellion [literally, "apostasy"] occurs and the man of lawlessness is revealed, the man doomed to destruction. He opposes and exalts himself over everything that is called God or is worshiped, and even sets himself up in God's temple, proclaiming himself to be God. (2 Thessalonians 2:3f)

Paul had already spoken about this matter to the Thessalonians, and takes for granted that they know what he means; hence he does not explain it for us. He goes on to say:

> . . .you know what is holding him back, so that he may be revealed at the proper time. For the secret power of lawlessness is already at work, but the one who now holds it back will continue to do so till he is taken out of the way. And then the lawless will be revealed, whom the Lord Jesus will overthrow with the breath of his mouth and destroy by the splendor of his coming. The coming of the lawless one will be in accordance with the work of Satan displayed in all kinds of counterfeit miracles, signs and wonders, and in every sort of evil that deceives those who are perishing. (2 Thessalonians 2:6-10)

What St. Paul calls "the lawless one" is apparently to be identified with what St. John calls the Antichrist (1 John 2:18, 22; 4:3; 2 John 7). Theologians debate whether the Antichrist should be understood as an individual person or as a figurative personification of the forces of evil. The individualist interpretation has predominated in the past, and perhaps still does today (although little attention is given to this whole topic in modern times). The Church has never given an official interpretation of this point.

THE PAROUSIA[1]

The "coming of the Son of Man" was equivalent to the establishment of the Kingdom of God in Daniel 7, and these notions are often used interchangeably in the Gospel accounts of Jesus' preaching. Hence the crowds, in the measure they regarded Jesus as the Messiah, expected the Kingdom to be established soon (see Luke 19:11). When he died without setting up a throne, they were thrown into consternation (Luke 24:21). And once the horrors of the crucifixion had been nullified by the marvel of the Resurrection, the disciples' expectations again revived, so that they asked, "Lord, are you at this time going to restore the kingdom to Israel?" (Acts 1:6). In truth, the coming of Christ is equivalent to the establishment of the Kingdom; however, after his first coming, the Lord had to return to the Father. Only his second coming will bring the Kingdom to its full realization.

The circumstances of the Lord's return are described in great detail in Jesus' discourse on the Mount of Olives, especially as reported in Matthew:

> . . .the sun will be darkened, and the moon will not give its light; the stars will fall from the sky, and the heavenly bodies will be shaken. At that time the sign of the Son of Man will appear in the sky, and all the nations of the earth will mourn. They will see the Son of Man coming on the clouds of the sky, with power and great glory. (24:29f)

Many dismiss this apocalyptic language as purely figurative and symbolic; be that as it may, it is striking that when Jesus ascended, finally disappearing from sight into the clouds, the angels who appeared and sent the disciples back into the city declared, "This

same Jesus, who has been taken up from you into heaven, will come back in the same way you have seen him go into heaven" (Acts 1:11). Even if one supposes all this to be figurative, it is clear that, whereas Jesus' first glorification took place quietly, before the eyes of the apostles alone, his return will be manifested before all the world, like lightning which "comes from the east and flashes to the west" (Matthew 24:27). *Now* his lordship can be recognized only by faith; but *then* there will be no ignoring it.

THE RESURRECTION

It comes as a surprise to many Christians to learn that Jesus does not have a doctrine on the immortality of the soul (although one can be derived from his teaching). He affirmed *the resurrection of the body*; this will take place at the end of time when the Son of Man returns in glory. "All who are in their graves will hear his voice and come out — those who have done good will rise to live, and those who have done evil will rise to be condemned" (John 5:28f). Hence St. Paul declares: "He who raised the Lord Jesus from the dead will also raise us with Jesus. . ." (2 Corinthians 4:14; see also 1 Thessalonians 4:16; John 5:29; etc.). Resurrection does not denote some wispy continuation of existence in a spiritualized form but the return of the body to life: "He who raised Christ from the dead will also give life to your mortal bodies" (Romans 8:11). The Apostles' Creed likewise affirms "the resurrection of the body."

The first Christians, expecting the imminent return of the Lord, did not concern themselves much with the present state of the departed. St. Paul had assured them that, at Christ's return, those who have died in Christ will rise first, and go to meet the Lord ahead of those that have not died (1 Thessalonians 4:16); what their state was in the meanwhile hardly mattered.

But as time went on and the Lord delayed his coming, the state of the departed became a topic of greater concern. Thus the immortality of the soul, a belief latent in the New Testament but prominent in Hellenistic philosophy, came to be insisted on, while the resurrection of the body drifted into the background. An excessive spiritualism that has led many Christians to identify the soul with the person, and to regard the body as a prison and an obstacle to holiness, encouraged this development. Finally, the rise of modern materialism obliged Christianity to maintain all the more energetically the spirituality and immortality of the soul. The essential "body-liness" of the human person is being rediscovered by modern philosophy; nevertheless, many Christians are still surprised and even embarrassed at belief in the bodily resurrection, and are inclined to seek some spiritualized reinterpretation of it.

Yet Scripture is plain-spoken not only in affirming bodily resurrection but also in in-

The raising of Lazarus.

sisting that the resurrection is a fundamental article of faith:

> . . .how can some of you say that there is no resurrection of the dead? If there is no resurrection of the dead, then not even Christ has been raised. And if Christ has not been raised, our preaching is useless and so is your faith. . . . For if the dead are not raised, then Christ has not been raised either. And if Christ has not been raised, your faith is futile; you are still in your sins. Then those also who have fallen asleep in Christ are lost. . . . But Christ has indeed been raised from the dead, the first fruits of those who have fallen asleep. (1 Corinthians 15:12-20)

END OF THE WORLD?

In what sort of setting will the resurrected pursue their future life? The Apocalypse (21:1) speaks of "new heavens and a new earth," but this can be understood either in the sense that the present world will be replaced by an entirely different one or that it will be profoundly renewed while remaining itself. Both of these interpretations are supported elsewhere in the New Testament. The first is in the Second Letter of Peter:

> The day of the Lord will come like a thief. The heavens will disappear with a roar, the elements will be destroyed by fire, and the earth and everything in it will be laid bare. . . . That day will bring about the destruction of the heavens by fire, and the elements will melt in the heat. But in keeping with his promise we are looking forward to a new heaven and a new earth, the home of righteousness. (3:10-13; see also Apocalypse 21:1)

This view has dominated popular Christian thought in the past, leading people to speak of the "end of the world" (a term which may have arisen due to a slight mistranslation of Matthew 24:3). On the other hand, however, St. Paul says:

> The creation waits in eager expectation for the sons of God to be revealed. For . . . creation itself will be liberated from its bondage to decay and brought into the glorious freedom of the children of God. (Romans 8:19-21)

This seems to imply the preservation and transformation of the present world. Modern theology generally seems inclined to favor a transformational eschatology; how-

432

ever, the language in which all these matters are presented in Scripture is so full of images that it is difficult to reach a decisive answer.

THE KINGDOM TO COME

It is likewise not easy to form an idea of the reward awaiting the faithful disciples of Jesus. "No eye has seen, no ear has heard, no mind has conceived what God has prepared for those who love him" (1 Corinthians 2:9). Jesus urged people to get ready for the Kingdom of God but did not elaborate on what life would be like in it. However, the term itself recalls all that the prophets had said about the perfect Kingdom that would be established by the Messiah, in which there would be no more suffering, no more injustice, but perfect peace and prosperity.

The Apocalypse (Book of Revelation) furnishes the richest depiction of the blessed life to come. Instead of "kingdom," the dominant image used is that of "the holy city, the new Jerusalem," in which God will dwell with men. There is no night there, and no need of the sun or of lamps to give light, "for the Lord God will give them light" (22:5).

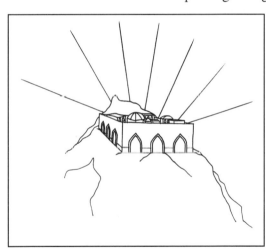

Likewise there is no temple in this city "because the Lord God and the Lamb are its temple" (21:22). God sits enthroned at the center of this city (22:1), surrounded by a throng of people singing his praises (4-7), while the "Lamb who was slain" stands before the throne sharing in the glory (5:6ff). There is perfect happiness: God "will wipe every tear from their eyes. There will be no more death or mourning or crying or pain, for the old order of things has passed away" (21:4).

The source of this blessedness is God himself: "Now the dwelling of God is with men, and he will live with them. They will be his people, and God himself will be with them and be their God" (21:3). This presence of God transforms and, in a sense, divinizes the creature: "Now we are children of God, and what we will be has not yet been made known. But we know that when he appears, we shall be like him, for we shall see him as he is" (1 John 3:2). The godlikeness established in this life by grace will then be perfect and complete.

• *Vision of God*

The principal factor will consist in our seeing God "face to face" (1 Corinthians 13:12) — something Moses yearned for but could not receive in this life (Exodus 33:18ff). At present we know God only "in a mirror dimly" (1 Corinthians 13:12, RSV), for all creatures are a reflection of him; but no creature can give an adequate idea of God. On the other hand, to know God in himself, without the intermediary of creatures, is absolutely beyond the natural power of any created intelligence. Not only human beings but even the angels, and for that matter the highest conceivable creature, all require a supernatural enlightenment to be able to "see" God directly. To see God as he is in himself belongs properly to God alone; for a creature it involves a participation in the divine life. This is the supreme realization of the life of children of God. The sharing in the divine nature that is begun on earth by grace comes to its full actualization in the vision of God in heaven.

The vision of God and union with him (which are one and the same thing) are enough to satisfy superabundantly all the longing of the human soul (hence the term *beatific vision*). The deepest desire of the human heart is for God; in fact, every desire of every creature is ultimately a desire for God. Whatever good attracts us in any object of our desire is only a reflection of the infinite Divine Good. But whereas animals, plants, etc., are not capable of the Divine Good in itself but only of those created goods that fulfill the needs of their nature, man has the unique ability to look beyond limited and particular goods to goodness as such, and to the One Good that embraces all values. For this reason, human beings alone, out of all material creation, are capable of receiving the communication of God. In what sense we naturally long for such a consummation is a delicate question, debated by theologians. But it is beyond debate that union with God in the beatific vision so fills and satiates a person that it leaves nothing to be desired; rather, it exceeds all expectations.

Although it is only by the spiritual faculties of our soul and not with bodily eyes that we will "see God," the resurrected body will share in the happiness filling the soul. It will be the happiness of a complete human being, not just that of a spirit. The body too will be transformed by the divine life that fills the human being. St. Paul insists that the condition of the risen body will be very different from the way we are now (1 Corinthians 15:35-37). It will be *imperishable*, no longer subject to sickness, suffering, or death. Instead of the weakness and "lowliness" under which it now labors, it will have power and glory (see Philippians 3:12). It will be a "spiritual body," which does not mean immaterial but transformed by the power of the Spirit. The splendor of Jesus' body at the Transfiguration (Matthew 17:1-8; Mark 9:2-8; Luke 9:28-35) gives us some notion of what our glorified bodies may be like.

Even though the happiness of heaven consists essentially in the vision of God, we will enjoy one another's company also. Heaven should not be imagined as a kind of drive-in cinema where all are engrossed in the same movie but each in his own automobile, cut off from the others. It will be like a kingdom, a city, or a home (John 14:2). People will be singing the praises of God together in concert (Apocalypse 5:9-14, etc.) and apparently even dancing (Apocalypse 4:10, 5:8, 5:14). Man is a social being, and the social aspects of his being, like all the rest, will attain their fulfillment and perfection in heaven. Since death will no longer occur, but life will be eternal, there will be no need for further reproduction of the species. "At the resurrection people will neither marry nor be given in marriage; they will be like the angels in heaven," Jesus declared to the skeptical Sadducees (Matthew 22:30; Mark 12:25; Luke 20:35). But there will be friendship and communion; love will have an intensity, purity, and serenity unknown on earth.

THE SAINTS NOW

St. Paul gave some hint about the present condition of the departed when he expressed the desire "to depart and to be with Christ" — a condition far better than "living in the body" (Philippians 1:22f; see also 1 Corinthians 5:1-9). This implies that the faithful departed are already with Christ, even though their bodies have not yet been raised. Similarly, in one of the apocalyptic visions of heaven, the seer perceives "under the altar the souls of those who had been slain because of the word of God. . ." (Apocalypse 6:9).

In line with these teachings, Christians began very early both to pray for the departed and to invoke their intercession. Evidence for this is found on tombstones from the first centuries. Long before a theology of the future life had begun to develop, the inscriptions carved on these stones expressed the spontaneous conviction of the Christian people that they had not lost touch completely with their loved ones.

• *The meaning of "saint"*

In the present language of the Church, those who have passed from this life into the next, and now enjoy the vision of God in eternal life, are called saints. It is true of course that St. Paul sometimes addresses all of his readers, that is, the faithful of this world, as saints (2 Corinthians 1:1; Philippians 1:1; Ephesians 1:1), for they have been consecrated to God by baptism, and sanctified by the presence of the Holy Spirit. However, we ordinarily do not know for sure about any individual person whether he is living in the state of grace or not; and in any case, even those who are now actually holy may some day lose their grace by sinning. St. Paul himself was concerned lest, after preaching salvation to others, he himself should be lost (1 Corinthians 9:2). Hence, sometimes instead of calling his readers saints, he used what may have been a more cautious expression, "called to be saints" (Romans 1:1; 1 Corinthians 1:2). In any case, such a usage has prevailed in the Church, in that the term *saint* is ordinarily reserved for those who have completed their time of trial on this earth and have entered into glory.

By and large, we do not know who they are; although, if a person seems to have led a good life, it is normal to presume that he or she is either in heaven or safely on the way through purgatory. From time to time, someone's holiness is so evident that the Church will, after careful investigation, "canonize" him or her as a saint. This is in effect an affirmation that the person is surely in heaven, and deserves to be venerated and invoked.

Such a judgment is not based solely on the way the person lived but also on signs that he is actually in heaven — namely, miracles worked through the saint's intercession. Before they are accepted as grounds for canonization, it must be demonstrated beyond all reasonable doubt that they are indeed miraculous, that is, impossible of explanation by any natural process; and that they came about in answer to prayer directed to the saint in question. As these points are exceedingly difficult to establish, canonization usually takes a long time and is quite difficult to achieve. On the other hand, the process has this benefit, that the miracles approved by the Congregation for the Causes of Saints are some of the most certain examples of miracles that we have.

• *Veneration of the saints*

Veneration of the saints is one of the grounds on which the Catholic Church has been most attacked; hence we must examine it carefully. What is most important for understanding it is that it be situated in the Catholic vision of the Church as the Body of Christ

— a living body in which all the members are in communion with one another; an organic body in which the members collaborate with one another for the good of all.

That being granted, the Church holds that those who have parted from this life, whether they are in heaven or in purgatory, have not been cut off from the Church but remain in living communion with their fellows on earth through Christ, the head, and through the Holy Spirit. In fact, it is the saints in heaven who are most fully and deeply anchored in the Church. Membership in Christ's Body attains its perfection when a person is joined with the head in glory.

The Letter to the Hebrews manifests this sense of our community with the saints in heaven and, moreover, witnesses to the beginning of veneration of the saints in the early Church. In order to encourage some Jewish Christians who were under pressure to abandon their Christian faith and revert to Judaism, it gives a long litany of the saints of the Old Testament — those justified by faith before the coming of Christ: Abel, Abraham, Isaac, Jacob, Moses, and innumerable others (Chapter 11). The author concludes, "since we are surrounded by such a great cloud of witnesses, . . . let us run with perseverance the race marked out for us. Let us fix our eyes on Jesus, the author and perfecter of our faith. . ." (Hebrews 12:1f). Note that this great cloud of witnesses encourages us to persevere in the race but does not take our eyes off Jesus.

The letter goes on to proclaim:

> You have come to Mount Zion, to the heavenly Jerusalem, the city of the living God. You have come to thousands upon thousands of angels in joyful assembly, to the church of the first-born, whose names are written in heaven. You have come to God, the judge of all men, to the spirits of righteous men made perfect, to Jesus, the mediator of a new covenant. . . . (12:22-24)

This text is pervaded with a sense of the fellowship that those still struggling in this life enjoy with both the angels and saints ("the spirits of righteous men made perfect"). And here again it is evident that this joyful assembly in no way detracts from the status of Jesus as unique mediator.

Veneration of the saints comprises three factors: (1) honoring them for the life they have led; (2) taking them as models for our own life; and (3) asking them to intercede with God on our behalf.

About the second point, imitation of their virtues, there can hardly be a problem. It is well attested in Scripture, especially in the Letter to the Hebrews: "Imitate those who through faith and patience inherit what has been promised" (6:12; see also 1 Thessalonians 2:14). "Remember your leaders who spoke the word of God to you. Consider the outcome of their way of life and imitate their faith" (Hebrews 12:7).

The paying of honor to the saints is not much attested in the New Testament, for an obvious reason. It was the New Testament teaching about eternal life and about the Church as the Body of Christ that gave chief impetus to this practice; but it took time for the implications of these beliefs to be drawn out and given liturgical expression. Nevertheless, the texts of Hebrews cited above are already pregnant with an atmosphere of veneration.

The virtues of the saints deserve to be honored by the rest of the Church just as much as, in fact far more than, the achievements of heroes, scientists, or artists. Not that the saints seek honor or are even gratified by it; true saints seek nothing but "the glory that comes from the only God" (John 5:44). But it is right and healthy for us to give "honor where honor is due" (Romans 13:7); it helps us establish a right standard of values, and encourages us to imitate the saints. Jesus once said, "My Father will honor the one who serves me" (John 12:26); surely those honored by the Father should be honored by us likewise.

The honor given to the saints is religious but not idolatrous. The virtues we honor in them are due to the grace of God, and are like palpable earthly reflections of the unspeakable holiness of the divinity. Therefore the veneration of the saints is ultimately referred to God, and is of a different order from that paid to God. Technical theological language (derived from the Greek) speaks of the honor paid to God as *latria* and that paid to the saints as *dulia*. In contemporary English, we speak of worshiping or adoring God, but we do not use such language of the saints.[2]

People accustomed to honor no one but God are understandably inclined, when they encounter the veneration of the saints, to sense it as idolatrous. This is the case of many Protestants. It is not just that intellectually they may be unaware of the distinction Catholics make between the two degrees of veneration; more importantly, their religious sentiments have been habituated to revolt against whatever bears any semblance of idolatry. For them to accept the Catholic practice of honoring the saints requires not only an intellectual conversion but a reeducation of their religious sentiments.

• *Intercession*

It is above all the intercession of the saints that is controverted. It is Catholic belief that, just as we intercede for one another in this life, so the saints in heaven intercede for us. Knowing our needs and our requests, they can act as spokespersons for us before the Lord. Such intercession pertains to the life of all of the People of God, to which they still belong.

God does not need the saints to inform him about us or direct his attention to us; rather, it is from him that they learn about us. Neither should we imagine that they are somehow more compassionate toward us than God is; all their love and mercy is nothing but a tiny, weak derivative of his. Yet Christ has gathered his followers into a community in which we depend on one another and assist one another not only physically but also spiritually. This community is not sundered by death. The faithful departed remain in living communion with us just as truly as when they were living on earth.

Actually, the question about the sense of intercession does not pertain particularly to the saints; the same problem exists concerning the prayers we make here below: God does not need them in order to be moved to help someone. But it is clear and certain that he wants us to intercede for one another. St. Paul frequently prays for his readers and asks for their prayers.

437

There is a striking biblical instance of God himself calling for the prayers of a saint in the story of Abraham's encounter with King Abimelech in Genesis 20. The king had wrongfully, though unwittingly, taken Abraham's wife Sarah. God spoke to the king in a dream, telling him to restore Sarah to Abraham, and adding, "for he is a prophet, and he will pray for you and you will live." Abraham was not yet of course a saint in heaven; however, if it is right for the saints on earth to pray for us, those in heaven can do so with still greater effectiveness, since their wills are now perfectly conformed to the divine will.

The intercession of the saints supposes that the saint is aware of what is going on here below, in particular of our prayers and needs, and that he or she is in a position to intercede for us. Obviously, the kind of natural communication that we have in this world is no longer possible with those who have died. Having no bodies as yet, and therefore no senses, those who are now in eternal life cannot see or hear us directly. (There are indeed well-authenticated stories of the departed appearing to people in this world, either to ask for prayers or to give aid and encouragement — for example, the saints who appeared to Joan of Arc. But these are exceptional and suppose that the separated soul assumes *the appearance* of a human body in order to manifest itself.)

It is in and by their vision of God that the saints perceive whatever God wills to make known to them about those they have known on earth or those who invoke them, for their happiness consists not merely in seeing God but in knowing all that it is becoming for them to know.

• *Images and relics*

It is especially when honor is shown to the relics or images of the saints that some people have the impression of idolatry. The use of *images* was forbidden in the Old Testament because of the proneness of those simple people to worship images as idols. In modern culture, abounding with images of all sorts, this is no longer so pressing a danger. And images are useful to help us keep Jesus, Mary, and the saints in mind; but it is the *persons* that are venerated, not the images in themselves. *Relics* come directly or indirectly from the body of the saint, which in life was an exceptionally holy member of the Body of Christ. Even though the soul has departed from them, they provide a very human contact with the person (touch is the sense of closest contact). And it has been the rich experience of the Church that God often uses relics as instruments of his power. It is God who does the healing; but just as he healed the sick by means of cloths touched by St. Paul (Acts 19:12) and even by the mere shadow of St. Peter (Acts 5:15); as he raised the dead by the bones of the prophet Elisha (2 Kings 13:21), he continues to do likewise today by the relics of the saints.

Finally, it must be repeated that the role attributed to the saints and the honor shown them do not in any way detract from the place of Christ. He is the unique head of the Church, which is his Body; all the virtue as well as all the efficacy of the members derives from him. But he has willed to associate his members actively with himself in the work of salvation, and he lets them share in the reflected light of his glory.

JUDGMENT

People are admitted into heaven as a reward for a good life, just as those who go to hell are being punished for the evil they have done. In other words, a person's condition in the next life is a recompense he has *merited* by his life in this world. We have already examined the sense in which merit is understood in Catholic theology (Chapter 21). It does not imply that we have a claim on God but that God rewards and punishes us according to the degree we have obeyed or disobeyed his will. It is an exercise of the justice of God, giving his creatures a recompense proportionate to their life on earth. He does not exalt some and reject others arbitrarily but *judges* them according to their deeds (1 Peter 1:17; etc.). The notion of God as judge of the whole earth appears very early in the Book of Genesis (18:25) and is maintained throughout the New Testament, with this modification, that God has given over the judgment to his Son (John 5:22, 27; 2 Timothy 4:1; etc.)

It is illustrated by one of the most famous of Jesus' parables:

> When the Son of Man comes in his glory, and all the angels with him, he will sit on his throne in heavenly glory. All the nations will be gathered before him, and he will separate the people one from another as a shepherd separates the sheep from the goats. [To one group he will say:] Come, you who are blessed by my Father; take your inheritance, the kingdom prepared for you since the creation of the world. [To the others:] Depart from me, you who are cursed, into the eternal fire prepared for the devil and his angels. (Matthew 25:31-41)

Whether this and kindred statements imply a moment when all mankind will be assembled together to receive publicly the judgment of God, as is usually pictured in what is called the General Judgment, is not important to determine. But what cannot be eliminated from such texts is the message that all will be judged according to their works, and requited accordingly.

HELL

We would like to believe that all human beings eventually enter the Kingdom of God. But the teaching of Jesus is plain and emphatic that this is reserved for those who believe in him (Chapter 20) and do the will of the heavenly Father; correspondingly, there is a hell for unbelievers and those who fail to do the Father's will. Jesus represents hell by various images. It is a prison and torture chamber (Matthew 5:25f). It is like being "thrown outside, into the darkness, where there will be weeping and gnashing of teeth" (Matthew 8:12, 13:42; see also 22:13, 25:30). It is a pit into which bodies are thrown (Matthew 5:29f; 18:9; Mark 9:45, 47; Luke 12:5), a place of fire (Matthew 3:10, 12; 5:22; 7:19; 18:9; Mark 9:43, 48f; Luke 3:9, 17). Apocalypse speaks of a "lake of fire" (20:14f), and Matthew describes a place where "both body and soul are destroyed" (10:28).

Gehenna was originally the name of a valley just outside Jerusalem, where human sacrifice had once been practiced by the Canaanites. Out of abhorrence for the place, the Jews burned refuse there, along with the bodies of dead animals and criminals. Hence it came to symbolize the final destiny of the wicked, which explains why Jesus speaks of hell as a place where "their worm does not die and the fire is not quenched" (Mark 9:48 = Isaiah 66:24).

Fire is one of the chief biblical images for the way God's enemies will be destroyed. Whether it is merely symbolic or whether hell involves real fire is debated; Catholic tradition tends to favor realism. The children of Fátima had a vision of hell which Lucia described thus:

> We saw a sea of fire. Plunged in this fire were demons and souls that looked like transparent embers, some black or bronze, in human form, driven about by the flames that issued from within themselves together with clouds of smoke. They were falling on all sides, just as sparks cascade from great fires, without weight or equilibrium, amid cries of pain and despair which horrified us so that we trembled with fear. . . . The demons could be distinguished by their likeness to terrible, loathsome and unknown animals, transparent as live coals.[3]

Whatever be the case about the fire, the chief suffering of hell consists in the deprivation of the vision of God. Far more than burning or other physical torments, the emptiness and utter frustration of one destined for union with God, and thirsting for this consummation with all the energy of his being, but definitively deprived of it, constitutes his supreme anguish.

Hell never comes to an end; no one is released from it. Jesus speaks of "eternal fire" (Matthew 3:10, 7:19, 18:8, 24:41, etc.) or "unquenchable fire" (Mark 9:43, 48) as well as the worm that "does not die" (Mark 9:48). St. Paul declares that the impious will be punished with eternal destruction (1 Thessalonians 1:9). The Apocalypse says, "They will be tormented day and night forever" (20:10).

The eternity of hell has troubled minds from the earliest ages of Christianity. Origen (c. 185-c. 254), one of the most brilliant thinkers in the history of the Church, conjectured that, after a certain period of punishment, all the damned would eventually be united with God. However, this idea was rejected throughout the Church, which has repeatedly affirmed the eternity of the final punishment.[4]

Many find it difficult to comprehend how any wrong done by a person in the limited span and confused circumstances of earthly life can deserve an eternity of punishment. But the gravity of sin is not measured by the damage it wreaks. In the actual situation of our grace-encompassed existence, sin is a rejection of God's love. Hence it is not God who banishes the sinner from his presence; rather, it is the sinner who refuses the divine embrace. God's merciful love pursues us unflaggingly to the end, like the Good Shepherd seeking the sheep that has strayed (Matthew 18:12f). Even in human society, there are people who, out of fear of entering into a love-relationship, imprison themselves in loneliness from which no one can deliver them. Similarly, the damned are cut off from God by their rejection of him, not his rejection of them.

We must likewise bear in mind that it is difficult for any of us fully to appreciate the evil of an offense against God because our sense of God has been dulled by sin. But faith in the justice of God assures us that there is no injustice in the way he punishes. If sin deserves hell, it must be more odious than we imagine.

• *Does anyone really go to hell?*

It is sometimes said, "We have to believe that hell exists, but not that anyone has actually gone there." This seems to be a strategy for avoiding effective belief in hell, rather than a sincere effort to follow the teaching of Jesus. He said, ". . .wide is the gate and broad is the road that leads to destruction, and many enter through it. But small is the gate 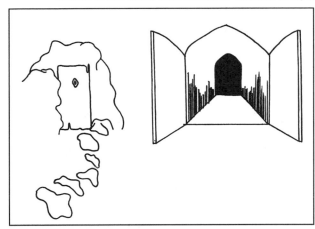 and narrow the road that leads to life, and only a few find it" (Matthew 7:13f). When someone asked him, "Lord, are only a few people going to be saved?" he replied, "Make every effort to enter through the narrow door, because many, I tell you, will try to enter and will not be able." He concluded, "There will be weeping there, and gnashing of teeth, when you see Abraham, Isaac and Jacob and all the prophets in the kingdom of God, but you yourselves thrown out" (Luke 13:23-30). Of Judas in particular, Jesus said, "It would have been better for him if he had not been born" (Matthew 26:24), which makes sense only on the supposition that Judas went to hell. At Fátima and elsewhere, Mary had said that many souls go to hell.[5] This accords with the teaching of Christ much better than the presumption that no one goes there.

• *No reincarnation*

The Christian doctrine of heaven and hell is absolutely incompatible with the Hindu belief in reincarnation. In both systems, the person undergoes a kind of judgment at the end of his life, which determines his future lot. Likewise both envisage an ultimate state which will consist either of happiness or of misery, which can no longer be altered. But in reincarnation, there is a series of trial lives, and how one behaves in his present life does not determine his ultimate destiny but only the conditions of his forthcoming incarnation. The Christian view is expressed in the Letter to the Hebrews:

> Just as man is destined to die once, and after that to face judgment, so Christ was
> sacrificed once to take away the sins of many people; and he will appear a second time
> . . . to bring salvation to those who are waiting for him. (11:27f)

Reincarnation is not just a harmless opinion; it minimizes the seriousness of this present life by holding out the possibility of future existences in which one can make up for present mistakes. In Christ's teaching, a sinner is always free to repent and turn back to God; but he must do so in this life, after which there will be no other opportunity.

PURGATORY

Those who die in grace are not all fit to enter immediately into union with the all-holy God. Some need to be purified. Purgatory designates the process of purification ("purging") which they undergo to prepare them for the beatific vision. It is primarily a process, not a place (if it is also a place, as is popularly believed, this itself would pertain to its penal character; for a pure spirit would be afflicted at being confined to a material place).

• *Not in Scripture?*

The objection is often made that purgatory is not mentioned in Scripture. This is true only of the word itself; Scripture speaks frequently of the *purification* which God's people will have to undergo. Purgatory is nothing other than the final phase of this purification.

Scripture affirms emphatically that nothing unholy or unclean can enter the presence of the thrice-holy God (see, for example, Isaiah 6:5; 38:8; 52:1, 11; etc.). This was inculcated also by many "visual lessons." For example, the Hebrew people were forbidden to go up on Mt. Sinai when God was manifesting himself to Moses (Exodus 19). Moses himself was told that he could not look upon the face of God and live (Exodus 33:23; see also 1 Kings 19:13; 2 Samuel 6:7). When Isaiah had a vision of Yahweh, he cried, "Woe to me, I am ruined! For I am a man of unclean lips, and I live among a people of unclean lips, and my eyes have seen the King, Yahweh the Almighty." Then a seraph touched his mouth with a burning coal and declared, "See, . . . your guilt is taken away and your sin atoned for" (Isaiah 6:1-7). The implications of these parabolic actions were summed up in the commandment "You must be holy, because I the Lord your God am holy" (Leviticus 11:44; 19:2), which the New Testament restates: "Be perfect, as your heavenly Father is perfect" (Matthew 5:48).

Moreover, the Kingdom which God promised to establish for his people was described as a perfect society, from which all evil would be banished, and into which no evildoer would be admitted (Isaiah 9:7; 11:6-9; 41:18-20; 51:6, 8; 54:11-14; 60:17-21; 65:17-25; etc.).

Thus there is no doctrine more evident or emphatic than God's demand that his people be holy and righteous. But if, in fact, they do not live up to this demand, what will he do? The principal answer of Scripture is that God will punish the unrighteous and cast them out of his Kingdom, preserving only the tiny remnant of those who have been faithful. But subordinate to that answer is a minor theme that *God is going to purify his people* and so make them worthy of their bond with him. Thus Yahweh declares: "I will thoroughly purge away your dross and remove your impurities" (Isaiah 1:25). Fire was the favorite symbol for this purifying action; it was not only an agent of destruction but also a means of purification. Yahweh himself, a "jealous God," was like "a consuming fire" (Deuteronomy 4:24; 9:3; Isaiah 33:14), and he promised not only to destroy the wicked but also to purify the faithful:

> In the whole land, two-thirds will be struck down and perish; yet one-third will be left in it. This third I will bring into the fire; I will refine them like silver and test them like gold. (Zechariah 13:8f; see also Isaiah 1:25, 4:5; Daniel 12:10; Zephaniah 3:1-13)

The smelter purifying gold and silver in his furnace was a common figure of Yahweh purifying his people (Ezekiel 22:20ff; Malachi 3:2f; see also 1 Peter 1:7).

John the Baptist spoke of the One who was to come after him, winnowing the harvest, gathering the wheat into barns, and burning the chaff with unquenchable fire (Luke 3:17). This can be understood not only of the judgment separating the evildoers from the righteous but also of the sifting out of good and bad elements in the individual person. In any case, Jesus spoke plainly when he said both that the fruitless branches would be cut down and burned and that those which bore fruit would be cleansed or purified in order that they might become still more fruitful (John 15:1-6). Finally St. Paul spoke of a fire that will test each man's work:

> No one can lay any foundation other than the one already laid, which is Jesus Christ. If any man builds on this foundation using gold, silver, costly stones, wood, hay or straw, his work will be shown for what it is, because the Day will bring it to light. It will be revealed with fire, and the fire will test the quality of each man's work. If what he has built survives, he will receive his reward. If it is burned up, he will suffer loss; he himself will be saved, but only as one escaping through the flames. (1 Corinthians 3:11-15)

Paul is speaking explicitly of people who are saved, and who have built on the foundation of Jesus Christ. Still fire will discriminate among their works, some of which will survive to be rewarded, while others are consumed. This is the key text for the doctrine of purgatory, but its full significance does not appear until it is read against the background of the other texts about the fire from God that both destroys the wicked and purifies the good.

• *Purification in this life*

St. Paul speaks also of a purification affecting the Church as a whole:

> . . .Christ loved the Church and gave himself up for her to make her holy, cleansing her by the washing with water through the word, to present her to himself as a radiant Church, without stain or wrinkle or any other blemish, but holy and blameless. (Ephesians 5:25-27)

Although the purifying effect of baptism and the Word of God are directly in view here, it hardly needs to be argued that the Church as it actually exists in the world is not yet free from blemishes; hence that its purification still needs to be completed.

The hardships endured by Christians in this life are a part of their continuing process of purification. The First Letter of Peter tells us that they are meant to prove the genuineness of our faith, "like gold tested in the fire" (1:6f). The Letter to the Hebrews uses the metaphor of a father disciplining his children:

> Endure hardship as discipline; God is treating you as sons. For what son is not disciplined by his father? . . . God disciplines us for our good, that we may share in his holiness. (12:7-10)

• *The "Purgative Way"*

The status of the faithful departed was hardly raised in the early Church, as we have seen. Spiritual masters quickly recognized, however, that purification was one of the basic requirements for spiritual growth. They named the first phase of this growth — that in which the majority of Christians find themselves — the "Purgative Way," in contrast with the "Illuminative" and "Unitive" ways of those who are more advanced. Purgatory is only the final step along this way for those who have not been adequately purified in this life. Other doctrines also, such as the distinction between venial and mortal sin, had to be clarified before the notion of purgatory could be rightly understood. It finally came to be proposed in the twelfth century,[6] and was promptly recognized as the logical application of the biblical doctrine of purification to the actual condition of the average Christian.

From what does a person need to be purified before he can enter the presence of God? In the first place, from what may be called inordinate affections. Even one who loves God above all else may still have an excessive craving for some things such as food and drink or may have too little concern for the sick or the poor. All this needs to be rectified and brought into perfect conformity with the will of God. (St. Catherine of Genoa speaks of "the rust of sin.")

Secondly, there is atonement from the sins of our past life. Even though we have repented of them and have been forgiven, the order of justice still requires that they be punished. This is not because God, like an angry parent or an injured victim, insists on having his revenge. It is not God that has been injured by our sins but ourselves and our fellows. But there seems to be a justice inscribed in the very nature of things that one who has done wrong should be punished for it. In fact, nature itself reacts against anyone who acts contrary to nature and thus punishes him, as is evident in the case of those who violate the laws of health, hygiene, or ecology. This is justice at a fundamental level, and a paradigm for that much more mysterious justice of God that requires atonement for all sin.

• *Our part in Jesus' atonement*

It was in view of this divine justice that Jesus was required to make atonement for the sins of the world. This, however, raises the immediate objection "Did not Jesus atone sufficiently for us all?" Here we touch on one of the characteristics of the Catholic view of the Christian life. Many other denominations affirm that, because Jesus has made total atonement, nothing remains for us to do but believe in him.

Catholic teaching, however, affirms that here too we are required to be collaborators with Jesus not because what he did was insufficient but because we are called to be conformed to him even in action. Jesus himself summoned everyone to prepare for the Kingdom of God by doing penance. (*Metanoia* did not mean merely inner conversion or repentance; it also expressed itself in penitential actions, such as fasting and the wearing of a penitential garb, "sackcloth and ashes.") After announcing that he himself had to die,

Jesus added, "If anyone would come after me, he must deny himself and take up his cross and follow me" (Mark 8:34; Matthew 16:24; Luke 9:23). St. Paul says bluntly, "I fill up in my flesh what is still lacking in regard to Christ's afflictions, for the sake of his body, which is the Church" (Colossians 1:24).

From this, it would also appear that it is not God's intention that anyone should need to pass through purgatory. It would seem that everyone has the opportunity of being purified of his sinfulness in this life, both by the endurance of trials and by penance voluntarily performed. But experience suggests that not all Christians respond earnestly to the call to penance, that many do not complete their purification in this world. Revelations given to numerous saints suggest that the great majority of people must endure purgatory, some for a very long time.[7]

About the nature of purgatory, we have little information. Fire is the chief image used by Scripture; how literally it should be understood is not clear. Numerous saints have been allowed to "visit" purgatory or have received visits from the souls detained there. The most important instance is St. Catherine of Genoa (1447-1510), who experienced a kind of purgatory in this life, on the basis of which she wrote a brief treatise, "Purgation and Purgatory." There seems to be general agreement that the sufferings of purgatory are far worse than any of the pains in this life, and are comparable only to those of hell. Yet the souls in purgatory have the joy of knowing that they are saved. Their worst suffering comes from an intense yearning for the vision of God, of which they are deprived until their purification is complete. The "fire" that consumes them is, according to St. Catherine, their own love for God which, finding itself held back by the impurities that remain, attacks the latter and burns them away. Likewise God's love for the soul becomes a kind of fire, burning away whatever it cannot inflame.

Epilogue: Mary, archetype of the Christian people

The prominence of the Virgin Mary in Catholic theology and piety has no true parallel in any other religion. There are of course critics who claim that the goddess cults of pagan polytheism are comparable to or even actual forerunners of the veneration of Mary. But this can be the view only of someone looking on from the outside, with no understanding of the inner soul of Catholic piety, which does not regard Mary as a goddess or even a demigoddess. In fact, the characteristic note of Marian veneration comes from the consciousness that she, a mere human being, was brought into an astonishingly intimate association with the Godhead.

It should also be noted that the mothers of other religious founders have not become cult objects in the religions of their sons. Confucius' mother is praised for the sacrifices she made to educate her son after her husband's death, but this has not won her religious veneration. Siddhartha Gautama's mother is quite ignored in Buddhist legend; his father is remembered but only as a kind of dramatic foil for the son, from whom he vainly attempted to hide the miseries of age, illness, and death. Muhammad's mother is said to have died when the prophet was only six years old, and so had not even an opportunity to win a ranking place in his religion.

Why then should Christianity give such high honors to the mother of its founder? It is because Jesus is not just the founder but the very substance of the Christian mystery: God become man. And Mary's motherhood associates her intimately with his divine person, and involves her intrinsically in the crucial reality of the Incarnation.

However, this simple statement needs considerable elaboration for its implications to become fully evident. In the first place, Mary has to be viewed in the perspective not only of the Incarnation but of all the great Christian doctrines, particularly grace and sin, predestination, the Church as the body of Christ, the economy of the sacraments, the place of the saints, and the role of the body. Trying to explain Mary without attention to these doctrines is like trying to get Americans to understand the Hindu reverence for cows. Unless one is willing to learn something of the total pattern of Hindu beliefs about the way human life fits into nature as a whole, and the way cattle are woven into the texture of human life at many levels, the idea that cows are sacred appears incomprehensible and ridiculous. In the same way, Catholic veneration of Mary cannot be understood except in the light of the entire complex of Catholic doctrines. She is like the point of convergence of them all. That is why she is being presented here as the epilogue to this book.

But even a complete theological background carries a person only part way. As in the case of many other Christian beliefs, those about Mary derive not only from truths and doctrines but from what may be called the great "sign-acts" of God. For example, her being a virgin-mother surely has a profound meaning but one not easily defined. It speaks powerfully to the Christian spirit, but what it says is difficult to put into words, and when formulated, difficult to demonstrate.

Our Lady of Guadalupe. — OSV Photo

• *Need of prayerful meditation*

Furthermore, the dogmas of the Church have seldom been arrived at by simple theological reflection or straight reasoning from the scriptural texts. Normally, the mysterious words and mighty deeds of Jesus were taken into the heart of the Christian people, meditated on prayerfully, assimilated into the spiritual life, and allowed to ferment over the course of many generations before they could be given an abstract, rational expression. Even the divinity of Christ was at first perceived quite implicitly. Not till the end of the first century do we find Ignatius speaking simply of Jesus Christ as "our God." Such a prayerful process was even more necessary in regard to Mary because the scriptural indications about her are much less abundant than those about Christ.

It is not only human reflection and prayer that are needed for this work; genuine understanding of any mystery of faith requires the light of the Holy Spirit, which is usually imparted little by little, with various insights given to different persons.

Finally, the understanding of Mary requires that we get to know her as a living human person — for Mary is indeed a person in living communion with us in the Body of Christ. Devotion to her is nourished and fostered by a life of communion with her. Even though one devoted to her does not ordinarily get a response in the form of visions or voices that can be perceived, nevertheless, he can have a mysterious but real sense of being blessed and helped by her.

In sum, devotion to Mary is like a very delicate but faithful expression of the quintessential spirit of Catholicism, as Karl Barth rightly perceived (*Church Dogmatics* 1/2, 138ff). A cold theological explanation will not adequately account for Catholic Marian piety. Nevertheless, there are objective theological principles, and these we will seek to indicate here.

MOTHER OF JESUS

We have already indicated the fundamental principle. Mary is a part — an intrinsic and important part — of the mystery of Jesus Christ, the Son of God who has become the Son of Man. This is the central truth and gigantic mystery of Christianity. Our God is not just gracious and merciful but extends his grace to us by sending his Son in our flesh. Mary is the one through whom he took on our nature. It is through her that we are related to him, with that relationship that makes us his brethren, and on which his saving work is founded. This principle needs to be considered from several angles.

First, Mary is not venerated apart from Jesus, as if by some independent title of her own. She is not a goddess erected as a consort to the One God, as in the objection noted above. She is a mere human being, and her link with the mystery of Jesus is based on one of the most primordial of human relationships — that of motherhood. In fact, a powerful incentive to our esteem for her comes from the wonder and awe that a mere human being should be brought into such an intimately human relationship with a divine person. This motif has inspired thousands of Christian artists to depict the Madonna and Child in every imaginable garb, posture, and circumstance, and Christian poets insatiably to invent new melodies and lyrics to sing of the Babe cuddled in Mary's arms and nourished at her breast.

What child is this, who, laid to rest,
On Mary's lap is sleeping?
Whom angels greet with anthems sweet,
While shepherds watch are keeping?
This, this is Christ the King,
Whom shepherds guard and angels sing:
Haste, haste to bring Him laud,
The Babe, the Son of Mary.

William Dix (an English Protestant poet, 1837-1898)

In good drama, not all the characters can be stars. Minor characters are necessary in order for the leads to stand out. In the drama of the Redemption, Mary's role is in part to be the human foil against which the divinity of Jesus can better be perceived.

Second, it is by the humanity of Jesus that the grace of God is imparted to us. But the Son of God did not create a completely new body for himself; he chose to receive his body from our race, "born of a woman" (Galatians 4:4, RSV), so that he might be not just our colleague but our brother — a true son of Abraham, son of Adam, Son of Man. For this, a mother was necessary; and Mary is the chosen one through whom Jesus became a blood relative to us.

• *Mother of God*

In Chapter 18, we noted that the early Church maintained the expression "Mother of God" not primarily to honor Mary but because of its implications for the unity of person in Jesus. Now it is time to ask, "What are its implications in regard to Mary?" If her son is indeed the Son of God, a divine person, what does being his mother imply about her? This question should not be dealt with in a purely theoretical fashion, as though we were asking what kind of mother did God *have* to have. All things are possible to God. He could have been born of a prostitute or of Mary Magdalene, had he so chosen. What we have to ask is, "What did he do in fact? Are there any indications in Scripture or elsewhere about the actual significance of Mary's motherhood?" We can approach these questions by viewing her in the perspective of the Hebrew people, to which she belonged.

Mary is the one who realized personally and eminently the vocation of the People of Israel — that of giving birth to the divine Messiah. The Hebrews are God's Chosen People not primarily because of the Covenant, the Law, the prophets, the Temple, and the Presence but because "from them is traced the human ancestry of Christ, who is God over all, forever praised!" (Romans 9:5). The "Virgin daughter of Sion," as Israel is often named by the prophets, is *really* personified in Mary.

Anyone intimately associated with Jesus cannot help but become the object of awe.

449

The places where God appeared to Abraham, Isaac, and Jacob were considered so holy that stone altars were erected to mark them; the woman in whose womb God lived for nine months is surely still more sacred. The places in which Jesus dwelt are spoken of as the *Holy Land*; people travel thousands of miles at great expense to visit Bethlehem, Nazareth, and Jerusalem, to walk by the Sea of Galilee, and to drink from Jacob's well. Mary — who was not merely an inanimate element of his environment but a living person consciously and willingly involved in his career — was surely more venerable.

• *Did Jesus deny Mary a blessing?*

The delicate question confronts us here, however, whether Mary's maternal relationship to Jesus has a properly religious and theological significance or merely a dramatic power to touch our sentiments. When a woman cried out to Jesus, "Blessed is the womb that bore you, and the breasts that nourished you," he replied, "Rather blessed are they who hear the word of God and keep it" (Luke 11:17-28; see also 8:21). Is he not denying that Mary should be honored for her motherhood?

In reply to this common objection, two things need to be said. In the first place, if there was ever anyone who heard the Word of God and kept it, it was Mary. She is the scriptural prototype of the faithful Christian. She was in fact the first one to hear and believe in the message of Jesus; for Gabriel's announcement that she was to bear a son who would be likewise the Son of God, and would sit on David's throne in a kingdom that would last forever, was nothing less than a summary of the Gospel. Moreover, her faith played a kind of structural role in the mission of Jesus that was unique. Other Christians believe in order to receive Jesus into their personal lives; Mary believed in order to receive him into the world. Our faith attaches us to the body of Jesus as members; her faith brought about the conception of that body. No one maintains that, because of her motherhood, Mary was saved without faith in Jesus. If she, like the brethren of Jesus (John 7:5), had failed to believe in him, her fleshly relationship with him would not have saved her. But in fact, she is presented by the Gospel as the eminent model of the faithful disciple. Elizabeth, speaking under the inspiration of the Holy Spirit, said of her, "Blessed is she who has believed that what the Lord has said to her will be accomplished!" (Luke 1:45). The Church rejoices in repeating these words to proclaim that Mary was preeminent in her faith. If those who hear the Word of God and keep it are blessed, then Mary is on these very grounds blessed among all women, the most blessed of all mankind.

• *Maternity not without significance*

However, this could lead to the conclusion that Mary was blessed for believing but not for being the mother of Jesus. Then it would still be true that her motherhood is without religious significance. And so we must add that the notion that a human or "carnal" relationship to Jesus is without significance in the regime of faith goes plainly counter to one of the fundamental themes of both Old and New Testaments.

The very concept of Israel as the Chosen People means that God has imparted a special blessing and a religious significance to a given human family. And not only are the children of Abraham "God's own people," but the offspring of Judah, the sons of Levi, the sons of David, and various other progenies also are designated by God for a special blessing and vocation. St. Paul declares that only by faith can we be true children of Abraham (Romans 4:11f), but he takes care to make it clear that this does not nullify the peculiar advantages of the fleshly descendants of the Patriarch. Their calling was a real grace (11:29), which God has not retracted. He has not rejected his people (11:1). They are still the natural olive tree, into which Gentile converts are grafted (11:17ff). Paul affirms that there is great advantage in being a Jew (3:2), and gives a long list of the blessings entailed (9:4ff). Neither Jew nor Gentile could be saved without faith in Jesus Christ; but for those who were faithful, being a Jew was a holy vocation and a grace. Similarly, we do not know the identity of the man called "James, the brother of the Lord," nor the exact degree

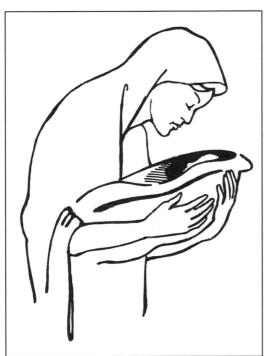

of his kinship to Jesus; yet there is no question but that this relationship was considered a significant title of honor in the early Church (Acts 12:17; 15:13-23; 21:18; Galatians 2:9, 12; 1 Corinthians 15:7; etc.).

So it was with that maiden in whom the vocation of Israel attained its culmination. She too was required to have faith in the Savior; but because she was faithful, her maternal relationship to the Savior gave her a unique place in salvation history.

Moreover, it is wrong to speak of the relationship between Mary and Jesus as merely physical or carnal. No human motherhood is that, unless it is radically deformed or defective. The physical bond between mother and child spontaneously engenders between them one of the deepest love relationships known to human life. If Jesus was a perfect human being, his love for his mother must likewise have been perfect. And if Mary was, at the very least, a good woman and a devout Israelite, her love for him would have been immense. Must we not then suppose that the love between them had an intimacy and depth unparalleled in human relations? But the mother-son relationship in this case involved God the Savior. It was God who loved Mary as a son loves his mother; it was God that she loved in loving her Son.

Here, however, we confront another objection. Jesus came for the salvation of the entire human race. Must his concern not have transcended the natural affection of a son for his mother? As great men sometimes sacrifice their family to their career, may not Jesus, in his concern for all of mankind, have foregone any particular love for his mother? Such a way of thinking would not only betray the sense of authentic love (which would abhor such a "sacrifice"), it would also subvert the dynamics of Jesus' redemptive activity. He did not take on merely a human body like a puppet through which he could speak to us; he embraced human nature and human life fully and in all earnestness. This includes human affections and emotions. He sanctified and elevated them; he did not suppress or distort them. For him to have disregarded his natural human relationships, and denied his natural affections, out of some kind of universal salvific vision would have been inhuman and therefore in contradiction to the very sense and truth of his becoming man. In fact he loved Jerusalem so much that he wept over its impending destruction; must he not have loved Mary far more? Likewise his tears at the death of Lazarus prompted observers to comment, "See how much he loved him!" (John 11:36). The sense of the Incarnation therefore leads us to affirm that Jesus loved Mary as only a perfect son could love an ideal mother; and his human love for her was the vehicle and expression of divine love.

Moreover, love was at the center of Jesus' redeeming mission. He came to us out of love; and he came primarily in order to elicit love from us. The fact that he persisted even when people rejected him does not mean that he disdained their affection; rather, it is a sign of the incredible faithfulness of his love. That someone responded to him with love was not therefore incidental to his purposes; it was their fulfillment. The one who loved him more than all others was by that fact the most important person in the world to him, and the crowning achievement of his grace. As Jesus looks out over the vast ocean of human faces, he must see Mary's countenance shining with a grace and a glory, with a precious value to him, unequaled and utterly unrivaled in anyone else.

Many find it hard to believe that someone who did "so little" could be so important. In the same way, the astronomers who first discovered the quasars could hardly believe in such powerful sources of energy. But the dimensions of the cosmos are not those of man; and neither are those of God. In his Kingdom, the most important persons are not those who have been elevated highest in the hierarchy, nor those who have founded the greatest movements, nor those who have been the most successful in preaching the Gospel, but those who love Jesus most tenderly and most fervently. On this scale, Mary ranks first and is in a class by herself.

IMMACULATE VIRGIN

Mary's *role* was to be Mother of God Incarnate; what about her person? What were the personal qualities of the woman who was brought into this incredibly intimate and human relationship with our God?

• *The virgin Mary*

The fundamental biblical datum is that, in conceiving Jesus, she remained a virgin. This appears at the Annunciation, when the angel Gabriel announced to her that she was to bear a son. Mary replied, "How will this be, since I know not man?" (Luke 1:34, RSV). In common biblical parlance, man and woman are said to "know" one another through carnal intercourse. Hence the NIV and other translations interpret the sense of Mary's reply by translating, ". . .because I am a virgin." The angel then declared:

> The Holy Spirit will come upon you, and the power of the Most High will over-
> shadow you. So the holy one to be born will be called the Son of God. (Luke 1:35; see
> also Matthew 2:20)

Some have compared this account to Hellenistic and Near Eastern myths of demigods who sprang from the union between a deity and a woman. But such fantasies of gods engaging in rape and seduction are not true parallels to the virgin birth, which does not involve carnal intercourse with a spirit but a sovereign action of divine power in total purity. Moreover, the unpretentious sobriety and simple reverence of St. Luke's account (confirmed by Matthew) as well as the spirit of holiness that pervades the narrative give additional assurance that this is a word of sober truth and a serious part of the Gospel.

Some have asked why make an issue of this doctrine, because the essential stature of Jesus Christ would not be affected by a denial of the virgin birth. It is certainly true that the Son of God could have taken on a human nature resulting from normal conjugal relations. However, God speaks to us through acts and gestures even more powerfully than through words. If he worked so spectacular a miracle to mark the entrance of his Son into the world, it is surely not without meaning. In our culture, which has vulgarized sex and turned virginity into a joke, this topic is delicate to deal with. Perhaps, however, reflection on it will have a cleansing and sanctifying influence on our sentiments.

Just as the title *Mother of God* is significant primarily in reference to Jesus Christ, and only secondarily in reference to Mary, the same is the case here. The virgin birth signifies first of all a new beginning in salvation history. It declares to us that the human race was unable to produce its own Savior; God had to provide one. However, the Savior was not to be a superman from outer space; according to the wisdom of the divine plan, he had to be human, a member of the human race who could assume the headship at which the first Adam had failed. Being born of a human mother but through a radical intervention by God rather than by the natural agency of a human father, Jesus was at one and the same time a true brother to us, and a new divine initiative.

Secondly, the fact that Jesus had no other Father but God is a sign for us of his eternal divine sonship. He was of course the Son of God from all eternity, and would have remained so had he been engendered by a human father. Nevertheless, the absence of an earthly father manifests graphically for us creatures of flesh and blood that mysterious divine sonship which is the ultimate secret of his person.

• *A sign of holiness*

As regards Mary herself, the virgin birth is a sign of holiness. Holiness can be taken in either a moral or physical sense; in both cases, its basic meaning is that of being set aside for God. A chalice is holy (in the physical sense) because it is reserved for use at the Eucharist. For someone to serve coffee or beer in it would be sacrilegious not because there is any evil in these beverages but because it would violate the exclusive dedication of this vessel to sacred use. The secular order is good and has its own rights and exigencies, but it is distinct from the sacred, or holy, order, which embraces things withdrawn from human usage and reserved for the worship of God. Similarly a church building is a holy place, and to use it for a dance hall or a shop would be offensive. Christmas and Easter as well as Sundays are holy days for those who, on those days, abstain from servile work and devote themselves to worship.

The distinction between sacred and secular does not deny that everything in the world belongs to God and ought to be used ultimately for the glory of God. That is indeed the right order of creation. But in order to keep himself mindful of God amid the press of creaturely affairs, man needs signposts, that is, times, places, and objects reserved exclusively for worship. That is why there is a distinct order of the sacred, or holy.

Mary's virginity is to be understood in the perspective of this physical or objective holiness. It is a sign of her total consecration to God. Her destiny and her vocation was to be mother of the divine Savior. She was like a tabernacle set aside to house him, similar to the tent in the desert kept as the dwelling place of Yahweh (see Chapter 15) or to the Temple of Solomon. For Mary to have had intimate intercourse with another human being would have been a kind of desecration of a locale far holier than the Temple. This does not imply that sexual relations are sinful or unclean but simply that whatever is set apart for God ought not to be given over to common human use.

Clearly it is not out of contempt or disdain for marriage that Jesus was born of a virgin (to say nothing of the fact that he remained one himself). God blessed marriage from the beginning, and Jesus made it a sacrament — a mysterious, sacred, efficacious sign of his love for the Church (see Ephesians 5:32). Not only did he attend the wedding feast at Cana, he intervened to make it succeed. Moreover, marriage is nowhere else held in such high esteem and even sacred veneration as in the Catholic Church, where likewise the biblical teachings on virginity (Matthew 19:10-12; 1 Corinthians 7) are the most faithfully respected.

Besides the physical holiness which can be found even in sanctuaries and sacred vessels, there is a moral holiness peculiar to persons. It consists in having one's heart *totally devoted* to God, not divided by attachments or any affections unsubordinated to the love of God. This is the holiness of the saints, far more precious than mere physical holiness. If God kept Mary holy in a physical sense, this is a sign that he intended her to be holy also in spirit, by a pure, sinless devotedness to him; and if he worked a miracle to preserve her virginity even in the conception of a child, surely he, the author of all grace, would have done just as much in the order of grace to preserve her from sin.

• *Full of grace*

That Mary was indeed holy in the moral sense is evident from the way she is greeted by the angel Gabriel. "Hail, full of grace," he salutes her or, as other translations put it, "favored one." It is impossible to capture in a single English translation all the meaning of the Greek word *kecharitomene* that is used here. Its root notion is grace *(charis)*. Literally it means "graced one," one on whom grace has been bestowed. It is, in effect, reiterated and explained in the following words of the angel, "you have found grace with God." Some translators prefer to render both of these passages in terms of *favor* rather than grace, in order to avoid all the connotations which have been attached to the latter term by centuries of theological debate. We prefer to keep the term *grace* because it is one of the central notions of the New Testament. But in the long run, it makes little difference which term is used, since God's favor is not simply an inefficacious benignity but confers on his creatures that effect which theologians speak of as grace.

In addressing Mary as the "graced one," the angel is declaring her to be holy with the holiness of the saints. God's spokesman is announcing that God is pleased with his hand-maiden. Thus Mary is the most certain instance of a saint; she is *the* biblical saint like no other. God himself has canonized her. Moreover, the angel speaks as though "graced one" were Mary's proper name, as if suggesting that she is *the* grace-filled person *par excellence*. Never before or since in sacred history has anyone been thus addressed by a heavenly messenger. When Moses received his call, he was told to take off his shoes because of his unworthiness to tread this holy ground. When Isaiah had a vision of God enthroned, he was riven by the consciousness of his own sinfulness, and a seraph had to purify his lips with a burning coal (Isaiah 6:5-6). A sense of unworthiness and fear is normal when a human being encounters a manifestation of God; Mary, however, is reassured that God is pleased with her. Shortly thereafter, Elizabeth, speaking under the inspiration of the Holy Spirit, calls her blessed because of her faith (Luke 1:45).

• *Perpetual Virginity*

The doctrines of the divine maternity and virgin birth do nothing but declare plainly and firmly the evident implications of the scriptural teaching. The same cannot be said of three further Marian doctrines: the *Immaculate Conception*, the *Perpetual Virginity*, and the *Assumption*. These have not been derived by some process of theological reasoning; it seems impossible to demonstrate them by objective logic. They are beliefs that germinated gradually in the hearts of Christians meditating on the New Testament portrait of Mary. The fact that they came eventually to be held with firm conviction by the Church at large was taken as a sign of the Holy Spirit's inspiration (Chapter 27), and they were defined as dogmas.

It would be impossible to document and weigh precisely all the factors that contributed to these beliefs. We can, however, indicate how the beliefs are rooted in Scripture and harmonize with the Gospel message as a whole.

On the subject of virginity, the New Testament declares merely that Mary was a virgin when she bore Jesus. The Church goes on to affirm that she remained a virgin the rest of her life. The Gospels do indeed mention "the brothers and sisters of Jesus" (Matthew 13:55; Mark 6:3); however, this is no decisive objection, since close relatives were commonly called brothers and sisters in the idiom of that time (St. Paul calls the whole Hebrew race "my brothers" in Romans 9:3). As a matter of fact, James and Joses, two "brothers of Jesus" mentioned in Mark 6:3, appear, from Mark 15:40, to have been sons of another mother (see Matthew 13:55; 27:56).

Mary's query to Gabriel "How will this be, since I do not know man?" indicates not only that she was in fact a virgin but that she intended to remain so; otherwise, she would not have had a problem, since she was already espoused to Joseph. Through the prophets, Yahweh had often called Israel his beloved spouse. Even before the "overshadowing" that left Mary with child, the Holy Spirit seems to have inspired her to consecrate herself to God as her unique spouse, anticipating what Jesus and St. Paul were later to teach about virginity, as a single-minded devotedness to the Lord, being better than marriage in view of the Kingdom of Heaven (Matthew 19:10-12; 1 Corinthians 7). If Mary had the firm intention of remaining a virgin, and if her virginity had been preserved by God miraculously even when she was called to be a mother, is it conceivable that she would subsequently have abandoned it? A further indication that Mary had no other children can be seen in the fact that Jesus, on the cross, entrusted her to the apostle John (John 19:26f). If she had other children, they would be expected to care for her (especially James, "the brother of the Lord," who became head of the Jerusalem Church).

• *Surpassing grace*

We saw above that Mary was clearly, on the testimony of Scripture, a holy person, a saint. Yet the firm conviction has grown in the Church that Mary was not merely one saint among many but the supreme saint, with a holiness transcending that of all others. This is based primarily on her vocation to be the Mother of God. Grace is given to everyone in proportion to his vocation; Mary's vocation far surpassed any other. Other Christians are called to serve the Church; Mary served Jesus, the founder and head of the Church. All grace comes from Jesus; Mary, being the one closest to him, would have received grace most abundantly. It cannot be objected that this closeness was merely physical or natural. Jesus used natural human contact to impart grace to those who encountered him with faith; and Mary, unlike the "brethren of Jesus," did indeed have faith in him. Her loving intimacy with him during the thirty years he lived in her home had to be a time of sanctification for her, unparalleled in the life of any other saint. The very flesh of Jesus is the Bread of Life by which the Church is nourished. But whereas the Church at large receives this bread only in sacramental form, Mary was in direct, unveiled, and almost uninterrupted contact with Jesus in the flesh (the flesh which she herself had given him!). Such indications lie at the root of the Church's conviction that Mary was "full of grace" in a way that transcends all comparison; that her grace had a kind of fullness or universality, in comparison with which the grace of any other saint has only a fragmentary or partial character. (Here recall St. Paul's teaching that each of us is only one organ among many in the Body of Christ [1 Corinthians 12].)

• *The Immaculate Conception*

How decisive are the above arguments? Left to his own reflections, an individual Christian might well hesitate to say. But the fact that the Church as a whole concurs in the conclusion enables each individual member to have certitude about it, as we saw in the preceding chapter. Instead of halting at this point, already so daring, the faith of the Church has pursued its reflection still further. In endeavoring to define as precisely as possible the grace given to Mary, it has come to affirm her Immaculate Conception. (This is not another name for the virgin birth, as people frequently mistake it; it refers to the conception of *Mary herself*.) It means that, whereas all the rest of Adam's offspring come into the world marked with original sin, Mary, by a unique privilege and grace, was conceived free from sin, that is, "immaculate." As a result, she was not subject to that conflict between the flesh and the spirit (Romans 7:15-24), with which even the greatest saints contend. The grace of God embraced her in the first instant of her existence and preserved her until the end of her life on earth, as a result of which she was taken directly into glory by another exceptional grace, that of the *Assumption*.

456

As evidence for the Immaculate Conception, beyond what has already been said about Mary's grace and holiness in general, we can add here two particular points. First, John the Baptist, the precursor of Jesus, was sanctified by the Holy Spirit even before his birth (see Luke 1:15, 41-44). Mary's far greater intimacy with Jesus would seem to call for an even more radical sanctification. Second, God worked a miracle to preserve Mary's physical integrity and virginity; must this not be a sign of an even more important spiritual integrity? He who, by his sovereign power, was able to preserve the one, was undoubtedly capable by his grace of bestowing the other.

We are not implying that, being sinless, Mary had no need to be redeemed by Christ. Rather, she was the finest fruit of his redemption. Where others are set free from the sin they have inherited or into which they have fallen, Mary was, *by the grace of Christ*, preserved from all taint of sin, according to the profound intuition of Duns Scotus.

As for St. Paul's teaching that "all have sinned and fall short of the glory of God" (Romans 3:23), this is true in general but admits of a privileged exception such as Mary.

• *The Assumption*

The Assumption is not so extraordinary a grace as it might at first seem. All human beings are destined for a bodily resurrection (whether for eternal life or for the living death of hell). Because we have been touched by sin, our resurrection is delayed until the end of

the world, when Jesus returns to "restore all things." But this was not God's original plan; it is a consequence of sin. If Mary was totally without sin, there was no reason for her resurrection to be delayed; it was normal for it to occur immediately at the end of her earthly life — which is what the Assumption means.

It should be noted, moreover, that it was from Mary that the Word Incarnate took that body in which he lived as man, by which he redeemed the world, through which he poured out the Holy Spirit, and which he gave as the Bread of Life. Mary's body was furthermore the Temple or, more precisely, the Ark of the Covenant, in which Jesus' body was tabernacled for nine months. Surely it is highly appropriate that the incorruptibility of Jesus' body should in some measure have irradiated that of his mother, preserving her from the ravages of that death which he had come to conquer.

THE MODEL DISCIPLE, ARCHETYPE OF THE CHURCH

Her eminence in grace and privileged association with Jesus Christ do not make Mary remote from the rest of the Church. On the contrary, she is the archetypical scriptural example of the perfect Christian. In her are depicted most purely and vividly the meaning of our own grace and the great Christian realities. Christianity is a mystery of the grace of the Holy Spirit given to us through Jesus Christ, gathering us into the community of the Church, and preparing us for resurrection into the coming Kingdom.

Grace means that God looks mercifully upon us not only to save us from the sin in which we are inextricably entangled but to sanctify us through the outpouring of his Holy Spirit, making us his children. Mary's Immaculate Conception is the eminent example of grace. Bestowed on her by a sheer act of divine goodness, before she was able to do anything meritorious of her own, it sanctified her perfectly, not just redeeming her from sin as in our case but preserving her from any taint of evil.

Jesus Christ is the one through whom grace is given. Through no one else, and in no other way, can it be obtained. And Jesus imparts grace through his human body, which is the Bread of Life for us (John 6:35, 48-58). Nowhere do we see more vividly than in the case of Mary that sanctification comes from Jesus, and specifically from contact with his body. From the Annunciation onward, her whole life was one of sanctifying contact with him. Even the Immaculate Conception was bestowed on her in view of Jesus' coming, so that she might be a worthy mother for him.

Our contact with Jesus is brought about through the *sacraments*, which are like the saving touch of Jesus imparted through his Body, the Church. Mary's contact with the body of Jesus, however, was not mediated through sacraments; it was direct. She did not need sacred signs to enable her to take part in the redemptive mysteries; she had an actual, physical part in them. And whereas even the apostles did not receive the Holy Spirit until after Jesus had been glorified, and so were not tuned in on the saving events taking place before their very eyes, Mary was overshadowed by the Holy Spirit from the moment that Jesus himself was conceived in her womb. She therefore was able to participate consciously and responsively in these saving mysteries because she did so in the Spirit of Jesus. Hence we can see in her the full and deep meaning of what we are doing in the sacraments. For example, the Eucharist is our way of joining in the offering which Jesus made of himself on Calvary; but Mary actually stood at the foot of the cross, associating herself with the action of her Son.

The principal act by which we accept Jesus and adhere to him is *faith*. Mary is hailed in Scripture as an example of faith, whereas even the apostles were frequently chided by Jesus for their lack of faith. Moreover, as above, Mary was the first person to receive the Gospel. She was therefore the first Christian, the first disciple of her Son. Faith unites all believers to the Body of Jesus; but for no one else is this so literally and physically true, as for Mary.

Besides receiving the grace of the Holy Spirit through faith, the disciple is obliged to cooperate with it by his *good deeds*. Mary's first response to the overshadowing of the Holy Spirit was to hasten to the aid of her elderly cousin Elizabeth, who was six months pregnant. Thereafter, Mary lived the ordinary life of a housewife and mother, caring for the child Jesus. If, to his other disciples, the King is going to say, "Come, ye blessed of My Father. . . . Whatever you did to the least of these, my brethren, you did unto me" (Matthew 25:40), what will he say to her who actually and literally cared for his physical body? Mary's care for Jesus manifests the profound meaning of all our works of charity.

Finally, the reward for our Christian life will be *resurrection* into the Kingdom of Eternal Life. Because of sin, our bodies must be separated from our souls in death and wait until Christ's Parousia, the Day of the Restoration (Acts 3:21) to be remade, sinless and glorious. But this "law of sin" (Romans 7:23) did not apply to Mary because of her total freedom from sin. At the completion of her earthly life, she was taken, in body as well as in soul, into the Kingdom of her Son, where she typifies the hope held out to us all.

Mary interests us therefore not only because of her association with Jesus but also as the supreme exemplar of our own Christian life. She is the scriptural model of the believing disciple. She is likewise the archetype or "ikon" (Bouyer) of the whole Church. What the grace of Christ brings about collectively in the People of God, was realized personally, eminently, and perfectly in her alone.

• *Spiritual motherhood*

Once this is realized, one is compelled to go a step farther. No one exists in the Church for himself alone; the grace we receive is meant to be shared in some way with others. All members of the Body are called to concern themselves with the other members, and to build up the Body not only by witness and example but also by being real channels of the Spirit to others. Like St. Paul, we all have some "charism of the Spirit" (Romans 1:11) to impart to one another. What must this have meant in regard to the unique grace of the Mother of God? As the most eminent grace in the entire People of God, it must be the most fruitful for others. As the one nearest to Christ, Mary has to be the one who most helps others draw near to him.

By a kind of spiritual interpretation which originated in the daring personal insights of a few individuals but has been confirmed by so many others and in such diverse ways as to become the common teaching of the Church, Mary's role in the Church is regarded as a kind of *spiritual motherhood*. The very fact that she gave birth to the Redeemer is already grounds for calling her "Mother of the Church" in some (metaphorical) sense, especially since she accepted her office consciously and freely, and cooperated by her own faith and obedience in the divine plan for redemption. But the probing reflections of devout faith have insisted that her motherhood involves something much more real and profound than that.

The Christian is not just a disciple of Jesus but a member of his Body, vitally identified with him, called to die and rise with him — mystically but very really. He is invited to adopt the sentiments of Christ (Philippians 2:5), to have the mind of Christ (1 Corinthians 2:16), clothe himself with Christ (Galatians 3:27), to live in Christ (Colossians 2:6), to let Christ live in him (Galatians 2:20). It is in full accord with the logic of this relationship for the disciple to regard the mother of Jesus as spiritually his mother. On the cross, with Mary and the Beloved Disciple standing at his feet, Jesus said to her, "Woman, there is your son," and to the disciple, "There is your mother" (John 19:26f). Here Mary's spiritual motherhood is declared in the case of one disciple at least, and it is commonly felt that the Beloved Disciple here represents all the others. Christians reading this text prayerfully have sensed that it was addressed to them. Throughout the centuries, in having recourse to Mary's intercession, the faithful have experienced her not just as a powerful advocate but as a true mother. This is often expressed in the maxim that, just as the Son of God came into the world through Mary, so he is reborn in each of our hearts through her.

Out of such considerations has arisen the firm and widespread conviction that Mary is mother of all the faithful in a mystical but real way that goes far beyond mere metaphor. Pope Paul VI, in closing the Second Vatican Council, solemnly declared her "Mother of the Church." The Council itself had already stated:

> . . .in a wholly singular way she cooperated by her obedience, faith, hope and burning charity in the work of the Savior in restoring supernatural life to souls. For this reason she is a mother to us in the order of grace.
>
> This motherhood of Mary in the order of grace continues uninterruptedly . . . until the eternal fulfillment of all the elect. . . . By her manifold intercession she continues to bring us the gifts of eternal salvation. By her maternal charity, she cares for the brethren of her Son, who still journey on earth surrounded by dangers and difficulties, . . .
>
> (Dogmatic Constitution on the Church, nos. 61 and 62)

• *Mediation of grace*

Mary's motherly role in the order of grace means concretely that the grace of Jesus is imparted to us through her. St. Bernard depicted her as the aqueduct bringing the living water from Jesus, the reservoir, to thirsty souls. Some theologians understand this in the sense that Mary is a kind of instrument used by Jesus in the sanctification of his disciples. Others interpret it merely in terms of intercession; just as, at Cana, Mary's request led Jesus to supply the wine needed for the wedding (John 2:1-11), so now, in response to her requests, he provides the wine of the Holy Spirit. In any case, Mary's mediation is always understood in the light of the firm dogma that Jesus is the unique source from whom all grace derives. Mary is not an alternative avenue to God alongside Christ, the Unique Mediator (1 Timothy 2:5), but simply one who has been assumed into intimate collaboration with him, as all of us are to a lesser degree.

Mary's intervention must not be imagined as interposing her between us and Jesus, thus making him more remote. (The metaphor of the aqueduct must not be taken literally in its application to spiritual realities.) The friends of Jesus do not act as walls keeping one another away from him; they create an atmosphere of love that helps to approach closer to him. Mary's personal grace was that of a most intimate relationship with the Son of God, and her effect on others is to introduce them into an intimacy with Jesus they would never have had on their own.

NOTES

PART 1

1. In this section, much use was made of the following works: *The Concise Encyclopedia of Living Faiths*, ed. Robert C. Zaehner (Boston, Beacon, 1959); Robert C. Zaehner, *Christianity and Other Religions* (New York: Hawthorn, 1964); John B. Noss, *Man's Religions*, 5th ed. (New York: Macmillan, 1974).

CHAPTER 1

1. We do not intend thereby to suggest the simplistic view that nature worship was the primitive form of religion. Evidence about the religion of prehistoric humans is tenuous, and scholars disagree about whether monotheism arose out of polytheism or degenerated into it. Without intending to take any stand on that question, we note simply that, in historic times, the great monotheistic religions have arisen out of a polytheistic milieu.

2. The early Romans seem to have taken courage as the principal virtue; the Latin word *virtus* meant originally "virility, manliness." In Christianity, love is paramount.

3. Zoroastrianism may also be considered a prophetic religion but hardly ranks among the major religious bodies today. See Zaehner, *Concise Encyclopedia*, p. 17.

CHAPTER 2

1. In modern usage, *heretic* means one who does not hold the doctrine of the universal Church; *schismatic* means one who, while holding the Catholic doctrine, refuses to submit to the authority of the hierarchy.

2. See Vatican II, "Dogmatic Constitution on Divine Revelation," ch. 2.

3. Whether Anglicans are to be called Protestants is a moot question. Originally the term was not applied to them, and some of them still object to it. Today, however, it is being more and more accepted, in view of the fundamental kinship between the British Reformers and those of the continent. We are following this usage here for the sake of simplicity, not in order to make any point.

4. According to Barrett's WCE, there were 7,889 Protestant denominations in 1980. In addition, there were 1,345 classified as "marginally Protestant," 10,965 "non-white indigenous," 485 "non-Roman Catholic," and 225 "Anglican" denominations, making a total of 20,909, most of which derived directly or indirectly from the Reformation. It should be borne in mind that, in computing denominations, Barrett tends to see a plurality where others might. For example, he counts 222 distinct denominations within the Roman Catholic Church! But even when this is taken into consideration, the figures are staggering.

5. It would not be true to say that, for Luther, good works were of no importance. He held that, if our faith is sincere, we will do good works spontaneously. But these good works do not merit a reward, as they do in Catholic thought.

6. The above account is based chiefly on Luther's *Commentary on Galatians*. It is true that somewhat different versions of his doctrine can be had from other writings. However, he himself said, when the Latin edition of his works was in preparation a couple of years before his death, "If they took my advice, they'd print only the books containing doctrine, like the Galatians." (Cited from Philip Watson's preface to the English translation of *A Commentary on St. Paul's Epistle to the Galatians* [Old Tappan, N.J.: Fleming J. Revell Co., 1953], p. 5.)

7. There are historical problems about some of the popes listed, such as whether Cletus and Anacletus were not the same man, and which among several claimants to a disputed papacy was valid. But these trifling details affect nothing other than the number 264, which might need to be raised or lowered slightly.

8. Muslims, however, are multiplying much more rapidly than Christians. David Barrett has estimated that, if the present rates continue, by the year 2000 there will be 1.2 billion Muslims and only 1.1 billion Catholics, this according to *World-class Cities and World Evangelization*, Appendix E (Birmingham, Ala.: New Hope, 1986).

CHAPTER 3

1. This text and much of the data in the foregoing two paragraphs are cited from C. Hayes, *A Political and Cultural History of Western Europe* (New York: Macmillan), I, ch. 11.

2. *Essay on Human Understanding*, IV, 18, par. 4.

3. *Ibid.*, par. 10.

4. See J. H. Randall, "The Religion of Reason," in *The Making of the Modern Mind* (Boston: Houghton Mifflin, 1926), pp. 281-307. This is also the source of the references below to Voltaire and d'Holbach.

5. Immanuel Kant, *Fundamental Principles of the Metaphysic of Ethics*, tr. T. K. Abbott, 10th ed. (London: Longmans, Green and Co., 1926), p. 21. See also his *Critique of Pure Reason* (1781) and *Critique of Practical Reason* (1788).

6. Charles Darwin, *Origin of Species* (Everymans Library ed.), p. 462.

7. *The Gay Science* (New York: Random House, 1974), p. 181.

8. Nietzsche's antipathy for the accepted moral values dated from his childhood, according to his own account in the Preface to *The Genealogy of Morals*. Interpretation of them as a hangover from theism is expressed most clearly in his posthumous writings, which are not readily available in English. See the summary in Hans Küng, *Does God Exist?* (London: Collins, 1980), p. 392ff.

9. *Beyond Good and Evil* (Gateway), p. 26.

10. Vatican II, "Constitution on the Church," no. 3.

11. See *God and Nature*, ed. David Lindberg and Ronald Numbers (Berkeley: University of California, 1986), p. 323.

12. On the history of this "warfare," see *ibid.*

13. Rudolf Bultmann, "New Testament and Mythology," in *Kerygma and Myth*, ed. H. W. Bartsch (New York: Harper, 1961), p. 5.

14. S. J. Gould, *The Panda's Thumb* (New York and London: Norton), especially pp. 20, 26.

PART 2

1. Plato, *Republic*, VI.

2. Aristotle, *Physics*, VIII, 5ff; *Metaphysics*, XII, 6-10.

3. St. Thomas Aquinas, *Summa Theologiae*, I, 1, 3. For modern expositions of this text, see Jacques Maritain, *Approaches to God* (New York: Harper, 1954) and R. Garrigou-Lagrange, *God, His Existence and Nature* (St. Louis, Mo.: Herder, 1934, 1936). See also William Bryar, *St. Thomas and the Existence of God* (Chicago: Regnery, 1951).

CHAPTER 4

1. See Jacques Maritain, *Preface to Metaphysics* (Freeport, N.Y.: Books for Libraries Press, 1979), ch. 7.

2. *Evolution from Space; A Theory of Cosmic Creationism*. Sir Fred Hoyle and N. C. Wickramasinghe (New York: Simon and Schuster, 1982).

3. *Ibid.*, p. 76.

CHAPTER 5

1. See Vatican II, "Declaration on the Relation of the Church to Non-Christian Religions," no. 56.

2. The prophet may see a vision or hear a word or perhaps receive some other form of communication.

3. It is not only by prophetic words but also by prophetic deeds that God has revealed himself. Hence salvation history — for example, the story of Israel's deliverance from Egypt — is itself a prophetic revelation about the saving power of God.

4. See Edward D. O'Connor, C.S.C., *Faith in the Synoptic Gospels* (Notre Dame, Ind.: University of Notre Dame Press, 1961).

5. This is not said as if to imply that Jesus was not God in person. That is one of the truths to be believed, and will be discussed in ch. 17.

CHAPTER 6

1. G. E. Wright, *Biblical Archaeology* (Philadelphia: Westminster Press, 1962), p. 10.

2. Rudolf Otto, *The Idea of the Holy* (New York: Oxford University Press, 1958), p. 65.

CHAPTER 7

1. The reason we cannot attribute to God the evils we find among creatures will be discussed in ch. 9.

2. See *Summa Theologiae*, I, 12 and 13. Note especially Article 12 of Question 12. See also *De Potentia* 7, 5, ad 2.

3. This can be seen by reflection on the way we measure time. To say a person is thirty years old means that the earth has revolved around the sun thirty times since he was born. If the earth did not move, we might take some other movement as the measure of time, as is done now with certain types of chemical change. But if nothing changed, there would be no meaning to "before" and "after"; there would be simply the existence of that which is.

4. People sometimes think of Father, Son, and Spirit as parts of the Blessed Trinity. Such an idea destroys the very notion of the Trinity, in which each person *is* the whole, not just a part of it. We shall see more about this in ch. 18.

5. For more on the meaning of Yahweh, see p. 257.

6. *The Phenomenon of Man* (New York: Harper, 1959), p. 60ff.

7. Bernadette Brooten, "Jewish Women's History in the Roman Period: A Task for Christian Theology," in *Christians Among Jews and Gentiles*, ed. G.W.E. Nikelsburg and G. W. MacRae, S.J. (Philadelphia: Fortress Press, 1986).

CHAPTER 8

1. The full text of this myth can be found in J. B. Pritchard, *Ancient Near Eastern Texts Relating to the Old Testament* (Princeton, N.J.: Princeton University Press, 1950), p. 60ff.

2. See John McKenzie, *The Two-edged Sword*, ch. 5 (Milwaukee: Bruce, 1956). R.A.F. MacKenzie, *Faith and History in the Old Testament* (New York: Macmillan, 1963), p. 57ff.

3. General audience of Sept. 19, 1979; *L'Osservatore Romano*, English edition, Sept. 24, 1979, p. 1. This talk was one in a long series of commentaries on the first two chapters of Genesis. They have been republished in English under the title, *Original Unity of Man and Woman* (Boston: St. Paul, 1981).

4. See Theodore Gaster, *Myth, Legend and Custom in the Old Testament* (New York: Harper and Row, 1969).

5. This seems to be the sense in which we are to understand the statement of Pius XII that "the first eleven chapters of Genesis, although properly speaking not conforming to the historical method used by the best Greek and Latin writers or by competent authors of our time, do nevertheless pertain to history in a true sense, which however must be further studied and determined by exegetes. . . . Therefore whatever elements of popular narrative may have been inserted into the Sacred Scriptures must in no way be considered on a par with myths or other such things, which

are more the product of an extravagant imagination than of that striving for truth and simplicity which, in the Sacred Books, including the Old Testament, is so apparent that our ancient sacred writers must be admitted to be clearly superior to the ancient profane writers" (*Humani Generis* 38; TCC 126f; TCT 142).

6. *Annales Veteris et Novi Testamenti* (London: 1650-1654).

7. *The Whole Works of the Rev. John Lightfoot*, vol. II (London: 1822). The date is proposed on p. 373 and the time of day on p. 335.

8. *Lucy, The Beginnings of Humankind* (New York: Simon and Schuster, 1981).

9. *Ibid.*, p. 103f.

10. The fact that we are using the terms *evil* and *bad* as synonymous may perplex some readers. The connotations and associations that generally accompany the term *evil* suggest something far worse than merely "bad." Also, *evil* is generally spoken of in a moral context. But the difference between bad and evil seems to be one of degree and connotation, not of essence. And as we shall see below, moral evil is only one particular form of evil, characterized by its being freely chosen. We will therefore follow the classical metaphysical tradition in taking *evil* and *bad* as synonymous.

11. We are leaving the supernatural order out of consideration here. It would complicate our definitions somewhat but would not alter the two types of evil being distinguished.

12. Angels likewise are capable of sin. They will be considered in ch. 13.

CHAPTER 9

1. See what is said in ch. 7 on God's immutability. Strictly speaking, nothing is changed in God by the fact of creation, but it seems to us that it is.

CHAPTER 10

1. In most of this book, we have used the term *human being* or an equivalent so as to avoid offense to those who object to speaking of *man* when women are included. However, good language demands that there be a single species name. For example, just as we compare birds and mammals, tigers and horses, so likewise we need to compare man and chimpanzee. Particularly in a chapter on human nature, it would be extremely cumbersome to be forever saying, "men and women, he or she," etc. One might wish that our language had developed otherwise, but we must use the language we have. (To change language is of course possible but not very easy, as is manifest from many infelicitous current attempts.) Mindful therefore of Hilaire Belloc's perspicacious dictum "Man embraces woman," we will continue to employ the traditional usage, taking "man" not in an exclusive but in an inclusive sense. There is no intention here of slighting woman's full human dignity and essential equality with the male of the species.

2. The data given in the following paragraphs is taken primarily from R. Lewins, *Human Evolution* (New York: Freeman, 1984), supplemented by Christian Montenant, Plateaux, and Roux, *How to Read the World: Creation in Evolution* (New York: Crossroad, 1985); Donald Johanson and M. Edey, *Lucy, The Beginnings of Humankind* (New York: Simon and Schuster, 1981); and other minor sources. We make no pretense of giving the latest scientific word in these matters, and we are very conscious of the danger inherent in the use of popular science by one who is not a scientist. But it is urgently necessary that theologians and scientists communicate, and our intention is merely to illustrate the kind of scientific positions on which the theologian is obliged to reflect.

3. Johanson and Edey, *Lucy, The Beginnings of Humankind*, p. 103f.

4. See T. H. Gaster, ed., *The New Golden Bough* (New York: Criterion, 1959), p. 148ff.

5. See Richard Leakey, *The Making of Mankind* (New York: Dutton, 1981), p. 135.

CHAPTER 11

1. The supernatural will be dealt with in ch. 21ff.

2. In the more nuanced view of St. Thomas Aquinas, nature itself is not spoken of as a law. Rather, human nature is the seat of inclinations by which we recognize certain things as good or bad for us. On the basis of the fundamental principle of the practical reason "Good is to be done and evil avoided," this recognition engenders in our minds the principles of natural law (*Summa Theologiae*, I-II, 94, 2).

3. The unpredictability of atomic particles postulated by Heisenberg is thought by some to provide a place for freedom. But this unpredictability, whether it comes from the limits of our observation or is intrinsic to the structure of matter itself, does not imply free choices made by particles!

CHAPTER 12

1. These citations follow the Flannery translation which, especially in the second citation, is more accurate than that of Abbott.

2. Translation by the present author.

3. In speaking of homosexuality as immoral, we refer to the act deliberately practiced, not to innate tendencies for which the subject is not to blame. The same applies to the other disorders mentioned here.

4. The Apostolic Exhortation *Familiaris Consortio*, published under the title *On the Family* (Washington, D.C.: United States Catholic Conference, 1982), is the richest official statement of Catholic marriage teaching ever published. It is the product of the 1980 Synod of Bishops, synthesized and interpreted by the Holy Father.

CHAPTER 13

1. DS 800, 3002.

2. See Apocalypse (Revelation) 12, cited earlier in this chapter.

3. On this, see Trevor Ling, *The Significance of Satan* (SPCK, 1961). His testimony is all the more impressive in that he personally does not believe the New Testament doctrine on this subject.

4. See John 6:70; Matthew 16:23; 1 John 3:8.

5. The Church's doctrine on Satan was presented by Pope Paul VI in an address to a general audience on Nov. 15, 1972. English translations can be found in *L'Osservatore Romano* (English ed.), Nov. 23, 1972, and (better) in *The Pope Speaks*, vol. 17 (1972), pp. 315-399. A summary of the teaching and practice of the Church, "Christian Faith and Demonology," was commissioned and published by the Congregation for the Doctrine of the Faith (English translation: *L'-Osservatore Romano*, English ed., July 10, 1975, pp. 6-10). John Paul II reiterated the doctrine in several Wednesday audiences during the summer of 1986.

6. See especially *Summa Theologiae*, I, 110-114 and *De malo*, 16.

CHAPTER 14

1. John A. Ryan, "Communism," in CE 4:182A.

2. When Paul says in v. 12, "all men sinned," even this seems to be meant in the sense, "all were accounted as sinners"; for in the abstruse rabbinic reasoning of vv. 13 and 14, not reproduced here, Paul seems to say that during the period from Adam to Moses, when the Law had not yet been given, men were not held accountable for breaking the Law; nevertheless, the fact that they died is a sign that they were judged to be sinners, that is, on the grounds of Adam's sin.

3. The Council of Trent, Session V (DS 1510:1516; TCT 371-376).

4. St. Augustine, *On the Merits and Remission of Sin, and on the Baptism of Infants* I, 16 (*The Anti-Pelagian Writings of St. Augustine* I, Edinburgh, 1872).

5. Anselm of Canterbury, *The Virginal Conception*, 2 and 23, tr. Joseph Colleran (New York: Magi, 1969).

6. *Hominisation: The Evolutionary Origin of Man as a Theological Problem* (New York: Herder and Herder, 1965), p. 103ff.

7. On this point, we need to be very cautious, however. The strong Augustinian tradition that, through original sin, the human race was not only deprived of grace but also wounded in its natural gifts, would seem to refer particularly to concupiscence.

8. Perhaps an exception ought to be made for slight pains, which would seem to be inseparable from the healthy functioning of the nervous system, as its way of deterring us from things that are harmful. But this hardly constitutes a serious problem.

CHAPTER 15

1. Van Imschoot. He points out further aspects of the uniqueness of Israel's Covenant relationship with God. "The idea that Yahweh has chosen for Himself this people from among all the nations has really made Israel into a people 'apart' (Nm 23:9) and has made their religion different from all those of the ancient East. In those religions the bond which unites each people with their gods originated from the nature of things; in the Old Testament and in Judaism this bond is born from an act of the will and intelligence of the personal God, since it is the result of a gratuitous choice and based solely on love; it began at a given moment of history and is attached to certain historical events, which appear as special interventions of Yahweh in the course of human things and as manifestations of His particular benevolence" *Theology of the Old Testament* (New York: Desclee, 1965), I, 254f.

2. Thus, for example, Arnold Toynbee in *An Historian's Approach to Religion* (London: Oxford, 1956), p. 13.

3. Exodus 1:11 mentions the city of Ramses as one of those built by the conscripted Hebrews. From other sources we know that it was built — that is, enlarged — by the pharaoh of the same name.

4. See K. A. Kitchen, *Ancient Orient and Old Testament* (Chicago: Inter-Varsity Press, 1966), p. 157.

5. See Roland de Vaux, *The Early History of Israel* (Philadelphia: Westminster Press, 1978), p. 464. For the historical and archaeological background of the Old Testament, this is one of the best sources available.

6. NIV: virgin.

7. *Apocalypse*, as pointed out earlier, means revelation. It refers to a type of literature which developed chiefly during the centuries just before and after the birth of Christ. It is marked by heavily symbolic visions in which things to come are revealed to those who know how to interpret the symbols. The Book of Daniel (chs. 7-12) is the chief Old Testament example, and the Apocalypse (or Book of Revelation) of John is the chief New Testament example; but there were many others, some included in the Bible, some not.

CHAPTER 16

1. The greek word *evangellion*, of which "gospel" is a translation, likewise meant "good news."

2. English translation: *The Quest of the Historical Jesus* (London: 1910).

3. See the conclusion to ch. 23.

4. See Adolf Harnack, *What Is Christianity?* 1900 (E. T. Harper, 1957).

5. See G. Mensching, "Vatername Gottes," in *Die Religion in Geschichte und Gegenwart* VI (Tübingen: Mohr, 1962); G. Van der Leeuw, *Religion in Essence and Manifestation*, I, ch. 20 (New York: Harper and Row, 1963).

6. See W. Kasper, *Jesus the Christ* (New York: Paulist, 1977), p. 79.

7. Jesus reprimanded people who looked for signs and wonders in order to believe (John 4:48), and he refused to work miracles for those who demanded them (Matthew 16:4). Nevertheless, it is clear that his miracles did much to win and sustain the faith of those who witnessed them (John 2:11; 5:36; 11:45-48; Matthew 11:4ff, etc.).

8. Many critics question whether the term *apostle* was given by Jesus and whether it was originally confined to the Twelve. This need not concern us; what matters is that there was a group chosen from among the general body of disciples and given a special commission and authority. St. Luke speaks also of a group of seventy (or seventy-two) other disciples who received a commission analogous to that of the Twelve; but we have not enough information to know how they fitted into the picture (Luke 10).

9. J. McKenzie, "Cross," in *Dictionary of the Bible* (Milwaukee: Bruce, 1965).

10. In Matthew 28:6, the angel at the tomb says to the women, "He has risen as he said" (see Matthew 28:7; Mark 16:9; Luke 24:6, 34).

11. See the text of 1 Corinthians 15:6, cited above, p. 275.

12. See Pliny the Younger, Letter to Tacitus (Aug. 24, 79 A.D.) and sequel, Lockwood, vol. II, nos. 29, 30, *Survey of Classical Roman Literature* (New York: Prentice Hall, 1934).

13. A fuller statement of his position, from 1968, appeared in English as *The Significance of the Message of the Resurrection for Faith in Jesus Christ* (Philadelphia: Fortress Press, 1970).

CHAPTER 17

1. John 4:26; 8:28; 18:5. The translations, struggling with the difficult problem of rendering these statements into intelligible English, do not always make it evident that his actual words are identical with those of Yahweh in Exodus 3:14, "You are to say to the Israelites, '*I am* has sent me to you.' "

2. Ch. 21 is manifestly a latter appendix.

3. The only text in which Jesus spontaneously calls himself the Christ occurs in his conversation with the Samaritan woman (John 4:28).

4. It is purely gratuitous to take this as an editorial invention of Mark.

5. That is why, for example, Matthew 16:16 has Peter say, "You are the Christ, the Son of the living God," where in Mark 8:29 and Luke 9:20 he says simply, "the Christ of God." The latter are more likely to be historically accurate.

6. The one recorded instance is John 10:36, and even it is somewhat indirect.

7. How this is to be reconciled with another statement, "The Father is greater than I" (John 11:28), will be dealt with in the next chapter.

8. Strictly speaking, no human language applies properly to God. Whatever we say about him is at best analogous. However, we say "proper" here for want of a better way to express the truth painfully hammered out by the Church (see ch. 18) that, whereas others are called sons of God because they are close to him, Jesus had really been born from God, and in the same nature as his Father.

CHAPTER 18

1. Pliny the Younger, Letter X, 96.

2. See ch. 6, p. 129.

3. As we have already seen, insistence on the genuineness of Jesus' flesh has been the backbone of the Church's constant opposition to all spiritualist movements inclined to treat the flesh as evil (ch. 10, p. 191).

4. Hans Küng, *On Being a Christian* (New York: Doubleday, 1976), pp. 216-219, 283, 340.

5. Matthew 16:21; 17:22f; 20:18f; Mark 8:31; 9:31; 10:33ff; Luke 9:22, 44; 18:31-33.

6. Matthew 23:38; 24:15-22; Mark 13:14-20; Luke 13:34f; 19:41-44; 21:20-24.

7. The references for this are too numerous to list in full, but among them are Matthew 24:43-51, Mark 13:35-36, and Luke 12:35-46.

CHAPTER 19

1. In the early centuries, some preachers represented Satan as the one to whom our ransom was paid, but this is just fantasy. Satan had no rights over us and Jesus did not pay him off.

CHAPTER 20

1. Jeremiah 3:32; 1 Maccabees 3:18; 4:11; 2 Maccabees 1:11; 2:17.

2. Literally: "The God of my salvation" — for example, Psalms 18:47; 24:5; 25:5; 27:9.

3. Psalms 33:16; 72:4, 13; 2 Samuel 14:4; 2 Kings 6:26f.

4. The Vatican Council itself did not by any means encourage this line of thought. The "Dogmatic Constitution on the Church" says that "it is in him [Christ] that it pleased the Father to restore all things" (no. 3). The "Decree on the Missionary Activity of the Church" says that Jesus Christ "has been constituted the head of a restored humanity" (no. 3). The "Declaration on the Relationship of the Church to Non-Christian Religions," while affirming the Catholic Church's respect for all that is true and holy in other religions, adds that it is "in duty bound to proclaim without fail Christ who is the way, the truth and the life (Jn 14:6). In him, in whom God reconciled all things to himself (2 Cor 5:18-19), men find the fullness of their religious life" (no. 2).

5. It is because this doctrine is so obvious and insistent that Luther coined his famous dictum, "Man is justified by faith alone." By attaching the *alone* to faith, he meant that nothing other than faith contributes to our justification; in particular, that charity and good works, although we ought to do them, do not help to justify us before God, nor merit an eternal reward. We have seen that the Church rejects this position as unbiblical (ch. 2; see also ch. 21, p. 346). But if Luther had said, "Man is justified *only by faith*" — in other words, that without faith justification is impossible — his position would have been unobjectionable. In any case, the very fact that his slogan obtained such wide acceptance is at least a graphic sign of how salvation is linked with faith in Christ by the New Testament.

6. See *Summa Theologiae*, II-II, 2, 7 ad 3.

7. Limbo is not a "third state" between heaven and hell. Technically speaking, it pertains to hell, since it involves exclusion from the Kingdom of God and the beatific vision. But as it involves no suffering, most people are reluctant to speak of it as hell. The word itself means the "edge" (that is, of hell), from the Latin *limbus*, fringe.

PART 5

1. NIV here translates "Counselor."

2. Literally, the text says even more bluntly that the Spirit "was not yet." Most translations, however, like the NIV cited here, interpret this to mean, "had not yet been given."

CHAPTER 21

1. According to Luther, grace does not involve any real effects in us. The Father simply imputes to us the justice and holiness that exist really only in Jesus Christ. Luther compares Christ to a hen covering its chicks with its wings; one looking on from above does not see the chicks but only the hen: "we shroud ourselves under the covering of Christ's flesh . . . lest God should see our sin. . . . God winketh at the remnants of sin yet sticking in our flesh, and so covereth them, as if they were no sin" (*Commentary on Galatians 3:6* [Old Tappan, N.J.: Fleming H. Revell Co., 1953]), p. 255. This gives the sense of Luther's famous description of the justified Christian, *"simul iustus et peccator"* — "sinful and just both together." If by this he had meant that our jus-

tice and holiness are incomplete, that we are partially good and partially bad, he would merely be expressing a truth recognized by everyone. But what Luther meant was that grace does not remove sin from us and confer real justice and holiness upon us; it merely imputes Christ's justice to people who retain fully their former sinfulness. It is the Catholic position that, just as the healing power of Jesus really cleansed the lepers, so his grace really cleanses us from the spiritual leprosy of sin.

2. One might wonder whether it is appropriate to speak of the painful consequences of our disorder as a punishment from God. This language is justified because, on the one hand, God designed the nature that reacts thus upon the one who violates it; on the other hand, he intends and uses these consequences as a way of teaching us not to sin again.

3. See Hosea 2; Isaiah 54:4f; Jeremiah 2:2; 3:20; Ezekiel 16 and 23. See also the Song of Songs.

4. See what is said above about the causality of God's knowledge, in ch. 9, no. 2.

CHAPTER 22

1. On the various uses of the word *faith*, see ch. 5.

2. *Summa Theologiae*, I, 1, 3, ad 2.

3. Similarly, Confucius proposed as an (unattainable?) ideal: "What I do not wish others to do unto me I also wish not to do unto others" (*Sayings* V, 12, tr. James Ware [New York: New American Library, 1955]).

CHAPTER 23

1. This is a literal translation of the term *palingenesis,* which the NIV translates by the more colloquial "rebirth."

2. The number seven derives chiefly from several passages of the Apocalypse (1:4; 3:1; 4:5; 5:6) that mention the seven spirits of God. The names come from Isaiah 11:2f. On the somewhat complicated history of this list, see the appendices to *The Gifts of the Spirit,* vol. 24 of *Summa Theologiae,* tr. and ed. Edward D. O'Connor, C.S.C. (Blackfriars, 1974).

3. Called "gratuitous gifts" (*gratiae gratis datae*) in the older scholastic terminology.

4. In the language of St. Paul, *charism* is not restricted to extraordinary or spectacular gifts; he mentions the charisms of serving, teaching, encouraging, and contributing to the needs of others. In modern usage, however, the term usually connotes something spectacular. See ch. 24, p. 375.

5. Matthew 17:15-21; Mark 16:17-18; Acts 8:6, 13, 18, 39; 11:27f; 13:1-4; 19:6; 21:4, 10-11; 1 John 4:1; Romans 12:4-8; 1 Corinthians 1:4-8; 1 Corinthians 12-13; Galatians 3:2f; Ephesians 3:11-16; Hebrews 2:4; 1 John 4:1; Apocalypse 10:11; 11:6.

6. Note what is said more generally in ch. 22 on faith as enabling us to receive the graces of Christ.

7. In 1879, Pope Leo XIII published an encyclical on the Holy Spirit, "the forgotten person of the Blessed Trinity" (*Divinum illud munus*). In 1986, partly in preparation for the Jubilee of the year 2000, Pope John Paul II published another, *Dominum et Vivificantem.*

CHAPTER 24

1. There were synonyms also, such as "God's chosen ones" (1 Peter 1:2) and "the saints," or "holy ones" (Colossians 1:2), which originally had been given to Israel.

2. Jeremiah 31:31.

3. Today the Church is often spoken of as "the new People of God." Might it not be better to speak of it as "the People of God renewed," to make clear that there is no question of one people having been replaced by another?

4. The original Hebrew expression "a kingdom of priests" has here become "a royal priest-

hood." This involves a shift of meaning that attributes to the addressee a royalty not intended by the original statement. Thus the People of the New Covenant is regarded not only as priestly (and prophetic) but also royal.

    5. Vatican II, "Dogmatic Constitution on the Church," no. 3.

    6. Plato, *The Republic*, bk. II.

CHAPTER 25

    1. By contrast, several elements of the New Testament have in effect been abandoned by most of Protestantism: forgiveness of sins by Church authorities (John 20:22f), the Church's power to bind and loose (Matthew 18:18), the indissolubility of marriage (Mark 10:10ff, etc.), the role of consecrated virginity (1 Corinthians 7), honor of the Mother of Jesus ("all generations will call me blessed" [Luke 1:48]), and of course being built on the Rock of Peter (Matthew 16:18; see also Luke 22:32).

    2. See especially the "Declaration on the Relationship of the Church to Non-Christian Religions," the "Decree on Ecumenism," and the "Dogmatic Constitution on the Church," nos. 8 and 13-17. The "Decree on Eastern Catholic Churches" is less important. The "Declaration on Religious Freedom" is also relevant, although not in the way often supposed.

    3. DS 3866-3873; TCT 266-280; TCC 398g.

    4. Apostolic Constitution "Humanae Salutis" convoking the Council (Dec. 25, 1961); Pope John XXIII's Opening Speech to the Council (Oct. 11, 1962), ed. Walter M. Abbott, S.J., *The Documents of Vatican II* (New York: America Press, 1966), pp. 768, 710. See the "Dogmatic Constitution on the Church," no. 22.

CHAPTER 26

    1. Vatican II, "Dogmatic Constitution on the Church," no. 48.

    2. Council of Trent, Session VII, Canon 1 (DS 1601; TCC 413; TCT 665).

    3. See Pius XII, *The Mystical Body of Christ* (DS 3802; TCC 398b; TCT 242).

    4. "Fully incorporated into the Church are those who, possessing the Spirit of Christ, accept all the means of salvation given to the Church together with her entire organization, and who — by the bonds constituted by the profession of faith, the sacraments, ecclesiastical government, and communion — are joined in the visible structure of the Church of Christ, who rules her through the Supreme Pontiff and the bishops" (Vatican II, "Dogmatic Constitution on the Church," no. 41).

    5. Limbo has traditionally been conceived as a state in which infants that have died without baptism are deprived of the beatific vision but do not suffer any pain. Some go so far as to say that such infants enjoy a perfect natural bliss. However, the whole notion of limbo seems to have originated as a stopgap for handling a problem to which we simply do not know the answer. Few theologians today are content with it, but no satisfactory alternative has been proposed. (The question of the fate of infants who die without baptism has become more acute in modern times because of the number of abortions and miscarriages. However, there is no firm teaching of the Church on this subject.)

    6. In many Protestant churches, the sacrament of confirmation has come to be simply a rite of rededication or reconsecration of those who, baptized as infants, are now asked to "confirm" as responsible persons the vows made for them in baptism.

    7. The Sunday readings are on a three-year cycle; the weekday readings, two-year.

    8. This is why not everyone can consecrate the Eucharist but only one who has been empowered to do so by the sacrament of holy orders. If the Eucharist were only a symbol, anyone should be able to celebrate it. Conversely, those who claim that anyone can "preside over" the Mass reduce it to nothing more than a banquet symbolic of friendship.

9. A popular account of such miracles is given by Joan C. Cruz in *Eucharistic Miracles* (Rockford, Ill.: TAN, 1987). A more critical account of most of these same miracles will be found in P. Browe, *Die eucharistischen Wunder des Mittelalters* (Breslau: 1938).

10. Sigrid Undset, *St. Catherine of Siena* (New York: Sheed and Ward, 1954), p. 153.

11. Protestants generally speak of their pastors as "ministers," not as "priests," precisely because they do not recognize a sacrificial character to the Eucharist.

12. *Pastoral Care of the Sick*, General Introduction, 6 (New York: Catholic Book Publishing Co., 1983). The ritual goes on to add, "If necessary, the sacrament also provides the sick person with the forgiveness of sins and the completion of Christian penance." The anointing of the sick is not meant directly for the forgiveness of sins, and should be preceded by the sacrament of reconciliation. However, in cases where this is not possible, the anointing takes its place.

13. For example, Aaron and his sons (Exodus 28:1); the Levites (Deuteronomy 18:1).

14. P. Delhaye, "Celibacy, history of," NCE 3.

15. Apostolic Exhortation *Declaration on the Question of the Admission of Women to the Ministerial Priesthood* (Vatican City, 1976).

16. Canon 968 of the old Code; 1024 of the new one.

17. According to the French review *Missi* (October 1975), up to the twelfth century there were slightly more men than women among those acknowledged as saints. Since then, however, there have been decidedly more women. And the process of canonization by the Vatican became established only during the twelfth and following centuries. Kenneth Woodward, in *Making Saints* (New York: Simon and Schuster, 1990), says, on the contrary, "Men [saints] outnumber women by about two to one" (p. 136). I am not in a position to resolve this contradiction; but his casual remark does not seem to match the carefully documented research reported in *Missi*. In any case, Woodward agrees that, at least in the twentieth century, the ratio has changed significantly in favor of women.

CHAPTER 27

1. Matthew 10:1-8; Mark 3:14-15; Luke 6:13; 9:1-2; 10:9, 17.

2. Matthew 10:40. See also Luke 10:16; John 13:20; Matthew 28:18-20.

3. DS 1776f; TCC 629f; TCT 842f.

4. Vatican II, "Dogmatic Constitution on the Church," no. 18.

5. *Ibid.*, no. 10.

6. We commonly describe the priest as the one who offers or celebrates the Eucharist (or the Mass). But since in truth all who participate in the Eucharist offer and celebrate, it seems better to describe the priest's role as that of consecrating.

7. Vatican II, "Dogmatic Constitution on the Church," nos. 21, 28.

8. *Ibid.*, no. 28.

9. The three priestly functions can be discerned in Moses' blessing of Levi, the head of the priestly tribe (Deuteronomy 33:7-11).

10. It is not possible to differentiate the three offices of prophet, king, and priest absolutely because they overlapped one another in various ways in the course of Israelite history.

11. This doctrine did not of course originate with that encyclical. It had been the teaching of the Church since patristic times, and was unanimously accepted by all Christian churches until the present century. Catholics did not begin publicly to question it until 1963.

12. Although teaching and governing are often associated with priesthood not only in Christianity but in Judaism and in many other religions, it is in worship that the definitive priestly function appears.

13. Although there are sacrificial overtones in the language used by Jesus at the Last Supper,

the Letter to the Hebrews is the only New Testament document to speak of Jesus explicitly as a priest.

14. See also John 21:15-19; Luke 24:34.

15. Philip Hughes, *Popular History of the Catholic Church* (New York: Macmillan, 1949; Doubleday paperback reedition), p. 16.

16. Matthew 18:17. See also 2 Corinthians 13:11; Ephesians 4:3; Philippians 1:27; 2:2; 4:2.

17. DS 2803; TCC 325; TCT 510.

18. DS 3903; TCC 334c; TCT 520.

19. There have been some notoriously evil popes, such as Alexander VI (1492-1503) who reigned during the youth of Martin Luther, but they have been very few. On the other hand, very many have been outstanding in holiness, generosity, and wisdom, those of the past one hundred thirty years being very notable examples. On the whole, the popes have been remarkable Christian leaders.

20. Pope Paul V, in 1618; see Edward D. O'Connor, C.S.C., *The Dogma of the Immaculate Conception* (Notre Dame, Ind.: University of Notre Dame Press, 1958), p. 306.

21. DS 125; TCC 829; TCT 3.

CHAPTER 28

1. A Greek term for the solemn visit of a king to a city or province. St. Paul uses it for Christ's future coming in glory.

2. In earlier English, these terms were not so restricted; people spoke of worshiping and adoring not only saints but even kings and lords. Yet that simply illustrates how language has changed; it does not imply that in those days saints were "worshiped" in the sense proper to God.

3. This vision occurred on the occasion of Mary's third apparition to the children, July 13, 1917. John Venancio, *Lucia Speaks on the Message of Fátima* (Washington, N.J.: Ave Maria Institute, 1968), p. 30.

4. In its ninth canon, the Synod of Constantinople (543), with the approval of Pope Vigilius, condemned the view that the punishment of hell would one day come to an end (DS 411; TCC 808; TCT 878). Since then, many Church documents have referred to the "eternal punishment" of hell.

5. Venancio, *Lucia Speaks. . .* , p. 35.

6. See Jacques Le Goff, *The Birth of Purgatory* (Chicago: University of Chicago Press, 1984).

7. The little volume of F. X. Schouppe, S.J., *Purgatory Explained by the Lives and Legends of the Saints* (London: Burns and Oates, 1926; reprinted by TAN, 1986) is not very critical in its citations, hence must be used with caution. Nevertheless, taken as a whole, it gives a general idea of these revelations.

INDEX

This is a *word* rather than a *topical* index. That is, except for a few entries that have been modified, references are to the pages on which the word appears, rather than to those on which the topic is discussed. Thus, when a word has several meanings (for instance, *communion*), all are listed together; and when one topic appears under several names (for example, *Satan, devil, demons*), these have distinct entries.

The most important references are indicated by **boldface** type.

Entries too long to be useful have either been eliminated (such as *God* or *Catholic*) or abridged by giving only the principal references, with the addition of *and passim* (for instance, *evil* and *goodness*).